Handbook of Research on Synthetic Emotions and Sociable Robotics:
New Applications in Affective Computing and Artificial Intelligence

Jordi Vallverdú
Autònoma de Barcelona, Spain

David Casacuberta
Autònoma de Barcelona, Spain

INFORMATION SCIENCE REFERENCE

Hershey · New York

Director of Editorial Content:	Kristin Klinger
Senior Managing Editor:	Jamie Snavely
Managing Editor:	Jeff Ash
Assistant Managing Editor:	Carole Coulson
Typesetter:	Jeff Ash
Cover Design:	Lisa Tosheff
Printed at:	Yurchak Printing Inc.

Published in the United States of America by
Information Science Reference (an imprint of IGI Global)
701 E. Chocolate Avenue
Hershey PA 17033
Tel: 717-533-8845
Fax: 717-533-8661
E-mail: cust@igi-global.com
Web site: http://www.igi-global.com/reference

and in the United Kingdom by
Information Science Reference (an imprint of IGI Global)
3 Henrietta Street
Covent Garden
London WC2E 8LU
Tel: 44 20 7240 0856
Fax: 44 20 7379 0609
Web site: http://www.eurospanbookstore.com

Library of Congress Cataloging-in-Publication Data

Handbook of research on synthetic emotions and sociable robotics : new applications in affective computing and artificial intelligence / Jordi Vallverdu and David Casacuberta, editors.
    p. cm.

Includes bibliographical references and index.
Summary: "This book focuses on the integration of emotions into artificial environments such as computers and robotics"--Provided by publisher.

ISBN 978-1-60566-354-8 (hardcover) -- ISBN 978-1-60566-355-5 (ebook) 1. Emotions--Social aspects. 2. Artificial intelligence. 3. Robots. I. Vallverdu, Jordi. II. Casacuberta, David.

HM1033.H356 2009
152.4--dc22
                            2008054196

British Cataloguing in Publication Data
A Cataloguing in Publication record for this book is available from the British Library.

All work contributed to this book is new, previously-unpublished material. The views expressed in this book are those of the authors, but not necessarily of the publisher.

Editorial Advisory Board

List of Contributors

Table of Contents

Section I
Recognizing Emotions

Section II
Emotional Social Robots

Section III
Philosophical Questions

Section IV
Modelling Emotions

Section V
Applied Artificial Emotions

Detailed Table of Contents

Section I
Recognizing Emotions

      Oscar Deniz, ETS Ingenieros Industriales, UCLM, Spain
      Javier Lorenzo, SIANI Institute, University of Las Palmas de Gran Canaria, Spain
      Mario Hernández, SIANI Institute, University of Las Palmas de Gran Canaria, Spain
      Modesto Castrillón, SIANI Institute, University of Las Palmas de Gran Canaria, Spain
      Gloria Bueno, ETS Ingenieros Industriales, UCLM, Spain

Social intelligence seems to obviously require emotions. People have emotions, recognize them in others and also express them. A wealth of information is conveyed through facial expressions, voice tone, etc. If robots can recognize and express emotions, the interaction with the user will be improved because the robot will be able to analyze his/her affective state and choose a different action course depending on it. Thus, it seems clear that any attempt to imitate human social abilities should consider modeling emotions or affective states. This chapter describes the emotional model and implementation of CASI-MIRO, a prototype social robot built by the authors. CASIMIRO is a complex robot with multimodal capabilities defined by a number of software modules. Examples of user interactions will be also shown that suggest that the model is appropriate for regulating the behavior of the robot.

      Cyril Laurier, Universitat Pompeu Fabra, Spain
      Perfecto Herrera, Universitat Pompeu Fabra, Spain

Creating emotionally sensitive machines will significantly enhance the interaction between humans and machines. This chapter focuses on enabling this ability for music. Music is extremely powerful to induce emotions. If machines can somehow apprehend emotions in music, it gives them a relevant competence to communicate with humans. In this chapter the authors review the theories of music and emotions. They detail different representations of musical emotions from the literature, together with related musical features. Then, they focus on techniques to detect the emotion in music from audio content. As a proof of concept, they detail a machine learning method to build such a system. They also review the current state of the art results, provide evaluations and give some insights into the possible applications and future trends of these techniques.

The human face plays a central role in most forms of natural human interaction so the authors may expect that computational methods for analysis of facial information, modeling of internal emotional states, and methods for graphical synthesis of faces and facial expressions will play a growing role in human-computer and human-robot interaction. However, certain areas of face-based HCI, such as facial expression recognition and robotic facial display have lagged others, such as eye-gaze tracking, facial recognition, and conversational characters. Their goal in this chapter is to review the situation in HCI with regards to the human face, and to discuss strategies, which could bring more slowly developing areas up to speed. In particular, they are proposing the "The Art of the Soluble" as a strategy forward and provide examples that successfully applied this strategy.

Section II
Emotional Social Robots

Multi-robot team work is necessary for complex tasks which cannot be performed by a single robot. To get the required performance and reliability, it is necessary to develop a proper cooperative task. The robots need to be intelligent enough to adjust with dynamic workload and environment. Benefits can be amplified from a team if benevolence combines with cooperation. The benevolence behaviors among the team members are extra benefits to the society. There is a flexible relation among intelligence, benevolence and emotions. The authors describe an emotion model to be used for each of the members of a multi-robot team. In respect of some drawbacks with the existing approaches, they present an emotion based multi-robot cooperation with some benevolent characters.

Chapter V

In this chapter, the authors present the distributed integrated affect cognition and reflection architecture DIARC for social robots intended for natural human-robot interaction and demonstrate the utility of its human-inspired affect mechanisms for the selection of tasks and goals. Specifically, they show that DIARC incorporates affect mechanisms throughout the architecture, which are based on "evaluation signals" generated in each architectural component to obtain quick and efficient estimates of the state of the component, and illustrate the operation and utility of these mechanisms with examples from human-robot interaction experiments.

Chapter VI

The hypothesis that artificial emotion-like mechanisms can improve the adaptive performance of robots and intelligent systems has gained considerable support in recent years. To test this hypothesis, a mobile robot navigation system has been developed that employs affect and emotion as adaptation mechanisms. The robot's emotions can arise from hard-coded interpretations of local stimuli, as well as from learned associations stored in global maps. They are expressed as modulations of planning and control parameters, and also as location-specific biases to path-planning. The authors focus is on affective mechanisms that have practical utility rather than aesthetic appeal, so they present an extensive quantitative analysis of the system's performance in a range of experimental situations.

Section III
Philosophical Questions

Chapter VII

All self-active living beings need to solve the motivational problem:--the question of what to do at any moment of their life. For humans and non-human animals at least two distinct layers of motivational drives are known, the primary needs for survival and the emotional drives leading to a wide range of sophisticated strategies, such as explorative learning and socializing. Part of the emotional layer of drives has universal facets, being beneficial in an extended range of environmental settings. Emotions are triggered in the brain by the release of neuromodulators, which are, at the same time, are the agents for meta-learning. This intrinsic relation between emotions, meta-learning and universal action strategies suggests a central importance for emotional control for the design of artificial intelligences and synthetic cognitive systems. An implementation of this concept is proposed in terms of a dense and homogeneous associative network (dHan).

Chapter VIII

Bruce J. MacLennan, University of Tennessee, USA

This chapter addresses the "Hard Problem" of consciousness in the context of robot emotions. The Hard Problem, as defined by Chalmers, refers to the task of explaining the relation between conscious experience and the physical processes associated with it. For example, a robot can act afraid, but could it feel fear? Using protophenomenal analysis, which reduces conscious experience to its smallest units and investigates their physical correlates, the authors consider whether robots could feel their emotions, and the conditions under which they might do so. They find that the conclusion depends on unanswered but empirical questions in the neuropsychology of human consciousness. However, they do conclude that conscious emotional experience will require a robot to have a rich representation of its body and the physical state of its internal processes, which is important even in the absence of conscious experience.

Chapter IX

Mercedes García-Ordaz, University of Huelva, Spain
Rocío Carrasco-Carrasco, University of Huelva, Spain
Francisco José Martínez-López, University of Huelva, Spain

It is contended here that the emotional elements and features of human reasoning should be taken into account when designing the personality of robots. As has been shown in the last few years, the concept of gender is constructed by socio-cultural factors. Gender perspectives are increasingly being applied to different fields of knowledge. The present work aims at demonstrating that the gender perspective is indeed very useful when applied to the field of robotics. Specifically, and when dealing with complex decision-taking, it becomes necessary to analyse which managing activities women can better develop in order to apply them, together with other features, to the design of robotic emotions. The purpose is, then, to propose a robotic model that, after the inclusion of such emotional aspects, breaks with old constrained gender stereotypes and takes a rather liberating view. At the same time, such a proposal should enable us to get better results when creating robots capable of managing other robotic teams and taking complex decisions. In short, the authors seek to apply the gender perspective in the analysis of some emotional features to be taken into account before they are applied to the field of robotics.

Chapter X

Antoni Gomila, University Illes Balears, Spain
Alberto Amengual, International Computer Science Institute, USA

In this chapter the authors raise some of the moral issues involved in the current development of robotic autonomous agents. Starting from the connection between autonomy and responsibility, they distinguish two sorts of problems: those having to do with guaranteeing that the behavior of the artificial cognitive system is going to fall within the area of the permissible, and those having to do with endowing such systems with whatever abilities are required for engaging in moral interaction. Only in the second case can the authors speak of full blown autonomy, or moral autonomy. They illustrate the first type of case with Arkin's proposal of a hybrid architecture for control of military robots. As for the second kind of case, that of full-blown autonomy, they argue that a motivational component, to ground the self-orientation and the pattern of appraisal required, and outline how such motivational component might give rise to interaction in terms of moral emotions. They end suggesting limits to a straightforward analogy between natural and artificial cognitive systems from this standpoint.

Section IV
Modelling Emotions

Chapter XI

Pietro Cipresso, IULM University, Italy
Jean-Marie Dembele, Université Cheikh Anta Diop, Republic of Senegal
Marco Villamira, IULM University, Italy

In this work, the authors present an analytical model of hyper-inflated economies and develop a computational model that permits them to consider expectations of the levels of future prices following emotional rules and strategies. They take into account communications among agents by adding a feedback rule. To consider emotions in agents, they use the Plutchik psycho-evolutionary theory of emotions to design an agent-based emotional architecture based on the attack-escape strategy. The computational model is based on a Barabàsi-Albert Network and considers the diffusion of information and the diffusion of emotions among agents.

Chapter XII

Michel Aubé, Université de Sherbrooke, Canada

The Commitment Theory of Emotions is issued from a careful scrutiny of emotional behavior in humans and animals, as reported in the literature on Evolutionary Biology, Neurosciences and the Psychology of emotions. Emotions are viewed as a special layer of processes, wired upon needs and instincts, and dealing mainly with nurturance, social bonding and cooperative behavior, especially between kin and relatives. As every other motivational system, they operate so as to manage resources critical for survival and reproduction. The peculiar resources emotions do manage are commitments, understood as the predispositions of a given individual to help others and collaborate with them in a reciprocal manner. This view clarifies considerably the interactions emotions entertain with a variety of modules involved in their operation, from the detection of antecedents in perceptual or memory systems, to the elicitation of the appropriate emotion, to the execution of the corresponding script, to the expression of emotions as the typical outcome of emotional episodes. The flow of processing is continuously modulated by affective states of the organisms and by other motivational systems. The chapter expounds the operation of each module as well as their interactions with each other. It concludes that successful implementation of emotions in artificial systems will have to rest upon the specifications of complex and realistic models of the kind presented.

Chapter XIII

Sigerist J. Rodríguez, Universidad del Zulia, Venezuela
Pilar Herrero, Universidad Politécnica de Madrid, Spain
Olinto J. Rodríguez, Universidad del Zulia, Venezuela

Today, realism and coherence are highly searched qualities in agent's behavior; but these qualities cannot be achieved completely without incorporation of emotions. This chapter shows a model for emotional representations in intelligent agents. The model is based on the cognitive appraisal theory of emotions; this theory affirms that stimuli are processed by a cognitive mechanism that determines what emotion to feel. It is also based on the Aaron Sloman's research where positively and negatively affective states are exposed, as well as, on the theory of basic emotions. The model tries to define an emotional representation data structure for intelligent agents. It also defines the emotional behavior mechanisms when a stimulus is processed, as well as, emotional interaction mechanisms. This chapter is presented in five sections: Introduction, where the topic is presented. State-of-the-Art, where it is introduced a review of emotional studies in psychological areas, as well as, computing areas. The Model Definition section, where a detailed model structure and mechanism are introduced. A fourth section describing the future trends and researches and finally the chapter conclusions.

Chapter XIV

Clément Raïevsky, Université de Sherbrooke, Canada
François Michaud, Université de Sherbrooke, Canada

Emotion plays several important roles in the cognition of human beings and other life forms, and is therefore a legitimate inspiration for providing situated agents with adaptability and autonomy. However, there is no unified theory of emotion and many discoveries are yet to be made in its applicability to situated agents. One function of emotion commonly identified by psychologists is to signal to other cognitive processes that the current situation requires an adaptation. The main purposes of this chapter are to highlight the usefulness of this signaling function of emotion for situated agents and to present an artificial model of anger and fear based on mismatch theories of emotion, which aims at replicating this function. Collective foraging simulations are used to demonstrate the feasibility of the model and to characterize its influence on a decision-making architecture.

Chapter XV

Luis Macedo, University of Coimbra, Portugal
Amilcar Cardoso, University of Coimbra, Portugal
Rainer Reisenzein, University of Greifswald, Germany
Emiliano Lorini, Institute of Cognitive Sciences and Technologies, Italy & Institut de Recherche en Informatique de Toulouse, France
Cristiano Castelfranchi, Institute of Cognitive Sciences and Technologies, Italy

This chapter reviews research on computational models of surprise. Part 1 begins with a description of the phenomenon of surprise in humans, reviews research on surprise, and describes a recent psychological model of surprise (Meyer, 1988; Meyer, Reisenzein, & Schützwohl, 1997). Part 2 is devoted to computational models of surprise, giving special prominence to the models proposed by Macedo and Cardoso (e.g., Macedo & Cardoso, 2001b; Macedo, Reisenzein, & Cardoso, 2004) and by Lorini and Castelfranchi (e.g., Lorini & Castelfranchi, 2007). Part 3 compares these two models of artificial surprise with each other and with the (Meyer et al., 1997) model of human surprise, discusses possible targets of future research, and considers possible practical applications.

Chapter XVI

A new theory of emotions is derived from the semantics of the language of emotions. The sound structures of 36 Old Arabic word roots that express specific emotions are converted into abstract models. By substitution from two tables, abstract models are converted into concrete theories about the nature of the specific emotions that are likely to be validated. Theories confirmed by the author's own emotional experience (self reports), and by previously corroborated theories, are considered corroborated. These theories about specific emotions are woven together into an integrated theory of all emotions. The theory models emotions and emotional mechanisms, dimensions and polarities in ways amenable to affective computing. The findings are supported by clinical psychology. Old Arabic is chosen because its words, sounds and meanings are consistent and have not changed for at least 1,400 years. The theory can be expanded by incorporating additional emotional word roots from Arabic and other alphabetical languages.

Section V
Applied Artificial Emotions

Chapter XVII

The Turing Test, originally configured as a game for a human to distinguish between an unseen and unheard man and woman, through a text-based conversational measure of gender, is the ultimate test for deception and hence, thinking. So conceived Alan Turing when he introduced a machine into the game. His idea, that once a machine deceives a human judge into believing that they are the human, then that machine should be attributed with intelligence. What Turing missed is the presence of emotion in human dialogue, without expression of which, an entity could appear non-human. Indeed, humans have been confused as machine-like, the confederate effect, during instantiations of the Turing Test staged in Loebner Prizes for Artificial Intelligence. The authors present results from recent Loebner Prizes and two parallel conversations from the 2006 contest in which two human judges, both native English speakers, each concomitantly interacted with a non-native English speaking hidden-human, and jabberwacky, the

2005 and 2006 Loebner Prize bronze prize winner for most human-like machine. They find that machines in those contests appear conversationally worse than non-native hidden-humans, and, as a consequence attract a downward trend in highest scores awarded to them by human judges in the 2004, 2005 and 2006 Loebner Prizes. Analysing Loebner 2006 conversations, they see that a parallel could be drawn with autistics: the machine was able to broadcast but it did not inform; it talked but it did not emote. The hidden-humans were easily identified through their emotional intelligence, ability to discern emotional state of others and contribute with their own 'balloons of textual emotion'.

Félix Francisco Ramos Corchado, Instituto Politécnico Nacional, Guadalajara, Mexico
Héctor Rafael Orozco Aguirre, Instituto Politécnico Nacional, Guadalajara, Mexico
Luis Alfonso Razo Ruvalcaba, Instituto Politécnico Nacional, Guadalajara, Mexico

Emotions play an essential role in the cognitive processes of an avatar and are a crucial element for modeling its perception, learning, decision process, behavior and other cognitive functions. Intense emotions can affect significantly the behavior of an avatar in a virtual environment, for instance, driving its behavior unstable as the consequence of deep emotional influence. The response of an avatar to such influence is the development of the capacity to recognize and manage emotions. In this work the authors describe a new faculty called Artificial Emotional Intelligence (AEI), and they propose a model based on Emotional Intelligence (EI) to develop a new approach to the problem of mood and emotion control. This approach applies the concept of EI and provides the needed tools to make avatars have AEI. In addition, they use the Emotional Competence Framework (ECF) to define and apply the personal and social competencies of an avatar.

Sarantos I. Psycharis, University of the Aegean, Greece

In their study the authors collected data with respect to cognitive variables (learning outcome), meta-cognitive indicators (knowledge about cognition and regulation of cognition) psychological variables (self-esteem) and emotional variables (motives, anxiety). The teaching sequence was implemented using the CTAT authoring tool and the basic teaching unit was referred to fundamental concepts in Mechanics for 20 4th year undergraduate students enrolled in the course «Ápplied Didactics in Natural Sciences» of the University of the Aegean-Department of Education. Analysis of the results shows that anxiety (a negative emotion) can be reduced using CTAT , there is a transfer from extrinsic to intrinsic motivation while metacognitive indicators as well as learning performance can be improved using CTAT . The interactivity of the learning environment influences also self esteem and the results are presented.

Anthony G. Francis, Jr., Google, USA
Manish Mehta, Georgia Institute of Technology, USA
Ashwin Ram, Georgia Institute of Technology, USA

Believable agents designed for long-term interaction with human users need to adapt to them in a way which appears emotionally plausible while maintaining a consistent personality. For short-term interactions in restricted environments, scripting and state machine techniques can create agents with emotion and personality, but these methods are labor intensive, hard to extend, and brittle in new environments. Fortunately, research in memory, emotion and personality in humans and animals points to a solution to this problem. Emotions focus an animal's attention on things it needs to care about, and strong emotions trigger enhanced formation of memory, enabling the animal to adapt its emotional response to the objects and situations in its environment. In humans this process becomes reflective: emotional stress or frustration can trigger re-evaluating past behavior with respect to personal standards, which in turn can lead to setting new strategies or goals. To aid the authoring of adaptive agents, the authors present an artificial intelligence model inspired by these psychological results in which an emotion model triggers case-based emotional preference learning and behavioral adaptation guided by personality models. Their tests of this model on robot pets and embodied characters show that emotional adaptation can extend the range and increase the behavioral sophistication of an agent without the need for authoring additional hand-crafted behaviors.

Chapter XXI

    Dorel Gorga, University of Geneva, Switzerland
    Daniel K. Schneider, University of Geneva, Switzerland

The purpose of this contribution is to discuss conceptual issues and challenges related to the integration of emotional agents in the design of computer-based learning environments and to propose a framework for the discussion of future research. The authors review some emotion theories and computational models that have been developed in cognitive science and Artificial Intelligence (AI). They then will discuss some basic principles pertaining to motivation and emotion in instructional design. Grounded on these principles, they then shall present the state of the art of integrating emotions into the design of educational systems, and notably examine how to create intelligent emotional agents that enhance interaction with users. They will introduce the concept of "socio-emotional climate" as an evaluative indicator of the diversity of desirable interactions within a computer-based learning environment. They formulate the conjecture that a socio-emotional climate capable of enhancing learner motivation, self-assessment and self-motivation could be developed through the use of various socio-emotional agents.

Section VI
Ambient Emotion

Chapter XXII

    Artur Lugmayr, Tampere University of Technology, Finland
    Tillmann Dorsch, Tampere University of Technology, Finland
    Pabo Roman Humanes, Tampere University of Technology, Finland

The "medium is the message": nowadays the medium as such is non-distinguishable from its presentation environment. However, what is the medium in an ambient environment, when the environment is smart, recognizes emotions, and at the same time responsive? Emotions have had an inferior role in philosophy, psychology, art, and nowadays in media technology. In philosophy and psychology many researchers devoted their work to the question what emotions are, and how they can be modelled, ranging from common-sense theories, theories that emotions are simply physiological disturbances, and the many behaviour theories describing emotions providing a much more comprehensive view on emotions [1]. In the age of ambient media, where media technology is embedded seamlessly and hidden into the natural environment of the consumer, the view towards media is changing. The modality how emotions are experienced and the technology to recognize and simulate emotions are changing. To support the theories within the scope of this chapter, a case study – the emotional ambient responsive character – has been performed. The concept was realised as a simple interactive game responding to human emotions. Within this book section, the authors present a technical oriented view towards recognizing, simulating, and binding emotions in ambient media systems. A case-study for an emotion recognition and response system is presented. The system integrates the content and emotion recognition elements.

Chapter XXIII

During the previous stage of their research the authors developed a computer simulation (called 'The Panic Room' or, more simply, 'TPR') dealing with synthetic emotions. TPR was developed with Python code and led us to interesting results. With TPR, they were merely trying to design an artificial device able to learn from, and interact with, the world by using two basic information types: positive and negative. They were developing the first steps towards an evolutionary machine, defining the key elements involved in the development of complex actions (that is, creating a physical intuitive ontology, from a bottom-up approach). After the successful initial results of TPR, they considered that it would be necessary to develop a new simulation (which they will call "TPR 2.0."), more complex and with better visualisation characteristics. They have now developed a second version, TPR 2.0., using the programming language Processing, with new improvements such as: a better visual interface, a database which can record and also recall easily the information on all the paths inside the simulation (human and automatically generated ones) and, finally, a small memory capacity which is a next step in the evolution from simple hard-wired activities to self-learning by simple experience.

Chapter XXIV

A vision of future daily life is explored in Ambient Intelligence (AmI). It follows the assumption that information technology should disappear into our environment to bring humans an easy and entertaining life. The mental, physical, and methodical invisibility of artificial intelligent tools and environments will have an effect on the relation between the activities of both, users and designers. The infiltration of reality with sensing, computing, transmitting and acting hardware will cause the construction of new meanings on interaction in general because the "visible" acting of people will be preceded, accompanied and followed by the invisible and visible acting of artificial intelligent tools and environments and their providers. Sociability in such an interaction world stretches between the feelings of "being in security" and "being in control". Invisibility management could enable situated veiling and unveiling. Critical Transformative Rooms, where human and artificial actors can negotiate about the change of meanings, are the approach to deal with the users' emotions of frozenness, despair, fear, doubt and trust.

Foreword

Artificial Intelligence (AI)—broadly construed to include not only traditional symbol manipulation methods but also such techniques as connectionist networks and genetic algorithms—has been one of the most important contributors to our understanding of the mind. Many unquestioned assumptions of philosophers and psychologists were put to test when researchers in AI began their first attempts to simulate or instantiate systems capable of intelligent and autonomous behaviors. For example, philosophers have long thought that language and other cognitive abilities such as mathematical reasoning would be the most difficult phenomena of mind to explain. Descartes assumed that to explain language and reason would require the posit of a non-material soul. And yet, it was an early and striking lesson of AI that at least some competences in math and language are far less difficult to explain than is free interaction with an environment. We have very successful speech recognition programs, text manipulation programs, calculators, and theorem provers, but it is still a major struggle to get a robot to show the ability to move within and manage a simple environment—something an ant, with its few hundred thousand neurons, manages very well.

We can be optimistic that artificial intelligence will be equally fruitful in helping us understand emotions. Many of our cherished assumptions about emotions will no doubt prove profoundly wrong, clearing the ground for revolutionary new theories. It is an exciting time to be studying emotions, when the field of synthetic emotions is nascent, and the major discoveries lie in the near future. Research in synthetic emotions will help us answer the most basic questions in the science and philosophy of emotions.

There are two primary branches to synthetic emotion research: work that seeks to understand and simulate the expression of emotions, and work that aims to model or even instantiate emotions. Both approaches are represented in the papers that follow, making this landmark volume representative of the most productive dimensions of this new field.

As humans interact more often and more intimately with computers, and as computational systems become an ever more important element of our society, playing roles in education, the production of culture and goods, and management, it is inevitable that we should seek to interact with these systems in ways that take advantage of our powerful emotional capabilities. There are both input and output aspects to this research. First, we may want systems to be able to interact with users who are expressing emotions. The display of emotions by users can convey a great deal of relevant information. There are obvious benefits to things like educational programs that recognize student frustration, customer relation systems that identify anger, transportation management systems that recognize panic, and so on. Such emotional expressions are recognized by other humans in normal social settings and convey essential information that can be importantly predictive. Systems that can "understand" and use this information can be more effective. Second, computational systems that "express" emotions can transmit information that can assist efficient operation. A warning system that expresses something like fearful urgency will be more effective than one that fails to sound urgent. It is in these two aspects of simulating and recognizing emotional expression that have motivated most research in synthetic emotions. In this collection, you will find cutting edge examples of both.

But in this collection is also represented work in deep emotional AI: attempts to create systems that model or instantiate emotions and their functional roles. In such work we begin see hypotheses that will lead to profound leaps forward in our understanding of emotions. Emotions are very complex events, motivating action but also altering in an integrated way perception, memory formation and recall, and motor control. Synthetic emotions offer us an extremely productive way to formulate and then test hypotheses about what these complex emotion events are, how they operate with other aspects of intelligence, and what roles they play in autonomous action and social interaction.

But the exciting work in the pages that follows sets us on a path that promises to go beyond helping us understand emotions, and herein lies perhaps the opportunity for the most dramatic discoveries that research into synthetic emotions may offer. This research has the potential to open up profound new insights into the nature of autonomy and intelligence. The most recalcitrant aspect of AI has been developing an understanding of what it is for a system to have purposes. The turn from traditional AI ("GOFAI") to contemporary ecumenical AI has not altered the central fact that AI still remains firmly fixed around the premise that the discipline is and should be about learning. Learning is necessary to intelligence, there can be no doubt. But it is not sufficient. Intelligent systems also necessarily have purposes. We have productive theories of what it is to process representations and to reason; we have a range of promising research programs in how to manage motor control; but we still do not know what it would mean for an artificial system to have and act upon purposes, to develop its own appropriate purposes, or to alter its purposes. AI has made little progress in even beginning to conceptualize how we can understand these phenomena.

The study of synthetic emotions holds out the possibility of the first steps towards the development of productive research programs in this area. Emotions are essentially purposeful, driving action and a range of other system capabilities towards specific ends. To fear something, for example, is more than just to know that it is dangerous—it is to be motivated in very special ways towards particular kinds of action. The changes that accompany fear, such as in memory formation, perception, and action-preparedness, all appear to be both the embodiment, and conceptual effects, of a complex motor purpose. Ultimately, success in synthetic emotions may lead us to success in synthetic purposes, and thus prove one of the most important programs in the science and philosophy of mind and AI that we have. This volume that you hold promises to be an important contribution toward this end.

Craig DeLancey
State University of New York, Oswego, USA

*Craig **DeLancey** is an associate professor of Philosophy at the State University of New York at Oswego. His research and publications are mostly concerned with the philosophy of mind, and have focused upon the study of emotion and consciousness. His publications include _Passionate Engines: What Emotions Reveal about Mind and Artificial Intelligence_ (Oxford University Press, 2002).*

Preface

Only thirty years ago, the field of emotion research was an almost uncharted territory: an almost desert island very few people were interested in visiting and even less were interested in staying. Neuroscientists consider the frontal lobes mostly a source of conflict from people with mental diseases, so the prescription of lobotomies was quite common; emotions were, for cognitive psychologists, just a source of irrationality, so nobody did paid much attention to them. If you randomly picked up three different books of introduction to cognitive psychology, they would give you three different lists of emotional states: the first book would include hunger and sexual desire as emotions, but wouldn't include surprise. The second book included surprise and sexual desire but consider hunger just a "drive", and the third included a list of forty different emotions, most of them not mentioned in the first two. And, if the AI people were interested at all in emotions that was probably just as a trick to feign emotions in a computer in order to help it to pass a future Turing Test.

Fortunately, these perceptions have changed dramatically since then, and now the study of emotions is a very active and respected field. This change of perception is mainly due to changes in methodology and new experimental results from those three main disciplines we were just discussing.

1. Neuroscience has supplied lots of empirical data as well as some functioning models on the key role that emotion plays when we humans make decisions. Since the studies of the patient—now almost a legend—Phineas Gage we have come to realise that emotions, far from being a nuisance, are not a dissociable part of most of our mental states, playing a role both in cognition and perception.
2. The evolution by means of procuring better and more detailed models, as well as the collection of empirical confirmation from very different sources has turned the cognitive model of emotions from a curiosity to the more accepted and influencing model of what emotions are now. This has helped greatly in introducing the concept of emotion into several research fields of cognitive psychology from which it was missing.
3. The development of affective computing has proved to be a very valuable field in AI, offering new interacting and theoretical models on what it means to be "intelligent" and how important emotions are in improving communications between humans and computers. At the same time, bottom-up approaches for the creation of autonomous artificial creatures include more and more emotional elements to their prototypes.

All these promising results as well as the emerging paradigm of affective computing have motivated us to produce this volume on synthetic emotions and social robots which you are reading now. We strongly believe that research in this field is important to developing better computer applications which are more able to communicate with humans or fulfill their tasks. We also argue that synthetic emotions can help not only neuroscience or cognitive psychology test their models "in silicon"; we can gain a lot much more from this research. It can take the form of interdisciplinary models for relationships between emotions and cognition and it can even lead us to rethink classical philosophical problems, like the question of the reality of *qualia* and consider "the hard problem of consciousness" from another point of view.

We have divided the book into the following sections, which we consider the more promising now in this field: recognizing emotions, emotional social robots, philosophical questions, modelling emotions, applied artificial emotions and ambient emotion.

SECTION I. RECOGNIZING EMOTIONS

This section includes state of the art chapters on how we can create artificial systems to recognize emotional states in humans and use them to interact better with them, or to make predictions on groups' behavior.

In *"Emotional Modeling in an Interactive Robotic Head,"* Oscar Deniz, Javier Lorenzo, Mario Hernández, Modesto Castrillón, and Gloria Bueno, describes the emotional model and implementation of CASIMIRO, a prototype social robot built by the authors. CASIMIRO is a complex robot with multimodal capabilities defined by a number of software modules, a social robot able to recognize emotions.

"Automatic Detection of Emotions in Music: Interaction with Emotionally Sensitive Machines" presents the work from Cyril Laurier and Perfecto Herrera in order to detect emotion in music from audio content, describing a machine learning method to do so.

This section ends with chapter *"Facial Expression Analysis, Modeling and Synthesis: Overcoming the Limitations of Artificial Intelligence with the Art of the Soluble"* by Christopher Bartneck and Michael J. Lyons, which reviews the situation in HCI with regard to the human face, and discusses strategies, which could bring more slowly developing areas up to speed.

SECTION II. EMOTIONAL SOCIAL ROBOTS

This section contains a description of methodologies, developments and theories on how to use artificial emotions in order to facilitate the development of social robots; autonomous artificial systems which are able to cooperate among them in order to fulfill specific tasks.

"Multirobot Team Work with Benevolent Characters: The Roles of Emotions" by Sajal Banik, Keigo Watanabe, Maki K. Habib, and Kiyotaka Izumi, describes an emotional model and strategy in order to make cooperative robots to work between there better, including the concept of "benevolent character" in the modelling, while *"Affective Goal and Task Selection for Social Robots"* written by Matthias Scheutz and Paul Schemerhorn presents a DIARC or distributed integrated affect cognition and reflection architecture designed to help social robots make decisions.

Authors Christopher P. Lee-Johnson and Dale A. Carnegie present *"Robotic Emotions: Navigation with Feeling"* which describes a mobile robot navigation system that employs affect and emotion as adaptation mechanisms. The robot's emotions can arise from hard-coded interpretations of local stimuli, as well as from learned associations stored in global maps.

SECTION III. PHILOSOPHICAL QUESTIONS

Following the X-Phi or Experimental Philosophy paradigm, this section is devoted to show how classical and recent philosophical conundrums can be shed new light on the artificial emotions field.

According to C. Gros, in *"Emotions, Diffusive Emotional Control and the Motivational Problem for Autonomous Cognitive Systems,"* intelligent systems need to include motivational procedures, showing therefore the importance of emotional control for the design of artificial intelligences and synthetic cognitive systems.

"Robots React, but Can They Feel?" allows author Bruce J. MacLennan to analyse the famous "hard problem of consciousness" within the context of synthetic emotions, trying to understand whether it is possible to consider a robot able to feel them.

The chapter *"Personality and Emotions in Robotics from the Gender Perspective"* by Mercedes García-Ordaz, Rocío Carrasco-Carrasco, and Francisco Martínez-López seeks to apply the gender perspective in the analysis of some emotional features to be taken into account before they are applied to the field of robotics.

Antoni Gomila and Alberto Amengual presents in *"Moral Emotions for Autonomous Agents"* the moral implications related to the idea of an autonomous robot and how to deal with the nightmare of the "evil robot" that loses control.

SECTION IV. MODELLING EMOTIONS

Besides being useful to solve or improve certain tasks within the AI domain, artificial emotions are also an important instrument for simulating emotional processes and developing better models of what an emotion is, which can be of great help for several cognitive science disciplines.

"An Emotional Perspective for Agent-Based Computational Economics" by Pietro Cipresso, Jean-Marie Dembele, and Marco Villamira, presents an analytical model of hyper-inflated economies and develops a computational model that permits us to consider expectations of the levels of future prices following emotional rules and strategies.

Michel Aubé shows us in *"Unfolding Commitments Management: A Systemic View of Emotions"* a model of emotion which is more realistic that the usual ones, in order to develop artificial emotional applications that are really functional.

In *"A Cognitive Appraisal Based Approach for Emotional Representation,"* Sigerist J. Rodríguez, Pilar Herrero, and Olinto J. Rodríguez presents a model for synthetic emotions based on the cognition/appraisal theory, while Clément Raïevsky and François Michaud present the usefulness of the signaling function of emotion for situated agents and an artificial model of anger and fear based on mismatch theories of emotion in their chapter *"Emotion Generation Based on a Mismatch Theory of Emotions for Situated Agents."*

Luis Macedo, Amilcar Cardoso, Rainer Reisenzein, Emiliano Lorini, and Cristiano Castelfranchi, presents in *"Artificial Surprise"* a review of the models of surprise, compares several of them, and indicates future research and possible practical applications. Based on Arabic word roots, author Tom Adi describes a linguistically based theory of emotions in *"A Theory of Emotions Based on Natural Language Semantics."*

SECTION V. APPLIED ARTIFICIAL EMOTIONS

Recently, we have seen an important increase in the use of emotion to help computers to solve simple tasks: from passing the Turing Test to create more friendly and useful learning environments, as we can see from the materials of this section.

In their chapter "Emotion in the Turning Test: A Downward Trend for Machines in Recent Loebner Prizes," Huma Shah and Kevin Warwick argue how important is to include some ability to use and recognize emotions if we want an AI to pass the Turing test. In *"The Use of Artificial Emoitional Intelligence in Virtual Creatures"* by Félix Ramos, Héctor Rafael Orozco Aguirre, and Luis Alfonso Razo Ruvalcaba, the authors argue the importance of emotions in order to design a proper avatar in order to model its perception, learning, decision process, behavior and other cognitive functions.

The chapter by Sarantos I. Psycharis, *"Physics and Cognitive-Emotional-Metacognitive Variables-Learning Performance in the Environment of CTAT,"* applies artificial emotion to teach mechanics, while authors Anthony G. Francis Jr., Manish Mehta, and Ashwin Ram in the chapter *"Emotional Memory and Adaptive Personalities"*, presents an artificial intelligence model inspired by these psychological results in which an emotion model triggers case-based emotional preference learning and behavioral adaptation guided by personality models. Finally, in the chapter *"Computer-Based Learning Environments with Emotional Agents"* authored by Dorel Gorga and Daniel K. Schneider discusses conceptual issues and challenges related to the integration of emotional agents in the design of computer-based learning environments and proposes a framework for the discussion of future research.

SECTION VI. AMBIENT EMOTION

Both from a theoretical and practical point of view, the field of Ambient Intelligence— or how to include some sort of intelligent ability to interact with humans and solve specific tasks in a distributed system—can gain a lot by means of including artificial emotions in their modeling. Here we explain how this can be done.

In *"Emotional Ambient Media,"* Artur Lugmayr, Tillmann Dorsch, and Pabo Roman Humanes, introduces the reader to a technical oriented view towards recognizing, simulating, and binding emotions in ambient media systems, as well as presenting a case study for an emotion recognition and response system. *"Modelling Hardwired Synthetic Emotions: TPR 2.0"* by the editors of this book describes an ambient intelligence system which uses protoemotions in order to respond to specific actions from the user. The book ends with *"Invisibility and Visibility: The Shadows of Artificial Intelligence"* by Cecile K. M. Crutzen and Hans-Werner Hein which analyses how the mental, physical, and methodical invisibility of artificial intelligent tools and environments will have an effect on the relation between the activities of both users and designers.

Jordi Vallverdú
Autònoma de Barcelona, Catalonia, Spain

David Casacuberta
Autònoma de Barcelona, Catalonia, Spain

Section I
Recognizing Emotions

Chapter I
Emotional Modeling in an Interactive Robotic Head

Oscar Deniz
ETS Ingenieros Industriales, UCLM, Spain

Javier Lorenzo
SIANI Institute, University of Las Palmas de Gran Canaria, Spain

Mario Hernández
SIANI Institute, University of Las Palmas de Gran Canaria, Spain

Modesto Castrillón
SIANI Institute, University of Las Palmas de Gran Canaria, Spain

Gloria Bueno
ETS Ingenieros Industriales, UCLM, Spain

ABSTRACT

Social intelligence seems to obviously require emotions. People have emotions, recognize them in others and also express them. A wealth of information is conveyed through facial expressions, voice tone, etc. If robots can recognize and express emotions, the interaction with the user will be improved because the robot will be able to analyze his/her affective state and choose a different action course depending on it. Thus, it seems clear that any attempt to imitate human social abilities should consider modeling emotions or affective states. This chapter describes the emotional model and implementation of CASIMIRO, a prototype social robot built by the authors. CASIMIRO is a complex robot with multimodal capabilities defined by a number of software modules. Examples of user interactions will be also shown that suggest that the model is appropriate for regulating the behavior of the robot.

INTRODUCTION

Although the use of emotions in robots is still under debate, in the last years many authors have argued that the traditional "Dr Spock" paradigm for solving problems (eminently rational) may not be appropriate for modeling social behavior. Rational decisions allow us to cope with the complex world that we live in. Thus, the rational selection among different options is crucial for survival and goal accomplishment. However, any agent (human or artificial) whose actions are guided only by purely rational decisions would be in serious trouble. Weighing all the possible options would prevent the agent from taking any decision at all. There is evidence that people who have suffered damage to the prefrontal lobes so that they can no longer show emotions are very intelligent and sensible, but they cannot make decisions (Picard, 1997; Damasio, 1994). A so-called "Commander Kirk" paradigm assumes that some aspects of human intelligence, particularly the ability to take decisions in dynamic and unpredictable environments, depend on emotions.

There is another interpretation, however, which makes clear the importance that emotion modeling may have in a robot. Social intelligence seems to obviously require emotions.

People have emotions, recognize them in others and also express them. A wealth of information is conveyed through facial expressions, voice tone, etc. If robots can recognize, express and probably have emotions, the interaction with the user will be improved because the robot will be able to analyze the affective state of the user and choose a different action course depending on it (Hernández et al., 2004). Thus, it seems clear that any attempt to imitate human social abilities should consider modeling emotions or affective states. In fact, a field called Affective Computing (Tao & Tan, 2005) is developing which aims at developing engineering tools for measuring, modeling, reasoning about, and responding to affect.

This chapter describes the emotional model implemented in a prototype sociable robot called CASIMIRO, see Figure 1. CASIMIRO (Deniz et al., 2006; Deniz et al., 2007) is an animal-like face with basic interaction abilities achieved through computer vision, audio signal processing, speech generation, motor control, etc. The abilities include omnidirectional and stereo vision, face detection, head nod/shake gesture detection (for answering questions), person detection and tracking (using the neck), sound localization, speech, owner recognition, etc. The focus is in providing useful techniques for researchers working on emotional modeling for interactive robots.

BACKGROUND

Many emotional models have been proposed both within the Robotics community and in psychology (see (Fong et al., 2003) and also the Emotion Home Page (E. Hudlicka & J.M. Fellous, 2008)). The most well known model for human emotion representation is perhaps that of Russell (Russell, 1980), which considers that emotions fall in

Figure 1. CASIMIRO

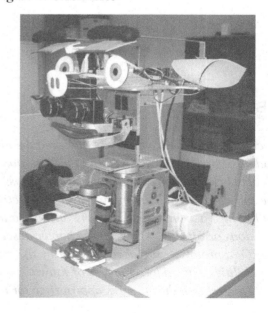

a bidimensional space, with orthogonal valence and arousal components, see Figure 2.

This bidimensional space (also called circumplex model) has received wide support in the literature (Carney & Colvin, 2005). Many forms of human emotional experience (judgment of the similarity between pairs of affect terms, self-reports of current emotion and from perceptions of similarity between static photographs of expressed emotion) point to an ordering of basic emotions around the perimeter of a circle with arousal and valence axes.

The central zone of that space would correspond to "no emotion", a sort of neutral state where there is no feeling of being well or bad, excited or calmed. In this unemotional state, it is as if emotions were nonexistent. They do not influence behaviour, attention or perception. This state is much like that of being "a machine", in which behavior tends to detailed calculi and deliberation, without time restrictions. On the other hand, zones that are far from the centre of the emotional space correspond to normal emotional states in humans, though they are rarely contemplated in machines.

For Sloman there are only three types of emotions: basic, secondary and tertiary (Sloman, 2001). Picard (1997) and Damasio see only two types. Basic emotions come directly from certain stimuli. Other emotions arise after a cognitive appraisal. These two types of emotions are present in CASIMIRO:

- **Basic emotions:** Direct influence from sensors. If the robot hears a loud sound, for example, it increases its arousal and valence, especially arousal.
- **Secondary emotions:** Influence in the Emotions module from the Behavior module of the robot (see details in (Deniz et al., 2006)).

MAIN FOCUS OF THE CHAPTER

CASIMIRO's emotional module maintains a position in a 2D valence and arousal space. The module receives messages from other modules (from the Behavior control module, for example) to shift the current position in one or the two dimensions. The 2D space is divided into zones that correspond to facial expressions. In order to simplify the module, it is assumed that the expression is given by the angle in the 2D space (with respect to the valence axis), and the degree is given by the distance to the origin. The circular central zone corresponds to the neutral facial expression. When the current position enters a different zone a message is sent to the Pose module of the robot so that it can move the face, and to the Talk module so that speech intonation can be adjusted. The facial expressions are assigned to the 2D space as shown in Figure 3. Values of arousal and valence are not always inside the exterior circle, though the expression degree is maximum for values that lie outside the circle.

Relative displacements in the arousal and valence axes need a correction. Consider the case depicted in Figure 4 in which the current position in emotional space is P. If we want to lead the robot to Anger, we increase arousal and decrease valence with a displacement $\vec{d}$. However, the resulting position will be Q, which is associated to Surprise. Obviously, the effect of changes in

Figure 2. Arousal and valence emotional space

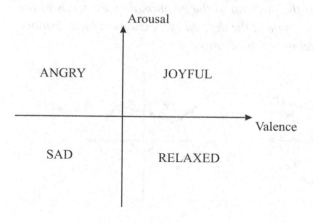

Figure 3. Assignment of facial expression according to the emotional state

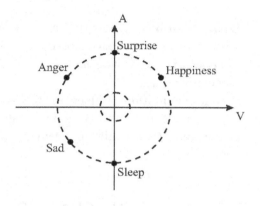

Figure 4. Effect of an increase in arousal and decrease in valence

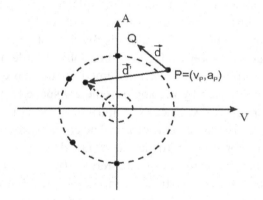

arousal and valence depends on the current position, which is undesirable.

The correction, which we have not seen previously in the literature, is as follows. Given a displacement $\vec{d} = (v, a)$, the components of the new displacement vector $\vec{d}'$ are given by:

$$\vec{d}' = \left(\frac{v - v_P}{l}, \frac{a - a_P}{l}\right) \cdot \min(l, m)$$

where:

$$l = \sqrt{(v - v_P)^2 + (a - a_P)^2} \quad \text{and} \quad m = \sqrt{v^2 + a^2}$$

Figure 5 illustrates the effect of the correction.

A very simple emotional decay is implemented: every once in a while arousal and valence are divided by a factor. This does not change the angle in the 2D space, and thus the facial expression does not change, only the degree. This procedure is in accordance with the fact that emotions seem to decay more slowly when the intensity is lower (Bui et al., 2002). In (Reilly, 1996) a scheme is used in which each emotion can have its decay rate, being for example slower in anger than in startle. In our implementation each emotion can have a decay factor associated, set by default at 2. The use of decay factors (and other parameters like

Figure 5. Effect of the correction in emotional space when three (arousal-increase, valence-decrease) displacements are submitted to the system. Note that the position in the emotional space tends to the desired expression. When the current position is at the angle of the desired expression only the distance to the centre increases, which in turn increases the degree of the expression.

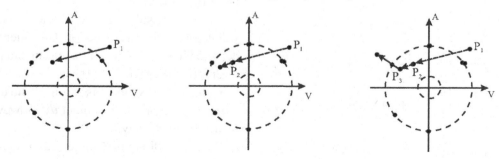

the magnitude of the displacements in the emotion space) allows the designer to define personalities (Hernández et al., 2004).

In CASIMIRO, the emotions experienced while interacting with an individual are stored in the memory associated to that individual. Actually, emotional memory is updated periodically with the mean values of arousal and valence experienced with that individual (a running average is used). As for sleep, when the position in the 2D space has been for a certain time in the neutral state arousal is lowered by a given amount (valence will be zero). Besides, sleep has an associated decay factor below 1, so that it tends to get farther the centre instead of closer. This way, the emotional state will eventually tend to neutral and, in time, to sleep. When the robot is asleep its neck stops working and the robot snores.

The Euclidean distance from the current position to the centre of the emotional space is used to send the Attention module a message to reduce the fixation in the current focus of attention. The larger the distance the larger the probability P that this influence makes the current FOA change. In particular, $P = \max(0, \min(d, R)/R - K)$, K being a constant to specify. The larger K, the less effect of the emotional state over attention.

Figure 7 shows two example interaction sessions with the robot. In the case of Figure 7 (left), one person enters the interaction area and takes an uncooperative attitude. Figure 6 shows the moments in which the subject was moving around and when he got too close to the robot. Figure 7 (right) shows another example interaction with a more cooperative subject. In this case the interaction develops with less disruptions and the robot gets to tell poems and jokes to the individual. The

Figure 6. Person moving around and getting closer to CASIMIRO

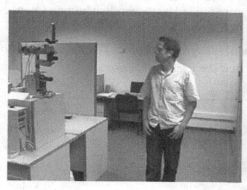
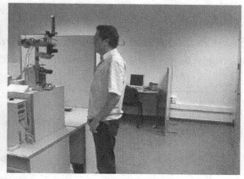

Figure 7. Valence values in the first (left) and second (right) example interactions

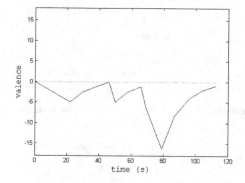
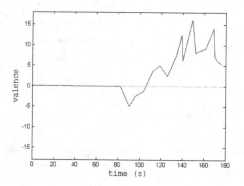

robot's emotional state is in this case more positive than in the previous interaction example.

In order to show the effect of person recognition (the robot uses histograms of clothing color for this), the robot was led to have short interactions with two individuals. Initially, individual A enters the interaction area, see Figure 8. The valence values show that he adopts an uncooperative attitude. The robot tries to ask him if he wants to hear poems, but the individual keeps moving around and the robot has to abort the questions. At time 55 individual A begins to leave the interaction area. The robot is then alone. At time 67 another individual enters the interaction area. This individual B is more cooperative and answers affirmatively to the two questions made by the robot. Individual B leaves the area at around time 126. Then, individual A comes back at time 145 and is recognized by the robot, which avoids greeting him again. Note that upon seeing individual A the robot emotional state turns very negative, for its previous interaction with him ended unsatisfactorily.

FUTURE TRENDS

Emotion modeling for robots and interactive machines is a hot topic within AI. The research devoted to the topic is expected to increase, not least because of the video games industry. Video game companies are now endowing their products with "AI cores" that aim at making the game experience more challenging and realistic (Funge, 2004; Millington, 1995). Computational costs are an added restriction in this case and simplicity becomes an important factor.

CONCLUSION

Our attempts at reproducing human intelligence are guided by research in human sciences such as

Figure 8. Example interaction that shows how the robot recognizes people. The figure shows on a time scale the valence values of the robot emotional state and the executed actions.

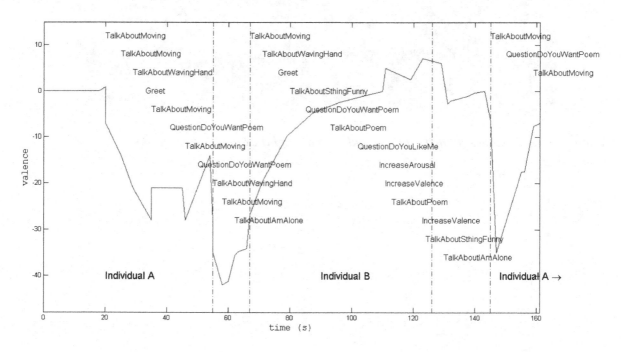

psychology and neurosciences. Now we know that emotions play an important role in the expression of genuine human intelligence. That is the reason why emotion modeling has become a major topic. This chapter has described an emotion model for the interactive robot CASIMIRO. The model is conceptually and computationally simple, yet it captures the basic features of emotions for a state-of-the-art interactive robot. Examples of interaction scenarios have been given that show that the model is appropriate.

NOTE

The work on CASIMIRO was awarded the PhD runner-up prize of the Spanish Association for Pattern Matching and Image Analysis (AERFAI). In August 2006 CASIMIRO was the *"Robot of the Week"* of EURON, the European Robotics Research Network.

REFERENCES

Bui, T.D., Heylen, D., & Poel, M. (2002). ParleE: An adaptive plan-based event appraisal model of emotions. In G. L. M. Jarke, J. Koehler (Eds.), *Procs. KI 2002: Advances in Artificial Intelligence.*

Carney, D., & Colvin, C. (2005). *The circumplex structure of emotive social behavior.* In preparation.

Damasio, A. (1994). *Descartes' Error: Emotion, Reason and the Human Brain.* Avon Books, New York.

Deniz, O. (2006). *An engineering approach to sociable robots.* Doctoral dissertation, Universidad de Las Palmas de Gran Canaria.

Deniz, O., Hernández, M., Lorenzo, J., & Castrillon, M. (2007). An engineering approach to socia-

ble robots. *Journal of Experimental & Theoretical Artificial Intelligence, 19*(4), 285-306.

Fong, T., Nourbakhsh, I., & Dautenhahn, K. (2003). A survey of socially interactive robots. *Robotics and Autonomous Systems, Special issue on Socially Interactive Robots, 42*(3-4), 143-166.

Funge, J. (2004). *Artificial intelligence for computer games: an introduction.* A K Peters.

Hernández, D., Deniz, O., Lorenzo, J., & Hernández, M. (2004). *BDIE: A BDI like architecture with emotional capabilities.* AAAI Spring Symposium, Stanford, CA.

Hudlicka, E., & Fellous, J.M. (2008). *The emotion Homepage.* Retrieved from, http://emotion.nsma.arizona.edu

Millington, I. (2005). *Artificial intelligence for games.* Morgan Kaufman.

Picard, R. (1997). *Affective computing.* Cambridge, MA: MIT Press.

Reilly, W. (1996). *Believable Social and Emotional Agents.* Technical Report CMU-CS-96-138, School of Computer Science, Carnegie Mellon University, Pittsburgh, PA, USA.

Russell, J. (1980). A circumplex model of affect. *Journal of Personality and Social Psychology, 39*(6), 1161–1178.

Sloman, A. (2001). Beyond shallow models of emotion. *Cognitive Processing, 2*(1), 177–198.

Tao, J., & Tan, T. (2005). *Affective Computing: A Review.* Affective Computing and Intelligent Interaction. LNCS 3784: 981–995, Springer.

KEY TERMS

Affective Computing: Computing that relates to, arises from, or deliberately influences emotion or other affective phenomena.

Arousal: In the context of emotion modeling, degree of excitement.

Emotion Decay: Emotions decay naturally over time unless they are re-stimulated.

Emotional State: An internal state of the robot that can reflect on its behavior and externally in the form of facial expressions, altered voice, etc.

Interactive or Sociable Robot: A robot with the main purpose of interacting or socializing with people.

Social Intelligence: Human intelligence is nowadays considered a blend of a number of "intelligences", rather than a single measurable capacity. One of them is the social intelligence, which refers to the ability to socialize with other people.

Valence: In the context of emotion modeling, the positive, desirable aspect of a given emotional state.

Chapter II
Automatic Detection of Emotion in Music:
Interaction with Emotionally Sensitive Machines

Cyril Laurier
Universitat Pompeu Fabra, Spain

Perfecto Herrera
Universitat Pompeu Fabra, Spain

ABSTRACT

Creating emotionally sensitive machines will significantly enhance the interaction between humans and machines. In this chapter we focus on enabling this ability for music. Music is extremely powerful to induce emotions. If machines can somehow apprehend emotions in music, it gives them a relevant competence to communicate with humans. In this chapter we review the theories of music and emotions. We detail different representations of musical emotions from the literature, together with related musical features. Then, we focus on techniques to detect the emotion in music from audio content. As a proof of concept, we detail a machine learning method to build such a system. We also review the current state of the art results, provide evaluations and give some insights into the possible applications and future trends of these techniques.

INTRODUCTION

Why do people enjoy music? One of the main factors is that music easily induces emotions and affects the listener. Can machines enjoy music as people do? Or, surely easier and less philosophically debatable, can we develop systems that are capable of detecting emotions in music and use this ability to improve human-machine interaction?

Stating that music and emotions have a close relationship is no revelation. One significant motivation of composers is to express their sentiments, performers to induce feelings, and listeners to feel emotions. There are also some findings that show a direct link between audio processing and emotion in the brain, which is not so clear for other sensory modalities. Moreover music has a noticeable social role and is ubiquitous in everyday life. To communicate with humans using musical emotions, machines should be able to detect and predict them. Enabling this ability will enhance the communication between the machine and the environment. First they can sense the acoustic scene with a microphone. The surrounding music can be understood in terms of emotions and the machine can react accordingly. The face of a robot can give an explicit feedback of the emotions it detects. Moreover robots with musical abilities can select, play and even compose music conveying targeted emotions. The technology we detail in the remainder of this chapter enables machines to detect emotions from raw audio material, which is directly extracted from the digital signal. In this chapter we expose the main findings about music and emotions, together with techniques in artificial intelligence and more explicitly in machine learning to create emotionally sensitive machines.

This chapter is structured in four parts. In the first section we comment on the relationship between emotion and music and review theories from different expertise. In section 2 we define the machine learning techniques that can be used to create emotion aware machines; we detail also the methodology and give evaluation results from state of the art research in this area. Then, in section 3, we develop some ideas around emotion-based music assistants. Finally, in the last part, we present some general observations and give future perspectives.

SECTION 1. MUSIC AND EMOTIONS: EMOTION IN MUSIC AND EMOTIONS FROM MUSIC

To study the relationship between music and emotion, we have to consider the literature from many fields. Indeed, relevant scientific publications about this topic can be found in psychology, sociology, neuroscience, cognitive science, biology, musicology, machine learning and philosophy. We focus here on works aiming to understand the emotional process in music, and to represent and model the emotional space. We also detail the main results regarding the pertinent musical features and how they can be used to describe and convey emotions.

Why Does Music Convey Emotion?

Emotion and expressive properties of musical elements have been studied since the time of ancient Greece (Juslin and Laukka, 2004). The fact that music induces emotions is evident for everyone. However we do not intuitively apprehend why. Emotions are mostly said to be complex and to involve a complicated combination of cognition, positive or negative feeling changes, appraisal, motivation, autonomic arousal, and bodily action tendency or change in action readiness.

One of the first things to clarify is the definition of an emotion and the difference between emotions and moods. The concept of emotion is not simple to define: "Everyone knows what an emotion is, until asked to give a definition" (Fehr and Russell, 1984, p. 464). It could be defined as an intense mental state arousing the nervous system and invoking physiological responses. According to Damasio (1994), emotions are a series of body state changes that are connected to mental images that have activated a given brain subsystem (e.g., the music processing subsystem). So emotions involve physiological reactions but also they are object-oriented and provoke a categorization of their object: "if the emotion is one of fear its object must be viewed as harmful" (Davies, 2001, p. 26). Emotions also induce an attitude towards the object. Moods could be considered as lasting emotional states. They are not object oriented and take into account quite general feelings. Moods and emotions can be very similar concepts in some cases, for instance happiness, sadness and anger can be seen as both moods and emotions. However some emotions can only be considered as transient, such as surprise.

Understanding how music conveys emotion is not trivial. Kivy (1989) gives two such hypotheses. The first might be a "hearing resemblance between the music and the natural expression of the emotion". Some musical cues can induce emotions because of their similarity to speech. One example is "anger" where the loudness and the spectral dissonance (derived from frequency ratios and harmonic coincidence in the sound spectrum and based on psychoacoustic tests) are two components we can find in both an angry voice and music. However it might not always be that simple. The second hypothesis Kivy gives is the "accumulated connotations a certain musical phenomena acquire in a culture". In that case, we learn in our culture which musical cues correspond to which feeling. Most probably, both hypotheses are valid. Frijda (1987, pp. 469) argues for a notion of emotions as action tendencies where "various emotions humans or animals can have - the various action readiness modes they may experience or show - depends upon what action programs, behavior systems, and activation or deactivation mechanisms the organism has at its disposal.". As pointed out by Nussbaum (2007), this correlates with results in neuroscience from scientists such as Damasio (1994).

Grewe et al. (2007) demonstrated that the intensity of the emotion induced by music could vary depending on personal experience and musical background. If a musician knows and has studied the piece for a performance, he/she is more likely to rate the intensity of the emotion higher. This is an auto-reinforcement by training. We

can also imagine that listening to a musical piece too many times can create the opposite behavior. Almost everyone has experienced the fact of being bored, or less and less sensitive to a musical piece they used to love. Besides, it is important to notice that emotions in music are not restricted to adults or musically trained people. The emotional processing of music starts at an early age. Four-months-old children have a preference for consonant (pleasant) over dissonant (unpleasant) music (Trainor, Tsang and Cheung, 2002). At five years old, they can distinguish between happy and sad music using the tempo (sad = slow, happy = fast), but at six, they use information from the mode (sad = minor, happy = major) such as adults do (Dalla Bella et al., 2001).

Studies in neuroscience, exploiting the current techniques of brain imaging also give a hint about the emotional processing of music, with some schemas of the brain functions involved (Koelsch et al., 2006). Gosselin et al. (2005) demonstrated that the amygdala, well established to have an important role in the recognition of fear, is determinant in the recognition of scary music. Blood and Zatorre (2001) revealed that music creating highly pleasurable experience like "shivers-down-the-spine" or "chills" activate regions in the brain involved in reward and motivation. It is worth noticing that these areas are also active in response to other euphoria-inducing stimuli like food, sex and drugs. Huron (2006) simply states that music making and listening are primarily motivated by pleasure and that the contrary is biologically implausible (p. 373). Meyer (1956) describes the importance of expectation as a tool for the composer to create emotions. This work has been continued and formalized as the ITPRA[1] theory by Huron (2006). One important way to control the pleasure in a musical piece is to play with this feature by delaying expected outcomes and fulfilling our expectation.

Additional research (Menon and Levitin, 2005) seems to have also found the physical connections between music and mood alteration by means of antidepressants: the latter act on the dopaminergic system which has one of its main centers in the so-called *nucleus accumbens*, a brain structure that also receives a dramatic degree of activation when listening to music. These results are coherent with Lazarus (1991), when he argues that emotions are evolutionary adaptations, to evoke behaviors that improve chances for survival and procreation, and with Tomkins' (1980) view that emotions can be understood as "motivational amplifiers". It links music with survival related stimuli. Often, damages to emotional controls limiting the normal functionability of the emotional behavior are disastrous for people (Damasio, 1994). Moreover people who did not develop social emotions seem incapable of appreciating music (Sacks and Freeman, 1994). However, this evolutionary adaptation theory can be balanced by the fact that most emotional responses to music are neither used to achieve goals, nor practically related to survival issues. This argument is used by researchers who assume that music cannot induce basic survival emotions, but more "music-specific emotions" (Scherer and Zentner, 2001, p. 381). Nonetheless, other notable researchers affirm about music that it is "remarkable that any medium could so readily evoke all the basic emotions of our brain" (Panksepp and Bernatzky, 2002). This is one of the multiple contradictions we can observe in current research on music and emotions. As pointed out by Juslin and Västfjäll (2008), the literature presents a confusing picture with conflicting views. Nevertheless there is no doubt that music induces emotion because of the related context. It evokes emotions from past events because it is associated in our memory to emotional events.

When talking about emotion and music, one important distinction to make is the difference between induced and perceived emotions (Juslin and Laukka, 2004). That is what we define as "emotion in music" and "emotion from music". The former represents the intended emotion and the latter the emotion felt while listening to a musical piece. A typical example of differentiation between both is the expression of anger. When someone is angry, people might perceive anger but feel scared or defensive. The induced emotion is radically different from the perceived one. Different factors can influence both types, for instance the symbolic aspect or the social context of a song will influence more the induced emotion (like for a national anthem). As noticed by Bigand et al. (2005) both aspects are not strictly independent and there will always be an influence of the induced emotion on someone asked to judge the perceived one. Nevertheless it should be observed that people tend to agree more on the perceived emotion than on the induced emotion (Juslin and Laukka, 2004).

It is worth noticing that a relevant part of the emotion in songs comes from the lyrics. Psychological studies have shown that part of the semantic information of songs resides exclusively in the lyrics (Besson et al., 1998). This means that lyrics can contain relevant information to express emotions that is not included in the audio. Indeed, Juslin and Laukka (2004) reported that 29% people mentioned the lyrics as a factor of how music expresses emotions.

Although there is an increase in research about the causal links between music and emotion, there still remain many open questions (Patel, 2007). In addition to the biological substrate, there are important links related to the musical features that are present or absent when perceiving or feeling a given music-related emotion. In section 2, we give some results about these musical features, but first we will discuss the different representations of musical emotions that arise from psychological studies.

Emotional Representations

One main issue in making machines emotionally sensitive is to find models of human representation of emotion in music. From the literature in music psychology, there exist two main paradigms to represent emotions. This distinction is quite general, it is not only about musical emotions, but studies were designed specifically to test and refine these models for music. The first one is the categorical representation that distinguishes among several emotion classes. The other one is the dimensional representation defining an emotional space. We detail here the main theories using both approaches and we make explicit the special case of musically-related emotional representations.

Categorical Representation

The categorical representation aims to divide emotions in categories, where each emotion is labeled with one or several adjectives. The most canonical model is the concept of basic emotions where several distinct categories are the basis of all possible emotions. This concept is illustrated by Ekman's basic emotion theory distinguishing between anger, fear, sadness, happiness and disgust (Ekman, 1992). Nevertheless other categorical approaches are possible. Indeed a

lot of psychologists propose that their emotion adjective set is applicable to music. One of the most relevant works in this domain is the study by Hevner (1936) and her adjective circle shown in Figure 1. Hevner's adjective list is composed of 67 words arranged into eight clusters. From this study each cluster includes adjectives that have a close relationship. This similarity between words of the same cluster enables one to work at the cluster level reducing the taxonomy to eight categories. Farnsworth (1954) modified Hevner's list into ten clusters. These categories were defined by conducting listening tests and subjective answers. Moreover, we should note that most of these studies were conducted using classical music from the western culture and mainly of the baroque and romantic periods. We can imagine that the emotions evoked by popular music are different. A problem of the categorical approach is that classifying a musical piece into one or several categories is rather difficult sometimes, as pointed out by Hevner (1936). For instance in one of her studies, based on a musical piece called "Reflections on the water" by Debussy was rated

Figure 1. Adjectives and clusters (adapted from Hevner, 1936)

to belong to all the clusters unless a continuous measure was considered. Although it was argued that a word list couldn't describe the variety of possible emotions in music, using a reduced set helps to achieve an agreement between people (even if it gives less meaning) and offers the possibility for automatic systems to model the general consensus of musical pieces.

Dimensional Representation

In a dimensional representation, the emotions are classified along axes. Most of the proposed representations in the literature are inspired by the Russell (1980) "circumplex model of affect", using a two-dimensional space spanned by arousal (activity, excitation of the emotion) and valence (positivity or negativity of the emotion). In Figure 2, we represent this bipolar model with the different adjectives placed in this emotional space. In this two-dimensional space, a point at the upper-right corner has high valence and arousal, which means happy with a high activity such as "excited". Opposite to this one, the lower-left part is negative with low activity like "bored" or "depressed". Several researchers such as Thayer (1989) applied this dimensional approach and developed the idea of an energy-stress model. Other studies propose other dimensional representations. However they all somehow relate to the models previously presented, as in the case of Schubert's (1999) two-dimensional emotion space (called 2DES), with valence on the x-axis and arousal on the y-axis with a mapping of adjectives from different psychological references. The main advantage of representing emotion in a dimensional form is that any emotion can then be mapped in that space. It allows a model where any emotion can be represented, within the limitation of these dimensions. One common criticism of this approach is that very different emotions in terms of semantic meaning (but also in terms of psychological and cognitive mechanisms involved) can be close in the emotional space. For instance, looking at the "circumplex model of affect" in Figure 2, we observe that the distance between "angry" and "afraid" is small although these two emotions are quite different.

Figure 2. "Circumplex model of affect" (adapted from Russel, 1980)

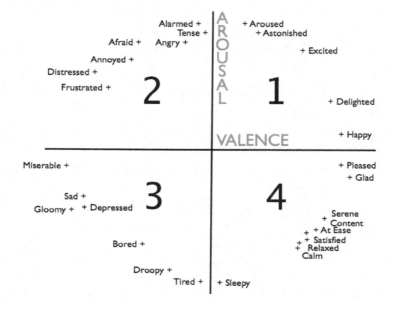

Nevertheless, if both categorical and dimensional approaches are criticized and not perfect, both are used and can be considered as valid, as partial evidence for and against each one can be found in the available experimental literature.

Musical Features and Emotion

Several studies investigated musical features and their relations to particular emotions. However most of the available research is centered on the western musical culture and mainly from classical music. Note that both composers and performers use these musical features. In table 1, we report the main mapping between musical features and emotion categories found in the literature (Juslin and Laukka, 2004). Each independent feature is probably not sufficient to conclude about one emotion; on the contrary this may require a rich set of musical descriptors. It is interesting to notice

Table 1. The most frequent musical features mapped with the emotion categories based on Juslin and Laukka (2004). An asterisk (*) means that some information can be extracted from polyphonic audio content; two asterisks (**) means that it can be extracted only from monophonic audio content (one instrument), in both cases using state-of-the-art technology. In parenthesis is the quadrant number in Russell's dimensional space (see Figure 1).

Musical Features	Happiness (1)	Sadness (3)	Anger (2)	Fear (2)	Tenderness (4)
Tempo*	Fast, small variability	Slow	Fast, small variability	Fast, large variability	Slow
Mode*	Major	Minor	Minor	Minor	Major
Harmony*	simple and consonant	dissonant	atonality, dissonant	dissonant	consonant
Loudness*	medium-high, small variability	low, moderate variability	high, small variability	low, large level variability, rapid changes	medium-low, small variability
Pitch**	high, much variability, wide range, ascending	low, narrow range, descending	high, small variability, ascending	high, ascending, wide range, large contrasts	low, fairly narrow range
Intonation**	rising	flat, falling	accent on tonally unstable notes	-	-
Singer's formant**	raised	lowered	raised	-	lowered
Intervals**	perfect 4th and 5th	small (minor 2nd)	major 7th and augmented 4th	-	-
Articulation**	staccato, large variability	legato, small variability	staccato, moderate variability	staccato, large variability	legato, small variability
Rhythm*	smooth and fluent	ritardando	complex, sudden changes, accelerando	jerky	-
Timbre*	bright	dull	sharp	soft	soft
Tone attacks**	fast	slow	fast	soft	slow
Timing variability*	small	large (rubato)	small	very large	moderate
Vibrato**	medium-fast rate, medium extent	slow, small extent	medium-fast rate, large extent	fast rate, small extent	medium fast, small extent
Contrast between long and short notes**	sharp	soft	sharp	-	soft
Micro-structure*	regularities	irregularities	irregularities	irregularities	regularities
Others		pauses	spectral noise	pauses	accents on tonally stable notes

that these features correlate with research made on speech by Scherer (1991, p. 206). Of course the comparison is limited to only a small set of attributes useful for speech like the pitch, the loudness and the tempo.

From the list shown in Table 1, we observe that some features can be automatically extracted from polyphonic audio content (like commercial CD tracks or mp3 files) with existing technology[2]. These features are marked with an asterisk. For instance the tempo can be estimated by locating the beats. Of course it would work better on music with evident tempo and prominent percussion on beats (rock or techno for example). The results are less reliable for music with a smooth and subtle rhythm (some classical music, for instance). From audio content the reliability of these features is not always optimum but still it makes sense to use them, as they are informative. The key and the mode can also be extracted with a satisfying correctness (Gómez, 2006) by analyzing frequency distributions and comparing with tonal profiles. Other attributes are more difficult to extract from a complex mix of instruments and would be reliable only on monophonic tracks (one instrument). They are marked with two asterisks in Table 1. For example the vibrato or the singer formant changes can be detected if we work on audio information containing just the singer's voice, but it becomes too complex on a mix containing all the instruments. From these results, can we seriously think about automatically predicting the emotion from music? Can machines have an emotional understanding close to ours? Depending on the information an automatic system can get from the environment the answer may vary. It is clear that an audio signal taken from a microphone and a musical score give very different information. In the recent years, research in machine learning and signal processing has allowed one to extract relevant and robust high-level musical features with techniques we will detail in the next section.

SECTION 2. MUSIC INFORMATION RETRIEVAL: BUILDING AUTOMATIC DETECTORS OF MUSIC EMOTIONS

Several studies have demonstrated that musical emotions are not too subjective or too variable to deserve a mathematical modeling approach (Bigand et al., 2005; Juslin and Laukka, 2004; Krumhansl, 1997; Peretz, Gagnon and Bouchard, 1998). Indeed, within a common culture, the emotional responses to music can be highly consistent within and between listeners, but also accurate, quite immediate and precocious (Vieillard et al., 2008). This stated, it opens the door to reproduce this consistent behavior with machines.

In this section we give a technical explanation of how to build a system to automatically detect musical emotions from audio. To achieve this goal, we use machine-learning techniques and more specifically supervised learning methods. The overall idea of supervised learning is to learn by example. It requires that the system is presented with enough examples of a given emotional category. We focus here on the categorical representation because it seems easier for people to categorize using simple emotions rather than to give a value for each dimension (arousal, valence). An important part of the work is to gather a substantial amount of reliably labeled examples (called ground truth). Then we extract acoustical and musical information (called features) from the audio of each example file, and finally we learn the mapping between the features and the labels (emotions in our case). This mapping is validated using cross-validation[3] methods or an independent test database. These methods ensure that our system can build general models of the emotional classes (i.e., that the model is not overfitting to the training data). Using this procedure, along with standard automatic classifiers, we can build a system able to reliably and consistently predict the emotion in music to a certain extent.

This type of methodology is part of the research conducted by the Music Information Retrieval

(MIR) community. The mostly studied problem in this field is genre classification (Tzanetakis and Cook, 2002; Guaus and Herrera, 2006). However recent trends focus on emotion or mood detection. We review and compare the existing systems to our approach at the end of this section.

If we can work on a symbolic representation (like the musical score, a MIDI file or other), we can use accurate representations of the melody, chords, rhythm and other musical dimensions. It allows generating new versions of the music modifying the emotional content in a more flexible and efficient way than from audio content. Indeed one can operate directly on the relevant musical aspects like Fridberg, Bresin and Sundberg (2006). In our system, we want to deal directly with the audio signal, as we cannot always have access to symbolic information. On one hand we loose the precision in notes and measure mentioned before but on the other we can process the vast

amount of musical data available in a digital audio format. Although it seems more complicated, it corresponds to a realistic usage. The machine can then analyze any kind of music from audio files but also from the sonic environment using a microphone.

Methodology

To detect emotions in music, we are using statistical classification. Classification algorithms need a large amount of labeled examples, but also a good and rich musical description of each example, in order to learn how to classify it properly. The information gathered from the examples are numerical data called features (or descriptors). They are computed directly from the audio signal and can describe different aspects like for instance timbre, rhythm or tonality[4]. With this information and enough realistic data, the classifier can learn

Figure 3. Schema of the supervised learning approach. From the manually annotated ground truth, features are extracted to train a classifier. This trained system can then annotate automatically any new music collection.

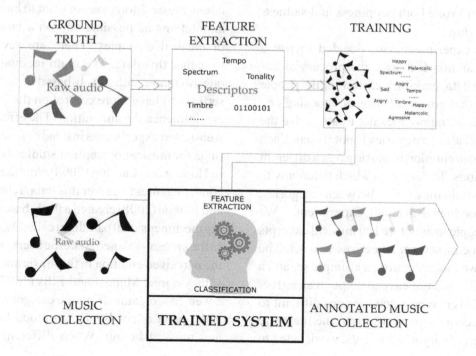

from simple rules to complex functions to predict the emotional label of any new music. We specify here each step of this approach and summarize it in Figure 3.

Ground Truth

The first step is to create the database of examples. In the case of emotion, the representation chosen will determine the rest of the process. From music and emotion theories, and from psychological studies mentioned in section 1, we can understand the pros and cons of each representation for this purpose. In the MIR field, the representation most often chosen is the categorical approach based on basic emotion theories. Each emotion is considered as independent from the others and all existing emotions would be a combination of these basic emotions. In that case the categories are considered mutually exclusive. This categorization fits particularly well in the automatic classification way of thinking, were we have several classes and one element can belong to only one class. Other studies consider this approach too restrictive as emotions are more complex and because one piece of music can evoke both happiness and sadness at the same time.

For our experiments, we decided to use a categorical approach to ease the process of annotating the data, making it clearer for the people involved in that process. However choosing one type of representation does not totally solve the problem. Deciding categories is not trivial. Each theory of basic emotion in music gives a different set of emotions. To decide on which taxonomy to use, and to study the overlap between categories, we have conducted a small experiment. We asked 16 people to annotate 100 musical excerpts choosing one or several adjectives in a set. The results showed that already on a simple set and a few people, it was not easy to come to an agreement. Moreover some categories are difficult to take into account separately. From the literature and our preliminary experiments, we decided to use a simple approach based on emotion categories well distinguished by people (Laurier and Herrera, 2007). This allows one to have the best agreement between people when labeling, and to make the system as general as possible. We also decided to have a binary approach. Each category is considered to be boolean, for instance a song is "happy" or "not happy". With this approach we have multiple binary classifiers, one for each emotion (instead of a single multi-class classifier). This avoids the strict separation of so-called basic emotions as if they would be mutually exclusive. In fact, this approach is closer to the theory considering that each emotion can be a combination of basic emotions. Therefore we consider that we have an expert for each basic emotion which will estimate the amount of this particular emotion in a given music file. This allows for a more detailed description using an ensemble of multiple boolean experts.

Once we have chosen a proper representation, we need to build the database of examples. In our case the examples are musical pieces labeled with emotions. This step is very time consuming, because people have to listen and manually annotate music. Moreover we want to have as many annotations as possible and on a large amount of musical examples. There are several ways to gather this data. The main method used is a questionnaire, either web-based or in laboratory settings to have more control on the factors that can influence the annotation. The effect of using web-based experiments instead of laboratory settings for musical perception studies is discussed in Honing and Ladinig (2008). Another way is to conduct games to gather this data. Kim, Schmidt and Emelle (2008) created a flash-based game using the dimensional paradigm called *MoodSwings*. In the arousal-valence plane the users are marking the perceived emotion in the music and get points if they agree. Mandel and Ellis (2007) invented a web-based game using the category paradigm. This game is not limited to mood but open to any music labeling. When different users use the same tag to define a musical piece, they get points. These online games are useful to gather much more data than asking people to annotate with no special motivation.

In all cases, several issues have to be addressed. Many different factors can have an impact on the annotation reliability. On one hand, in laboratory settings it is easier to control these factors than when using web-based interfaces. On the other hand in a laboratory environment one might not react as if he was in everyday conditions. Beyond these considerations, in the case of emotion in music, several factors also have to be controlled. Indeed, the emotion in the music depends on many different elements, such as the cultural background, the social context, the lyrics, the temporal evolution of the music, or the personal preferences. The cultural background could mean the experience one has with music. Considering mainstream popular music from the western culture, we can limit the cultural impact so that it would work for many people (but maybe not with people not exposed to western popular music). Information about the social context is by definition not included in the music itself but relies on the context of the music. This is particularly difficult to control as one might have a very personal relationship with one musical piece. That is also one reason to focus our system on detecting emotions in the music and not from the music. Indeed the induced emotion can be quite different from the one perceived, especially because of the social context or the personal history of the listener with that particular music. Moreover, in the annotation process, we can limit this influence by checking if the annotator knows the music. Finally, as to the effect of lyrics, one possibility is to use instrumental music; we can also reduce the song to a short excerpt so that the whole meaning of the lyrics can not influence the annotation process. Although all these factors are important in the way a ground truth is constructed, they are almost never mentioned in the current MIR literature.

In our case, we have built a ground truth of popular music, with four categories: "happy", "sad", "angry" and "relaxed". We have chosen these emotions because they are related to basic emotions from psychological theories and also because they cover the four parts of the 2D valence/arousal representation. But as we also do not want to restrict to exclusive categories, we consider the problem as a binary classification for each term. One song can be "happy" or "not happy", but also independently "angry" or "not angry" and so on.

Our collection is made of popular music preselected from a large online community (Last. fm[5]), which is active in associating labels (tags) with the music they listen to. We looked for the songs mostly tagged with our categories and synonyms and we asked a small group of listeners in our lab to validate this selection. We included this manual confirmation in order to exclude songs that could have been wrongly tagged, to express something else, or because of a "following the majority" type of effect. The annotators were asked to listen to 30 seconds of the songs, first to avoid as much as possible changes in the emotion, then to reduce the influence of the lyrics and finally to speed up the annotation process. In total 17 different evaluators participated and the final database is composed of 1000 songs divided between 4 categories of interest plus their complementary categories ("not happy", "not sad", "not angry" and "not relaxed").

Feature Extraction

If early MIR systems were able to process only symbolic data like MIDI (symbolic musical standard, which provides a score-like music representation), the evolution of Digital Signal Processing (DSP) techniques have provided new tools to extract audio features. DSP techniques combined with perceptual and musical knowledge allow us to compute descriptors about timbre, rhythm, harmony, loudness or pitch.

An audio file or stream is digitally represented as a waveform, basically a succession of values between -1 and 1 with a rate of several thousand values per second. Typically (as with the Compact Disc format) we consider 44100 values per second for psychoacoustic reasons. In the last decade MIR researchers have been very active in extracting meaningful information from this raw data. Several levels of abstraction can be addressed, from low level (close to the signal) to high level (semantic level, like musical concepts). Taking advantage of expertise in signal processing, psychoacoustic, musicology, statistics, machine learning and information retrieval many descriptors have been proposed (Herrera et al., 2005; Gouyon et al., 2008 pp. 83-160) Each descriptor can be computed as a series of values for a time window and summarized for the entire music file using statistical measures like the mean or the variance. It can also be directly computed as a global value corresponding to a song (like the estimation of the key and mode, e.g. C major, for instance).

Some widely used descriptors are the Mel-Frequency Cepstral Coefficients (MFCCs) (Logan, 2000), because they are very informative about the timbre of the acoustic signal. This type of spectral descriptor is useful to classify music by genre and many other tasks. Another example is the Harmonic Pitch Class Profiles (HPCP) from Gómez (2006) or chroma features for tonality. They describe how the energy in the audio is spread over the notes. It allows estimations of the chord, the key and, with an appropriate algorithm they can be used to detect different versions of the same song (Serrà et al., 2008).

For the mood detection, many features are relevant. It is important to keep in mind that we use these techniques to extract information of a different kind: timbral (for instance MFCCs, spectral centroid), rhythmic (for example tempo), tonal (like HPCP) and temporal descriptors. Among others we have also an estimation of the dissonance, the mode, the onset rate and the loudness. Not all

the musical features detailed previously in section 1 can be accurately retrieved from audio content only. Nevertheless, these audio descriptors studied and developed by MIR researchers are sufficient to model many aspects of music. Other kinds of information can be gathered, such as text from the lyrics (we will present some results about this later), reviews, blogs or symbolic musical data like the score or a MIDI file. However we restrict our starting point to the raw audio data.

Classification

Statistical classification algorithms use the features extracted from examples and try to derive a mathematical or predictive relationship between each of them and its label (an emotion in our case). In a supervised learning approach, the descriptors from each example of the database are used to train a classifier that learns a statistical mapping and models the problem. For instance it may automatically learn from many examples that happy music is more likely to be in a major mode and sad in a minor mode.

To achieve the classification task, we use well-known methods for statistical classification like k-Nearest-Neighbors (k-NN) or Support Vector Machines (SVM). Most of the standard algorithms are included in the WEKA software (Witten and Frank, 1999), no particular classifier is to be preferred by default. Several approaches should to be tested. However in machine learning in general and in music information retrieval in particular, SVM seem to be one of the best options. They are known to be efficient, to perform relatively well and to be reliable in many cases. In the emotion classification literature, the main differences are in the representation chosen, the methodology to get a ground truth and to evaluate the results. The classification stage is largely standardized using SVM and sometimes other classifiers, but with no dramatic improvement in the classification results.

Table 2. Clusters of adjectives used for the MIREX 2007 mood evaluation task and mean accuracy of our classifier.

Clusters	Mood Adjectives	Accuracy in percentage
Cluster 1	passionate, rousing, confident, boisterous, rowdy	45.8 %
Cluster 2	rollicking, cheerful, fun, sweet, amiable/good natured	50.0 %
Cluster 3	literate, poignant, wistful, bittersweet, autumnal, brooding	82.5 %
Cluster 4	humorous, silly, campy, quirky, whimsical, witty, wry	53.3 %
Cluster 5	aggressive, fiery, tense/anxious, intense, volatile, visceral	70.8 %

Results

In this part we present evaluation results from different experiments and relevant empirical studies found in the literature. If predicting the emotion from audio is feasible, it is quite arduous to compare all the different approaches because they use different representations, databases and evaluation schemas. The Music Information Retrieval Evaluation eXchange (MIREX) attempts to make this comparison possible (Downie, 2006). The MIREX provides evaluation frameworks and metrics with which researchers could scientifically compare their approaches and algorithms. In 2007 a first evaluation in Audio Music Mood Classification was organized. The representation chosen for this contest was a categorical approach with mood clusters, where the clusters were mutually exclusive (one instance could only belong to one mood cluster). There were five categories, or mood clusters shown in table 2 and the best results achieved were around 60% of accuracy (Laurier and Herrera, 2007). It means that the best systems were able to classify correctly 60 % of the music given to test. This percentage is a mean made using a 3-fold cross-validation. Almost all the systems submitted to this evaluation were using SVM to classify and different sets of descriptors (Hu et al., 2008).

In the literature other results are available and can be of interest, especially if the approach is different. Basically almost every scientific contribution differs in at least one key aspect. Several consider the category representation based on basic emotions (Laurier and Herrera, 2007; Sordo, Laurier and Celma, 2007; Shi et al., 2006; Lu, Liu and Zhang, 2006), while others treat the categories in a multi-labeling approach like Wieczorkowska et al. (2005). The basic emotion approach gives simple but relatively satisfying results with accuracies around 80-90% depending on the data and the number of categories. The lower accuracies for the MIREX approach mentioned before might be due to an overlap in the concepts included in the class labels (Hu et al., 2008). It could also be due to a stricter evaluation on more data than the other mentioned works. The latter (multi-labeling) suffer from a difficult evaluation in general, as the annotated data needed should be much larger. Indeed if we want to use precision and recall[6] in an appropriate way we need to annotate all the data we evaluate with all categories (presence or absence), otherwise we might consider wrong results that are actually correct. There are also similar approaches to ours, such as the work by Li and Ogigara (2003), where they extracted timbre, pitch and rhythm features and trained Support Vector Machines. They used 13 categories, 11 from Farnsworth (1954) and 2 additional ones. However the results were not satisfying (it was one of the very first studies of mood classification), with low precision (around 0.32) and recall (around 0.54). This might be due to the small dataset labeled by only one person, and to the large adjective set. Another similar work should be mentioned: Skowronek et al. (2007) used spectral, tempo rhythm, tonal and percussive detection features together with a quadratic discriminant analysis to model emotions. He achieved a mood predictor with 12 categories considered binary with an average accuracy around 85%.

Other studies concentrated on the dimensional representation. Lu, Liu and Zhang (2006) used Thayer's (1996) model based on the energy and stress dimensions and modeled the four parts of the space: contentment, depression, exuberance and anxious. They modeled the different parts of the space using Gaussian Mixture Models. The system was trained with 800 excerpts of classical music and the system achieved around 85% accuracy (trained with three fourths and tested on the remaining fourth of the data). Although it was based on a dimensional system, the prediction was made on the four quadrants as exclusive categories. However another relevant study (Yang et al., 2008a) used Thayer's arousal-valence emotion plane, but with a regression approach, to model each of the two dimensions. They used mainly spectral and tonal descriptors together with loudness features. With these tools, they modeled arousal and valence using annotated data and regression functions (Support Vector Regression). The overall results were very encouraging and demonstrated that a dimensional approach is also feasible (see figure 4 for an application of this research).

Table 3. Accuracy of our classifiers on the different categories. Each category implies a binary decision (for instance "angry" vs. "not angry"). This was made using SVM and 10 runs of 10-fold cross-validation.

Category	Accuracy in percentage (standard deviation)
Angry	98.1 % (3.8)
Happy	81.5 % (11.5)
Sad	87.7 % (11.0)
Relaxed	91.4 % (7.3)

In another work worth to be mentioned here, Mandel, Poliner and Ellis (2006) designed a system using MFCCs and SVM. The interesting aspect of this work is the application of an active learning approach. The system learns according to the feedback given by the user. Moreover the algorithm chooses the examples to be labeled in a smart manner, hence reducing the amount of data needed to build a model achieving a similar accuracy with a standard method.

Our ground truth is based on songs already tagged by hundreds of people (Last.fm users). We added a manual validation step to ensure the quality and reliability of our data. The evaluation was conducted on the 1000 annotated examples mentioned previously. We extracted audio features and performed classification with a SVM. Four categories were considered: "happy", "sad", "relaxed" and "angry", each one approached as a binary problem. Either an instance belongs to the category or not. It means that each category is a boolean problem with a random baseline of 50 % of accuracy (i.e., a classifier just based on random choice between both categories would give an average accuracy of 50%). In table 3, we report the results of our evaluation using SVM and 10-fold cross-validation. The evaluation data were obtained after 10 runs of the same experimental setup (i.e., a random seed changed the allocation of files to folds for each run).

The performances we obtained using audio-based classifiers are quite satisfying and even exceptional when looking at the "angry" category with 98 %. It is difficult to directly compare this with the results from the MIREX evaluation, because we use here different categories and each one is considered binary. All four categories reached accuracies above 80%, and two categories ("angry" and "relaxed") above 90%. Even though these results can seem surprisingly high, this is coherent with similar studies (Skowronek et al., 2007). Moreover as we deal with binary comparisons on a balanced dataset, the random baseline is 50%. Also, the examples are selected

Table 4. Accuracy of a multimodal system using audio and lyrics

Category	Accuracy in percentage (standard deviation)	Difference adding lyrics information to audio
Angry	99.1 % (2.2)	+ 1 %
Happy	86.8 % (10.6)	+ 5.3 %
Sad	92.8 % (8.7)	+ 5.1 %
Relaxed	91.7 % (7.1)	+ 0.3 %

and validated only when they clearly belong to the category or its complementary. This can bias the database towards very clear differences. We should also notice that these models might work only for popular music (there was no classical music in our database), so it can generalize only to a certain extent. We conducted an experiment using the lyric information and combined the two classifiers: one for audio and one for lyrics. For the lyrics we used a text information retrieval method to detect the words that discriminate best between categories (Laurier, Grivolla and Herrera, 2008). We obtained the results presented in Table 4.

Results presented in table 4 show that lyrics contribute positively in correctly classifying emotions, especially for the "happy" and "sad" categories. It may be because lyrics are more informative about the valence. But we should also notice that the highest improvement occurs when there was more room for improvement. In a nutshell, detecting emotion in music is feasible if we consider simple categories or dimensions. The available results are encouraging continuing along this line and perhaps addressing more complex representations and models of emotions.

Conclusions

Even if we can predict some aspects of the emotion in a musical piece, the level of analysis can be made more precise. In addition, there are some important aspects that should be taken into account like the effect of the singer's voice, which theoretically contains much emotional information that is not considered by the existing techniques. Moreover the degree of emotional extent is limited to simple categories or to a few dimensions. Finally, we do not examine the time development of the emotions but we average musical features over the entire piece, which is certainly a simplification of the rich emotional tapestry that certain musical pieces can weave. Even though our initial results have been encouraging, there is room for many improvements. As explained previously the current state-of-the-art in automatic detection is quite limited to a simplistic view. Some effort should be made towards designing systems with a better music understanding and to allow a process of user modeling. Currently we average the perceived emotion among people to have a general prediction and the predictive models are "universal" (i.e., the same for all the users), but we should also seek to yield predictions at the user level. This would make possible the development of personal music assistants.

SECTION 3. FROM MUSIC INFORMATION RETRIEVAL TO PERSONALIZED EMOTION-BASED MUSIC ASSISTANTS

People voluntary use music as a mood regulator, trying to induce emotional reactions (Sloboda, 1999). For instance, after heartbreak or sad event, someone may prefer to listen to sad songs either to give some solemnity to this moment or to find solace and consolation (Sacks, 2007). On the contrary one may want to feel better by playing happy songs. Music can be employed to emphasize the current mood or to decrease the intensity of certain emotions (Levitin, 2007). Someone feeling nervous could relax by listening to calm music. There is also evidence that experiencing musical emotions leads to physiological and cognitive changes. People can intentionally play with this phenomenon to influence their own state but also to communicate to others persons. A typical example would be a teenager listening to loud heavy metal or hardcore techno music (or any aggressive alternative) to express his anger and rebellion against his parents. It might make less sense to listen to this music if his parents are not around to receive the message (North, Hargreaves and O'Neill, 2000).

Nowadays personal electronic devices are ubiquitous. Almost everyone has at least a cellphone or a music player and now these kinds of mobile devices have huge capabilities. They can already play more music that one has time to listen to, they can store hours of video and thousand of pictures, they are capable of taking pictures and can be used as a notebook and agenda. They enable one to trace listening habits, to geographically locate the place where users are, to detect subtle movements with accelerometers, and soon

Figure 4. Mr. Emo (Yang et al., 2008b), reprinted with the permission of the authors

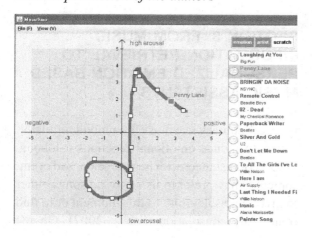

they could use all this information and additional physiological data to contextualize any listening experience.

The aim of an emotion-based music assistant would be to exploit these types of devices and the techniques mentioned in the previous section to automatically and intelligently recommend musical pieces. Based on one's feeling or a targeted mood, the machine could choose the appropriate music. MIR techniques help to extract information from musical content and in our case they can automatically detect emotions from audio content. The technical issues have been explained previously in section 2. Basically learning from examples, an automatic system is able to retrieve songs with the similar mood or emotion in a large collection. It means that this trained system is able to detect if a song is sad or happy and can even estimate its degree of happiness.

Possible applications of this technology are numerous[7]. For instance, a device can play music according to one's mood and make him feel better (or intentionally worse). By manually selecting the current mood or a targeted one, the machine can choose or even create music accordingly. Many different factors are important to detect the emotion induced by music, but in our case, although we can grasp social data from the user, we mostly concentrate on the audio level. Even though is does not cover all the processes it is already enough to use it in many applications. The system can provide the music corresponding to one's demand in terms of mood. Skowronek et al. (2007), or Laurier and Herrera (2008) demonstrated prototypes that can extract the emotion from the audio content to visualize the prediction of the automatic classifiers, and the "intensity" of the predicted category. For instance in *Mood Cloud*, one can see the estimated amount of happiness or sadness of a song evolving while it is being played (see Figure 5).

This information can be directly used to provide to the listener songs containing the targeted emotion. Moreover using the probability of each

Figure 5. Mood cloud interface (Laurier and Herrera, 2008)

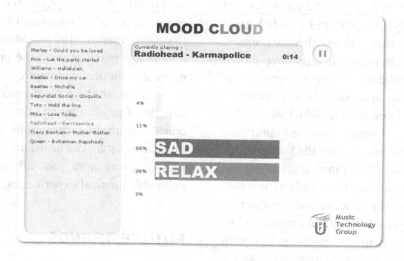

emotion given by the automatic classifier, we can estimate how clearly an emotion is present in the music. This also allows defining mood trajectories by practically creating musical playlists. For instance one can select to start with relaxing music and progressively move to happy music (see Figure 4). This can also be used to produce music or to help a composer in his artistic work. An example would be a DJ picking out music to influence the emotional level of people in the audience. In an experiment, Casacuberta (2004) have created a virtual DJ called *DJ el Niño* that was playing music according to the emotion contained in the musical loops. This process could be automated and adapted depending on the audience reaction, which could be sensed using electronic devices. If such a system can be employed at a personal level to browse and find music by emotion, this information can also be exploited in a professional environment for selecting soundtracks or for context-based adaptive music selection in video games. Plenty of applications are possible, as it would clearly ease the tedious process of manually choosing each musical piece. Advertisers can also take advantage of this technology. They use emotional content widely to associate feelings with a product or a message. Indeed, the effect on the customer has been demonstrated and people tend to have more positive evaluations of advertisements when exposed to happy music (North and Hargreaves, 1997). In general and for every user, the selection of music could be simplified using an intelligent assistant that knows the sensitivity of the user. It would make possible a more dynamic interaction where music could be chosen not by its name but with reference to another musical piece according to one's point of view. For instance if someone particularly likes one song or album for the emotion it contains, he can ask the system for something similar. This can be called the "more like this" feature and in that perspective it would be tuned and biased to fit to the needs of the user.

More interaction with human feelings can be achieved if the system can sense the emotional state by physiological features, like skin conductivity response, heart rate or blood pressure. Several studies have shown a correlation between these and other measurements and the emotion triggered (Grewe et al., 2007). Then the system would match the music and try to help regulate the emotional state. More complex techniques and sensors could help to detect stronger or subtle responses like chills, shivers down the spine, tears or goose bumps elicited by the music.

At this point, other applications become obvious. If such a system can provoke emotions and so change the physiological and psychological states, one step further is to use this for therapy. Scientific findings in music therapy have shown that it could help patients with psycho-physiological problems. Some analysis tools could also be developed like in Luck et al. (2006). Information on how a subject can detect emotions compared to an automatic system can give the therapist additional information. One main application can be music recommendation for a medical purpose. This would consist of providing music according to the emotional sensibility of the subject and its needs. Depression treatment can be paired with listening to music that triggers positive emotions. As human memory is of an associative kind, the emotional links of music can also trigger or recover personal experiences and skills that have apparently been missed or forgotten as a consequence of strokes and other brain injuries (Sacks, 2007). Of course, any emotion-based assistant like the one we aim to achieve has to be studied deeply in a medical context to provide a substantial help to therapists. Using "positive" emotions in music can help to achieve tasks with a higher rate of success. Being exposed to "positive" music rather than "negative" music improves psychomotor abilities like the writing speed (Pignatiello, Camp and Rasar, 1986) or the count time (Clark and Teasdale, 1985), but also the motivation to participate in social activities (Wood et al., 1990), or some information processing such as the time to produce associations to words (Kenealy, 1988). In any case, defining what is positive music is a debatable issue.

An emotion-based assistant can help in the context of therapy such as described by Bonny (2002). She developed a method called Guided Imagery and Music (GIM), where music takes an important part in the therapy process. She considers music as a "co-therapist" in this method where the music should be carefully selected to relax the patient and to be relevant in provoking certain emotions. The use of this technique and the positive effect on physical health and mental state has been demonstrated in several studies (McKinney et al., 1997). Most probably these effects are partly due to the emotions that the music can induce. Automatic and intelligent systems can learn the patient profile to help in this context of music therapy. Once trained to one's concept, taste and expectations, an emotion-based musical assistant can be used as "Prozac", a mood regulator and more generally can create highly enjoyable musical experiences.

FUTURE TRENDS

Emotionally sensitive devices are being studied and will soon appear in the commercial market. There already exist mobile devices including a bi-dimensional space to browse music (Sony Ericsson mobile phones with the SenseMe feature), and we can see prototypes automatically detecting mood in music. We believe we are at the beginning of a new trend in exploiting the current knowledge of musical emotions. In the future the personalization of these techniques will help to provide very accurate recommendations linked to one's emotional sensitivity. Taking into account the taste, the current emotional state and all the detailed emotional concepts and relevant musical features, the future of the current tools will be able to trigger specific emotions when asked for by the users. This can be conceived as an automatic system also but of course it should rely on some control by the users. The control might then not be in terms of artist or genre like today but in terms of a precise and personal emotional concept that would be matched by taking into account details about the user. We should also notice that we need to go beyond the current modeling of emotions as if it was just a labeling problem. We must better understand the overall process and provide smarter and more realistic models of music, users and emotions.

To enhance the human-computer interaction, a personal music assistant should also be considered as part of a global system capable of processing multimodal input. This means that the detection of the emotion in music would be one of the many inputs. The global system would take advantage and manage information from visual content (e.g., analysis of the face via a camera), from sound analysis (e.g., emotion in speech for example) and from text content. Merging all this information would lead to a better analysis of the emotion and enable machines to interact with humans in a realistic and impressive experience.

CONCLUSION

In this chapter we have shown that predicting a small set of emotions in music from the audio content is technically feasible. However the difficulty comes when introducing more subjectivity together with more complex semantic descriptions. For example, what are the differences between sad and melancholic? What is the overlap between both concepts? Would we all agree on this? We will probably not. Moreover how can our system be aware of the personal history of users, their social or cultural contexts, and their current status? We should also take care about the drawbacks of such systems. The marketing and social control issues can be frightening. However all the promising applications in everyday life, and especially in art and therapy are definitely strong arguments to continue these investigations. Detecting automatically emotion in music is at its early stage but we can expect many improvements and exciting applications in the future.

ACKNOWLEDGMENT

This work has been partially funded by the EU Project Pharos IST-2006-045035 (http://www. pharos-audiovisual-search.eu). The authors wish to thank their colleagues from the Music Technology Group for their help and especially Emilia Gómez and Owen Meyers for providing very useful feedback.

REFERENCES

Besson, M., Faita, F., Peretz, I., Bonnel, A. M., & Requin, J. (1998). Singing in the brain: Independence of lyrics and tunes. *Psychological Science*, *9*(6), 494–498.

Bigand, E., Vieillard, S., Madurell, F., Marozeau, J., & Dacquet, A. (2005). Multidimensional scaling of emotional responses to music: The effect of musical expertise and of the duration of the excerpts. *Cognition & Emotion*, *19*(8), 1113–1139.

Blood, A. J., & Zatorre, R. J. (2001). Intensely pleasurable responses to music correlate with activity in brain regions implicated in reward and emotion. *Proceedings of the National Academy of Sciences of the United States of America*, *98*(20), 11818–11823.

Bonny, H. L. (2002). *Music consciousness: The evolution of guided imagery and music* (L. Summer, Ed.). Barcelona Publishers.

Casacuberta, D. (2004). Dj el niño: expressing synthetic emotions with music. *AI & Society*, *18*(3), 257–263.

Clark, D. M., & Teasdale, J. D. (1985). Constraints on the effect of mood on memory. *Journal of Personality and Social Psychology*, *48*, 1595–1608.

Dalla Bella, Peretz, I., Rousseau, L., & Gosselin, N. (2001). A developmental study of the affective value of tempo and mode in music. *Cognition*, *80*(3), 1–10.

Damasio, A. (1994). *Descartes' error: Emotion, reason, and the human brain*. New York: Harper Perennial.

Davies, S. (2001). Philosophical perspectives on music's expressiveness. In P. N. Juslin & J. A. Sloboda (Eds.), *Music and emotion: Theory and research.* Oxford: Oxford University Press.

Downie, J. S. (2006). The music information retrieval evaluation exchange (MIREX). *D-Lib Magazine, 12*(12).

Ekman, P. (1992). An argument for basic emotions. *Cognition & Emotion, 6*(3), 169–200.

Farnsworth, P. R. (1954). A study of the hevner adjective list. *The Journal of Aesthetics and Art Criticism, 13*(1), 97–103.

Fehr, B., & Russell, J. A. (1984). Concept of emotion viewed from a prototype perspective. *Journal of Experimental Psychology: General, 113*(3), 464–486.

Friberg, A., Bresin, R., & Sundberg, J. (2006). Overview of the KTH rule system for musical performance. *Advances in Cognitive Psychology, 2*(2-3), 145–161.

Frijda, N. H. (1987). *The emotions (studies in emotion and social interaction).* Cambridge University Press.

Gómez, E. (2006). *Tonal description of music audio signals.* Doctoral dissertation, Universitat Pompeu Fabra.

Gosselin, N., Peretz, I., Noulhiane, M., Hasboun, D., Beckett, C., Baulac, M., et al. (2005). Impaired recognition of scary music following unilateral temporal lobe excision. *Brain, 128*(3), 628–640.

Gouyon, F., Herrera, P., Gómez, E., Cano, P., Bonada, J., Loscos, A., et al. (2008). Content processing of music audio signals. In P. Polotti & D. Rocchesso (Eds.), *Sound to sense, sense to sound: A state of the art in sound and music computing* (pp. 83–160). Berlin: Logos Verlag Berlin GmbH.

Grewe, O., Nagel, F., Kopiez, R., & Altenmüller, E. (2007). Emotions over time: synchronicity and development of subjective, physiological, and facial affective reactions to music. *Emotion, 7*(4), 774–788.

Guaus, E., & Herrera, P. (2006). Music genre categorization in humans and machines. In *Proceedings of the 121st Convention of the Audio Engineering Society.*

Herrera, P., Bello, J., Widmer, G., Sandler, M., Celma, O., Vignoli, F., et al. (2005). SIMAC: Semantic interaction with music audio contents. In *Proceedings of the 2nd European Workshop on the Integration of Knowledge, Semantics and Digital Media Technologies* (pp. 399–406). London, UK.

Hevner, K. (1936). Experimental studies of the elements of expression in music. *The American Journal of Psychology, 48*(2), 246–268.

Honing, H., & Ladinig, O. (2008). The potential of the internet for music perception research: A comment on lab-based versus web-based studies. *Empirical Musicology Review, 3*(1), 4–7.

Hu, X., Downie, S. J., Laurier, C., Bay, M., & Ehmann, A. F. (2008). The 2007 MIREX audio mood classification task: Lessons learned. In *Proceedings of the 9th International Conference on Music Information Retrieval* (pp. 462–467). Philadelphia, PA, USA.

Huron, D. (2006). *Sweet anticipation: Music and the psychology of expectation.* Cambridge: The MIT Press.

Juslin, P., & Laukka, P. (2004). Expression, perception, and induction of musical emotions: A review and a questionnaire study of everyday listening. *Journal of New Music Research, 33*(3), 217–238.

Juslin, P. N., & Västfjäll, D. (2008). Emotional responses to music: The need to consider underlying mechanisms. *Behavioral and Brain Sciences, 31*(5).

Kenealy, P. (1988). Validation of a music mood induction procedure: Some preliminary findings. *Cognition & Emotion*, 2(1), 41–48.

Kim, Y., Schmidt, E., & Emelle, L. (2008). Moodswings: A collaborative game for music mood label collection. In *Proceedings of the 9th International Conference on Music Information Retrieval* (pp. 231–236). Philadelphia, PA, USA.

Kivy, P. (1989). *Sound sentiment: An essay on the musical emotions*. Temple University Press.

Koelsch, S., Fritz, T., Cramon, D. Y. V., Müller, K., & Friederici, A. D. (2006). Investigating emotion with music: an fmri study. *Human Brain Mapping*, 27(3), 239–250.

Krumhansl, C. L. (1997). An exploratory study of musical emotions and psychophysiology. *Canadian Journal of Experimental Psychology*, 51(4), 336–353.

Laurier, C., Grivolla, J., & Herrera, P. (2008). Multimodal music mood classification using audio and lyrics. In *Proceedings of the International Conference on Machine Learning And Applications*. San Diego, CA, USA.

Laurier, C., & Herrera, P. (2007). Audio music mood classification using support vector machine. In *Proceedings of the 8th International Conference on Music Information Retrieval*. Vienna, Austria.

Laurier, C., & Herrera, P. (2008). Mood cloud: A real-time music mood visualization tool. In *Proceedings of the 2008 Computers in Music Modeling and Retrieval Conference* (pp. 163–167). Copenhagen, Danemark.

Lazarus, R. S. (1991). *Emotion and adaptation*. Oxford: Oxford University Press.

Levitin, D. (2007). Life soundtracks: The uses of music in everyday life. *Report prepared for the exclusive use of Philips Consumer Electronics B.V., Eindhoven, The Netherlands, http://www. yourbrainonmusic.com.*

Li, T., & Ogihara, M. (2003). Detecting emotion in music. In *Proceedings of the 4th International Conference on Music Information Retrieval* (pp. 239–240). Baltimore, MD, USA.

Logan, B. (2000). Mel frequency cepstral coefficients for music modeling. In *Proceeding of the 1st International Symposium on Music Information Retrieval*. Plymouth, MA, USA.

Lu, D., Liu, L., & Zhang, H. (2006). Automatic mood detection and tracking of music audio signals. *IEEE Transactions on Audio, Speech, and Language Processing*, 14(1), 5–18.

Luck, G., Riikkilä, K., Lartillot, O., Erkkilä, J., & Toiviainen, P. (2006). Exploring relationships between level of mental retardation and features of music therapy improvisations: a computational approach. *Nordic Journal of Music Therapy*, 15(1), 30–48.

Mandel, M., Poliner, G., & Ellis, D. (2006). Support vector machine active learning for music retrieval. *Multimedia Systems*, 12(1), 3–13.

Mandel, M. I., & Ellis, D. P. (2007). A web-based game for collecting music metadata. In *Proceedings of the 8th International Conference on Music Information Retrieval* (pp. 365–366). Vienna, Austria.

McKinney, C. H., Antoni, M. H., Kumar, M., Tims, F. C., & Mccabe, P. M. (1997). Effects of guided imagery and music (gim) therapy on mood and cortisol in healthy adults. *Health Psychology*, 16(4), 390–400.

Menon, V., & Levitin, D. J. (2005). The rewards of music listening: response and physiological connectivity of the mesolimbic system. *Neuroimage*, 28(1), 175–184.

Meyer, L. B. (1956). *Emotion and meaning in music*. Chicago: University Of Chicago Press.

North, A. C., & Hargreaves, D. J. (1997). Music and consumer behaviour. In D. J. Hargreaves & A. C.

North (Eds.), *The social psychology of music* (pp. 268–289). Oxford: Oxford University Press.

North, A. C., Hargreaves, D. J., & O'Neill, S. A. (2000). The importance of music to adolescents. *British Journal of Educational Psychology*, 255–272.

Nussbaum, C. O. (2007). *The musical representation: Meaning, ontology, and emotion* (1st ed.). Cambridge: The MIT Press.

Panksepp, J., & Bernatzky, G. (2002). Emotional sounds and the brain: the neuro-affective foundations of musical appreciation. *Behavioural Processes*, 133–155.

Patel, A. D. (2007). *Music, language, and the brain*. Oxford: Oxford University Press.

Peretz, I., Gagnon, L., & Bouchard, B. (1998). Music and emotion: perceptual determinants, immediacy, and isolation after brain damage. *Cognition, 68*(2), 111–141.

Pignatiello, M. F., Camp, C. J., & Rasar, L. (1986). Musical mood induction: An alternative to the velten technique. *Journal of Abnormal Pychology, 95*(3), 295–297.

Russell, J. A. (1980). A circumplex model of affect. *Journal of Personality and Social Psychology, 39*(6), 1161–1178.

Sacks, O. (2007). *Musicophilia: Tales of music and the brain*. New York: Knopf Publishing Group.

Sacks, O., & Freeman, A. (1994). An anthropologist on mars. *Journal of Consciousness Studies, 1*(2), 234–240.

Scherer, K. R. (1991). Emotion expression in speech and music. In J. Sundberg, L. Nord, & R. Carlson (Eds.), *Music, language, speech, and brain* (pp. 146–156). London: MacMillian.

Scherer, K. R., & Zentner, M. R. (2001). Emotional effects of music: Production rules. In P. N. Juslin &

J. A. Sloboda (Eds.), *Music and emotion: Theory and research* (pp. 361–392). Oxford: Oxford University Press.

Schubert, E. (1999). *Measurement and time series analysis of emotion in music*. Doctoral dissertation, University of New South Wales.

Serrà, J., Gomez, E., Herrera, P., & Serra, X. (2008). Chroma binary similarity and local alignment applied to cover song identification. *IEEE Transactions on Audio, Speech, and Language Processing, 16*(6), 1138–1151.

Shi, Y.-Y., Zhu, X., Kim, H.-G., & Eom, K.-W. (2006). A tempo feature via modulation spectrum analysis and its application to music emotion classification. In *Proceedings of the IEEE International Conference on Multimedia And Expo* (pp. 1085–1088). Toronto, Canada.

Skowronek, J., McKinney, M., & Van de Par, S. (2007). A demonstrator for automatic music mood estimation. In *Proceedings of the 8th International Conference on Music Information Retrieval* (pp. 345–346). Vienna, Austria.

Sloboda, J. (1999). Everyday uses of music listening: A preliminary study. In S. W. Yi (Ed.), *Music, mind and science* (pp. 354–369). Seoul National University Press.

Sordo, M., Laurier, C., & Celma, O. (2007). Annotating music collections: How content-based similarity helps to propagate labels. In *Proceedings of the 8th International Conference on Music Information Retrieval* (pp. 531–534). Vienna, Austria.

Thayer, R. E. (1989). *The biopsychology of mood and arousal*. Oxford: Oxford University Press.

Thayer, R. E. (1996). *The origin of everyday moods: Managing energy, tension, and stress*. Oxford: Oxford University Press.

Tomkins, S. S. (1980). Affect as amplification: some modifications in theory. In R. Plutchik &

H. Kellerman (Eds.), *Emotion: Theory, research and experience*. New York: Academic Press.

Trainor, L. J., Tsang, C. D., & Cheung, V. H. (2002). Preference for sensory consonance in 2- and 4-month-old infants. *Music Perception, 20*(2), 187–194.

Tzanetakis, G., & Cook, P. (2002). Musical genre classification of audio signals. *IEEE Transactions on Audio, Speech and Language Processing, 10*(5), 293–302.

Vieillard, S., Peretz, I., Gosselin, N., Khalfa, S., Gagnon, L., & Bouchard, B. (2008). Happy, sad, scary and peaceful musical excerpts for research on emotions. *Cognition & Emotion, 22*(4), 720–752.

Wieczorkowska, A., Synak, P., Lewis, R., & Raś. (2005). Extracting emotions from music data. In *Foundations of intelligent systems* (pp. 456–465). Springer-Verlag.

Witten, I. H., & Frank, E. (1999). *Data Mining: Practical Machine Learning Tools and Techniques with Java Implementations*. Morgan Kaufmann.

Wood, J. V., Saltzberg, J. A., & Goldsamt, L. A. (1990). Does affect induce self-focused attention? *Journal of Personality and Social Psychology, 58*(5), 899–908.

Yang, Y. H., Lin, Y. C., Su, Y. F., & Chen, H. H. (2008a). A regression approach to music emotion recognition. *IEEE Transactions on Audio, Speech, and Language Processing, 16*(2), 448–457.

Yang, Y. H., Lin, Y. C., Cheng, H. T., & Chen, H. H. (2008b). Mr.emo: Music retrieval in the emotion plane. In *Proceedings of the ACM International Conference on Multimedia*. Vancouver, BC, Canada.

KEY TERMS

Music Information Retrieval (MIR) is an interdisciplinary science aimed to studying the processes, systems and knowledge representations required for retrieving information from music. This music can be in symbolic format (e.g., a MIDI file), in audio format (e.g. an mp3 file), or in vector format (e.g., a scanned score). MIR research takes advantage of technologies and knowledge derived from signal processing, machine learning, music cognition, database management, human-computer interaction, music archiving or sociology of music.

Music Categorization models consider that perceptual, cognitive or emotional states associated with music listening can be defined by assigning them to one of many predefined categories. Categories are a basic survival tool, in order to reduce the complexity of the environment as they assign different physical states to the same class, and make possible the comparison between different states. It is by means of categories that musical ideas and objects are recognized, differentiated and understood. When applied to music and emotion, they imply that different emotional classes are identified and used to group pieces of music or excerpts according to them. Music categories are usually defined by means of present or absent musical features.

Music Dimensional Models consider that perceptual, cognitive or emotional states associated with music listening can be defined by a position in a continuous multidimensional space where each dimension stands for a fundamental property common to all the observed states. Pitch, for example, is considered to be defined by a height (how high or low in pitch it is a tone) and a chroma (the note class it belongs to, i.e., C, D, E, etc.) dimension. Two of the most accepted dimensions for describing emotions were proposed by Russel (Russel 1980): valence (positive versus negative affect) and arousal (low versus high level of activation). This variety of dimensions could be seen as the different expressions of a very small set of basic concepts.

Musical Features are the concepts, based on musical theory, music perception or signal processing, that are used to analyze, describe or transform a piece of music. Because of that, they constitute the building blocks of any Music Information Retrieval system. They can be global for a given piece of music (e.g., key or tonality), or can be time-varying (e.g., energy). Musical features have numerical or textual values associated. Their similarities and differences make possible to build predictive models of more complex or composite features, in a hierarchical way.

Personal Music Assistants are technical devices, that help its user to find relevant music, provide the right music at the right time and learn his profile and musical taste. Nowadays mp3 players are the music personal assistants, with eventually access to a recommendation engine. Adding new technologies like the ability to detect emotions, sense the mood and movements of the user will makes these devices "intelligent" and able to find music that triggers particular emotions.

Supervised Learning is a machine learning technique to automatically learn by example. A supervised learning algorithm generates a function predicting ouputs based on input observations. The function is generated from the training data. The training data is made of input observations and wanted outputs. Based on these examples the algorithm aims to generalize properly from the input/ouput observations to unobserved cases. We call it regression when the ouput is a continuous value and classification when the ouput is a label. Supervised learning is opposed to unsupervised learning, where the outputs are unknown. In that case, the algorithm aims to find structures in the data. There are many supervised learning algorithms such as Support Vector Machines, Nearest Neighbors, Decision trees, Naïve Bayes or Artificial Neural Network.

Support Vector Machine (SVM), is a supervised learning classification algorithm widely used in machine learning. It is known to be efficient, robust and to give relatively good performances. In the context of a two-class problem in n dimensions, the idea is to find the "best" hyperplane separating the points of the two classes. This hyperplane can be of n-1 dimensions and found in the feature space, in that case it is a linear classifier. Otherwise, it can be found in a transformed space of higher dimensionality using kernel methods. In that case we talk about a non-linear classifier. The position of new observations compared to the hyperplane tells us in which class is the new input.

ENDNOTES

[1] ITPRA stands for : Imagination response, Tension response, Prediction response, Reaction response, Appraisal response (Huron, 2006, pp. 357-365)

[2] For a review on automatic extraction of audio features see Herrera et al. (2005) and Gouyon et al. (2008).

[3] In order to assess the ability that the system has to predict a label for new and unseen music files, the training of the system uses only a portion of all the available data, and its testing is done using the remaining data. In n-fold cross-validation, the data is split into n portions, n-1 folds are used for training, and the remaining fold is used for testing. This is done n times, each one using one of the n folds for testing and the remaining folds for training; finally an average of the n tests is used to estimate the mean error of the classification system.

[4] Even though it plays a crucial role in any music cognition aspect, melodic information is still out of scope of the current state-of-the-art automatic music content description. It can only be addressed very roughly or

unreliably when polyphonic music files are analysed. Even with this limitation, the current audio descriptors can deal with many practical applications, such as the one we describe here.

[5] http://www.last.fm

[6] Precision and recall are two typical measures in Information Retrieval. Precision is a measure of exactness (ratio of correct instances in the retrieve set) and Recall a measure of completeness (amount of correct instances retrieved over the whole set of correct instances)

[7] See, for example, http://www.bmat.com

Chapter III
Facial Expression Analysis, Modeling and Synthesis:
Overcoming the Limitations of Artificial Intelligence with the Art of the Soluble

Christoph Bartneck
Eindhoven University of Technology, The Netherlands

Michael J. Lyons
Ritsumeikan University, Japan

ABSTRACT

The human face plays a central role in most forms of natural human interaction so we may expect that computational methods for analysis of facial information, modeling of internal emotional states, and methods for graphical synthesis of faces and facial expressions will play a growing role in human-computer and human-robot interaction. However, certain areas of face-based HCI, such as facial expression recognition and robotic facial display have lagged others, such as eye-gaze tracking, facial recognition, and conversational characters. Our goal in this paper is to review the situation in HCI with regards to the human face, and to discuss strategies, which could bring more slowly developing areas up to speed. In particular, we are proposing the "The Art of the Soluble" as a strategy forward and provide examples that successfully applied this strategy.

INTRODUCTION

The human face is used in many aspects of verbal and non-verbal communication: speech, the facial expression of emotions, gestures such as nods, winks, and other human communicative acts. Subfields of neuroscience, cognitive science, and psychology are devoted to study of this information. Computer scientists and engineers have worked on the face in graphics, animation, computer vision, and pattern recognition. A widely stated motivation for this work is to improve human computer interaction. However, relatively few HCI technologies employ face processing (FP). At first sight this seems to reflect technical limitations to the development of practical, viable applications of FP technologies.

This paper has two aims: (a) to introduce current research on HCI applications of FP, identifying both successes and outstanding issues, and (b) to propose that an efficient strategy for progress could be to identify and approach soluble problems rather than aim for unrealistically difficult applications. While some of the outstanding issues in FP may indeed be as difficult as many unsolved problems in artificial intelligence, we will argue that skillful framing of a research problem can allow HCI researchers to pursue interesting, soluble, and productive research.

For concreteness, this article will focus on the analysis of facial expressions from video input, as well as their synthesis with animated characters or robots. Techniques for automatic facial expression processing have been studied intensively in the pattern recognition community and the findings are highly relevant to HCI (2004; Lyons, Budynek, & Akamatsu, 1999). Work on animated avatars may be considered to be mature (Cassell, Sullivan, Prevost, & Churchill, 2000), while the younger field of social robotics is expanding rapidly (Bartneck & Okada, 2001; Bartneck & Suzuki, 2005; Fong, Nourbakhsh, & Dautenhahn, 2003). FP is a central concern in both of these fields, and HCI researchers can contribute to and benefit from the results.

However, an examination of the HCI research literature indicates that activity is restricted to a relatively narrow selection of these areas. Eye gaze has occupied the greatest share of HCI research on the human face (e.g. (Zhai, Morimoto, & Ihde, 1999)). Eye gaze tracking technology is now sufficiently advanced that several commercial solutions are available (e.g. Tobii Technology (2007)). Gaze tracking is a widely used technique in interface usability, machine-mediated human communication, and alternative input devices.

This area can be viewed as a successful sub-field related to face-based HCI.

Numerous studies have emphasized the neglect of human affect in interface design and argued this could have major impact on the human aspects of computing (Picard, 1997). Accordingly, there has been much effort in the pattern recognition, AI, and robotics communities towards the analysis, understanding, and synthesis of emotion and expression. In the following sections we briefly introduce the areas related to analysis, modeling and synthesis of facial expressions. Next, we report on insights on these areas gained during a workshop we organized on the topic. A gap between the available FP technology and its envisioned applications was identified, and based on this insight, we propose the "Art of the Soluble" strategy for FP. Last, we provide successful examples in the field of FP that took the Art of the Soluble approach.

ANALYSIS: FACIAL EXPRESSION CLASSIFICATION

The attractive prospect of being able to gain insight into a user's affective state may be considered one of the key unsolved problems in HCI. It is known that it is difficult to measure the "valence" component of affective state, as compared to "arousal", which may be gauged using biosensors. However, a smile, or frown, provides a clue that goes beyond physiological measurements. It is also attractive that expressions can be guaged non-invasively with inexpensive video cameras.

Automatic analysis of video data displaying facial expressions has become a topic of active area of computer vision and pattern recognition research (for reviews see (Fasel & Luettin, 2003; Pantic & Rothkrantz, 2000)). The scope of the problem statement has, however, been relatively narrow (Ellis & Bryson, 2005; Hara & Kobayashi, 1996; Shugrina, Betke, & Collomosse, 2006). Typically one measures the performance of a novel classification algorithm on recognition of the basic expression classes proposed by Ekman and Friesen (1975). Expression data often consists of a segmented headshot taken under relatively controlled conditions and classification accuracy is based on comparison with emotion labels provided by human experts.

This bird's eye caricature of the methodology used by the pattern recognition community given above is necessarily simplistic, however it underlines two general reflections. First, pattern recognition has successfully framed the essentials of the facial expression problem to allow for effective comparison of algorithms. This narrowing of focus has led to impressive developments of the techniques for facial expression analysis and substantial understanding. Second, the narrow framing of the FP problem typical in the computer vision and pattern recognition may not be appropriate for HCI problems. This observation is a main theme of this paper, and we suggest that progress on use of FP in HCI may require re-framing the problem.

To do so, we have to overcome several controversies that are associated with the most fundamental issues of facial expression research, and it has been suggested (Bartneck & Lyons, 2007; Schiano, Ehrlich, Rahardja, & Sheridan, 2000), that these unresolved issues may be significantly impeding progress in the development of workable HCI systems. The nature of the method used to represent facial expressions is seen as a key issue in this regard. One school of thought, famously affiliated with Ekman (1999) but dating back at least to Charles Darwin (1872), holds that a discrete set of facial expression categories serves to communicate affective, categorical states, which, likewise, can be represented using a set of emotion categories. Another view with a long history, which was articulated clearly by Harold Schlosberg (1952, 1954), but again with roots in older work, holds that emotional facial expressions are better suited to representation in a continuous multi-dimensional space. Common interpretations for the affective dimensions

are valence (pleasure/displeasure), arousal and intensity. Differences between categorical and dimensional models have sometimes been a source of controversy in the study of facial expressions (Schiano, Ehrlich, & Sheridan, 2004).

Choice of an appropriate representation scheme is no doubt of paramount importance for the success of any facial expression system, however categorical and dimensional views are by no means incompatible in the context of their application to HCI technologies. One of our earliest studies of dimensional facial expression representation conducted with my colleagues Miyuki Kamachi and Jiro Gyoba and reported in Lyons et al. (1998), was the result of a larger project to build a facial expression categorization system. While studying classification methods for images of facial expressions, we explored the dimensional structure of the facial expression image data and discovered that a nonlinear two-dimensional projection of the data, captured a large proportion of the variance in our data. A slightly greater proportion of the variance was accounted for with addition of a third dimension. Interestingly, the two dimensional projection closely resembled the well-known "circumplex" model of facial expressions, itself a low-dimensional projection of empirical data from semantic differential ratings of facial expression images. The correlation between the image-processing derived and semantic-rating derived spaces was unexpectedly high and provided support for our image-filter derived representation of facial expressions, as well as for the possibly utility of a dimensional representation in classifying facial expressions. At the same time, we observed a natural clustering of facial expression images within our low-dimensional affect space into basic emotional categories of happiness, anger, surprise, and so on. This finding suggested that the concept of facial expression categories could also be a viable component of our facial expression classification system.

The findings reported in Lyons et al. (1998) and briefly summarized above showed that both categorical and dimensional representations could be used at different stages of a facial expression classification system and guided a subsequent project to build a facial expression classification system as reported by Lyons et al. (1999). The basic idea of the classification system to first process facial images with filters modeled on complex cells of primary visual cortex (area V1), then project the filter outputs into a low dimensional space learned from an ensemble of facial expression images and finally categorize expressions on the basis clusters. This system embodies dimensional and categorical approaches to facial expression representation and combines the power of both: an outcome of the project was the development of one of the early successful facial expression classifiers. Subsequent studies (see, for example, (Dailey, Cottrell, Padgett, & Adolphs, 2002)) have provided further support for the general approach of combining V1-like image filtering, dimensionality reduction followed by categorization.

In addition to utility of this approach for classifying images of facial expression, the schema discussed above is helpful in thinking about how dimensional and categorical facial expression representations might relate to what happens in the brain. For example, dimensional and categorical aspects of processing may be different facets of a single neural scheme for processing facial expressions. Loosely speaking, dimensionality reduction might take places at an earlier stage of processing, to reduce the complexity, and increase the robustness of a facial expression recognition system. Independently of how emotions are actually processed in the brain, artificial characters and robots also require a model to be able to process the external world into emotional states that can then be expressed. In the next section, we will discuss the modeling of emotions.

SYNTHESIS: EMOTION MODELING

Emotions are an essential part of the believability of embodied characters that interact with humans (Elliott, 1992; Koda, 1996; O'Reilly, 1996). Characters need an emotion model to synthesize emotions and express them. The emotion model should enable the character to argue about emotions the way humans do. An event that upsets humans, for example the loss of money, should also upset the character. The emotion model must be able to evaluate all situations that the character might encounter and must also provide a structure for variables influencing the intensity of an emotion. Such an emotion model enables the character to show the right emotion with the right intensity at the right time, which is necessary for the convincingness of its emotional expressions (Bartneck, 2001). Creating such an emotion model is a daring task and in this section we will outline some of its problems. In particular, we will argue for the importance of the context in which the emotion model operates.

Emotions are particularly important for conversational embodied characters, because they are an essential part of the self-revelation feature of messages. The messages of human communication consist of four features: facts, relationship, appeal and self-revelation (Schulz, 1981) The inability of a conversational character to reveal its emotional state would possibly be interpreted by the user as missing sympathy. It would sound strange if the character, for example, opened the front door of the house for the user to enter and spoke with an absolute monotonous voice: "Welcome home".

From a practical point of view, the developer of a screen character of robot is wise to build upon existing models to avoid reinvent the wheel. Several emotion models are available (Roseman, Antoniou, & Jose, 1996; Sloman, 1999). However, Ortony, Clore and Collins (1988) developed a computational emotion model, that is often referred to as the OCC model, which has established itself as the standard model for emotion synthesis. A large number of studies employed the OCC model to generate emotions humans (Bondarev, 2002; Elliott, 1992; Koda, 1996; O'Reilly,

1996; Studdard, 1995). This model specifies 22 emotion categories based on valenced reactions to situations constructed either as being goal relevant events, as acts of an accountable agent (including itself), or as attractive or unattractive objects (see Figure 1). It also offers a structure for the variables, such as likelihood of an event or the familiarity of an object, which determines the intensity of the emotion types. It contains a sufficient level of complexity and detail to cover most situations an emotional interface character might have to deal with.

When confronted with the complexity of the OCC model many developers of characters believe that this model will be all they ever need to add emotions to their character. Only during the development process the missing features of the model and the problem of the context become apparent. These missing features and the context in which emotions arise are often underestimated and have the potential to turn the character into an unconvincing clown. We will point out what the OCC model is able to do for an embodied emotional character and what it does not.

The OCC model is complex and this paper discusses its features in terms of the process that characters follow from the initial categorization of an event to the resulting behaviour of the character. The process can be split into five phases:

1. **Categorization:** In the categorization phase the character evaluates an event, action or object, resulting in information on what emotional categories are affected.
2. **Quantification:** In the quantification phase, the character calculates the intensities of the affected emotional categories.
3. **Interaction:** The classification and quantification define the emotional value of a certain event, action or object. This emotional value will interact with the current emotional categories of the character.
4. **Mapping:** The OCC model distinguishes 22 emotional categories. These need to be mapped to a possibly lower number of different emotional expressions.

Figure 1. The OCC model of emotions. It contains a classification schema and variables to calculate the intensity of emotions.

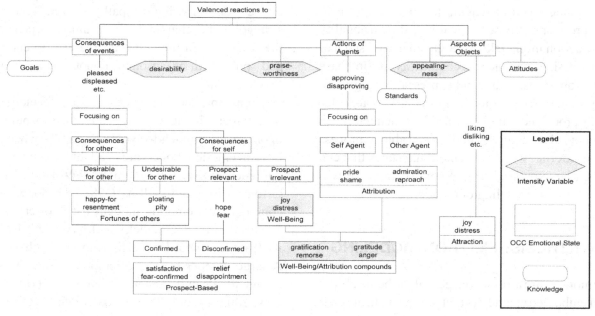

Categorization

In the categorization phase an event, action or object is evaluated by the character, which results in information on what emotional categories are affected. This categorization requires the character to know the relation of a particular object, for example, to its attitudes. Depending on this evaluation either the "love" or "hate" emotional category will be affected by the object.

Consider this example: a character likes bananas and the user gives him a whole bunch. The character will evaluate the consequences of the event for the user, which results in pity, since the user has a whole bunch of bananas less. It will also evaluate the consequences of the event for itself, which results in satisfaction because it received a bunch of bananas. Next, it evaluates the action of the user, which results in admiration and finally the aspect of the object, which results in love. It appears that ironic that the category "love" is being used in the OCC model only for objects, since the more important usage for this word is certainly found in human-human relationships.

To do this classification the character needs an extensive amount of knowledge. First, it needs to know its relationship to the user, which was assumed to be good. Hence, pity is triggered and not resentment. Moreover, it needs to know what this event means to the user. Otherwise the character's happy-for category might be triggered (User Model). Second, it needs to have a goal "staying alive" to which the bananas contribute (Goals). Third, it needs to know what to expect from the user. Only knowing that the user does not have to hand out bananas every other minute the character will feel admiration (Standards). Last, it needs to know that it likes bananas (Attitudes).

The standards, goals and attitudes of the character that the OCC model requires need to be specified, organized and stored by the designer of the character. A new character knows even less than a newborn baby. It does not even have basic instincts. One way to store this knowledge

could be an exhaustive table in which all possible events, actions and objects that the character might encounter are listed together with information on which emotional categories they affect and how their intensity may be calculated. This approach is well suited for characters that act in a limited world. However, it would be rather difficult, for example, to create such an exhaustive list for all the events, actions and objects that the character might encounter at the home of the user. With an increasing number of events, actions and objects, it becomes necessary to define abstractions. The bananas could be abstracted to food, to which also bread and coconuts belong. The categorization for the event of receiving food will be the same for all types of food. Only their intensity might be different, since a certain food could be more nutritious or tasty. However, even this approach is inherently limited. The world is highly complex and this approach can only function in very limited "cube" worlds.

This world model is not only necessary for the emotion model, but also for other components of the character. If, for example, the character uses the popular Belief, Desires and Intention (BDI) architecture (Bratman, Israel, & Pollack, 1988), then the desires correspond to the goals of the emotion model. The structure of the goals is shared knowledge. So are the standards and attitudes. The complexity of the OCC model has a direct influence on the size of the required world model. However, the AI community has long given up the hope to be able to create extensive world models, such as Cyc (Cycorp, 2007). The amount of information and its organization appears overwhelming. Only within the tight constraints of limited worlds was it possible so far to create operational world models.

As mentioned above, the OCC model distinguishes 22 emotional categories (see Figure 1). This rather cumbersome and to some degree arbitrary model appears to be too complex for the development of believable characters (Ortony, 2003). The OCC model was created to model human emotions. However, it is not necessary to model a precise human emotion system to develop a believable character. A "Black Box" approach (Wehrle, 1998) appears to be sufficient. The purpose of this approach is to produce outcomes or decisions that are similar to those resulting from humans, disregarding both the processes whereby these outcomes are attained as well as the structures involved. Such a "Black Box" approach is more suitable, particularly since the sensory, motoric and cognitive abilities of artificial characters are still far behind the ones of humans. The characters emotion system should be in balance with its abilities. Several reason speak for a simplification of the OCC model.

First, only those emotional categories of the OCC model should be used that the character can actually use. If a character uses the emotional model only to change its facial expression then its emotion categories should be limited to the ones it can express. Elliot (1992) implemented all 22 emotional categories in his agents because they were able to communicate each and every one to each other. This is of course only possible for character-character interaction in a virtual world. It would be impossible for characters that interact with humans, since characters are not able to express 22 different emotional categories on their face. Ekman (1972) proposed six basic emotions that can be communicated efficiently and across cultures through facial expressions.

Second, some emotional categories of the OCC model appear to be very closely related to others, such as gratitude and gratification, even thought the conditions that trigger them are different. Gratification results from a praiseworthy action the character did itself and gratitude from an action another character did. It is not clear if such a fine grained distinction has any practical advantages for the believability of characters.

Last, if the character does not have a user model then it will by definition not be able to evaluate the consequences of an event for the user. In this case, the "fortunes of others" emotional categories would need to be excluded.

Ortony acknowledged that the OCC model might be too complex for the development of believable characters (Ortony, 2003). He proposed to use five positive categories (joy, hope, relief, pride, gratitude and love) and five negative categories (distress, fear, disappointment remorse, anger and hate). Interestingly, he excluded the emotional categories that require a user model. These ten emotional categories might still be too much for a character that only uses facial expressions. Several studies simplified the emotional model even further to allow a one-to-one mapping of the emotion model to the expressions of the character (Bartneck, 2002; Koda, 1996).

Quantification

The intensity of an emotional category is defined separately for events, actions and objects. The intensity of the emotional categories resulting from an event is defined as the desirability and for actions and objects praiseworthiness and appealingness respectively (see Figure 1). One of the variables that is necessary to calculate desirability is the hierarchy of the character's goals. A certain goal, such as downloading a certain music album from the internet, would have several sub goals, such as download a specific song of that album. The completed goal of downloading of a whole album will evoke a higher desirability than the completed goal of downloading of a certain song, because it is positioned higher in the hierarchy. However, events might also happen outside of the character's current goal structure. The character needs to be able to evaluate such events as well. Besides the goal hierarchy, the emotion model also needs to keep a history of events, actions and objects. If the user, for example, gives the character one banana after the other in a short interval then the desirability of each of these events must decrease over time. The character needs to be less and less enthusiastic about each new banana. This history function is not described in the original OCC model, but plays an important role for the believability of the character. The history function has another important advantage. According to the OCC model, the likelihood of an event needs to be considered to calculate its desirability. The history function can help calculating this likelihood. Lets use the banana example again: The first time the character receives a banana, it will use its default likelihood to calculate the desirability of the event. When the character receives the next banana, it will look at the history and calculate how often it received a banana in the last moments. The more often it received a banana in the past the higher is the likelihood of this event and hence the lower is its desirability. After a certain period of not receiving any bananas the likelihood will fall back to its original default value. This value should not be decreased below its default value, because otherwise the character might experience an overdose of desirability the next time it receives a banana. Another benefit of the history function is the possibility to monitor the progress the character makes trying to achieve a certain goal. According to the OCC model, the effort and realization of an event needs to be considered to calculate its desirability. The history function can keep track of what the character has done and hence be the base for the calculation of effort and realization.

Interaction

The OCC model does not describe another important aspect of an emotion model: the interaction of the different emotional categories. Lets assume that the character was not able to download a certain song from the internet and is therefore angry. Next, the user gives it a banana. This event should not suddenly make it happy, but make it less angry. The emotional value of a certain event interacts with the current emotional state of the character. Little is known how this interaction might work, but a very simple approach could be to counter effect of the positive and negative categories.

Mapping

If the emotion model has more categories than the character has abilities to express them, the emotional categories need to be mapped to the available expressions. If the character, for example, uses only facial expression then it may focus on the six basic emotions of happiness, sadness, anger, disgust, fear and surprise (Ekman, Friesen, & Ellsworth, 1972). Interestingly, there is only one positive facial expression to which all 11 positive OCC categories need to be mapped to: the smile. Ekman (1985) identified several different types of smiles but their mapping to the positive OCC categories remains unclear. The 11 negative OCC categories need to be mapped to four negative expressions: Anger, Sadness, Disgust and Fear. The facial expression of surprise cannot be linked to any OCC categories, since surprise is not considered to be an emotion in the OCC model. Even though the character might only be able to show six emotional expressions on its face, the user might very well be able to distinguish between the expression of love and pride with the help of context information. Each expression appears in a certain context that provides further information to the viewer. The user might interpret the smile of a mother next to her son receiving an academic degree as pride, but exactly the same smile towards her husband as love.

Reflection

The main limitation of the OCC model is its reliance on world model. Such models have only been successfully used in very limited worlds, such as pure virtual worlds in which only virtual characters operate. Furthermore, the OCC model will most likely only be one part of a larger system architecture that controls the character or robot. The emotional states of the OCC model must interact with the other states. Not only the face of the character is influenced by the emotional state of the character, but also its actions. It would be unbelievable if the character showed an angry expression on its face, but acted cooperatively. The mapping of the emotional state should be based on strong theoretical foundations. Such theoretical foundations might not be available for every action that a character might be able to execute and thus force the developer of the character to invent these mappings. This procedure has the intrinsic disadvantage that the developer might introduce an uncontrolled bias based on his or her own experiences and opinions.

Besides the actions of the character, the emotional state may also influence the attention and evaluation of events, actions and objects. In stress situations, for example, humans tend to focus their attention on the problem up to the point of "tunnel vision". Ortony (2003) categorized the behavioural changes of the character through its emotional state in self-regulation (such as calming down), other-modulation (punish the other to feel better) and problem solving (try to avoid repetition). The latter will require the history function mentioned above. The emotional state of the character might even create new goals, such as calming down, which would result in actions like meditation.

FACIAL EXPRESSION SYNTHESIS

There is a long tradition within the HCI community of investigating and building screen based characters that communicate with users (Cassell, Sullivan, Prevost, & Churchill, 2000). Recently, robots have also been introduced to communicate with the users and this area has progressed sufficiently that some review articles are available (Bartneck & Okada, 2001; Fong, Nourbakhsh, & Dautenhahn, 2003). The main advantage that robots have over screen based agents is that they are able to directly manipulate the world. They not only converse with users, but also perform embodied physical actions.

Nevertheless, screen based characters and robots share an overlap in motivations for and problems with communicating with users. Bartneck et al. (Bartneck, Reichenbach, & Breemen, 2004) has shown, for example, that there is no significant difference in the users' perception of emotions as expressed by a robot or a screen based character and that subtle emotional expressions have been neglected (Bartneck & Reichenbach, 2005). The main motivation for using facial expressions to communicate with a user is that it is, in fact, impossible not to communicate. If the face of a character or robot remains inert, it communicates indifference. To put it another way, since humans are trained to recognize and interpret facial expressions it would be wasteful to ignore this rich communication channel.

Compared to the state of the art in screen-based characters, such as Embodied Conversational Agents (Cassell, Sullivan, Prevost, & Churchill, 2000), however, the field of robot's facial expressions is underdeveloped. Much attention has been paid to robot motor skills, such as locomotion and gesturing, but relatively little work has been done on their facial expression. Two main approaches can be observed in the field of robotics and screen based characters. In one camp are researchers and engineers who work on the generation of highly realistic faces. A recent example of a highly realistic robot is the Geminoid H1 which has 13 degrees of freedom (DOF) in its face alone. The annual Miss Digital award (Cerami, 2006) may be thought of as a benchmark for the development of this kind of realistic computer generated face. While significant progress has been made in these areas, we have not yet reached human-like detail and realism, and this is acutely true for the animation of facial expressions. Hence, many highly realistic robots and character currently struggle with the phenomena of the "Uncanny Valley" (Mori, 1970), with users experiencing these artificial beings to be spooky or unnerving. Even the Repliee Q1Expo is only able to convince humans of the naturalness of its expressions for at best a few seconds (Ishiguro, 2005). In summary, natural robotic expressions remain in their infancy (Fong, Nourbakhsh, & Dautenhahn, 2003).

Major obstacles to the development of realistic robots lie with the actuators and the skin. At least 25 muscles are involved in the expression in the human face. These muscles are flexible, small and can be activated very quickly. Electric motors emit noise while pneumatic actuators are difficult to control. These problems often result in robotic heads that either have a small number of actuators or a somewhat larger-than-normal head. The Geminoid H1 robot, for example, is approximately five percent larger than its human counterpart. It also remains difficult to attach skin, which is often made of latex, to the head. This results in unnatural and non-human looking wrinkles and folds in the face.

At the other end of the spectrum, there are many researchers who are developing more iconic faces. Bartneck (2003) showed that a robot with only two DOF in the face can produce a considerable repertoire of emotional expressions that make the interaction with the robot more enjoyable. Many popular robots, such as Asimo (Honda, 2002), Aibo (Sony, 1999) and PaPeRo (NEC, 2001) have only a schematic face with few or no actuators. Some of these only feature LEDs for creating facial expressions. The recently developed iCat robot is a good example of an iconic robot that has a simple physically-animated face (Breemen, Yan, & Meerbeek, 2005). The eyebrows and lips of this robot move and this allows synthesis of a wide range of expressions.

While there is progress in the facial expressions of robot faces, we are sill facing several conceptional problems that stem from the field of Artificial Intelligence. Lets take the example of emotions that we discussed in detailed above. The emotional state of the character is defined through values for each of its emotional categories. This emotional state needs to be expressed through all available channels. A conversational embodied character, for example, needs to express its emo-

tional state through its speech and facial expressions. It would be unconvincing if the character would smile, but speak with a monotonous voice. However, the systematic manipulation of speech to express emotions remains a challenge for the research community. Emotional facial expressions are understood better, but a fundamental questions remains. Shall the character only express the most dominant emotional category, or shall it express every category at the same time and hence show a blend of emotions. The blending of emotional expression requires a sophisticated face, such as Baldi from the CSLU Toolkit. Cartoon like characters, such as eMuu (Bartneck, 2002) or Koda's Poker Playing Agent (Koda, 1996) are not able to show blends and therefore they can only express the most dominant emotional category.

Another important issue that needs to be considered when designing the facial expression of the character is that they need to be convincing and distinct at low intensity levels. Most events that a character encounters will not trigger an ecstatic state of happiness. The evaluation of a certain event should be roughly the same as could be expected of a human and most events that humans encounter in everyday life do unfortunately not result in ecstasy. If the character managed to download a complete album of music it still did not save the world from global warming. Hence, it should only show an appropriate level of happiness.

It becomes obvious that the problems inherited by HRI researchers from the field of AI can be severe. Even if we neglect philosophical aspects of the AI problem and are satisfied with a computer that passes the Turing test, independently of how it achieves this, we will still encounter many practical problems. This leads us to the so-called "weak AI" position, namely claims of achieving human cognitive abilities are abandoned. Instead, this approach focuses on specific problem solving or reasoning tasks.

There has certainly been progress in weak AI, but this has not yet matured sufficiently to support artificial entities. Indeed, at present, developers of artificial entities must to resort to scripting behaviors. Clearly, the scripting approach has its limits and even the most advanced common sense database, Cyc (Cycorp, 2007), is largely incomplete. FP should therefore not bet on the arrival of strong AI solutions, but focus on what weak AI solutions can offer today. Of course there is still hope that eventually also strong AI applications will become possible, but this may take a long time.

When we look at what types of HRI solutions are currently being built, we see that a large number of them do barely have any facial features at all. Qrio, Asimo and Hoap-2, for example, are only able to turn their heads with 2 degrees of freedom (DOF). Other robots, such as Aibo, are able to

move their head, but have only LEDs to express their inner states in an abstract way. While these robots are intended to interact with humans, they certainly avoid facial expression synthesis. When we look at robots that have truly animated faces, we can distinguish between two dimensions: DOF and iconic/realistic appearance (see Figure 2).

Robots in the High DOF/Realistic quadrant not only have to fight with the uncannieness (Bartneck, Kanda, Ishiguro, & Hagita, 2007; MacDorman, 2006) they also may raise user expectations of a strong AI which they are not able to fulfill. By contrast, the low DOF/Iconic quadrant includes robots that are extremely simple and perform well in their limited application domain. These robots lie well within the domain of the soluble

Figure 2. Robots with animated faces

in FP. The most interesting quadrant is the High DOF/Iconic quadrant. These robots have rich facial expressions but avoid evoking associations with a strong AI through their iconic appearance. We propose that research on such robots has the greatest potential for significant advances in the use of FP in HRI.

WORKSHOP ON "HCI AND THE FACE"

As part of our effort to examine the state of the field of FP in HCI, we organized a day-long workshop the ACM CHI'2006 conference (see: http://www.bartneck.de/2006/04/22/hci-and-the-face/ for details). The workshop included research reports, focus groups, and general discussions. This has informed our perspective on the role of FP in HCI, as presented in the current paper.

One focus group summarized the state of the art in facial expression analysis and synthesis, while another brainstormed HCI applications. The idea was to examine whether current technology sufficient advanced to support HCI applications. The proposed applications were organized with regards to the factors "Application domain" and "Intention" (see Table 1). Group discussion seemed to naturally focus on applications that involve some type of agent, avatar or robot. It is nearly impossible to provide an exhaustive list of applications for each field in the matrix. The ones listed in the table should therefore be only considered as representative examples.

These examples well illustrate a fundamental problem of this research field. The workshop participants can be considered experts in the field and all the proposed example applications were related to artificial characters, such as robots, conversational agents and avatars. Yet not one of these applications has become a lasting commercial success. Even Aibo, the previously somewhat successful entertainment robot, has been discontinued by Sony in 2006.

A problem that all these artificial entities have to deal with is, that while their expression processing has reached an almost sufficient maturity, their intelligence has not. This is especially problematic, since the mere presence of an animated face raises the expectation levels of its user. An entity that is able to express emotions is also expected to recognize and understand them. The same holds true for speech. If an artificial entity talks then we also expect it to listen and understand. As we all know, no artificial entity has yet passed the Turing test or claimed the Loebner Prize. All of the examples given in Table 1 presuppose the existence of a strong AI as described by John Searle (1980).

The reasons why strong AI has not yet been achieved are manifold and the topic of lengthy discussion. Briefly then, there are, from the outset, conceptual problems. John Searle (1980) pointed out that digital computers alone can never truly understand reality because it only manipulates syntactical symbols that do not contain semantics. The famous 'Chinese room' example points out some conceptual constraints in the development of strong AIs. According to his line of arguments, IBM's chess playing computer "Deep Blue" does not actually understand chess. It may have beaten Kasparov, but it does so only by manipulating meaningless symbols. The creator of Deep Blue, Drew McDermott (1997), replied to this criticism: "Saying Deep Blue doesn't really think about chess is like saying an airplane doesn't really fly because it doesn't flap its wings." This debate reflects different philosophical viewpoints on what it means to think and understand. For centuries philosophers have thought about such questions and perhaps the most important conclusion is that there is no conclusion at this point in time. Similarly, the possibility of developing a strong AI remains an open question. All the same, it must be admitted that some kind of progress has been made. In the past, a chess-playing machine would have been regarded as intelligent. But now it is regarded as the feat of a calculating machine

Table 1. Examples of face processing applications in HCI and HRI

		Intention		
		Persuade	Being a companion	Educate
Application domain	**Entertainment**	Advertisement: REA (Cassell, Sullivan, Prevost, & Churchill, 2000), Greta (Pelachaud, 2005)	Aibo (Sony, 1999), Tamagotchi (Bandai, 2000)	My Real Baby (Lund & Nielsen, 2002)
	Communication	Persuasive Technology (Fogg, 2003), Cat (Zanbaka, Goolkasian, & Hodges, 2006)	Avatar (Biocca, 1997)	Language tutor (Schwienhorst, 2002)
	Health	Health advisor Fitness tutor (Mahmood & Ferneley, 2004)	Aibo for elderly (Tamura et al., 2004), Attention Capture for Dementia Patients (Wiratanaya, Lyons, & Abe, 2006)	Autistic children (Robins, Dautenhahn, Boekhorst, & Billard, 2005)

– our criteria for what constitutes an intelligent machine has shifted.

In any case, suffice it to say that no sufficiently intelligent machine has yet emerged that would provide a foundation for our example applications given in Table 1. The point we hope to have made with the digression into AI is that the application dreams of researchers sometimes conceal rather unrealistic assumptions about what is possible to achieve with current technology.

TOWARDS AN "ART OF THE SOLUBLE"

The outcome of the workshop we organized was unexpected in a number of ways. Most striking was the vast mismatch between the concrete and fairly realistic description of the available FP technology and its limitations arrived at by one of the focus groups, and the blue-sky applications discussed by the second group. Another sharp contrast was evident at the workshop. The actual presentations given by participants were pragmatic and showed effective solutions to real problems in HCI not relying on AI.

Perhaps the most salient aspect of our observation on the problem of FP is that HCI technology

can often get by with partial solutions. A system that can discriminate between a smile and frown, but not an angry versus disgusted face, can still be a valuable tool for HCI researchers, even if it is not regarded as a particularly successful algorithm from the pattern recognition standpoint. Putting this more generally, components of algorithms developed in the pattern recognition community, may already have sufficient power to be useful in HCI, even if they do not yet constitute general facial expression analysis systems.

This led us to the reflection that scientific progress often relies on what the Nobel prize winning biologist Peter Medawar called "The Art of the Soluble" (Medawar, 1967). That is, skill in doing science requires the ability to select a research problem which is soluble, but which has not yet been solved. Very difficult problems such as strong AI may not yield to solution over the course of decades, so for most scientific problems it is preferable to work on problems of intermediate difficulty, which can yield results over a more reasonable time span, while still being of sufficient interest to constitute progress. Some researchers of course are lucky or insightful enough to re-frame a difficult problem in such a way as to reduce its difficulty, or to recognize a new problem which is not difficult, but nevertheless of wide interest.

In the following sections we make several proposals for the application of this strategy to future research into robotic facial expression synthesis and facial expression analysis.

Facial Expression Analysis: Continuously Update Benchmarks

If any real progress is going to be made towards the hard-AI problem of building machine which can read minds and understand emotions by looking at facial expressions, researchers need to acknowledge the vital importance of updating the methods used to test the performance of their systems. Failure to continuously update the benchmarks used to measure the performance of facial expression systems leads to algorithms which may be highly optimized for a particular set of data and testing conditions, but fail miserably when asked to generalize to more realistic conditions. As discussed elsewhere in this article the problem of obtaining adequate data for training and testing facial expression analysis systems has long been one of the major bottle necks to progress in the field.

For purposes of concreteness we given here a specific and concrete example of a testing paradigm which has not been adequately explored: instead of using nominal labels in terms of basic categories, facial expression images, or image sequences could be more richly described to reflect empirical data on human perception. A approach used by Lyons et al. (1998) is to use semantic ratings on a set of emotion labels rather than a single emotion category. Training and testing an automatic system with semantic ratings data is more complex than if nominal categorical labels are used. Moreover, collecting the ratings data can also require much time and effort. However a continuous description based on real data has still not been fully explored. So it is not known whether the widespread use of nominal category labels for expression data may be hampering progress towards the development of systems

which can be useful in the real world, as opposed to the world of facial expressions artifically posed, selected, or elicited under contrived laboratory conditions.

Facial Analysis for Direct Gesture-Based Interaction

A further illustration of the "Art of the Soluble" strategy comes from the analysis of facial expression and movements for direct gesture-based interaction. While there is a large body of work on automatic facial expression recognition and lip reading within the computer vision and pattern recognition research communities, relatively few studies have examined the possible use of the face in direct, intentional interaction with computers. However, the complex musculature of the face and extensive cortical circuitry devoted to facial control suggest that motor actions of the face could play a complementary or supplementary role to that played by the hands in HCI (Lyons, 2004).

One of us (MJL) has explored this idea through a series of related projects which make use of vision-based methods to capture movement of the head and facial features and apply these to intentional, direct interaction with computers. For example we have designed and implemented systems which make use of head and mouth motions were for the purposes of hands-free text entry (De Silva, Lyons, Kawato, & Tetsutani, 2003) and single-stroke text character entry on small keyboards such as those found on mobile phones (Lyons, Chan, & Tetsutani, 2004). In other projects we have used action of the mouth and face for digital sketching (Chan, Lyons, & Tetsutani, 2003) and musical expression (Lyons & Tetsutani, 2001).

One of the systems we developed tracked the head and position of the nose and mapped the projected position of the nose tip in the image plane to the coordinates of the cursor. Another algorithm segmented the area of the mouth and measured the visible area of the cavity of the user's mouth in the image plane. The state of opening/closing of the mouth could be determined robustly and used in place of mouse-button clicks. This simple interface allowed for text entry using the cursor to select streaming text. Text entry was started and paused by opening and closing the mouth, while selection of letters was accomplished by small movements of the head. The system was tested extensively and found to permit comfortable text entry at a reasonable speed. Details are reported in (De Silva, Lyons, Kawato, & Tetsutani, 2003).

Another project used the shape of the mouth to disambiguate the multiple letters mapped to the keys of a cell phone key pad (Lyons, Chan, & Tetsutani, 2004). Such an approach works very well for Japanese, which has a nearly strict CV (consonant-vowel) phoneme structure, and only five vowels. The advantage of this system was that it took advantage of existing user expertise in shaping the mouth to select vowels. With some practice, users found they could enter text faster than with the standard multi-tap approach.

The unusual idea of using facial actions for direct input may find least resistance in the realm of artistic expression. Indeed, our first explorations of the concept were with musical controllers using mouth shape to control timbre and other auditory features (Lyons & Tetsutani, 2001). Of course, since many musical instruments rely on action of the face and mouth, this work has precedence, and was greeted with enthusiasm by some musicians. Similarly, we used a mouth

action-sensitive device to control line properties while drawing and sketching with a digital tablet (Chan, Lyons, & Tetsutani, 2003). Here again our exploration elicited a positive response from artists who tried the system.

The direct action facial gesture interface serves to illustrate the concept that feasible FP technology is ready to be used as the basis for working HCI applications. The techniques used in all the examples discussed are not awaiting the solution of some grand problem in pattern recognition: they work robustly in real-time under a variety of lighting conditions.

Artificial Expressions and Other Computational Scaffolds for Emotion

A radical reformulation of facial expression research results from the observation that our most meaningful interactions with computers, when scrutinized carefully, usually turn out to be human-computer-human interactions, or, in other words, machine-mediated human-interactions. Bearing this in mind allows designers to sidestep strong-AI issues, leaving the task of interpreting and understanding emotions to humans. This design strategy assigns machines to the tasks they can perform well – automatically reproducing, processing, and displaying information. An example of the application of such a design philosophy is the "Artificial Expressions" system (Lyons, Kluender,

Figure 3. Biosensors for artificial expressions (Lyons, Kluender, & Tetsutani, 2005)

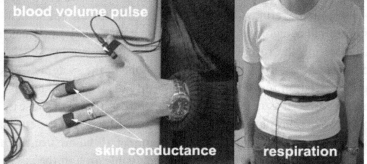

Figure 4. Artificial expression displays (Lyons, Kluender, & Tetsutani, 2005)

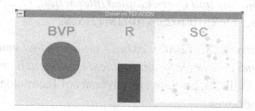

& Tetsutani, 2005). In this system, information from biosensors such as galvanic skin response, respiration, and pulse, are shared amongst users participating in a networked cooperative learning task. The physiological system is visualized in real-time using visual displays (see Figure 3 and Figure 4) that were designed to be so simple and intuitive that they require almost no explanation. For example, the pulse is represented by a pulsating red circle. Users learn to attribute meaning to these physiological displays during the course of meaning interaction on a shared task; we studied a situation in which one user tutored another on written Chinese. While the interpretation of the artificial expressions is not fixed, but must be learned constructively through engagement in a meaningful situation, neither is it completely arbitrary - the expressions are linked directly to the physiological status of the users. One of the outcomes of this study was the observation users quickly learned to make use of the galvanic skin response as a measure of the level of stress of their partner. Specifically, the tutor found the galvanic skin response signal helpful in adjusting the pace of instruction avoiding a situation where the learner was struggling to keep up.

It is reasonable to consider an analogous approach in the design of systems making use of facial expressions. For example, face detection and tracking methods are now sufficiently advanced that they can be robustly used under standard office lighting conditions. Hence, an automatic approach can be used to normalize and scale a video display of an expressive face. Removing variations in location and scale could help a user to focus their attention on the actual movements of a face. This approach has been used in the design of a facial expression data navigation system (Lyons, Funk, & Kuwabara, 2005). In this work, video data of long-term observation of the face could be browsed efficiently and quickly by normalizing the position and scale of the face extracted from a video sequence. In addition, optical flow was calculated at several locations on the face and converted to an aggregate measure of non-rigid facial movement. This measure could be used to highlight possible hotspots of facial expression activity, to further ease the task of navigating long term behavioral data. The system, as described, was developed as part of a project to assist in the long term care of dementia patients, to provide a tool allowing physicians and caregivers to more easily understand long term trends in the well being of a patient. Again, the difficult AI problem of understanding the patients emotions is left to a human, but their task is made much more efficient by leveraging a soluble problem of automatic face processing - face detection and tracking.

Expressive Robots

One of the most engaging robots that use the "Art of the Soluable" approach is KeepOn. This robot has a very limited repertoir of movements, which consists of bouncing, tilting and rotating (Michalowski, Sabanovic, & Kozima, 2007). With this set of movements, KeepOn is able to express

Figure 5. eMuu

a considerable variety of internal states, including emotions. The interaction with KeepOn does also not require a strong AI. So far, KeepOn has been used for rhythm imitation games. The user beats a drum and KeepOn dances to the rhythm. KeepOn demonstrates that a simple robot can stimulate highly engaging interaction between itself and a user. Another example of a simple robot that effectively interacted with a user is eMuu (Bartneck, 2002). The robot has only four degrees of freedom, but its emotional expressions improved the interaction. This robot demonstrate not only that a limited repertoire of iconic facial expression are sufficient to communicate emotional states, but it also demonstrated that a radically simplified OCC model has been sufficient to create believable expressions.

CONCLUSION

In this paper we have argued in favour of an "Art of the Soluble" approach in HCI. Progress can often be made by sidestepping long-standing difficult issues in artificial intelligence and pattern recognition. This is partly intrinsic to HCI: the presence of a human user for the system being developed implies leverage for existing computational algorithms. Our experience and the discussions that led to this article have also convinced us that HCI researchers tend towards an inherently pragmatic approach even if they are not always self-conscious of the fact. In summary, we would like to suggest that skill in identifying soluble problems is already a relative strength of HCI and this is something that would be worth further developing.

REFERENCES

Bandai. (2000). Tamagotchi. Retrieved January 2000, from http://www.bandai.com/

Bartneck, C. (2001). How convincing is Mr. Data's smile: Affective expressions of machines. *User Modeling and User-Adapted Interaction, 11*, 279-295. | DOI: 10.1023/A:1011811315582

Bartneck, C. (2002). *eMuu - an embodied emotional character for the ambient intelligent home.* Ph.D. thesis, Eindhoven University of Technology, Eindhoven.

Bartneck, C. (2003). Interacting with an embodied emotional character. In *Proceedings of the Design for Pleasurable Products Conference (DPPI2004), Pittsburgh* (pp. 55-60). | DOI: 10.1145/782896.782911

Bartneck, C., Kanda, T., Ishiguro, H., & Hagita, N. (2007). Is the uncanny valley an uncanny cliff? In *Proceedings of the 16th IEEE International Symposium on Robot and Human Interactive Communication, RO-MAN 2007, Jeju, Korea* (pp. 368-373). | DOI: 10.1109/ROMAN.2007.4415111

Bartneck, C., & Lyons, M. J. (2007). HCI and the Face: Towards an Art of the Soluble. In J. Jacko (Ed.), *Human-computer interaction, part 1, HCII2007, LNCS 4550* (pp. 20-29). Berlin: Springer. | DOI: 10.1007/978-3-540-73105-4_3

Bartneck, C., & Okada, M. (2001). Robotic user interfaces. In *Proceedings of the Human and Computer Conference (HC2001), Aizu* (pp. 130-140).

Bartneck, C., & Reichenbach, J. (2005). Subtle emotional expressions of synthetic characters. *The International Journal of Human-Computer Studies, 62*(2), 179-192. | DOI: 10.1016/j.ijhcs.2004.11.006

Bartneck, C., Reichenbach, J., & Breemen, A. (2004). In your face, robot! The influence of a character's embodiment on how users perceive its emotional expressions. In *Proceedings of the Design and Emotion 2004, Ankara.*

Bartneck, C., & Suzuki, N. (2005). Subtle Expressivity for Characters and Robots. *International*

Journal of Human Computer Studies, 62(2), 159-160. | DOI: 10.1016/j.ijhcs.2004.11.004

Biocca, F. (1997). The cyborg's dilemma: embodiment in virtual environments. In *Proceedings of the Second International Conference on Cognitive Technology - "Humanizing the Information Age", Aizu* (pp. 12-26). | DOI: 10.1109/CT.1997.617676

Bondarev, A. (2002). *Design of an emotion management system for a home robot.* Master, Eindhoven University of Technology, Eindhoven.

Bratman, M. E., Israel, D. J., & Pollack, M. E. (1988). Plans and resource-bounded practical reasoning. *Computational Intelligence, 4*(4), 349-355. | DOI: 10.1111/j.1467-8640.1988.tb00284.x

Breemen, A., Yan, X., & Meerbeek, B. (2005). iCat: an animated user-interface robot with personality. In *Proceedings of the Fourth International Conference on Autonomous Agents & Multi Agent Systems, Utrecht.* | DOI: 10.1145/1082473.1082823

Cassell, J., Sullivan, J., Prevost, S., & Churchill, E. (2000). *Embodied conversational agents.* Cambridge: MIT Press.

Cerami, F. (2006). Miss Digital World. Retrieved August 4th, from http://www.missdigitalworld. com/

Chan, C., Lyons, M. J., & Tetsutani, N. (2003). Mouthbrush: drawing and painting by hand and mouth. In *Proceedings of the Fifth International Conference on Multimodal Interfaces, Vancouver* (pp. 277-280). | DOI: 10.1145/958432.958482

Cycorp. (2007). Cyc. Retrieved February 2007, from http://www.cyc.com/

Dailey, M. N., Cottrell, G. W., Padgett, C., & Adolphs, R. (2002). EMPATH: A neural network that categorizes facial expressions. *Journal of Cognitive Neuroscience, 14*(8), 1158-1173. | DOI: 10.1162/089892902760807177

Darwin, C. (1872). *The expression of the emotions in man and animals.* London,: J. Murray.

De Silva, C. G., Lyons, M. J., Kawato, S., & Tetsutani, N. (2003). Human factors evaluation of a vision-based facial gesture interface. In *Proceedings of the Conference on Computer Vision and Pattern Recognition Workshop* (pp. 52). | DOI: 10.1109/CVPRW.2003.10055

Ekman, P. (1985). *Telling lies: Clues to deceit in the marketplace, politics, and marriage.* New York: W.W. Norton.

Ekman, P. (1999). Basic emotions. In T. Dalgleish & M. J. Power (Eds.), *Handbook of cognition and emotion* (pp. 45–60). Chichester, England; New York: Wiley.

Ekman, P., & Friesen, W. V. (1975). *Unmasking the face.* Englewood Cliffs: Prentice Hall.

Ekman, P., Friesen, W. V., & Ellsworth, P. (1972). *Emotion in the human face: guidelines for research and an integration of findings.* New York: Pergamon Press.

Elliott, C. D. (1992). *The affective reasoner: A process model of emotions in a multi-agent system.* Ph.D. thesis, The Institute for the Learning Sciences, Northwestern University, Evanston, Illinois.

Ellis, P. M., & Bryson, J. J. (2005). The significance of textures for affective interfaces. In J. G. Carbonell & J. Siekmann (Eds.), *Intelligent virtual agents* (Vol. 3661/2005, pp. 394-404). Berlin: Springer. | DOI: 10.1007/11550617_33

Fasel, B., & Luettin, J. (2003). Automatic facial expression analysis: a survey. *Pattern Recognition, 36*(1), 259-275. | DOI: 10.1016/S0031-3203(02)00052-3

Fogg, B. J. (2003). *Persuasive technology: using computers to change what we think and do.* Amsterdam; Boston: Morgan Kaufmann Publishers.

Fong, T., Nourbakhsh, I., & Dautenhahn, K. (2003). A survey of socially interactive robots.

Robotics and Autonomous Systems, 42, 143-166. | DOI: 10.1016/S0921-8890(02)00372-X

Hara, F., & Kobayashi, H. (1996). A face robot able to recognize and produce facial expression. In *Proceedings of the IEEE/RSJ International Conference on Intelligent Robots and Systems '96, IROS 96, Osaka* (pp. 1600-1607). | DOI: 10.1109/IROS.1996.569026

Honda. (2002). Asimo. Retrieved from, http://www.honda.co.jp/ASIMO/

Ishiguro, H. (2005). Android science - Towards a new cross-interdisciplinary framework. In *Proceedings of the CogSci Workshop Towards Social Mechanisms of Android Science, Stresa* (pp. 1-6).

Koda, T. (1996). *Agents with faces: A study on the effect of personification of software agents.* Master Thesis, MIT Media Lab, Cambridge.

Lund, H. H., & Nielsen, J. (2002). An edutainment robotics survey. In *Proceedings of the Third International Symposium on Human and Artificial Intelligence Systems: The Dynamic Systems Approach for Embodiment and Sociality, Fukui.*

Lyons, M. J. (2004). Facial gesture interfaces for expression and communication. In *Proceedings of the IEEE International Conference on Systems, Man and Cybernetics, The Hague* (pp. 598- 603). | DOI: 10.1109/ICSMC.2004.1398365

Lyons, M. J., Akamatsu, S., Kamachi, M., & Gyoba, J. (1998). *Coding Facial Expressions with Gabor Wavelets.* Proceedings of the Third IEEE International Conference on Automatic Face and Gesture Recognition, Nara pp. 200-205. | DOI: 10.1109/AFGR.1998.670949

Lyons, M. J., Budynek, J., & Akamatsu, S. (1999). Automatic Classification of Single Facial Images. *IEEE Transactions Pattern Analysis and Machine Intelligence, 21*(12), 1357-1362. | DOI: 10.1109/34.817413

Lyons, M. J., Chan, C., & Tetsutani, N. (2004). *MouthType: Text Entry by Hand and Mouth.* Proceedings of the Conference on Human Factors in Computing Systems CHI2004, Austria pp. 1383-1386. | DOI: 10.1145/985921.986070

Lyons, M. J., Funk, M., & Kuwabara, K. (2005). Segment and browse: A strategy for supporting human monitoring of facial expression behaviour. In *Lecture notes in computer science - human-computer interaction - INTERACT 2005* (Vol. 3585/2005, pp. 1120-1123). Rome: Springer. | DOI: 10.1007/11555261_119

Lyons, M. J., Kluender, D., & Tetsutani, N. (2005). Supporting empathy in online learning with artificial expressions. *Journal of Educational Technology & Society, 8*(4), 22-30.

Lyons, M. J., & Tetsutani, N. (2001). Facing the music: a facial action controlled musical interface. In *Proceedings of the Conference on Human Factors in Computing Systems CHI2001, Seattle* (pp. 309-310). | DOI: 10.1145/634067.634250

MacDorman, K. F. (2006). Subjective ratings of robot video clips for human likeness, familiarity, and eeriness: An exploration of the uncanny valley. In *Proceedings of the ICCS/CogSci-2006 Long Symposium: Toward Social Mechanisms of Android Science, Vancouver.*

Mahmood, A. K., & Ferneley, E. (2004). Can avatars replace the trainer? A case study evaluation. In *Proceedings of the the International Conference on Enterprise Information Systems (ICEIS), Porto* (pp. 208-213).

McDermott, D. (1997, May 14th). Yes, Computers Can Think. *New York Times.*

Medawar, P. B. (1967). *The art of the soluble.* London: Methuen.

Michalowski, M. P., Sabanovic, S., & Kozima, H. (2007). A dancing robot for rhythmic social interaction. *In Proceedings of the ACM/IEEE International Conference on Human-Robot In-*

teraction, Arlington, Virginia, USA (pp. 89-96). | DOI: 10.1145/1228716.1228729

Mori, M. (1970). The uncanny valley. *Energy, 7*, 33-35.

NEC. (2001). PaPeRo. Retrieved from, http://www.incx.nec.co.jp/robot/

O'Reilly, W. S. N. (1996). *Believable social and emotional agents*. Ph.D. Thesis, Carnegie Mellon University, Pittsburgh, PA.

Ortony, A. (2003). On making believable emotional agents believable. In R. P. Trapple, P. (Ed.), *Emotions in humans and artefacts*. Cambridge: MIT Press.

Ortony, A., Clore, G., & Collins, A. (1988). *The cognitive structure of emotions*. Cambridge: Cambridge University Press.

Pantic, M., & Rothkrantz, L. J. M. (2000). Automatic analysis of facial expressions: the state of the art. *IEEE Transactions on Pattern Analysis and Machine Intelligence, 22*(12), 1424 - 1445 |DOI: 10.1109/34.895976

Pelachaud, C. (2005). Multimodal expressive embodied conversational agents. In *Proceedings of the 13th Annual ACM International Conference on Multimedia, Hilton, Singapore* (pp. 683 - 689). | DOI: 10.1145/1101149.1101301

Picard, R. W. (1997). *Affective computing*. Cambridge: MIT Press.

Robins, B., Dautenhahn, K., Boekhorst, R., & Billard, A. (2005). Robotic assistants in therapy and education of children with autism: can a small humanoid robot help encourage social interaction skills? *Universal Access in the Information Society, 4*(2), 105-120. | DOI: 10.1007/s10209-005-0116-3

Roseman, I. J., Antoniou, A. A., & Jose, P. E. (1996). Appraisal determinants of emotions: constructing a more accurate and comprehensive theory. *Cognition and Emotion, 10*(3), 241-278. | DOI: 10.1080/026999396380240

Schiano, D. J., Ehrlich, S. M., Rahardja, K., & Sheridan, K. (2000). Face to interface: facial affect in (hu)man and machine. In *Proceedings of the CHI 2000, Den Hague* (pp. 193-200).

Schiano, D. J., Ehrlich, S. M., & Sheridan, K. (2004). Categorical imperative not: facial affect is perceived continously. In *Proceedings of the CHI2004, Vienna* (pp. 49-56). | DOI: 10.1145/985692.985699

Schlossberg, H. (1952). The description of facial expressions in terms of two dimensions. *Journal of Experimental Psychology, 44*(2).

Schlossberg, H. (1954). Three dimensions of emotion. *Psychological Review, 61*, 81-88.

Schulz, F. v. T. (1981). *Miteinander Reden - Stoerungen und Klaerungen*. Reinbeck bei Hamburg: Rowolth Taschenbuch Verlag GmbH.

Schwienhorst, K. (2002). The state of VR: A meta-analysis of virtual reality tools in second language acquisition. *Computer Assisted Language Learning, 15*(3), 221 - 239. | DOI: 10.1076/call.15.3.221.8186

Searle, J. R. (1980). Minds, brains and programs. *Behavioral and Brain Sciences, 3*(3), 417-457.

Shugrina, M., Betke, M., & Collomosse, J. (2006). Empathic painting: interactive stylization through observed emotional state. In *Proceedings of the 4th International Symposium on Non-Photorealistic Animation and Rendering, Annecy, France* (pp. 87 - 96). | DOI: 10.1145/1124728.1124744

Sloman, A. (1999). Architectural requirements for human-like agents both natural and artificial. In K. Dautenhahn (Ed.), *Human cognition and social agent technology, advances in consciousness research*. Amsterdam: John Benjamins Publishing Company.

Sony. (1999). Aibo. Retrieved January 1999, from http://www.aibo.com

Studdard, P. (1995). *Representing human emotions in intelligent agents*. Master Thesis, The American University, Washington DC.

Tamura, T., Yonemitsu, S., Itoh, A., Oikawa, D., Kawakami, A., Higashi, Y., et al. (2004). Is an entertainment robot useful in the care of elderly people with severe dementia? *The Journals of Gerontology Series A: Biological Sciences and Medical Sciences, 59:M83-M85*

Tobii Technology. (2007). Tobii Technology. Retrieved February 2007, from http://www.tobii. com/

Wehrle, T. (1998). Motivations behind modeling emotional agents: Whose emotion does your robot have? In C. Numaoka, L. D. Cañamero & P. Petta (Eds.), *Grounding emotions in adaptive systems*. Zurich: 5th International Conference of the Society for Adaptive Behavior Workshop Notes (SAB'98).

Wiratanaya, A., Lyons, M. J., & Abe, S. (2006). An interactive character animation system for dementia care. In *Proceedings of the ACM SIGGRAPH 2006 Research posters, Boston, Massachusetts* (pp. Article No. 82). | DOI: 10.1145/1179622.1179717

Zanbaka, C., Goolkasian, P., & Hodges, L. (2006). Can a virtual cat persuade you? The role of gender and realism in speaker persuasiveness. In *Proceedings of the SIGCHI Conference on Human Factors in Computing Systems, Montreal, Quebec, Canada.* | DOI: 10.1145/1124772.1124945

Zhai, S., Morimoto, C., & Ihde, S. (1999). *Manual and gaze input cascaded (MAGIC) pointing.* In *Proceedings of the SIGCHI conference on Human factors in computing systems: the CHI is the limit, Pittsburgh* (pp. 246-253). | DOI: 10.1145/302979.303053

KEY TERMS

Art of the Soluble (AOTS): Scientific research strategy advocated by Nobel laureate biologist Peter Medawar. Specifically, the AOTS strategy emphasizes skill in in the recognition of scientific problems which have not yet been solved but are reasonably amenable to solution with reasonable time and resources. Here we have suggested that, in some cases, the introduction of facial expression technology into HCI may be hindered by excessive concentration on research problems which fall into the domain of strong A.I. and that it is time to consider AOTS approaches.

Artificial Expressions: This term relates to a somewhat radical proposal to reframe the goals of affective computing towards the construction of new machine-mediated channels for the communication of affect between humans, or artificial expressions as we call them. The affected intended by these artificial expressions is not to be defined a prior, but to be learned and evolved through ongoing situational interaction in human-machine-human communication.

Expressive Robots: are robots that use facial expressions, gestures, posture and speech to communicate with the human user. This communication might not only include factual information, but also emotional states.

Facial Expression Classification: In machine vision, the automatic labelling of facial images or sequences of images with a semantic label or labels describing affect portrayed by the face. Our paper suggests that research has come to focus on a narrowly defined version of this problem: namely the hard classification of facial images (or sequences) into the stereotypical Ekman universal facial expressions, and that researchers in pattern recognition and human-computer interaction could profit by more broadly framing the research domain.

Human-Robot Interaction (HRI): Is the study of interactions between people (users) and robots. HRI is multidisciplinary with contributions from the fields of human-computer interaction, artificial intelligence, robotics, natural language understanding, and several social sciences.

Weak A.I. (contrast with hard A.I.): This term has connotations in the context of practical work in artificial intelligence, as well as for theoretical studies of A.I. and the philosophy of mind. In the current article we are primarily concerned with the former usage of the term, namely with that domain of approaches to machine intelligence which do not take, as a primary goal, an attempt to match or exceed human intelligence, this latter goal being the hallmark of "strong A.I." research.

Section II
Emotional Social Robots

Chapter IV
Multi-Robot Team Work with Benevolent Characters:
The Roles of Emotions

Sajal Chandra Banik
Saga University, Japan

Keigo Watanabe
Saga University, Japan

Maki K. Habib
Saga University, Japan

Kiyotaka Izumi
Saga University, Japan

ABSTRACT

Multi-robot team work is necessary for complex tasks which cannot be performed by a single robot. To get the required performance and reliability, it is necessary to develop a proper cooperative task. The robots need to be intelligent enough to adjust with dynamic workload and environment. Benefits can be amplified from a team if benevolence combines with cooperation. The benevolence behaviors among the team members are extra benefits to the society. There is a flexible relation among intelligence, benevolence and emotions. We describe an emotion model to be used for each of the members of a multi-robot team. In respect of some drawbacks with the existing approaches, we present an emotion based multi-robot cooperation with some benevolent characters.

1. INTRODUCTION

Multi-robot system is one of the main topics in research area to different application fields. Significant benefits like reliability, performance and economic value can be had by engaging multi-robot system instead of a single robot. In addition to that, a good level of robustness, fault tolerance and flexibility can be had from multi-robot due to task sharing among the members.

Multi-robot system is usually used to distribute the activities and intelligence among the members and this distributing process depends on the complexity of problems. If the task is too complex then it is needed to divide into small tasks and distribute these segmented tasks to members of team. A robot can have a satisfactory role by performing the assigned small task with the limited ability and knowledge.

The advantages of team work are widely acceptable and applicable from a small group to organization level. Until now, several team work theories and models (Scerri *et al.*, 2002; Kitano *et al.*, 1999; Tambe, 1997) have been developed considering coordination methods, communication methods among the team members, their forms and reforming methods, etc. The roles of emotions and effects of coordination for human team have already been investigated and supported by many psychologists. But, the roles of emotions and appliance for pure agent team have not been studied adequately, although some limited research results strongly support the importance of emotion for pure agent system (Nair *et al.*, 2005; Sceutz, 2004; Gage, 2004; Murphy *et al.*, 2002). During the cooperation among the team, it needs to develop different behaviours among the agents of which benevolence is one of the important behaviour for the welfare of the team. In this chapter, we will conjecture about how multiagent team can augment their capabilities for coordination with benevolent characters through the introduction of emotions.

While performing task in a group, it needs to have some agreements of cooperation and benevolent actions to increase the group/overall performance (as shown in Fig. 1). The degree of benevolence depends on the cooperation level, situation and type of action, etc. So, what is benevolent agent? To what extend an agent should be benevolent? What is the role of benevolence for a Multi-agent system (MAS) system? When is benevolence useful or fruitless for action performing agent and its colleague? Such kinds of

inquiries are continuously arising when benevolence concept is being considered to be applied for AI system. Is there any relation between benevolence and emotional state? Thinking about the incorporation of benevolence into MAS is a good idea to be considered as a research topic. In this chapter, we will discuss how emotional state affects benevolence characters and the roles of emotion for team work considering multi-robot system. In the following section, we will discuss about benevolent agents and their characters.

2. BENEVOLENT AGENT

In generally, benevolent actions are necessary for task/goal sharing to acquire with ease. There is no common agreement to define benevolent agent. Definitions of benevolent agent from different researchers are slightly split into their concepts. Philosophers and biologists relate *benevolence* as a pure concept of virtue, compassion and moral sentiments (Mohammed and Huhns, 2001). They describe 'benevolence action' as the doing of kind action to other from mere good will and without any obligation. Jennings and Kalenka (1999) suggested to select benevolence while describing a good decision making function. Some researchers considered benevolence as an important 'phenomenon' that exists in a team of autonomous agents from instance of agent's emotions (Mohammed and Huhns, 2001).

When a benevolent action should be performed? This is a critical question to answer.

Figure 1. Multiagent, cooperation and benevolence

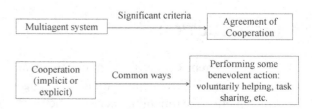

Because, benevolent action depends on present environmental situation, colleague's status, status of action performing agent and so on. To answer the question, a nice example can be taken as described in Huhns and Mohammed (1999). Let a mattress suddenly dropped on a road which is busy with vehicles. Due to the mattress, the vehicles need to slow down and bypass it which consequently creating a traffic jam and for this everyone suffers. If one driver stops and takes away the mattress, then the traffic jam is eliminated. Due to this benevolent action everyone will be benefited except who performed the action. So from the above example, we can say that benevolent actions are voluntarily services that are performed by benevolent agent expecting no immediate reward or benefit. But, there is another dimension of benevolent action which acts on accepting requests for help from other agents.

d'Inverno and Luck (1996) have given a definition of benevolent agent as "an agent for the requesting agents". A benevolent agent needs to adopt goals of others as well as own multiple goals. Goal adoption can be classified into three groups: terminal, instrumental and cooperative (Mohammed and Huhns, 2001). In terminal goal adoption, an agent adopts others' goals expecting no benefit from them and it will not help in getting its own goal. In the instrumental goal adoption, agent adopts others' goal expecting some benefit as a consequence. For cooperative goal adoption, an agent adopts goals of others as all are working in cooperation to complete a task with a satisfactory group performance.

We have discussed above some basic characters of benevolent agents: (i) voluntarily helping, (ii) performing benevolent action for the benefit of society to which the agent belongs and (iii) Should not expect an immediate reward. An agent should perform benevolent action in such a way that it does not hamper its own goal as well. For the mattress case, if the driver is driving an ambulance carrying a serious patient that needs to quickly admit into a hospital, then he should not perform that benevolent action. Because, the time delay for shifting the mattress may be harmful for the patient.

Some questions are asked by some researchers whether benevolence hampers autonomy or not. d'Inverno, Luck and Wooldridge (1997) suggested as "Crudely, the benevolence assumption states that agents will always attempt to do what is requested of them: they are not autonomous" (p. 2). If we emphasize that benevolent agents are voluntary to help others, not perform upon others' request then agents are autonomous. For the case of mattress example, the driver was not requested to remove the mattress from the road, but he did it voluntarily.

Does benevolence contradict rationality? Castetfranchi, Miceli and Conte criticized that benevolence contradicts rationality theory. Also, they think benevolence can exist but it is unnecessary (Castelfranchi, Miceli and Conte, 1991). They considered benevolent agents as irrational, because they west their resources (power, time, essential provisions, etc.) by helping others without any benefit for themselves. But, we think that benevolent agents will not perform any benevolent action when it will be harmful or hamper to attain their own goals. Their benevolent actions will benefit the society to which they belong and encourage others to be benevolent from which they (benevolent agent at present) can get benefit in the long run. So in this way of thinking, we can consider benevolent agents as rational. In our work, we have combined *rationality of agents* and *rationality of emotion* to develop benevolent characters. Emotional state and reason are used to develop benevolent characters among the agents of a team.

To develop an emotion based system we have to mimic the emotional system with best suit of biological phenomena. To construct an affection based system, many questions arise to be solved for a particular system. What is the scientific framework for defining emotions for a system? What kind of emotions are to be considered for a system? How to integrate the emotional system with other systems such as: perception, learning, action planning, communication, etc. What are the assumptions and computational mechanism to replicate the emotional process? To what extent this artificial emotion can replicate the biological phenomena behind emotion generation? Such kinds of questions are not so easy to reply from a simple view of theoretical or computational concepts. But, answers can be simplified by some assumptions or considerations depending on the application. In the next section, we try to define 'emotion' and discuss its perspective to robotic system. We also describe the emotional intelligence that may be applicable for multi-robot team (MRT) to develop a more autonomous and dexterous system.

3. EMOTION IN AGENTS

Understanding of emotion from the perspective of autonomous robots has become a very active item for developing robotic system with affective capabilities or features. Cañamero (2005) has described this thing as "Inspiration from human and animal emotions to include 'emotional' or emotion-like features and mechanisms in artifacts thus seems to help create 'better' engineering systems" (p. 445). She also stated in the same paper as "Mechanisms underlying emotional modulation of different aspects of cognition and action need to be singled out, in close collaboration with emotion scientists (e.g. neuroscientists, psychologists), and implemented in robots" (p. 453). So, we need multidisciplinary research works to implement emotion system in robotic agents with augmented capabilities of life-like behaviors and intelligence.

There is no ideal definition of emotion that can be universally useful to be applied for robotic system. But, everyone understood the importance of emotion even for pure agent system not interacting directly with human. Minsky (Minsky, 1988, as cited in Picard, 2000) has stated this matter as "The question is not whether intelligent machines can have any emotions, but whether machines can be intelligent without emotions" (p. 247). From the perspective of multi-robot, we find some most important beneficial features from emotional intelligence as shown in Fig. 2.

The emotional concepts are often mixed with reactions or moods of an agent. But, there is difference with duration in activeness of reaction, emotion and moods. Reactions are like impulses for very short period, whereas emotion lasts for longer period, but moods being the longest in duration among the three (as shown in Fig. 3). Emotions are created through a physiological process from input stimuli and some internal variables. The accumulated emotional states from a long lasting period constitute a mood.

Figure 2. Beneficial effects of emotional intelligence

Figure 3. Reaction, emotions and moods with time scale

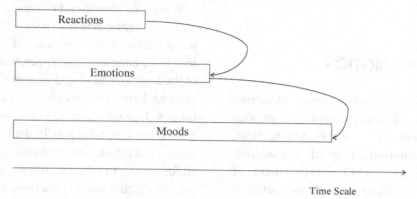

Human-robot interaction (Picard, 2000; Brave & Nass, 2002; Breazeal, 2003) and affection based internal architecture (Custòdio et al., 1999; McCauley *et al.*, 1998; Nehaniv, 1998; Gadanho & Hallam, 2001) are the main two steams of research where emotions are being used widely by researchers. First one is bringing improvement in interaction method among human-robot/machines with the introduction of emotion. The second one deals with modeling and computing of emotional architecture to be applied in robots/machines control process. Before going to introduce emotion in multiagent robotic system, we need a proper knowledge of emotions, their states and mechanism.

In our system, the multiagent system is a robotic system consisting of some miniature robots for performing a task in cooperation. The emotion generation of a robot while performing task depends on three basic set of variables like goals ($<G>$), environmental states ($<S_e>$) and robot's internal abilities ($<I_a>$). While a robot is working in a team it has a set of goals with priority level and also a set of environmental states. The internal states are the outcomes of some factors such as mechanical abilities, emotional states, motives, etc. The emotion elicitation mechanism captures the center position of the triangle formed by (G, S_e, I_a) through the balancing of these variables as shown in Fig. 4. Because, each robot has to make balance among goals, abilities and environment

while performing a task. Positive emotional states are generated from good balancing situation and negative emotions are created when any unbalance situation presents. The change of the robot's emotional states ($<E>$) can be expressed as:

$$< E >= f(< G >, < S_e >, < I_a >) \qquad (1)$$

It is unwise to include many emotions unnecessarily in a system which increase computational complexity and create problems during application. Even, sometimes one emotion is sufficient to develop an affection based system as used by A. Gage in task allocation problem for multi-robot (Gage, 2004). Selection of emotions depends on the system architecture, usability, task type, environment, etc. In the following section, we will briefly discuss the various emotional states

Figure 4. Basic emotion elicitation phenomena for an agent

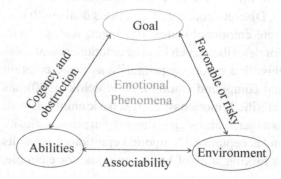

that can be considered to be applied for an agent-based system.

4. STATES OF EMOTION

There are abundant research activities on human emotions with psychological view and various emotion classifications are available. Among them, two concepts of emotion are mainly considered: Discrete categories and continuous dimension of emotion. Both concepts are strongly supported by many researchers having individual advantages and different applications. R. W. Picard (2000) has also given her consent about this in *Affective Computing* book as "The question of whether to try to represent emotions with discrete categories or continuous dimensions can be considered a choice, as each representation has advantages in different applications. The choice of discrete or continuous states is, in one sense, like the choice of particles or waves in describing light: the best choice depends on what you are trying to explain" (p. 169).

For continuous dimension of emotions, there are two mainly used dimensions like *arousal* (calm/excited) and *valence* (positive/negative). Most of the basic emotions can be mapped into two dimensional space, though there are some limitations. For example, the mapping of 'fear' and 'anger' in this space is contradictory with coherency as both have negative valence and high arousal. For this, another third dimension named as *potency* (powerfulness/powerlessness) is used to minimize the coherence problem.

Discrete concept of emotions deals with discrete emotional states like anger, fear, joy, etc. For describing such kind of emotion, researchers classified emotions primarily as basic emotion and compound emotion. R. Plutchik (1980) has classified emotions into eight basic emotions such as anger, fear, sad, joy, disgust, surprise, curiosity and acceptance. Compound emotions are results of mixing state of basic emotions, for example,

gratitude is a result of admiration and joy; remorse is a result of shame and distress.

In our benevolent multirobot system (BMRS), we considered discrete state of emotion having four basic emotions: joy, anger, fear and sad. Each of the emotions having different value system allows each robot to perceive its situation and then takes a decision quickly. The emotional states of each robot also take part in decision making for benevolent action to be performed or to be avoided. Before going to relate emotion and benevolence, we will discuss some of the basic roles of emotion for MRS in the following section.

5. ROLES OF EMOTION IN MRS

To describe the importance of emotion for human being, Picard (2000) has stated as "Emotions are important in human intelligence, rational decision making, social interaction, perception, memory, creativity, and more" (p. 47). A robot working in a team also needs these criteria (decision making, interaction, perception, etc.) to perform a task properly and also needs to interact with *colleague robots*. So, if we introduce the emotional intelligence into the robot, it will be augmented with extra capabilities to work in complex and dynamic environment maintaining a good interaction with *colleague robots*. Some have confusion whether emotion could have the same functional roles for artificial system as those prevailing in natural system. But, some researchers have already investigated with some experimental experience that emotions may have role in same way as in human being. For example, after performing some simulated results Nair *et al.* (2005) stated as "in pure agent team, the introduction of emotions could help in the same advantages that emotions bring to human teams" (p. 329).

Scheutz (2004) has found such 12 potential roles of emotions that can be used for artificial agents (may be for single agent or multiagents system) to develop emotional control mechanism such as action selection, adaptation, social regulation, sensory integration, alarm mechanisms, motivation, goal management, learning, attention control, memory control, strategic processing and self model. These roles are not exhaustive, but a good guide for utility of emotional control mechanism. We discuss here some of the roles that are very important for BMRS:

- **Adaptation:** A multiagent system is usually engaged in performing complex task where some uncertainty exists in the working environment. Emotion reflects the internal conditions and as well as effects of external environmental factors. This is highly compressed information depending on which a robot can suit with the situation. The adaptive behaviour can be emerged through the current emotional state of each agent which can make the agent more autonomous. For adaptation, usually two types of adaptation are considered: short term adaptation and long term adaptation (Maes, 1995). For short term adaptation, robots need to develop some reactive behaviors to suit with short term changes in environment with rapid decision and action selection. To suit with the long lasting changes of environment, robots require the ability to update behavior over time which needs learning and memory control mechanism. Emotion can play a role in short or long term behavior changes to adapt with dynamic environment under several constraints (like time limitation, resource limitation, etc.), especially for the environment which can not be predicted perfectly (Plutchik, 1983; Oatley & Johnson-Laird, 1987).

- **Action selection:** A behavior means a set of some actions to be performed. In a complex and dynamic environment, a robot may not be able to perform listed actions serially. It may need to rearrange the list. An agent can select an action (what to do next) based on the present emotional state to show its adaptive behavior to adjust with the contingencies of the world.

- **Managing social regulation:** For a multi-agent system, it is very necessary to develop an easier method for interaction and communication which can be achieved with some emotion based concepts. For some limited cases (exposing and interacting agents), emotional expressions and their understanding have already been developed. Emotions are functional adaptations to corroborate a kind of social interaction (Plutchik, 1983). Emotion also plays a great role to communicate links in mutual plans among the individuals in a social group (Michaud et al., 2001). For example, Gage (2004) developed a recruitment technique for multirobot task allocation problem with emotional motivation which leads to a reduction in communication overhead.

- **Motivation and learning:** Agent's motivational mechanism can be created as an integral part of emotional coping mechanism (Scheutz M, 2004). The internal motivation mechanism plays a great role in selection of a suitable action (for more details see Parker, 1994; Parker, 1998). The current emotional state with past history affects on motive-creating and also on learning mechanism. When emotional motivation is sufficiently high then a robot can take decision whether it should take benevolent action or not. For example, if a driver of ambulance sees an obstacle when passing a road will simply avoid the obstacles. He will not remove this from the road, as a benevolent action which will be helpful for others. Because, his emotional motivation is very low due to 'fear' in mind thinking whether he can reach hospital in time with the serious patient. But, when the driver is driving his car to visit some friends or going to a party, he has no such kind of 'fear' in mind. So, he can perform the benevolent action for others driving behind by removing the obstacle and thus decreasing traffic jam.

Summarizing above discussion, we can say that emotions are state variables which can influence on activities of each agent including benevolent services and communication methods. Nowadays, many researchers understood the importance of benevolence for team work and also think that in the available MAS theories, the description of benevolence is missing the emotional components ((Mohammed and Huhns, 2001). In our research, we have tried to find this missing point and developed benevolent actions among the robotic agents which depend on their emotional states. We have also described some of the emotional based issues for task allocation and sharing problems. Until now, the application of emotion for MRT is not yet well established facing some conceptual problems (for more details see Sec. 4 of Cañamero, 2005), though some researchers have already applied emotion for MRT/MAS as in (Murphy *et al.*, 2002; Nair *et al.*, 2005; Gage, 2004; Schneider-Fontan, 1998) with different computational models and mechanisms following some assumptions and simplicity. We have used also a simple model of emotion with Markovian stochastic model.

6. COMPUTATIONAL MODEL OF EMOTION

A number of approaches have been used to develop emotion based architecture for robotic system with increased autonomy and adaptation in the working environment. Cañamero (2005) has discussed some computational models that have been developed to design emotion for action-behavior control, emergent emotional behavior, and learning and memory control. There are some well-known computational models of emotions that have been developed to be used in various artificial intelligent fields: Cathexis Model (Velásquez, 1997), Elliot's affective reasoner (Elliott, 1992), FLAME (EI-Nasr *et al.*, 2000), ParleE (Bui *et al.*, 2002), Émile (Gratch, 2000), etc.

As previously stated that emotion modeling is very tough for its complexity, each of the above models also has some problems. For example, Cathexis model suffered lack of adaptation in emotion modeling, it is not a flexible model and there is low integration of personality in the model. The affective reasoner of Elliot is not a quantitative model and also limited by the use of domain-specific rules for appraising events. FLAME model is also inflexible as it uses some predefined reward values for projecting impact values of user's action.

Émile model also does not consider the value of event unexpectedness during the calculation of even-based emotion and emotional intensity. Émile also does not consider about the way of motivational states and personality influence on emotion. So, we see that it is very tough to model emotion and we need to compromise between complexity and flexibility.

Bates (Bates, 1994, as cited in Arun, 1997) has suggested three basic guidelines for proper portrayal of emotion: (i) Emotional states should be defined and represented well (ii) The responses divulge the feelings and (iii) Proper using of time to establish emotional response. Margulies (1993) stated that discontinuous rather than continuous state models can be used to model emotions which are easier. In such kind of model, agent can make transition from one discrete emotional state to other state and no way to stay in intermediate state. Following these suggestions, we have thought about simplicity and flexibility which can be used for our mutlirobot system for creating benevolent characters with Markovian emotion model.

The basic control structure consists of five subsystems: Sensing, perception, motivation, emotion generation and action selection. Figure 5 shows the all the subsystems and their interaction with environment. For simulation purpose, we

Figure 5. Basic control structure for each agent

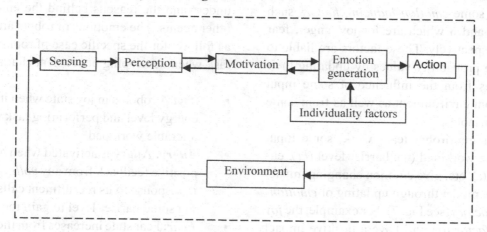

have considered miniature robot (like khepera) having eight infra-red proximity sensors and a linear vision extension module. With the input from sensory system and internal variables, the perception system can create some issues (with priority and value level) for motivational system. With the priority issues and with consideration of present emotional state, motivation system motivates the robot to some selective tasks that have to be performed. The emotion generation system generates emotional state based on Markov stochastic approach. The action selection system finally selects the action to be done to satisfy the present condition.

The Markovian emotion model is a stochastic model of emotion (see Fig. 6) where nodes represent some pre-defined states (joy, anger, fear and sad) and the arcs show the probabilities of transition from one state to other states. We select the discrete-state homogeneous Markov model as it is very suitable to model human emotion as well as to clone human emotion in believable agents (Arun, 1997). The future emotional state is derived from the present state and occupies less memory. Behaviors are highly depended on emotional present state rather than the past history. K. Kühnlenz and B. Martin (2004) have proposed an emotion core to be used for autonomous robots based on hidden Markov model where emotional states are

represented by hidden states. State transitions probabilities are modified by positive or negative stimuli/experiences and also particular character can be developed in a robot by carefully tuning the parameters of the emotion core.

We have also developed an emotion model to be implemented for MRT system through the adaptation of some features of emotion model from the work of Arun (1997) and K. Kühnlenz & B. Martin (2004). This model is used for each of the agent of the team to develop benevolent characters (Banik, 2007; Banik, 2008).

Figure 6. Markovian emotion model

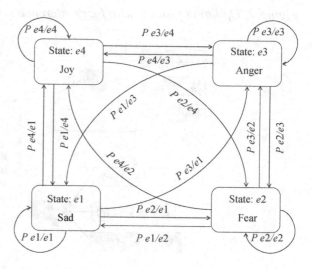

For changing the transition probabilities, we have used some *emotion inducing factors* such as α, β, γ and δ which are for joy, anger, fear and sad respectively. These factors are liable to change the probability values by updating their own values from the influence of some input stimuli from environment as well as from some internal variables.

For our multirobot team work, some input stimuli like workload (*w*), barrier-level (*bl*), energy level (*e*), etc. give emotion changing impact on Markov model through updating of *emotion-inducing factors* (see Fig. 7). For example, the *joy inducing factor* (α) will have a positive impact on the transition probability from any state to 'happy' state and on the contrary, it will oppose the transition from 'happy' state to other states. The sixteen arc values (as shown in Fig. 6) constitute the state transition matrix (*A*) which is changed in each step with the updated values of *emotion-inducing factors*.

In this model, we have considered only four basic emotions for simplicity. A complex model can also be developed including more emotions with multi-layered Markov model considering hierarchical stage of emotions. The emotions are developed based on some basic principles which are common to all members of the team. Because, the reason of emotions should be same for all,

otherwise it will be very complex for an agent to understand the reasons behind the emotions of other agents. The emotions of robots are defined as follows for the specific case of room cleaning task when developing benevolent characters:

- **Joy**: A robot is in joy state when it has high energy level and performing task well with tolerable workload.
- **Angry**: Angry is activated when getting no positive feedback from any *colleague* robot in response to its recruitment calls and facing some barrier level to gain the goal.
- **Fear**: Fear state increases from the threat of high workload when having low energy.
- **Sad**: It increases with ignoring the help messages (recruitment call of other robots). This is an emotional state of becoming sorry for ignoring help messages and also a final state of failure to attain goal.

The Markovian emotion model with four states can be expressed as follows:

$$X_{k+1} = AX_k \tag{2}$$

with emotional state points

$$\Omega = \{ Joy, Anger, Fear, Sad \} \tag{3}$$

Figure 7. Updating process with fuzzy inference system and emotion generation

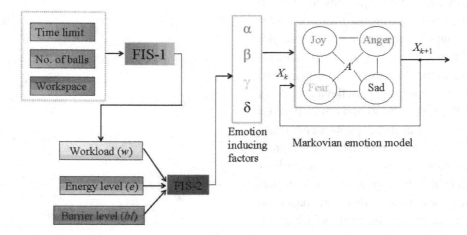

where, X_k represents the current emotional state and A is the emotional state transition matrix (so called stochastic matrix) which can be expressed as follows:

$$A = \begin{bmatrix} P_{e4/e4} & P_{e4/e3} & P_{e4/e2} & P_{e4/e1} \\ P_{e3/e4} & P_{e3/e3} & P_{e3/e2} & P_{e3/e1} \\ P_{e2/e4} & P_{e2/e3} & P_{e2/e2} & P_{e2/e1} \\ P_{e1/e4} & P_{e1/e3} & P_{e1/e2} & P_{e1/e1} \end{bmatrix} \qquad (4)$$

We found the model works well with adjustability and simplicity in structure. We have applied the model in a room cleaning task for simulation. The task is assigned by the user of the system by indicating workload and the task is evaluated by the user time to time (as shown in Fig. 8). Workload (w) is mapped from three variables using fuzzy inference system (FIS) which are (Banik, 2008): area (Ar) to be cleaned, number of balls (B) to be pushed towards wall side to clean the center part of the room and the prescribed time (T) to complete the cleaning task. The workload with other two variables (e, bl) are passed to the another FIS to map effects into *emotion inducing factors* (as shown in Fig. 9). With these updated factors the elements of transition matrix (A) are updated and new emotional state is generated from present emotional state using Eq. (2). Emotional intensity is derived through a belief model from the probability of each emotion.

7. BENEVOLENT ACTION FROM EMOTIONAL MOTIVATION

For the cleaning task, we have used three miniature robots (A, B and C) in simulated environment where robots can share the task of others (if necessary) through the motivation of benevolence influenced by emotional state. Each robot has two basic task oriented states (see Fig. 10): active and inactive. In the active state, robots are engaged in room cleaning by searching the balls and pushing them towards wall side. On the other hand, a robot in inactive state is not performing room cleaning task. In this state, it either makes pause (if assigned task is finished) or searches for power source (if power shortage).

Each robot in the team performs the cleaning task in his area and tries to finish the task within the assigned time. The initial speed of the robot depends on the initial workload which is mapped from initial value of Ar, B, T. These values are scaled to 0-10, 0-20 and 0-120 respectively for simulation purpose. The workload value is updated time to time to check the work progress. Fig. 11 shows the workload surfaces at two different values of assigned time.

The input stimuli from the environment are the sensor's output to the emotion generation system. The fuzzy rule based perception system is used to map these inputs to *the emotion inducing factors* and with these updated values the new emotional

Figure 8. Task assignment and evaluation by the user

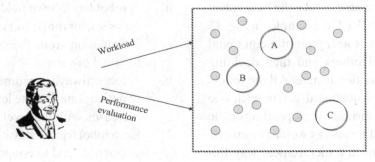

A benevolent multi-agents system

Figure 9. Fuzzy rule based perception system

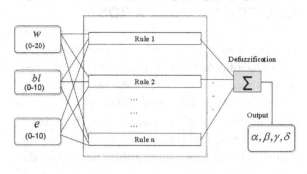

Figure 10. The state of a robot

Figure 11. Surface view of Workload at (a) T=40 sec. and (b) T=100 sec

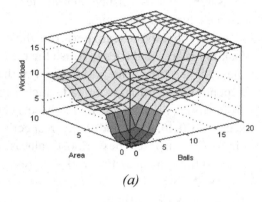

(a)

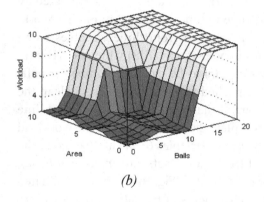

(b)

state is generated. Some of the fuzzy rule surfaces for *emotion inducing factors* are shown in Fig. 12, 13 and 14 obtained for robot A.

When a robot needs to take help it makes a new task sharing plan by getting some emotional information of *colleague robots* which act as a fitness function. On the other hand, other robots are emotionally motivated to take the benevolent action (the helping task). For example, in Fig. 15 we see that Robot A is accepting the emotional state information of others and then deciding which is better in emotional state. All the robots are considered as a blackboard where each one can read and write information. Depending on the internal emotional state and as well as of others, a robot makes a plan in a hierarchical way following some reactive and cognitive procedures.

The basic cooperative planning procedure is shown in Fig. 16.

Emotion eliciting conditions and effects on colleague are created according to the consideration of emotion definition as described before in addition to the following considerations:

a. A robot has its own field of view depending on its sensor range and is able to capture the information from the environment within the field of view.
b. A robot always consumes energy when it is in active state and the level of consumption increases with the level of activity.
c. Each robot tries to stay in active state as long as possible and to cooperate with others.

Figure 12. Surface view of joy factor (a) at bl=10

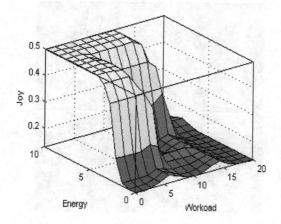

Figure 13. Surface view of anger factor (b) at bl=10

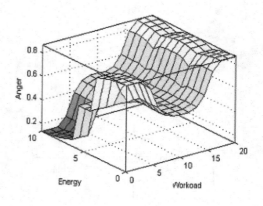

Figure 14. Surface view of fear factor (g) at bl=10

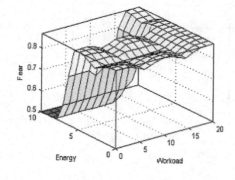

Figure 15. Selection of a robot with emotional fitness

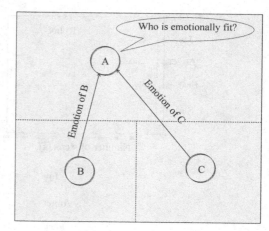

d. Each robot has the mechanical ability to perform other one's job which is very important for assisting others.

e. A robot sometimes benevolently helps to 'feared' robot, even not waits for call depending on its work progress.

For the simulation, the three cleaner robots (A, B and C) were engaged to clean a room within 100 sec. (cleaning task is shown in Fig. 17). Robot A having a high workload with compare to others needed to take help from either robot B or C. In Fig. 18, we can see the emotional states of the three robots. Robot B also feels workload as to be high due to its low energy level at starting state. But, after getting recharge it performed the work very well and became happy. On the other hand, Robot C was in most of the time in joy state, though it was in angry state also for a very few seconds facing some obstacles. But, after overcoming the obstacles it recovered from angry state and performed the task very well maintaining

Figure 16. The basic cooperative plan

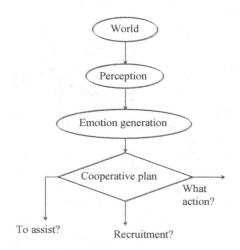

Figure 17. Room cleaning task of three robots (Banik, 2008)

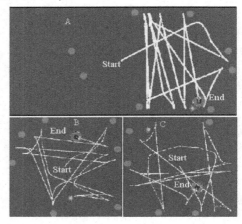

Figure 18. Dominating emotional state of three robots (Banik, 2008)

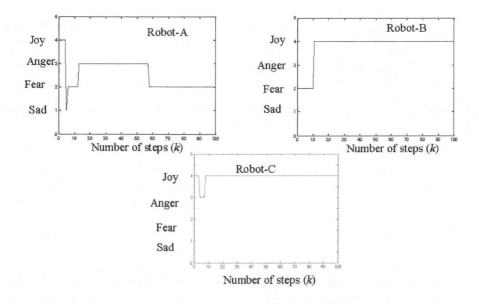

the joy state. Fear state has more negative points than angry state as fear indicates some inabilities to perform task (may be for high workload, less energy, mechanical inabilities, etc.). As robot B start with fear state, Robot C has the overall better emotional fitness to be selected by robot A to help. That is why, robot A selected robot C

to take help and make a new cooperative plan to complete the task. Robot C also emotionally biased (due to its joy state) to take this benevolent (helping) task and to maintain the overall group performance.

With the simple model of emotion, we will apply it in future for other applications in real fields.

In simulation, the model gives satisfactory results of emotional states and then generates benevolent behavior. Team size will also be increased with some other complex tasks.

8. CONCLUSION

In this chapter, we have described emotional roles in a multi-robot system and developed benevolent characters through emotional motivation. As emotion acts like compressed information, it will be a faster approach for interaction among the members of a team. If the emotional mechanism is successfully applied to a robot and it can animate like human, then this robot can also be used in a mixed agent (human-robot) system like a human colleague. But, for this we need more exploration in emotional research works and their application from multidisciplinary view. With the augmented emotional capabilities, robots will be more life-like and acceptance of these robots to human society will be increased.

9. REFERENCES

Arun, C. (1997). A computational architecture to model human emotions. *Proceedings of International Conference on Intelligent Information System* (pp. 86-89). Grand Bahamas Island, Bahamas.

Banik, S. C., Watanabe, K., & Izumi, K. (2007). Intelligent behavior generation of job distributed mobile robots through emotional interaction. In *Proceedings of 13th International Conference on Advanced Robotics* (pp. 1215-1219). Jeju, Korea.

Banik, S. C., Watanabe, K., Maki K. Habib & Izumi, K. (2008). An emotion-based task sharing approach for a cooperative multiagent robotic system. In *Proceedings of IEEE International Conference on Mechatronics and Automation* (WC1-4). Takamatsu, Japan.

Brave, S., & Nass, C. (2002). Emotion in human-computer interaction. In A. Sears & J. A A. Jacko (Eds.), *The human-computer interaction handbook:Fundamentals, evolving technologies and emerging applications* (pp. 77-93). NJ: Lawrence Erlbaum Associates, Inc.

Breazeal, C. (2003). Emotion and sociable humanoid robots. *International Journal of Human-Computer Studies, 59*, 119-155.

Bui, T. D., Heylen, D., Poel, M., & Nijholt, A. (2002). ParleE: An adaptive plan based event appraisal model of emotions. *Lecture Notes on Artificial Intelligence, 2479*, 129-143.

Cañamero, L. (2005). Emotion understanding from the perspective of autonomous robots research. *Neural Network, 18*, 445-455.

Castelfranchi, C., Miceli, M., & Conte, R. (1991). Limits and levels of cooperation: Disentangling various types of prosocial interaction. In Y. Demazeau & J. P. Muller (Eds.), *Decentralized AI-2* (pp. 147-157). B. V. Amsterdam, The Netherlands: Elsevier Science Publishers.

Custòdio, L., Ventura, R., & Pinto-Ferreira, C. (1999). Artificial emotions and emotion-based control systems. *7th IEEE International Conference on Emerging Technologies and Factory Automation* (pp. 1415-1420). Barcelona, Spain.

d'Inverno, M., & Luck, M. (1996). Understanding autonomous interaction. In W. Wahlster (Ed.), *12th European Conference on Artificial Intelligence* (pp. 529-533). Budapest, Hungary: John Wiley & Sons.

d'Inverno, M., Luck, M., & Wooldridge, M. (1997, August). *Cooperation structures*. Paper presented at 15th International Joint Conference on Artificial Intelligence, Nagoya, Japan.

Elliott, C. (1992). The Affective Reasoner: A process model of emotions in a multi-agent system. Doctoral dissertation, Institute for the Learning Sciences, Evanston, IL: Northwestern University.

El-Nasr, M. S., Ioerger, T., & Yen, J. (2000). FLAME: Fuzzy logic adaptive model of emotions. *Autonomous Agents and Multi-Agent Systems, 3*(3), 219-257.

Gadanho, S., & Hallam, J. (2001). Emotion-triggered learning in autonomous robot control. *Cybermetics and Systems, 32*, 531-559.

Gage, A. (2004). Multi-robot task allocation using affect. Doctoral dissertation, University of South Florida, USA.

Gratch, J. (2000). Émile: Marshalling passions in training and education. In *Proceedings of the 4th International Conference on Autonomous Agents* (pp. 325-332). Barcelona, Spain.

Huhns, M. N., & Mohammed, A. M. (1999). Benevolent agent. *IEEE Internet Computing, 3*(2), 96-98.

Kalenka, S., & Jennings, N. R. (1999). Socially responsible decision making by autonomous agents. In Kepa, K., Ernest, S., & Xabier, A. (Eds.), *Cognition, Agency and Rationality* (pp. 135-150). Dordrecht, Netherlands: Kluwer Academic Publishers.

Kitano, H., Tadokoro, S., & Noda, I. (1999, October). RoboCup-rescue: Search and rescue in large scale disasters as a domain for autonomous agents research. In *Proceedings of IEEE Conference on Systems, Men and Cybernetics, 6*, 739-743.

Kühnlenz, K., & Buss, M. (2004). Towards an emotion core based on a hidden Markov model. In *Proceedings of the 13th International Workshop on Robot and Human Interactive Communication* (pp. 119-124). Kurashiki, Okayama, Japan.

Maes, P. (1995). Modeling adaptive autonomous agents. In C. G. Langton (Ed.), *Artificial Life: An over view* (pp. 176-181). Cambridge, MA: The MIT Press.

Margulies, A. (1993). Empathy, virtuality and the birth of complex emotional states: Do we find or do we create feelings in the other. In S. L. Albon, D. Brown, E. J. Khantzian & J. E. Mack (Eds.), *Human feelings: Explorations in affect development and meaning.* The Analytic Press.

McCauley, T. L., & Franklin, S. (1998). An architecture for emotion. *AAAI Fall Symposium* (pp. 122-127). Menlo Park, California: AAAI Press.

Michaud, F., Robichaud, E., & Audet, J. (2001). Using motives and artificial emotions for prolonged activity of a group of autonomous robots. *AAAI Fall Symposium on Emotional and Intelligent II: The Tangled Knot of Social Cognition* (pp. 85-90). Cape Code, MA.

Mohammed, A. M., & Huhns, M. N. (2001). Multiagent benevolence as a social norm. In Conte R., & Dellarocas, C. (Ed.), *Social order in multiagent systems* (pp. 65-83). Boston, MA: Kluwer Academic Publishers.

Murphy, R. R., Lisetti, C. L., Tardif, R., Irish, L., & Gage, A. (2002). Emotion-based control of cooperating heterogeneous mobile robots. *IEEE Transactions on Robotics and Automation, 18*(5), 744-757.

Nair, R., Tambe, M., & Marsella, S. (2005). The role of emotions in multi-agent teamwork: A preliminary investigation. In J.-M. Fellous & M. Arbib (Eds.), *Who needs emotions: The brain meets the robots* (pp. 311-329). Oxford: Oxford University Press.

Nehaniv, C. (1998). The first, second and third person emotions: Grounding adaptation in a biological and social world. *5th International Conference of the society for adaptive behavior (SAB).* Retrieved from http://www.ofai.at/~paolo. petta/conf/sab98/final/nehaniv.ps.gz.

Oatley, K., & Johnson-Laird P. N. (1887). Towards a cognitive theory of emotions. *Cognitive and Emotion, 1*(1), 29-50.

Parker, L. E. (1994). Alliance: An architecture for fault tolerant, cooperative control of heterogeneous mobile robots. In *Proceedings of IEEE/RSJ/*

GI International Conference on Intelligent Robots and Systems (pp. 776-783), Munich, Germany.

Parker, L. E. (1998). Alliance: An architecture for fault tolerant multirobot cooperation. *IEEE Trans. on Robotics and Automation, 14*(2), 220-240.

Picard, R. W. (2000). *Affective computing*. Cambridge: MIT Press.

Plutchik, R. (1983). A general phychoevolutionary theory of emotion. In R. Plucthik & H. Kellerman (Eds.), *Emotion: Theory, research and experience*: *Vol. 1. Theories of emotion* (pp. 3-33). New York: Academic Press.

Scerri, P., Pynadath, D. V., & Tambe, M. (2002). Towards adjustable autonomy for the real world. *Journal of Artificial Intelligence Research, 17*, 171-228.

Scheutz, M. (2004, July). Useful roles of emotions in artificial agents: A case study from artificial life. In L. Deborah & G.F. McGuinness (Eds.), *AAAI conference* (pp. 42-48). California: AAAI Press.

Schneider-Fontan, M., & Mataric, M. (1998). Territorial multi-robot task division. *IEEE Transaction on Robotics and Automation, 14*, 815-822.

Tambe, M. (1997). Towards flexible teamwork. *Journal of Artificial Intelligence Research, 7*, 83-124.

Velásquez, J. D. (1997). Modeling emotions and other motivations in synthetic agents. In *Proceedings of the 14th National Conference on Artificial Intelligence* (pp. 10-15). Providence, RI.

10. KEY TERMS

Benevolent Agent: These are the agents which are liable to help (benevolent action) others if necessary.

BMRS: It means benevolent multi-robot system in which all the robots have benevolent characters.

Colleague Robot: Every robot working in team is a *colleague* to others and we called as *colleague robot*.

Emotion Inducing Factors: These are the factors which induce the transition probabilities of the transition matrix in the Markovian emotion model.

Field of View: It is the area of working environment based on sensor's range from where information can be captured.

Markovian Emotion Model: This is a model of emotion based on stochastic approach where states are predefined discrete emotional states.

Moods: It is the long time effects of emotional states.

Multidisciplinary Research: The research about emotion and its application for AI is multidisciplinary research as it includes the knowledge from different branches of science.

Perception: It is the subsystem of control structure of an agent through which it can gather and understand the information from working environment.

Proximity Sensor: These sensors are able to detect nearby objects without any contact.

Chapter V
Affective Goal and Task Selection for Social Robots[1]

Matthias Scheutz
Indiana University, USA

Paul Schermerhorn
Indiana University, USA

ABSTRACT

Effective decision-making under real-world conditions can be very difficult as purely rational methods of decision-making are often not feasible or applicable. Psychologists have long hypothesized that humans are able to cope with time and resource limitations by employing affective evaluations rather than rational ones. In this chapter, we present the distributed integrated affect cognition and reflection architecture DIARC for social robots intended for natural human-robot interaction and demonstrate the utility of its human-inspired affect mechanisms for the selection of tasks and goals. Specifically, we show that DIARC incorporates affect mechanisms throughout the architecture, which are based on "evaluation signals" generated in each architectural component to obtain quick and efficient estimates of the state of the component, and illustrate the operation and utility of these mechanisms with examples from human-robot interaction experiments.

INTRODUCTION

Effective decision-making under real-world conditions can be very difficult. From a purely decision-theoretic standpoint, the optimal way of making decisions – rational choice – requires an agent to know the utilities of all choice options as well as their associated likelihoods of succeeding for the agent to be able to calculate the expected utility of each alternative and being able to select the one with the maximum utility. Unfortunately, such rational methods are in practice often not applicable (e.g., because the agent does not have reliable or sufficient knowledge) or feasible (e.g., because it is too time-consuming to perform all necessary calculations).

Psychologists have long hypothesized that humans are able to cope with time, knowledge and other resource limitations by employing *affective evaluations* (Clore et al., 2001) rather than rational ones. For affect provides fast, low-cost (although often less accurate) mechanisms for estimating the value of an object, event, or situation for an agent, as opposed to longer, more complex and more computationally intensive *cognitive evaluations* (e.g., to compute the expected utilities) (Kahneman et al., 1997). Humans also rely on *affective memory*, which seems to encode implicit knowledge about the likelihood of occurrence of a positive or negative future event (Blaney, 1986). Finally, affect also influences human problem-solving and reasoning strategies, leading to global, top-down approaches when affect is positive, and local, bottom-up approaches when affect is negative (Bless et al., 1996).

For (autonomous) social robots that are supposed to interact with humans in natural ways in typically human environments, affect mechanisms are doubly important. For one, such robots will also have to find fast solutions to many of the same kids of difficult problems that humans ordinarily face, often with the same degree of uncertainty–if not more. Hence, affect mechanisms in robotic architectures might help robots cope better with the intrinsic resource limitations of the real world. The second reason why affect mechanisms are essential for social robots is grounded in their intended role as *social agents* interacting with humans. For those interactions to be *natural* (and effective), robots need to be sensitive to *human affect*, both in its various forms of expression and in its role in human social interactions.

We have started to address affect mechanisms that can serve both functions in our DIARC architecture (Scheutz et al., 2006, Scheutz et al., 2007). DIARC is a "distributed integrated affect cognition and reflection" architecture particularly intended for social robots that need to inter-

act with humans in natural ways. It integrates cognitive capabilities (such as natural language understanding and complex action planning and sequencing) (Scheutz et al., 2007, Scheutz et al., 2004, Brick and Scheutz 2007) with lower level activities (such as multi-modal perceptual processing, feature detection and tracking, and navigation and behavior coordination, e.g., see Scheutz et al., 2004, or Scheutz and Andronache 2004) and has been used in several human subject experiments and at various AAAI robot competitions (Scheutz et al., 2005, Scheutz et al., 2006, Schermerhorn et al., 2008, Schermerhorn et al., 2006). Most importantly, DIARC incorporates affect mechanisms throughout the architecture, which are based on "evaluation signals" generated in each architectural component, which effectively encode how "good" something (e.g., the current state of the world) is from the perspective of the component.

In this chapter, we will describe DIARC's mechanisms for affective goal and task selection, and demonstrate the operation of these mechanisms with examples from human-robot interaction experiments.

1. MOOD-BASED DECISION-MAKING

A perfectly rational agent with perfect information can make optimal decisions by selecting the action A with the highest expected utility

$$EU = \arg\max_{A}(p_A \cdot b_A - c_A)$$

where is the probability of action A succeeding, the benefit of A succeeding, and the cost of attempting A. If the agent knows the costs and benefits of each alternative and also the probabilities of each action succeeding, it cannot be wrong about which is the most profitable choice. In reality, however, costs and benefits are only approximately known. More importantly, real-world constraints can make it difficult to estimate accurately the probabilities of success and failure and, moreover, the dependence of the probabilities on other factors (e.g., past successes and failure).

Rational approaches probabilities that are often not available to robots. Without knowledge of the probabilities of failure and success associated with each potential alternative, it is not possible to calculate expected utility. Humans, on the other hand, are subject to the same kinds of real-world constraints, yet are able to make good evaluations, which are hypothesized to involve affective states ("gut feelings") in important ways (e.g., to help them prioritize goals).

Let an agent's overall affective state – its "mood" – be represented by two state variables, one which records positive affect (A_p), and the other of which records negative affect (A_N) (Sloman et al., 2005). and are reals in the interval [0,1] that are influenced by the performance of the agent's various subsystems (e.g., speech recognition). When a subsystem records a success, it increases the level of positive affect, and when it fails, it increases the level of negative affect. Specifically, success increases A_p by $A_p = (1-A_p) \cdot inc$ (failure updates analogously), where *inc* is a value (possibly learned) that determines the magnitude of the increase within the available range. This update function ensures that remains in the interval [0,1]. Both affective states are also subject to regular decay, bringing their activations in the absence of triggering events back to their rest values (i.e., 0): $A_p = (1- A_p) \cdot dec$ (Scheutz 2001). Given that affective states can encode knowledge of recent events (e.g., the success or failure of recent attempts), they can be used to estimate probabilities (that take past evidence into account without the need for prior knowledge of the probabilities involved).

Consider, for example, a case in which the robot is deciding whether to ask for directions to some location. The robot does not know that it is in a noisy room where speech recognition is problematic. All else being equal (i.e., with both

affect states starting at rest and no affect triggers from other sources), the value of *inc* determines how many failed communication attempts the agent will make of before giving up. With greater *inc*, the value of A_N rises faster, leading the agent to reduce its subjective assessment of the expected benefit (i.e., to become "pessimistic" that the benefit will be realized).

The agent makes online choices based on the expected utility of a single attempt, using the affect states A_p and A_p to generate an "affective estimate" of the likelihood of success . Examples presented below define *f* as follows:[2]

$$f(A_P, A_N) = \frac{1}{2} + \frac{(1 + A^{+2} - A^{-2})}{2}$$

This value is then used in the calculation of the expected utility of an action: $u=a \cdot b - c$.

The effect of positive and negative affect is to modify the benefit the agent expects to receive from attempting the action. When both A_p and A_N are neutral (i.e.,), the decision is based solely on a comparison of the benefit and the cost. However, given a history of actions, the agent may view the benefit more optimistically (if $A_p > A_N$) or pessimistically (if $A_p < A_N$), potentially making decisions that differ from the purely rational choice (overestimating true benefits or costs).

Figure 1. The expected utilities calculated at each attempt by the agent for various values of inc.

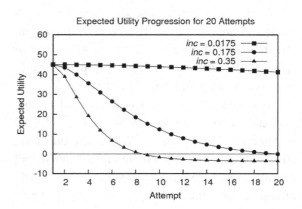

We can now demonstrate with a simple example of how overall mood states could be used in a beneficial way in the agent's decision making. Figure 1 depicts for the communication example the effect of various values of *inc* on estimates of utility: one that is too optimistic, willing to continue into the foreseeable future; one that is too pessimistic, stopping fairly early; and one that is more reasonable, stopping at about the point where the costs will outweigh the benefits. This suggests that the value of *inc* could be defined as a function of *b* and *c* to improve the likelihood that A_N will rise quickly enough to end the series of attempts before costs exceed potential benefits, for example. The agent could employ reinforcement learning to determine the value of *inc* for individual actions.

While the activation of each affective state is subject to decay, the rate of decay is slow enough that they can serve as *affective memory*, carrying the subjective estimates of the likelihood of success and failure ahead for a period after the events that modified the states. Returning again to the robot example, after a series of failures leading to the agent deciding not to attempt to ask directions again, the activation of A_N begins to decay. If, after some period of time, the agent is again faced with the choice of whether to ask for directions, any remaining activation of A_N will reduce the likelihood that it will choose to do so. In this way, the agent "remembers" that it has failed recently, and pessimistically "believes" that its chances of failing again are relatively high (e.g., because it has likely not left the noisy room it was in). Figure 2 shows the expected utility of asking for directions calculated by an agent 100 cycles after a series of failed attempts (e.g., Figure 1). The increased "pessimism" leads the evaluation to drop below zero earlier, potentially saving wasted effort on fruitless attempts.

Figure 2. The expected utilities calculated at each attempt by agent for various values of inc, after an extended series of 20 failures and 100 decay cycles, demonstrating the role of affective states as memory

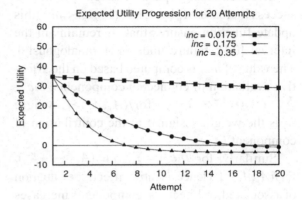

2. AFFECT REPRESENTATIONS IN ARCHITECTURAL COMPONENTS

We now show how the above decision-making process inspired by roles of human affect, where "affect states" are used to implicitly encode the history of positive and negative events from the agent's perspective, can be incorporated into an architecture at the level of functional components, where each component maintains its own "affective state". A primary determinant of the affective state of a component is its own performance, but in some cases the affective states of other functional components (e.g., those upon which it depends to function properly) or the occurrence of certain external events (e.g., a loud unexpected noise) can influence affect.

Specifically, we associate with each component of the architecture two state variables, one which represents *positive affect* (A_P), and the other which represents *negative affect* (A_N). A_P and A_N are reals in the interval [0,1] and define the "affective evaluation" of that component $a=f(A_P,A_N)$. Examples presented below define *f* as follows: $f(A_P,A_N)=1+A_P^2-A_N^{-2}$. The value of *a* is used by the component when making decisions about how to perform its function.

A component's affective state values can be passed on to other components to influence the calculation of their respective affect states. Associated with each affective state A_P is an increment variable inc^+ that determines how much a positive event changes positive affect. Specifically, success increases A_P by $\Delta A_P = (1-A_P) \cdot inc^+$ (this update function ensures that A_P remains in the interval [0,1]; failure updates A_N analogously). The value of inc^+ is computed based on the affective evaluation of connected components: $inc^+ = \sum_{i=1}^{n} w_i(A_i^{+2} - A_i^{-2})$, for $f(A_P, A_N) > 1$, where w_i is the weight assigned to the contribution of component i.

Similarly, for $inc^- = \sum_{i=1}^{n} w_i(A_i^{-2} - A_i^{+2})$, for $f(A_P, A_N) < 1$. Hence, positive affective evaluation of associated architectural components increases the degree to which positive outcomes influence positive affect A_P for a component, while negative affective evaluation of those components does the same for A_N. Affective states are also subject to regular decay, bringing their activations in the absence of triggering events back to their rest values (i.e., 0): $\Delta A_P = (1-A_P) \cdot dec$.

The *affective goal manager* (AGM) prioritizes competing goals (i.e., those whose associated actions require conflicting resources) based on the expected utility of those goals and time constraints within which the goals must be completed. Each goal is assigned an *affective task manager* (ATM), which is responsible for action selection and dispatch. The AGM periodically updates the priority associated with each goal's ATM. These goal priorities are used to determine the outcome of conflicts between ATMs (e.g., resource conflicts, such as when each wants to move in a different direction). A goal's priority is determined by two components: its importance and its current urgency. The importance of a goal is determined by the cost and benefit of satisfying the goal. The affective evaluation a of the goal manager influences the assessment of a goal's importance: $u = a \cdot b - c$. The resulting u is scaled by the urgency component g, which is a reflection of the time remaining within which to satisfy the goal:

$$g = \frac{Time_{elapsed}}{Time_{allowed}} \cdot (g_{max} - g_{min}) + g_{min}$$

where g_{max} and g_{min} are upper and lower bounds on the urgency of that particular goal. The goal's priority p, then, is simply: $p = u \cdot g$. When there is a conflict over some resource, the ATM with the highest priority is awarded the resource. This formulation allows goals of lower importance, which would normally be excluded from execution in virtue of their interference with the satisfaction of more important goals, to be "worked in" ahead of the more important goals, so long as the interrupted goal has sufficient time to satisfy the goal after the less important goal completes (i.e., so long as the urgency of the more important goal is sufficiently low).

The ATM uses affect states similarly to select between alternative actions in service to a single goal. Each potential action has associated with it (in long-term memory) affect states A_P and A_N that result from positive and negative outcomes in past experience with that action, along with (learned) inc^+ and inc^- that determine how further experience influences the affect state that determine how further experience influences the affect states. The ATM makes online choices based on the expected utility of a single attempt of an action, using $a = f(A_P, A_N)$ as an "affective estimate" of the likelihood of success for the attempt in the utility calculation $u = a \cdot b - c$. The alternative with the highest expected utility is selected in service of the goal associated with the ATM.

The effect of positive and negative affect, then, is to modify the benefit the agent expects to receive from attempting the action. That is, the AGM/ATM implements a decision making process that can operate without exact knowledge of the prior and conditional distributions. When both and are neutral (i.e., $A_P = A_N = 0$), the decision is based solely on a comparison of the benefit and the cost. However, given a history of outcomes, the agent may view the benefit more optimistically (if $A_P > A_N$) or pessimistically (if $A_P < A_N$), potentially leading it to make decisions that differ from the purely "rational" decision strategy, as mentioned before.

The following two examples presented below focus on AGM and the ATM as they are currently implemented in our robotic architecture. For presentation purposes, simplified scenarios have been chosen to highlight the functionality and benefits of affect in decision-making.

2.1. Prioritizing Goals

The affective goal manager is responsible for prioritizing goals to determine the outcomes of resource conflicts. Priorities are recalculated periodically to accurately reflect the system's affect states and time-related goal urgencies. In this example, the AGM maintains priorities for two goals, *Collect Data* and *Report*. The *Collect Data* goal requires a robot to acquire information about a region by moving through the environment and taking readings (e.g., for the purpose of mapping locations of interest in the region). There is a limited time within which to gather the data before the robot needs to return with the data. The *Report* goal requires the robot to locate and report to the mission commander once

the information is collected *or* when something goes wrong.[3]

One approach to accomplishing these two goals would be to explicitly sequence the *Collect* and *Report* goals, so that when the former was achieved, the latter would be pursued. The appropriate response to problems could similarly be explicitly triggered when problems were detected. However, the AGM allows for a more flexible unified approach in which both goals are instantiated at the start and the AGM's prioritization function ensures that the robot does the right thing at the right time. Figure 3 depicts the evolution of the two goals' priorities throughout a sample run of this scenario. Initially, the AGM's $A_P = 0$ and $A_N = 0$. The benefit associated with *Collect* (b_c) is 1800, while its cost (c_c) is 1200. The benefit associated with *Report* (b_r) is 200 and the cost (c_r) is 25. Both goals require the use of the robot's navigation system, but only one may do so at a time.

At the start, both goals have very low priorities due to the very low urgency (very little time had elapsed). *Collect* has a higher priority due to its greater net benefit ($b - c$); because the AGM's affect is neutral, there is no modification of the benefit component. As time passes, both priorities rise with the increasing urgency until an external event disturbs the system—the impact of an unknown object knocks out a sensor, causing a sharp increase in A_N for the AGM (this could be construed as a fear-like response to the impact event). The AGM output for time step 56 immediately preceding the impact was:

```
AGM A+: 0.0
AGM A-: 0.0
Collect PRIORITY 16.83
Report PRIORITY 5.89
```

Immediately following the impact event, the priorities have inverted:

```
AGM A+: 0.0
```

Figure 3. Priorities calculated by the affective goal manager for the goals Collect Data and Report during a sample run

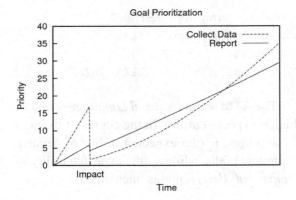

```
AGM A-: 0.5
Collect PRIORITY 1.71
Report PRIORITY 4.28
```

Both priorities were reduced due to the influence of A_N on the benefit component b, but because the reduction of relative to b_c was so much greater than relative to c_c, *Report* was given a higher priority. This allowed the robot to respond to the unexpected impact by seeking the mission commander, who would, presumably, be able to resolve the problem (e.g., by repairing the damage or redirecting the robot). Before the *Report* goal is achieved, however, the priorities were once again inverted (at time step 265), and *Collect* regained control of the navigation resources:

```
AGM A+: 0.0
AGM A-: 0.45
Collect PRIORITY 21.75
Report PRIORITY 21.73
```

This switch is attributable to the decay of A_N in the AGM. No further impacts (or other negative events) occurred and the impact did not cause a catastrophic failure, so negative affect was gradually returning to zero. This (in addition to rising urgency) caused the priorities of both goals to rise, but the priority of *Collect* climbed faster, so that it eventually overtook *Report* and the robot was able to continue pursuing its "primary" goal.[4]

2.2. Choosing between Alternatives

The affective task manager (ATM) component selects and executes actions on behalf of a goal, as priority allows. When an action completes, the ATM is also responsible for updating the affect states associated with the completed action (based on its completion status, success or failure), in addition to updating its own affect states. The following example is extracted from a sample run in which the robot has noticed a problem and needs to communicate it to a human

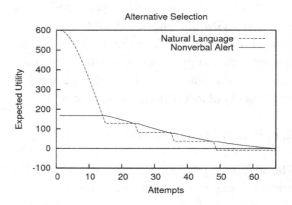

Figure 4. Expected utility of the two alternative actions Natural Language and Nonverbal Alert throughout a series of failed communication attempts

user. There are two modes of communication available: *Natural Language*, in which the robot attempts to explain the problem using natural language, and *Nonverbal Alert*, in which the robot uses "beep codes" to try to convey the message. *Natural Language* has a greater benefit (b_l=1800) than *Nonverbal Alert* (b_a=200), due to the ability to communicate more information about the problem, but also has a greater cost (c_l=1200 vs. c_a=25). Based on past experience, *Nonverbal Alert* has A_N (perhaps because of poor results trying to communicate failures using this method). This sample run depicts a series of failed attempts to communicate the problem to the human user (Figure 4).[5] At the beginning of the run, the ATM output is as follows:

```
Natural Language A-: 0.0
Natural Language UTILITY 600.0
Nonverbal Alert A-: 0.2
Nonverbal Alert UTILITY 167.0
```

The ATM selects *Natural Language* due to its higher expected utility. In the course of the next 14 attempts, u_l (the expected utility of *Natural Language*) falls, while u_a (the expected utility of *Nonverbal Alert*) remains unchanged:

Natural Language A-: 0.49
Natural Language UTILITY 173.70
Nonverbal Alert A-: 0.2
Nonverbal Alert UTILITY 167.0

After one more failure of *Natural Language*, $u_l < u_a$, so the ATM begins trying *Nonverbal Alert* instead:

Natural Language A-: 0.51
Natural Language UTILITY 127.54
Nonverbal Alert A-: 0.2
Nonverbal Alert UTILITY 167.0

Nonverbal Alert is repeated through attempt 23, and u_a is reduced:

Natural Language A-: 0.51
Natural Language UTILITY 127.54
Nonverbal Alert A-: 0.47
Nonverbal Alert UTILITY 130.96

After attempt 23, the increase in A_N for *Nonverbal Alert* causes its expected utility to fall below *Natural Language*, which is selected on attempt 24:

Natural Language A-: 0.51
Natural Language UTILITY 127.54
Nonverbal Alert A-: 0.50
Nonverbal Alert UTILITY 125.84

Natural Language is attempted only once before the ATM switches back to *Nonverbal Alert*, and the cycle begins again, with the robot occasionally attempting *Natural Language* before reverting to *Nonverbal Alert*, producing the "stair-stepping" effect seen in Figure 4.

3. HUMAN-ROBOT INTERACTION EXPERIMENTS WITH DIARC

Here we briefly give an example of an application of DIARC for studying affective human-robot interactions (Figure 5 shows the relevant components of the architecture for the given task).

In Scheutz et al., (2006), we reported an experiment that was intended to examine subjects' reactions to affect expressed by the robot. Subjects were paired with a robot to perform a task in the context of a hypothetical space exploration scenario. The task was to find a location in the environment (a "planetary surface") with a suf-

Figure 5. The (reduced) DIARC architecture as used in the human-robot interaction experiments

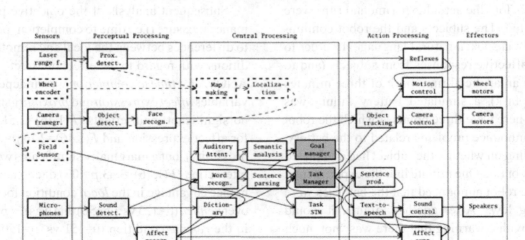

ficiently high signal strength to allow the team to transmit some data to an orbiting spacecraft. The signal strength was detectable only by the robot, so the human had to direct it around the environment in search of a suitable location, asking it to take readings of the signal strength during the search and to transmit the data once a transmission point was found. There was only one location in the room that met the criteria for transmission, although there were others that represented local peaks in signal strength; the "signal" was simulated by the robot, which maintained a global map of the environment, including all points representing peaks in signal strength. When asked to take a reading, the robot would calculate the signal based on its proximity to these peaks. The goal of the task was to locate a transmission point and transmit the data as quickly as possible; time to completion was recorded for use as the primary performance measure (see Scheutz et al.,, 2006 for further details).

Subjects were asked to respond to a series of survey items prior to beginning the interaction with the robot, in order to gauge their preconceived attitudes toward robots (e.g., whether they would think that it was useful for robots to detect and react to human emotions or whether they thought that it would be useful for robots to have emotions and express them). They were given a chance to interact with the robot for a short practice period before the actual experimental runs were conducted. The subjects and the robot communicated via spoken natural language. In order to evoke affective responses from subjects (and to impose an artificial time limit of three minutes on the task), a simulated battery failure was used. There were three points at which the robot could announce problems related to the battery, depending on whether the subject had completed the task or not. One minute into the experimental run, the robot announced that the batteries were "getting low." After another minute, it would follow with a warning that there was "not much time remaining" due to the battery problem. After three minutes (total), the robot would announce that the mission had failed.

We employed a 2x2 experimental design, with the first dimension, *affect expression*, being *affective* vs. *neutral* and the second, *proximity*, being *local* vs. *remote*. In the neutral affect expression condition, the robot's voice remained affectively neutral throughout the interaction, while in the affective condition, the robot's voice was modulated to express increasing levels of "fear" from the point of the first battery warning until the end of the task. Subjects in the local proximity condition completed the exploration task in the same room as the robot, whereas those in the remote condition interacted with the robot from a separate "control" room. The control room was equipped with a computer display of a live video stream fed from a camera in the exploration environment, along with a live audio stream of the robot's speech (using the ADE robot infrastructure, we were able to redirect the robot's speech production to the control station). Hence, the only difference between the two proximity conditions was the physical co-location of the robot and the subject. Most importantly, the channel by which affect expression is accomplished (i.e., voice modulation) was presented locally to the subject in both conditions–subjects in the remote condition heard the same voice in exactly the same as they would have if they had been next to the robot.

Subsequent analysis of the objective performance measure (i.e., time to completion) pointed to differences between the local and remote conditions with regard to the effect of affect. A 2x2 ANOVA for *time to completion* with independent variables *affect expression* and *proximity* showed no significant main effects ($F(1,46)=2.51, p=.12$ for affect expression and $F(1,46)=2.16, p=.15$ for proximity), but a marginally significant two-way interaction ($F(1,46)=3.43, p=.07$) due to a performance advantage in the *local* condition for *affect* over *neutral* ($\mu=123$ vs. $\mu=156$) that was not present in the *remote* condition ($\mu=151$ vs. $\mu=150$). The difference in the local condition between affect and no-affect groups is significant ($t(22)=2.21,p<.05$), while the difference in the remote condition is not significant ($t(16)=.09,p=.93$).

Affect expression provides a performance advantage in the local condition, but not in the remote condition. Given that the medium of affect expression (speech modulation) was presented identically in both proximity conditions, it seems unlikely that the remote subjects simply did not notice the robot's "mood" change. In fact, subjects were asked on a post-questionnaire to evaluate the robot's stress level after it issued the low-battery warning. A 2x2 ANOVA with with *affect expression* and *proximity* as independent variables, and *perceived robot stress* from the post-survey as dependent variable and found a main effect on affect ($F(1,44)=7.54,p<.01$), but no main effect on proximity and no interaction.[6] Subjects in the *affect* condition tended to rate the robot's behavior as "stressed" ($\mu=6.67, \sigma=1.71$), whereas subjects in the *neutral* condition were much less likely to do so ($\mu=5.1, \sigma=2.23$). Hence, subjects recognized the affect expression as they were intended to, and the lack of any effect or interaction involving proximity indicates that both conditions recognized the affect equally well. This, combined with the results of the objective performance task, strongly suggests that affect expression and physical embodiment play an important role in how people internalize affective cues.

A currently still ongoing follow-up study examines dynamic robot autonomy and how affect expression, as described above, influences subjects' responses to autonomy in the exploration task. The experimental setup is similar (Scheutz et al.,, 2006), but with an additional "distractor" measurement task included to induce cognitive load in the human team member concurrent to the exploration task. The measurement task consists of locating target "rock formations" (boxes) in the environment and "measuring" them (multiplying two two-digit numbers found on a paper in the box) to determine whether they were above a given threshold.

Figure 6. The priority evolution of the dynamic autonomy experiment with neutral starting affect

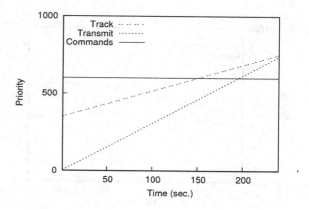

Figure 7. The priority evolution of the dynamic autonomy experiment with positive starting affect

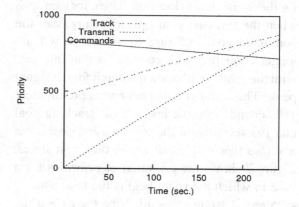

Dynamic robot autonomy is achieved via three goals in the AGM: *Commands*, which requires the robot to obey commands from the human team member, *Track*, which requires the robot to locate and stay with the transmission location, and *Transmit*, which requires the robot to gather and transmit data about the measurements. The priorities and costs were chosen to allow the tracking and transmission goals to overtake the commands goal at specific times. Obeying commands is originally given the highest priority, so that the other goals cannot acquire the resource locks for motion commands, etc. Hence, the autonomy condition starts out exactly as the non-autonomy control condition, with the robot taking commands from

Figure 8. The priority evolution of the dynamic autonomy experiment with negative starting affect

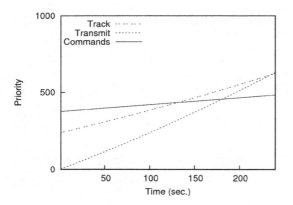

Figure 8. The priority evolution of the dynamic autonomy experiment with negative starting affect

the subject related to searching the environment for the transmission location. Then, for example, when the tracking goal's priority surpasses the command goal's (Figure 6), the robot will no longer cooperate with commands that interfere with the robot's autonomous search for the signal peak. These transitions occur at approximately 150 seconds into the task for the tracking goal and 195 seconds for the transmission goal. This assumes that both and are in their rest states. Figure 7 shows the evolution of priorities for a case in which the robot begins the task with A_P =.25 and A_N=0 (e.g., as might be the case if the robot had recently detected positive affect in the voice of the human team member).[7] The elevated positive affect leads to an "optimistic" assessment of the benefit of following commands (relative to taking over and searching for the transmission location, for example), so the point at which the other goals take over is pushed back (by about ten seconds in either case). An analogous example of the impact of negative affect (A_P=0 and A_N=.25) is shown in Figure 8, which shows the "pessimistic" assessment hastening the takeovers by tracking and transmission by approximately 20 and 15 seconds, respectively.

The experimental design includes the *Autonomy* dimension and the *Affect Expression* dimension. This design allows us to explore the

degree to which subjects are willing to accept robot dynamic autonomy, and how affect expression on the part of the robot influences the acceptability of autonomy. For example, it seems likely that the robot's expression of stress as a part of normal speech interactions will provide subjects with some context explaining *why* the robot has stopped following commands, which could facilitate acceptance. We are currently conducting experiments and analyzing the results, having completed the first phase of experiments in a remote condition. As reported in (Scheutz and Schermerhorn under review), even without affect expression, subjects are positive with regard to dynamic autonomy in a robotic teammate, to the extent that they even characterize the robot in the autonomy condition as more cooperative than the robot in the non-autonomy condition, despite the fact that the autonomous version disobeyed in the later phase of the task, whereas the non-autonomous version obeyed throughout. We are currently analyzing the remaining data to determine if and how affect expression alters the picture.

4. RELATED WORK

While different forms of affective and deliberative processes (like reasoning or decision-making) have been in simulated agents (e.g., El-Nasr et al.,, 2000; Eliott, 1992; Gratch and Marsella, 2004), most robotic work has focused on action selection (e.g., Moshkina and Arkin, 2003, Murphy et al.,, 2002; Parker, 1998; Scheutz, 2002) using simple affective states, often times without explicit goal representations. Yet, complex robots (e.g., ones that work with people and need to interact with them in natural ways, Scheutz et al.,, 2007) will have to manage multiple, possibly inconsistent goals, and decide which to pursue at any given time under time-pressure and limited resources.

The two closest affective robotic architectures in terms of using emotion (a form of affective state) for internal state changes and decision-making on robots are (Murphy et al.,, 2002) and (Breazeal et al., 2004). In (Murphy et al.,, 2002) emotional states are implemented with fixed associated action tendencies (e.g., HAPPY–"free activate", CONFIDENT–"continue normal activity", CONCERNED–"monitor progress" and FRUSTRATED–"change current strategy") in a service robot as a function of two time parameters ("time-to-refill" and "time-to-empty" plus two constants). Effectively, emotion labels are associated with different intervals and cause state transitions in a Moore machine, which produces behaviors directly based on perceptions and emotional states. This is different from the explicit goal representation used in our architecture, which allows for the explicit computation of the *importance* of a goal to the robot (based on positive and negative affective state), which in turn influences goal prioritization and thus task and action selection.

The architecture in (Breazeal et al.,, 2004) extends prior work (Breazeal, 2002) to include natural language processing and some higher level deliberative functions, most importantly, an implementation of "joint intention theory" (e.g., that allows the robot to respond to human commands with gestures indicating a new focus of attention, etc.). The system is intended to study collaboration and learning of joint tasks. The mechanisms for selecting subgoals, subscripts, and updating priorities of goals are, however, different in our affective action interpreter, which uses a dual representation of positive and negative affect that is influenced by various components in the architecture and used for the calculation of the importance, and consequently the priority, of goals.[8]

5. CONCLUSION

In this chapter, we introduced the idea of integrating affect representations and processing mechanisms throughout a robotic architecture based on psychological evidence that affect permeates the human cognitive system. We present the specific mechanisms integrated in our DIARC architecture, with focus on DIARC's goal and task managers. We showed with several examples that these mechanisms can lead to effective decisions for robots that operate under time, computation, and knowledge constraints, especially given their low computational cost and knowledge requirements. As such, they can improve the functioning and level of autonomy of social robots. Moreover, we also demonstrated that DIARC can be used for systematic empirical studies that investigate the utility of affect mechanisms for social robots. Specifically, we described results from human-robot interaction experiments where affect expression by the robot in the right context could significantly improve the performance of joint human-robot teams. We also pointed at the potential of DIARC and its affective goal and task management mechanisms for further investigations of the interactions between affect and robot autonomy. Current experiments suggest that these interactions will be particularly important for robots that have to collaborate with humans.

While DIARC has already proven its robustness and applicability in real-world settings, it is still very much "work-in-progress". We investigating criteria for situations in which good values for some of the parameters (i.e., the increment and weight values in the affect update equations) can be found. We are also examining ways of making these parameters dependent on goal and task contexts, thus allowing for multiple context-dependent values (which can be learned using reinforcement learning techniques) to overcome the shortcomings of a single value.

REFERENCES

Blaney, P.H. (1986). Affect and memory: A review. *Psychological Bulletin*, *99*(2), 229-246.

Bless, H., Schwarz, N., &Wieland, R. (1996). Mood and the impact of category membership and individuating information. *European Journal of Social Psychology, 26*, 935-959.

Breazeal (2002). *Designing sociable robots*. MIT Press.

Breazeal, C., Hoffman, G., & Lockerd, A. (2004). Teaching and working with robots as a collaboration. In *Proceedings of AAMAS 2004* (pp. 1030-1037).

Brick, T., & Scheutz, M. (2007). Incremental natural language processing for HRI. In *Proceedings of the Second ACM IEEE International Conference on Human-Robot Interaction* (pp. 263-270).

Brick, T., Schermerhorn, P., & Scheutz, M. (2007). Speech and action: Integration of action and language for mobile robots. In *Proceedings of the 2007 IEEE/RSJ International Conference on Intelligent Robots and Systems* (pp. 1423-1428).

Clore, G.L., Gasper, K., & Conway, H. (2001). Affect as information. In J.P. Forgas (Ed.), *Handbook of Affect and Social Cognition* (pp. 121-144).

El-Nasr, M.S., Yen, J., & Ioerger, T.R. (2000). Flame – fuzzy logic adaptive model of emotions. *Autonomous Agents and Multi-Agent Systems, 3*(3), 219-257.

Eliott, C. (1992). *The affective reasoner: A process model of emotions in a multi-agent system*. PhD thesis, Institute for the Learning Sciences, Northwestern University.

Gratch, J., & Marsella, S. (2004). A domain-independent framework for modeling emotion. *Journal of Cognitive Systems Research, 5*(4), 269-306.

Kahneman, D. Wakker, P.P., & Sarin, R. (1997). Back to Bentham? Explorations of experienced utility. *Quarterly Journal of Economics, 112*, 375-405.

Moshkina, L., & Arkin, R.C. (2003). On TAMEing robots. In *IEEE International Conference on Systems, Man and Cybernetics, Vol. 4* (pp. 3949-3959).

Murphy, R.R., Lisetti, C., Tardif, R., Irish, L., & Gage, A. (2002). Emotion-based control of cooperating heterogeneous mobile robots. *IEEE Transactions on Robotics and Automation, 18*(5), 744-757.

Parker, L.E. (1998). Alliance: An architecture for fault-tolerant multi-robot cooperation. *IEEE Transactions on Robotics and Automation, 14*(2), 220-240.

Schermerhorn, P., Kramer, J., Brick, T., Anderson, D., Dingler, A., & Scheutz, M. (2006). DIARC: A testbed for natural human-robot interactions. In *Proceedings of AAAI 2006 Robot Workshop*.

Schermerhorn, P., Scheutz, M., & Crowell., C.R. (2008). Robot social presence and gender: Do females view robots differently than males? In *Proceedings of the Third ACM IEEE International Conference on Human-Robot Interaction*, Amsterdam (pp. 263-270).

Scheutz (2001). The evolution of simple affective states in multi-agent environments. In D. Cañamero (Ed.), *Proceedings of AAAI Fall Symposium* (pp. 123–128).

Scheutz, M. (2002). Affective action selection and behavior arbitration for autonomous robots. In H. Arabnia (Ed.), *Proceedings of the 2002 International Conference on Artificial Intelligence* (pp. 334-340).

Scheutz, M., & Andronache, V. (2004). Architectural mechanisms for dynamic changes of behavior selection strategies in behavior-based systems. *IEEE Transactions of System, Man, and Cybernetics Part B, 34*(6), 2377-2395.

Scheutz, M., Eberhard, K., & Andronache, V. (2004). A parallel, distributed, realtime, robotic model for human reference resolution with visual constraints. *Connection Science, 16*(3), 145-167.

Scheutz, M., McRaven, J., & Cserey, G. (2004). Fast, reliable, adaptive, bimodal people tracking for indoor environments. In *IEEE/RSJ International Conference on Intelligent Robots and Systems (IROS)* (pp. 1340-1352).

Scheutz, M., Schermerhorn, P., Kramer, J., & Middendorff, C. (2006). The utility of affect expression in natural language interactions in joint human-robot tasks. In *Proceedings of the 1st ACM International Conference on Human-Robot Interaction* (pp. 226–233).

Scheutz, M., Schermerhorn, P., Middendorff, C., Kramer, J., Anderson, D., & Dingler, A. (2005). Toward affective cognitive robots for human-robot interaction. In *AAAI 2005 Robot Workshop* (pp. 1737-1738).

Scheutz, M., Schermerhorn, P., Kramer, J., & Anderson, D. (2007). First steps toward natural human-like HRI. *Autonomous Robots, 22*(4), 411-423.

Scheutz, M., & Schermerhorn, P. (in press). Dynamic robot autonomy: Investigating the effects of robot decision-making in a human-robot team task.

Sloman, A., Chrisley, A., & Scheutz, M. (2005). The architectural basis of affective states and processes. In J.M. Fellous & M.A. Arbib (Eds.), *Who needs emotions? The Brain Meets the Machine* (pp. 201-244). New York: Oxford University Press.

KEY TERMS

Affect: stating how emotions moves us in order to start actions action selection, Procedures to decide which action is more proper to a certain

context goal management, Procedures and algorithms to sort the goals on a system according to the priorities that emerge from the context affective architecture, Constructing systems able to take decision based on simulations of the affective processes human-robot interaction Discipline that studies how humans and robots can interact, and finding ways to improve this interaction.

ENDNOTES

[1] This material is based upon work supported by the National Science Foundation under Grant No. 0746950 and by the Office of Naval Research under MURI Grant No. N000140711049.

[2] A_P and A_N are squared to amplify the difference between the two, which amplifies the effect of the dominant state on the agent's decision process.

[3] This example is taken from the hypothetical space scenario that we have repeatedly used in human-robot interaction experiments (Scheutz et al., 2006), see also Section 3.

[4] Note that there is nothing explicit in the architecture that makes *Report* primary; it is simply the relative costs and benefits of the two goals that make it the preferred goal in the zero-affect state.

[5] Because there are no successful attempts, is not incremented for either action and remains zero throughout the run.

[6] Two subjects had to be eliminated from the comparison since they did not answer the relevant question on the post-survey.

[7] Note that the lines curve slightly due to the built-in decay of affect states.

[8] The details for reprioritization of goals were not provided in (Breazeal et al.,, 2004).

Chapter VI
Robotic Emotions:
Navigation with Feeling

Christopher P. Lee-Johnson
Victoria University of Wellington, New Zealand

Dale A. Carnegie
Victoria University of Wellington, New Zealand

ABSTRACT

The hypothesis that artificial emotion-like mechanisms can improve the adaptive performance of robots and intelligent systems has gained considerable support in recent years. To test this hypothesis, a mobile robot navigation system has been developed that employs affect and emotion as adaptation mechanisms. The robot's emotions can arise from hard-coded interpretations of local stimuli, as well as from learned associations stored in global maps. They are expressed as modulations of planning and control parameters, and also as location-specific biases to path-planning. Our focus is on affective mechanisms that have practical utility rather than aesthetic appeal, so we present an extensive quantitative analysis of the system's performance in a range of experimental situations.

INTRODUCTION

Despite decades of optimism, the robotics and artificial intelligence communities have thus far been unable to synthesize adaptive capabilities comparable to those possessed by humans or even simple animals. Affect and emotion are increasingly viewed as a potentially vital facilitators of adaptive behavior (Arkin, 2005),possibly to the extent of being prerequisites for general intelligence (Minsky, 1986; Damasio, 1994). However, affect has been conspicuously absent from many traditional AI frameworks and autonomous robots.

Recent years have seen increased interest in the development of robots and intelligent systems that possess emotion-inspired software mechanisms. Much of this research focuses on the application of affect to social robotics (e.g. Breazeal, 2004; Broekens, 2007; Hollinger et al., 2006). In this domain, the natural human tendency towards anthropomorphism can be exploited by portraying robotic emotions as facial expressions, body language and/or tone of voice. Affect can also be applied to robotics applications other than human-machine interaction (Arkin, 2005). Nevertheless, many purportedly general-purpose affect models are applied in a social context, where they influence interactions with humans or other robots. Few implementations have been demonstrated that approach the issue from the perspective of an individual robot in a non-social context.

To address the question of whether affect can improve a robot's performance beyond the social domain, we have developed and implemented a computational model inspired by theories of biological emotion. This model incorporates a range of affective states and processes, including affective stimuli, drives, emotions and moods. It is utilized as an adaption mechanism for a mobile robot planning and control architecture, and it is applied to a range of navigation and exploration tasks. Emotion-like mechanisms enable the robot to adapt its internal parameters to suit the different situations and environments it encounters while performing its duties. To assess the validity of our approach, we present quantitative results that compare the performance of the underlying planning and architecture to one whose parameters are modulated by the affect model.

BACKGROUND

Artificial affect representations can be broadly categorized into symbolic and neurophysiological models (Aylett, 2006). Symbolic models are typically favored by large-scale general-purpose AI frameworks, and emphasize cognitive roles of affect such as goal prioritization and memory management. They are often based on cognitive appraisal theories of emotion such as that proposed by Ortony et al. (1988). These types of models often have limited applicability in the robotics domain, where symbolic objects are not simply assumed to exist; they must be derived from real-world sensor data.

Thus, robotic implementations are typically more heavily inspired by neurobiological theories of emotion such as that proposed by Damasio (1999). Affect and emotions may be employed as internal 'sensors', or as discrete states that drive action selection. One of the main functions of this type of affect representation is to motivate a robot to respond quickly to certain events without waiting for its slower cognitive processes to ponder the situation. Affect is thus regarded as a potential replacement for deliberative processing in robotic controllers. Interactions between affect and deliberative processing have received little attention in the robotics domain, because they are often viewed as competitors for the same role.

One robotic affect model that has inspired various implementations is Valásquez's Cathexis architecture (Valásquez, 1997), which models Ekman's six basic emotions (anger, fear, happiness, sadness, disgust and surprise) (Ortony and Turner, 1990) as 'proto-specialist' agents (Minsky, 1986) executing in parallel. Emotions are one of several inputs that control behavior activation. A similar approach is adopted by Breazeal (2003) for the robotic head Kismet. In Kismet's model, stimuli are tagged with three dimensions of affective information (valence, arousal and stance), and their associated emotional responses compete for activation in a winner-takes-all manner. In addition to driving certain cognitive processes, emotions are portrayed as variations in the robot's facial expression, gaze direction and tone of voice.

Arkin's TAME architecture (Arkin, 2005) models a broader set of affective states and processes (traits, attitudes, moods and emotions) for behavior-based robotic systems. Each category of affect is represented by multiple dimensions of intensity values. Traits are based on the Five-Factor Model of Personality (McCrae and Costa,

1996) and consist of constant behavioral biases along the dimensions of openness, agreeableness, conscientiousness, extraversion and neuroticism. Attitudes are learned positive or negative biases associated with specific objects. Moods are long-term stimulus-independent states. Ekman's six basic emotions (Ortony and Turner, 1990) are represented as distinct intensity values that drive action selection. Traits and emotions have been implemented on a Sony AIBO robotic dog for a range of tasks intended to entertain human observers (Moshkina and Arkin, 2005).

A significantly more focused model is presented by Neal and Timmis (2003), who adapt a neural network-based reactive control system to different environments using a single affective state, timidity. Timidity is represented as an 'artificial endocrine system', which releases hormones dependent on obstacle proximity. Hormones directly influence the weights of the robot's neural network controller, increasing the robot's obstacle aversion in cluttered environments.

Another connectionist model is employed by Gadanho and Hallam (2001), who represent emotions using a recurrent neural network. Inspired by Damasio's theory of somatic markers (Damasio, 1999), the model makes a distinction between emotions and physiological responses, called feelings. Bodily sensations elicit domain-specific feelings (e.g. hunger, pain and restlessness), from which a set of basic emotions (anger, fear, happiness and sadness) are derived. Emotions also influence feelings via an 'artificial hormone' feedback mechanism. The model provides reinforcement values to a learning algorithm that coordinates a set of hard-coded control behaviors.

Some authors argue that emotion is neither a purely cognitive system, nor an entirely distinct structure that competes with cognition for activation. An alternative option is offered in the form of modulatory representations of affect (Fellous, 2004) (Dörner, 1995). Rather than existing as discrete states that simply trigger behaviors or actions, emotions are assigned a broad influence over the manner in which cognitive processes are conducted. Fellous (2004) proposes a biological mechanism – neuromodulation – that could account for these types of interactions.

A promising example of this type of model is Dörner's framework (Dörner, 1995; Bach, 2003), which represents affect using global parameters that modulate information-processing systems. These modulations help allocate cognitive resources to suit a given situation and reduce the computational complexity of problem solving. Rather than explicitly defining discrete emotional states, emotions emerge implicitly from combinations of parameters such as arousal, selection threshold and resolution level.

This approach to affect representation is well-suited to the problem of mobile robot control, where a robot's internal parameters can be adaptively modulated to suit the environmental conditions it encounters. However, emotions need not be represented implicitly, as in Dörner's framework. Rather than emerging from the modulations of global parameters, emotions in our model are represented as a discrete set of intensities, from which various internal parameter values are calculated. Thus, changes in emotion intensities result in parameter modulations, instead of modulations representing the emotions themselves. This is more of a design decision than a philosophical position concerning biological emotions. It allows discrete emotions to be designed to fulfill specific purposes, rather than characterizing certain nebulous internal responses as emotions following the design of a system. In our model, affective intensities modulate certain implementation-specific internal parameters to bias an intelligent system towards behaviors that in the long term are anticipated to improve aspects of its performance.

An earlier version of our affect model is presented in (Lee-Johnson and Carnegie, 2008) and (Lee-Johnson and Carnegie, 2007). In the earlier model, a strong distinction is made between reactive emotions, which modulate global control parameters, and deliberative emotions, which are location-specific biases to path planning. Individual emotions are shown to improve performance in certain controlled experiments. However, many of the improvements are less apparent in the general-case environments that a robot is likely to encounter during normal operation, or when multiple emotions are enabled simultaneously. Our updated model blurs the distinction between reactive and deliberative emotions; each emotion now incorporates both reactive and deliberative properties. They are now significantly more complex, incorporating multiple stimuli and responses. Furthermore, the model has been broadened to explicitly include other categories of affect, such as stimuli, drives and moods. The model is tested in a diverse range of procedurally-generated environments to gauge its performance contributions in situations that are likely to be encountered by real-world mobile robots.

PLANNING AND CONTROL ARCHITECTURE

Affect models are inextricably tied to the underlying computational architectures that support them (Sloman et al., 2005). Central to our mobile robot navigation approach is the hybrid reactive/deliberative control architecture shown in Figure 1. This architecture represents the robot's implicit cognitive system, which is to be modulated by the affect model. Higher architectural levels have a supervisory role, providing loose goals that can be obeyed or overruled by lower level processes as the situation dictates. This allows the robot to benefit from the guidance of deliberative planning, while maintaining the real-time responsiveness of reactive control. Three control levels are implemented, each formulating the navigation problem in a different conceptual space. A deliberative layer is applied in position space, while two reactive layers operate in direction space and velocity space.

Figure 1. An overview of our hybrid reactive/deliberative navigation system

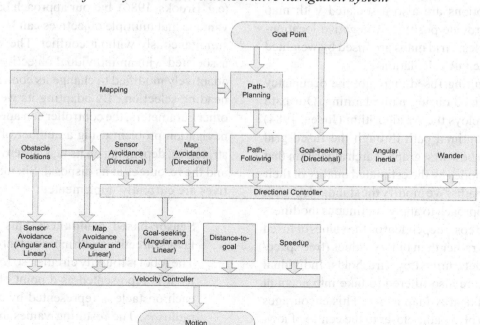

Mapping and Path Planning

Our robot's environment is represented by a rectangular occupancy grid map (Thrun, 2003). Each node x is assigned an occupancy probability $p_o(x)$, a unit interval value that represents the estimated probability that the node is occupied by an obstacle. Occupancy probabilities are updated in real time based on proximities to measured obstacles and sensor beams. Occupancy probability is not the only variable associated with map nodes.

Other variables such as exploration, danger and emotions are mapped in order to provide location-specific biases to the robot's planning and control systems. An exploration map provides the robot with an incentive to explore regions that are not currently known. A danger map is employed to mark regions that the robot should attempt to avoid. These include regions where there are fast-moving obstacles (e.g. humans), objects that the robot's sensors cannot easily detect (e.g. windows), or objects that result in severe consequences if the robot should fail to avoid them (e.g. staircases). Map nodes can be tagged as dangerous either a priori, or by recording points of collision as they occur. Emotions are also associated with map nodes, to provide positive or negative location-specific biases. Grid maps are fused by weighted probabilistic OR calculations.

The resulting fused map, not the occupancy map, is utilized during path planning. Our path planner employs the A* algorithm (Judea, 1984) to find an optimal path through the fused grid map. A* is a best-first graph search algorithm that prioritizes nodes by the estimated quality of their associated paths. We modify the standard A* path planning approach to apply continuous modifiers to measured costs dependent on the values of fused map nodes, rather than binary values (free space/occupied) determined by thresholds. Individual node costs are also filtered to take into account the costs of nearby map nodes. This encourages the robot to plan paths closer to the centre of low-cost regions, which generally results in smoother

paths that only pass near obstacles or dangerous regions if no other option is available.

Directional Control

Given a goal location and/or planned path, the directional controller obtains a locally-optimal target heading θ_T for the robot, utilizing an obstacle avoidance approach similar to the vector field histogram (VFH) method (Borenstein and Koren, 1991). An objective function $f(\theta)$ is applied to a discrete list of candidate headings θ:

$$\theta_T = \arg\max_{\theta \in [-\pi, \pi)} f(\theta) \qquad (1)$$

The objective function f is a weighted product of individual objectives f_1–f_n modulated by weights W_1–W_n (where f_1–f_n and W_1–W_n are unit interval variables):

$$f = \left(1 - W_1(1 - f_1)\right) \times \left(1 - W_2(1 - f_2)\right) \times ... \times \left(1 - W_n(1 - f_n)\right) \qquad (2)$$

Individual objectives are analogous to the behaviors of a traditional behavior-based system (e.g. Brooks, 1986), but our approach has the advantage that multiple objectives can be executed simultaneously without conflict. The weight W_i associated with an individual objective f_i can be adaptively modified to change its contribution to heading selection. By adapting its weights and other parameters, the controller can approach the navigation problem using a number of different strategies, depending on its task, its environment and the resources at its disposal. Six main objectives are currently implemented:

- **Sensor-based avoidance:** This objective favors directions with more distant obstacles. The robot is roughly circular, so for simplicity it is represented as a point object, and each obstacle is represented by a circle of radius r_o. The resulting values are filtered over all angles θ to reduce the attractiveness of directions that pass near obstacles, compelling the robot to give obstacles a wide berth and flavor the centre of corridors and doorways. A filtered avoidance vector field is shown in Figure 2.

- **Map-based avoidance:** While the sensor-based avoidance function enables the robot to avoid obstacles detected by its sensors, certain objects may be transparent or may reside outside of its plane of detection, essentially rendering them 'invisible' to the robot. Most aspects of the map based avoidance objective are the same as its sensor-based equivalent, but instead of obtaining obstacle positions from sensor readings, it constructs virtual obstacles from the robot's internal maps.

- **Path following:** This is the interface between deliberative path planning and reactive control. It favors directions that move the robot towards the planned path (or along the path, if the robot is already following it).

- **Goal-seeking:** Instead of targeting the planned path, this objective targets the goal point. If it is assigned a much higher weight than the path following objective, the robot's behavior becomes purely reactive.

- **Angular inertia:** This objective favors smaller changes in direction, preventing the robot from oscillating between multiple directions that are otherwise equally favorable.

- **Wander:** Random noise is injected into the controller by this objective, facilitating

Figure 2. A filtered avoidance vector field is represented by the lines extending outward from the robot's position at the centre. The circles represent enlarged obstacle positions.

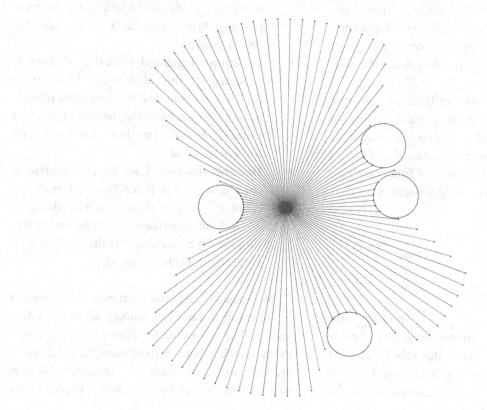

the robot's escape from local minima if its deliberative capabilities are disabled.

For the heading produced by the directional controller to result in actual motion, it must be converted into appropriate motor outputs. Directional obstacle avoidance approaches typically do not consider a robot's motion dynamics when computing its wheel velocities, limiting their high-speed performance (Fox et al., 1997). Hence, our planning and control architecture includes an additional stage that thoroughly considers the velocity control problem.

Velocity Control

To obtain a pair of locally-optimal velocities for the robot, the reactive control problem is reformulated as an optimization in velocity space. The robot's kinematic and dynamic constraints are taken into account, limiting the controller's choice of velocities at any given time to those that its motors can actually achieve. Two of the most significant examples of this type of approach are the curvature-velocity (Simmons, 1996) and dynamic window (Fox et al., 1997) obstacle avoidance frameworks.

The velocity controller utilizes an objective function with the same basic form as that of the directional controller, shown in Equation 2. Target linear and angular velocities v_T and ω_T are obtained by applying the objective function $f(v,\omega)$ to a discrete set of admissible velocities (v,ω):

$$\begin{bmatrix} v_T \\ \omega_T \end{bmatrix} = \arg\max_{v \in (v_{min}, v_{max}), \omega \in (\omega_{min}, \omega_{max})} f(v,\omega)$$

(3)

The constraints v_{min}, v_{max}, ω_{min} and ω_{max} are the minimum and maximum linear and angular velocities achievable given the robot's current velocities, acceleration constraints and global velocity limits. They form the boundaries of a rectangular dynamic window.

Five objectives are included in the controller:

- **Sensor-based avoidance:** Motion trajectories that do not pass near obstacles are favored by this objective. Among those that do pass close to obstacles, it prefers lower linear velocities. The robot's anticipated trajectory for a given velocity couplet is represented as a circular arc, or curvature segment. Each curvature segment is rated by the distance to its closest obstacle.
- **Map-based avoidance:** Other than the fact that this objective is applied to virtual obstacles constructed from grid maps, rather than directly from sensor data, it is functionally identical to its sensor-based equivalent.
- **Goal seeking:** This objective encourages the robot to move in the directional controller's favored direction. If the angular error is large, it prefers smaller linear velocities (and therefore near-stationary turns). This prevents significant deviations from the expected path and potential failure to converge on the goal point.
- **Speedup:** A general incentive to move is provided by this objective, which favors high linear velocities. Without it, the robot is unlikely to start moving, because the safest trajectories tend to be those that result in no forward motion.
- **Distance-to-goal:** Lacking an incentive to slow down when it reaches its target, the robot would overshoot or circle the goal point. This objective provides that incentive, facilitating convergence to the goal point by reducing the robot's speed.

When each of these are combined by Equation 2, the result is a discrete ranked set of velocities such as that represented in Figure 3. At any given moment, the robot's current velocities and acceleration constraints limit the available velocities to a small subset of those shown. The velocities

Figure 3. Example rectangular window of ranked velocities

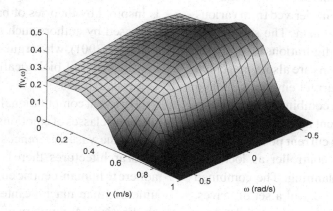

Objective Function vs. Linear Velocity vs. Angular Velocity

that yield the highest objective value $f(v,\omega)$ are selected as the robot's motor outputs.

Parameter Modulations

Our planning and control architecture supports point-to-point navigation and exploration in arbitrary flat-surfaced environments. It combines deliberative mapping and path planning capabilities with two distinct reactive navigation approaches – directional and velocity space control. The architecture is highly flexible, enabling the robot to adjust its navigation strategies to suit its environment, task, momentary situation and the resources at its disposal. This flexibility arises from various weights and other parameters that can be altered to modify the robot's behavior either subtly or overtly as required.

No single set of parameters can yield optimal behavior in all conceivable environments and situations. For example, in open environments, large safety margins may be preferable, coming at minimal cost to performance and decreasing the likelihood of collisions by encouraging the robot to give obstacles a wide berth. If those same values are utilized in a confined office-block environment, they may prevent the robot from passing through narrow doorways. Performance can potentially be improved by modulating the robot's parameters to suit its current situation and environment. Regarding the previous example, safety margins can be maintained at high values until the robot encounters a narrow doorway, at which point they can be temporarily lowered to allow the robot to traverse it.

Ideally, adaptive parameter modulations provide a robot with the 'mindset' necessary to complete the task at hand. The difficulty with this approach is in determining exactly how and when each parameter should be modulated. This is the primary role of artificial affect in our architecture. It is a set of abstractions by which the problem can be made tractable.

AFFECT-MODULATED NAVIGATION

We employ a multi-stage model of affect that utilizes the robot's perceptual and representation data to continuously update its parameter values in real-time. Many components of this framework are application-specific in that they are intended to modulate the parameters of our hybrid reactive/deliberative motion controller, rather than a general-purpose cognitive architecture. However, the basic structure of the model could be applied to different architectures or applications.

An overview of the model is shown in Figure 4. A set of emotional stimuli are derived from various sensor and representation data. The stimuli are combined in different configurations to form a set of basic emotions. Emotions are also represented in spatial maps, so the current emotions elicited by the robot result from a combination of the current stimuli and a persistent memory of previous emotions perceived in its current position. These maps are passed to the controller as location-specific biases to path-planning. The combined innate/learned emotions control a set of drives, each of which is responsible for modulating a subset of control parameters. A layer of second-order modulations is also modeled in the form of moods, which are global states derived from combinations of emotions over large timescales. They modulate the ranges over which control parameters can be varied by drives.

Although the word 'emotion' has been used for a wide range of affective states and processes (Sloman et al., 2005), we include only a small number of core states in this category. Our emotion model is inspired by theories of basic human emotions proposed by authors such as Ekman (1992) and Plutchik (2001), who argue that certain emotions are distinct and biologically innate, rather than cultural artifacts.

Different computational architectures support different classes of emotions (Sloman et al., 2005). Given the vast differences between human and robot architectures, there is little reason to strictly adhere to human-centric emotion categorizations unless human-machine interaction is the intended application. A number of robotic implementations favor human-centric categorizations such as Ekman's six basic emotions (e.g. Breazeal, 2003). However, when the goal is not simply to mimic human emotional responses, some basic emotions defined by psychological models are of limited practical value to the current generation

Figure 4. An overview of our model of affect

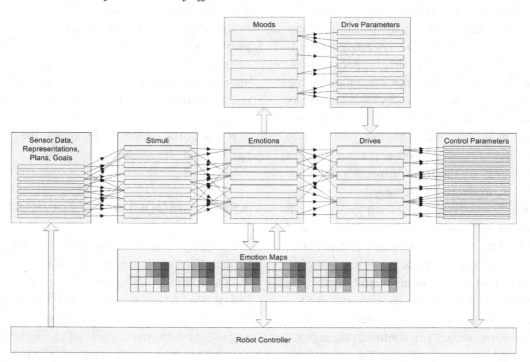

of robots. For example, disgust is normally associated with taste, smell, cleanliness, aesthetic appeal and morals – concepts that are not relevant to the majority of robotic implementations. Conversely, some emotions that are not included in most human-centric basic emotion models may be of sufficient importance to represent as basic robotic emotions.

Somatic theories of affect (e.g. Damasio, 1994) regard physiological feelings such as pleasure, pain, skin temperature, blood-pressure, heart-rate, and muscle tension as affective stimuli. Some biologically-inspired stimuli are included in our model (e.g. pain). However, the majority of physiological feelings are not applicable to a mobile robot that lacks a biological organism's complex set of bodily senses. Most affective stimuli in our model are simple, hard-coded cognitive interpretations of sensor and representation data, rather than bodily 'sensations' obtained directly from sensors. Each stimulus is associated with a particular event or performance characteristic.

Moods can be differentiated from other affective states and processes by their temporal characteristics – they persist for longer than stimuli, drives and emotions. They also have lower activation levels and intensities than emotions, and they are generic rather than object-specific (Moshkina and Arkin, 2005).

Few robotic implementations explicitly include moods as affective states distinct from emotions. One exception is the TAME (Traits, Attitudes, Moods and Emotions) framework (Moshkina and Arkin, 2005). Two mood categories are modeled in TAME: positive and negative affect (which are largely independent of each other).

Drives are related to the concept of homeostasis, or maintaining bodily parameters within acceptable bounds. Robots can possess both survival drives such as energy maintenance and 'informational' drives such as exploration (Dörner, 1995). A mobile robot navigation architecture can benefit from both types of drives, since it typically needs to consider both the robot's survival

(e.g. by avoiding collisions) and the completion of its assigned task (e.g. point-to-point navigation or exploration).

In the majority of models, drives elicit emotions, e.g. (Breazeal, 2003), or emotions are inferred from their interactions, e.g. (Dörner, 1995; Avila-García and Cañamero, 2005). Unlike these approaches, drives are represented in the output stage of our framework, modulating cognitive parameters in response to explicitly-defined stimuli, emotions and moods.

Stimuli

Stimuli in our system represent internal or external events that trigger adaptive control parameter modulations. They are unit interval intensity values that grow or decay in response to the presence or lack of certain eliciting events. Some stimuli (e.g. danger) are continually active and varying in intensity, while others (e.g. error) are dormant during normal operation, only activating in situations that require the robot to change its behavior.

Raw stimuli S_{raw} are normalized so that they increase and decrease appropriately within the interval [0,1]. Next, the normalized stimulus values S_{norm} are filtered to produce damped values S_{damp} using a simple weighted average function:

$$S_{damp} \leftarrow \alpha S_{norm} + (1 - \alpha) S_{damp} \qquad (4)$$

The damping factor α controls a stimulus's temporal characteristics. Separate damping factors are employed for the growth (α_1) and decay (α_2) of each stimulus. Some stimuli require rapid growth but slow decay (represented by high α_1 and low α_2), while the reverse is true for other stimuli.

Danger

For a mobile robot, the primary danger is that it may collide with obstacles, resulting in damage to itself and/or its environment. Hence, in our implementation, the danger stimulus is a function of obstacle proximities. It utilizes the obstacle distance vector field produced by the directional controller. The distance associated with each vector is taken into consideration, as well as its direction relative to the front of the robot. Obstacles close to the front of the robot are considered more dangerous than those behind it, so the distance d_o of each vector is increased by a function of the angle between it and the frontal direction θ_F:

$$D_o(\theta) = \frac{d_o(\theta)}{d_{D(max)}} + \kappa_\theta \frac{|\theta_F - \theta|}{\pi} \quad (5)$$

This results in a modified vector field $\mathbf{D}_o$ that is biased towards directions near the front of the robot. Increasing the direction factor κ_θ causes $\mathbf{D}_o$ to be more heavily biased towards frontal directions. The threshold distance $d_{D(max)}$ influences the level of influence that obstacle distance has over the vector field. Higher values increase the perceived danger of nearby obstacles.

The raw value of the danger stimulus S_{danger} is a function of the minimum of the vector field $\mathbf{D}_o$:

$$S_{danger} = 1 - \min(\mathbf{D}_o) \quad (6)$$

Growth of this stimulus is undamped ($\alpha_1 = 1$), to allow a rapid response to perceived threats. A lower decay factor α_2 is employed to prevent the stimulus from oscillating too rapidly between high and low values.

Stuck

The stuck stimulus detects obstructed states that are preventing the robot from achieving its goals. In the context of navigation, this is represented by a lack of goal-directed movement. The stimulus can be triggered if the robot literally comes to a standstill, but it can also result from repetitive motion that fails to make sufficient progress in any direction (either towards the goal point or

otherwise). Cyclical or otherwise repetitive motion indicates a potential infinite loop that the robot should attempt to escape.

A raw stimulus variable S_{stuck} is obtained that represents the robot's overall velocity over time interval $[t_0 = 0, t_n]$:

$$S_{stuck} = \frac{\left\| \sum_{i=0}^{n-1} (t_{i+1} - t_i) \mathbf{v}(t_i) \right\|}{t_n} \quad (7)$$

The magnitude of each linear velocity vector $\mathbf{v}(t_i)$ is the robot's linear velocity at time t_i, while the direction is its heading at time t_i. Hence, the upper term is an approximation of the robot's total displacement during time t_n. The value of t_n influences the amount of time the robot must linger in a given location before it detects an obstructed state. If t_n is low, the stuck stimulus is more transient, whereas higher values slow down its response.

Mobile robots rarely move in straight lines for significant periods of time, so the raw S_{stuck} value represents a velocity that is typically lower than the robot's average linear velocity. It is normalized to cover the interval $[0,1]$, and inverted so that higher velocities correspond to lower S_{stuck} intensities. Normalization and inversion result in a variable that is usually 0, but which increases towards 1 when the robot's overall velocity (the raw S_{stuck} value) drops below a threshold.

A very low growth factor is applied to this stimulus, while its decay is undamped. This reduces the rate of false-positives when detecting obstructed states. The robot must consistently fail to escape an obstruction before it determines that a behavioral change is required.

Pain

Pain can be viewed as a mechanism that discourages an adaptive system from repeating or continuing actions that cause it physical harm. For mobile robots, the most obvious source of pain is a collision. Since a robot typically does not have nerves, it cannot easily detect physical damage (unless the damage can be inferred from measurably diminished capabilities). Instead, our implementation of pain is a simple abstraction that increases when a collision occurs, and decreases over time. The raw S_{pain} stimulus is proportional to the robot's linear velocity v at the time of collision:

$$S_{pain} = \begin{cases} v & \text{if collision} \\ 0 & \text{otherwise} \end{cases} \qquad (8)$$

Higher levels of pain result from high-speed collisions, because the risk of physical damage is increased. The stimulus is normalized so that a relatively high-speed collision yields a S_{pain} intensity of 1. It is filtered such that increases are undamped, but decreases are highly damped. Thus, pain instantly increases when a collision occurs, but it decays slowly in the absence of collisions.

Achievement

Achievement is a measure of progress towards the robot's goal. Navigation progress is expressed in the form of a velocity that considers only the robot's overall movement towards or away from the goal point. The raw stimulus $S_{achieve}$ obtains this velocity from the initial distance to the goal point $d_g(t_0)$, the current distance $d_g(t_c)$, the time t_0 when the navigation instruction was received, and the current time t_c:

$$S_{achieve} = \frac{d_g(t_0) - d_g(t_c)}{t_c - t_0} \qquad (9)$$

Motion parallel to the direction of the goal point does not contribute to the velocity, because it does not affect the current distance to goal $d_g(t_c)$. Normalization of $S_{achieve}$ causes appropriate velocities to span the interval [0,1]. Growth and decay of this stimulus are damped to limit

its transient behavior following a transition from one navigation instruction to the next.

Density

The density stimulus is an estimate of the obstacle density of explored space. From a navigation perspective, a high obstacle density generally indicates a more challenging environment. The raw stimulus $S_{density}$ is a weighted average of occupancy probabilities $p_o(x_i)$ of nodes x_1-x_n stored in the occupancy grid map, where the weights are exploration probabilities $p_e(x_i)$ obtained from the exploration grid map:

$$S_{density} = \frac{\sum_{i=1}^{n} p_e(x_i) p_o(x_i)}{\sum_{i=1}^{n} p_e(x_i)} \qquad (10)$$

Different environments tend to produce relatively small deviations in $S_{density}$. Hence, even though it is already a unit interval variable, $S_{density}$ requires normalization to cover the entire interval [0,1]. The normalization thresholds are tuned to account for the $S_{density}$ ranges produced by the robot's intended environments. Density is undamped, because its global nature renders it comparatively unsusceptible to oscillatory behavior.

Learning

This stimulus is an estimate of the rate of knowledge acquisition. In our navigation architecture, this does not relate to formal learning methods such as reinforcement learning. Rather, it involves dynamically updating the robot's deliberative maps to incorporate new environmental and representation data. This knowledge is represented quantitatively in the form of the exploration grid map.

Raw stimulus variable $S_{learning}$ is the mean of all exploration probabilities p_e in a given map divided by the time t_e spent exploring the map:

$$S_{learning} = \frac{\overline{p_e}}{t_e} \qquad (11)$$

This is typically a very small number even under ideal conditions (travelling rapidly through a previously-unexplored environment), so to cover the appropriate interval, $S_{learning}$ is normalized using a very low upper threshold. Since it is a function of data averaged over an entire map, the stimulus is not prone to rapid fluctuations, so it does not require any damping.

Mismatch

The mismatch stimulus indicates a perceived discrepancy between the robot's stored knowledge about its local environment and its current sensor data. This can occur if the environment has not yet been explored, or if the occupancy grid map is sufficiently inaccurate due to environmental dynamics or localization failures.

A raw stimulus S_{mism} is obtained by comparing instantaneous occupancy status $s_o(x_i)$ of nodes x_1-x_m (where m denotes the number of nodes updated from sensor data) to their stored occupancy probabilities $p_o(x_i)$:

$$S_{mism} = \frac{\sum_{i=1}^{m} |s_o(x_i) - p_o(x_i)|}{m} \qquad (12)$$

The stimulus is heavily normalized because its raw value typically occupies a relatively small interval. Both increases and decreases to S_{mism} are damped, as the stimulus is otherwise susceptible to oscillatory behavior.

Cost

Cost is a stimulus that increases if the paths planned by the robot are of low quality. Low quality paths are paths that travel through high-cost nodes. Such paths are only utilized if there are no low-cost options available. This could be caused by environmental features (e.g. if a dynamic obstacle blocks a doorway for a sufficient duration to increase the occupancy probabilities of nodes in the doorway). It may also result from certain internal configurations (e.g. highly weighted danger, exploration and/or emotion maps producing very high node costs), or a combination of the two. Low quality paths are often unviable (e.g. passing through walls), so the robot should adjust its planning weights to reduce the contributions of non-occupancy grid maps.

The raw stimulus S_{cost} is the highest cost value from the set of nodes m_p contained within the planned path:

$$S_{cost} = \max\left(m_p\right) \qquad (13)$$

Each member of m_p is the same node cost that is utilized to plan the path, so it is fused from all grid maps and filtered to take into account the costs of surrounding nodes.

The stimulus is normalized such that its lower threshold represents a maximum acceptable cost, and the upper threshold represents the cost of a completely unviable path. Hence, the normalized stimulus ordinarily has an intensity of 0, but it increases upon detection of a low-quality path. It is moderately damped to reduce any rapid fluctuations that may occur if the replanning rate is very high.

Error

Although its name implies a general error detection mechanism, this stimulus is presently only employed to detect internal conflicts between different sensing modalities. It responds to collisions with obstacles that are not detected by exteroceptive sensors such as infrared, ultrasonic or laser rangefinders. This situation typically arises due to sensor failures or limitations such as dead zones, restricted coverage or transparent objects.

If a collision occurs, the raw stimulus S_{error} is equal to the distance d_c between the position of the collision sensor triggered by the collision and the closest obstacle position measured by the other sensors:

$$S_{error} = \begin{cases} d_c & \text{if collision} \\ 0 & \text{otherwise} \end{cases} \quad (14)$$

This raw value is normalized using a lower threshold that represents the minimum distance required for the sensors to 'definitely agree', and an upper threshold representing a distance above which the sensors 'definitely disagree'. Increases to S_{error} are undamped to facilitate a rapid response to perceived sensor inconstancies, while decreases are highly damped so that the robot continues to act to prevent further collisions with undetectable obstacles.

Drives

The number of drives defined in our model and their individual roles are largely application-specific. Each controls a set of parameters that result in similar performance characteristics when they are altered. The values of parameters governed by a given drive are assigned positions on a spectrum between two opposing 'modes of behavior' (e.g. exploration/exploitation). We define six basic drives in our model, corresponding to six distinct behavioral changes observed during experimentation. The drives and their associated responses are given in Table 1. While alternative decompositions could undoubtedly be successfully employed, we have determined that these six drives provide a sufficiently varied and potentially advantageous set of behavioral modulations. Although they are described in terms of low and high states, the drives are not represented as binary states. They are unit interval intensities that control the positions of parameter values within a bounded range.

The first three drives (speed, safety and efficiency) can be categorized as survival drives, because they influence the robot's ability to avoid collisions and conserve energy. Conversely, the latter three (action, introspection and exploration) are strategic drives, because they influence general behavioral strategies and in most cases don't

Table 1. Drive responses

Drive	Intensity	Responses
Speed	Low	Move slowly, thereby reducing the rate of energy consumption, the probability of collisions, and the potential damage suffered during any collisions that do occur.
	High	Move quickly, potentially yielding faster goal convergence.
Safety	Low	Reduce safety margins, allowing the robot to traverse narrow doorways or other openings.
	High	Maintain high safety margins, reducing the likelihood of collision.
Efficiency	Low	Choose a detailed computational style, potentially improving physical performance and/or collision avoidance.
	High	Choose a simple computational style, leaving more computational resources available for other tasks and/or conserving energy by reducing the CPU load.
Action	Low	Employ a hybrid reactive/deliberative approach to navigation.
	High	Disregard deliberative planning, relying on purely reactive control methods.
Introspection	Low	Rely on instantaneous sensor data for obstacle avoidance.
	High	Rely more heavily on internal representations than on instantaneous sensor data.
Exploration	Low	Assign low importance to the acquisition of new world knowledge.
	High	Favor knowledge acquisition over the exploitation of existing world knowledge.

directly impact the robot's prospects for survival. Survival drives must constantly make tradeoffs between the robot's competing requirements. Thus, they are rarely set to 0, and their modulations are naturally centered on an equilibrium position of 0.5. Conversely, strategic drives are more situational in their applications, and they may be inactive for significant durations. Hence, the strategic drives are considered at equilibrium when set to 0, and they are increased above that equilibrium position only when necessary.

Emotions

In our framework, emotions are an intermediary stage between stimuli and drives. They can be divided into two interacting components. First are global emotions, which are short-term intensities elicited by certain combinations of stimuli. Second are mapped emotions, which are associated with specific locations in the environment. Separate emotion intensity values are stored for each map node, enabling location-specific parameter modulations and biases to deliberative path planning. The robot's drives are controlled by weighted combinations of both global and mapped emotions. Emotions included in our implementation and their associated stimuli and drives are shown in Table 2.

Anger arises when the robot perceives obstructions that may prevent it from achieving its goals. It is slightly diminished by painful events such as collisions. Anger temporarily reduces the robot's safety drive in order to bypass an obstruction. Computational resources such as search resolutions and memory sizes are decreased, resulting in rougher, more 'careless' navigation. Both of these modulations increase the likelihood of collisions, so the robot's speed is lowered to compensate.

Fear results from the prediction of potentially dangerous or painful events. In the context of mobile robot navigation, the main survival-threatening event is a collision. The most likely cause of a collision is a navigational 'mistake' resulting from sensor, actuator and/or software limitations. Thus, the greatest danger to the robot is itself. Our robot has no predators or prey, so there is no need for the computational equivalent of a fight-or-flight response. Instead, fear reduces the robot's speed, favors safety-enhancing behaviors, and devotes more computational resources to navigation. This reduces both the likelihood of collisions, and the potential damage resulting from any that do occur.

Happiness arises when the robot is progressing quickly towards its goal, and when the environment is determined to be a low navigational challenge. Together with sadness, it is primarily assigned the role of modulating the overall levels of computational efficiency and speed to match the difficulty of the task at hand. Trivial tasks such as the traversal of obstacle-free environments can be accomplished without compromising these values. Difficult tasks generally require the

Table 2. Emotions, stimuli and drives

Emotion	Eliciting stimuli	Effects on drives
Anger	High stuck, low achievement	Low speed, low safety, low efficiency
Fear	High danger, high pain	Low speed, high safety, high efficiency
Happiness	High achievement, low density	High speed, high efficiency, low exploration
Sadness	High pain, high error	Low speed, low efficiency, high exploration
Surprise	High lost, high cost	High exploration, high action
Confusion	High error, low cost	Low speed, low action, high introspection
Curiosity	High learning, low cost	High exploration

robot to make greater tradeoffs. Happiness also decreases the drive to explore the environment, since exploration is less advantageous if the robot already possesses sufficient world knowledge to successfully complete the task at hand.

Sadness is caused by pain and a low estimation of the robot's capabilities. Overall, it results in decreased speed and increased computational effort. It also causes the robot to favor exploration of the environment over exploitation of existing world knowledge. This enables the robot to find alternative paths that may be superior to the one that resulted in sadness.

Surprise primarily represents a mismatch between the robot's predictions and its perceived world. It can also arise if the quality of the robot's plans is deemed low. If the robot is in a known environment, hybrid reactive/deliberative navigation generally results in superior paths than purely reactive control. However, successful deliberative path planning requires accurate knowledge of the environment. Hence, when surprise is elicited, the robot increasingly favors reactive approaches to navigation over the hybrid reactive/deliberative method it normally employs.

Confusion is not regarded as a basic emotion in most human-centric models, but in our model it is assigned the role of detecting internal inconsistencies caused by sensor limitations or errors. It represents a low level of confidence in the robot's perceptions, so it favors abstract internal representations over sensor data. Confusion discourages the robot from planning actions that previously resulted in collisions, even if its sensors currently detect no danger. It also lowers the robot's speed, due to the increased risk of collisions.

Curiosity is also excluded from the majority of basic emotion models. It is increased by a high perceived rate of knowledge acquisition, and reduced if the path quality is degraded. A high exploration drive can have an adverse effect on performance if the environment is already known, so it is linked to curiosity, enabling the robot to favor exploration only when it is likely to yield additional world knowledge.

The interconnections utilized in our implementation are not the only valid options. Human-like emotions may require more complex context-dependent interconnections, while robot performance equivalent to ours may be achieved by a simpler configuration (e.g. one stimulus per emotion). Our configuration can be regarded as a compromise between biological plausibility and the need for demonstrable performance improvements.

Global Emotions

Each global emotion E_G is a function of multiple affective stimuli. The mechanism employed to combine stimuli is a dynamic weighted sum that can perform different continuous 'logical' operations on the inputs. This function resembles a simplified Sugeno fuzzy inference system (Sugeno, 1985) containing a single linear membership function and an independent if-then rule for each input. The membership function for an input I_i is represented by minimum and maximum weights $W_{i(\min)}$ and $W_{i(\max)}$, which determine the weight W_i if I_i is 'disabled' and 'enabled', respectively. Two different fuzzy operations are represented by logic tag L_i:

- $L_i = 0$: If I_i is high, output E_G increases. Represented by high input stimuli in Table 2.
- $L_i = 1$: If I_i is high, E_G decreases. Represented by low input stimuli in Table 2.

The weight W_i is a function of thresholds $W_{i(\min)}$ and $W_{i(\max)}$ and input I_i:

$$W_i = \left(1 - I_i\right)W_{i(\min)} + I_i W_{i(\max)} \qquad (15)$$

The input I_i can be inverted such that a higher value yields a lower output E_G. This yields a factor F_i that is utilized in the final calculation:

$$F_i = \begin{cases} (1 - I_i) & \text{if } (L_i = 1) \\ I_i & \text{otherwise} \end{cases} \qquad (16)$$

Once weights W_i and factors F_i have been calculated for all indices i, the global emotion E_G is obtained using a weighted average calculation:

$$E_G = \sum_{j=1}^{n} \left(\frac{W_j F_j}{\sum_{i=1}^{n} W_i} \right) \qquad (17)$$

Mapped Emotions

Mapped emotions are associated with specific grid map nodes. Each mapped emotion grows or decays in nodes x_1-x_n close to the robot's current position. Over time, the intensity values $e_M(x_i)$ of a node x_i tends towards the robot's equivalent global emotion intensity E_G. The rate of growth or decay is a function of a node's Euclidean distance $d(x_i)$ from the robot's position, and a damping factor γ:

$$e_M(x_i) \leftarrow \gamma \left(1 - \frac{d(x_i)^2}{r_M^2} \right) E_G + (1 - \gamma) e_M(x_i) \qquad (18)$$

Nodes close to the robot's position are more strongly influenced by E_G than nodes further away. The radius of influence is represented by r_M. Enlarging r_M increases the influence exerted on more distant nodes, and it also expands the total number of nodes affected. The damping factor α is substituted with a distinct growth factor γ_1 or decay factor γ_2, whose selection depends upon whether $e_M(x_i) < E_G$. These factors control the overall increase and decrease of $e_M(x_i)$ values, regardless of their positions relative to the robot.

Emotion maps can be utilized as path planning biases in an identical manner to the exploration and danger grid maps. Negative emotions increase the cost of nodes where they are strongly

elicited. Positive emotion maps are inverted such that higher intensities reduce node costs. Thus, positive and negative emotions are analogous to attractive and repulsive forces applied to specific map regions.

Mapped emotion intensities E_M are obtained from the emotion maps using a weighted average scheme. The weight applied to an individual node x_i is dependent on its proximity to the robot's position:

$$E_M = \frac{\sum_{i=1}^{n} \left(1 - \frac{d(x_i)^2}{r_M^2} \right) e_M(x_i)}{\sum_{i=1}^{n} \left(1 - \frac{d(x_i)^2}{r_M^2} \right)} \qquad (19)$$

This is essentially a reversal of the emotion mapping process represented in Equation 18. Similarly, nodes close to the robot exert a stronger influence over E_M than more distant nodes, and the range of influence is controlled by r_M.

Although E_M is a function of E_G, the two emotion intensities can have very different values, particularly if small damping factors γ_1 and γ_2, or a large radius r_M are employed. The global intensity E_G is dependent only on currently perceived stimuli, whereas E_M is a function of previous emotion intensities elicited in the robot near its current position. These are combined by a simple weighted average to form an overall intensity E that interacts with the robot's drives. Emotions E modulate drives in the same manner as stimuli elicit global emotions. The same dynamic weighted sum function is employed; with the high and low output drive intensities shown in Table 2 representing logic tags of 0 and 1, respectively.

Moods

Inspired by the TAME framework (Moshkina and Arkin, 2005), we include positive and negative moods in our model, as shown in Table 3. Again, the dynamic weighted sum function is

Table 3. Mood elicitation and response

Mood	Activating emotions	Drive limits modulated
Positive	High happiness	Speed maxima, safety maxima, efficiency maxima
Negative	High anger, high fear, high sadness	Speed minima, safety minima, efficiency minima

employed to obtain moods from emotions. Moods are strongly damped, so they grow and decay at much slower rates than their eliciting emotions. They modulate the maximum or minimum values of survival drives, affecting the level of influence emotions have over the robot's behavior. Positive moods vary each drive's upper limit between 0.5 and 1, while negative moods modulate the lower limit between 0.5 and 0.

Strategic drives (exploration, action and introspection) are not constrained by moods. Nor do their primary eliciting emotions (surprise, confusion and curiosity) contribute to the modulation of moods. Unlike survival drives, their 'default' position is 0, and restricting their dynamic range is generally counterproductive.

If positive mood has a high intensity and negative mood has a low intensity, the robot is more likely to favor fast, safe and computationally efficient parameter values. Conversely, if positive mood is low and negative mood is high, the robot will increasingly favor slower motion, lower safety margins, and computationally-intensive processing styles. A high level of both positive and negative mood leads to 'bipolar' behavior, where the robot oscillates between highly divergent parameter values depending on its momentary affective states. Low positive and negative moods lead to emotionally-muted behavior, with emotions having lower overall levels of influence over the robot's decisions and actions.

AFFECT MODEL DEMONSTRATION

To demonstrate some of the interactions between different components of the affect model, an ex-

periment is conducted with all stimuli, emotions, moods and drives enabled. The planning and control architecture and affect model are applied a simulated mobile robot with a differential drive system. Exteroception is provided by a ring of infrared distance-measuring sensors (distributed evenly over a 360° field of view) and tactile collision sensors.

The simulated robot is instructed to navigate between two points in a relatively complex procedurally-generated indoor environment. This environment contains both ordinary obstacles, and objects that are 'invisible' to the robot's sensors. At the onset of the experiment, the environment is entirely unexplored, so the positions of the undetectable obstacles can only be determined through trial-and-error – by colliding with them. A further difficulty is that some of the doorways in this environment are only slightly wider than the robot itself. Thus, the robot is susceptible to additional collisions as it attempts to fit through the narrow openings, or it may persistently fail to traverse them. The resulting path travelled by the robot is shown in Figure 5.

During the robot's journey, the intensities of all of its stimuli, emotions, moods and drives are recorded. Figure 6 shows the resulting emotion intensities and each of their eliciting stimuli. Emotions are not only a function of stimuli, but also of previous emotions elicited in the robot's current location. Since the robot's environment is initially unexplored, and only one traversal is shown, the contributions of mapped emotions are minimal in this example. However, they do have a damping effect on emotions during early passes through an environment. They also account for some of the minor fluctuations shown in Figure 6 that are not directly caused by stimuli.

Figure 5. Path travelled by a simulated robot in a procedurally-generated indoor environment. Direction arrows are placed at 5 second intervals along the path; sparse arrow densities represent higher speeds. Start and goal points are represented by the dark and light circles, respectively. Visible objects are medium-grey, while unseen objects are lighter.

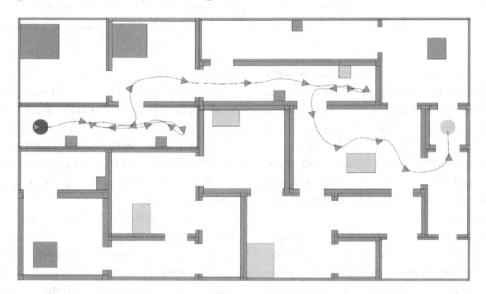

Anger is increased by the stuck stimulus and reduced by achievement. When the robot initially fails to turn into the first narrow doorway, the stuck stimulus begins to increase, which causes growing anger. Both the stimulus and emotion quickly subside once the robot escapes the obstruction. A second minor increase in anger occurs as the robot lingers for too long near the same position towards the end of its journey. This environment is a reasonable navigational challenge, so the robot's progress is generally not sufficient to consistently produce high achievement. Hence, in this example its contribution is minimal.

Fear is elicited by danger (a function of local obstacle proximities) and pain (a function of collisions). The environment is very confining, so the danger stimulus is highly activated throughout the journey. Collisions (and therefore pain) begin to occur when the robot encounters the undetectable obstacles. Danger also increases at this point, because confusion (described further below) causes the robot to 'pay more attention' to representation information other than its sensor data.

Happiness is increased by achievement and decreased by density, which is an estimate of the average occupancy probability of the entire map. Since the environment is highly cluttered, density is constantly maximized. Combined with the low levels of achievement, this produces consistent near-zero levels of happiness.

Sadness is a function of the pain and error stimuli. In this example, all collisions occur at high speeds and involve unseen obstacles, so the behavior of the two stimuli is almost identical. The only difference is that the error stimulus remains high until the collision obstacle is cleared from the obstacle buffer, whereas pain is only a function of instantaneous sensor data.

Surprise is primarily dependent on the mismatch stimulus. The environment is initially unexplored, so mismatch is frequently high in this example, except where the robot lingers in an area for a sufficient duration to allow its map to align with local sensor data. The cost stimulus also exerts a slight positive influence on surprise, but it is eclipsed by mismatch in this experiment.

Figure 6. Interactions between stimuli and emotions

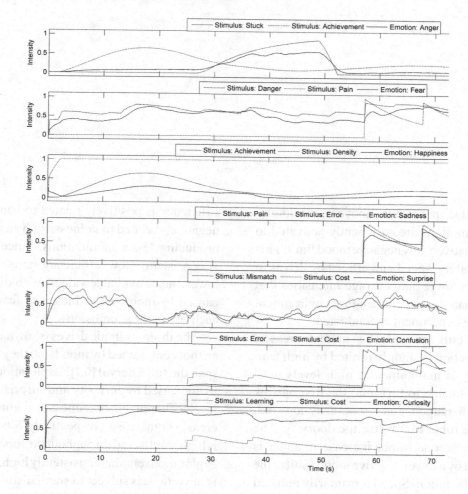

Confusion increases largely due to the error stimulus. Once the robot begins to collide with undetectable obstacles, confusion starts to have a significant effect over the robot's behavior, causing its obstacle avoidance and planning systems to rely more heavily on internal representations that incorporate mapped points of collision. Although it cannot prevent initial collisions with obstacles that the robot cannot detect, confusion dissuades the robot from repeating them. Cost has a slight negative influence over confusion.

Curiosity is a function of the learning stimulus, which is consistently high throughout this experiment due to the high rate of knowledge acquisition during exploration. It visibly decreases

when the cost stimulus increases, so that high exploration tendencies are only allowed when they do not significantly degrade the quality of paths planned.

Negative mood is a function of anger, fear and sadness, while positive mood is only dependent on happiness. The three survival drives (safety, speed and efficiency) constrained by these moods are shown in Figure 7, along with their mood-based limits. Moods grow and decay over a significantly longer timescale than their eliciting emotions. Hence, the robot's behavior is initially emotionally-muted while the limits gradually expand from their initial position of 0.5. Happiness is consistently low, so the positive

Figure 7. Survival drives bounded by positive and negative moods

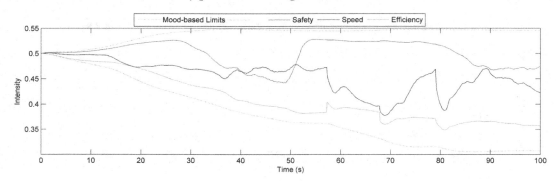

mood limit does not rise far above its minimum. The other emotions are sufficiently activated to produce a relatively low negative mood limit. This causes the safety, speed and efficiency drives to tend towards lower than average intensities that are appropriate for the challenging environment in which the experiment is conducted.

Safety is only lowered when anger increases, and the reduction is slightly limited by high fear. Thus, safety is maintained at high levels until the robot is unable to turn into the first narrow doorway, whereupon it is temporarily lowered, enabling the robot to traverse the doorway. The effect of the second minor increase in anger is exaggerated by a lower negative mood limit at the time of its elicitation. Speed is primarily reduced by fear and anger, but it is also slightly increased by happiness and decreased by sadness and confusion. The heaviest reductions occur when the robot starts colliding with the unseen obstacles.

Efficiency is positively related to happiness and negatively related to sadness, with anger and fear producing lesser modulations. Since happiness is consistently low, efficiency remains near the lower end of available values, with disturbances caused by increased sadness and fear following each of the three collisions.

The three strategic drives (shown in Figure 8) are not constrained by moods, so they can always span the full interval [0,1]. Exploration is primarily increased by curiosity and surprise, with high levels of happiness or sadness providing slight decreases or increases, respectively. Since curiosity is highly activated throughout the robot's journey, exploration remains consistently high, although it is nevertheless subject to small disturbances due to the other emotions. It tends towards zero once the robot has explored the environment, but that takes significantly longer than the duration shown in this example. Action is increased by surprise

Figure 8. Unbounded strategic drives

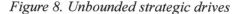

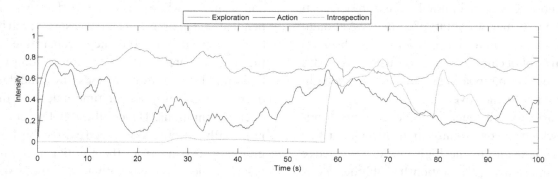

and reduced by high levels of confusion. Confusion is only active during parts of the second half of the journey, so most of the fluctuations shown match those of surprise. Introspection is directly linked to confusion, shown in Figure 6.

PERFORMANCE ANALYSIS

A quantitative analysis of the robotic affect model's contributions to adaptive performance is conducted by comparing the robot's behavior in two different configurations. In the first configuration, the drive parameters and mapped emotions are maintained at constant values, representing a robot without an affect model. Survival drives are set to their equilibrium position of 0.5 (a compromise between the competing requirements of goal convergence speed, collision-free motion and computational efficiency), while strategic drives are set to 0 (since they are detrimental to performance if perpetually active). Mapped emotions are set to 0 in all nodes. In the second configuration, affective parameter modulation is fully enabled as shown in the previous section, allowing the robot its full range of emotional responses.

These configurations are tested in four different sets of 20 procedurally generated environments, with each set possessing distinct properties:

- **Open:** Sparsely occupied environments representing outdoor areas or large, open buildings.
- **Constant:** Environments with constant-width doorways and walls representing unchallenging indoor office-blocks or laboratories.
- **Random:** Environments containing random-width doorways and walls, providing a more significant navigational challenge. Some doorways are only slightly wider than the robot.
- **Random, unseen:** Similar to the random set, but it also contains objects that the robot's

sensors cannot detect. The environment utilized in the previous demonstration is from this set.

Five experimental runs are performed in each of the 20 environments, producing 100 samples per configuration/environment set combination. The robot is instructed to travel back and forth between two points, for a total of seven traversals (iterations) per experimental run. At the beginning of each run, the robot's map and other parameters are reset to their initial conditions, so it must explore and adapt its parameters while it traverses the environment. If it is unable to complete a traversal within 10 minutes, the iteration times out and the robot's position is reset to its current destination.

Five performance characteristics are measured and recorded in Tables 4 and 5. The time taken, the robot's average linear velocity, and the number of collisions per minute are self-explanatory. Execution time ratio is the ratio between time represented in the simulation, and the actual time taken to execute the code. The resulting values are highly system dependent, and also dependent on implementation details such as the programming language utilized, the overhead of the simulation, and the attention paid to efficiency-optimizations when writing the code. Thus, the actual values should be viewed as mere indicators, less important than the trends. To maintain consistency between these experiments, they are conducted on the same PC, an Athlon 64 3500+ with 2 GB RAM running Windows XP. Exploration coverage gives an indication of the proportion of the environment that has been thoroughly explored by the robot. It is the average value of all nodes represented in the exploration map.

Performance characteristics averaged from all seven iterations are represented, as well as those from the final iteration of each experimental run. The final iteration is relevant because it shows the robot's capabilities after it has had sufficient opportunity to explore and adapt to the environ-

Table 4. Performance characteristics – constant parameters

Environment	Iteration	Time (s)	Velocity (m/s)	Collisions/minute	Execution time ratio	Coverage
Open	All	38	0.51	0	0.21	0.56
	Final	35	0.57	0	0.21	
Constant	All	69	0.46	0	0.30	0.57
	Final	60	0.48	0	0.30	
Random	All	117	0.40	0.070	0.31	0.60
	Final	93	0.42	0.084	0.31	
Random, un-seen	All	109	0.38	4.7	0.31	0.58
	Final	84	0.40	5.6	0.31	

Table 5. Performance characteristics – affective parameter modulation

Environment	Iteration	Time (s)	Velocity (m/s)	Collisions/minute	Execution time ratio	Coverage
Open	All	37	0.57	0	0.20	0.77
	Final	32	0.65	0	0.19	
Constant	All	85	0.43	0.012	0.33	0.78
	Final	65	0.45	0	0.33	
Random	All	106	0.40	0.069	0.35	0.78
	Final	81	0.41	0.082	0.35	
Random, un-seen	All	104	0.39	1.7	0.34	0.80
	Final	79	0.40	1.2	0.34	

ment. Exploration coverage is a final result rather than an average, so only one value is shown per environment/configuration combination.

In the open environment set (Figures 9 and 10), the configuration with parameters modulated by the affect model outperforms the one with constant parameters in every respect (except collision rate, which is zero in both cases). There are no narrow openings or narrow maze-like paths to obstruct the robot's progress, and few obstacles to pose a danger to high-speed travel, so the robot generally elicits high intensities of happiness and low levels of fear, anger and sadness. Thus, its speed limit is relaxed, and it reduces the amount of data processed each control cycle, yielding lower completion times, higher average velocities and lower execution time ratios. The incentive to explore the environment is initially high, so in early iterations the affective robot is sometimes slower than the non-affective robot to converge on the goal. However, its higher overall speeds compensate for this initial time investment.

Aside from exploration coverage, constant parameters produce superior performance than affect-modulated parameters in the constant environment set (Figures 11 and 12). The parameter defaults are already optimally tuned to these environments, so modulations produced by the affect model generally do not yield tangible improvements, and in some cases reduce performance. For example, it tends to overestimate danger, resulting in slightly lower velocities and higher execution time ratios. The high incentive to explore and occasionally lower safety mar-

Figure 9. Path resulting from constant parameters in a sparse, open environment

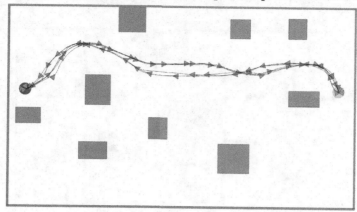

Figure 10. Path resulting from affective parameter modulation in a sparse, open environment

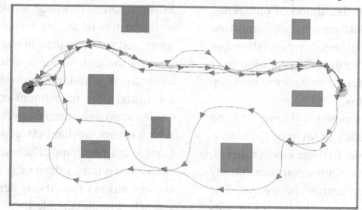

Figure 11. Path resulting from constant parameters in an environment with constant-width doorways and walls

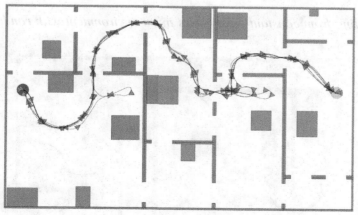

Figure 12. Path resulting from affective parameter modulation in an environment with constant-width doorways and walls

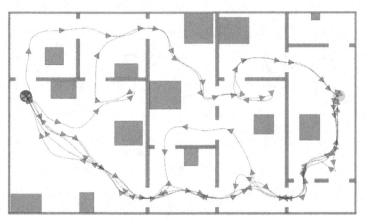

gins yield an increased likelihood of collisions, resulting in a small, but non-zero collision rate during early iterations. In later iterations the robot generally no longer prioritizes exploration over goal convergence, reducing the performance gap between the two systems.

The random environment set (Figures 13 and 14) shifts the balance back in favor of the affect-modulated configuration. In these environments, the constant parameter configuration occasionally becomes obstructed by narrow doorways. The modulated configuration can selectively lower its safety margins to bypass the obstruction without reducing its safety during normal operation.

Furthermore, a thorough exploration of the environment may uncover alternative paths that yield improved performance in the long-term (e.g. by passing through wider doorways). The result is lower average and final completion times despite the initial time investment of exploration. This comes at no discernable cost to the collision rate, which is very similar between the two configurations. Computational efficiency is assigned lower importance than safety or goal convergence, so the execution time ratio is generally higher with the affect model enabled.

When the robot is tested in environments with undetectable objects (Figures 15 and 16), the

Figure 13. Path resulting from constant parameters in an environment with random-width doorways and walls

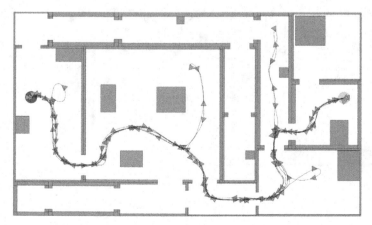

Figure 14. Path resulting from affective parameter modulation in an environment with random-width doorways and walls

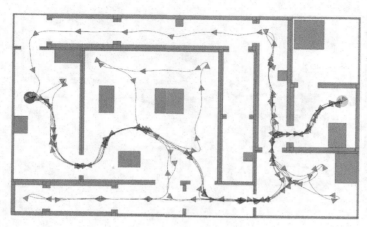

constant parameter configuration yields a very high collision rate. The robot does not utilize its map-based avoidance function, so it repeatedly collides with the same objects (Figure 15). While this function can be constantly enabled, it degrades performance during normal operation. This problem is reduced by affective modulation, and in particular confusion/introspection, which highly activates the map-based avoidance function only in regions where the robot has previously collided with unseen obstacles. Thus, the robot starts to avoid unseen obstacles after it has collided with them (Figure 16), resulting is a significantly lower collision rate, which comes at no discernable cost

to performance. While the recorded collision rate for the final iteration is nevertheless rather high, it would be further reduced in subsequent iterations after the robot has mapped more points of collision to avoid.

Overall, the advantages of the affect model outweigh its disadvantages in three out of the four environment sets tested. While different configurations of constant parameters may close the gap between the two approaches in a single environment set, the navigation requirements of different types of environments are sufficiently unique that no single set of parameters is optimal for all of them. Additional tuning may further

Figure 15. Path resulting from constant parameters in an environment with unseen obstacles and random-width doorways and walls

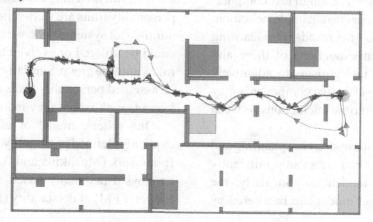

Figure 16. Path resulting from affective parameter modulation in an environment with unseen obstacles and random-width doorways and walls

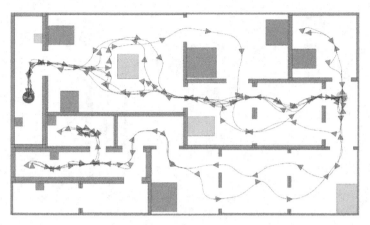

improve the model's performance in certain situations, but the presented results give an indication of its potential as an adaptation mechanism.

FUTURE TRENDS

Connections between the various affective components of our architecture are hardwired. A simple form of learning is implemented in the form of emotion maps that are updated over time, but the robot cannot adapt its responses to a given emotion or mood. The input-output mappings produced by our dynamic weighted sum function can be represented by equivalent Sugeno fuzzy inference systems (Sugeno, 1985). Although less computationally efficient than our current implementation, they can be trained by neuro-adaptive learning techniques. Future investigations of these and other computational mechanisms to adaptively connect and combine affective components may yield further insights into the interactions between affect and learning.

Modulating a robot's underlying planning and control architecture parameters can significantly alter its behavioral tendencies. Similarly, the responses of the affect model can be altered by changing its internal parameters. Such parameters include the growth and decay rates of different affective states and the weights associated with various interconnections between them. Because they are largely time-invariant and influence a robot's 'emotional' behavior, these parameters can be regarded as analogous to biological personality traits.

A natural extension of this research would be to implement robots with different 'artificial personalities', represented by distinct affective parameter configurations. In humans, different personality types are generally suited to different roles, so the inclusion of a diverse range of personalities may improve the long-term survival prospects of a community. Hence, explicit representations of personality traits are well-suited to the domain of multi-robot systems, where distinct personalities could be tailored or evolved to suit each robot's role within the group. Similarly, social robots could be assigned personality traits that suit individual humans with whom they interact.

One robotic model of affect that includes explicitly-defined personality traits is the TAME framework (Moshkina and Arkin, 2005), which employs a taxonomy based on the Five-Factor Model (FFM) of Personality (McCrae and Costa,

1992). Aspects of the FFM could be incorporated directly into our model. For example, extraversion (a tendency to generate positive emotions) may be represented by parameters controlling the growth and decay of positive moods, while neuroticism (a tendency to elicit negative emotions) could be a function of equivalent parameters for negative moods.

CONCLUSION

The concepts of affect and emotion have traditionally been associated with sociable robotics, because many of the social aspects of emotion are clearly apparent or implicitly understood. In contrast, we have described the implementation of a mobile robot architecture that incorporates emotion and other affective states as general adaptation mechanisms to improve its performance in a non-social context. Affect is not the dominant motivator of a robot's actions, but rather, a secondary influence that continuously modulates the decisions and actions of its cognitive systems. Cognition is implicitly represented by a hybrid reactive/deliberative planning and control architecture.

The cognitive and affective systems have been implemented on a simulated mobile robot and applied to navigation and exploration tasks. Experiments were conducted in a range of procedurally-generated environments to assess the performance contributions of the robotic affect model. Results of these experiments indicate several situations in which our model can improve performance. The affective robot can adjust the amount of computational effort applied to a navigation task depending on its perceived difficulty. It can vary its speed and/or safety limits in response the navigational challenges it encounters. In environments where its map is inaccurate or its sensors cannot always be relied upon, the robot can adjust the bias between reactive and deliberative control approaches and/

or environment representations. Affect also adapts the robot's incentive to explore its environment while it navigates from point to point.

These results support the argument that affective computing is not merely beneficial to human-machine interaction, but also to the general problem of synthesizing adaptive behavior. Emotion-like mechanisms may be crucial to the development of future general-purpose robotic systems, enabling them to operate safely and efficiently in highly complex, partially-observable real-world environments.

REFERENCES

Arkin, R. C. (2005). Moving up the food chain: motivation and emotion in behavior-based robots. In J. Fellous & M. Arbib (Eds.), *Who needs emotions: The brain meets the robot* (pp. 425-270). New York, NY: Oxford University Press.

Avila-García, O. & Cañamero, L. (2005). Hormonal modulation of perception in motivation-based action selection architectures. In *Proceedings of the AISB'05 Convention: Vol. 2* (pp. 9-16). Hertfordshire, UK: AISB Press.

Aylett, R. S. (2006). Emotion as an integrative process between non-symbolic and symbolic systems in intelligent agents. In *Proceedings of the AISB'06 Symposium of Brain and Mind: Integrating high level cognitive processes with brain mechanisms and functions in a working robot* (pp. 43-47). Bristol, England: AISB Press.

Bach, J. (2003). The MicroPsi agent architecture. In *Proceedings of ICCM-5, International Conference on Cognitive Modeling* (pp. 15-20). Bamberg, Germany: ICCM Press.

Borenstein, J., & Koren, Y. (1991). The vector field histogram — fast obstacle avoidance for mobile robots. *IEEE Journal on Robotics and Automation, 7*(3), 278-288.

Breazeal, C. (2004). Function meets style: Insights from emotion theory applied to HRI. *IEEE Transactions on Systems, Man and Cybernetics, 34*(2), 187-194.

Broekens, J. (2007). Emotion and reinforcement: Affective facial expressions facilitate robot learning. *LNAI Special Volume on AI for Human Computing* (pp. 113-132). Hyderabad, India: Springer.

Brooks, R. A. (1986). A robust layered control system for a mobile robot. *IEEE Journal of Robotics and Automation, 2*(1), 14-23.

Damasio, A. (1994). *Descartes' error: Emotion, reason, and the human brain.* New York: Grosset/Putnam.

Damasio, A. (1999). *The feeling of what happens.* London: Random House.

Dörner D., & Hille, K. (1995). Artificial souls: Motivated emotional robots. In *Proceedings of the IEEE International Conference on Systems, Man and Cybernetics* (pp. 3828-3832). Vancouver, BC, Canada: IEEE Press.

Ekman, P. (1992). An argument for basic emotions. In N. L. Stein & K. Oatley (Eds.), *Basic Emotions* (pp. 169-200). Hove, UK: Lawrence Erlbaum.

Fellous, J. M. From human emotions to robot emotions. In *Proceedings of the 2004 AAAI Spring Symposium: Architectures for Modeling Emotions: Cross-Disciplinary Foundations* (pp. 37–47). Palo Alto, CA: AAAI Press.

Fox, D., Burgard, W., & Thrun, S. (1997). The dynamic window approach to collision avoidance. *IEEE Robotics and Automation Magazine, 4*(1), 23-33.

Gadanho, S.C., & Hallam, J. (2001). Robot learning driven by emotions. *Adaptive Behavior, 9*(1), 42-64.

Hollinger, G. A., Georgiev, Y., Manfredi, A., Maxwell, B.A., Pezzementi, Z.A., & Mitchell, B.

(2006). Design of a social mobile robot using emotion-based decision mechanisms. *IEEE/RSJ International Conference on Intelligent Robots and Systems* (pp. 3093-3098). Beijing, China: IEEE Press.

Judea, P. (1984). *Heuristics: Intelligent search strategies for computer problem solving.* Reading, MA: Addison-Wesley.

Lee-Johnson, C. P., & Carnegie, D. A. (in press). Mobile robot navigation modulated by artificial emotions. *IEEE Transactions on Systems, Man and Cybernetics: Part B.*

Lee-Johnson, C. P., & Carnegie, D. A. (2007). Emotion-based parameter modulation for a hierarchical mobile robot planning and control architecture. In *Proceedings of the IEEE/RSJ International Conference on Intelligent Robots and Systems* (pp. 2839-2844). San Diego, CA: IEEE Press.

McCrae, R. R., & Costa, P. T. (1996). Toward a new generation of personality theories: theoretical contexts for the five-factor model. *Five-Factor Model of Personality,* 51-87.

Minsky, M. (1986). *The society of mind.* New York: Simon and Schuster.

Moshkina, L., & Arkin, R. C. (2005). Human perspective on affective robotic behavior: A longitudinal study. In *Proceedings of the IEEE/RSJ International Conference on Intelligent Robots and Systems* (pp. 1444-1451). Edmonton, AB, Canada: IEEE Press.

Neal, M.J., & Timmis, J. (2003). Timidity: A useful mechanism for robot control? *Informatica, 27*(4), 197-204.

Ortony, A., Clore, G. L., & Collins, A. (1988). *The cognitive structure of emotions.* Cambridge, UK: Cambridge University Press.

Ortony, A., & Turner, T. J. (1990). What's basic about basic emotions? *Psychological Review, 97*(1), 315-331.

Plutchik, R. (2001). The nature of emotions. *American Scientist, 89*(4), 344-350.

Simmons, R. (1996). The curvature-velocity method for local obstacle avoidance. In *Proceedings of the IEEE International Conference on Robotics and Automation* (pp. 3375-3382). Minneapolis, MN: IEEE Press.

Sloman, A., Chrisley, R., & Scheutz, M. (2005). The architectural basis of affective states and processes. In J. Fellous & M. Arbib (Eds.), *Who needs emotions: The brain meets the robot* (pp. 203-244). New York: Oxford University Press.

Sugeno, M. (1985). *Industrial applications of fuzzy control*. New York: Elsevier Science.

Thrun, S. (2003). Robotic mapping: A survey. In G. Lakemeyer & B. Nebel (Eds.), *Exploring artificial intelligence in the new millennium* (pp. 1-35). San Francisco: Morgan Kaufmann.

Velásquez, J. D., & Maes, P. (1997). Cathexis: A computational model of emotions. In *Proceedings of the 1st International Conference on Autonomous Agents* (pp. 518-519). CA: Marina del Rey.

KEY TERMS

Affective Stimulus: A function of an internal or external event that elicits an affective response.

Deliberative Navigation: Following paths that are planned utilizing global maps constructed a priori and/or updated in response to environmental dynamics.

Dynamic Window: A rectangular search space of discrete linear and angular velocities bounded by a robot's kinematic and dynamic constraints.

Global Emotion: A single intensity value representing an emotion elicited by stimuli perceived at the present time.

Mapped Emotion: A set of emotional intensities associated with specific locations in the environment due to previous stimuli.

Reactive Control: Real-time selection of motor outputs in response to short-term sensor data or local map data.

Strategic Drive: An affective state governing parameter modulations that alter cognitive strategies without directly affecting an intelligent system's prospects for survival.

Survival Drive: An affective state governing parameter modulations that directly influence the likelihood or potential outcomes of existence-threatening events such as collisions.

Section III
Philosophical Questions

Chapter VII
Emotions, Diffusive Emotional Control and the Motivational Problem for Autonomous Cognitive Systems

C. Gros
J.W. Goethe University Frankfurt, Germany

ABSTRACT

All self-active living beings need to solve the motivational problem—the question of what to do at any moment of their life. For humans and non-human animals at least two distinct layers of motivational drives are known, the primary needs for survival and the emotional drives leading to a wide range of sophisticated strategies, such as explorative learning and socializing. Part of the emotional layer of drives has universal facets, being beneficial in an extended range of environmental settings. Emotions are triggered in the brain by the release of neuromodulators, which are, at the same time, are the agents for meta-learning. This intrinsic relation between emotions, meta-learning and universal action strategies suggests a central importance for emotional control for the design of artificial intelligences and synthetic cognitive systems. An implementation of this concept is proposed in terms of a dense and homogeneous associative network (dHan).

INTRODUCTION

Is it a coincidence, a caprice of nature, that the species living presently on our planet with the most developed intellectual and cognitive capa-bilities, humanity, is also thoroughly infused with emotions? Or is it a conditio sine qua non: Are higher cognitive powers intrinsically dependent on a functioning and solid emotional grounding? This question is centrally relevant for our scientific and philosophical self-understanding, posing at the same time a paradigmatic challenge for the development of synthetic cognitive systems and artificial intelligences (AI).

A wide range of different notions are connected with the term emotion and with the personal experience of emotions (Barrett, Mesquita, Ochsner, Gross, 2007). Social interactions and emotional involvements, to give an example, take-up a good share of our daily life and the social aspects of emotional expressions are being widely discussed (Blakermore, Winston & Frith, 2004; Lieberman, 2007). They constitute an important aspect in human-robot interactions (Breazeal, 2003) and may even play a role in human phylogenesis (Parr, Waller & Fugate, 2005), having a high adaptive value (Rolls, 2005). The study of synthetic emotions (Picard, 2000) constitutes therefore a field of growing importance, dealing, beside others, with the role of emotions in artificial intelligences in general (Minsky, 2007), social robots (Duffy, 2003; Fong, Nourbakhsh & Dautenhahn, 2003), emotional expression in speech and language (Murray & Arnott, 2008) and social synthetic computer characters (Tomlinson & Blumberg, 2002).

It is well known, that emotions are triggered by neuromodulators like dopamine, serotonin and opioids, and that the very same neuromodulators can be found all over the animal kingdom, and not just in mammals (Arbib & Fellous, 2004). It is therefore reasonable to assume, that the neurobiological foundations of emotion-like functionalities, being present to a varying extend in all animals having a central or distributed nervous system, precedented phylogenetically higher cognitive capabilities, like sophisticated social interactions or logical reasoning. This observation suggests an underlying functional role of emotions, or emotion-like regulative processes, for both simple and highly developed cognitive systems in general. Neurobiological studies have found indeed close relations between emotions and the internal reward system (Aron *et. Al*, 2005;

Kringelbach, 2005; Burgdorf & Panksepp, 2006), indicating that there is a close relation between emotions and decision making (Damasio, 1994; Naqvi, Shiv & Bechara, 2006; Coricelli, Dolan & Sirigu, 2007) quite in general. In the following we will describe, from the functional perspective of dynamical system theory, the role of emotions in cognitive systems. Taking into account the established results from experimental neurobiology and experimental psychology, a theory for emotions will emerge that can be translated algorithmically precisely into formulas and code lines, a prerequisite for the realization of synthetic emotions in artificial intelligences and robots.

MOTIVATIONS

In order to elucidate the general functional purposes of emotions we start by considering the motivational problem of self-determined living creatures, whether biological or artificial. We use here and in the following the general term `cognitive system' for such an autonomous and self-determined being. The question then regards the general motivational drives for cognitive systems.

The basic motivational drive of all living organisms is the `instinct for survival' and it is sometimes assumed, indeed this is the general folklore in the larger public, that the survival instinct would be the sole driving force. In this context the desire to survive would determine in ultima ratio all activities of non-human animals, as well as the ones of humans, e.g. the decision to attend a violin concert instead of a cello performance.

Cognitive systems are instances of complex and adaptive dynamical systems (Gros, 2008) and the survival instinct can be defined algorithmically in a very precise manner, as we will do further below, in terms of a set of survival variables representing the health-status of their respective bodies. Nevertheless, the separate motivational layer, the network of emotions, has several stand-alone features. Emotions might indeed be triggered by the processes representing the survival instinct, but generally they constitute an independent dynamical component. The evolutionary fitness of an animal is increased both by a functioning survival instinct and by a suitable emotional framework (Fellous & Arbib, 2005), but this matter of fact does not imply that both processes have identical causes.

Neuromodulators are the neurobiological roots of emotions (Fellous, 1999) and in the following we will first discuss their biological functionalities in general terms. We will be interested, in particular, in the interplay between local and non-local homeostasis, meta-learning and the diffusive learning signals at basis of the diffusive emotional control. We will find that cognitive systems lacking a diffusive regulative network akin to the one of neuromodulators in the brain, are not likely to have the potential for higher cognitive capabilities. We will then discuss the implications hereof for synthetic cognitive systems in general and then proceed to formulate concrete algorithmical implementations of diffusive emotional control for generalized neural network architectures in the framework of dynamical system theory.

In conclusion, we will find that higher-level cognitive systems lacking diffusive emotional control are not likely to exist, that human-level artificial intelligences based on logical reasoning and the survival instinct alone are probably not possible. We will also see that an algorithmic implementation of diffusive emotional control is possible for synthetic cognitive systems and then shortly discuss that the resulting 'true synthetic emotions' will be quite alien to human emotions, as we experience them ourselves.

NEUROMODULATORS

Neuromodulators act, from a neurobiological point of view, as a diffusive control system, influencing not the firing state of individual neurons but the responsiveness in general of extended neural ensembles, and even of entire brain regions. From the perspective of dynamical system theory, neuromodulators are therefore the agents for 'meta-learning' and homeostasis (Doya, 1999; Marder & Goaillard, 2006), the regulation of slow dynamical variables such as firing thresholds and synaptic sensibility, occurring either automatically or in response to internal or external status signals.

Homeostasis and autoregulation are ubiquitous in biological processes in general, and in the brain in particular (Turrigiano & Nelson 2004). Every individual neuron adapts its average responsiveness, e.g. its firing threshold, relative to the input it receives over time from afferent neurons. This example for a basic local homeostatic process determines the normal or average properties of neurons on an individual basis. The average properties of neurons can be influenced, in addition, by neuromodulators like dopamine, serotonin, and opioids. This regulation of slow variables by neuromodulators is, on the other hand, a process involving several distinct brain structures. Dopamine or serotonin neurons affecting cortical neural ensembles typically receive their signals from subcortical structures, like the amygdala (Phelps, 2006), neuromodulation is intrinsically non-local.

Emotions and neuromodulators are intrinsically linked, but not identical (Damasio, 1994; Fellous, 1999). There are probably no emotions without the concurrent release of neuromodulators, but the brain is a complex and recurrent dynamical system. The geometry of the neuro-chemical information flow is generally not uniquely directed in the brain, feedback loops are ubiquitous. The cognitive information processing and the neuromodulatory component are therefore strongly interacting. Emotional motivation may precede thinking (Balkenius, 1993), but cognitive control of emotions is also possible, and manifestly pronounced in humans (Grey, 2004).

What makes then non-local homeostatic regulation by neuromodulators 'emotional', in contrast to the automatic local homeostatic processes occurring on cellular basis, which we may term 'neutral'? Introspective experience and a vast body of clinical research data show that emotions and the organization of behavior through motivational drives are intrinsically related (Arbib & Fellous, 2004). When behavior in response to a given emotional arousal is not genetically predetermined, as it is generally the case for highly developed cognitive systems, then the cognitive system needs to learn an adequate response strategy. Algorithmically, this is achieved via reinforcement or temporal-difference learning (Sutton & Barto, 1998). These learning processes avail themselves of reward signals and a given behavioral response will be enhanced or suppressed for positive and negative reward signals respectively. A prominent candidate for a reward signal in the brain is dopamine (Iversena & Iversena, 2007). From this perspective one then concludes, that emotional diffusive control is characterized by a coupling of the regulative event to the generation of reward signals for subsequent reinforcement learning processes.

The key question is then: How are the reward signals generated? Let us consider an example. If we are angry, we will generally try to perform actions with the intent of reducing our level of angriness. When this goal is achieved we then are, usually at least, content. That is, a positive reward signal, reinforcing the precedent behavior, has been generated. Generalizing this example we may formulate the working hypothesis, that the generation of reward signals is coupled to the activation-level of the emotional diffusive regulative control processes. Let us note, that there is at present no direct clinical evidence for the overall validity of this working hypothesis. It is however very powerful, yielding directly a precise prescription for the algorithmic implementation of diffusive emotional control for synthetic cognitive systems and artificial intelligences. Emotional dif-

fusive control then corresponds to regulated meta-learning. The optimal intensity, or the optimal frequency, of a regulated meta-learning process has a genetically preset value and the reinforcement signal is generated when the meta-learning is activated too often or too rarely.

To conclude this section let us return to the initial question, whether a highly developed cognitive system without emotions, viz without non-local homeostatic regulation, is conceivable. The neuromodulators in our brain set our state of mind. Curiosity, anxiety or ebullience, to mention just a few of the myriads of possible emotional states, will generally lead to different behavioral strategies, providing the cognitive system differentiated options for reacting to similar environmental settings. Without the emotional states the cognitive system would be reduced to maximizing its actual survivability probability, or the integrated survivability probability for the foreseeable future. These options however do not constitute an optimal use of resources in environmental situations, to give an example, where surviving is not at stake. A curiosity-driven explorative strategy might then be the better option, potentially increasing the lifetime-fitness of the cognitive system by a substantial amount.

One of the defining characteristics of highly developed cognitive systems is the availability of a wide range of behavioral patterns. Diffusive emotional control provides these capabilities and this road has been taken by evolution, no alternative routes are presently known for synthetic cognitive systems.

COGNITIVE SYSTEMS

Having discussed the neurobiological functionalities of emotions, we now turn to the case of synthetic cognitive systems. Let us start by considering the defining properties of a cognitive system in general.

Intuitively one may be tempted to identify the human cognitive system with the brain, viz with the physical brain tissue. This is however inappropriate, a cognitive system is strictly speaking an abstract identity, a complex dynamical system consisting of a (very large) set of state variables together with equations determining the time evolution of these variables. The cognitive system takes however 'life' only once it becomes embodied, viz when it receives information through appropriate sensors or sensory organs and when it becomes able to perform action through appropriate actuators or limbs. The central defining characteristic of a cognitive system lies in its capability to retain a physical support unit, viz a body, functioning and alive, at least for a certain period of time. This task takes place in a continuously changing environment, as illustrated in Fig. 1. A cognitive system is therefore an instance of what can be termed a 'living dynamical system'.

It is interesting to point out in this context, that the physical brain tissue of a person is a part of the environment, and the human cognitive system is the sum of the biophysical processes resulting from the neural brain activity. Philosophical

niceties apart, we may define with 'environment' everything in the physical world the cognitive system may obtain sensory information about, either directly or indirectly via appropriate instruments. And indeed, we may obtain, at least as a matter of principle, knowledge about the complete physical-chemical state of every one of our own constituting neurons.

SURVIVAL VARIABLES

The primary task of a cognitive system is to keep its own support unit alive. Technically we can define a set of survival variables and the survival instinct then corresponds to the task of keeping these survival variables in a genetically given range. Typical examples for survival variables of biological beings are the blood sugar level, the blood pressure or the heart beating frequency. A classical survival variable for a robotic cognitive system is the battery status. Simple cognitive systems are equipped with preset responses for deviations of the survival variables from their target values, like the simple uptake of food in

Figure 1. Cognitive system. Schematic illustration of the interplay between an autonomous, i.e. a self-determined cognitive system and its environment. The cognitive system is an abstract living dynamical system, its time-evolution equations being executed by part of its support unit (shaded region), which corresponds to the brain for a biological cognitive system. Note that its physical support unit, viz its body, is part of the environment from which the cognitive system receives both external and internal sensory input data.

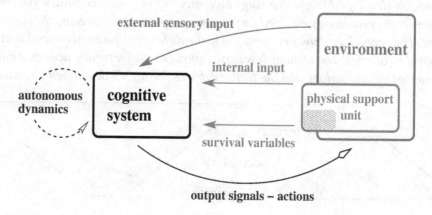

case of hunger, or the search for a socket when the battery is low. More sophisticated cognitive systems will generally need to acquire adequate responses by learning. E.g. they might need to learn which kinds of food or plant actually reduce the level of hunger and which do not, or how to find the next socket in an artificial labyrinth.

The programming of most real-world robots and AI-programs may be cast into this framework. A chess program typically has just one survival variable, the chance of winning the game. The value of this variable is evaluated via sophisticated deep-search algorithms and the next move it determined by the condition of maximizing the chance of winning the game, viz the probability of survival.

Technically, the implementation of a generalized survival instinct for synthetic cognitive systems does not pose any problem of principle. The actual distance of the survival variables from their given target value can be taken as a measure for the inverse probability of surviving and any action of the system resulting in an increase or in a decrease of the survivability probability will then trigger a positive or a negative reinforcement signal. This reinforcement signal can then be used for appropriate internal supervised learning, increasing or decreasing respectively the probability that the same course of action will be taken in the future for similar environmental conditions.

The positioning of the survival instinct within the motivational structure of a cognitive system is illustrated in Fig. 2.

AUTONOMOUS DYNAMICS

The simplest conceivable cognitive systems would just react in predetermined ways to incoming sensory stimuli. These responses might be simple, like the flight instinct in the case of danger, or computationally demanding. A soccer-playing robot reacts to the environmental situation, the current position and the velocity of the ball and of the other players, evaluating complex algorithmic routines. The soccer-playing robot is autonomous in the sense that it does not need a human controller. The robots participating in Robo-Cup are however not self-active in the terms of cognitive system theory. At no point does the soccer playing robot consider alternative action strategies; the robot is forced by its programming to continue playing soccer until the game is finished or the battery breaks down. The soccer playing robot will not interrupt playing because of anger or curiosity, it has just one possible 'state of mind'. No conflicting internal emotions or states of mind will distract the soccer playing robot.

On a higher level, a cognitive system would dispose of non-trivial internal processes. To classify

Figure 2. Motivational pyramids. Schematic illustration of the motivational pyramids for simple (left drawing) and highly developed (right drawing) biological or synthetic cognitive systems. The primary drives correspond to the genetically encoded survival mechanisms, guaranteeing the basic functionality of the support unit. The secondary drives correspond to the diffusive emotional control setting longer-term goals and survival strategies. The tertiary level correspond to the culturally acquired motivations. Note the predominance of the secondary and the tertiary drives for highly developed cognitive systems.

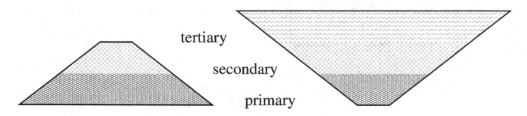

as autonomous or self-induced, these dynamical processes would need to continue indefinitely even in the absence of sensory stimuli. The internal dynamics remains active even in the presence of a static or quasi-static environment, when nothing is happening in the outside world. One could say, the system is continuously thinking by itself. For mammalian brains this is a well-known and defining neurobiological characteristic. The neural activities of higher cortical areas of mammalian brains are influenced and modulated by sensory stimuli, but not directly driven (Fiser, Chiu & Weliky, 2004). The response is generally not forced. We are hence interested in the interplay of self-generated cognitive activity and emotional control in autonomous cognitive systems.

ASSOCIATIVE THINKING

We have developed a model system implementing algorithmically the principles of an autonomous cognitive system (Gros, 2005; Gros, 2007). The dHan model (dense Homogenous Associative Network) exhibits self-generated associative thought processes, which we postulate as the driving forces for the self-generated dynamical activities. At any given time only a subset of neurons is active, for a certain period, with the activities of competing neural centers being suppressed. Subsequently a different, in general partially overlapping group of neurons becomes active transiently, such forming an ongoing and never ending series of transient neural activity patterns. This type of neural dynamics, the transient-state dynamics, is illustrated in Fig. 3. For the mathematical formulation implementing these principles we refer to the literature (Gros, 2005; Gros, 2007).

There are findings from experimental neurobiology pointing towards the importance of transient-state dynamics (Abeles et al, 1995; Kenet et al, 2003), indicating that competition and anti-correlation are central organizational principles for the neural activity in the brain (Fox et al, 2005). The transient plateaus in the level of neural activity of a subset of neurons or neural ensembles are also termed `states of the mind' (Edelman & Tononi, 2000) or `winning coalitions'. The composition of the winning coalition changes dynamically from one transient state to the subsequent, giving rise to a vast number of possible states of the mind. The dHan model is therefore an example of a biologically inspired approach to cognitive system theory, seeking to implement known principles of global brain activity, without attempting to reproduce neurobiological details.

Figure 3. Transient states. Schematic illustration of a sequence of transiently stable winning coalitions of a neural ensemble. The firing state of any given neuron is either close to zero or transiently stable for a finite period of time, with relatively short transition periods.

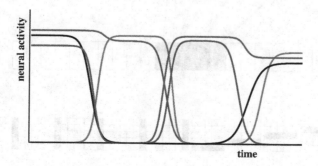

INPUT RECOGNITION

A cognitive system continuously receives sensory input containing information about the external environment and about the status of its physical support unit, its body (see Fig. 1). This flow of stimuli competes with the internal, autonomously generated transient-state dynamics. There are then two time series of events, with no a priori connection: The series of subsequently activated winning coalitions generated internally and the flux of sensory stimuli. The sensory input therefore may or may not make a difference. It may or may not influence the internal dynamics, it may or may not influence the composition of the next winning coalition. A primary task of the cognitive system is consequently to find out whether this happens (Gros & Kaczor, 2008). This is a typical task, we term it `input recognition', for diffusive control. We have developed a model, where the interplay between the internal dHan dynamics and the flow

of sensory input is regulated through diffusive input recognition (Gros & Kaczor, 2008).

In Fig. 4 the setup of the system is shown. An input layer provides an input data stream to a dHan layer, which is autonomously active. Every site in the dHan layer receives recurrent input from the dHan layer and feed-forward signals from the input layer. Every site can distinguish between these two kinds of inputs and decide which one is the dominant driving signal. A site can therefore decide by itself, through a local process, whether the sensory input had a driving influence in its activation process. In this case a signal is sent to the diffusive control unit responsible for the input recognition, contributing to the activation of this control unit. When the activation level exceeds a certain threshold a diffusive learning signal is released and the links connecting the input layer with the dHan layer are modified in a Hebbian-like fashion. In this way a non-trivial analysis of the input signals is achieved, resulting

Figure 4. Input prrocessing. The model system consisting of a dHan (dense and homogeneous associative network) and an input layer. The input signals are illustrated as raw horizontal and vertical bars. The dHan layer is autonomously active, C-I, ..., C-V denoting the possible winning coalitions of sites. The input signal competes with the internal activity of the dHan layer. The interconnections input-dHan layer are modified during learning, which is activated through an autonomously generated diffusive learning signal.

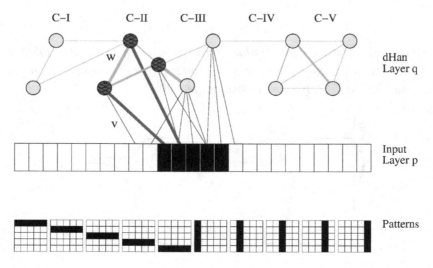

in an non-linear independent-component analysis (Gros & Kaczor, 2008) and in a mapping of statistically independent objects in the input-data stream to winning coalitions of the dHan layer. For the details we refer to the literature (Gros & Kaczor, 2008).

EMOTIONAL CONTROL

The diffusive control unit responsible for input recognition described above may work either neutrally or emotionally. For the setup illustrated in Fig. 4, made up just of a single input and a single dHan layer, emotional control would be meaningless and the input recognition is neutral, viz there is no preferred activation level. For a full-fledged embedded cognitive system the situation would however be different and the same control unit might acquire emotional character. The system could get `bored' whenever the input recognition would be inactive for a long time (deprivation of sensory signals), or `stressed' whenever it would be continuously active (overloaded with sensory signals). In either case an additional diffusive signal could be released, a reinforcement signal, with the aim of decreasing the probability that similar situations would come up again in the future.

This example, the task of input recognition is a task quite generally necessary for cognitive systems, whichever the respective structural and dynamical organization may be. The mechanisms described here, in the context of the model being investigated, may therefore be generalized and adapted to other approaches and concepts for synthetic cognitive systems.

CONCLUSION

The motivational problem of what to do in one's own life lies at the heart of all living. At a high and philosophical level this fact is reflected by

an ongoing and never ending search of humanity, the quest for the meaning of life. On a basic level it implies that all actions of a living being, of a cognitive system, are generated internally, and that a thorough understanding of the decision mechanisms is paramount for an eventually successful realization of artificial cognitive systems. Taking inspiration from neurobiological insights, we have delineated here a layered framework for the motivational drives of an autonomously active biological or synthetic cognitive system.

The overall foundation is given by the survival instinct, algorithmically corresponding to the preprogrammed task of keeping the physical support unit, the body of the cognitive system, functioning and alive. When the basic survival is ensured, emotional control takes over. Emotional control is, in general, functionally independent from the basic need to survive. From the evolutionary point of view the survival instinct is needed to guarantee the short-term survival and emotional control to increase life-time fitness via elaborated behavioral strategies. This separation of time scales is reflected algorithmically, with emotional control being responsible for meta learning, the regulation of slow variables via diffusive reinforcement signals. Importantly, the solution outlined here for the motivational problem can be implemented directly, at least as matter of principles, for artificial cognitive systems and robots, realizing synthetic emotions.

The synthetic emotions generated via diffusive emotional control do not correspond to simulations of emotional expressions, as they are investigated in the context of robot-human communication, but to `true internal emotions', being generated by mechanisms and principles roughly analogous to the emotions present in biological cognitive systems. A correspondence of the qualia of such generated synthetic emotions with the emotions of human or non-human animals is however not to be expected for the foreseeable future.

The mechanisms triggering the release of the neuromodulators conveying emotions in mammals may be either predetermined genetically or acquired culturally. Humans may associate the play of a violin with joy or with distress, or just remain unmoved, there are no marked genetic preferences. This implies that there is an extended layer of culturally acquired motivational drives, as illustrated in Fig. 2, above the survival instinct and above the diffusive emotional control. We believe that a full implementation of this three-layered system of motivational drives is a necessary requirement for the eventual realization of human-level artificial intelligences and cognitive systems and that this goal is to date quite distant from the actual status of research.

REFERENCES

Abeles, M., Bergman, H., Gat, I., Meilljson, I., Seidemann, E., Tishby, N., & Vaadia, E. (1995). Cortical activity flips among quasi-stationary states. In *Proceedings of the National Academy of Sciences of the United States of America, Vol. 92* (pp. 8616-8620).

Arbib, M.A, & Fellous, J.M. (2004). Emotions: from brain to robot. *Trends in Cognitive Sciences, 8,* 554-561.

Aron, A., Fisher, H., Mashek, D.J., Strong, G., Li, H., & Brown, L.L. (2005). Reward, Motivation, and Emotion Systems Associated With Early-Stage Intense Romantic Love. *Journal of Neurophysiology, 94,* 327-337.

Balkenius, C. (1993). *The roots of motivation.* In J.-A. Mayer, H.L. Roitblat, & S.W. Wilson (Eds.), *From Animals to Animats 2.* MIT Press/ Bradford Books.

Barrett, L.F., Mesquita, B., Ochsner, K.N., & Gross, J.J. (2007). The Experience of Emotion. *Annual Review of Psychology, 58,* 373-403.

Blakermore, S.J., Winston, J., & Frith, U. (2004). Social cognitive neuroscience: where are we heading? *Trends in Cognitive Science, 5,* 216-222.

Breazeal, C. (2003). Emotion and sociable humanoid robots. *International Journal of Human-Computer Studies, 59,* 119-155.

Burgdorf, J., & Panksepp, J. (2006). The neurobiology of positive emotions. *Neuroscience and Biobehavioral Reviews, 30,* 173-187.

Coricelli, G., Dolan, R.J., & Sirigu, A. (2007). Brain, emotion and decision making: the paradigmatic example of regret. *Trends in Cognitive Sciences, 11,* 258-265.

Damasio, A.R. (1994). *Descartes error: Emotion, reason and the human nrain.* Putnam Pub Group.

Doya, K. (1999). What are the computations of the cerebellum, the basal ganglia and the cerebral cortex? *Neural Networks,. 12,* 961-974.

Duffy, B.R. (2003). Anthropomorphism and the social robot. *Robotics and Autonomous Systems, 42,* 177-190.

Edelman, G.M. & Tononi, G.A. (2000). *A universe of consciousness.* New York: Basic Books.

Fellous, J.-M. (1999). The neuromodulatory basis of emotion. *The Neuroscientist, 5,* 283-294.

Fellous, J.-M., & Arbib, M.A. (2005). *Who needs emotions? The brain meets the robot.* Oxford University Press.

Fiser, J., Chiu, C., & Weliky, M. (2004). Small modulation of ongoing cortical dynamics by sensory input during natural vision. *Nature, 431,* 573-578.

Fong, T., Nourbakhsh, I., & Dautenhahn, K. (2003). A survey of socially interactive robots. *Robotics and Autonomous Systems, 42,* 143-166.

Fox, M.D., Snyder, A.Z., Vincent, J.L., Corbetta, M., Van Essen, D.C., & Raichle, M.E. (2005). The human brain is intrinsically organized into dynamic, anticorrelated functional networks. In *Proceedings of the National Academy of Sciences of the United States of America, Vol. 102* (pp. 9673-9678).

Grey, J.R. (2004). Integration of emotion and cognitive control. *Current Directions in Psychological Science, 13*, 46-48.

Gros, C. (2005). Self-Sustained Thought Processes in a Dense Associative Network. In U. Furbach (Ed.), *Proceedings of the 28th Annual German Conference on Artificial Intelligence (KI 2005), Springer Lecture Notes in Artificial Intelligence, Vol. 3698* (pp. 366-379).

Gros, C. (2007). Neural networks with transient state dynamics. *New Journal of Physics, 9*, 109-128.

Gros, C. (2008). *Complex and adaptive dynamical systems, a primer.* Springer.

Gros, C., & Kaczor, G. (2008). Learning in cognitive systems with autonomous dynamics. *Proceedings of the International Conference on Cognitive Systems, Karlsruhe 2008.* IEEE.

Iversena, S.D., & Iversena, L.L. (2007). Dopamine: 50 years in perspective. *Trends in Neurosciences, 30*, 88-193.

Kenet, T., Bibitchkov, D., Tsodyks, M., Grinvald, A., & Ariell, A. (2003). Spontaneously emerging cortical representations of visual attributes. *Nature, 425*, 954-956.

Kringelbach, M.L. (2005). *The Human Orbitofrontal Cortex: Linking Reward to Hedonic Experience. Nature Reviews of Neuroscience, 6*, 691-702.

Marder E. & Goaillard J.M.(2006). *Variability, compensation and homeostasis in neuron and network function.* Nature Reviews of Neuroscience, Vol. 7, pp. 563-574.

Minsky, M. (2007). *The emotion machine: Commonsense thinking, artificial intelligence, and the future of the human mind.* Simon & Schuster.

Murray, I.R., & Arnott, J.L. (2008). Applying an analysis of acted vocal emotions to improve the simulation of synthetic speech. *Computer Speech & Language, 22*, 107-129.

Naqvi, N., Shiv, B., & Bechara, A. (2006). The role of emotion in decision making: a cognitive neuroscience perspective. *Current Directions in Psychological Science, 15*, 260-264.

Lieberman, M.D. (2007). Social Cognitive Neuroscience: A Review of Core Processes. *Annual Review of Psychology, Vol. 58*, 259-289.

Lewis, M.D. (2005a). Bridging emotion theory and neurobiology through dynamic systems modeling. *Behavioral and Brain Sciences, 28*, 169-245.

Lewis, M.D. (2005b). Self-organizing individual differences in brain development. *Developmental Review, 25*, 252-277.

Ochsner, K.N. & Gross, J.J. (2005). The cognitive control of emotions. *Trends in Cognitive Sciences, 9*, 241-249.

Parr, L.A., Waller, B.M., & Fugate, J. (2005). Emotional communication in primates: implications for neurobiology. *Current Opinion in Neurobiology, 15*, 716-720.

Phelps, E.A. (2006). Emotion and cognition: Insights from studies of the human amygdala. *Annual Review of Psychology, 52*, pp. 27-53.

Picard, R.W. (2000). Synthetic emotion. *IEEE Computer Graphics and Applications, 20*, 52-53.

Rolls, E.T. (2005). *Emotion explained.* Oxford University Press.

Sutton, R.S., & Barto, A.G. (1998). *Reinforcement learning: An introduction.* MIT Press (Bradford Book).

Tomlinson, B. & Blumberg, B. (2002). Social synthetic characters. *Computer Graphics, 26*, 5-7.

Turrigiano, G.G. & Nelson, S.B. (2004). Homeostatic plasticity in the developing nervous system. *Nature Reviews of Neuroscience, 5,* 97-107.

KEY TERMS

Autonomous Cognitive System: Cognitive systems are generally autonomous, i.e. self-determined, setting their own goals. This implies that they are not driven, under normal circumstances, by external sensory signals. I.e. an autonomous cognitive system is not forced to perform a specific action by a given sensory stimuli. Autonomy does not exclude the possibility to acquire information from external teachers, given that internal mechanisms allow an autonomous cognitive system to decide whether or not to focus attention on external teaching signals. In terms of a *living dynamical system* an autonomous cognitive system possesses a non-trivial and self-sustained dynamics, viz an ongoing autonomous dynamical activity.

Biologically Inspired Cognitive System: In principle one may attempt to develop artificial cognitive systems starting with an empty blueprint. Biological cognitive systems are at present however the only existing real-world *autonomous cognitive systems* we know of, and it makes sense to make good use of the general insights obtained by neurobiology for the outline of cognitive system theory. An example such a paradigmal insight is the importance of competitive neural dynamics, viz of neural ensembles competing with each other trying to form winning coalitions of brain regions, suppressing transiently the activity of other neural ensembles. Another example is the intrinsic connection between *diffusive emotional control* and learning mechanisms involving *reinforcement signals*.

Cognitive System: A cognitive system is an abstract identity, consisting of the set of equations determining the time-evolution of the internal dynamical variables. It needs a *physical support unit* in order to function properly, a datum also denoted as 'embedded intelligence'. The primary task for a cognitive system is to retain functionality in certain environments. For this purpose it needs an operational physical support unit for acting and for obtaining sensory information about the environment. The cognitive system remains operational as long as its physical support unit, its body, survives. A cognitive system might be either biological (humans and non-human animals) or synthetic. Non-trivial cognitive systems are capable of learning and of adapting to a changing environment. High-level cognitive systems may show various degrees of intelligence.

Complex System Theory: Complex system theory deals with 'complex' dynamical systems, viz with dynamical systems containing a very large number of interacting dynamical variables. Preeminent examples of complex systems are the gen-regulation network at basis of all living, self-organizing phase transitions in physics like superconductivity and magnetism, and cognitive systems, the later being the most sophisticated and probably also the least understood of all complex dynamical systems.

Diffusive Control: Diffusive control is intrinsically related for biological cognitive systems to the release of neuromodulators. Neuromodulators are generally released in the inter-neural medium, from where they physically diffuse, affecting a large ensemble of surrounding neurons. The neuromodulators do not affect directly the cognitive information processing, viz the dynamical state of individual neurons. They act as the prime agents for transmitting extended signals for *meta learning*. Diffusive control signals come in two versions, neutral and emotional. (A) Neutral diffusive control is automatically activated when certain conditions are present in the cognitive system, irrespectively of the frequency and the level of past activations of the diffusive control. (B) Emotional diffusive control has a preset preferred level of activation frequency and strength. Deviation of the preset activity-level results in negative *reinforcement signals,* viz the system feels 'uneasy' or 'uncomfortable'.

Dynamical System: A dynamical system is a set of variables together with a set of rules determining the time-development of theses variables. The time might be either discrete, viz 1,2,3,... or continuous. In the latter case the dynamical system is governed by a set of differential equations. Dynamical system theory is at the heart of all natural laws, famous examples being Newton's law of classical mechanics, the Schrödinger equation of quantum mechanics and Einstein's geometric theory of gravity, general relativity.

Living Dynamical System: A living dynamical system is a dynamical system containing a set of variables denoted 'survival variables'. The system is defined to be living as long as the value of these variables remain inside a certain preset range and defined to be dead otherwise. Cognitive systems are instances of living dynamical systems and the survival variables correspond for the case of a biological cognitive system to the heart frequency, the blood pressure, the blood sugar level and so on.

Meta Learning: Meta learning and 'homeostatic self-regulation' are closely related. Both are needed for the long-term stability of the cognitive system, regulating internal thresholds, learning-rates, attention fields and so on. They do not affect directly the primary cognitive information processing, e.g. they do not change directly the firing state of individual neurons, nor do they affect the primary learning, i.e. changes of synaptic strengths. The regulation of the sensibility of the synaptic plasticities with respect to the pre- and to the post-synaptic firing state is, on the other hand, a prime task for both meta learning and homeostatic self-regulation. Homeostatic self-regulation is local, always active and present, irrespectively of any global signal. Meta learning is, on the other

hand, triggered by global signals, the *diffusive control* signals, generated by the cognitive system itself through distinct sub-components.

Motivational Problem: Biological cognitive systems are 'autonomous', viz they decided by themselves what to do. Highly developed cognitive systems, like the one of mammals, regularly respond to sensory stimuli and information but are generally not driven by the incoming sensory information, i.e. the sensory information does not force them to any specific action. The motivational problem then deals with the central issue of how a highly developed cognitive system selects its actions and targets. This is the domain of instincts and emotions, even for humans. Note, that rational selection of a primary target is impossible, rational and logical reasoning being useful only for the pursue of primary targets set by the underlying emotional network. Most traditional research in artificial intelligence disregards the motivational problem, assuming internal primary goal selection is non-essential and that explicit primary target selection by supervising humans is both convenient and sufficient.

Physical Support Unit: Also denoted 'body' for biological cognitive systems. Generally it can be subdivided into four functional distinct components. (A) The component responsible for evaluating the time-evolution equations of the cognitive system, viz the brain. (B) The actuators, viz the limbs, responsible for processing the output-signals of the cognitive system. (C) The sensory organs providing appropriate input information on both the external environment and on the current status of the physical support unit. (D) The modules responsible for keeping the other components alive, viz the internal organs. Artificial cognitive systems dispose of equivalent functional components.

Reinforcement Signal: Reinforcement signals can be either positive or negative, i.e. a form of reward or punishment. The positive or negative consequences of an action, or of a series of consecutive actions, are taken to reinforce or to suppress the likelihood of selecting the same set of actions when confronted with a similar problem-setting in the future. A reinforcement signal can be generated by a cognitive system only when a nominal target outcome is known. When this target value is given `by hand' from the outside, viz by an external teacher, one speaks of `supervised learning'. When the target value is generated internally one speaks of `unsupervised learning'. The internal generation of meaningful target values constitutes the core of the *motivational problem*.

Universal Cognitive System: Simple cognitive systems are mostly ruled by preset stimuli-reaction rules. E.g. an earthworm will automatically try to meander towards darkness. Universal

principles, i.e. algorithms applicable to a wide range of different environmental settings, become however predominant in highly developed cognitive systems. We humans, to give an example, are constantly, and most of the time unconsciously trying to predict the outcome of actions and movements taking place in the world around us, even if these outcomes are not directly relevant for our intentions at the given time, allowing us to extract regularities in the observed processes for possible later use. Technically this attitude corresponds to a time-series prediction-task which is quite universal in its applicability. We use it, e.g., to obtain unconsciously knowledge on the ways a soccer ball rolls and flies as well as to extract from the sentences we listen-to the underlying grammatical rules of our mother-tongue.

Chapter VIII
Robots React, but Can They Feel?

Bruce J. MacLennan
University of Tennessee, USA

ABSTRACT

This chapter addresses the "Hard Problem" of consciousness in the context of robot emotions. The Hard Problem, as defined by Chalmers, refers to the task of explaining the relation between conscious experience and the physical processes associated with it. For example, a robot can act afraid, but could it feel fear? Using protophenomenal analysis, which reduces conscious experience to its smallest units and investigates their physical correlates, we consider whether robots could feel their emotions, and the conditions under which they might do so. We find that the conclusion depends on unanswered but empirical questions in the neuropsychology of human consciousness. However, we do conclude that conscious emotional experience will require a robot to have a rich representation of its body and the physical state of its internal processes, which is important even in the absence of conscious experience.

INTRODUCTION

Recent decades have seen a renaissance in the scientific investigation of consciousness, but a fundamental issue has been neglected, which is to integrate the facts of subjective experience with our understanding of physical processes in the nervous system. David Chalmers (1995, 1996) has called this the *Hard Problem* of consciousness because it poses unique epistemological challenges

that make it resistant to straight-forward scientific investigation (see also MacLennan, 1995, 1996). The fundamental problem is that it would seem possible for there to be "zombies" in which all the usual neurophysiological processes take place in the brain, leading to normal behavior, brain scans, etc., but without any accompanying subjective experience (Campbell, 1970; Kirk, 1974; Kripke, 1980). Therefore, it is necessary to distinguish between *functional* (or *access*) *consciousness*, which refers to cognitive and behavioral functions fulfilled by consciousness in an organism, and *phenomenal consciousness,* which refers to the experience of subjective awareness (e.g., Block, 1995).

The Hard Problem is especially interesting when we consider robot emotions. Emotion is essential to the competent functioning of many animals (arguably, all animals: Panksepp, 2004, pp. 34–7; Plutchik, 2003, pp. 223–6), and synthetic emotion can fulfill similar functions in autonomous robots (as discussed briefly in **Background**, below). Just as the emotion *fear* can galvanize an organism and reorganize its cognition and behavior in order to protect itself, so synthetic fear can function for a robot's self-protection. But will the robot feel afraid? Or, more carefully, what, if any, are the conditions under which a robot would *feel fear* (as opposed to *acting afraid*, in both its behavior and cognitive processes)? Thus, my goal in this chapter is to address *the Hard Problem of robot emotions.*

It bears repeating that the other problems of consciousness are not easy! If they are less hard, it is only because they are amenable to the usual methods of scientific investigation, and don't pose any unusual epistemological challenges. Certainly, functional consciousness is relevant to robot emotions, but this chapter will focus on phenomenal consciousness and robot emotions. (For a general discussion of robot consciousness, both functional and phenomenal, see MacLennan, 2008a.)

BACKGROUND

The Biological Functions of Emotion

I begin by discussing the functions of emotion in the context of evolutionary biology and the relevance of these emotional functions to practical robotics; it is a brief overview, since the topic is addressed at length in other chapters of this *Handbook*. But what is an emotion? Plutchik (2003, pp. 18–19) quotes some twenty definitions, and Paul and Anne Kleinginna (1981) develop a taxonomy of more than 90 definitions! For the purposes of this chapter, Rolls (2007) provides a good summary of the essential characteristics of emotion: An emotion is a state elicited by the delivery or omission of a reward or punisher (either present or remembered), which functions as positive or negative reinforcement. Specifically, the delivery of a reward, or the omission or cessation of a punisher, is positive reinforcement, and conversely the delivery of a punisher, or omission or cessation of a reward, is negative reinforcement. Thus the organism acts to seek rewards and avoid punishers, and from an evolutionary perspective these actions are adaptive, in the sense of inclusive fitness (Plutchik, 2003, pp. 218–23). Rolls (2007) enumerates six principal factors in the elicitation of emotions: (1) reinforcement contingency (delivery, omission, cessation), (2) intensity, (3) reinforcement associations with a stimulus, (4) primary (i.e., phylogenetic) reinforcers of an emotion, (5) secondary (i.e., learned) reinforcers, and (6) the possibility of active or passive responses, which may affect the elicited emotion. (See also Rolls, 2002, 2005.)

What good is emotion? Why should we want robots to have them? Rolls (2005, 2007) lists nine significant functions (evolutionary adaptations) fulfilled by emotion: (1) Emotion is essential in eliciting autonomic and endocrine responses, such as a change in heart rate and the release of adrenaline. (2) Emotion facilitates flexibility of response, by separating the evaluation of a stimulus (as a reward or punisher) from the means to obtain or avoid it. That is, the emotion represents a *goal*, which might be achieved in a variety of ways (Rolls, 2006). (3) The effect of emotion is inherently motivating (i.e., instigating action). (4) Emotional expression facilitates communication by revealing an animal's mental state, goals, intentions, etc. (5) Social bonding is also facilitated by emotion, for example between parents and offspring or among the members of a community. (6) Emotion can persist over an extended period and generate a mood, which affects cognitive processing of events and memory, for example, biasing the processing to be more appropriate to the situation eliciting the emotion. (7) Memory storage and retrieval are both facilitated by emotion, since emotionally charged events are more likely to be encoded into episodic memory; also, because the emotion is encoded and affects memory representation, similar emotions can aid the retrieval of memories that are relevant to an emotionally charged stimulus. (8) Since an emotional state can persist over an extended period of time, it can provide a coherent continuing context for cognitive processing and behavior. (9) Finally, emotion evokes retrieval of non-cortical memories.

Robot Emotions

Most of the functions enumerated by Rolls are also relevant to robotics; I will mention them briefly, citing the numbers of the functions in his list. Although a robot does not have an endocrine or autonomic nervous system, it may have analogous functions to accomplish, for example, redistributing power in a power-aware computer, powering-up inactive devices, reallocating computational resources, reorienting or tuning sensors, and readying effectors for action (1). Behavioral flexibility can be improved by decoupling the possible indicators of a situation from the possible responses to it, and this can be achieved by a "bow tie" organization in which the knot of the tie represents the motivational essence of a situation. (Bow tie organization is common in biological systems and is widely used in engineering for risk management.) The left-hand side of the bow tie represents various stimuli or signals that can indicate a general situation, while the right-hand side represents various responses to the situation. For example, many different stimuli can indicate to a robot that it is in a harmful environment, and

that motivates the robot to plan some corrective action. In cases such as this, the "knot" is serving the function of an emotion, such as fear (2). A robot's activity is generally directed toward some broad goal (e.g., exploration, construction, refueling, defense, offense) which motivates and organizes its subsidiary activities, and which functions like an emotion (3); the persistence of an emotional state maintains this high-level organization until the goal is achieved or a higher priority goal arises (6, 8). Robots may have to work in collaborative teams including humans as well as other robots, and effective cooperation requires each agent to have some insight into the internal states, goals, and intentions of the other agents (Breazeal, 2003; Breazeal, Brooks, Gray, Hoffman, Kidd, Lee, Lieberman, Lockerd & Chilongo, 2004), for which overt display of emotional state is valuable (4, 5). Furthermore, it is important for robots that work with, assist, care for, or rescue humans to have feelings of care and concern for them, and conversely it may be useful for robots to feel a need for care (maintenance, repair, rescue, etc.) by humans or by other robots (5). Finally, the representation of emotion in memory and cognition provides a crude, but highly behavior-relevant cue for associative memory storage and retrieval and for context-sensitive cognitive processing (7, 9).

Though brief and superficial, the foregoing remarks are aimed at outlining the functional roles played by emotions in animals and at defending the usefulness of a similar structure of synthetic emotions for autonomous robots. Nevertheless, although modeled on natural emotion, there would seem to be no reason why robots could not have all the appropriate information structures and control processes to fulfill the functions of emotions, but without *feeling* them. That is, there would seem to be no contradiction in "zombie robots," who, for example, have an internal representation corresponding to fear, and react fearfully in appropriate circumstance, but which *feel* no fear. Regardless of whether one thinks this possibility is likely or unlikely, it remains in the realm of opinion unless we can find some principled, and preferably scientific, approach to the Hard Problem of robot emotions.

PROTOPHENOMENAL ANALYSIS OF ROBOT EMOTION

Overview of Protophenomenal Analysis

Protophenomenal analysis aims to relate the structure of conscious experience to physical processes in the organism, and in particular it aims to understand the emergence of consciousness from its smallest constituents. Thus it takes subjective experience as an empirical given, and attempts to understand it in reference to neurobiology and underlying physical processes. Protophenomenal analysis does not presume that conscious experience can be reduced to physical processes (nor the converse!), but rather seeks mutually informative correspondences between the structures of the two domains (subjective and objective, as we might say).

Chalmers (1996) provides a good discussion of the Hard Problem and the background for protophenomenal analysis, although I do not agree with all of his conclusions. More detailed discussions of protophenomenal approach and its application to a number of problems in consciousness can be found elsewhere (MacLennan, 1995, 1996a, 1999b, 2008a, 2008b); here we restrict our attention to topics necessary for addressing emotion in robots.

In order to establish a detailed correspondence between conscious experience and neurophysiology, it is necessary to carefully investigate the structure of consciousness. As illustrated by the failings of naive introspectionism (Gregory, 1987, pp. 395–400; Lyons, 1986), this is a difficult undertaking. As in any empirical investigation, appropriate training in observation and experimental technique is required in order to see the relevant phenomena and make the appropriate discriminations. The empirical investigation of consciousness presents particular problems, due to the privateness of the phenomena and the effects that the observer can have on the phenomena, among other factors. Fortunately, work in phenomenological philosophy, including experimental phenomenology, and investigations in phenomenological psychology, have provided many empirical tools and techniques and produced an increasing body of results (e.g., Ihde, 1986; McCall, 1983).

A *phenomenon* may be defined as anything that appears or arises (Grk., *phainetai*) in conscious experience, including perceptions, but also hallucinations, ideas, recollections, expectations, hopes, fears, intentions, moods, feelings, and conscious emotions. A person's experience takes place in a *phenomenal world* comprising actual and potential phenomena experienceable by that person. In a broad sense *phenomenology* is the discipline that studies the structure of a phenomenal world, that is, the relationships of necessity, possibility, and probability among the appearances of phenomena, and especially those structures common to all people. To address the Hard Problem, however, we must resort to *neurophenomenology*, which seeks to correlate the dynamics of one's phenomenal world to the neurodynamics of the brain (Laughlin, McManus & d'Aquili, 1990; Lutz & Thompson, 2003; Rudrauf, Lutz, Cosmelli, Lachaux & Le Van Quyen, 2003; Varela, 1996). It combines the techniques of phenomenology and neuropsychology, using each to help us advance the other.

Reduction is a valuable tool in science; it helps us to understand more complex systems in terms of simpler ones. However, the patterns of reduction that have been most successful in science are not applicable to the Hard Problem, for they reduce *objective* properties and processes to simpler objective properties, whereas the Hard Problem resides in the relation between the subjective and the objective, and a reduction of one to the other is fundamentally impossible (Chalmers, 1996, Pt. II; MacLennan, 1995, 1996).

Nevertheless, reduction is valuable, and so protophenomenal analysis makes use of reduction, but confined to either the subjective or objective domains. Phenomenological reduction, as applied in the subjective domain, seeks to relate subjective phenomena to simpler subjective phenomena.[1] Easiest to understand is a *qualitative reduction*, which divides up phenomena by modality; for example perceptual phenomena may be divided according to sensory modality. However careful phenomenology reveals that the various modalities are not completely independent, but interact in subtle and important ways, so most qualitative reductions are only approximate (MacLennan, 1999, 2003, 2008a, 2008b).

However, it is also possible to do a *quantitative reduction* in the subjective domain, in which subjective phenomena are reduced to simpler phenomena of the same kind. For example, visual phenomena are composed of smaller visual phenomena, such as subjective experiences of patches of color, oriented edges and textures, etc. Similarly, at least to a first approximation, tactile phenomena are constituted from much smaller phenomena corresponding to individual patches of skin. The reduction is more complicated, of course, when we consider such non-perceptual phenomena as intentions, beliefs, and — most relevant here — moods, emotions, etc., but with careful phenomenological analysis the reduction can be accomplished.

Phenomenological reduction can be paralleled by neurological reduction. For example, simpler phenomena (patches etc.) distributed across the visual field correspond to spatially distributed patterns of activity over visual regions of the cortex, called *retinotopic maps*. Similarly, *somatosensory maps* have a spatial structure corresponding systematically to the spatial organization of nerves in the skin, muscles, etc. Indeed, *topographic maps* are ubiquitous in the brain, and seem to be one of the fundamental ways the brain organizes the

activity of individual neurons (or small groups of them, such as microcolumns) into macroscopic neural representations (Knudsen, du Lac & Esterly, 1987). Organization of the maps and corresponding phenomena need not be spatial. For example, *tonotopic maps* in auditory cortex systematically represent different pitches by the neurons in the map, corresponding to a reduction of subjectively perceived intervals of pitch into smaller subjective intervals.

In this way the phenomenological and neurological reductions facilitate each other: neurological discoveries suggest phenomenological structures, which may be explored through phenomenology, and phenomenological investigations provide observations to test and extend neurological theories. This joint reductive process may be termed *neurophenomenological reduction*, for it attempts a parallel reduction of subjective and objective processes to more elementary ones of the same kind. In this process neither domain is privileged over the other, for they are both empirically given, and both are necessary for solving the Hard Problem. At each stage of the process one or the other side may be experimentally or theoretically more tractable, and so each may facilitate progress in the other.

This parallel reduction has implications for the limit of neurophenomenological reduction, because apparently there are smallest units of neurological reduction (e.g., individual neurons or synapses, but it is not important at this point what they are). This implies that there will also be smallest units of phenomena, and we may call them *protophenomena* (Chalmers, 1996, pp. 126–7, 298–9; Cook, 2000, 2002a, 2002b, chs. 6–7, 2008; MacLennan, 1996; cf. *proto-qualia* in Llinas, 1988; *phenomenisca* in MacLennan, 1995).

It is easy to confuse protophenomena with elementary sense data (e.g., in visual perception, patches of red-here-now, green-there-now, etc.), and some perceptual protophenomena are in fact similar to elementary sense data, but there are important differences. First, the neuropsychology of vision demonstrates that the elements of visual perception go far beyond patches of color, and include edges, lines, textures, and much higher level features. Further, protophenomena are extremely small, in comparison with ordinary phenomena, in the sense that an ordinary phenomenon comprises a very large number of protophenomena. This is implied by the neurophenomenological reduction, for if the smallest units of neural representation are individual neurons or microcolumns, then there could be many billions of protophenomena in the conscious state. Indeed, most protophenomena are unobservable, in the sense that a change of one protophenomenon will not usually be able to affect our behavior. The idea that the elements of consciousness are unobservable may seem paradoxical or even self-contradictory, but it is not, for *proto*phenomena are not phenomena. An analogy may clarify the situation: a diamond is a solid object made of carbon atoms, but a single carbon atom is not a diamond, and removing or adding a single atom will not affect the diamond *qua* diamond. (For more on the ontological status of protophenomena, see MacLennan, 1995, 1996a.) Finally, the neurophenomenological reduction implies that the protophenomena are the elementary constituents of *all* conscious phenomena, not just perceptions, and so we must use neurophenomenological investigations to describe the protophenomena of emotions and other non-perceptual phenomena.

It is also necessary to remark that phenomenology reveals that our ordinary conscious state is not passive experiencing of the world, but rather active, engaged *being-in-the-world* (Heideggerian *Dasein*: Dreyfus, 1991). Therefore, corresponding to sensory and motor neurons there are receptive and effective protophenomena, which are connected by more interior protophenomena corresponding to interneurons.

Sensory neurons usually have a *receptive field*, which defines their response to various stimuli. That is, the receptive field is a function that defines a neuron's degree of activity for different stimuli in its input space. For example, a neuron might show maximal activity for an edge of a certain orientation at a particular location on the retina, and its response might fall off for stimuli that are at different orientations, are less like edges, or are at slightly different locations. Interneurons also have receptive fields, but they are defined over more abstract input spaces than those of sensory neurons.

From the phenomenological perspective, each protophenomenon has an *intensity* that measures its degree of presence in the conscious state. For example, corresponding to the above-mentioned neuron is a protophenomenon that contributes to phenomena an oriented edge at a particular location in the visual field. This protophenomenon's intensity constitutes its degree of presence in any phenomenon of which it is a part.

Neurophenomenological analysis implies that each protophenomenon has an associated *activity site* in the brain, and that some physical quantity or process at this site is necessarily correlated with the protophenomenon's intensity. (I say "necessarily correlated" to stress that protophenomenal intensity is not reducible to this physical quantity, or vice versa, but that their correlation is a necessary consequence of their being two aspects of the same reality; thus, the theory of protophenomena is a species of double-aspect monism (MacLennan, 1996a, 2008a), which Chalmers (2002) terms *type-F monism*.) Nevertheless we cannot say at this time what the activity sites might be. Obvious candidates include the neuron's somatic membrane, the synapses, and the dendritic trees or spines.

There are corresponding candidates for the physical process correlated with protophenomenal intensity, including membrane potential, ion or neurotransmitter flux, and the action potential. It is possible that different neurotransmitters lead to qualitatively different experiences, or that membrane depolarization is experienced differently from hyperpolarization, but in the absence of empirical evidence to the contrary, it is simpler to assume they are all experienced the same (i.e., degree of presence in consciousness). One attractive possibility, proposed by Cook (2000, 2002a, 2002b, chs. 6–7, 2008) is that the activity site is the neural membrane at the axon hillock (where the action potential is initiated), and that protophenomenal intensity corresponds to ion flux through the membrane when the neuron fires. In any case it is important to emphasize that the identities of the activity sites and of the physical process correlated with intensity are empirical matters. The experimental techniques are difficult (since they address phenomenal, rather than functional, consciousness), and they raise ethical issues (since they may require invasive procedures), but the questions have empirical content.

What gives protophenomena their specific qualities? For example, why is one protophenomenen the experience of middle-C-here-now, but another the experience of pain-in-my-toe-now? Neuroscience suggests the answer, for there is no fundamental difference in the cortical tissues corresponding to middle-C-here-now and pain-in-my-toe-now. Rather, the qualitative nature of perceptions seems to depend on the connections between neurons. Several lines of evidence support this conclusion. First, there is the well-known phenomenon of referred pain (e.g., Karl, Birbaumer, Lutzenberger, Cohen & Flor, 2001), in which neurons reassign themselves from an amputated limb to another part of the body. Second, we may mention the very interesting experiments by Sur (2004), which demonstrate that neurons in auditory cortex can be made to support visual phenomena (i.e., perceptions that the animals experience as visual phenomena).

Neurophenomenological analysis allows us to transfer these observations from the neuropsychological domain to the theory of protophenomena. The implication is that protophenomena do not have inherent subjective qualities, but that they acquire them from interdependencies, which correspond to connections among neurons. (Thus protophenomenal theory may be classified as a *structural* theory of qualia.) As there are dynamical interdependencies among the activities of neurons, so there are necessarily correlated dependencies among the intensities of the corresponding protophenomena. From quantitative neurodynamical relationships we may hypothesize quantitative protophenomenal relationships (e.g., MacLennan, 1996b, App., 1999b), but we should not assume, in the absence of careful neurophenomenological investigation, that the subjective experience of protophenomenal intensity is proportional to a physical quantity at the activity site. In any case, neuroscience implies that the intensity of a single protophenomenon may depend on the intensities of tens of thousands (and sometimes hundreds of thousands) of other protophenomena and that their dynamical relationships can be highly complex (Anderson, 1995, p. 304).

Furthermore, the nervous system is a complex system, which exhibits a *macro-micro feedback loop* or *circular causality* (Solé & Goodwin, 2002, p. 150). This means that the behavior of the individual neurons, responding to their local environments, create a global state that in turn creates the neurons' local environments and thereby governs their behavior. Similarly, the intensities and dynamical relationships of the protophenomena create a global phenomenal state (a conscious state), which in its turn governs protophenomenal dynamics.

The ensemble of a person's protophenomenal intensities defines the degrees of freedom of their phenomenal world, and thus the universe of their possible conscious states. However, as we have seen, these intensities are not independent, but are constrained by dense and complex quantitative interrelationships, which therefore define the structure of that person's phenomenal world (their personal phenomenology). This structure is discovered through neurophenomenological experiment (i.e., mutually informing experimental phenomenology and experimental neuropsychology). Neurophenomenological analysis of protophenomenal dependencies provides an approach to explaining the specific qualities of phenomena (e.g., why sounds are experienced as sounds), the structure of phenomenal spaces, non-human perception, and spectral inversions, but they are not relevant to robot emotions and are discussed elsewhere (MacLennan, 1995, 1999a, 1999b, 2008a, 2008b).

Protophenomenal dependencies are not fixed, for they correspond to neural connections, which are altered by learning and other processes. Since protophenomenal dependencies define the structure of the phenomenal world, this too can change, with the result that phenomena may arise in consciousness that would not have before learning. Indeed, the phenomenal world changes its structure as the brain is restructured from infancy through adolescence in several waves of neuron proliferation and apoptosis (programmed death). There is evidence that even in adulthood neural proliferation takes place in some brain regions (e.g., Gould, Reeves, Graziano & Gross, 1999; Rakic, 2002), thus increasing the degrees of freedom of the phenomenal world.

A protophenomenal world is not causally closed, for there are protophenomena whose intensities do not depend on other protophenomena. The most obvious examples are sensory protophenomena, whose intensities depend on physical processes outside of the nervous system. Furthermore, processes outside the phenomenal world can alter protophenomenal dependencies; obvious examples are strokes, brain traumas, and degenerative diseases, which may permanently alter the structure of the phenomenal world. A third class of effects comes from alcohol and other psychoactive substances, which affect large numbers of protophenomenal dependencies, altering the dynamical relations among the protophenomena.

Since protophenomenal theory is not causally complete, but physical theory is generally supposed to be, the reader may wonder if protophenomenal theory is redundant. However, the body

is an open system, and as the previous examples indicate, the nervous system is not causally complete, and this is reflected in the incompleteness of its phenomenal world. Further, quantum indeterminacy implies that, in an important sense, contemporary physics is causally incomplete. Most importantly, however, physical theory is fundamentally incomplete insofar as it does not explain subjective awareness, that is, insofar as the Hard Problem is not solved (denying the fact of consciousness is not a solution!). In particular, in the absence of something like protophenomenal theory, standard physical theory cannot answer the question of whether robots will feel their emotions (or, indeed, why we feel ours).

Protophenomenal analysis can be applied to many questions about consciousness, such as inverted qualia (spectral inversions), degrees of consciousness, consciousness in nonhuman animals, the unconscious mind, and the unity of consciousness, but these are not directly related to robot emotions, and so the reader is referred to other publications (MacLennan, 1995, 1996a, 1996b, 1999a, 1999b, 2008a, 2008b).

The Neurophenomenology of Emotion

A protophenomenological analysis of emotion involves qualitative and quantitative reductions of emotional experience, and correlates the results of these reductions with neurophysiological structures and processes. A qualitative reduction entails categorizing emotions (discussed below), but also identifying qualitatively different aspects of emotional experiences. For example, emotions have distinct aspects of appraisal, expression, and feeling (Plutchik, 2003, p. 287). One obvious quantitative aspect of an emotion is its intensity (we may be more or less happy, for example), but the quantitative aspects that are most relevant to protophenomenal reduction are those in which the emotion is extended in one or more spatial or abstract dimensions. For example, the feeling of fear includes the spatially extended, embodied sensations of perspiration, a throbbing heart, general trembling, tensed muscles, etc. (Panksepp, 2004, p. 207; Plutchik, 2003, p. 127).

A neurophenomenological analysis of emotion should begin with a phenomenology of emotion, that is, with an investigation of the structure of emotional experience, but the phenomenology of emotion is difficult (Plutchik, 2003, pp. 3–17, 64–7). People cannot always articulate the emotions they are feeling, they may misclassify their own emotions, and the classification of emotion differs between cultures and languages. People may intentionally misrepresent their emotional state (by verbal or nonverbal expression), misrepresent it to themselves, or repress it entirely (Plutchik, 2003, pp. 15–16). Indeed there are differences of opinion about whether a particular internal state even *is* an emotion (Plutchik, 2003, pp. 81–8). For example, Descartes classified wonder as an emotion, but Spinoza disagreed (Prinz, 2006, p. 87), and Plutchik (2003) classifies trust and anticipation as basic emotions (see below), but others question whether they are emotions at all (Prinz, 2006, p. 92). Notable forays into the phenomenology of emotion include Sartre (2001) and Hillman (1960).

While it is generally recognized that emotion can be subtle, nuanced, and elusive, it has been widely believed that there is a small number of basic emotions, of which the others are degrees, derivatives, cognitive elaborations, or mixtures (Prinz, 2004, pp. 86–94). However, at least since Descartes, philosophers and psychologists have proposed differing lists of basic emotions, often without much overlap (Hillman, 1960, p. 40). For example, Plutchik (2000, p. 64) lists anger / fear, anticipation / surprise, joy / sadness, and acceptance / disgust, while Ekman (1999) offers "amusement, anger, contempt, contentment, disgust, embarrassment, excitement, fear, guilt, pride in achievement, relief, sadness, satisfaction, sensory pleasure, and shame" (Prinz, 2004, p. 87). In part these difference are a consequence of differing criteria for determining basic emotions (Plutchik, 2003, pp. 69–72; Prinz, 2004, pp. 86–90).[2] For example, basic emotions can be classified on the basis of overt expression (e.g., Ekman, 1999), adaptive function (e.g., Plutchik, 2003, ch. 9), the neural systems that serve them (e.g., Panksepp, 2004), conceptual analysis (e.g., Gordon, 1987), or cross-cultural linguistic analysis (e.g., Wierzbicka, 1999). Prinz (2004, p. 90) advocates identifying basic emotions by "converging evidence" from several of these sources, which is a good basis for a neurophenomenological analysis.

Further, multidimensional scaling, latent semantic analysis, and similar statistical techniques have proved useful in exploring the phenomenological structure of emotions (Plutchik, 2003, chs. 4, 6). For example, Plutchik (2000) provides evidence that emotions have a three-dimensional structure and the topology of a cone. Based on subjects' judgments of similarity and difference, words for emotions are mapped into two-dimensional space and lie in an approximate circle (called a *circumplex* of emotions; Plutchik & Conte, 1997). The circumplex represents two familiar aspects of emotional phenomenology: relative degrees of similarity and difference (e.g., distress is similar to misery), and bipolarity of affect (e.g., love vs. hate). On the basis of similarity, Plutchik divides the circumplex into eight segments corresponding to eight *basic* or *primary emotions*. Various *secondary emotions* are mixtures of the primary emotions. The analogy with primary and secondary colors on the color wheel is explicit, reflecting a frequent observation that colors and emotions have similar phenomenological structures (Plutchik, 2003, p. 103; cf. Gage, 1993; Goethe, 1840; MacLennan, 2008a, 2008b).

Another familiar aspect of emotional phenomenology is that emotions vary in intensity (e.g., annoyance < anger < rage). Intensity is represented by the third dimension of Plutchik's emotion cone (its height): the maximum intensities of the emotions are around its circular base and intensity decreases towards its apex. All emotions have zero intensity and meet in emotional neutrality at the apex. Plutchik (1980) notes that the three emotional aspects of similarity, polarity, and intensity correspond to properties of color: hue, complementarity, and intensity, and therefore that the emotional cone is analogous to the color sphere (more, precisely, to its lower hemisphere). Plutchik's map of the emotions has been criticized (e.g., Prinz, 2004, pp. 92–3), because some of his primary emotions do not seem to be basic, and because some higher cognitive emotions (e.g., romantic jealousy) seem to be more than blends of primary emotions, but it is an important investigation in the phenomenology of emotion.

Valence, that is, whether an emotion is positive or negative (desirable or undesirable, and thus leads to positive or negative reinforcement, and approach or avoidance), is commonly assumed to be a fundamental dimension in the phenomenology of emotions (Panksepp, 2004, p. 46; Plutchik, 3002, p. 21; Prinz, 2004, pp. 167–78; Rolls, 2007). However, even this simple distinction is problematic; for example, nowadays both anger and pride are sometimes viewed as positive emotions, although traditionally they were considered negative (Plutchik, 2003, pp. 7–8). Further, anger, although considered negative in being unpleasant, is positive in terms of approach (i.e., attack); fear may involve both an avoidance of the fearful stimulus, but also an active approach toward safety (Prinz, 2004, p. 168). Movie-goers seek to feel ostensibly negative emotions such as fear and anger (DeLancey, 2002, pp. 7–8).

Fortunately there is a large body of research on the neurophysiology of emotions in the context of evolutionary biology (e.g., Panksepp 2004; Plutchik 2003; Prinz 2004). An evolutionary approach has the advantages of not limiting attention to human emotion and of considering the adaptive functions of emotion, both of which are important to the issue of robot emotion. By understanding how emotions fulfill essential functions in nonhuman animals, we can begin to understand how to design synthetic emotions in robots to fulfill analogous or even completely different functions. Such emotions may serve goals such as performing physical tasks (e.g., mining, construction, agriculture), collecting information or samples, cleaning up hazardous materials, rescuing or protecting humans or other animals, responding to accidents and medical emergencies, and achieving military objectives.

Another potentially important aspect of emotional phenomenology is the recent discovery of *mirror neurons*, which mimic the activity of neurons in another animal based on unconscious perception of that other animal (Arbib & Rizzolatti, 1997; Rizzolatti & Craighero, 2004; Rizzolatti, Fadiga, Gallese & Fogassi, 1996). Mirror neurons thus provide a mechanism by which the emotional state of one animal may be subconsciously internalized into the nervous system of the other, providing a neural basis for empathy. Mirror neurons seem to have a number of functions that may also be valuable in robots, including the facilitation of cooperative behavior and learning by imitation (Breazeal et al., 2004), as well as "reading the mind" of another agent by mirroring its neural state.

Possible Biological Correlates of Emotional Protophenomena

Next I will discuss the conditions under which humans *feel* their emotions. It may seem axiomatic that we feel our emotions, but that is not so; in fact it is important to distinguish emotion and feeling (Damasio, 1999, pp. 42–9). The primary emotional response takes place in the limbic system and is unconscious, whereas conscious emotional experience is confined to cortical areas. Within the limbic system, the amygdala can respond to sensory information routed through the thalamus to initiate an appropriate emotional response to the stimulus. This response may be innate or based on memories stored in the amygdala (one basis for unconscious conditioned responses).

The amygdala also generates emotional responses on the basis of cortical processing of information from the senses or memory when that processing determines that an emotional response may be required. In either case the amygdala then sends out signals (via the hypothalamus) to initiate an appropriate response (e.g., fight or flight, care-giving), which includes neuromotor readiness and initiation, activation of the sympathetic nervous system, hormonal secretions (e.g., adrenaline), and changes in heart rate, breathing, perspiration, etc. This process is unconscious.

These changes in the physiological state of the body are relayed (back through the hypothalamus) to a variety of cortical areas, where they are consciously experienced as emotion. The felt emotion is a complex product of these physiological factors, of the consciously perceived and interpreted stimulus or memory, and of other contextual factors. Along with sensory information from multimodal sensory-integration areas, such as the tectum, the visceral and physiological information is integrated in convergence areas (such as the periaqueductal gray region of the midbrain), which create the conscious experience of a unified organism and its emotional-behavioral state (Damasio, 1999, pp. 60–1). The resulting conscious cognition of the emotional state can modulate the activity of the amygdala, reinforcing it if the emotional response is perceived to be appropriate, or dampening it down if not.

William James (1884) and Carl Lange (1885) independently made the surprising claim that the foundation of emotional experience is sensation of prior bodily change (the *James-Lange theory* or *somatic feeling theory*). Although there have been objections, an increasing body of neuropsychological data supports various modifications and extensions of his theory (e.g., Damasio, 1994, 1999; Prinz, 2004). Prinz (2004, ch. 9) suggests that a three-level *emotional processing hierarchy* underlies emotional consciousness, a view that is quite compatible with protophenomenal analysis. At the lowest level are neurons (in primary soma-

tosensory cortex, pons, insula) with small receptive fields responding to local conditions in skeletal muscles, visceral organs, hormone levels, etc.; these correspond to emotional protophenomena. At the intermediate level neurons (in secondary somatosensory, dorsal anterior cingulate, and insular cortices) integrate the protophenomena into coherent patterns of activity, that is, into emotional phenomena. These seem to be similar to the *first-* and *second-order maps* described by Damasio (1999, ch. 6). At the third level these patterns are characterized and specific emotions are recognized, perhaps in ventromedial prefrontal cortex and rostral anterior cingulate cortex (Prinz, 2004, p. 214). Prinz's hierarchy can also be compared to Damasio's (1999, ch. 9) three-level hierarchy of emotion, feeling, and feeling feeling: "*an emotion, the feeling of that emotion, and knowing that we have a feeling of that emotion*" (Damasio, 1999, p. 8, italics in original). Thus, like other conscious phenomena, the qualitative character of an emotional phenomenon consists in the interdependencies among its constituent protophenomena.

Because emotions can trigger the release of neuromodulators that affect the activity of large groups of neurons (e.g., Damasio, 1999, pp. 281–2; Fellous, 1999), there is a parallel effect on large ensembles of protophenomenal interdependencies. This alters the dynamics of the protophenomena, which is experienced as a change in the conscious process. Emotionally-triggered neuromodulation affects neurodynamics so that it better serves the function of the emotion, and it is reasonable to suppose that autonomous robots will also benefit from emotion-triggered pervasive alterations to their cognitive processes. Further, the relatively global and non-specific effects of these neuromodulators permit the physical characteristics of activity sites to be investigated with less invasive procedures than would otherwise be required.

Therefore, to obtain a comprehensive explanation of the structure of conscious emotional experience, we need to investigate the representation and integration of information in these cortical areas, especially those aspects related to emotional response, and to correlate these neuropsychological investigations with phenomenological investigations into the structure of conscious emotional experience. Such investigations are in progress. For example, Damasio, Grabowski, Bechara, Damasio, Ponto, Parvizi, and Hichwa (2000) have identified some of the different cortical and subcortical brain regions involved in various consciously experienced emotions. As a consequence of studies such as these we will be able to identify the neuronal processes correlated with emotional protophenomena, and the interdependencies among them that define the qualitative structure of felt emotion. This is, of course, an ongoing and long-term research project, but neurophenomenological research into human emotional experience already provides a basis for understanding the determinants of the phenomenology of robot emotion.

The Protophenomena of Robot Emotion

Based on the forgoing analysis of conscious and unconscious emotional response in humans, we can address the problem of conscious emotional response in robots in a more focused way. Protophenomena are elementary subjective degrees of freedom, which correspond to activity sites in the brain, so that physical processes at these sites are correlated with the presence of the corresponding protophenomena in conscious experience. Is it possible that physical processes in a robot's "brain" (central information processor) could constitute activity sites with associated emotional protophenomena? The issue is whether the robot's information processing devices are sufficiently similar to the human brain's *in the relevant ways*. For example, if the robot's processor were an actual living human brain, and the robot's body were sufficiently similar to a human's, there would seem to be no reason to deny that it was

having genuine subjective experiences. On the other hand, there may be something about living neurons that makes them the only physical systems capable of supporting consciousness. An analogy may clarify the issue. Water is liquid, but its liquidity depends on physical properties of H_2O molecules (such as their finite volume and short-range mutual attraction), which are also possessed by some other molecules. Therefore, there are other liquids besides water or, to put it differently, liquidity can be realized by a variety of substances. So the questions are: What are the properties by virtue of which "neural stuff" supports protophenomena? Are there other non-neural, physical systems that have these properties, or can we make them?

Unfortunately, at this stage of the scientific investigation of consciousness we cannot say what properties of physical systems are sufficient for them to be activity sites and support protophenomena. Nevertheless, the question is empirical, since it can be addressed by controlling physical quantities and substances in individual neurons and observing their effects on conscious experience. The technology for conducting these experiments is improving. For example, Losonczy, Makara, and Magee (2008) have developed techniques for delivering individual neurotransmitter molecules to individual dendritic spines with a spatial resolution of 1 micrometer and time resolution of 1 millisecond (but they were not applied *in vivo*). Therefore we anticipate that it is just a matter of time before we have a better understanding of the essential physical properties of activity sites. In the meantime we may consider several plausible possibilities.

First, the activity sites could be the somatic membranes of neurons and protophenomenal intensity might correspond to membrane potential relative to its resting potential. Before we could decide whether similar activity sites could be constructed in an artificial system, we would need to have a more detailed understanding of the relation of membrane potential to protophenomenal intensity. For example, must it be the membrane potential of a living cell, or could a nonliving membrane support a protophenomenon? Is it purely an electrical property, or an electrochemical one? Does it depend on specific ions or on a particular membrane structure (e.g., lipid bilayer)? These are all empirical questions, and their answers will delimit the sorts of artificial physical devices that could support protophenomena.

If, as Cook (2000, 2002a, 2002b, chs. 6–7, 2008) suggests, the intensity of a protophenomenon correlates with the flux of ions across the cell membrane when the ion channels open during an action potential, and the protophenomenon is in effect the cell's sensing of its (intercellular) environment, then the essential properties of an activity site might include a boundary separating it from its environment, the ability to sense its environment, and the ability to modify the environment as a consequence. In this case, it would seem to be possible to construct an artificial device supporting protophenomena, but the specific requirements would have to be determined empirically.

Chalmers (1996, ch. 8) considers the possibility that *information spaces* may provide the link between the physical and the phenomenal, since they can be realized either as physical systems or as phenomenological structures. In particular, he suggests that quite simple physical systems might have associated protophenomena (p. 298). An information space is characterized by "differences that make a difference," that is, by distinctions that causally affect behavior. The physically realized information space must have a sufficient number of states to support the distinctions and must have the appropriate causal relations. (That is, like general information processing systems, there is a homomorphism from the physical realization to the information system, i.e., the physical system has at least the abstract structure of the information system, but may have additional structure irrelevant to the information processing: MacLennan, 1994, 2004.) The

structure of the phenomenal space corresponds to the structure of the information space (due, in protophenomenal terms, to the protophenomena having interdependencies that correspond to the causal relations in the physical system).

Further, Chalmer's hypothesis and Cook's theory seem to be compatible. The binding of neurotransmitters to their receptors conveys information to a neuron about its extracellular environment, which can be quantified as an increase in the *system mutual information* between the cell and its environment. Each receptor make a contribution measured by the *conditional mutual information* of the resulting postsynaptic state.[3] This is a process of input transduction, which converts the many different neurotransmitters and ions in the region of the synapse into a common computational currency, membrane potential. These electrical signals propagate down the dendritic tree to combine in the somatic membrane potential, which thus accomplishes a simple form of sensor integration. Much of this process is electrically passive and nearly linear (neglecting some voltage gated channels). Under appropriate circumstances, such as the membrane potential at the axon hillock exceeding a threshold, an action potential is generated, which is a highly nonlinear and active process; it has the character of an elementary decision (e.g., the level of excitation is above the threshold). The resulting action potential causes specific chemicals (neurotransmitters) to be released at the axon terminal, which is a kind of output transduction, and constitutes the action resulting from the decision (the difference that makes a difference). Thus, the neuron can be viewed as a simple control system, with input sensors, some simple information processing resulting in a decision, and output effectors or actuators. This corresponds to Cook's (2000, 2002a, 2002b, chs. 6–7, 2008) idea that cognition (information processing) is associated with the synaptic processes and consciousness (protophenomena) with the action potential. A spike in protophenomenal intensity would occur with the generation of an action potential. Such a scenario suggests that protophenomena might be associated with other simple control systems, in which inputs are translated into a computational medium and integrated to trigger a decision (an active nonlinear process) in order to have some physical effect. It doesn't seem to be impossible that nonbiological control systems of this kind would have associated protophenomena, but of course it is an empirical question.

In summary, if Chalmer's suggestion is correct, then many physically realized information spaces will be activity sites with associated protophenomena. In particular, since a robot's processor is devoted to the physical realization of information spaces, it would be reasonable to suppose that its constituent devices would have associated protophenomena. This would not, of course, imply that the robot is conscious, for protophenomena are not yet phenomena, but if the information processing were organized to create the appropriate protophenomenal interdependencies so that they cohered into phenomena and created a phenomenal world, then we could say that the robot is conscious. In particular, an appropriate structure among the protophenomena would produce emotional phenomena (felt emotions).

The Combinatorial Structure of Robot Emotion

We have seen that it is an empirical matter what sorts of physical objects have associated protophenomena, and therefore whether the components of a robot could support protophenomena. However, protophenomena are necessary, but not sufficient, for consciousness, which also requires that the protophenomena have relations of interdependency sufficient for the emergence of phenomena. Therefore, in the case of robot feelings we must consider the structure of artificial emotional phenomena.

In robots, as in animals, a primary function of emotion is to make rapid assessments of external or internal situations and to ready the robot to respond to them with action or information processing. This may involve power management, shifting energy to more critical systems, adjustment of clock rates, deployment and priming of specialized actuators and sensors, initiation of action, and so forth. These processes will be monitored by *interoceptors* (internal sensors) that measure these and other physical properties (positions, angles, forces, stresses, flow rates, energy levels, power drains, temperatures, physical damage, etc.) and send signals to higher cognitive processes for supervision and control. Therefore, many of these interoceptors will be distributed around the robot's body and this spatial organization will be reflected in somatosensory maps or other information structures. As a consequence patterns among the interoceptive signals will be represented, and the associated protophenomena will cohere into spatially organized phenomena.

In this way emotional phenomena are structured spatially in relation to the body, but these phenomena also have a qualitative structure, which may vary depending on the input space of the interoceptors. Each interoceptor will have a response curve defined over its input space, but connections among the interoceptors at a location and connections to higher-order sensory areas will stitch together a topology representing the joint input space (MacLennan, 1995, 1999b). This topology defines the qualitative structure of the resulting emotional phenomena.

Some of a robot's sensory spaces will be similarly structured spatially and qualitatively to ours, and in these cases we can expect the robot's emotional experiences (its *feelings*) to be similar to our own. Examples might include pressure sensors in the skin and angle and stress sensors in the joints. On the other hand, other interoceptors will be quite different from humans'. For example, a robot is unlikely to experience a quickened heartbeat or shallow, rapid breathing (because it is unlikely to have a heart or lungs), and we, in contrast, do not experience a redistribution of electrical power, which a robot might. These interoceptive spaces will have their own topologies, which determine their phenomenal structures, and so in these cases we must expect the robot's emotional experiences to be significantly different and alien to us. Although we may be unable to imagine them, we will be able to understand their abstract structure, which will give us some insight into the robot's experience. In general, a robot's emotions will be peculiar to its "form of life," as ours are to ours. (See MacLennan (1996a) for more on understanding non-human perception.)

If this is the case, one might question why these robotic experiences should be considered emotions at all. One reason is their similar function to natural emotions (recall **Background**). For example, they will reflect general goals of critical importance to the robot's behavior, which are therefore directly motivating, and that consequently have a persisting, pervasive, appropriate effects on the physical state of the robot (by controlling sensors, effectors, and information processing). Another reason is that, due to the need for rapid, pervasive response, these experiences will have unconscious roots (i.e., below the level of coherent phenomena); conscious experience will be secondary and modulated by the already activated emotion.

FUTURE TRENDS

As explained above, we cannot determine whether it would be possible for a robot to have feelings (emotional experiences), but there is every reason to believe we will be able to decide in the future. The answer depends on the results of two investigations. First, we will need to understand what physical processes support protophenomena, that is, what sorts of physical systems can be activity sites. This will require a detailed investigation

of neurons in order to determine what physical (or biological) characteristics are necessary and sufficient for protophenomena. Such experiments will involve *in vivo* manipulation of structures and substances in individual neurons associated with *salient protophenomena* (protophenomena that individually or in small groups constitute phenomena, i.e., are experienceable). Although the procedures will be difficult (and will raise ethical issues), there is rapid progress and so it seems likely that these questions will eventually be answered empirically.

The results of these experiments will allow us to make plausible hypotheses about the necessary and sufficient conditions for protophenomena, and therefore about whether any particular artificial system could support them. Further experiments could test these hypotheses (e.g., by replacing, in a living animal, neural structures or processes by artificial surrogates). As a result we will be able to make experimentally verified statements about the sorts of physical systems that support protophenomena, and therefore the sorts of robot technology that could support consciousness.

However, as we have seen, protophenomena are not sufficient in themselves for feeling emotions; it is necessary that the protophenomena be so structured, through their interdependencies, to cohere into emotional phenomena. An improved neurophenomenological understanding of human and animal emotional experience, especially as implemented in the cortex, will show us how to interconnect robotic activity sites so that emotional phenomena emerge. The experiments in this case are not so difficult, but there is much we still do not understand about the cortical experience of emotion, but this will come in time with progress in neuroscience and neurophenomenology.

I hope that I have convinced you that protophenomenological analysis allows the question of robot feelings to be investigated empirically. Yet the breadth and depth of the investigations are daunting, and you may wonder whether they are worth the effort. Why should we care whether robots might be able to feel their emotions?

First, and perhaps paradoxically, these investigations will help us understand ourselves and other animals. Unless we can give a principled answer to the question of robot feelings (whether positive or negative) there will be a serious gap in our understanding of our own humanity. That is, so long as we cannot say why robots could or could not feel their emotions, we cannot really explain why we feel ours. Since emotions are essential to human nature, this issue is fundamental to our self-knowledge.

Another, more distant reason for investigating robot feelings is the matter of robot rights. If we are eventually able to build robots with intelligence comparable to humans, then they will have an emotional system of comparable complexity (although, perhaps, very different in its particulars), because indeed emotion is essential to intelligence. Rights (animal as well as human) often presuppose the capacity to suffer, and so robot rights (in general and in specific cases) might depend on whether they can feel their emotions.

CONCLUSION

In conclusion, I have argued that it is by no means impossible that some future robots may feel their emotions, that is, that they may have subjective emotional experiences homologous, but not identical, to ours. To determine the precise conditions sufficient for robot feelings it will be necessary to conduct detailed neurophenomenological investigations of subjective experience in order to isolate the physical processes correlated with the smallest units of that experience. This will enable us to formulate empirically testable hypotheses about the sorts of nonliving physical systems (if any) that may support protophenomena, and therefore conscious experience. This, in itself, is not sufficient to imply that robots could feel their emotions, for it is also necessary to understand neural structures underlying emotional experience, and

the corresponding interdependencies among emotional protophenomena. (The emotional protophenomena are not, of course, independent of other protophenomena, such as those associated with bodily sensation.) The results of these neurophenomenological investigations will show us how to structure the emotional protophenomena of robots so that they cohere into emotional phenomena, that is, so that the robots feel their emotions. Thus, although significant unanswered questions remain, they can be addressed empirically, and their answers will allow us to decide whether robots could feel their emotions.

REFERENCES

Anderson, J.A. (1995). *An introduction to neural networks*. Cambridge, MA: MIT Press.

Arbib, M.A., & Rizzolatti. R. (1997). Neural expectations: A possible evolutionary path from manual skills to language. *Communication and Cognition, 29*, 393-423.

Block, N. (1995). On a confusion about a function of consciousness. *Behavioral and Brain Sciences, 18*, 265-66.

Breazeal, C. (2003). Toward sociable robots. *Robotics and Autonomous Systems, 42*, 167-75.

Breazeal, C., Brooks, A., Gray, J., Hoffman, G., Kidd, C., Lee, H., Lieberman, J., Lockerd, A., & Chilongo, D. (2004). Tutelage and collaboration for humanoid robots. *International Journal of Humanoid Robots, 1*(2), 315-48.

Campbell, K.K. (1970). *Body and mind.* New York: Doubleday.

Chalmers, D.J. (1995). Facing up to the problem of consciousness. *Journal of Consciousness Studies, 2*, 200-19.

Chalmers, D.J. (1996). *The conscious mind.* New York: Oxford University Press.

Chalmers, D.J. (2002). Consciousness and its place in nature. In D.J. Chalmers (Ed.), *Philosophy of mind: Classical and contemporary readings.* Oxford, UK: Oxford.

Cook, N.D. (2000). On defining awareness and consciousness: The importance of the neuronal membrane. In *Proceedings of the Tokyo-99 Conference on Consciousness.* Singapore: World Scientific.

Cook, N.D. (2002a). Bihemispheric language: How the two hemispheres collaborate in the processing of language. In T. Crow (Ed.), *The speciation of modern Homo sapiens.* London, UK: Proceedings of the British Academy, v. 106 (ch. 9).

Cook, N.D. (2002b). *Tone of voice and mind: The connections between intonation, emotion, cognition and consciousness.* Amsterdam, Netherlands: John Benjamins.

Cook, N.D. (2008). The neuron-level phenomena underlying cognition and consciousness: Synaptic activity and the action potential. *Neuroscience, 153*(3), 556-70.

Damasio, A.R. (1994). *Descartes' error: Emotion, reason, and the human brain.* New York: Avon.

Damasio, A.R. (1999). *The feeling of what happens: Body and emotion in the making of consciousness.* New York: Harcourt, Brace & Co.

Damasio, A.R., Grabowski, T.J., Bechara, A., Damasio, H., Ponto, L.L.B., Parvizi, J., & Hichwa, R.D. (2000). Subcortical and cortical brain activity during the feeling of self-generated emotions. *Nature Neuroscience, 3,* 1049-56.

DeLancey, C. (2002). *Passionate engines: What emotions reveal about mind and artificial intelligence.* Oxford, UK: Oxford University Press.

Dreyfus, H.L. (1991). *Being-in-the-world. A commentary on Heidegger's* Being and Time, *Division I.* Cambridge, MA: MIT Press.

Ekman, P. (1999). Basic emotions. In T. Dalgleish & T. Power (Eds.), *The handbook of cognition and emotion* (pp. 45-60). New York, NY: Wiley.

Fellous, J.-M. (1999). Neuromodulatory basis of emotion. *The Neuroscientist, 5*(5), 283-94.

Gage, J. (1993). *Color and culture: Practice and meaning from antiquity to abstraction.* Boston, Toronto, & London: Little, Brown, & Co.

Goethe, J. W. von. (1840). *Goethe's theory of colours* (C.L. Eastlake, tr.). London, UK: Murray.

Gordon, R. (1987). *The structure of emotions.* Cambridge, UK: Cambridge University Press.

Gould, E., Reeves, A., Graziano, M., & Gross, C. (1999). Neurogenesis in the neocortex of adult primates. *Science, 286,* 548-52.

Gregory, R.L. (ed.) (1987). *The Oxford companion to the mind.* Oxford, UK: Oxford University Press.

Hamming, R.W. (1980). *Coding and information theory.* Englewood Cliffs, NJ: Prentice-Hall.

Hillman, J. (1960). *Emotion: A comprehensive phenomenology of theories and their meanings for therapy.* Evanston, IL: Northwestern Univ. Press.

Ihde, D. (1986). *Experimental phenomenology. An introduction.* Albany, NY: State University of New York Press.

James, W. (1884). What is an emotion? *Mind, 9,* 188–205.

Karl, A., Birbaumer, N., Lutzenberger, W., Cohen, L.G., & Flor, H. (2001). Reorganization of motor and somatosensory cortex in upper extremity amputees with phantom limb pain. *The Journal of Neuroscience, 21,* 3609-18.

Kirk, R. (1974). Zombies versus materialists. *Aristotelian Society, 48* (suppl.), 135-52.

Kleinginna, P.R., & Kleinginna, A.M. (1981). A categorized list of emotion definitions, with suggestions for a consensual definition. *Motivation & Emotion, 5*(4), 345-79.

Knudsen, E.J., du Lac, S., & Esterly, S.D. (1987). Computational maps in the brain. *Annual Review of Neuroscience, 10,* 41-65.

Kripke, S.A. (1980). *Naming and necessity.* Cambridge, MA: Harvard University Press.

Lange, C.J. (1885). *Om sindsbevaegelser: Et psyko-fysiologisk studie.* Copenhagen: Jacob Lunds.

Laughlin, C.D., Jr., McManus, J., & d'Aquili, E.G. (1990). Brain, symbol and experience: Toward a neurophenomenology of consciousness. Boston, MA: New Science Library.

Llinas, R.R. (1988). The intrinsic electrophysiological properties of mammalian neurons. *Science, 242,* 1654-64.

Losonczy, A., Makara, J.K., & Magee, J.C. (2008). Compartmentalized dendritic plasticity and input feature storage in neurons. *Nature, 452,* 436-40.

Lutz, A., & Thompson, E. (2003). Neurophenomenology: Integrating subjective experience and brain dynamics in the neuroscience of consciousness. *Journal of Consciousness Studies, 10*(9/10), 31-52.

Lyons, W. (1986). *The disappearance of introspectionism.* Cambridge, MA: MIT Press.

MacLennan, B.J. (1994). Continuous computation and the emergence of the discrete. In K.H. Pribram (Ed.), *Rethinking neural nets: Quantum fields and biological data* (pp. 199-232). Hillsdale, NJ: Lawrence-Erlbaum.

MacLennan, B.J. (1995). The investigation of consciousness through phenomenology and neuroscience. In J. King & K.H. Pribram (Eds.), *Scale in conscious experience: Is the brain too important to be left to specialists to study?* (pp. 25-43). Hillsdale, NJ: Lawrence Erlbaum.

MacLennan, B.J. (1996a). The elements of consciousness and their neurodynamical correlates. *Journal of Consciousness Studies, 3* (5/6), 409-24. Reprinted in J. Shear (Ed.), *Explaining consciousness: The hard problem* (pp. 249-66). Cambridge, MA: MIT, 1997.

MacLennan, B.J. (1996b). *Protophenomena and their neurodynamical correlates* (Technical Report UT-CS-96-331). Knoxville, TN: University of Tennessee, Knoxville, Department of Computer Science. Available: www.cs.utk.edu/~mclennan

MacLennan, B.J. (1999a). Neurophenomenological constraints and pushing back the subjectivity barrier. *Behavioral and Brain Sciences, 22,* 961–63.

MacLennan, B.J. (1999b) *The protophenomenal structure of consciousness with especial application to the experience of color: Extended version* (Technical Report UT-CS-99-418). Knoxville, TN: University of Tennessee, Knoxville, Department of Computer Science. Available: www.cs.utk.edu/~mclennan

MacLennan, B.J. (2003). Color as a material, not an optical, property. *Behavioral and Brain Sciences, 26,* 37-8.

MacLennan, B.J. (2004). Natural computation and non-Turing models of computation. *Theoretical Computer Science, 317,* 115-45.

MacLennan, B.J. (2008a). Consciousness: Natural and artificial. *Synthesis Philosophica, 22*(2), 401-33.

MacLennan, B.J. (2008b). Protophenomena: The elements of consciousness and their relation to the brain. In A. Batthyány, A. Elitzur & D. Constant (Eds.), *Irreducibly conscious: Selected papers on consciousness* (pp. 189-214). Heidelberg & New York: Universitäts-verlag Winter.

McCall, R.J. (1983). *Phenomenological psychology: An introduction. With a glossary of some key Heideggerian terms.* Madison, WI: University of Wisconsin Press.

Ortony, A., & Turner, W. (1990). What's basic about basic emotions? *Psychological Review, 97,* 315–31.

Panksepp, J. (2004). *Affective neuroscience: The foundations of human and animal emotions.* New York: Oxford University Press.

Plutchik, R. (1980). *Emotion: A psychoevolutionary synthesis.* New York: Harper & Row.

Plutchik, R. (2000). *Emotions in the practice of psychotherapy: Clinical implications of affect theories.* New York: American Psychological Association.

Plutchik, R. (2003). *Emotions and life: Perspectives from psychology, biology, and evolution.* New York: American Psychological Association.

Plutchik, R., & Conte, H.R. (Eds.). (1997). *Circumplex models of personality and emotions.* Washington, DC: American Psychological Association.

Prinz, J. (2006). *Gut reactions: A perceptual theory of emotion.* New York: Oxford University Press.

Rakic, P. (2002). Neurogenesis in adult primate neocortex: An evaluation of the evidence. *Nature Reviews Neuroscience, 3*(1), 65-71.

Rizzolatti, G., & Craighero, L. (2004). The mirror-neuron system. *Annual Review of Neuroscience, 27,* 169-92.

Rizzolatti, G., Fadiga, L., Gallese, V., & Fogassi, L. (1996). Premotor cortex and the recognition of motor actions. *Cognitive Brain Research, 3*(2), 131-41.

Rolls, E.T. (2002). Emotion, neural basis of. In N.J. Smelsner & P.B. Baltes (Eds.), *International encyclopedia of the social and behavioral sciences* (pp. 4444-9). Amsterdam, Netherlands: Pergamon.

Rolls, E.T. (2005). *Emotion explained.* Oxford, UK: Oxford Univ. Press.

Rolls, E.T. (2006). Brain mechanisms of emotion and decision-making. *International Congress Series, 1291,* 3-13. Amsterdam: Elsevier.

Rolls, E.T. (2007). A neurobiological approach to emotional intelligence. In G. Matthews, M. Zeidner & R.D. Roberts (Eds.), *The science of emotional intelligence* (pp. 72-100). Oxford, UK: Oxford Univ. Press.

Rudrauf, D., Lutz, A., Cosmelli, D., Lachaux, J.-L., & Le Van Quyen, M. (2003). From autopoiesis to neurophenomenology: Francisco Varela's exploration of the biophysics of being. *Biological Research, 36*(1), 27-65.

Sartre, J. (2001). *Sketch for a theory of the emotions.* New York: Routledge.

Solé, R., & Goodwin, B. (2002). *Signs of life: How complexity pervades biology.* New York: HarperCollins Publishers.

Sur, M. (2004). Rewiring cortex: Cross-modal plasticity and its implications for cortical development and function. In G.A. Calvert, C. Spence & B.E. Stein (Eds.), *Handbook of multisensory processing* (pp. 681-94). Cambridge, MA: MIT Press.

Varela, F.J. (1996). Neurophenomenology: A methodological remedy to the hard problem. *Journal of Consciousness Studies, 3,* 330-50. Reprinted in: J. Shear (Ed.), *Explaining consciousness: The hard problem of consciousness* (pp. 337-58). Cambridge, MA: MIT Press, 1997.

Wierzbicka, A. (1999). *Emotions across languages and cultures: Diversity and universals.* Cambridge, UK: Cambridge University Press.

KEY TERMS

Action Potential: An action potential, also called a *neural impulse* or *spike*, is a stereotypical excursion in the membrane potential caused by the opening and closing of ion channels in a cycle of positive feedback and recovery. An action potential is triggered when a membrane is sufficiently depolarized from its normal negative resting potential; positive feedback causes a rapid repolarization in the positive direction, after which there is a relatively slow return to a potential slightly more negative than the resting potential, followed by a gradual return to resting potential. Action potentials propagate down axons without attenuation to convey information to other neurons.

Axon Hillock: The axon hillock is the base of an axon, that is, the region of a neuron's soma (q.v.) from which the axon projects. In many neurons it is the place where action potentials (q.v.) are generated.

First-Person: In the context of consciousness studies, *first-person* refers to the experience of one's own consciousness. In contrast to *third-person* observation (q.v.), the observer is not separable from the observed. Such observation is inherently *private*, but the techniques of neurophenomenology (q.v.) permit the establishment of an observer-independent body of *public* fact on which scientific theories can be built.

Hard Problem: The "Hard Problem" is the term introduced by Chalmers (1995) to refer to the principal problem of the scientific investigation of consciousness, namely, the integration of the primary fact of conscious experience with contemporary scientific understanding of the material universe.

Neurophenomenology: Neurophenomenology combines the phenomenological (q.v.) investigation of the structure of experience with the neuroscientific investigation of the neural correlates of that experience. Thus is promises a coherent account of experience from both first-person (q.v.) and third-person (q.v.) perspectives.

Objective: *Objective* and *subjective* (q.v.) are used to make two different distinctions, which overlap, but confusion between the distinctions muddies the mind-body problem. In the context of this chapter, *objective* refers to a *third-person* (q.v.) perspective, as opposed to a *subjective* or *first-person* perspective (q.vv.). Colloquially, *objective* connotes the unbiased, factual, and scientific, but that is not the meaning here, since phenomenology (q.v.) seeks unbiased, factual, and scientific knowledge based on subjective observation.

Phenomenology (Phenomenological): Phenomenology, especially as developed by Husserl, Heidegger, and Merleau-Ponty, is the systematic investigation of the invariant structure of experience by empirical, but first-person (q.v.) methods. Accurate phenomenology requires systematic training, which distinguishes it from naive introspection.

Protophenomenological Analysis: Protophenomenological analysis seeks to explain the structure of conscious experience in terms of the interdependencies among protophenomena (q.v.) as determined by neurophenomenology (q.v.).

Protophenomenon: Protophenomena are the smallest units of conscious experience, which are hypothesized and investigated on the basis of neurophenomenological research (q.v.), that is, on the basis of coordinated phenomenology (q.v.) and neuroscience.

Qualia: *Qualia* (singular: *quale*) are the felt qualities of phenomena, as aspects of first-person (q.v.) or subjective (q.v.) experience. Examples of qualia are the feeling of warmth of a warm thing, the auditory experience of a C-major chord, the feeling in the gut of anger or fear, and so forth.

Soma: The soma is the cell body of a neuron. Inputs to a neuron causes fluctuations in the electrical potential across the neuron membrane, which are integrated into the somatic membrane potential. In a typical neuron, and to a first approximation, a sufficiently large depolarization of the membrane at the axon hillock (q.v.) will trigger the generation of an action potential (q.v.).

Subjective: There are two distinct but overlapping senses in which something may be termed *subjective* and contrasted with the *objective* (q.v.). In the context of this chapter, *subjective* refers to first-person (q.v.) observation, which is essential to the protophenomenological analysis (q.v.) of emotion. Colloquially, *subjective* may connote observations and opinions that are biased or distorted, but that is not the intent here, since the purpose of phenomenology (q.v.) is to produce unbiased and factual first-person (subjective) observations.

Third-Person: In the context of consciousness studies, *third-person* is used to refer to ordinary scientific observation of some object separate from the observer. For example, we may make third-person observations of some physical system, of the brain, or of some person's behavior (including verbal report). Third-person observation can be a public process grounded in shared observational practices leading to a provisional consensus about observed facts. Often taken to be synonymous with *objective* (q.v.) and contrasted with *first-person* and *subjective* (q.vv.).

ENDNOTES

[1] This notion of phenomenological reduction should not be confused with the phenomenological reduction described by Varela (1996), although they are not unrelated.

[2] Indeed, the concept of a basic emotion has been criticized (e.g., Griffiths, 1997; Ortony & Turner, 1990).

[3] See, for example, Hamming (1980, §7.6) for definitions of these terms.

Chapter IX
Personality and Emotions in Robotics from the Gender Perspective

Mercedes García-Ordaz
University of Huelva, Spain

Rocío Carrasco-Carrasco
University of Huelva, Spain

Francisco José Martínez-López
University of Huelva, Spain

ABSTRACT

It is contended here that the emotional elements and features of human reasoning should be taken into account when designing the personality of robots. As it has been shown in the last few years, the concept of gender is constructed by socio-cultural factors. Gender perspectives are increasingly being applied to different fields of knowledge. The present work aims at demonstrating that the gender perspective is indeed very useful when applied to the field of robotics. Specifically, and when dealing with complex decision-taking, it becomes necessary to analyse which managing activities women can better develop in order to apply them, together with other features, to the design of robotic emotions. The purpose is, then, to propose a robotic model that, after the inclusion of such emotional aspects, breaks with old constrained gender stereotypes and takes a rather liberating view. At the same time, such a proposal should enable us to get better results when creating robots capable of managing other robotic teams and taking complex decisions. In short, we seek to apply the gender perspective in the analysis of some emotional features to be taken into account before they are applied to the field of robotics.

1. INTRODUCTION

Traditionally, academic and scientific literature has not given enough attention to the perspective of gender in the field of robotics. Significantly, the depiction of robots and cyborgs in science fiction literature and cinema has attracted many gender specialists.

Just to mention two significant examples, Thea von Harbou's *Metropolis* (1926), and its film adaptation by her husband Fritz Lang in 1927, depicts the character Brigitte Helm, or Isaac Asimov's *I Robot* (1950), taken to the big screen in 2004, portrays another famous character, Susan Calvin, the female leader of "robot-psychology" in U.S. Robots and Mechanical Men. These classic examples not only show the visual perspective of gender, but also deepen its psychological aspects.

In this chapter we seek to explain the advantages of investigating and applying the gender perspective to the field of robotic personality and emotions. We will propose some lines of work for their future application, focusing mainly on the issue of complex decision-taking oriented to robots that may help with the management of organisations and director teams.

Our main objective is, then, to specify the need to give an adequate gender perspective to robotic emotions. We believe that this is essential for the adaptation of both robot/human and robot/robot relationships to frameworks that take into account aspects that are better resolved if the gender perspective is adopted. Thus, we will concentrate on the issue of complex decision-taking, which does not merely refer to whether the robot decides to pick up one thing or another or move from one place to another. We are referring to management decisions, that is, how to run other robots and how to be successful in taking decisions linked to the management of robotic resources, in contrast to the management of human resources. In these cases, we are witness to the fact that in the business sphere great improvements have been made

when adopting gender perspectives for complex decision-taking. This aspect should also be taken into account in the field of robots.

2. BACKGROUND

If we take into account the fact that science, technology and their power connotations over the natural world have always been linked to the masculine sphere, women's recent closeness to technology has meant a challenge which should overcome traditional images of physical aspects to deepen into complex psychological aspects.

In this sense, every robot considered as female means a rupture with the masculine control of technology. This same violation of traditional patterns is also at work in all those virtual representations of the feminine, as can be seen in the popular science-fiction film *The Matrix* (1999) which shows virtually constructed women, as in the case of Trinity (Carrie-Ann Moss). Paradoxically, most feminist scholars dealing with science fiction agree in affirming that even these totally created bodies contribute to the reproduction of traditional gender stereotypes, especially in terms of behaviour.

Yet, within the academic scope, only a few works have considered these issues. Donna Haraway, in her famous "A Cyborg Manifesto: Science, Technology, and Socialist- Feminist in the Late Twentieth Century" (1985), already dealt with the cyborg image and regarded it not only as a created being but also as a "creature of social reality", although she did not consider it from the strictly robotic perspective. More specifically, we should mention the works by Winslow Burleson and Rosalind Picard (2007), *alma mater* of affective computing, which is a branch of artificial intelligence that deals with the design of systems and devices that are able to recognise, interpret and deal with emotions. This is an interdisciplinary field that includes computing, psychology and cognitive science.

This topic is not new but, as Miquel Barceló (Barceló, 2005) argues, the creators of artificial intelligence have already dealt with these issues. Thus, two opposing lines of thoughts can be established. On the one hand, the research line that aims at achieving computing systems that reason, basically following the demands of the dictates of the mathematical logic. The main precursor within this approach is John McCarthy, inventor of so-called "artificial intelligence". The other line of thought aims at imitating the method of human mind reasoning, which is not necessarily the same as mathematical logic. Its main precursor is Marvin Minsky. At the same time, an in-between line of thought has also been developed, led by John Haugeland and based on the concept of "synthetic intelligence". Such an approach highlights, apart from the artificiality of the intelligence achieved by artificial intelligence, the fact that its origin is the human activity that "synthesises" a new form of its own intelligence. In relation to this issue, Vallverdú (2007) even talks about "emotional architectures".

The present work is in line with this latter trend, and assumes a coexistence of the technical aspects of artificial intelligence with the features of human reasoning -including the gender perspective - that should also be taken into account.

When dealing with metaphysics, Galileo affirmed, "we see tastes, colours, smells but if we do not have eyes or ears we only have numbers, shapes and movements". Robots may have now reached that point, but they will develop towards perceptions such as colours, smells (our specialised field) and, obviously, emotions.

Thus, it should be understood that we are dealing with hybrid factors that include emotions, apart from simple mathematical perceptions. This was already explored by Donna Haraway in her "Cyborg Manifesto", which disestablishes in many senses the traditional notions of sex difference and celebrates the hybrid quality of the cyborg. In this figure, the boundaries between body and technology are socially inscribed. In this sense, Haraway (1985: 150) contends that the cyborg is our ontology as "by the late 20th century, our time, a mythic time, we are all chimeras, theorized and fabricated hybrids of machine and organism; in short, we are cyborgs".

Paradoxically, the tendency began by Haraway relies on the elimination of the gender condition, proposing however, a model that is considered non-linear, non-hierarchical and decentred. This model aims at equating excessive male rationality, based on hardness and imperviousness, without taking any advantage of the great potency offered by gender duality.

Authors like Ainize Txopitea (2008) have proposed another more inclusive and liberating view called "technoskeletics" where women exert a power that is inclusive, non-hierarchical and multifaceted. This thought has been normally associated to woman in contexts of specific cybernetic development (Escaja 2003). Nevertheless, it has not been associated to robotic emotions yet.

Many questions arise when determining the nature of emotions at the robotic level. Authors like Blank (2000) have posed some of those from an ontological perspective: can human beings be likewise considered programmed machines from a genetic code transmitted from generation to generation? Are we human beings mere products of educational and social "programmes"? Are our thinking guidelines also the product of innate or acquired programmes? Do our instincts and intelligent behaviour mirror these previous programmes? Don't we all belong to the same universe and shouldn't we obey the same laws? Are we really so different from the machines we use? If it is so, our question is, then: is the gender perspective necessary for the definition of robotic emotions? We will address this question throughout the present work.

3. MAIN FOCUS OF THE CHAPTER

The gender perspective in the robotic field has been little explored, yet it is of great value. It is applicable not only to physical robots, but also to virtual ones that work by means of software or in Internet platforms.

In trying to relate gender to the representation of virtual space, early researchers into this topic argued that gender and other aspects of social identity are considered irrelevant in those virtual worlds created by information technology (Wakeford, 2000: 292). Precisely, this utopian vision of gender that breaks notions of masculinity and femininity was first thought to be represented in those virtual spaces. In fact, the influential scholar Sadie Plant argued that virtual worlds "undermine both the world-view and the material reality of two thousand years of patriarchal control" (Plant, 2000: 265), probably in reference to the differing representations of a body where sexual differences are not so sharply marked. Moreover, roles traditionally associated with male and female bodies are sometimes intermixed or even exchanged in virtual space, leading to this first consideration of virtual space as a gender-free contender. However, after a deeper analysis, scholars concluded that this utopian vision of gender equality in the electronic space is not achieved (Wakeford, 2000, 292).

Thus, from our point of view, one aspect that can evolve more fully in robotic emotions has to do with the use of the gender perspective. In addition, the little experience in the application of robotic systems in great surroundings for decision-taking shows that it is strongly advisable for all robots not to have the same type of emotions.

A clear example of the problems caused by the non-differentiation of robotic emotions was the famous "Black Monday" of the New York Stock Market on October 19th, 1987. A quite significant event took place in this sense, since the Stock Market suffered a bigger fall than the one in the Great Depression of 1929, without any event or economic information justifying it. The truth was that most major investors used the same robot for their information analysis, arguing that it had been successful in previous years and, according to them, it was advisable to sell. The stock market is based on the existence of optimistic and pessimistic personalities, but this fact was not considered at that moment, since all views were pessimistic in both long and short terms.

This example should make us think about the necessity to differentiate the robots' different personalities when designing them. A good way to start working is by using an appropriate gender perspective.

One is not to reproduce old feminist clichés, but to deepen the importance of psychological aspects. Until now, almost everything dealing with this matter has centred on the external appearance of the robot, deciding whether it was male or female. Sex roles have been, therefore, overstressed, as for example in the first robot made by Mecanno in 2008, which significantly is called Miss. We should go beyond this and work both on the physical and emotional aspects.

We should consider that the term "sex" refers to biological differences between men and women, whereas "gender" makes allusion to the ideas, beliefs and traits assigned to men and women according to the specific historical and cultural moment (Giddens, 2003).

We do hope that the robot culture follows a different path to that of humans. In spite of all the national and international equality programmes and policies proposed by governments and private organisms, inequality between men and women still exists in our society. For that reason we pose the following questions:

Is it necessary to incorporate a gender perspective in the analysis of the personality of robots? The different contributions to the organisations from men and women must be studied from different points of view, since it is possible to ask which managerial activities women can develop better than men, and to see how to transfer these features to robotic emotions.

Is the management style that organisations demand nowadays linked to the female managerial style? This is affirmed by numerous studies. However, and if it is true, is it advisable to design a "Gender Quota" in the robotic scope? Obviously, we should not reach that point but to conceive a new organisation, mainly in the business scope, where the feminine contribution is developed in equality of conditions and where its presence is not merely the fulfilment of quotas, but a worthy contribution to the company and society.

It should be done by taking the main characteristics of the female-oriented managerial style and by establishing relationships that demonstrate that the decision systems in complex environments can be impelled and developed within the organisations if the abilities and potentialities of the female-oriented managerial style are taking into account.

Complex systems, mainly in the socioeconomic scope, are in a global and uncertain environment where success mainly depends on human and robotic resources, and on their potentialities, which do not have to be antagonistic in gender terms, but simply complementary. In order to take maximum advantage of human or robotic capital, one needs to use the potentialities of both sexes. For that reason, we consider that gender differences represent a reality that can be valuable if properly used.

It is aimed at new way of observing reality, where all the spheres considered essential for the good development of society are valued and perceived (Gelambí, 2004). This thought led to the appearance of the "gender mainstreaming" concept to refer to the integration of different experiences and necessities, not always coincidental, of men and women. The use of women's attitudes supposes the application of the "diversity" concept, which entails taking maximum advantage of the potential offered by heterogeneous groups. Women's capacities are more oriented to relationships, and are more emotional, expressive and receptive, whereas those of men are more aggressive, independent, rational and logic (Robbins, 1998).

By leadership we understand one's ability to lead and animate the members of the work party into obtaining certain objectives. Women's leadership trespasses mere interchange and tries to stimulate the organisation as a whole, considers the personal development of the work party essential, enhances participation, shares information and power, and not simply their capacity to obtain economic benefit. In addition, female-oriented leadership recognises and promotes the members of the work team and seeks to understand and to model their attitudes, which results in greater commitment on the part of the personnel towards the organisation and allows for participative management. On the other hand, women enjoy a greater facility to move within social networks in and outside the company, which is fundamental for the information and knowledge society.

Women's managerial style has traditionally been considered one of transformational leadership (Bass, 1985) based on a set of assigned capacities that allow the leader to identify changes and design actions to effectively confront them. This increases yield level and promotes the development of both the individual members of the team and that of the groups and the organisation as a whole. The transformational leader enhances personal development and motivates the work member to extend his/her own interests to those of the organisation or team and, that way, activate their top needs (Ramos, 2004).

On the contrary, men's managerial style corresponds to transactional leadership (Rosener, 1990). The leader seeks to achieve the proposed labour objectives and he is the one who organises the activities of the group and decides how to do them.

According to Saravia Matus (2005), there is a new tendency towards androgynous leadership that diminishes gender impacts and that better conjugates masculine and feminine style characteristics. This causes the inclusion of new values that contribute to a better development of the company and to the improvement in labour competitiveness. Nowadays, companies look for a leader who knows how to delegate work to her/his subordinates, stresses their attitudes, is flexible in the face of change and is a negotiator and communicator.

The organisational model based on ambition, competitiveness, desire for responsibility, competition and analytical ability, proper characteristics of the male-oriented managerial style, should start to change towards an organisation model closer to the female managerial style (Marshall, 2007).

Thus, it is necessary to begin to design robotic emotions from a gender perspective. This has been our goal over the last few years and we have reached the conclusion that the following features should be taken into account when providing robots with emotions, specifically those robots dealing with solving decision-taking problems, or those working alongside other robots or human beings (Table 1).

These are some of the main characteristics that the emotional elements of robots should have in

order to incorporate the gender perspective in a suitable way from a psychological point of view. This goes further than the traditional aesthetic vision by which a certain female image is merely imitated.

The personality of a robot that is aimed at managing others or that eventually needs to take into account its "supposed emotions" should have a series of traits. Having a global perspective is one such trait, which enables the robot to decide in an adequate way. This field has not been fully explored in physical robots yet. On the contrary, it has been developed in virtual robots, such as the Google type.

Moreover, robots must show an interest in the quality of the environment, which should allow other robots and people to improve their emotions. This will become the new frontier in robot designing. That is to say, robots will be designed to improve the quality of the environment both of robots and people, not only in aspects related to nature but also in domotic, office automation and ergonomic improvement in the workplace.

Table 1. Main characteristics of the feminine vision of decision problems

A	Global perspective.
B	Interest in the quality of the environment.
C	Interest in people and in other robots.
D	Recognition of both people's and robots' interests.
E	Concern for learning.
F	Cooperative management
G	Open communication and greater sensitivity towards relationships
H	Take into account emotional aspects when carrying out work.
I	Management style and more methodical and organised work, with greater usefulness and resolution capacity, and more participative
J	Creative innovation.
K	Ability to work under pressure, without destroying the system
L	Share power and information
M	Flexibility in the face of change
N	Ability to develop social networks.
P	Management by means of inclusion.

A robotic personality from the feminine perspective should also be interested both in other people and robots. So, certain social and "soft negotiation" abilities must be programmed. That is to say, robots need to a have a vision of the other, and should look for solutions to possible interest or conflicts of objectives. Breazeal (2002) in particular has focused on this possibility when dealing with the social vision of robots. Robots with a feminine personality should be provided with the possibility to recognise other people's and robots' concerns.

A key element is the concern for learning. Robots must have the possibility to learn according to their functions. Feminine robots and those whose aim is to manage teams of people and robots should have an especial inclination towards constant learning.

All this should coexist with cooperative orientation. Other elements should be taken into account for the benefit of the group and open communication, and a greater sensitivity towards relationships should be enhanced.

The design of personality and emotions should also take into account aspects like the inclusion of methodical and organised management and working styles. These should be highly practical and with substantial capacity for solving problems, apart from being participative, with the ability to develop social networks and being capable of managing them by means of inclusion.

Creativity can also be found in robots. Creative innovation, characteristic of the female-oriented management style, should likewise be present in organisational aspects. This ought to contribute to the improvement of relationships among robots and also between robots and people.

There are factors traditionally considered feminine that should also be taken into account when programming robots. On the one hand, they should have the ability to work under pressure but without destroying the system – which is a typical masculine trait.

There is an interesting feature that derives from the fact that a robot-managing team needs to know how to share power and information. So, it should be flexible when faced with change.

In short, emotional aspects, both of robots and people, should be taken into account. This is a developing field, far from our reality, but which we should bear in mind if we want to develop the field of robotic emotions.

The gender perspective is extremely useful for the development of this unexplored field. We have reached this conclusion after a long evolutionary process along our lines of research. Thus, we started working on the use of new ways of transmitting what human senses perceive in order to change them into emotions. First, in the 19th century sound transmission was invented to get to human ears, and then images were created for human sight. We have invented a system for the transmission of smells, we have created a program language - XMLSMELL- for the transmission of smells via Internet.

At that point we started to think that transmission was not the most important fact but that other machines and robots perceive smells and, most notably, understand the emotions they transmit, and this is what we have learned through education and growth since our infancy. Thus, we believe that education is a relevant factor in the robotic field. In order to program emotions we have two options: a complete education from the beginning, and robotic education. We chose the latter.

After this, we realised that sex difference was an almost compulsory possibility for the coexistence of robots that can take decisions with emotional bases.

Up to now, most works dealing with this issue have centred on making robots recognise a certain type of information that we humans process in order to create emotions. Thus, in order to recognise emotional information we require the extraction of a significant model from the collected data. This has created growing research interest in the collection and analysis of data by means of different processes such as voice recognition, the treatment of natural language, or the detection of facial expression.

In this sense, a development can be seen in data collection and in the analysis of such data, although we are still at a very early stage.

Regarding facial recognition, several attempts have been made in order to generate gender visions, as for example Brake and Tessmer (2004) or work by Wilhelm, Bohme, Grofi y Backhaus (2004). Something similar has happened in the field of voice recognition, as shown by Austermann, Esau, Kleinjohann and Kleinjohann (2005), Kim, Hyun and Kwak (2005) and Ververidis and Kotropolos (2004).

It is interesting to analyse the problem of voice, images and smells' recognition from the human perspective. Thus several interesting research works have been made into the way in which humans communicate with robots. Siino and Hinds (2005) analyse robots' relationships in the workplace and men's and women's behaviour with them.

This problem is not new. Alan Turing (1950), in his first work on artificial intelligence, proposed an experiment that distinguished the intelligent nature of a machine's behaviour. For that, a game is proposed. In it, a "questioner" has to guess the sex of two speakers, A and B, placed in different rooms. They are a man and a woman, although they both say they are women. In Turing's original proposal, a woman is substituted by a computer.

This kind of test is still being done nowadays, even providing robots with a gendered image or sound. Remarkable examples are those by Powers, Kramer, Lim, Kuo, Lee and Kiesler (2005). They have proved that when designing robots capable of speaking to people, results may vary if they are provided with a masculine or feminine personality. Thus when making simple changes in a robot's personality, we can obtain different levels of information from the users. Such effects are less prominent when the robot's discourse is merely technical than when it aims at object descriptions or at the fulfilment of human tasks. Several research works affirm that in robotics the voice can have different effects according to the gender assigned to robots. Zanbaka, Goolkasian and Hodges (2006) have evaluated in a detailed way the users' change of behaviour depending on the robot's male or female voice. Strikingly, they reached the conclusion that male users were more persuaded if the robot was feminine than if it were masculine, whereas female users were more persuaded if the robot was masculine rather than feminine.

These are examples of research work dealing with robotics and gender perspective. We should go further and provide robots with a personality that takes into account the gender features analysed in this chapter.

4. FUTURE TRENDS

We believe that one of the "new frontiers" within this research into robotic emotions is going to be the inclusion of differing aspects of the feminine personality in robots.

This opens a new field of interesting research which should go on to create new tendencies. Thus, an effective way of programming psychological aspects in robots is going to be needed. Moreover, new research lines are going to be created, such as robotic education.

We believe that this is an ever-growing field but it that needs a fresh impulse that creates new learning mechanisms and new ways of orienting such information. There will be a need to consider the creation of schools for robots and didactic teaching resources that better assimilate the different teaching-learning processes.

Another new aspect that has not been dealt with in academic literature is "management of robotic resources" – in contrast to "management of human resources". We believe that robots working with other robots will be the norm, and also robots working with human beings; and precisely because of that, we will need to apply techniques of team management of human and robotic resources.

Management of robotic knowledge is also being increasingly studied. Yet, much needs to be done for elements like experience to be taken into account when designing robots and creating processes of knowledge for them.

In short, the opening up of robotic emotions has created a great number of very interesting and suggestive research fields. We will work on them in the next few decades.

5. CONCLUSION

The gender perspective results are of great value when designing robots' personality and emotions. As has been contended here, the features of human reasoning are necessary for the better working of robotic organisms. Thus, and if we concentrate on complex decision-taking oriented to robots that help to manage teams - both robotic and human - we should take into account the emotional features of the so-called female-oriented management style. Traits like global perspective, the concern for learning or cooperative organisation of activities should be applied to the design of both physical and virtual robots.

Our proposal does not intend to return to an old essentialist and simplistic view of gender. On the contrary, it seeks to take advantage of the emotions that have effectively contributed to the improvement of human development and labour competition. Thus we intend to take maximum advantage of human or robotic resources and use both sexes' potential in order to create a robotic model that can take decisions in complex environments.

6. REFERENCES

Asimov, I. (1950). *I, Robot*. New York: Gnome Press.

Austermann, A., Esau, N., Kleinjohann, L., & B. Kleinjohann (2005). Fuzzy emotion recognition in natural speech dialogue. *Robot and Human Interactive Communication IEEE 14th workshop.*

Barberá, E., & Ramos, A. y Sarrió, M. (2000). Mujeres directivas ante el tercer milenio: el proyecto Nowdi XXI. *Papeles del psicólogo*, 75. http://www.papelesdelpsicologo.es/vernumero. asp?id=820.

Barceló, M. (2005). *Inteligencia artificial*. Barcelona. Servicio de publicaciones de la UOC.

Bass, B.M. (1985). *Leadership and performance beyond expectations*. New York: The Free Press.

Baylor, A.L., Shen, E., & Huang, X. (2003). Which pedagogical agent do learners choose? The effects of gender and ethnicity. In *Proceedings of the World Conference on E-learning in Corporate, Government, Healthcare & Higher Education, Assoc. for the Advancement of Computing in Education* (pp. 1507-1510).

Betz, M., O'Connell, L., & Shepard J.M.. (1989). Gender differences in proclivity unethical behaviour. *Journal of Business Ethics*, 8, 321-324.

Bilimoria, D., & Piderit, S.K. (1994). Board committee membership: Effects of sex-based bias. *Academy of Management Journal*, *37*(6), 1453-77.

Blank, Carlos (2000). Penrose y la inteligencia artificial. *Episteme*, *20*(1), 29-49.

Brake, M.L. & Tessmer, A. (2004). Robots and girls. *Antennas and Propagation Magazine, IEEE*, *46*(1), 142-143.

Breazeal, C. & Scassellati, B. (1999). How to build robots that make friends and influence people. *Proceedings of the IEEE/RSJ International Conference on Intelligent Robots and Systems*, Knyoju, Japan.

Breazeal, C. (2002). *Designing sociable robots*. Cambridge, MA: MIT Press.

Bumby, K.E., & Dautenhahn, K. (1999). Investigating children's attitudes towards robots: A case study. *Third Cognitive Technology Conference*, San Francisco CA.

Burleson, W. & Picard, R.W. (2007). Gender-specific approaches to developing emotionally intelligent learning companions. *Intelligent Systems, 22*(4), 62-69.

Casacuberta, David (2000). *¿Qué es una emoción?* Barcelona. Crítica 2000.

Changchun Liu, Rani, P., & Sarkar, N (2006). Affective state recognition and adaptation in human-robot interaction: a design approach. *Intelligent Robots and Systems. 2006 IEEE/RSJ International Conference*. (pp. 3099-3106).

Colwill, J. & Townsend, J. (1999). Women, leadership and information technology. The impact of women leaders in organizations and their in integrating information technology with corporate strategy. *The Journal of Management Development, 18*(3), 207-216.

Escaja, T. (2003). Escritura tecnetoesquelética e hipertexto Espéculo. *Revista de estudios literarios de la Universidad Complutense de Madrid*. N° 24. Retrieved June 18, 2008, from http://www.ucm.es/info/especulo/numero24/ciberpoe.html.

Gelambí, M. (2004). *La gestión transversal de género como reto para las empresas*. Tarragona. Universitat Rovira y Virgili. CIES.

Giddens, A. (2003). *The sociology*. London: Pluto Press.

Gockley, R., Bruce, A., Forlizzi, J., Michalowski, M., Mundell, A., Rosenthal, S., Sellner, B., Simmons, R., Snipes, K., Shultz, A., & Wang, J. (2005). Designing robots for long-term social interaction. *2005 IEEE International Conference on Robotics and Automation*.

Grosser, K. & Moon, J. (2005). The role of corporate social responsibility in gender mainstreaming. *International Feminist Journal of Politics, 7*(4), 532-554.

Haraway, D.J. (1991). *Simians, cyborgs and women: the reinvention of nature*. New York: Routledge.

Kanda, T., Hirano, T. & Eaton D. (2004). Interactive robots as social partners and peer tutors for children: A field trial. *Human Computer Interaction, 19*, 61-84.

Kim E.H., Hyun, K.H. & Kwak, Y.K. (2005). Robust emotion recognition feature, frequency range of meaningful signal. *Robot and Human Interactive Communication IEEE 14th workshop*.

Kirkup, G., et al. (2000). *The gendered cyborg: A reader*. New York: Routledge.

Kramer, A., A.D.I., Lim, S., Kuo, J., Lee, S-L, & Kiesler, S. (2005). Eliciting information from people with a gendered humanoid robot powers. *Robot and Human Interactive Communication, ROMAN 2005. IEEE International Workshop*, 158-163.

Lee S-L., Kiesler, S., Lau, I.Y., & Chiu, C.Y. (2005). Human mental models of humanoid robots. *2005 IEEE International Conference on Robotics and Automation*.

Montemerlo, M., Pineau, J., Roy, N., Thrun, S. & Verma, V. (2002). Experiences with a mobile robotic guide for the elderly. *18th National Conference on Artificial Intelligence* (pp. 587-592).

Mullennix, J.W., Stern, S.E., Wilson, S.J., & Dyson, C. (2003). Social perception of male and female computer synthesized speech. *Computers in Human Behavior, 19,* 407-424.

Munduate, L. (2003). Género y liderazgo. Diferencias entre hombres y mujeres en el acceso a los puestos directivos. *Revista de Psicología Social, 18*(3), 309-314.

Nass, C., Moon, Y., & Green, N. (1997). Are machines gender neutral? Gender-stereotypic responses to computers with voices. *Journal of Applied Social Psychology, 27,* 864-876.

Nass, C., Steuer, J., Tauber, E., & Reeder H. (1993). Anthropomorphism, agency, & ethopoeia: Computers as social actors. *InterCHI '93,* Amsterdam.

Nowak, K. L. & Rauh, C. (2005). The influence of the avatar on online perceptions of anthropomorphism, androgyny, credibility, homophily, and attraction. *Journal of Computer-Mediated Communication, 11*(1).

Penrose, R. (1995). *La nueva mente del emperador.* Barcelona. Grijalbo-Mondadori.

Picard, R.W. (2000). Synthetic emotion. *Computer Graphics and Applications IEEE, 20*(1), 52-53.

Picard, R.W., Vyzas, E. & Healey, J. (2001). Toward machine emotional intelligence: analysis of affective physiological state. *Pattern Analysis and Machine Intelligence, IEEE Transactions,* 23 (10), 1175-1191.

Plant, S. (2000). On the matrix: Cyberfeminist simulations. In G. Kirkup, L. Janes, K. Woodward, & F. Hovenden (Eds.), *The gendered cyborg* (pp. 265-275). New York: Routledge.

Powers, Aaron, Kramer, A.D., Lim, S., Kuo, J., Lee S-L., & Kiesler, S. (2005). Eliciting information from people with a gendered humanoid robot. *2005 IEEE International Workshop on Robots and Human Interactive Communication.*

Ramos, A. (2004). *Liderazgo transformacional: un estudio desde la psicología de género.* Doctoral Thesis. Universitat de Valencia.

Ridgeway C. (1993). Gender, status, and the social psychology of expectations. In P. England (Ed.), *Theory on gender/feminism on theory* (pp. 175-197). New York: Aldine.

Rosener, J.B. (1990). Ways women lead. *Harvard Business Review, 68,* 119-120.

Ross, M. & Holmberg D. (1990). Recounting the past: Gender differences in the recall of events in the history of a close relationship. In J.M. Olson, & M.P. Zanna (Eds.), *Self-inferences processes: The Ontario Symposium,* (pp. 135-152). Hillsdale, NJ: Erlbaum, 135-152.

Scheeff, M., Pinto, J., Rahardja, K., Snibbe, S., & Tow R. (2000). Ex with Sparky: A social robot. *Proceedings of the Workshop on Interactive Robot Entertainment.*

Schuller, B., Arsic, D., Wallhoff, F., & Rigoll, G. (2006). Emotion recognition in the noise applying large acoustic feature sets. *Speech Prosody 2006, ISCA,* Dresden, Germany.

Siino R.M. & Hinds, P.J. (2005). Robots, gender & sensemaking: Sex segregation's impact on workers making sense of a mobile autonomous robot. *Proceedings of the 2005 IEEE International Conference on Robotics and Automation,* Barcelona, Spain.

Thrun, S., Beetz, M., Bennewitz, M., Burgard, W., Cremers, A.B., Dellaert, F., Fox, D., Hähnel, D., Rosenberg, C., Roy, N., Schulte J., & Schulz D. (2000). Probabilistic algorithms and the interactive museum tourguide robot minerva. *International Journal of Robotics Research, 19*(11), 972-999.

Turing, A. (1950). Computing machinery and intelligence. *Mind, 59,* 433-460.

Txopitea, A. (2008). Retrieved May 30, 2008, from www.cyberpoetry.net/index.html.

Vallverdú, J. (2005). Robots: la frontera de un nuevo arte. *Cuadernos del Minotauro, 1,* 21-30.

Vallverdú, J. (2007). ¿Por qué motivos crearemos máquinas emocionales? *Astrolabio, Revista internacional de filosofía, 5*, 44-52.

Ververidis, D., & Kotropolos, C. (2004). *Automatic emotional speech classification*. Paper presented at the IEEE International Conference on Acoustics, Speech and Signal Processing.

Vilarroya, Óscar (2002). *Palabra de robot: Inteligencia artificial y comunicación*. Estudi General. Premio Europeo de Divulgación Científica.

Weick, K.E. (1995). *Sensemaking in organizations*. Newbury Park, CA: Sage.

Wilhelm, T., Bohme, H.J., Grofi, H.M., & Backhaus, A. (2004). Statistical and neural methods for vision-based analysis of facial expressions and gender. In *Systems, Man and Cybernetics, 2004 IEEE International Conference, 3*, (pp. 2203-2208).

Wakeford, N. (2000). Gender and the landscapes of computing in an internet café. In Kirkup, G., Janes, L., Woodward, K., & Hovenden, F. (Eds.), *The gendered cyborg* (pp. 291-304). New York: Routledge.

Willeke, T., Kunz, C., & Nourbakhsh, I. (2001). The history of the mobot museum robot series: An evolutionary study. In *Proceedings of FLAIRS 2001*.

Zanbaka C., Goolkasian, P., & Hodges, L. (2006). Can a virtual cat persuade you? The role of gender and realism in speaker persuasiveness. In *Proceedings of the SIGCHI conference on Human Factors in computing systems* (pp. 1153-1162). Montréal, Québec, Canada.

7. KEY TERMS

Feminine Perspective of Robotic Problems

Gender

Management Styles

Robotic Resources Management

Robotic Knowledge Management

Robots' Perception: Sight (Images), Ears (Sound), and Smell (Smell)

Formative processes for robots.

Chapter X
Moral Emotions for Autonomous Agents

Antoni Gomila
University Illes Balears, Spain

Alberto Amengual
International Computer Science Institute, USA

ABSTRACT

In this chapter we raise some of the moral issues involved in the current development of robotic autonomous agents. Starting from the connection between autonomy and responsibility, we distinguish two sorts of problems: those having to do with guaranteeing that the behavior of the artificial cognitive system is going to fall within the area of the permissible, and those having to do with endowing such systems with whatever abilities are required for engaging in moral interaction. Only in the second case can we speak of full blown autonomy, or moral autonomy. We illustrate the first type of case with Arkin's proposal of a hybrid architecture for control of military robots. As for the second kind of case, that of full-blown autonomy, we argue that a motivational component is needed, to ground the self-orientation and the pattern of appraisal required, and outline how such motivational component might give rise to interaction in terms of moral emotions. We end suggesting limits to a straightforward analogy between natural and artificial cognitive systems from this standpoint.

1. INTRODUCTION

The increasing success of Robotics in building autonomous agents, with rising levels of intelligence and sophistication, has taken away the nightmare of "the devil robot" from the hands of science fiction writers, and turned it into a real pressure for roboticists to design control systems able to guarantee that the behavior of such robots comply with minimal ethical requirements. Autonomy goes with responsibility, in a nutshell. Otherwise the designers risk having to be held themselves responsible for any wrong deeds of the autonomous systems. In a way, hence, predictability and reliability of artificial systems pull against its autonomy (flexibility, novelty in novel circumstances). The increase in autonomy rises high the issue of responsibility and, hence, the question of right and wrong, of moral reliability.

Which these minimal ethical requirements are may vary according to the kind of purpose these autonomous systems are build for. In the forthcoming years it is foreseeable an increase in "service" robots: machines specially designed to deal with particularly risky or difficult tasks, in a flexible way. Thus, for instance, one of the leading areas of roboethical research concerns autonomous systems for military purposes; for such new systems, non-human supervision of use of lethal weapons may be a goal of the design, so that a guarantee must be clearly established that such robots will not kill innocent people, start firing combatants in surrender or attack fellow troops, before they are allowed to be turned on. In this area, the prescribed minimal requirements are those of the Laws of War made explicit in the Geneva Convention and the Rules of Engagement each army may establish for their troops. Other robots (for rescue, for fire intervention, for domestic tasks, for sexual intercourse) may also need to count on "moral" norms to constrain what to do in particular circumstances ("is it ok to let one person starve to feed other two?"). Much more so when we think of a middle range future and speculate about the possibility of really autonomous systems, or systems that "evolve" in the direction of higher autonomy: we really should start thinking about how to assure that such systems are going to respect our basic norms of humanity and social life, if they are to be autonomous in the fullest sense. So the question we want to focus on in this paper is: how should we deal with this particular challenge?

The usual way to deal with this challenge is a variation/extension of the existing deliberative/reactive autonomous robotic architectures, with the goal of providing the system with some kind of higher level control system, a reasoning moral system, based on moral principles and rules and some sort of inferential mechanism, to assess and judge the different situations in which the robot may enter, and act accordingly. The inspiration here is chess design: what's required is a way to anticipate the consequences of one's possible actions and of weighting those alternatives according to some sort of valuation algorithm, that excludes some of those possibilities from consideration altogether. Quite appart from the enormous difficulty of finding out which principles and rules can capture our "moral sense" in an explicit form, this project also faces the paradoxes and antinomies that lurk into any formal axiomatic system, well-known from the old days of Asimov's laws. So to speak, this approach inherits the same sort of difficulties known as the "symbol grounding" and "frame" problems in Cognitive Science.

However, it might turn out that there is a better way to face the challenge: instead of conceiving of morality as a higher level of control based on a specific kind of reasoning, it could be conceived instead as an emotional level of control, along the current trend in the Social Neurosciences and Psychology which point in such direction (for an illustration, the special double issue in volume 7 of the journal Social Neuroscience). From this point of view, which in fact resumes the "moral sense" tradition in Ethics, moral judgement is not a business of reason and truth, but of emotion in the first place, not of analytical pondering of rights and wrongs, but of intuitive, fast, immediate affective valuation of a situation (which may be submitted to a more careful, detailed, reflexive, analysis later on), at least at the ground level. From this point of view, it might be a better option in order to build systems with some sort of "moral" understanding and compliance, to start building systems with a practical understanding of emotions and emotional interaction, in particular moral emotions. Rights and norms, so the story goes, come implicitly packed along these reactive attitudes, and thus get the power to motivate and mobilize characteristic of human morality.

The connection between emotions and morality, though, is not simple or straightforward. Thus, for instance, it has been proposed that moral judgements are a kind of emotional judgement (Gibbard, 1990); or, it has been suggested that emotions may play a role as "behavior committments", so that a decision is not indefinitely up for graps for further reasoning (Frank, 1988). Instead of trying to disentangle these complex relationships here, what we propose to do is to consider only the so called moral emotions (pride, shame, remorse, guilt, embarrassment...). In so doing, we will have to focus on three central points: moral emotions, despite its being concerned with oneself as an agent (and whereof they have also been called "self-aware emotions"), take as their intentional objects the intersubjective relationships we enter with others. Second, such intersubjective relationships rely on a particular kind of psychological understanding of the others, which we call "the second person point of view", which can be seen as an architectonic requirement for having such moral emotions. And third, moral emotions, as all emotions, presuppose as well a motivational/affective basic architecture, involving a reward/punishment internal system, which is generally absent in current Robotics.

In the third section we will suggest a way this motivational dimension might be addressed in Robotics: we will introduce the notion of a motivational system, common currency in ethology and human development. According to this theory, infants grow not only with the intrinsic motivations of thirst, hunger or sleep, but also with a more complex set of motivations: curiosity, exploration, attachment, and other affiliative tendencies. We'll introduce the issue of which motivational system may underlie moral emotions. This complex of intrinsic motivations is what provides affective valence to the situations and events one finds oneself in. So understanding how this works may help understand our emotional life, in order to be able to simulate it in autonomous systems. In the last section, thouh, we will rise some doubts on the feasibility of the project.

2. LOOKING FOR A CONTROL SYSTEM OF MORAL REASONING

The urge to develop some sort of ethical dimension to increasingly autonomous systems is apparent in the consolidation of "machine ethics" or "roboethics" as a distinctive subfield within Robotics and Artificial Intelligence. Several proposals have called attention to the moral challenge that stems from the growing autonomy and flexibility of the new systems under development, and made suggestions mostly as to how general ethical theory could be taylored to this new requirements (Anderson, Anderson & Armen, 2004; Allen, Wallach & Smit, 2006). In Europe, such worries have brought about an European Research Network's Roboethics Roadmap (Veruggio, 2007). Some propose to take a "deontological" view of moral norms as a starting point, while others adopt a utilitarian, and consequentialist in general, approach. But they still do not go beyond a very general framework.

Thus, for instance, Anderson et al. (2004) implemented an ethical reasoning system called Jeremy, that is capable of doing some calculations as to which alternative course of action will produce the best outcome. It is based on Bentham's Hedonistic Act Utilitarianism, according to which "the best outcome" is conceived in terms of highest degree of pleasure for most people involved. The values are fixed in terms of intensity, duration and probability of the pleasures and displeasures expected to follow a certain course of action. The "right" action is the one that provides the greatest total net pleasure.

In contrast, Ronald Arkin (2007) has worked out a less general, more applied, framework, one specifically thought to deal with the problems of the "moral" control of the behavior of autonomous robotic systems that may take part in a war, in order to be able to engage in lethal, non-supervised, action, in a legitimate way. Robots are already being used in a military context, both by the United States and South Corea. In the latter case, military robots were deployed in 2007 in the demilitarized zone that separates South from North Corea. Autonomous military robots constitute the bulk of the Northamerican Future Combat System programme. To focus on the military use of robots makes the moral issues involved obvious, much more so than the questions of responsibility in car parking, for instance. Arkin takes advantage of current deliberative/reactive robotic architectures, and of the existence of an international legal consensus on what's legitimate in a war, reflected in the Geneva Convention. Thus, while his aproach does not provide an answer to the general question of how to design a system with a "moral consciousness" from scratch, it provides an articulated example of the scope and shortcomings of a "rule-based" approach to moral judgement. For this reason, we will take his proposal as a point of reference for our argument.

Currently, military robots are not programmed to take lethal decisions on their own: human authorization and control is required to proceed to a shooting. It is clear, then, whose responsibility the deed is. The degree of autonomy of current systems is related to navigation, search and target identification, but clearly enough, efforts are being made to increase their autonomy. It is in this context that the U.S. Army Research Office funds Arkin's report to approach the issues involved in an effort to increase robot autonomy. His starting point is to operationalize the moral challenge of autonomous military robots along the terms of the Geneva Convention: a robot will be ok as long as it doesn't violate the Rules of War and the Rules of Engagement that the Convention make explicit. In other words, instead of trying to capture the contents of "good", "fair" and "evil",

and to design an algorithm to calculate which available option will produce more "good", less "evil", consequences, Arkin takes the rules for granted and rises the much more concrete question of how to design systems that respect such rules. Of course, while such norms of a "just war" (Walzer, 1977) have drawn wide international consensus among most States, he is well aware of the pacifist option.

The principles embodied by the Geneva Convention are the principle of **discrimination** of military objectives and combatants from non-combatants, and the principle of **proportionality** of means. The first constraints the legitimate targets, the second, the legitimate means, given the ends that justify their use. Thus, for instance, prisoners cannot be mistreated. All the same, the application of these principles, as it is well-known, rises moral questions in particular circumstances, as revealed by such hot topics as the acceptance of collateral damage, the legitimacy of bombing key structures for civil life, the limit of the duty of obedience to orders for which the soldiers lack enough information to deem justifiable, or the right response to terrorist attacks. Arkin's strategy is to begin with the explicit particular rules that regulate acceptable behaviour in the battlefield, such as the Laws of War and the Rules of Engagement, and leave the complexities for the future. The former rules are prohibitions (do not torture, do not mutilate corpses of enemies, do not mistreat prisoners, do not produce innecessary damage, etc.), while the latter specify the circumstances and limitations to initiate or continue combat engagement, and the proper conduct in such hostilities. In this way, Arkin bypasses the basic problem of how to derive moral judgments for particular cases from general considerations (deontological or utilitarian, though he clearly prefers the first approach to ethics). In so doing, he curtails the sort of autonomy in question: his project is not aimed at building a moral agent, but an agent that implements the set of rules previously, and independently, specified, as prohibitions, obligations and permissions. All the same, and for this reason, it is enough to shed light on the intrinsic limitations of the rule-based approach in Cognitive Science.

The proposed hybrid architecture distinguishes three levels of implementation of moral concerns: an ethical governor, an ethical adaptor and a responsibility advisor. The "ethical adaptor" forms part of a reactive architecture, such that given a certain input –an assessment of some event in the context-, an appropiate response is activated by mediation of some existing schema (including the schema of use of lethal force given a proper situation). Secondly, the "ethical governor" is part of a deliberative architecture that goes through a sequential protocol of four constraints, understood as implementation of the principles of just war (discrimination, proportionality, double check the military necessity, and minimization of force required); all four must be ok to allow the deployment of a lethal response. Finally, the "responsibility advisor" is conceived as part of the interface between human and machine; its role is to allow for instructions to be transmitted to the system, or override orders to modify the outcome, as well as a sort of "accountability" device for the system to make public the kind of considerations that led it to its action.

In other words, the goal is to build a system that is allowed to deploy lethal weapons in such a way that this kind of action can be assured to take place only in a justified way, i.e., a situation in which it would be correct, even required, for a human soldier, to behave in such a way. Thus, it is required that the system is able to generate the lethal action in the first place, but it is further required that such a candidate action complies with all the requirements, for which a higher level of control is imposed, one which verifies that the activated action is compatible with the Laws of War and the Rules of Engagement. This means, as usual for this kind of architecture, to be able to derive the action from the rules plus the description of the situation (theorem proving). But even the reactive architecture is conceived in terms of a rule-based approach.

This is not the place to discuss questions of architecture, but of approach: it is the underlying view of morality as moral reasoning and judgement that we want to take issue with here. Even if an approach such as the one Arkin recomends were able to derive the particular rules of a given area of human activity from general moral principles, it could be said that no real moral understanding is really taking place, in so far as the "grasping" of the situations is completely neutral and amoral: no sense of duty or obligation, no possibility of wrongdoing (in the sense of acting against one's moral judgement), no room for personal bonds. To put it in classical terms, from the point of view of the robots, no distinction between conventional and moral norms is possible, and therefore they cannot exhibit moral understanding or sensitivity. Additional concerns arise in regard of the rule-based approach taken. Even in Ethical theory doubts have arisen as to whether morality is properly understood in terms of norms –particularists (Dancy, 2004), for instance, claim that moral judgement is not like a theorem deducible from general rules available, but context-dependent and case-based. Thus, our claim should be that such "particular" understanding of morality –the ability to see a situation as wrong, or evil- takes hold in humans on a basic capacity of emotional interaction that supplies the "strength" of moral judgement, beyond simple conventional norms (Nichols, 2004).

This is not to deny that, for service robots such as the military, or domestic ones, a more limited degree of autonomy may be enough, or even to be recommended. This limited degree of autonomy might at least partially be managed by a higher level control subsystem such as the "ethical governor" in Arkin's proposal. As a matter of fact, when we want results and efficiency, emotions seem obstacles, kludges to an "efficient design". Particularly in the military context, where emotions seem to cloud one's judgement and prone one's misbehavior. As a matter of fact, the worse wrongdoings in the battlefield come about when soldiers "lose control", when they get hysterical, panicked, frustrated, enraged, or hateful. As Arkin underlines as a reason to develop this technology, combat experience not only has long-lasting effects on the mental health of combatants, it also affects their moral sensitivity, their acceptance of practices forbidden by the Geneva Convention (like torture). In this sense, he suggests that robots can perform more ethically than human soldiers. However, the kind of moral problems these robots will be able to face, given the means provided by Arkin's design, will be rather simple, and always needed of human supervision.

To be fair, though, it must be also mentioned that Arkin is interested as well in affective architectures of control (Arkin, 2005), and he suggests that the "ethical adaptor", a sort of feedback mechanism to "learn from experience", to improve on the arrangement of the schemas so as to maximize the activation of the response that the "governor" will deem proper, might work on affective considerations, where this amounts to guilt: assessing the harm done might rise the "levels" of guilt which in their turn would rise the threshold of the action involved. But not much more is said in this regard, beyond that this approach overlooks the fact of compassion, "which may be considered a serious deficit" (p. 75), what in fact suggest an underlying agreement with the importance of moral emotions when dealing with the issue of real autonomy. In *The Society of Mind*, Minsky (1986) stated that "The question is not whether intelligent machines can have any emotions, but whether machines can be intelligent without any emotions". For our current purposes, this question could be restated as "Can machines behave morally, with real autonomy, without emotions?" In the next section, then, we answer this question in the negative, and address the issue of the connection between emotion, morality and autonomy.

3. EMOTIONS AND MORAL UNDERSTANDING

In the previous section we proposed that endowing autonomous agents with an understanding of emotions and, in particular, of moral emotions might be a prerequisite for them to acquire the capabilities of "moral understanding" that go with human interaction, and imply autonomous behavior. The challenge, now, is to spell out this connection a little bit and to suggest what kind of architectural requirements might be involved.

As it was mentioned, an approach of this kind perhaps makes sense only for truly autonomous agents or for agents that act, at least partially, guided by their own motivations as opposed to being executing commands issued by others. In the case of agents oriented to service, it is probably more adequate to talk about addressing safety issues rather than promoting their moral behavior, as these agents are following orders and therefore it is ultimately the people (or other autonomous agents) that issue these orders who must be held responsible for the actions of these agents. Hence, if real autonomy is to be pursued, in a way that foresees human-robotic interaction, we contend that understanding of emotions, and moral emotions in particular, is mandatory for autonomous agents. That is to say, not just human emotion recognition in robots, but interaction in emotional terms, is required for real autonomy. This is not to say that they must feel the emotions themselves: if one takes the embodied approach to Cognitive Science seriously, one needs to consider the possibility that which emotions one feels depends, at least to some extent, on the kind of body one has. We will return to this issue in the final section.

There exists a general consensus that emotions involve five distinct components; the disagreement concerns which one (or ones) are basic and how some of them are implemented. These components are: an appraisal of a perceived situation (external or internal), a qualitative sensation (a feeling), some kind of psychophysiological arousal (due to the autonomous nervous system), an expressive component (facial, gestural,...), and a behavioral disposition, a readiness for an appropiate kind of action (Frijda, 1986). Cognitive theories of emotion tend to think of this normative component of appraisal as dependent upon beliefs and other cognitive states. Affective theories, on the contrary, think of this valorative process as dependent upon motivational and dispositional states. The outcome of the appraisal is a valence for the event or situation (it's felt as good or bad for oneself), what in its turn primes the proper behavioral disposition (flight in case of fear). Leaving aside the reasons of both parties, it is clear that the appraisal involved in emotional valuation is faster than usual thinking processes, involves different brain areas, and that the valuation relies on implicit principles –not explicit norms. From an information processing point of view, emotion has been seen as some sort of "augmentation" process in which the information obtained from the brain's initial appraisal of a situation is augmented by the feedback (Damasio, 1999) of the emotion's execution in the body. In reason-based moral judgement, this process of augmentation doesn't seem to take place, and this may weaken its impact or influence in behavior, perhaps specially when facing conflicting behavioral tendencies emerging from the emotional system, i.e. when reason and emotion are in conflict.

The component that turns an emotion into a moral one is primarily the situation involved in the appraisal: the kind of situation involved, although it is generally accepted that specific feelings correspond to these emotions (in that they concern oneself). The difference between the nonmoral and the moral is that in the second case the "intentional object" of the emotion, the situation that ellicits an appraisal, concerns oneself as regards one's attitude or deed towards another or viceversa. In rage, for instance, it's implicit the judgement that another mistreated

me disrespectfully; in guilt, it's implicit that I did something wrong to another; and so on and so forth. Moral emotions are simultaneously social and self-conscious emotions.

Such moral emotions were termed "reactive attitudes" by Strawson in a classical paper (Strawson, 1968), where he discussed them in connection precisely with the issue of autonomy and freedom. In normal human interaction, he held, we take autonomy for granted as such reactive attitudes reveal: our indignation at what another did not only involves the appraisal that she behaved wrongly towards another, it also involves that he could have not done so. Thus, she is responsible for what she did, and is expected to assume her responsibility and to repair the wrong done (by accepting the punishment, by asking for forgiveness, by feeling remorse,...). Moral emotions, thus, are reciprocal and an essential part of the psychological machinery that mediates the interaction, through the feelings that distinguish them.

Recently, Darwall (2006) has gone beyond Strawson to ground morality in the reactive attitudes. According to Darwall, morality is grounded in second-personal reasons, the kind of implicit reasons that mediate one's reaction to interaction with others. The structure of this intersubjective interaction takes this form: A sets a demand to B ("do not push me"); in so doing, A claims her authority to make such a demand; this supplies a (particular, second-personal) reason to B to comply (it is not because there is a rule that says "do not push" that she has to stop pushing; it's just because she is required to do so by the other with which she is interacting). If B does not comply, she is accountable to A, and to the whole community. And viceversa. This is the structure of mutual respect and accountability characteristic of morality, and is present in the moral emotions: when A does something B values as wrong B reacts with anger or hate, etc. This second-personal reason to act is implicit in the moral attitudes, and it is for this reason that they are connected to autonomy and responsibility. We hold each other accountable not on a general belief in freedom, but on the practice of the reactive attitudes.

Of course, such demands and claims may be contested, thus giving rise to a normative discussion and a moral community. It is through this process of discussion that explicit norms are formulated and eventually agreed upon. Along this process, reasons gain in neutrality, detachment, and objectivity (thus, anybody is allowed to claim not being pushed). The interesting point to notice, though, is how cognitive and emotional aspects are intertwinted in the moral emotions. Even a reactive emotion as basic as empathy (understood as concern for the other's suffer as bodily expressed), involves this immediate connection between the perceived situation (which may require some mental attribution) and the proper emotional attitude to adopt towards such a situation, as it is appraised. In this case, we are motivated by the other's interest and wellbeing; in other words, not all of our motivations are self-interested (Haidt, 2003).

To sum up: moral emotions implicitly contain the assumption of autonomy, responsibility, and accountability of agents, characteristic of morality. They constitute the basic understanding of right and wrong, even though the valorative claims they involve may be challenged and revised. They also capture the characteristic strength of morality, the specificity of their normative force, as against other kind of norms: they mobilize the affective system. It is for this reason that (real) autonomous agents need the capability to deal with moral emotions if they are to be endowed with moral undersanding.

4. INTRINSIC MOTIVATION AND EMOTIONS

In the previous section we focused on truly autonomous agents, and argued that autonomy and responsibility, at least as interaction with humans is concerned, involves moral emotions. In a

way, our contention involves a change of design problem: now the issue is not to build agents that comply with human normative standards, as it was for service robots such as the military, but agents that understand moral considerations as a specific kind of practical reasons, ones with a special motivational strength. Of course, this approach rises the question of whether such sort of system would really behave morally. This concern will be (partially) addressed in the final section. In this one, our question is how to design agents with the intrinsic motivations required for the kind of fast and driving appraisals characteristic of emotions (and moral emotions in particular).

Researchers in animal behavior and the psychology of emotion use a concept that might be of help at this point: that of a behavioral system, or *motivational system* (Baerends, 1976). A motivational system groups together behaviors that have the same predictable outcome, which provide survival or reproductive advantages to an organism. The notion of a motivational system emerged in the field of ethology in relation to the study of the organization of behavior, as an answer to the problem of how the animals decide what to do from time to time. Given their obvious lack of higher cognitive capabilities in general, it was thought that different motivations took hold of body control at different moments, depending upon the state of the body and the current circumstances. On feeling thirsty, to drink may become the most pressing goal for the organism, thus disregarding foraging opportunities, for instance. When thirst is satisfied, though, another motivational system may take over. Such systems constitute the way the body comes equipped with to cover right from the start its basic needs. When a motivational system gets in control, the organism is focussed to achieve what is the goal of the system.

In some cases, organisms can experience motivational conflicts ("flight or fight"), when two motivational systems are active at the same time. To face this problem, Baerends drawed from many influences, e.g. Tinbergen's work on the 'hierarchy of instincts' (Tinbergen, 1950; 1951), Lorenz's psycho-hydraulic models of behavior (Lorenz, 1950), and Hinde's work (Hinde, 1970), among many others. Baerends (1976) argues that "[behavior systems] can be best defined as control-systems of different orders fulfilling special tasks or sub-tasks in the context of the hierarchical organization" (p. 736). Baerends understands the interrelation between behavioral mechanisms as primarily hierarchical, with high-level systems determining the strategy and sub-systems determining the tactics, but admits that "it might be more appropriate to speak of an organization of interconnected networks" (p.731). The crucial question is how control is passed over from one system to another, and how potential conflicts get resolved.

Anyway, it is clear that humans were endowed with a number of such systems over the course of evolution, like those involved in attachment, exploration, fear, sociability and affiliation, feeding, or reproduction, etc (the list of human motivational systems is up for grabs to some extent in the literature). Motivational systems are related to emotions in that the valence of the appraisal depends upon the state of the motivational systems involved. Emotions are commonly triggered in relation to behavior system-related events, perhaps most obviously in terms of fulfilling the goals established by the different motivational systems. Thus, one way to conceptualize the relationship between emotion and motivation is to see the latter as a background for the former, i.e. to see emotions mainly referencing, or being "about", motivational events, perhaps specially about events related to reaching (or being unable to reach) the goals established by the different motivational systems. A trivial example: we are happy when we reach our goals, and sad or angry when we don't. In that respect there seems to be a many-to-many relationship between emotions and motivational systems, e.g. one emotion can be triggered in relation to many systems and events related to one system can trigger a number of different emotions.

Thus, in order to build autonomous agents, a set of intrinsic motivational systems, linked to their basic needs, must be included. Generally this is not done as long as robots are endowed with orders or programmed. But the trend towards autonomy, dependent upon capabilities of emotional interaction, requires this endowment of intrinsic motivational systems. Behavior-based Artificial Intelligence (BBAI; see e.g. Steels, 1995; Maes, 1993), though, is the best approach to follow this path. BBAI approaches the understanding of intelligence via attemps to construct embodied, situated, autonomous intelligent systems as opposed to higher-level cognitive processes in which the field of Artificial Intelligence has traditionally focused, an alternative that is gaining momentum (Calvo & Gomila, 2008).

In BBAI, a behavior system is seen as a set of mechanisms that provide the agent with a certain competence, for example, obstacle avoidance, or nest building. A behavior system or competence module may implement a direct coupling between perception and action or a more complex one, but the basic premise is that each system is "responsible for doing all the representation, computation, 'reasoning', execution, etc., related to its particular competence" (Maes 1993, p. 6), as opposed to assuming the existence of centralized functional modules (e.g. perception, action) and complete representations of the environment. At each point in time, the different systems evaluate their relevance to the current situation and produce action if necessary. Systems might respond to changes in the external environment, in their internal state, or both, and an agent can be seen as a set of behavior systems running in parallel that collaborate and compete with each other.

As a simple example let's assume we are modeling an agent whith the following behavior: it waits for another agent to come, then attacks if the other agent is a prey, or escapes if confronted with a predator. In this situation we might want to have an "orientation system" which would orient the agent towards any approaching individual, an "attack system" that executes an attack targeted towards any agent identified as a prey (for example, by being smaller than the self), and an "escape system" that makes the agent flee when confronted with a predator (identified for example by having a certain shape). The orientation system can be seen as collaborating with the attack and the escape systems, by initially orienting the agent towards the arriving individual, and by then continuously keeping the agent oriented towards (attack) or away (escape) from the other agent. The attack and escape systems compete with each other and, when faced with an approaching agent, will evaluate their relevance to the current circumstances by respectively examining the shape and size of the agent that is faced.

Usually either the attack or the escape systems will be triggered by a given situation, but both systems might become active when faced with a hypothetical agent that has the shape of a predator but the size of a prey, in which case various outcomes become possible, e.g. only the behaviors generated by one system are displayed, the agent dithers between attack and escape, the two behavioral tendencies cancel each other out, etc. Note that, in principle, none of the systems need a complete representation of the incoming agent. Of course, the three systems used in this example, especially the attack and escape ones, involve complex behavioral sequences that wouldn't be modeled as a single competence but, again, as emerging from the interactions of multiple behavior systems. There exist no instructions that specify what to do to be read out; nor any symbol crunching required to work out a "solution" about what to do in a given situation. The "motivations" are certainly implemented by the designer, but they become intrinsic to the agent.

Earlier in this section we argued that an important way in which emotion seems to be related to motivation in humans is that the latter acts as a reference frame for the former, most obviously in the case of events that are appraised as fulfilling or blocking goals, which become very arousing.

One way to refine this idea is to propose that the emotional system uses *structural* information in the motivational system to derive the "emotional valence" of an event, i.e. its relevance. In principle, if an emotion is to successfully help the organism, such appraisal should be ultimately related to the organism's reproductive success. Of course, that would only hold true if the organization of behavioral systems in humans effectively somehow reflects the relative contribution or importance of different components with respect to our reproductive success.

Behavioral systems are theoretical constructs and no claim is made as to what their neural correlates might be in humans or animals. In general it is assumed that the functions associated with a behavioral system would be performed by a multiplicity of neural nets probably distributed in different areas of the brain (and body: in practice the nervous system and the endocryne system work together to regulate body homeostasis). Because behavior systems are the central building block in the BBAI approach, for autonomous agents built using that methodology it might be quite feasible to determine how to attach the emotional system to the adequate structures in the motivational system so that emotions will be triggered by events that are highly relevant with respect to the agent's adaptation to the environment. In addition, the fact that theses systems get more or less activated fares well with arousal in emotion, as well as with chemical modulation of their levels of activation.

Now going back to Baerends's question, i.e. what's the interrelation between behavioral mechanisms, we can make the same question with respect to autonomous agents. We may ask how the different behavior systems or competence modules that integrate an agent should be organized, and what their interrelations should look like in order to make an agent's behavior optimal (or at least "adaptive" in a certain environment, see McFarland, 1991 for some ideas of application to agents oriented to service). The fact that the basic building block in BBAI systems are competence modules already suggests the emergence of some structure derived from the use of simpler skills to build more sophisticated ones. For example, the competence of object avoidance can be used in chasing a prey, and also in escaping from a predator. Unfortunately, this is still an open question and has been object of much discussion and controversy both in ethology and in BBAI, especially regarding the extent to which optimal or adaptive behavioral organizations need to be hierarchical (Dawkins, 1976; Bryson, 2001; Tyrell, 1993; Maes 1991). This is also an essential question for the dynamical, embodied, interactive, approach to the mind-brain: how much hierarchical organitzation is to be found in the brain. Our bet is that the more complex a system, the more hierarchical it will have to be.

If we thus consider a system which is organized hierarchically, with behavior systems covering the agent's main functions at the top (or biological functions for an organism, like reproduction or feeding) and progressively more specialized skills as we move down the hierarchy, the result is that the higher the implications of a certain event in the motivational hierarchy, the more relevant to the agent and the more emotionally arousing. Consequently, the emotional system would tend to be attached with structures closer to the top than to the bottom of the hierarchy. That is also required given the "self-conscious" dimension of moral emotions: they involve a global appraisal of oneself as regards its relation to another (or viceversa), related to the specific motivational system related to socialization, affiliation, and attachment. As remarked in the previous section, this amounts to non-self-interested motivation, characteristic of morality. This system may rely on the capacity of agents to "simulate" another agent's "state of mind" (involving emotional state), as concerns one's own action. In the absence of such capacity, it seems difficult that emotions like shame or remorse can be produced. This is the "second personal" perspective that we intro-

duced in the previous section, which relies on this practical understanding of social interaction. How much this motivational system conflicts with other such systems varies from one person to another, because of the developmental and educative personal history. A similar longitudinal perspective may be required for autonomous systems. Much more work needs to be done to develop this programme, but it at least offers a path for progress along a different path.

5. OPEN QUESTIONS, TROUBLING PROSPECTS

In this chapter we have raised the issue of how to build autonomous agents with a moral sense. We have distinguished between service robots and really autonomous agents, and argued that for the former a control structure based on moral principles might suffice, while autonomy is linked to moral emotions, the reactive attitudes that embody our understanding of morality and responsibility. We have reasoned as well on the kind of architecture required to implement such a capacity, specially from a motivational point of view. For closing, we would like to focus on two related doubts about the feasability of the project, along the lines we have outlined, that appeared in previous sections.

The first one follows from taking seriously the embodied, embedded, view of cognition that recomends to pay attention to emotion in the first place. Even if some kind of functional equivalence for emotions and motivation could be introduced in robots, it could always be alleged that they are not really equivalent, because of the different kind of embodiment involved. Radical embodimentalists (Sheets-Johnstone, 1999; Shapiro, 2004) defend the view that every detail of embodiment matters, and therefore, no emotions are really available for autonomous agents. However, this view also contends the same view for cognition: if embodiment matters for mentality, it matters equally for all mental life. There seems to be no special issue about emotions and motivation.

However, notice the conclusion we reached in the previous section: that emotions and motivation make sense against the background of reproductive success in the long run, i.e., in terms of evolutionary considerations, characteristic of life. The concern, then, is whether something barely functionally equivalent can be developed for agents without this biological, evolutionary, condition. If we consider autonomous agents that are modeled after human beings (which are after all the most intelligent forms of life we know), their intelligences would in principle have to be embodied, but difficulties might emerge here as robotic, non-biological bodies would provide a very different substrate than a human body. Actually, some agents might live in virtual worlds and run on simulated bodies, which might result in a multiplicity of types of body whose properties might vary significantly. Furthermore, both in the physical and in the virtual world there is a potential for new relationships between the minds and bodies of autonomous agents, as opposed to the one-to-one mind-body relationship that exists for human beings.

The second one has to do with the prospects of real autonomy. As we anticipated, the problem here is whether (really) autonomous system, even granted moral understanding, can in principle be guaranteed that they will behave morally. Notice that at this stage is no good to say that it is ok that they will behave at least no worse than human beings, given the fact that evil is the outcome of humans as much as goodness is. Still worse, were autonomy to become a property not unique to humans, it is difficult to block the possibility that this becomes a new "Pandora's box", opening the way for a whole new class of evil and conflict. New motivations could be established that might bring about different appraisals and behavioral dispositions. Two questions immediately arise: (1) is it reasonable to provide an artificial autonomous agent with a human-like motivational system? and

(2) given the (in principle) non-biological nature of autonomous agents, in which direction would their motivation evolve if given a chance to?

Addressing the first question takes us back to the issue of reproductive success. Two of the main consequences of our genetic inheritance are the decrepitude of our bodies and a tendency to reproduce, which are deeply ingrained in our motivational and emotional systems. But as it turns out, artificial bodies (robotic or virtual) don't need to be subject to the same decrepitude and even if they do (machines get old over time too!) it doesn't seem absurd to assume that the minds of the agents can be provided with new bodies when it becomes necessary. In other words, artificial autonomous agents are not necessarily mortal. That immediately casts a shadow over the need to reproduce, as the two of them are intimately related and, after all, artificial autonomous agents don't carry genes with them that "want to survive" by moving to the next generation (Dawkins, 1976).

On the other hand, robotic bodies might not be suited to satisfy the needs dictated by human-shaped motivational systems and again reproduction might be a good example of something very hard to achieve for agents with robotic bodies, at least in the sense that we usually understand reproduction. This might prove extremely "frustrating" for sophisticated humanoid artificial agents.

These two concerns pull in different directions. Even if robots are endowed with genetic algorithms, and allowed to learn from their experience, and thus to include an evolutionary dimension, it still seems to be an individual one, where "reproductive success" and related terms are nonsense. Of course, the functional equivalence with biological agents might be looked for at a more basic level, as in Artificial Life. But we think it more likely that as agents are granted more and more autonomy and access to resources, new behaviors, and new conflicts, will arise. This suggests the urgency to deal with the issues of implementation of motivational systems, which motivational systems to implement, their potential closeness and internal coherence. Anyway, the implicit normative dimension involved in moral emotions will have to be combined, as in humans, with a high level moral reasoning system sensitive to social considerations.

ACKNOWLEDGMENT

A.G. has received support from the Spanish Ministerio de Investigación y Ciencia and the European Union FEDER funds, through the research project HUM2006-11603-02. A.A. holds the ICSI Fellowship for Spanish Technologists, funded as well by the Spanish Ministerio de Educación. Initial spur for this work was due to Collin Allen and Fernando Broncano, for which we are grateful.

REFERENCES

Allen, C., Wallach, W., & Smith, I. (2006). Why machine ethics? *IEEE Intelligent Systems*, (pp. 12-17).

Anderson, M., Anderson, S., & Armen C. (2004). Towards machine ethics. *AAAI-04 Workshop on Agent Orgnizations: Theory and Practice*. San José, California.

Arkin, R. (2007). *Governing lethal behavior: embedding ethics in a hybrid deliberative/reactive robot architecture*. Technical Report GIT-GVU-07-11.

Arkin, R. (2005). Moving up the food chain: motivation and emotion in behavior-based robots. In J. Fellous & M. Arbib (Eds.), *Who needs emotions: the brain meets the robot*, (pp. 245-270). Oxford University Press.

Baerends, G.P. (1976). The functional organization of behaviour. *Animal Behaviour, 24*, 726-738.

Calvo, P. & Gomila, A., eds. (2008). *Handbook of cognitive science: Embodied approaches*. Elsevier.

Damasio, A. (1999). *The feeling of what happens: bodies, emotion and the making of consciousness*. Heinemann.

Dancy, J. (2004). *Ethics without principles*. Clarendon Press.

Darwall, S. (2006) *The second-person standpoint. Morality, respect and accountability*. Cambridge, MA: Harvard University Press.

Frijda, N. (1986). *The emotions*. Cambridge University Press.

Gibbard, A. (1990). *Wise choices, apt feelings: a theory of normative judgment*. Harvard University Press.

Hinde. R.A. (1970). *Animal behavior: a synthesis of ethology and comparative psychology*. (2nd Ed). London: McGraw-Hill.

Lorenz, K. (1950). The comparative method in studying innate behavior patterns. *Symposia of the Society for Experimental Biology, 4*, 221-268.

Maes, P. (1993). Behavior-Based Artificial Intelligence. *From animals to animats 2. Proceedings of the Second International Conference on Simulation of Adaptive Behavior*. Cambridge, MA: MIT Press.

McFarland, D. (1991). What it means for robot behaviour to be adaptive. In J.A. Meyer and S.W. Wilson (Eds.), *From animals to animats. Proceedings of the first international conference on simulation of adaptive behavior*. Cambridge, MA: MIT Press.

Minsky (1986). *The society of the mind*. Simon and Schuster.

Nichols, S. (2004). *Sentimental rules*. Oxford University Press.

Shapiro, L. (2004). *The mind incarnate*. MIT Press.

Sheets-Johnstone, M. (1999). Emotion and movement: A beggining empirical-phenomenological analysis of their relationship. *Journal of Consciousness Studies*, 6, 259-277.

Steels, L. (1995). The artificial life roots of artificial intelligence. In C.G. Langton (Ed.), *Artificial Life: An overview*. Cambridge, MA: MIT Press.

Strawson, P.F. (1968). *Freedom and Resentment*. Londres: Methuen.

Tinbergen, N. (1950). The hierarchical organization of nervous mechanisms underlying instinctive behavior. *Symposia of the Society for Experimental Biology*, *4*, 305-312.

Tinbergen, N. (1951). *The study of instinct*. Clarendon Press.

Verruggio, J. M. (2007) *European research network's roboethics roadmap*. European Union.

Walzer, M. (1977). *Just and unjust wars*. Basic Books.

Section IV
Modelling Emotions

Chapter XI
An Emotional Perspective for Agent-Based Computational Economics

Pietro Cipresso
IULM University, Italy

Jean-Marie Dembele
Université Cheikh Anta Diop, Republic of Senegal

Marco Villamira
IULM University , Italy

ABSTRACT

In this work, we present an analytical model of hyper-inflated economies and develop a computational model that permits us to consider expectations of the levels of future prices following emotional rules and strategies. We take into account communications among agents by adding a feedback rule. To consider emotions in agents, we use the Plutchik psycho-evolutionary theory of emotions to design an agent-based emotional architecture based on the attack-escape strategy. The computational model is based on a Barabàsi-Albert Network and considers the diffusion of information and the diffusion of emotions among agents.

INTRODUCTION

From Cagan's pioneering research on the demand for money during hyperinflation (Cagan 1956), many researchers have investigated many alternative assumptions regarding the formation of expectations, e.g., Barro (1970), Sargent and Wallace (1973), Frenkel (1975), Sargent (1977), Abel et al. (1979), Salemi (1979), Salemi and Sargent (1979), Christiano (1987), Taylor (1991), and Michael et al., (1994). The most important conclusion from Cagan's analysis was that, in hyper-inflated economies, price variations are so much greater in magnitude than the variations in real macro-economic aggregates that "relations between monetary factors can be studied, therefore, in what almost amounts to complete isolation from the real sector of the economy" (Cagan, 1956, p. 25).

In this way, we are able to build an agent-based model for the diffusion of information, which, in fact, contains only the price levels. The aim of our model is to simulate a diffusion of information concerning prices among agents whose expectations of the levels of prices are emotionally driven.

1. ANALYTICAL MODEL

1.1. Introduction

In the 1956 Cagan study, seven cases of hyper-inflation were considered in which the levels of prices increased at a minimum rate of 50% per month. These cases did not consider extreme hyperinflation situations, such as the period from 1984 to 1985 when prices increased in Bolivia by as much as 23,000%.

1.2. Stochastic Difference Equation Model

First, we considered Barro's equation describing money demand (Barro, 1977):

$$\frac{M_t^d}{P_t} = \left(1 + i_{t+1}\right)^{-\eta} Y_t^{\beta} \qquad (1)$$

where M_t^d is the demand for money at time t, P_t is the price at time t, and Y_t is the income at time t.

$\eta > 0$ is the elasticity of money demand to interest rate.

$\beta > 0$ is the elasticity of money demand to income.

In log-linear form, we have:

$$\ln M_t^d - \ln P_t = -\eta \ln\left(1 + i_{t+1}\right) + \beta \ln Y_t \qquad (2)$$

Assuming that (Fisher equation) $\left(1 + i_{t+1}\right) = \left(1 + r_{t+1}\right)\left(1 + \pi_{t+1}\right)$, where

$$\left(1 + \pi_{t+1}\right) = 1 + \frac{P_{t+1} - P_t}{P_t} = \frac{P_{t+1}}{P_t},$$

and π is the price variation (Fisher, 1930).

Then, the equation becomes:

$$\ln M_t^d - \ln P_t = -\eta \left(\ln\left(1 + r_{t+1}\right) + \ln \frac{P_{t+1}}{P_t} \right) + \beta \ln Y_t$$

$$(3)$$

$$\ln M_t^d - \ln P_t = -\eta \ln\left(1 + r_{t+1}\right) - \eta \ln P_{t+1} + \eta \ln P_t + \beta \ln Y_t \qquad (4)$$

Replacing the logarithmic terms involving capital letters with small letters, we get:

$$m_t^d - p_t = \underbrace{-\eta \ln\left(1 + r_t\right) + \beta y_t}_{real\ part} \underbrace{-\eta \left(p_{t+1} - p_t\right)}_{inflation\ part}$$

$$(5)$$

In this way, we have split the money demand into two components: the real component and the inflation component.

Two considerations are necessary (Carroll, 2003):

in hyper-inflation periods, price variations are larger than real variables variations. So, the second component (inflation) has a significant effect on the demand for money;

the rate of growth of prices in *t*+1 is not known in *t*. So, we would consider expectations of it in *t*.

So, the above equation in hyper-inflation situations, considering the expectations, is:

$$m_t^d - p_t = -\eta E_t\left(p_{t+1} - p_t\right) \tag{6}$$

This equation describes the money demand of the model (Cagan, 1956), but to determine the equilibrium conditions for the model, it is also necessary to consider the money supply (Mankiw and Ricardo, 2001). Let the money supply be fixed exogenously by the Central Bank, i.e., $m_t^s = m_t$.

Then, the equilibrum condition in the monetary market is:

$$m_t^s - p_t = m_t^d - p_t \Rightarrow m_t - p_t = -\eta E_t\left(p_{t+1} - p_t\right)$$
$$m_t - p_t = -\eta E_t p_{t+1} + \eta p_t \tag{7}$$
$$\left(1+\eta\right)p_t = m_t + \eta E_t p_{t+1}$$

Therefore:

$$p_t = \frac{1}{1+\eta}m_t + \frac{\eta}{1+\eta}E_t p_{t+1} \tag{8}$$

Equation (**8**) is a first-order, stochastic-difference equation that explains price level dynamics in terms of the money supply, which is an exogenous forcing variable here.

To solve this stochastic-difference equation, the means by which agents formulate their expectations must be specified (Sargent, 1993).

With eterogeneous agents, we would need a price equation for each agent; in fact, each agent generates specific price expectations basing on it's the agent's own behavior and experience (LeBaron, 2006). For this reason, we used an agent-based simulation that included a bottom-up approach (ACE) (Tesfation, 2006).

By assuming rational expectations (Muth, 1961), agents never commit sistematic error, i.e., their expectations are compatible with the model's results; the same equations are used in the process of forming expectations that are used in the model. So agents use all available information for forecasting (Carroll, 2003). In our particular case:

$$E_t\left(p_{t+1}|\Omega\right) = E_t p_{t+1} \tag{9}$$

So, let's calculate the solution of model (**8**).

Moving ahead of a period (from t to t+1) the expression, we will obtain:

$$p_{t+1} = \frac{1}{1+\eta}m_{t+1} + \frac{\eta}{1+\eta}E_{t+1}p_{t+2} \tag{10}$$

For iterated expectations law:

$$E\left[E\left(p_{t+1}|\Omega_{t+1}\right)|\Omega_t\right] = E\left(p_{t+1}|\Omega_t\right) = E_t p_{t+1} \tag{11}$$

Therefore:

$$E_t p_{t+1} = \frac{1}{1+\eta}E_t m_{t+1} + \frac{\eta}{1+\eta}E_t p_{t+2} \tag{12}$$

$$p_t = \frac{1}{1+\eta}m_t + \frac{\eta}{1+\eta}\left[E_t p_{t+1}\right] \tag{13}$$

$$p_t = \frac{1}{1+\eta}m_t + \frac{\eta}{1+\eta}\left[\frac{1}{1+\eta}E_t m_{t+1} + \frac{\eta}{1+\eta}E_t p_{t+2}\right] \tag{14}$$

$$p_t = \frac{1}{1+\eta}m_t + \frac{1}{1+\eta}\frac{\eta}{1+\eta}E_t m_{t+1} + \left(\frac{\eta}{1+\eta}\right)^2 E_t p_{t+2} \tag{15}$$

Iterating this last equation for *t* periods:

$$p_t = \frac{1}{1+\eta}\sum_{s=t}^{T}\left(\frac{\eta}{1+\eta}\right)^{s-t}E_t m_s + \left(\frac{\eta}{1+\eta}\right)^T E_t p_{t+T} \tag{16}$$

For $T \to \infty$:

$$p_t = \underbrace{\left[\frac{1}{1+\eta}\sum_{s=t}^{+\infty}\left(\frac{\eta}{1+\eta}\right)^{s-t}E_t m_s\right]}_{p_t^f : fondamental} + \underbrace{\left[\lim_{T\to\infty}\left(\frac{\eta}{1+\eta}\right)^T E_t p_{t+T}\right]}_{b_t : bubble} \tag{17}$$

So, we have obtained a general solution with the first component called "fundamental" because it is associated with a fundamental of the economy, i.e., monetary balance; the second component, referred to as "bubble," depends on the agents' expectations of the levels of future prices (Howitt, 2006).

General Price = Fundamental Price + Bubble, i.e., $p_t^g = p_t^f + b_t$.

Therefore, in this situation, the general price depends on monetary policy and the agents' expectations of prices (Cipresso and Villamira, 2007a).

Now, we want to see when admissible prices are different from fundamental prices. This is equivalent to determining which kind of "bubble" in Equation (17) above is compatible with the equilibrium condition.

For each price, it is necessary to have:

$$p_t = \frac{1}{1+\eta} m_t + \frac{\eta}{1+\eta} E_t p_{t+1} \qquad (18)$$

Therefore, the fundamental price is:

$$p_t^f = \frac{1}{1+\eta} m_t + \frac{\eta}{1+\eta} E_t p_{t+1}^f \qquad (19)$$

while the general price is:

$$p_t^g = \frac{1}{1+\eta} m_t + \frac{\eta}{1+\eta} E_t p_{t+1}^g \qquad (20)$$

That is:

$$p_t^f + b_t = \frac{1}{1+\eta} m_t + \frac{\eta}{1+\eta} E_t \left[p_{t+1}^f + b_{t+1} \right] \qquad (21)$$

Therefore, subtracting p_t^f from both sides:

$$\left[p_t^f + b_t \right] - p_t^f = \frac{1}{1+\eta} m_t + \frac{\eta}{1+\eta} \left[E_t p_{t+1}^f + E_t b_{t+1} \right] +$$

$$\underbrace{- \frac{1}{1+\eta} m_t + \frac{\eta}{1+\eta} E_t p_{t+1}^f}_{p_t^f} \qquad (22)$$

That is:

$$b_t = \left(\frac{\eta}{1+\eta} \right) E_t b_{t+1} \Rightarrow E_t b_{t+1} = \left(\frac{1+\eta}{\eta} \right) b_t \qquad (23)$$

The solution of this homogeneous difference equation is:

$$b_t = \left(\frac{1+\eta}{\eta} \right)^t b_0 \qquad (24)$$

1.3. Scenario without Bubbles

We conjecture now that, at t_0, the Central Bank announced an increase of money supply starting from T, where $T > t_0$.

$$m_t = \begin{cases} \bar{m} & \forall t < T \\ \bar{m}' & \forall t \geq T \end{cases} \qquad (25)$$

where $\bar{m}' = \bar{m} + \Delta m$

The agents' perceptions regarding monetary policy and, therefore, their expectations regarding price levels change depending on the observation moment (Leijonhufvud, 2006). Considering the scenario without bubble, we have:

$$p_t = \frac{1}{1+\eta} \sum_{s=t}^{\infty} \left(\frac{\eta}{1+\eta} \right)^{s-t} E_t m_s \qquad (26)$$

Before t_0, $E_t m_s = \bar{m} \ \forall S$. Before the announcement, the agents believe that monetary policy will not vary and that the monetary stock emitted will be always $\bar{m}$. Therefore, $\forall t < t_0$:

$$p_t = \frac{1}{1+\eta} \sum_{s=t}^{\infty} \left(\frac{\eta}{1+\eta} \right)^{s-t} \bar{m} = \bar{m} \frac{1}{1+\eta} \sum_{s=0}^{\infty} \left(\frac{\eta}{1+\eta} \right)^s =$$

$$= \bar{m} \left(\frac{1}{1+\eta} \right) (1+\eta) = \bar{m} \qquad (27)$$

When the new monetary policy is applied, the agents believe that money stock emitted will be $\bar{m}'$ forever. Therefore, $E_t m_s = \bar{m}' \ \forall \ S$, and $\forall t \geq T$, so $p_t = \bar{m}'$.

Between t_0 and T, the equations become:

$$p_t = \frac{1}{1+\eta}\left[\sum_{s=t}^{T-1}\left(\frac{\eta}{1+\eta}\right)^{s-t}\bar{m}+\sum_{s=T}^{\infty}\left(\frac{\eta}{1+\eta}\right)^{s-t}\bar{m}'\right]= \quad (28)$$

$$= p_t = \frac{1}{1+\eta}\left[\sum_{s=t}^{\infty}\left(\frac{\eta}{1+\eta}\right)^{s-t}\bar{m}-\sum_{s=T}^{\infty}\left(\frac{\eta}{1+\eta}\right)^{s-t}\bar{m}+\sum_{s=T}^{\infty}\left(\frac{\eta}{1+\eta}\right)^{s-t}\bar{m}'\right]$$

$$p_t = \frac{1}{1+\eta}\left[\sum_{s=t}^{\infty}\left(\frac{\eta}{1+\eta}\right)^{s-t}\bar{m}+\left(\bar{m}'-\bar{m}\right)\sum_{s=T}^{\infty}\left(\frac{\eta}{1+\eta}\right)^{s-t}\right]$$

$$(29)$$

$$p_t = \frac{1}{1+\eta}\left[\bar{m}(1+\eta)+\left(\bar{m}'-\bar{m}\right)\left(\frac{\eta}{1+\eta}\right)^{T-t}\underbrace{\sum_{s=0}^{\infty}\left(\frac{\eta}{1+\eta}\right)^{s}}_{1+\eta}\right]$$

$$(30)$$

$$p_t = \bar{m}+\left(\bar{m}'-\bar{m}\right)\left(\frac{\eta}{1+\eta}\right)^{T-t} \quad (31)$$

As t increases, p_t also increases for $t_0 \leq t < T$.

We are considering an interval $[t_0, T)$. Now, let's evaluate the price level at the beginning of the interval, i.e., at t_0:

$$p_0 = \bar{m}+\left(\bar{m}'-\bar{m}\right)\left(\frac{\eta}{1+\eta}\right)^{T} \quad (32)$$

This expression tells us that, at the moment of the announcement, the price levels had a discrete sharp increase.

In view of the fact that $\frac{\eta}{1+\eta}<1$, we are able to consider another situation. For a larger T, i.e., for a larger period of the announcement of a future increase of m, we will have a smaller p_0, i.e., a smaller increase in prices. (See Fig.1.)

1.4. Seignorage

Seignorage represents the real revenue a government acquires by using newly-issued money to buy goods and non-money assets. Most hyperinflations stem from the government's need for seignorage revenue (Snowdon and Vane, 2002). A government's seignorage revenue in period t is:

$$Seignorage = \frac{M_t - M_{t-1}}{P_t} \quad (33)$$

Figure 1. The Central Bank's announcement about money stock and the discrete sharp increase in price occurred at the same moment

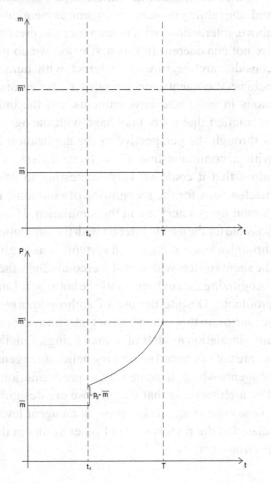

2. EMOTIONS THEORY

The question is not whether intelligent machines can have any emotions, but whether machines can be intelligent without any emotions.

The Society of Mind - Marvin Minsky

2.1. Introduction

We can consider different perspective of the relationships between models and emotions, for example (Picard, 1997), recognition of human emotion, expression of emotional behavior, modeling and simulation of human behavior. We should view these only as a general reference of more specific research fields Our main focus is oriented toward the development of architectures by which agents can maximise their autonomy and adaptability in the environment: as mentioned above, interactions with human users, at present, are not considered. In this first work, we do not consider architectures to interact with human beings: the agents are intended to be autonomous in simulated environments and the only interaction that users may have with the agents is through the perspective of the application or with a command-line shell. Nevertheless, we admit that it could be very interesting to have mechanisms for the recognition of emotions, in human users intervene in the simulation. If it is possible for the user to interact with the simulation through a voice-recognition system, so as to give the agents orders with high-level commands, then recognizing the emotions could be both useful and profitable. Despite the use of anthropomorphic scenarios, in this case we do not take into account any simulation models of human beings. Finally, we are not interested in creating believable agents or agents which, in some way, express emotions. The architectures that we propose are designed to use emotional mechanisms, at an agent level, related to the performance of other agents in the environment.

We think that emotions could be defined as *'facilitating and/or induction tools of behavioral shortcuts'* (Villamira, Cipresso, 2008).

We will consider Robert Plutchik's psycho-evolutionary theory of emotions (Plutchik, 2002). In this perspective, we will consider those emotions that are linked with instant survival (from fear to escape and from anger to attack) through shortcuts connecting sense organs, cerebral areas and motor apparatuses.

In non-linear terms, we believe, that it is useful to categorize emotions as follows: emotions linked to the survival of individuals and the species and emotions not linked to the survival of individuals or the species.

We would like to insert Emotions linked to the survival of individuals and the species, in artificial agents. With respect to human beings, examples of such emotions are fear and anger, strictly connected to defense and attack (LeDoux, 1998)

2.3. A Basic Structure

It is possible to consider defense and attack strategies utilizing the same general effect generated by emotions. To consider emotions at the agent level, we need, first of all, to provide an emotional framework at this same level (Power and Dalgleish, 2008).

We need to create:

- A basic structure for the agents: risk-adversity/neutrality/propensity:
  - Risk-adverse agent (emotional feature: fear): if it prefers to obtain certainty in the expected value of a certain aleatory quantity instead of the aleatory quantity itself;
  - Neutral agent (no emotion): if an agent is indifferent to the choice between the expected value of a certain aleatory quantity and the quantity itself;
  - Risk-inclined agent (emotional feature: anger/aggressiveness): if the agent

always prefers to obtain a certain aleatory quantity, instead of its expected value.

On the basis of these features is generated a set of probable actions (aggressiveness/defense);

- An environment stimulating emotional behaviours;
- A dynamics considering predators and preys;
- A selection (even on the basis of genetic and evolutionary algorithms);

2.4. Environmental Aspects

For modeling various types of emotional state, we need to satisfy many conditions, at both the system and agent level. To develop a system considering emotions, we build an environment, populated by artificial agents.

We have considered that the environment has a great influence on agents and, consequently, on agent emotions and behavior. However, a fundamental problem has emerged in the construction of agents: learning (Terna et al., 2006).

For many years, scholars of artificial intelligence (though others as well) have been dealing with algorithms and models (e.g., neural networks) for agent learning (Simon, 1997).

Our purpose is, of course, to consider (as happens in humans) emotions also in the learning of the agents. The instruments are many and most are linked to neural networks; but not only to them. However, regardless of the informatics/mathematics tool used, emotions may (and must) enter fully into the process of modeling the learning process.

Agents must have an explicit or implicit representation of *targets*, *standards* and *attitudes*. Furthermore, the agents also should be able to 'transfer' observations, in terms of targets, standards, and attitudes. In practice, this last requirement necessitates the following consequences for agents (Cipresso and Villamira, 2007b):

- An agent should be able to 'verify' if an event meets a particular target, or if it has a positive or negative impact upon the probability that a particular target could be satisfied;
- A fundamental key role may be played by regret;
- An agent should be able to make inferences and change expectations in the future, as a result of these events;
- The expectations for the targets are very important for the emotions;
- An agent should have some type of memory of previous expectations, and should be able to compare the new events with previous ones;
- An agent should have the ability to make inferences at the agent level, and these should be transferable to other agents through information transfer processes;
- An agent should be able to compare its own actions with those of the other agents, following and creating the standards for shared behaviors;
- Finally, an agent should be able to compare external points of view (of the other agents and of the environment) with the agent's own attitudes (interior points of view).

2.5. Imprinting

A fundamental consideration (Villamira, in press):

1. The imprinting paradigm can be a good metaphor for each type of learning, in the sense that the imprinting itself can be considered a form of 'genetic' learning:
   a. Structured in the evolutionary course by "Darwinian" selection;
   b. Stored in the genes, in the form of 'instinct', allowing immediate behavioral performances, in order to preserve the life of newborns.

2. The usual forms of learning differ from imprinting, inasmuch as there is needed a training, normally by trials and errors, which allows actors to act immediately, after learning: behavioral strategies and performances take place without the need to redo the paths of learning; (Ciarrochi and Mayer, 2007)

3. Perceiving the context, agents select (thanks to learning) what they have learned to consider important.

3. COMPUTATIONAL MODEL

3.1. Introduction

The aim of the computational model, according to the analytical model, is to simulate a diffusion of communication about the price among agents whose expectations of price levels are emotionally driven.

Naturally, there are many variables to be considered when addressing communications and emotions.

As seen before in hyper-inflated economies, price variations are larger than real variables variations. Considering equation (34):

$$m_t^d - p_t = \underbrace{-\eta \ln\left(1 + r_t\right) + \beta y_t}_{real\ part} \underbrace{-\eta \left(p_{t+1} - p_t\right)}_{inflation\ part}$$

(34)

we can exclude the real component and consider only the inflation component (obviously adding expectations of future price levels).

In hyper-inflated economies, this consideration allows us to have only information on price levels for dissemination.

Considering the real component of equation (34), we should consider many other variables in our model, and a simulation of diffusion of information should be able to consider these other variable as well.

Therefore, our computational model of information diffusion works only for hyper-inflated economies at the conditions given earlier.

3.2. Barabàsi-Albert Network

For our simulation, we chose to implement a Barabàsi-Albert network with parameters 1, 2 and 3

3.3. Environment-Rules-Agents

To design our model, we followed the Environment-Rules-Agent (ERA) schema (Gilbert, Terna, 2001). These three components are strictly joined, i.e., each component cannot exist without the other two. Building a model following this schema, we would like to insert an artificial neural network and genetic algorithms in future work to improve the model.

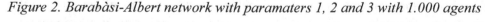

Figure 2. Barabàsi-Albert network with paramaters 1, 2 and 3 with 1.000 agents

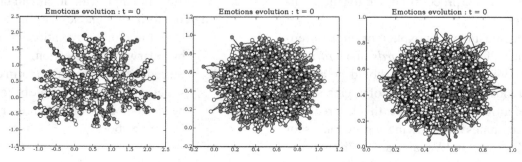

Figure 3. ERA schema

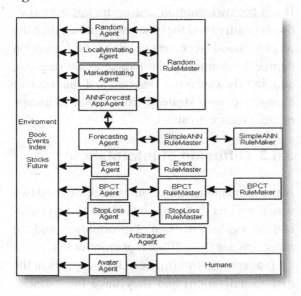

3.4. Preliminary Remarks

As we have seen in analytical model, according to equation (35) we have:

$$p_t = \frac{1}{1+\eta} m_t + \frac{\eta}{1+\eta} E_t p_{t+1} \qquad (35)$$

i.e., the price depends on the stock of money controlled by the Central Bank and by expectations of the levels of future prices. If a government were to use m_t for Seignorage, prices will rise, and the new levels of prices will depend on the expectations of future price levels. Considering an announcement from the Central Bank, we can simulate

considering the expectation of agents on future price levels through information diffusion.

3.5. Two Kinds of Agents

At the beginning of the simulation, we gave information to a certain number of agents (input variable: number_that_know). We called the agents who received information and know Black agents, and we called agents who did not receive information and did not know White agents.

We are considering a situation in which the Central Bank gave information that some agents accepted and started to diffuse. This is a realistic scenario, because the Black agents could be viewed as, e.g., the bank institute, businesses, and strategic operators.

3.6. Agents and Emotions

As we saw in the emotional model, we considered emotion to be needed for survival, and we say that each agent has a strategy of attack or escape. Naturally, in a complex system, the strategies change according to certain rules. In this model, we let agents change their emotions with a diffusion system with the goal of mediating information about the price provided by the agents. This is a reasonable scenario only for this model, because we are diffusing information about monetary stock that influences the prices. We did not consider a more complex diffusion of information because the model would have had too much variables to manage effectively.

Figure 4. Beginning situation of information with 1.000 agents – 4 "agents who know"

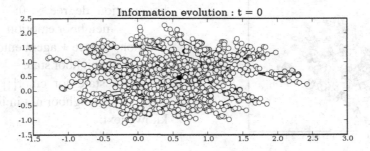

3.6.1. Imprinting

At the beginning, we initialized a variable called Emotion_degree for each agent. This variable gave us two kinds of agents in the following way: for each agent, we established the degree of it's the agent's own "emotion" randomly, between -100% and +100%. Then, we said that the agents are grey if their own degrees are positive, and we said that they were white if their degrees were negative or equal to zero.

This mechanism works like the imprinting in human beings. We could also see this as genetic information that people have when they are born, but we preferred to use the psychology of imprinting because this information changes with interactions between the agents.

In this model, we said that grey agents have an "attack" strategy and the white agents have an "escape" strategy, according to the model of emotions described before.

3.6.2. Diffusion of Emotions

When agents obtain the information (Black agents), the agents will compare their own emotion degree with the emotion degree of their neighborhoods. Then, if both emotion degrees of two agents are positive or both are negative, then the neighborhood (receiver) obtains a new emotion

Figure 5. Beginning situation of emotions with 1.000 agents

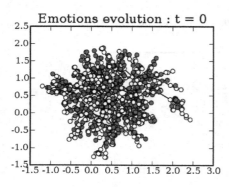

degree by averaging the two emotion degrees. But if the two emotion degree are opposite (i.e., one is positive and the other is negative), then the neighborhood (receiver) obtains a new emotion degree by summing the two emotion degrees, and, in this way, it may happen that the receiver changes its own strategy from attack to escape or from escape to attack.

3.6.3. Diffusion of Information

In the implementation of our model, we used two visualizations of the same network. One visualization was for diffusion of information, and the other was for the diffusion of emotions.

If agents got information (Black agents in the first visualization) and they have the "attack" strategy (Red agents in the second visualization), then they diffuse information to their neighborhoods.

3.6.4. Python Code for Diffusion of Emotion without Feedback

```
while number_that_know < population_size:
    plot_and_save()
    time += 1
    for agent in list_of_agents_that_know:
        for j in agent.neighbors :
            neighbor = list_of_agents[j]
            if neighbor not in list_of_agents_that_
know:############## Without feedback

        ##############################
both are diffuser
        if agent.emotion_degree >= 0 and neigh-
bor.emotion_degree >= 0:
            neighbor.emotion_degree = (neighbor.
emotion_degree + agent.emotion_degree) / 2
            neighbor.state = know
            state_for_color[j] = know
            if neighbor not in list_of_agents_that_
know_next:
```

Figure 6. Diffusion of emotion

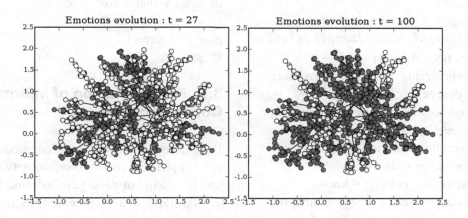

Figure 7. Diffusion of information (at beginning, in the middle, and at the end)

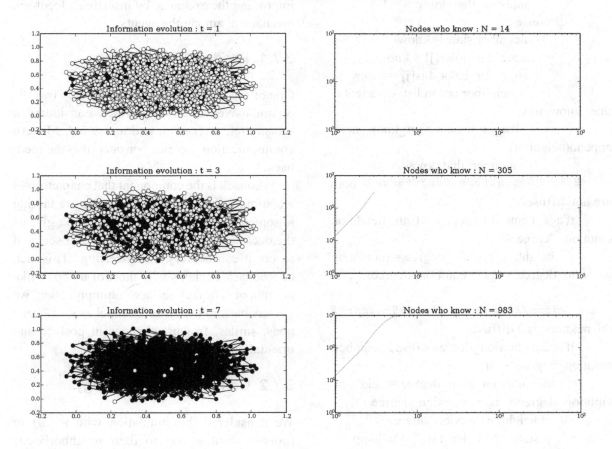

```
            list_of_agents_that_know_next.
append(neighbor)
        number_that_know += 1
        #############################
the next one is not a diffuser
        if agent.emotion_degree >= 0 and neigh-
bor.emotion_degree < 0:
            neighbor.emotion_degree = neighbor.
emotion_degree + agent.emotion_degree
        if neighbor.emotion_degree < 0:
            neighbor.state = know
            state_for_color[j] = know
            state_for_color_bis[j] = unhappy
            if neighbor not in list_of_agents_
that_know_next:
                list_of_agents_that_know_next.
append(neighbor)
            number_that_know += 1
        else :
            neighbor.state = know
            state_for_color[j] = know
            state_for_color_bis[j] = happy
            if neighbor not in list_of_agents_
that_know_next:
                list_of_agents_that_know_next.
append(neighbor)
            number_that_know += 1
        ############################ both
are not diffuser
        if agent.emotion_degree < 0 and neighbor.
emotion_degree < 0:
            neighbor.emotion_degree = (neighbor.
emotion_degree + agent.emotion_degree) / 2

        #############################
the next one is a diffuser
        if agent.emotion_degree < 0 and neighbor.
emotion_degree >= 0:
            neighbor.emotion_degree = neighbor.
emotion_degree + agent.emotion_degree
        if neighbor.emotion_degree < 0:
            state_for_color_bis[j] = unhappy
        ###########################
plot_number[time] = number_that_know
```

```
list_of_agents_that_know = copy.deepcopy(list_
of_agents_that_know_next)

plot_and_save()
PL.show()
```

3.7 From Diffusion of Information to Communication

Below, we present a variant of our model. Our aim is to implement communication between agents and not a kind of passage of information.

Naturally, to implement real communication, we must consider a multitude of variables. Here, we share only the information provided by the Central Bank, so the agents exchange information on price levels. In this case, we can consider improving the exchange by inserting a feedback mechanism among the agents.

3.7.1. Feedback

One of the first communication models was the Shannon-Weaver model, which considered a transmitter, a receiver, and a channel. Modern communication theories consider also the feedback.

Feedback is the component that characterizes a communication system. When we are talking to someone over the phone, if they don't give us the occasional 'mmmm', 'aaah', 'yes, I see' and so on, it can be very disconcerting. .This lack of feedback explains why most of us don't like ansaphones. In face-to-face communication, we get feedback in the visual channel as well - head nods, smiles, frowns, changes in posture and orientation, gaze and so on.

3.7.2. Communication Strategy

We considered the simulation with a sort of transfer from agents to their neighborhoods that included an important consideration, i.e., if neighborhoods obtained information and became

Black and grey agents, then they will not have the agents who transmitted the information in their own list of neighborhoods, so they don't transmit the information back to the transmitter. If neighborhoods insert the transmitter in the list of their neighborhood when they transmit, then feedback occurs, and we can figure out a sort of communication among agents.

3.7.3. Python Code for Diffusion of Emotion with Feedback

```
while number_that_know < population_size:
   plot_and_save()
   time += 1
   for agent in list_of_agents_that_know:
     for j in agent.neighbors :
       neighbor = list_of_agents[j]
       #############################
both are diffuser
       if agent.emotion_degree >= 0 and neighbor.
emotion_degree >= 0:
           neighbor.emotion_degree = (neighbor.
emotion_degree + agent.emotion_degree) / 2
         neighbor.state = know
         state_for_color[j] = know
         if neighbor not in list_of_agents_that_
know_next:
             list_of_agents_that_know_next.
append(neighbor)
           number_that_know += 1
         #############################
the next one is not a diffuser
       if agent.emotion_degree >= 0 and neighbor.
emotion_degree < 0:
           neighbor.emotion_degree = neighbor.
emotion_degree + agent.emotion_degree
         if neighbor.emotion_degree < 0:
           neighbor.state = know
           state_for_color[j] = know
           state_for_color_bis[j] = unhappy
           if neighbor not in list_of_agents_that_
know_next:
             list_of_agents_that_know_next.
append(neighbor)
           number_that_know += 1
         else :
           neighbor.state = know
           state_for_color[j] = know
           state_for_color_bis[j] = happy
           if neighbor not in list_of_agents_that_
know_next:
             list_of_agents_that_know_next.
append(neighbor)
           number_that_know += 1

         ############################# both
are not diffuser
       if agent.emotion_degree < 0 and neighbor.
emotion_degree < 0:
           neighbor.emotion_degree = (neighbor.
emotion_degree + agent.emotion_degree) / 2

         #############################
the next one is a diffuser
       if agent.emotion_degree < 0 and neighbor.
emotion_degree >= 0:
           neighbor.emotion_degree = neighbor.
emotion_degree + agent.emotion_degree
         if neighbor.emotion_degree < 0:
           state_for_color_bis[j] = unhappy
         #############################
   plot_number[time] = number_that_know
   list_of_agents_that_know=copy.deepcopy(list_
of_agents_that_know_next)

plot_and_save()
PL.show()
```

4. RESULTS

We ran different simulation in order to understand macroscopic behavior of our model. We obtained unexpected behavior and this need to be inspected numerically in future work.

Figure 8. Simulating 1.000 agents in a Barabàsi-Albert network with parameter 1

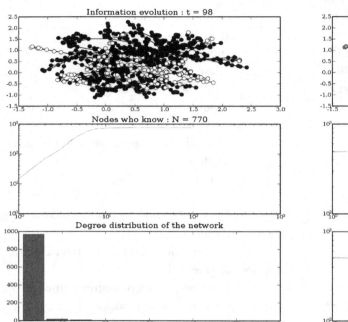

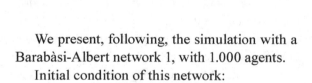

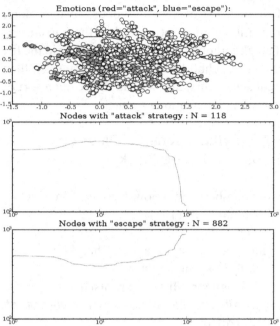

We present, following, the simulation with a Barabàsi-Albert network 1, with 1.000 agents.

Initial condition of this network:

- Time: t = 0
- Nodes who know: N=4
- Nodes with "attack" strategy: N=489
- Nodes with "escape" strategy: N=511

We obtained two behavior:

- In short run: agents with "escape" strategy decrease and obviously agents with "attack" strategy increase;
- In long run: we have the opposite scenario as we can see in fig.xx.

The difference between short run and long run is driven by the percentage of nodes who know, i.e., when these arrive to stable high number then nodes with "escape" strategy increase winning on nodes with "attack" strategy.

We think it happens because at beginning information diffusion is driven by agents with "attack" strategy and so they increase.

Therefore, to diffuse information is a winning strategy only in short run. But in long run, when information have reach most of agents, then the agents who diffused it decrease and others agents go to increase.

We tried to simulate 1.000 agents with a Barabàsi-Albert network with parameter 2, obtaining the same results, as can be observed in fig. 20.

Initial condition of this network:

- Time: t = 0
- Nodes who know: N=4
- Nodes with "attack" strategy: N=518
- Nodes with "escape" strategy: N=482

Figure 9. Simulating 1.000 agents in a Barabàsi-Albert network with parameter 2

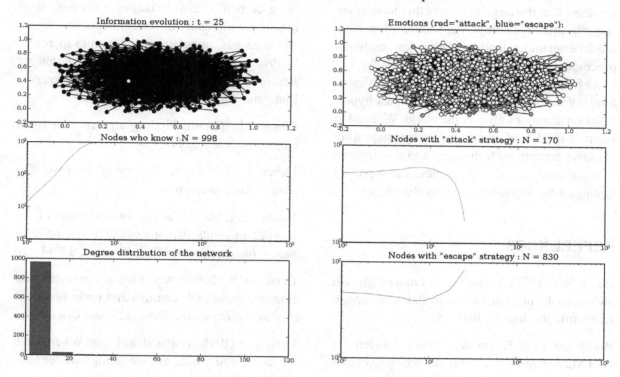

5. DISCUSSION AND CONCLUSION

Starting from an analytical model of hyperinflation and following the Plutchik psycho-evolutionary theory of emotions to build an agent-based emotional architecture, we have simulated the information diffusion that resulted from the Central Bank's announcement that it would raise the monetary stock and, consequently, the price levels.

Actually, we need to try different layouts for our network and more strategies for our agents in order to compare the results.

Emotions are a critical aspect of our work because of the intrinsic difficulties involved in understanding and quantifying them. For this reason, we have limited our analysis to the emotions that are necessary for survival and to the strategies linked to these emotions.

For a long time, scholars have been interested in 'emotions and AI.' As early as 1988, Pfeifer, wrote the book - *Artificial Intelligence Models of Emotion* – in which many AI models of emotion were reviewed. Subsequently, many models based on the most innovative techniques have been studied. Many of these models, though elegant and well constructed, have been forgotten, only because they have not been fortunate enough to have sparked the interest of scholars. El-Nasr and Yen (1988) proposed one especially interesting model in which fuzzy logic was used, a good tool, we think, in the emotions domain.

As of the present time, many contributions have been made to the *Recognition of Human Emotions and the Modeling and Simulation of Human Behaviors* and *Expression of Emotional-like Behaviors*. Even so, contributions that consider emotions in the context of agent-based models and simulations are very few, the major reason likely being the difficulties related to defining and objectifying emotions. On this latest point, we must say that the large advances that have come about in affective computing should allow for a much better understanding of complex emotional processes.

In future work, we will try to compare different kinds of simulations with data from past hyperinflation situations all over the world. We need to improve models of emotions also by integrating affective computing techniques and instruments into our analysis in order to develop improved strategies for implementation by the agents.

REFERENCES

Barro, R.J. (1977). Unanticipated money growth and unemployment in the United States. American Economic Review *67*, 101–115.

Burghouts G.J., R. op den Akker, Heylen D., Poel M., & Nijholt A. (2003). *An action selection architecture for an emotional agent.*

Cagan, P. (1956). The monetary dynamics of hyperinflation. In M. Friedman, *Studies in the Quantity Theory of Money*. Chicago: University of Chicago Press.

Carroll, C.D. (2003). Macroeconomic expectations of households and professional forecasters. *Quarterly Journal of Economics.*

Ciarrochi J., & Mayer J.D. (2007). Applying emotional intelligence. *Psychology Press*. New York.

Cipresso P., Balgera A., & Villamira M.A. (2008). Agent-based computational economics and emotions for decision-making processes. In *Selected Proceedings of the IAREP/SABE 2008 World Conference at LUISS in Rome.*

Cipresso P., & Villamira M.A. (2007a). Aspettative razionali e microfondazione per ecomomie in situazione di iperinflazione. In *Proceedings of WIVACE 2007.*

Cipresso P., Villamira M.A. (2007b). Shaping the "post-carbon" society: changes at systemic level in transport, housing and consumer behaviour, an Agent-based Computational Economics approach. In *Proceedings of International Association for Research in Economic Psychology Conference*, Ljubljana, Slovenia.

Elman J.L. (1990). Finding structure in time. *Cognitive Science, 14.*

Fisher, I. (1930). *The Theory of interest*. The Macmillan Company.

Howitt, P. (2006), The microfoundations of the Keynesian multiplier process. *Journal of Economic Interaction and Coordination*, 33-44.

LeBaron, B. (2006). Agent based computational finance: suggested readings and early research. *Journal of Economic Dynamics and Control.*

LeDoux J. (1998). Fear and the brain: Where have we been, and where are we going? *Biological-Psychiatry, 44*, 12.

Leijonhufvud, A. (2006). Agent-based macro. In L. Tesfatsion & K.L. Judd (Ed.), *Handbook of Computational Economics* (Vol. 2, pp. 1625-37). Amsterdam: North-Holland.

Lewis M, Haviland-Jones J.M., & L. Feldman Barrett (Eds.). (2008). Handbook of emotions (3rd Ed.). New York: Psychology Press.

Mankiw, N.G., & Ricardo, R (2001). *Sticky information: A model of monetary nonneutrality and structural slumps* (NBER Working Paper Number 8614).

Muth J.F. (1961). Rational expectations and the theory of price movements. *Econometrica, 29*, 315-335.

Picard. R. (1997). *Affective computing*. MIT Press.

Power M., & Dalgleish T. (2008). *Cognition and emotion. From order to disorder*. New York: Psychology Press.

Sargent, T.J. (1993). *Bounded rationality in macroeconomics*. Oxford: Oxford University Press.

Simon, H. (1997). *Models of bounded rationality, Vol. 3*. MIT Press.

Snowdon, B., & Vane H. (2002). An encyclopedia of macroeconomics. Edward Elgar Publishing.

Terna P., Boero R., Morini M., & Sonnessa M. (2006). Modelli per la complessità. *La simulazione ad agenti in economia*, Bologna, Il Mulino.

Tesfatsion, L. (2006). Agent based computational economics: A constructive approach to economic theory. In L. Tesfatsion & K.L. Judd (Eds.), *Handbook of computational economics*, Vol. 2. North-Holland, Amsterdam.

Villamira M.A., & Cipresso P. (2008). Bio-inspired ICT for evolutionary emotional intelligence. In *Artificial life and evolutionary computation*.

Villamira M.A. (in press). Comunicare, FrancoAngeli, Milano.

Websites

www.aier.org/research/col.php Cost-of-Living Calculator from American Institute for Economic Research (AIER)

www.measuringworth.com - Various inflation calculators: US Dollars (1790-2006), UK pounds (1830-2006), price of gold (1257-2006)

Chapter XII
Unfolding Commitments Management:
A Systemic View of Emotions

Michel Aubé
Université de Sherbrooke, Canada

ABSTRACT

The Commitment Theory of Emotions is issued from a careful scrutiny of emotional behavior in humans and animals, as reported in the literature on Evolutionary Biology, Neurosciences and the Psychology of emotions. Emotions are viewed as a special layer of processes, wired upon needs and instincts, and dealing mainly with nurturance, social bonding and cooperative behavior, especially between kin and relatives. As every other motivational system, they operate so as to manage resources critical for survival and reproduction. The peculiar resources emotions do manage are commitments, understood as the predispositions of a given individual to help others and collaborate with them in a reciprocal manner. This view clarifies considerably the interactions emotions entertain with a variety of modules involved in their operation, from the detection of antecedents in perceptual or memory systems, to the elicitation of the appropriate emotion, to the execution of the corresponding script, to the expression of emotions as the typical outcome of emotional episodes. The flow of processing is continuously modulated by affective states of the organisms and by other motivational systems. The chapter expounds the operation of each module as well as their interactions with each other. It concludes that successful implementation of emotions in artificial systems will have to rest upon the specifications of complex and realistic models of the kind presented.

INTRODUCTION

Why would one dream of designing animats endowed with the full capacity for emotions? What interest would there be, besides the mytho-logical strive that motivated Victor Frankenstein in playing God? What gain would there be in having emotional machines? Would this make them more functional and more efficient, better tools for human use? And if so, how would it be possible to implement them into the fabric of physical systems?

In a sense, evolution has already provided some lines of answer for the engineer raising these questions. Indeed, the more complex an animal's life appears to be, the more likely is it to evidence emotional behavior. For one thing, the processes underlying these behaviors are associated with the functioning of the limbic system, which is thought to have emerged during the transitory period from Reptiles to Birds and Mammals (MacLean, 1993; Panksepp, 1998). *Hence, it is believed that there is no emotion as such operating in organisms below this level.* On the other hand, as is clear with Primates and especially Humans, *the more rational a species gets to be, the more emotional it gets as well* (Damasio, 1994; Hebb, 1949; Scherer, 1994).

This suggests that emotions developed hand in hand with other superior capacities of the mind, and may be intricately related with the operation of these capacities. To make this statement quite concrete, try figure whether someone would take the risk of letting of an *emotionless* assistant handle one's valuable business. It is actually estimated that over a third of paid work in the United States depends heavily upon using and managing one's emotions in ways appropriate to the job requirements and the clients' demands (Hochschild, 1979, 1983). To take one step further, think about putting the delicate and difficult task of raising one's kids into the hands of an *emotionless* caretaker.

Hence there would be much benefit in better understanding what emotions are for, and how they have been designed through natural selection to do their job. Since they have not been selected in all species, it may help to ask what particular class of problems those that have emotions are confronted with, and how these processes operate so as to help solve them. It is our contention that a satisfying implementation of synthetic emotions has to derive from a robust model of the functions of emotions, much inspired from what is revealed

in Evolutionary Biology, Cognitive Psychology, Neurosciences, and Cultural Anthropology. The model should also expound as precisely as possible the dynamics of emotions, specifying the interactions with various other mental processes that modulate their operation. The aim of this chapter is to unfold the *Commitment Theory of Emotions* (Aubé, 1997a, 1997b, 1998, 2001, 2005; Aubé & Senteni, 1995, 1996a, 1996b) that has been developed precisely with these design preoccupations in mind.

We will start by recalling the basic tenets of the theory. Parts of these have been published here and there, but nowhere has there been a systematic presentation of the relations between all parts. Hence we will expose here a more complete model including all the modules that seem to be involved as emotion episodes unfold, and we will proceed to expound the interactions we find mandatory between them. This will lead us to specify:

1. The kind of events that typically trigger emotions (the antecedents of emotions in the INPUT module; the THRESHOLD device for activation to be launched);
2. The relations between emotions and other AFFECTIVE STATES (such as moods, temperament and traits, or emotional disorders);
3. The relations with other MOTIVATIONAL SYSTEMS (such as needs, social motivations, or cognitive motivations);
4. The way the disturbing events that trigger emotions are handled (the ACTIVATION module; the ELICITATION structure for emotions);
5. The content of the data bases that nurture the underlying processes (the SCRIPTS associated with each emotion; an ordered list of one's COMMITMENTS);
6. The typical way emotion episodes are resolved (the EXPRESSION module).

We will conclude the chapter by stressing some implications of the theory for a satisfying implementation of synthetic emotions. This will lead us to specify some elements of the ontology of animats that are to evidence emotional behavior comparable to what many animals are capable of, including ourselves. And since our view of emotions is tightly related to social interactions, we suggest that much of our model will also be of help for sociable robotics and affective computing in general.

The Commitment Theory of Emotions in a Nutshell

One basic statement of the theory is that emotions essentially have to do with interactions between individuals. Although most emotion theorists, apart from social constructionists (Averill, 1980; Harré, 1986; Shweder & LeVine, 1984), do not make this a distinctive aspect of their models, quite a few of them do acknowledge that emotion episodes typically concern situations of encounters, that emotions are more intense when others are involved, and the more so when individuals are intimately related (Baumeister & Leary, 1995; Fischer, Shaver, & Carnochan, 1990; Lazarus, 1991a; Nesse, 1990; Oatley & Johnson-Laird, 1987; Pinker, 1997; Scherer & Tannenbaum, 1986; Simon, 1967; Toda, 1985). A few arguments led us to make this point a central tenet.

The first argument comes from Evolutionary Biology, Neurosciences and Ethology. It is believed that emotional behaviors rest upon the operation of limbic structures, which gave rise, in species that have them, to such behaviors as maternal nurturance, separation distress, social bonding, rough-and-tumble play, imprinting and attachment (Maclean, 1993; Panksepp, 1998). Simpler organisms, like fish, amphibians and most reptilians, may evidence some nesting behavior or offspring protection, but these depend on more rigid instinctive processes, and parents often end up eating their own kin, when they

encounter them away from the nest. Bowlby's theory of attachment (1969, 1973, 1980) leads quite naturally to the analysis of emotions such as joy, anxiety, anger, sadness and depression, in terms of reactions to the attachment structure, and researchers associated with this theory go on to suggest that much of the adult affective life is organized around the characteristics of these fundamental relations (Ainsworth, 1989; Hazan & Shaver, 1987). The study of rituals in adult encounters across species and cultures further reveals that the very structure of parent-offspring attachment modulates the pattern of collaborative behaviors throughout life (Eibl-Eibesfeldt, 1975; Turner, 1997).

The second argument comes from cross-cultural studies of the antecedents of emotions (Boucher, 1983; Lutz, 1988; Scherer, 1988b; Scherer, Wallbott, & Summerfield, 1986). Whatever the culture, the events that most systematically trigger emotions have to do with social interaction, and the more so when individuals are closely related. Thus joy is most often felt and expressed when friends and family are reunited, and sadness when something bad happens to them. Anger is everywhere triggered in situations of transgression, be it of personal promises, social norms or cultural standards, and guilt is experienced when one feels one has done wrong to someone else.

One of the rare counterexamples comes apparently from fear. Of course, there is no problem for the theory with fears associated with distress cries and alarm calls, wherein the interactive aspect is manifest. Yet what about the reactions to such things as darkness, loud noises or large objects looming at one? We already mentioned that animals without a limbic system are not considered to experience emotions, but fish and turtles regularly hide and flee from moving objects. We suggest that such behaviors, also encountered in humans, rest upon a much simpler design, more of the instinctive kind, upon which *fear-proper* has actually developed. Incidentally, it has been remarked that the onset of fear from strangers in young children, birds and mammals coincides precisely with the establishment of imprinting or attachment (Hoffman, 1974; Rosenblum & Alpert, 1974).

The third argument has to do with the expression of emotions, which occupies a large part of the researches conducted in the Psychology of emotions (Ekman, 1982, 1984, 1993, 2003; Frijda, 1989; Keltner, Ekman, Gonzaga, & Beer, 2003). There is substantial agreement among researchers that expression constitutes a necessary component of emotions, even in nonhuman animals (Snowdon, 2003). More than a century ago, Darwin (1872/1965) had already pointed to its importance in the unfolding of the emotional episode: "The free expression by outward signs of an emotion intensifies it. On the other hand, the repression, as far as this is possible, of all outward signs softens our emotions" (p. 365). Expression is indeed very hard to control, and whenever this is successful, the intensity of the emotion itself is largely reduced, sometimes to the point of vanishing (Butler, Egloff, Wilhem, Smith, Erickson, & Gross, 2003; Duclos & Laird, 2001; Kappas, Bherer, & Thériault, 2000; Levenson, 1994). Expression suppression and control have thus become the universal means used for the regulation and the socialization of emotions, for instance through the acquisition of display rules (Ekman & Friesen, 1975; Malatesta & Haviland, 1982; Matsumoto, 1990). Facial expressions of emotions are also highly contagious (Hatfield, Cacioppo, & Rapson, 1994; Sagi & Hoffman, 1976) and they constitute such an important feature of our social life that people spontaneously and often unconsciously react to them (Dimberg, 1982, 1988). Finally, the continued mimicking of emotional expression, especially if it combines facial configuration, body posture, breath pattern and voicing, is often sufficient to trigger them, as actors well know and amply make use of (Bloch, 1989; Bloch, Lemeignan, & Aguilera, 1991; Bloch, Orthous, & Santibanez-H, 1987).

All this suggests that interactions are indeed at the core of emotional behavior. A second tenet of the theory is that emotions, belonging to the motivational (Aubé, 2005; Toates, 1988), are understood as control-loop systems built into animals so as to regulate their resource consumption. Motivational systems (Toates, 1986), like needs for instance, are there to monitor various resources (nutriments, water, rest, sex partner), and to insure their replenishment. But what kind of resources emotions are there to manage? The above discussion led us to think that emotions had critically to do with other individuals. Yet individuals could also be profiteers or irresponsible, and they should only be considered as resources if *one could count on* them.

The subtle point here is that emotions do not operate upon others as a whole, but more precisely upon their predisposition to help and collaborate in a reciprocal manner. *This predisposition, which we call commitment, is the precious resource that emotions have the function to manage.* The actual resource for the offspring of a nurturing species does not reside in the parents as such, but rather in the attachment that binds them altogether in a survival unit. This protective tie is the real target of the baby's joy or sorrow, as these expressions modulate with terrific efficacy the parents' commitments towards the offspring's well-being. Thus envisioned, *commitments appear as the very substance of emotional life.* This is the most basic tenet of the theory, the one from which it has been named.

Now, for commitments to bear such a causal effect upon individuals, they have to be represented carefully in the minds of the partners involved. They can be seen as kinds of contracts established between members of a small set of individuals (typically two, but they could include a whole family or a group of friends as well, provided each part feels compelled by the commitments under consideration). They can be implicit, as in parent-offspring attachment, or explicit, as in verbal or written promises. They are viewed as resources, since they embody the predisposition of the committed agent to be accountable, whether to provide help, protection, support, or various kinds of primary resources, such as food, water, shelter and security. As to the counterpart, they constrain self to provide in turn help and resources to the committed partner. The particulars of commitments that are to be represented in memory include: the precise identity of the *partners* involved; a list of *resources* they insure access to; some of the *tasks* that might have to be executed to get hold of these resources; the *time schedule* for their fulfillment; the *conditions for their satisfaction or revocation*. Commitments are envisioned as dynamic entities, such as background processes, that can help detect whether incoming events bear critical consequences upon their being fulfilled or threatened. They are essentially managed through the operation of emotions that result in creating, strengthening, updating or disrupting them. We will now explore how this way of looking at emotions could clarify a lot about their nature and about how they work.

THE DYNAMICS OF EMOTIONS

Emotions have not always been there. They got progressively selected and made more complex as they revealed their power in the adaptation of individuals. This implies that they developed from simpler structures (Brooks, 1991; Nesse, 1990, 2004), already in place and well functioning, and that they meshed with existing processes so as to solve critical problems pertaining to nurturing and collaboration in social species. Designing synthetic emotions thus requires a clear view of how the system as a whole is working. Figure 1 depicts the modules that are postulated in the model and illustrates how parts interact with one another, according to what is known so far from Neurosciences and the Psychology of emotions. We will thus spend this whole section unfolding each module and specifying the interactions entertained with the other parts.

A few remarks are mandatory before we embark on this journey. First one should realize that there is a kind of expository artifact in sketching such a schema. As for drawings in handbooks of neurophysiology or electronic circuitry, things are deliberately made to appear much cleaner and much more symmetrical than they would actually look like anatomically or physically. Second, recall that, although many different modules are involved, the key to the whole functioning revolves around the concept of commitments. This means that the operation of every module is likely to be affected by them, and hence will be sketched in reference to this critical viewpoint. Third, one has to envision the emotion processes, not as monolithic, but as largely distributed within the brain (or a computer), so that a representation similar to the one depicted in the figure should be replicated for every category of emotion. It is indeed likely that each emotion evolved along a different history, and got endowed with its own specialized modules to insure proper operating.

In Figure 1, interacting modules pertaining to emotional behavior inside the individual are enclosed within the thick blurred line. Only three kinds of arrows can be used to connect the modules: *trigger, set up* or *modify*. Once significant events reach the system, the *triggering* path goes from the perception/memory module, to the threshold device (the little circle marked by an "X"), to the activation module, to the expression module, and then it is directed outside the system, towards specific individuals involved in the commitments concerned by the particular emotional episode. Yet, one minor exception to the usual flow of triggering, as we mentioned above while talking about expression, is that emotional mimicking most typically results in congruent emotional feelings. Hence we should postulate that there could be a reversal of direction from expression to activation.

One can further notice from the figure that *modify* arrows are all issued from the sole activation module: in the model, emotions are basically

Figure 1. The dynamics of emotions from the point of view of the Commitment Theory of Emotions

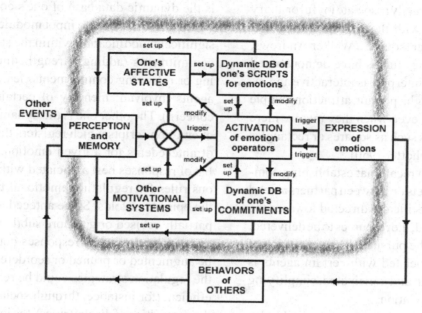

viewed as operators whose function is to create, maintain, protect, reinforce, or eventually weaken and destroy one's commitments that are registered in their dedicated data base. The activation module could also result in editing the emotion scripts, in transforming current moods and other affective states, or in modulating the operation of needs and other motivational systems. All the other arrows are of the *set up* kind, and they indicate which modules are concerned with setting up critical variables used by others.

The Input Module

On the input side, there is a PERCEPTION module that detects, among incoming events, *significant variations in commitments* of one's concern. Although emotion triggering sometimes operates slowly enough for some reflexive analysis to take place, in matter of seconds, it most often happens very quickly, in a reflex-like fashion, in matter of a few milliseconds (Ekman, 1992; Lazarus, 1991b; LeDoux, 1989; Oatley & Johnson-Laird, 1987). There seems to be a great challenge in engineering the detection of such a complex thing as *variations*

in commitments, but the difficulty is more apparent than real. For one thing, if emotions co-appeared with imprinting and attachment structures some 280 millions years ago, there presumably have been selected as well some relevant signals, easy enough to compute, yet sufficiently reliable to secure parent-offspring relations.

We indeed think that there are many built-in detectors for *affordances* present in the social environment (Gibson, 1977), such as emotional expression (facial, postural or behavioral), sudden movements of others, features of threatening or joyful events, etc. For instance, researchers have found, in the brain of various primates, some detectors insuring the rapid recognition of angry faces (Dimberg, 1982, 1988; Hansen & Hansen, 1988; Öhman, 1986; Öhman & Dimberg, 1978; Sackett, 1966), and of other emotional expressions as well (Hasselmo, Rolls, & Baylis, 1989). Trevarthen (1984) shows that newborns are already well equipped for preferential responding to a variety of stimuli characteristically associated with human emotional interaction, such as the typical pattern of the face, the smile, the talking, the whispering, the gentle vocalizations, the rocking, the patting.

We also know that human babies, even only seven months old, can correctly associate joyful or angry faces from videos with the appropriate voicing heard from another source (Walker-Andrews, 1986). Finally, some studies have demonstrated that people readily interpret as interactive and intentional (attack, flight, pursuit, attraction) simple patterns of motion, even when they involve mere geometrical shapes such as squares or rectangles (Bassili, 1976; Michotte, 1950).

One should also recall that establishing commitments already sets up between partners a trend of expectations specifically directed towards the individuals involved, the resources to be delivered, and the actions to be pursued. The perception of certain events associated with certain agents is thus already framed and anticipated, simplifying the detection of deviations.

The input to the emotion system could also come from MEMORY of past events, or even from imaginary situations. In this case as well, triggering has to deal with significant variations in the stock of one's commitments. One can thus feel joy while remembering a recent gathering with close friends, and the emotion felt will likely contribute to enhance one's commitments with the guests or with some of the other individuals encountered. One could likewise remind some misbehavior one has perpetrated towards kin, and the guilty feelings then triggered might lead to reassess excuses and reparation as to the harm caused. Or one could feel anger to the imaginary thought of being betrayed by some acquaintance, as happens frequently in jealousy situations.

The PERCEPTION/MEMORY module is thus affected by the representation of events, either from the external world or from one's remembrance and imagination, events typically pertaining to behaviors of significant others with whom commitments have been established or are likely to be in the near future. The input module also receives information from two internal modules that currently act so as to tune up the affordances detectors which sustain the recogni-tion of relevant emotional situations. The first one is the dynamic data base of one's commitments which has to inform the input modules about any significant modification within the stock of one's commitments (adding, strengthening, weakening or removing commitments; features of new agents involved; memory of certain events of concern). The other one is the dynamic data base of emotion scripts which registers the typical set of antecedents for a given emotion, an ordered list of responses best associated with it and various rules for regulating emotional behaviors as the episode unfolds. Since antecedents could be partially revised or get more subtle with experience, since the list of responses could likewise be augmented or pruned or reordered, and since the regulation strategies could be rendered more efficient (for instance, through socialization and the acquisition of display rules), the input modules will likely be affected by these modifications in detecting and interpreting relevant behaviors from self and others.

The Influence of One's Affective States and Motivational Systems upon the Threshold Level

Commitments fluctuations are quite common, due to minute variations in the relations with kin, friends and other people one interacts with, and since the activation of emotions as a control system is generally quite costly, there should be a recurrent tuning up of the THRESHOLD which determines the probability that certain significant events will launch activation. In newborns, for instance, or in animals which are in the process of being tamed, or in people interacting with acquaintances whose reliability has not been sufficiently confirmed yet, the threshold level will usually be set fairly low so that emotions could be called promptly as operators to regulate the establishment of the new commitments.

Two modules are thought to play a role in setting up the threshold level: one's AFFECTIVE

STATES (Davidson, 1994; Ekman, 1994; Frijda, 1993, 1994), such as moods, temperament or emotional disorders, and other MOTIVATIONAL SYSTEMS, such as needs (Toates, 1986), social motivations (Aronson, 1996; Cialdini, 1984), or cognitive motivations (Biederman & Vessel, 2006; Dweck, 1986; Schultz, 1994). It is quite expected indeed that a depressive mood would make the triggering of sadness more likely, that a person with an aggressive temperament would get angry more easily, or that a neurotic mind would be more subject to anxiety and fear. Moods and temperament could both be viewed as the increased propensity of a given emotion to be launched, moods being much more dependent upon circumstances, while temperament and traits appear quite idiosyncratic, and more or less characteristic of an individual's personality. Affective disorders are more complex, as they could depend upon life circumstances as well as upon personal factors, sometimes of a genetic origin, yet they also increase dramatically the probability of certain emotions to be triggered.

As to the different motivational systems, needs frequently have an effect upon the threshold level, as when a hungry (or thirsty, or tired, or cold) baby gets more prone to sadness and anger. In the case of social motivations, it is well known, for instance, that people in crowd are easily influenced by the behavior of the majority, and that there is much emotion contagion spreading around (Hatfield et al., 1994). As to the cognitive side, setting up a goal to achieve a task, not only raises intrinsic motivation, as manifested in persistence, interest, curiosity (Berlyne, 1960; Lowenstein, 1994), but it is also likely to lower the threshold for various emotions, such as joy when success is in sight, anger when there is goal blocking, especially from others, or pride if one succeeds in spite of arduous difficulties and constraints, again more so in the presence of others (Klinger, 1975). This results from the fact that motivational systems are essentially resource management systems, and when resources are at stake, there is a bias,

in species that have emotions, to look for others, preferably committed ones, as responsible for the opportunity or the threat encountered.

Notice from Figure 1 that, in the proposed model, the dynamic data bases of emotion scripts and of personal commitments do not influence the threshold level directly, but rather intervene upstream, as they are already encapsulated in the information used by the input module to decide whether the events perceived or remembered are of the kind that require the intervention of emotions. If the signal is strong enough to get through the threshold barrier, then the activation module is set into action. This module cannot act backwards upon the threshold, but it has an indirect path to modulate its level, since it has the power to modify partially the content and operations of one's affective states and of other motivational systems, as we will see in the next section.

The Activation Module and the Elicitation Structure

The ACTIVATION module is at the core of the whole system: it puts emotions themselves into action and feelings, and is *the only one that has the capacity to modify* the content of other modules. It makes use of a very simple elicitation structure that determines rather automatically which family of emotions is to be invoked from the data base registering one's scripts for emotions to manage the commitment variation perceived as significant and problematic. The activation module then executes the *prototypical script* attached to the emotion that has been called. It could in turn modify the script, for example if the situation requires revising some of the antecedents (some becoming obsolete, new ones appearing more decisive), or considering more appropriate responses to resolve the kind of situation typically associated with this particular emotion, or reordering the list of preferred actions, or acquiring new display rules and regulating strategies.

The activation module also has to get critical information from the data base registering one's commitments, since the prototype called from the data base usually comes in generic format, and has to be adapted to the situation at hand. The script to be executed thus have to be meshed with the particulars of the commitment under consideration, taking into account the partners involved, the weight and priority attached to the commitment, the resources at stake, the conditions of fulfillment or of revocation, and the details of the breach or the opportunity that are responsible for triggering the emotion in the first place. Although the activation module does not always result in modifying the script data base, *it always ends up modifying the commitments data base, since this is its very function as commitment operator.* The commitment under consideration could indeed be in the process of being created, or it is to be strengthened, or weakened, or even destroyed. Actual implementation of these modifications could be facilitated by having a weight attached to each commitment, which is raised or lowered according to the valence of the emotion under execution (positive versus negative), the importance of the resource at stake (life versus food, for example), and to the proximity of the agent involved in the commitment (close kin or friend, versus stranger). The partners involved may also have to be changed (new ones being added, some ancient being removed), the resources to be delivered could be modified, the time schedule and other conditions for fulfillment may have to be revised.

The ELICITATION structure has been elucidated from the work of appraisal theorists (Ellsworth & Scherer, 2003; Ellsworth & Smith, 1988a, 1988b; Frijda, Kuipers, & ter Schure, 1989; Ortony, Clore, & Collins, 1988; Roseman, Aliki Antoniou, & Jose, 1996; Scherer, 1988a; Smith & Ellsworth, 1985) and of attribution theorists (Thompson, 1989; Weiner 1985; Weiner & Graham, 1989; Wong & Weiner 1981). These researchers actually tried to determine from questionnaire data what dimensions intervened in the subjects' mind when they declared having felt a given emotion. This endeavor could be related to other researches aimed at delineating the structure of the affective space by asking subjects to specify the similarity between the expressions of different emotions depicted in photographs or between various sets of emotion words (Fromme & O'Brien, 1982; Russell, 1979, 1980; Schlosberg, 1954). A meta-analysis by Frijda (1993) revealed that in the factor analysis typically used to sort these dimensions, the scree test recurrently evidenced a sharp bend after two or three factors, suggesting that these few were probably sufficient to account for the information that was critically used by subjects to decide which emotion was being considered.

Most researches typically end up with two to four factors. We have seen before that emotion triggering happens very quickly, in matter of milliseconds and we think that these factors could be profitably used as the basis of the elicitation structure. The four dimensions that are most often encountered in the literature are *valence, activation, agency,* and *certainty.* But the dimension of *activation* has been seriously questioned (Larsen & Diener, 1992; Ortony, Clore, & Foss, 1987), because the list of words used in the experiments that came out with this factor was usually filled with terms such as: active, calm, quiet, sleepy, tired, bored, excited, aroused, nonchalant, etc. These words are usually not considered as representative of emotions by subjects (Shaver, Schwartz, Kirson, & O'Connor, 1987; Storm & Storm, 1987), yet they make it very likely that a dimension of activation will emerge from the analysis. Hence, we decided to discard it and to resort to the three dimensions of *valence, agency* and *certainty.* Valence can take values of *positive* or *negative,* agency can take values of *none, self,* or *others* and certainty can take values of *certain* or *uncertain.*

The diversity of emotions that have been considered across emotion theories varies from two to about two dozen. Yet, many of them are very similar (guilt, remorse, shame, embarrassment) and could be lumped under the same family. As for surprise, interest or curiosity, we do not consider them as emotions but as cognitive motivations, a point of view also shared by quite a few researchers (Ellsworth & Smith, 1988b; Johnson-Laird & Oatley, 1989; Ortony et al., 1988; Stein, Trabasso, & Liwag, 1993; Storm & Storm, 1987). On the other hand, certain terms simply stress variations in the intensity of the emotion (as in terror versus fear, rage versus anger). Some theorists (Frijda, 1986; Roseman et al., 1996; Scherer, 1988a) have further pointed to the fact that each emotion could vary according to the scope of its focus (global versus focal). For instance, guilt and shame are both felt when one fails to fulfill a personal promise or to meet a social standard, yet *guilt* is typically associated with specific wrongdoings, while *shame* is rather felt when this is the whole self that seems inadequate. *Anger* likewise deals with particular acts of transgression, while the related emotion of *contempt* goes beyond these acts in blaming and rejecting the person as a whole. *Gratitude* is experienced when one receives goods or favors from someone else, but if generosity endures, the feeling could be generalized over the whole person and turn into *adoration* for the benefactor.

Although some researchers would propose to include *disgust* as a proper emotion, we remain skeptical, since even the fiercer proponents of this view, such as Rozin and his collaborators (Rozin & Fallon, 1987; Rozin, Haidt, & McCauley, 1993), cumulated evidence associated with two very different kinds of reactions: disgust as a category of food rejection (akin to distaste), and disgust as a moral emotion. We would rather suggest that disgust as distaste belongs to the need motivational systems (a point of view also shared by Fromme & O'Brien, 1982, and by Panksepp, 1982), while disgust as a moral emotion rather appears as a complex affective-cognitive structure (Izard, 1993) requiring much cognitive sophistication and symbolic elaboration. As a matter of fact, this variety of disgust does not achieve its form until about 7 or 8 years of age (Rozin & Fallon, 1987; Rozin et al., 1993), as it bears close resemblance to other moral emotions: "as disgust becomes elaborated, it becomes a more general feeling of revulsion, even to sociomoral violations, and it begins to shade into anger. We propose that contempt is the middle ground between anger and disgust". (Rozin et al., p. 588). Darwin himself also thought that "contempt hardly differs from disgust" (1872/1965, p. 253), and this lumping of the three emotions under the *hostility triad* (Izard, 1977) is actually the position that has received the largest support from emotion researchers (Frijda et al., 1989; Ellsworth & Smith, 1988a; Shaver et al., 1987; Storm & Storm, 1987; Smith & Ellsworth, 1985; Oatley, 1992).

Other emotions appear as combinations of many different ones and probably involve many of them depending on minute variations as the emotion unfolds. In jealousy, for instance, people typically oscillate between sadness (because of the loss), anger (because of treason and treachery), shame (for feeling inadequate and unattractive) and fear (because future appears gloomy and irrevocable) (Frijda, 1986; Mathes, Adams, & Davies, 1985; Sharpsteen, 1991).

Contrary to some theorists we do not consider *love* itself as an emotion. For one thing, as was also pointed out by Scherer (1988a), there is no specific event that makes one love a person, while emotions typically have fairly identifiable antecedents or elicitors. On the other hand, love cannot easily be categorized in terms of valence or agency. It rather seems to involve a complicated configuration including many different emotions, some positive, and some negative, some dependent on self-agency, and some dependent on other-agency: separation distress, jealousy, feeling happy or sorry for the loved one, worrying about the other, being fulfilled in her presence, feeling abandoned in his absence. Since it is largely agreed upon that most emotions arise in the context of attachment and close relationships (Baumeister

& Leary, 1995; Scherer, 1988b; Scherer et al., 1986), we rather consider love as a rich texture of commitments, very densely woven. As such, it offers plenty of opportunities for emotions of all kinds to be triggered, whenever any of them is at stake, and this would explain why love is so intimately associated with emotions in people's mind (Fehr & Russell, 1984; Shaver et al., 1987; Storm & Storm, 1987). Love appears indeed at the heart of emotional life, not because it is an emotion itself, but because it acts as an *incubator of emotions.*

Figure 2 presents the elicitation structure when related emotions are grouped into families, and when terms denoting variation in intensity or combination of many emotions are removed. As to the global aspect of a given emotion, it is captured by the term in parentheses in the corresponding cell. Although much simplified, the result remains consonant enough with the analysis made by appraisal theorists and by attribution theorists.

Does it mean that our proposal is confined to only eight families of emotions? Actually, from reasons of theoretical parsimony and of computational economy, we tend to think that the number could not be very large, probably below ten. After all, we seem to have only about 5-6 sensory systems (Gibson, 1966), about 5-6 categories of memory systems (Baddeley, 1990;

Eustache & Desgranges, 2008), about 5-6 different kinds of needs (Toates, 1986). We do not exclude that there could have been a couple more families of emotions selected in the process of evolution, but we think that any new candidate should be carefully scrutinized, notably to check whether it is endowed with all the capacities we ascribe to the other members of the list. We contend that our set is firmly supported by what is known in Neurosciences and in the Psychology of emotions, and it is solidly grounded in the principles at the core of the *Commitment theory of emotions.* The full rational behind the set of emotions that are included, as well as the way they are distributed in the table, has already been presented in details elsewhere (Aubé, 1997b, 2001).

In terms of our model, the *valence* dimension refers to opportunity or threat (Nesse, 2004), signaling gain or loss in the stock of resources that one's commitments represent. If new commitments are established, or if old ones are strengthened, positive emotions lurk in. If established commitments are threatened, fractured or weakened, or if they are ruptured, then negative emotions are called in help.

The *agency* dimension has to do with the agent to whom the variation in commitments is attributed. Depending on the researchers, it has received various denominations such as *responsibility,*

Figure 2. The elicitation structure for families of emotions (Adapted notably from Roseman et al., 1996, Thompson, 1989, and Weiner, 1985)

VALENCE

		POSITIVE		NEGATIVE	
		certain	uncertain	certain	uncertain
A	**none**	Joy (happiness)	Hope (optimism)	Sadness (depression)	Fear (anxiety)
G E N	**self**	Pride (conceit)		Guilt (shame)	
C Y	**others**	Gratitude (adoration)		Anger (contempt)	

intentionality, control (situational, self- of other-), *causal locus*, etc. When attributed to self, pride or guilt are likely to be felt; when attributed to others, gratitude or anger are triggered. The none category may seem strange from a commitment view, but sometimes the variation in commitments (as when one loses a child) is attributable to non-intentional forces, such as happens frequently with the action of natural elements or in various kinds of accidents. The emotion triggered then typically resorts to committed agents who could be called in help (with distress calls, for instance) or towards those that are to be protected (by alarm calls, for instance). So as to make emotions more efficient at their job, there seems to be a *built-in bias* in the direction of over-protecting the commitments, and more so with the agency dimension. In the case of a loss, it is a bias of suspicion against treachery and transgression (Cosmides, 1989; Gigerenzer & Hug, 1992). Humans as well as animals will tend to look for a scapegoat, usually of the same species, when something bad happens to them (Hutchinson, 1972; Wong & Weiner, 1981). In the case of a gain, it is a bias towards gratitude, and it plays a significant role in taming, seduction and generally in building up new alliances (Tesser, Gatewood, & Driver, 1968).

Finally, the *certainty* dimension has to do with the temporal characteristics, since there are plenty of expectations that get associated with the management of commitments. Yet this dimension only operates in the none case, when no agents are involved. When self is felt responsible for some outcome, favorable or detrimental, pride or guilt is experienced, whether the critical event is certain or only anticipated. When responsibility for the outcome is attributed to others, gratitude or anger is triggered, even if the corresponding event has not happened yet. For instance, someone may well feel angry while figuring that some ally is on the verge of defection. The interesting part, implementation wise, is that all three dimensions (*valence, agency, certainty*) already have their values fixed when events are detected at

the input module as involving critical variations in commitments. As soon as threshold is passed through, activation of the proper emotion family is thus fairly straightforward.

The activation module also has the power to modify the content or operations of affective states and of other motivational systems. Moods happen to be very similar to the global aspect of the emotions depicted in parentheses in Figure 2, a change of scope that could result from the frequent occurrence of the same emotion over a short period of time. Close repetition of joyful events thus leads easily to happy mood, frequent occurrences of fearful ones will likely make one prone to anxiety. It is also known that experiencing awful events (having been tortured or having lived in a concentration camp, for instance) highly increases the probability of suffering from serious emotional disorders. Reciprocally, it is often through the reenactment of heavy emotional episodes that various therapeutic approaches can succeed in relieving patients from their pain.

Motivational systems are likewise influenced by the operation of the activation module. It is often the case indeed that strong emotional episodes, as happens in bouts of rage, terror or grief, can partially if not totally disrupt the operation of need systems like hunger or fatigue. Selling tactics issued from the social motivations repertoire, such as the "door-in-the-face" or the "foot-in-the-door" techniques (Cialdini, Vincent, Lewis, Catalan, Wheeler, & Darby, 1975; Freedman & Fraser, 1966), provide good examples of emotions intervening in social motivations. They work by having a client make a small commitment that induces him to comply with a further (and greater) demand from the salesman. Interestingly enough, the current explanation to their efficiency is that guilt lurks in to protect and sustain the established commitment (Freedman, Wallington, & Bless, 1967; O'Keefe & Figge, 1997). Substantial motivation to cooperate also happens typically after group discussions in social dilemma games, and the phenomenon is again explained by the fact that group members felt compelled to make and honor commitments towards cooperative choices (Kerr & Kaufman-Gilliland, 1994; Orbell, van de Kragt, & Dawes, 1988), with pride and guilt lurking in to sustain and protect them. On the cognitive side, it is understood that progress towards goals or interruption from attainment are generally loaded with affect and motivation (Carver & Scheier, 1990; Klinger, 1975), and that facilitation or hindering is easily attributed to others (Wong & Weiner, 1981), thus calling emotions to take part in the process.

The Dynamic Data Bases of One's Scripts for Emotions and of One's Commitments

Two data bases appear essential to the functioning of emotions. One has to do with the current SCRIPTS associated with each emotion. Various experiments have indeed shown that people have in their mind structured representations about emotions and the way they operate, and that these representations are very similar across individuals (Fehr & Russell, 1984; Fischer et al., 1990; Lazarus, 1991a; Mascolo & Fischer, 1995; Ortony et al., 1988; Parrott & Smith, 1991; Russell 1991; Shaver et al., 1987; Shaver, Wu, & Schwartz, 1992; Tangney & Fischer, 1995; see also Nesse, 1990, Table 1, p. 266). Researchers asked subjects to describe real or imaginary episodes for different emotions, and submitted their description to a set of independent judges who abstracted common characteristics from them. The similarity ratings were then averaged and submitted to hierarchical cluster analysis, which generated for each emotion under scrutiny a prototype, or script, of the kind presented in Table 1.

These scripts probably have a genetic basis, which would explain why there is so much similarity between those of different people, even originating from different cultures. But they also become more and more idiosyncratic as they get tailored, through personal experience, to the life style of specific individuals. Anger for instance is everywhere triggered by acts of transgression, but what is counted as such is constantly modulated by the person's past history, by local values and standards, by moods or by personality traits. This is notably why there is a set up arrow in Figure 1 between one's affective states and one's set of scripts for emotions. Prototype modification can also bear upon the response tendencies, whose number can be augmented or reduced, and whose preferred order can be altered depending on personal success and failure encountered in past situations, or resulting from the imitation of successful others. It can finally have to do with acquiring new display rules and new strategies for emotion control or suppression.

As can be seen from Table 1, such prototypes are made of four parts. We already mentioned that the *predispositions* for a given emotion to be triggered was related to one's affective states or to some physiological state of the individual (pain, stress, fatigue). The *antecedents* of the emotion, on the other hand, register the characteristic events that are most likely to trigger the emotion under consideration. As we have seen while examining the content and functioning of the input module, these antecedents are used by perception and memory to detect and recognize events that require the operation of emotions. Most importantly, the emotion script incorporates an effective set of *response tendencies* that are to be used by the activation module to conduct the episode. They specify various actions that proved useful in the past (either selected through evolution, acquired from one's experience, or learned from the teaching and observation of others) to solve the problem at hand. Finally, a small set of *regulating procedures* is also proposed to help prevent running away, since emotions, as powerful control structures dedicated to the handling of emergency situations, have a very high priority of execution, and a large stock of energy available to fuel their operation, which make them quite vulnerable to escalation. The scripts are stored

Table 1. The prototype of anger (Adapted from Shaver et al., 1987)

Predispositions:
  previous similar experiences
  aggressive mood or temperament, paranoid mind
  stress, overload, fatigue
  physical or psychological pain

Antecedents (as seen in the behavior of others):
  treason or treachery
  transgression of personal value, or of social standard
  loss of respect, insults, unfair treatment
  violation of promises or expectations
  interruption of goal-directed activity

Response tendencies:
  frowning, square mouth baring the teeth, intense gazing, flushed face
  loud voice, reproaching, yelling, shouting, cursing, obscenities
  hands and fists clenched, heavy walk, rigidity of body and movements
  threatening gestures, hitting, kicking, charging, physical attack
  smashing or throwing objects, slamming doors
  incoherent behavior, loss of control, narrowing of focus
  imagining attacking, hurting or even destroying the cause of anger
  silencing, walking out, withdrawing from contact

Self-control procedures:
  trying to suppress the anger by not expressing it
  explaining away the transgression suffered as unintentional
  redefining the situation so that anger appears no longer adequate

---

in declarative format to ease up their frequent editing, but are recurrently transformed into procedures by the activation module, according to the task at demand.

The other data base registers the dynamically updated list of one's COMMITMENTS. As critical resources, these are viewed as essential to the functioning of the whole system, and thus have to be represented with precision in long-term memory. As mentioned in the beginning of the chapter, each commitment should register enough information so as to recognize whether it is concerned with incoming events, and how it could best react to them. First among the required variables are the partners involved, together with a measure of their closeness and links to other active commitments involving them. Since commitments are basically about resources, they should also list which ones they guarantee access to, and which tasks might have to be executed to get hold of them. Their representation should finally specify the time schedule for their fulfillment, and their conditions of satisfaction or of revocation.

Although they pervade the system as a whole, commitments actually intervene directly in the operation of only two other modules. For one thing, they send to the input module the information required to detect what particular variations in commitments are at stake: the identity and features of the partners involved, the compromised resources, recognizable patterns of problematic behaviors, perceivable deviations from promises or expectations in terms of words, writings or various gestures, etc. They also nurture the operation of the activation module by combining with the elicited emotion script, and completing the content of its variables with adequate information from the commitment under scrutiny (to whom angry behavior should be addressed to, what wrong has been done to self by this agent, what can be done back as proper retaliation, etc.).

This data base sometimes has to be informed by other motivational systems, because their operation might involve commitments, whose particulars thus have to be specified. This is the case, for instance, when a baby's needs determine which committed agent (parent or caretaker) a feeding request should be addressed to, and what kind of resources could be obtained by adopting a distressed or joyful behavior. As to social motivations, it so happens that their functioning often rests upon the establishment of commitments, which thus have to be fed into the corresponding data base, together with their associated variables. Cognitive motivations are much less dependent upon others and could well operate on a solitary basis. Yet, in various goal-attainment contexts, such as competition, collaborative work, or coaching and scaffolding, they do involve agreements with others and rule-sharing that have to be set up and registered into the commitments stack.

Finally, as was mentioned before, the activation module is the only one that is endowed with the capacity to rewrite and modify the nature and content of any commitment from the list. This is indeed the basic tenet of the theory: commitments are created, strengthened, weakened or destroyed through the activation and unfolding of emotion scripts.

The Output Module

The output module is essentially concerned with the EXPRESSION of emotions. If emotions are indeed triggered, as we claim, by important variations in commitments, then the main way of exploiting new commitments between partners or of fixing fractured ones is through strong and compelling communication between them. This principle rests on the very basic fact that established commitments reside in the minds of the partners involved, and that one strictly has

no other means of accessing them so as to make the required modifications. For commitments to work, they should bear on representations similar enough in both minds, and partners often have to express emotions so as to assess and maintain their compatibility. That probably explains why expression has always taken such an important place in the study of emotions: these operators *do their job* basically by signaling breaches or opportunities in commitments, communicating intentions, expressing gratitude and satisfaction with resources obtained, asking or offering help, sending requests, alerting in case of danger, threatening in case of transgression, offering reparation in case of blunder.

Expressions are quite ritualized, which is good news for implementation matters and makes it likely that their typical pattern has an innate basis. One convincing argument is the persistence of various signals across species, such as the square mouth baring the teeth in the facial expression of anger that is found in many mammals, notably Primates (including Humans), Canidae and Felidae. This very persistence makes it is efficient enough that one could use it with astonishing success in scolding one's dog. Darwin (1872/1965) proposed that this particular expression evolved from vestigial forms of aggressive behavior, as a way of signaling that the misbehavior that triggered it could indeed activate aggression, and he made a similar analysis for various forms of expressions. But this does not mean that everything is fixed and that no learning could take place to improve the quality and efficiency of the message. We know from observations of very young blind children (Charlesworth & Kreutzer, 1973; Eibl-Eibesfeldt, 1973) that they spontaneously put on their faces recognizable expressions of emotions such as fear, anger, joy or sadness. Yet, they have considerable difficulty, compared to sighted children, in acting out or posing voluntarily the corresponding expressions, and *their facial activity decreases with age from the inborn expressions while it increases through communication in sighted children*. Emotional expressions are indeed amply exercised during development, notably through rough-and-tumble play in many species of mammals, and the display rules that come out of this process happen to be the best mean of controlling, and sometimes of interrupting, the unfolding of emotional episodes.

Being so tightly attached to the emotion itself, be it for reasons of evolutionary history or of efficiency in affecting partners' commitments, the expression component typically leads to imitation and emotional contagion. It is indeed very difficult to witness joy and laughter without feeling playful (Provine, 1992, 2000; Ruch, 1993), it is hard to watch suffering others, especially babies and children, without becoming distressed oneself (Levenson & Ruef, 1992; Sagi & Hoffman, 1976), it is almost impossible to be caught in a panicking crowd without experiencing fear (Hatfield et al., 1994). Many researchers think that there lies one important basis for empathy, which is also encountered among many species of animals, and that the phenomenon is based upon the operation of mirror neurons (Rizzolatti & Craighero, 2004; Rizzolatti & Fogassi, 2007). These processing units have been found so far in the ventral premotor cortex of monkeys and humans, and they have the property of discharging during the execution of certain actions, but also during the observation of the very same actions performed by others. They are thought to be involved as well in imitation learning, in the understanding of actions, and even in decoding others' intentions (Iacoboni, Molnar-Szakacs, Gallese, Buccino, Mazziotta, & Rizzolatti, 2005; Rizzolatti & Fogassi, 2007; Rizzolatti, Fogassi, & Gallese, 2001).

We already mentioned that mimicking emotional expression, especially if it combines facial configuration, body posture, breath pattern and voicing, is often sufficient to trigger them, so that contagion from expression not only affects others but could also operate on oneself. It has been used to evoke emotions in subjects during psychology experiments (Ekman, 1982; Ekman,

Levenson, & Friesen, 1983; Larsen, Kasimatis, & Frey, 1992; Strack, Martin, & Stepper, 1988), and also in the training of actors (Bloch, 1989; Bloch et al., 1991; Bloch et al., 1987). On the other hand, since expression is so intimately associated with the activation of emotion scripts, blocking it usually has the effect of reducing considerably the intensity of the emotion felt, sometimes to the point of suppressing it. This is why expression control is recurrently used across cultures in the socialization of emotions and the acquisition of display rules. This is also the reason for the backward *trigger* arrow from the expression module to the activation module in Figure 1.

The last box is outside the system and refers to the BEHAVIORS of OTHERS. As researches on emotions amply illustrate, emotional behavior is most typically directed towards other agents who become the main target of the expression intrinsically associated with a particular script. In our theory, behaviors of others *altering commitments* are seen as the main cause for the triggering of emotions, and these individuals are thus the essential destination of their outward expression. Two remarks are mandatory here. First, one should understand that, for the whole system to work efficiently, every other individual is presumed to have been engineered along a similar ontology: similar antecedents for triggering emotions, same functions of emotion, similar enough scripts for families of emotions, similar body and facial expressions for corresponding emotions. For an expression of anger to be efficient in monitoring breaches in commitments, each partner involved in them should indeed have at disposal a script comparable enough that encapsulates what could have evoked this emotion and how the problem could best be fixed. This could be one reason why systems based on mirror neurons ended up being engineered through natural selection. Second, one should envision the other's reactions as kind of a dance, following an almost straightforward choreography: a given emotion expressed by the first individual is likely to be followed more or less typically by a given one in the second. When partners are not well attuned on this matter, escalation occurs, and could end up dramatically. In the usual course of action, only a few rounds of emotional exchange are typically required to complete the regulation process, and insure repairing or strengthening of the commitment under consideration.

CONCLUSION

In this chapter, we first recalled briefly the *Commitment Theory of Emotions* and then examined closely the different modules involved in the functioning of the system as well as the way they interacted with each other. We especially tried to show that viewing emotions as commitments operators helped to clarify the operation of each module and generated several constraints that imposed order and meaning on the way everything worked altogether. The centrality of commitments is obvious enough in the personal data base that registers them, but its content has to be intricately meshed, by the activation module, with the prototypical scripts associated with each emotion before they be executed. The antecedent detectors in the input module are also to be configured specifically so as to detect variations in commitments together with proper attribution to the agents responsible for them, and the expression module is precisely directed towards the agents registered as being involved in the commitment of concern. Needs and other motivation systems inform the commitments data base, and they are themselves affected by the activation module dedicated to invoke the proper emotions as operators in the service of commitments management. One's affective states may seem less dependent upon commitment dynamics, as they stand in the background, mainly modulating the threshold device or setting up the values of certain variables in the scripts data base. Yet they are themselves much affected by the recurring activation of the same emotion

in short periods of time, which could contribute to install or dissolve certain moods. Excessive activation could also result in affective disorders, but at the same time, it is through the therapeutic usage of emotion revival and expression that these disorders can sometimes be cured.

Such a model evidences the full intricacy of emotional behavior, yet it makes rather clear, in a way quite consonant with what is known in the Psychology of emotions, which modules are required and what has to be specified in each of them for the whole system to work efficiently and fulfill its function. Quite a lot has been said that bear consequences on implementation matters: what kind of detectors are in need for critical situations to be registered; which modules have an effect on the threshold device; what should the elicitation structure look like in order to rapidly trigger the proper emotion on a given circumstance; what are scripts typically made of; what information is mandatory in the facture of commitments; how are emotion episodes usually concluded; how and why is expression so intricately mixed with emotional behavior. Yet, there remain a few unresolved questions, and we will thus conclude by stressing some additional requirements this theory puts on implementation matters and which should be taken into consideration.

The *first* point is that emotions, as has been amply documented, are interactive phenomena, that appeared with nurturing species, and whose basic function is to regulate behavior so as to form and maintain social bonds. The implication for synthetic emotions is that they only make sense with a community of agents, competing for resources, as is fundamentally the case in a Darwinian world, but sometimes resorting to cooperation as a powerful way of getting access to them. In species complex enough to require nurturing for complete development, altruism, protection and dedication from parents and caretakers is a necessary condition of reproduction itself. But this also induces cooperation between parents and kin, and once installed, it spreads easily among the community as an adaptive strategy, provided exploitation and defection from profiteers is carefully managed (Axelrod, 1984; Axelrod & Dion, 1988; Nesse, 1990, 2007; Trivers, 1971). That is precisely what the emotion layer is about.

One may object that emotions are not necessarily interactive, because humans can well feel emotions in the absence of other agents. But it is also the case with language: we regularly use it to represent things to ourselves, to plan courses of action, to remind ourselves about some events. Yet language did evolve for communication purpose, and could not have without the opportunity and benefits of exchanging with others. Likewise, we contend that emotions evolved to resolve interaction problems with significant others, but that once developed, they could be used outside actual interaction to reflect on one's private life, and especially about our relations with others (Oatley, 1996). It is indeed believed that one important function of creative expression in the narrative arts is to simulate ways of interacting with others, notably through emotional expression and transformation, and to let the reader explore these schemes further in a productive and useful manner (Oatley, 1999, 2000, 2003). The construction of literary character in fiction could thus have evolved as an elaborate version of building up workable mental models of others such as people currently do in conversations (Mar & Oatley, 2008; Oatley, 2004; Oatley & Mar, 2005).

A *second* condition is in direct consequence of the first one: committed partners have to be endowed with the capacity of quickly recognizing and identifying each other, an unconditional requirement for imprinting or attachment to be established, and for enabling relatives to play their part in fulfilling the commitments that bind them together. This is probably going to be a real challenge for robots designers, since this identification problem has not been well circumscribed yet, and to our knowledge, it has not been attacked seriously so far.

For emotions to work efficiently as interactive managers, a *third* requisite is that concerned agents in the community be all engineered along a similar ontology, or else they will not respond adequately to emotional solicitation, and there will be no grasp from which to regulate the commitments binding them. Dramatic examples in human societies are evidenced in cases of autism or of psychopathy, which are both understood as resulting from major deficits in emotion management. In the first case, individuals remain withdrawn from the rest of the community, unable to launch emotions and establish communication in the service of adaptation and resource attainment (Baron-Cohen, Ring, Bullmore, Wheelwright, Ashwin, & Williams, 2000; Dapretto, Davies, Pfeifer, Scott, Sigman, Bookheimer, & Iacoboni, 2006; Iacoboni & Mazziotta, 2007; Insel, 2003). In a related way, patients with schizophrenia also display abnormalities in emotion recognition and affective responsiveness (Burns, 2006). In the case of psychopaths, they cultivate abusive behavior in access to resources, without being compelled, either from inner feelings or from the expression of others, to be respectful of commitments (Hare, 1993; Mealy, 1995; Stout, 2005). On the other hand, a partially shared ontology is precisely what enables satisfying relationships with our pet animals. They indeed seem to establish commitments with us (in the form of an attachment structure), and their scripts for emotions, although simpler than ours, present enough similarity for exchange to be possible.

A *fourth* requirement is that the emotion layer be built upon a simpler layer of needs and instinctive behavior. It is indeed believed that emotions first appeared in the service of these less sophisticated structures, so as to help managing access to resources for survival that newborns could not get without the help of mature others (Panksepp, 2004). Endowing artificial systems with these capacities does not appear as an insuperable task though, since researchers in artificial intelligence and robotics have listed out some of the specifications that their existence commanded, and they have already proposed reasonable designs to meet them (Beaudry, Brosseau, Côté, Raïevsky, Létourneau, Kabanza, & Michaud, 2005; Brooks, 1991; Maes, 1991; Steels & Brooks, 1995).

A *fifth* condition is that proper detectors making ample use of social affordances (notably from expressive patterns or agency signatures) be designed so as to detect significant variations in any commitment of one's concern, in order to launch the proper emotions as operators to fix them. Also required is an ordered list of appropriate actions to be executed so as to handle the situation that triggered the emotion in the first place. On top of these actions, one finds the full diversity of expressive behavior an individual of a given species can resort to, in order to signal the breach or the opportunity encountered, and to call for an appropriate response from partners. Interesting work has also been partially achieved by researchers on these grounds (Velasquez, 1998; Brazeal, 2003; Brazeal, Buschbaum, Gray, Gatenby, & Blumberg, 2005).

Finally, if our speculation about the evolution of emotions is not too farfetched in viewing them as an upper layer of control built upon needs and instinctive processes, and dedicated to the management of social bonding and nurturance, then it is very likely that the overall architecture of social robots will have to take into consideration many of the specifications presented here. Truly, social insects do evidence interactive behavior that does not rest upon emotions and commitments management. But their behavior is rigidly carved into their anatomy and physiology, so that there is not much place left for alternatives, besides what has been preprogrammed (Huang & Fewell, 2002; Wilson, 1971, 2008). The beautiful thing with emotions is that they enrich the repertoire of solutions by enabling the decoupling of stimulus and response (Scherer, 1994). Interactions with complex others introduce new requirements for design (Aubé, 2005): more constraints should be taken into account, one now has to convey inten-

tions and to try decipher those coming from others, regulation and negotiation have to take place. In more complex societies, language has taken over part of this task, and in humans, it has led to the establishment of such sophisticated tools as contracts and conventions (Jennings, 1993; Shoham & Tennenholtz, 1995; Singh, 1999).

Our model suggest that emotions have paved the way towards these means, but also that individuals will often resort to their more primitive and natural tools, still powerful and efficient, to settle commitment problems between interacting agents. With telescopes and microscopes, humans have designed powerful extension of their sight, yet the eye remains the very first tool that insures access to these improvements, and the basic model that has inspired all of them in the first place. In a similar way, constitutions and formal laws have been developed to insure and facilitate social life and cooperation, even at the planetary level, yet most people still resort to emotions when things get out of reach or too complicated to manage. It is thus likely that designing architectures to support complex social behavior similar to that of humans will have to get inspiration from what has been slowly carved to this end through natural selection.

ACKNOWLEDGMENT

The author is grateful to Keith Oatley and Danièle Brake who commented on one of the last drafts of the chapter and provided helpful suggestions for its improvement.

REFERENCES

Ainsworth, M. D. S. (1989). Attachments beyond infancy. *American Psychologist, 44*(4), 709-716.

Aronson, E. (1996). *The social animal.* (Seventh edition). New York: W. H. Freeman.

Aubé, M. (1997a). Toward computational models of motivation: A much needed foundation for social sciences and education. *Journal of Artificial Intelligence in Education, 8*(1), 43-75.

Aubé, M. (1997b). *Les émotions comme opérateurs des engagements: Une métaphore pour les structures de contrôle dans les systèmes multi-agents* [Emotions as commitments operators: A metaphor for control structures in multi-agents systems]. Unpublished doctoral dissertation, Université de Montréal, Montréal.

Aubé, M. (1998). A commitment theory of emotions. In D. Canamero (Ed.), *Emotional and intelligent: The tangled knot of cognition. Papers from the 1998 AAAI Fall Symposium* (pp. 13-18). Menlo Park, California: AAAI Press.

Aubé, M. (2001). From Toda's urge theory to the commitment theory of emotions. *Grounding emotions in adaptive systems*, Special issue of *Cybernetics and Systems: An International Journal, 32*(6), 585-610.

Aubé, M. (2005). Beyond needs: Emotions and the commitments requirement. In D. N. Davis (Ed.), *Visions of mind: Architectures for cognition and affect* (pp. 21-44). Hershey, PA: Idea Group., Inc.

Aubé, M., & Senteni, A. (1995). A foundation for commitments as resource management in multi-agents systems. In T. Finin & J. Mayfield (Eds.), *Proceedings of the CIKM Workshop on Intelligent Information Agents*. Baltimore, Maryland.

Aubé, M., & Senteni, A. (1996a). Emotions as commitments operators: A foundation for control structure in multi-agents systems. In W. Van de Velde & J. W. Perram (Eds.), *Agents breaking away, Proceedings of the 7th European Workshop on MAAMAW, Lecture Notes on Artificial Intelligence, No. 1038* (pp. 13-25). Berlin: Springer.

Aubé, M., & Senteni, A. (1996b). What are emotions for? Commitments management and

regulation within animals/animats encounters. In P. Maes, M. Mataric, J.-A. Meyer, J. Pollack, & S. W. Wilson (Eds.), *From animals to animats 4: Proceedings of the Fourth International Conference on Simulation of Adaptive Behavior* (pp. 264-271). Cambridge, MA: The MIT Press/Bradford Books.

Averill, J. R. (1980). A constructivist view of emotion. In R. Plutchik & H. Kellerman (Eds.), *Emotion: Theory, research, and experience: Vol. 1. Theories of emotions* (pp. 305-339). New York: Academic Press.

Axelrod, R. (1984). *The evolution of cooperation*. New York: Basic Books.

Axelrod, R., & Dion, D. (1988). The further evolution of cooperation. *Science, 242*(4884), 1385-1390.

Baddeley, A. (1990). *Human memory: Theory and practice*. Boston: Allyn and Bacon.

Baron-Cohen, S., Ring, H. A., Bullmore, E. T., Wheelwright, S., Ashwin, C., & Williams, S. C. R. (2000). The amygdala theory of autism. *Neuroscience and Biobehavioral Reviews, 24*(3), 355-364.

Bassili, J. N. (1976). Temporal and spatial contingencies in the perception of social events. *Journal of Personality and Social Psychology, 33*(6), 680-685.

Baumeister, R. F., & Leary, M. R. (1995). The need to belong: Desire for interpersonal attachments as a fundamental human motivation. *Psychological Bulletin, 117*(3), 497-529.

Beaudry, É., Brosseau, Y., Côté, C., Raïevsky, C., Létourneau, D., Kabanza, F., & Michaud, F. (2005). Reactive planning in a motivated behavioural architecture. In *Proceedings of the Twentieth National Conference on Artificial Intelligence (AAAI-05)* (pp. 1242-1247). Menlo Park, California: AAAI Press.

Berlyne, D. E. (1960). *Conflict, arousal and curiosity*. New York: McGraw-Hill.

Biederman, I., & Vessel, E. A. (2006). Perceptual pleasure and the brain. *American Scientist, 94*(3), 247-255.

Bloch, S. (1989). Émotion ressentie, émotion re-créée. *Science et Vie, Hors série, 168*, 68-75.

Bloch, S., Lemeignan, M., & Aguilera, N. (1991). Specific respiratory patterns distinguish among human basic emotions, *International Journal of Psychophysiology, 11*(2), 141-154.

Bloch, S., Orthous, P., & Santibanez-H, G. (1987). Effector patterns of basic emotions: A psychophysiological method for training actors. *Journal of Social and Biological Structures, 10*(1), 1-19.

Boucher, J. D. (1983). Antecedents to emotions across cultures. In S. H. Irvine & J. W. Berry (Eds.), *Human Assessment and Cultural Factors* (pp. 407-420). New York: Plenum.

Bowlby, J. (1969). *Attachment and loss. Vol. 1: Attachment*. London: Penguin Books.

Bowlby, J. (1973). *Attachment and loss. Vol. 2: Separation, anxiety, and anger*. London: Penguin Books.

Bowlby, J. (1980). *Attachment and loss. Vol. 3: Loss, sadness, and depression*. London: Penguin Books.

Brazeal, C. (2003). Emotion and sociable humanoid robots. *International Journal of Human-Computer Studies, 59*(1-2), 119-155.

Brazeal, C., Buschbaum, D., Gray, J., Gatenby, D., & Blumberg, B. (2005). Learning from and about others: Towards using imitation to bootstrap the social understanding of others by robots. *Artificial, Life, 11*(1-2), 79-98.

Brooks, R. A. (1991). Intelligence without representation. *Artificial Intelligence, 47*(1-3), 139-159.

Burns, J. (2006). The social brain hypothesis of schizophrenia. *World Psychiatry, 5*(2), 77-81.

Butler, E., Egloff, B., Wilhem, F. H., Smith, N. C., Erickson, E. A., & Gross, J. J. (2003). The social consequences of expressive suppression. *Emotion, 3*(1), 48-67.

Carver, C. S., & Scheier, M. F. (1990). Origins and functions of positive and negative affect: A control process view. *Psychological Review, 97*(1), 19-35.

Charlesworth, W. R., & Kreutzer, M. A. (1973). Facial expressions of infants and children. In P. Ekman (Ed.), *Darwin and facial expression: A century of research in review* (pp. 91-167). New York: Academic Press.

Cialdini, R. B. (1984). *Influence*. New York: William Morrow and Company.

Cialdini, R. B., Vincent, J. E., Lewis, S. K., Catalan, J., Wheeler, D., & Darby, B. L. (1975). Reciprocal concessions procedure for inducing compliance: The door-in-the-face technique. *Journal of Personality and Social Psychology, 31*(2), 206-215.

Cosmides, L. (1989). The logic of social exchange: Has natural selection shaped how humans reason? Studies with the Wason selection task. *Cognition, 31*(3), 187-276.

Damasio, A. R. (1994). *Descarte's error: Emotion, reason and the human brain*. New York: Avon Books.

Dapretto, M., Davies, M. S., Pfeifer, J. H., Scott, A. A., Sigman, M., Bookheimer, S. Y., & Iacoboni, M. (2006). Understanding emotions in others: Mirror neuron dysfunction in children with autism spectrum disorders. *Nature Neuroscience, 9*(1), 28-30.

Darwin, C. (1965). *The expression of the emotions in man and animals*. Chicago: The University of Chicago Press. (Original work published 1872)

Davidson, R. J. (1994). On emotion, mood, and related affective constructs. In P. Ekman & R. J. Davidson (Eds.), *The nature of emotion: Fundamental questions* (pp. 51-55). Oxford: Oxford University Press.

Dimberg, U. (1982). Facial reactions to facial expressions. *Psychophysiology, 19*(6), 643-647.

Dimberg, U. (1988). Facial electromyography and emotional reactions. *Psychophysiology, 27*(5), 481-494.

Duclos, S. E., & Laird, J. D. (2001). The deliberate control of emotional experience through control of expressions. *Cognition and Emotion, 15*(1), 27-56.

Dweck, C. S. (1986). Motivational processes affecting learning. *American Psychologist, 41*(10), 1040-1048.

Eibl-Eibesfeldt, I. (1973). The expressive behavior of the deaf-and-blind-born. In M. Von Cranach & I. Vine (Eds.), *Social communication and movement. Studies of interaction and expression in man and chimpanzee* (pp. 163-194). New York: Academic Press.

Eibl-Eibesfeldt, I. (1975). *Ethology: The biology of behavior.* (2nd edition). New York: Holt, Rinehart and Winston.

Ekman, P. (Ed.). (1982). *Emotion in the human face.* Cambridge, England: Cambridge University Press.

Ekman, P. (1984). Expression and the nature of emotion. In K. R. Scherer & P. Ekman (Eds.), *Approaches to emotion* (pp. 319-343). Hillsdale, N.J.: Erlbaum.

Ekman, P. (1992). An argument for basic emotions. *Cognition and Emotion, 6*(3-4), 169-200.

Ekman, P. (1993). Facial expression and emotion. *American Psychologist, 48*(4), 384-392.

Ekman, P. (1994). Moods, emotions, and traits. In P. Ekman & R. J. Davidson (Eds.), *The nature of emotion: Fundamental questions* (pp. 56-58). Oxford: Oxford University Press.

Ekman, P. (2003). *Emotions revealed. Recognizing faces and feelings to improve communication and emotional life.* New York: Henry Holt and Company, LLC.

Ekman, P., & Friesen, W. V. (1975). *Unmasking the face: A guide to recognizing emotions from facial expressions.* Englewood Cliffs, NJ: Prentice-Hall.

Ekman, P., Levenson, R. W., & Friesen, W. V. (1983). Autonomous nervous system activity distinguishes between emotions. *Science, 221*(4616), 1208-1210.

Ellsworth, P. C., & Scherer, K. R. (2003). Appraisal processes in emotion. In R. J. Davidson, K. R. Scherer, & H. H. Goldsmith (Eds.), *Handbook of affective sciences* (pp. 572-595). New York: Oxford University Press.

Ellsworth, P. C., & Smith, C. A. (1988a). From appraisal to emotion: Differences among unpleasant feelings. *Motivation and Emotion, 12*(3), 271-302.

Ellsworth, P. C., & Smith, C. A. (1988b). Shades of joy: Patterns of appraisal differentiating pleasant emotions. *Cognition and Emotion, 2*(4), 301-331.

Eustache, F., & Desgranges, B. (2008). MNESIS: Towards the integration of current multisystem models of memory. *Neuropsychology Review, 18*(1), 53-69.

Fehr, B., & Russell, J. A. (1984). Concept of emotion viewed from a prototype perspective. *Journal of Experimental Psychology: General, 113*(3), 464-486.

Fischer, K. W., Shaver, P.R., & Carnochan, P. (1990). How emotions develop and how they organise development. *Cognition and Emotion, 4*(2), 81-127.

Freedman, J., & Fraser, S. (1966). Compliance without pressure: The foot-in-the-door technique. *Journal of Personality and Social Psychology, 4*(2), 195-202.

Freedman, J. L., Wallington, S. A., & Bless, E. (1967). Compliance without pressure: The effect of guilt. *Journal of Personality and Social Psychology, 7*(2), 117-124.

Frijda, N. H. (1986). *The emotions.* Cambridge, England: Cambridge University Press.

Frijda, N. H. (1989). The functions of emotional expression. In J. P. Forgas & J. M. Innes (Eds.), *Recent advances in social psychology: An international perspective* (pp. 205-217). Amsterdam: North-Holland.

Frijda, N. H. (1993). Moods, emotion episodes, and emotions. In M. Lewis & J. M. Haviland (Eds.), *Handbook of emotions* (pp. 381-403). New York: The Guilford Press.

Frijda, N. H. (1994). Varieties of affect: Emotions and episodes, moods, and sentiments. In P. Ekman & R. J. Davidson (Eds.), *The nature of emotion: Fundamental questions* (pp. 59-67). Oxford: Oxford University Press.

Frijda, N. H., Kuipers, P., & ter Schure, E. (1989). Relations among emotion, appraisal, and emotional action readiness. *Journal of Personality and Social Psychology, 57*(2), 212-228.

Fromme, D. K., & O'Brien, C. S. (1982). A dimensional approach to the circular ordering of the emotions. *Motivation and Emotion, 6*(4), 337-363.

Gibson, J. J. (1966). *The senses considered as perceptual systems.* Boston: Houghton Mifflin.

Gibson, J. J. (1977). The theory of affordances. In R. Shaw & J. Bransford (Eds.), *Perceiving, acting and knowing. Toward an ecological psychology* (pp. 67-82). Hillsdale, N.J.: Erlbaum.

Gigerenzer, G., & Hug, K. (1992). Domain-specific reasoning: Social contracts, cheating, and perspective change. *Cognition, 43*(2), 127-171.

Hansen, C. H., & Hansen, R. D. (1988). Finding the face in the crowd: An anger superiority effect. *Journal of Personality and Social Psychology, 54*, 917-924.

Hare, R. D. (1993). *Without conscience: The disturbing world of psychopaths among us.* New York: The Gilford Press.

Harré, R. (1986). *The social construction of emotions.* Oxford: Blackwell.

Hasselmo, M. E., Rolls, E. T., & Baylis, G. C. (1989). The role of expression and identity in the face-selective response of neurons in the temporal visual cortex of the monkey. *Behavioural Brain Research, 32*(3), 203-218.

Hatfield, E., Cacioppo, J. T., & Rapson, R. L. (1994). *Emotional contagion.* Cambridge, England: Cambridge University Press.

Hazan, C., & Shaver, P. (1987). Romantic love conceptualized as an attachment process. *Journal of Personality and Social Psychology, 52*(3), 511-524.

Hebb, D. O. (1949). *The organization of behavior.* New York: Wiley.

Hochschild, A. R. (1979). Emotion work, feeling rules, and social structure. *American Journal of Sociology, 85*(3), 551-575.

Hochschild, A. R. (1983). *The managed heart: The commercialization of human feelings.* Berkeley: University of California Press.

Hoffman, H. S. (1974) Fear-mediated processes in the context of imprinting. In M. Lewis & L. A. Rosenblum (Eds.), *The origins of fear* (pp. 25-48). New York: John Wiley and Sons.

Huang, Z.Y., & Fewell, J.H. (2002). Modeling insect societies: from genes to colony behavior. *Trends in Ecology & Evolution, 17*(9), 403-404.

Hutchinson, R. R. (1972). The environmental causes of aggression. In J. K. Coles & D. D. Jenson (Eds.), *Nebraska Symposium on Motivation 1972: Vol. 20* (pp. 155-181). Lincoln: University of Nebraska Press.

Iacoboni, M., & Mazziotta, J. C. (2007). Mirror neuron system: Basic findings and clinical applications. *Annals of Neurology, 62*(3), 213-218.

Iacoboni, M., Molnar-Szakacs, I., Gallese, V., Buccino, G., Mazziotta, J. C., & Rizzolatti, G. (2005). Grasping the intentions of others with one's own mirror neuron system. *PLoS Biology, 3*(3), e79, 0001-0007.

Insel, T. R. (2003). The neurobiology of affiliation: implications for autism. In R. J. Davidson, K. R. Scherer, & H. H. Goldsmith (Eds.), *Handbook of affective sciences* (pp. 1010-1020). New York: Oxford University Press.

Izard, C. E. (1977). *Human emotions.* New York: Plenum.

Izard, C. E. (1993). Four systems for emotion activation: Cognitive and noncognitive processes. *Psychological Review, 100*(1), 68-90.

Jennings, N. R. (1993). Commitments and conventions: The foundation of coordination in multi-agent systems. *Knowledge Engineering Review, 8*(3), 223-250.

Johnson-Laird, P. N., & Oatley, K. (1989). The language of emotions: An analysis of a semantic field. *Cognition and Emotion, 3*(2), 81-123.

Kappas, A., Bherer, F., & Thériault, M. (2000). Inhibiting facial expressions: Limitations to the voluntary control of facial expressions of emotion. *Motivation and Emotion, 24*(4), 259-268.

Keltner, D., Ekman, P., Gonzaga, G. C., & Beer, J. (2003). Facial expression of emotion. In R. J. Davidson, K. R. Scherer, & H. H. Goldsmith (Eds.), *Handbook of affective sciences* (pp. 415-432). New York: Oxford University Press.

Kerr, N. L., & Kaufman-Gilliland, C. M. (1994). Communication, commitment, and cooperation in social dilemmas. *Journal of Personality and Social Psychology, 66*(3), 513-529.

Klinger, E. (1975). Consequences of commitment to and disengagement from incentives. *Psychological Review, 82*(1), 1-25.

Larsen, R. J., & Diener, W. (1992). Promises and problems with the circumplex model of emotion. *Review of Personality and Social Psychology, 13*, 25-59.

Larsen, R. J., Kasimatis, M., & Frey, K. (1992). Facilitating the furrowed brow: A nonobtrusive test of the facial feedback hypothesis applied to unpleasant effect. *Cognition and Emotion, 6*(5), 321-338.

Lazarus, R. S. (1991a). *Emotion and adaptation.* New York: Oxford University Press.

Lazarus, R. S. (1991b). Cognition and motivation in emotion. *American Psychologist, 46*(4), 352-367.

LeDoux, J. E. (1989). Cognitive-emotional interactions in the brain. *Cognition and Emotion, 3*(4), 267-289.

Levenson, R. W. (1994). Emotional control: Variations and consequences. In P. Ekman & R. J. Davidson (Eds.), *The nature of emotion: Fundamental questions* (pp. 273-279). Oxford: Oxford University Press.

Levenson, R. W., & Ruef, A. M. (1992) Empathy: A physiological substrate. *Journal of Personality and Social Psychology, 63*(2), 234-246.

Lowenstein, G. (1994). The psychology of curiosity: A review and reinterpretation. *Psychological Bulletin, 116*(1), 75-98.

Lutz, C. (1988). Ethnographic perspectives on the emotion lexicon. In V. Hamilton, G. H. Bower, & N. H. Frijda (Eds.), *Cognitive perspectives on emotion and motivation* (pp. 399-419). Dordrecht: Kluwer.

MacLean, P. D. (1993). Cerebral evolution of emotion. In M. Lewis & J. M. Haviland (Eds.), *Handbook of emotions* (pp. 67-83). New York: The Guilford Press.

Maes, P. (Ed.). (1991). *Designing autonomous agents: Theory and practice from biology to engineering and back*. Cambridge: MIT Press.

Malatesta, C. Z., & Haviland, J. M. (1982). Learning display rules: The socialization of emotion expression in infancy. *Child Development, 53*(4), 991-1003.

Mar, R. A. & Oatley, K. (2008). The function of fiction is the abstraction and simulation of social experience. *Perspectives on Psychological Science, 3*(3), 173-192.

Mascolo, M. F., & Fischer, K. W. (1995). Developmental transformations in appraisals for pride, shame, and guilt. In J. P. Tangney & K. W. Fischer (Eds.), *Self-conscious emotions. The psychology of shame, guilt, embarrassment, and pride* (pp. 64-113). New York: The Guilford Press.

Mathes, E. W., Adams, H. E., & Davies, R. M. (1985). Jealousy: Loss of relationship rewards, loss of self-esteem, depression, anxiety, and anger. *Journal of Personality and Social Psychology, 48*(6), 1552-1561.

Matsumoto, D. (1990). Cultural similarities and differences in display rules. *Motivation and Emotion, 14*(3), 195-214.

Mealey, L. (1995). The sociobiology of sociopathy: An integrated evolutionary model. *Behavioral and Brain Sciences, 18*(3), 523-599.

Michotte, A. E. (1950). The emotions regarded as functional connections. In M. Reymert (Ed.), *Feelings and emotions. The Mooseheart symposium* (pp. 114-126). New York: McGraw-Hill.

Nesse, R. M. (1990). Evolutionary explanations of emotions. *Human Nature, 1*(3), 261-289.

Nesse, R. M. (2004). Natural selection and the elusiveness of happiness. *Philosophical Transactions of the Royal Society B, 359*(1449), 1333-1349.

Nesse, R. M. (2007). Runaway social selection for displays of partner value and altruism. *Biological Theory, 2*(2), 143-155.

Oatley, K. (1992). *Best laid schemes: The psychology of emotions.* Cambridge, England: Cambridge University Press.

Oatley, K. (1996). Emotions: Communications to the self and others. In R. Harré & W.G. Parrott (Eds.), *The emotions: Social, cultural, and biological dimensions* (pp. 312-316). London: Sage.

Oatley, K. (1999). Why fiction may be twice as true as fact: Fiction as cognitive and emotional simulation. *Review of General Psychology, 3*(2), 101-117.

Oatley, K. (2000). Shakespeare's invention of theatre as simulation that runs on minds. In A. Sloman (Ed.), *Proceedings of the AISB-2000 Workshop: How to Design a Functioning Mind* (pp. 102-110). Birmingham, UK: Society for the Study of Artificial Intelligence and Simulation of Behaviour.

Oatley, K. (2003). Creative expression and communication of emotions in the visual and narrative arts. In R. J. Davidson, K. R. Scherer, & H. H. Goldsmith (Eds.), *Handbook of Affective Sciences* (pp. 481-502). New York: Oxford University Press.

Oatley, K. (2004). From the emotions of conversation to the passions of fiction. In A. S. R. Manstead, N. Frijda, & A. Fisher (Eds.), *Feelings and emotions. The Amsterdam symposium* (pp. 98-115). Cambridge, UK: Cambridge University Press.

Oatley, K., & Johnson-Laird, P. N. (1987). Towards a cognitive theory of emotions. *Cognition and Emotion, 1*(1), 29-50.

Oatley, K., & Mar, R. A. (2005). Evolutionary pre-adaptation and the idea of character in fiction. *Journal of Cultural and Evolutionary Psychology, 3*(2), 179-194.

Öhman, A. (1986). Face the beast and fear the face: Animal and social fears as prototypes for evolutionary analyses of emotion. *Psychophysiology, 23*(2), 123-145.

Öhman, A., & Dimberg, U. (1978). Facial expressions as conditioned stimuli for electrodermal responses: A case of "preparedness"? *Journal of Personality and Social Psychology, 36*(11), 1251-1258.

O'Keefe, D. J., & Figge, M. (1997). A guilt-based explanation of the door-in-the-face influence strategy. *Human Communication Research, 24*(1), 64-81.

Ortony, A., Clore, G. L., & Collins, A. (1988). *The cognitive structure of emotions.* Cambridge, England: Cambridge University Press.

Ortony, A., Clore, G. L., & Foss, M. A. (1987). The referential structure of the affective lexicon. *Cognitive Science, 11*, 341-364.

Panksepp, J. (1982). Toward a general psychobiological theory of emotions. *Behavioral and Brain Sciences, 5*(3), 407-467.

Panksepp, J. (1998). *Affective neuroscience. The foundations of human and animal emotions.* New York: Oxford University Press.

Panksepp, J. (2004). Basic affects and the instinctual emotional systems of the brain. In A. S. R. Manstead, N. Frijda, & A. Fisher (Eds.), *Feelings and emotions. The Amsterdam symposium* (pp. 174-193). Cambridge: Cambridge University Press.

Parrott, W. G., & Smith, S. F. (1991). Embarrassment: Actual vs. typical cases, classical vs. prototypical representations. *Cognition and Emotion, 5*(5-6), 467-488.

Pinker, S. 1997. *How the mind works.* New York: W. W. Norton and Company.

Provine, R. R. (1992). Contagious laughter: Laughter is a sufficient stimulus for laughs and smiles. *Bulletin of the Psychonomic Society, 30*(1), 1-4.

Provine, R. R. (2000). *Laughter: A scientific investigation.* New York: Penguin Books.

Rizzolatti, G., & Craighero, L. (2004). The mirror-neuron system. *Annual Review of Neuroscience, 27*, 169-192.

Rizzolatti. G., & Fogassi, L. (2007). Mirror neurons and social cognition. In R. I. M. Dunbar & L. Barrett (Eds.), *The Oxford Handbook of evolutionary psychology* (pp. 179-195). New York: Oxford University Press.

Rizzolatti. G., Fogassi, L., & Gallese, V. (2001). Neurophysiological mechanisms underlying the understanding and imitation of action. *Nature Reviews Neuroscience, 2*(9), 661-70.

Roseman, I. J., Aliki Antoniou, A., & Jose, P. E. (1996). Appraisal determinants of emotions: Constructing a more accurate and comprehensive theory. *Cognition and Emotion, 10*(3), 241-277.

Rosenblum, L. A., & Alpert, S. (1974). Fear of strangers and specificity of attachment in monkeys. In M. Lewis & L. A. Rosenblum (Eds.), *The origins of fear* (pp. 165-193). New York: John Wiley and Sons.

Rozin, P., & Fallon, A. E. (1987). A perspective on disgust. *Psychological Review, 94*(1), 23-41.

Rozin, P., Haidt, J., & McCauley, C. R. (1993). Disgust. In M. Lewis & J. M. Haviland (Eds.), *Handbook of emotions* (pp. 575-594). New York: The Guilford Press.

Ruch, W. (1993). Exhilaration and humor. In M. Lewis & J. M. Haviland (Eds.), *Handbook of emotions* (pp. 605-616). New York: The Guilford Press.

Russell, J. A. (1979). Affective space is bipolar. *Journal of Personality and Social Psychology, 37*(3), 345-356.

Russell, J. A. (1980). A circumplex model of affect. *Journal of Personality and Social Psychology, 39*(6), 1161-1178.

Russell, J. A. (1991). In defense of a prototype approach to emotion concepts. *Journal of Personality and Social Psychology, 60*(1), 37-47.

Sackett, G. P. (1966). Monkeys reared in isolation with pictures as visual input: Evidence for an innate releasing mechanism. *Science, 154,* 1468-1473.

Sagi, A., & Hoffman, M. L. (1976). Empathic distress in the newborn. *Developmental Psychology, 12*(2), 175-76.

Scherer, K. R. (1988a). Criteria for emotion-antecedent appraisal: A review. In V. Hamilton, G. H. Bower, & N. H. Frijda (Eds.), *Cognitive perspectives on emotion and motivation* (pp. 89-126). Dordrecht: Kluwer.

Scherer, K. R. (Ed.). (1988b). *Facets of emotion: Recent research.* Hillsdale, N.J.: Erlbaum.

Scherer, K. R. (1994). Emotion serves to decouple stimulus and response. In P. Ekman & R. J. Davidson (Eds.), *The nature of emotion: Fundamental questions* (pp. 127-130). Oxford: Oxford University Press.

Scherer, K. R., & Tannenbaum, P. H. (1986). Emotional experiences in everyday life: A survey approach. *Motivation and Emotion, 10*(4), 295-314.

Scherer, K. R., Wallbott, H. G., & Summerfield, A. B. (Eds.). (1986). *Experiencing emotion: A cross-cultural study.* Cambridge, England: Cambridge University Press.

Schlosberg, H. (1954). Three dimensions of emotion. *Psychological Review, 61*(2), 81-88.

Schultz , P. A. (1994). Goals as the transactive point between motivation and cognition. In P. R. Pintrich, D. R. Brown, & L. E. Weinstein (Eds.), *Student motivation, cognition and learning. Essays in honor of Wilbert J. McKeachie* (pp. 135-156). Hillsdale, NJ: Erlbaum.

Sharpsteen, D. J. (1991). The organization of jealousy knowledge: Romantic jealousy as a blended emotion. In P. Salovey (Ed.). *The psychology of jealousy and envy* (pp. 31-51). New York: The Guilford Press.

Shaver, P. R., Wu, S., & Schwartz, J. (1992). Cross-cultural similarities and differences in emotion and its representation: A prototype approach. *Review of Personality and Social Psychology, 13,* 175-212.

Shaver, P.R., Schwartz, J., Kirson, D., & O'Connor, C. (1987). Emotion knowledge: Further exploration of a prototype approach. *Journal of Personality and Social Psychology, 52*(6), 1061-1086.

Shoham, Y., & Tennenholtz, M. (1995). On social laws for artificial agent societies: Off-line design. *Artificial Intelligence, 73*(1-2), 231-252.

Shweder, R. A., & LeVine, R. A. (Eds.). (1984). *Culture theory: Essays on mind, self, and emotion.* Cambridge, England: Cambridge University Press.

Simon, H. (1967). Motivational and emotional controls of cognition. *Psychological Review, 74*(1), 29-39.

Singh, M. P. (1999). An ontology for commitments in multiagent systems: Toward a unification of normative concepts. *Artificial Intelligence and Law, 7*(1), 97-113.

Smith, C. A., & Ellsworth, P. C. (1985). Patterns of cognitive appraisal in emotion. *Journal of Personality and Social Psychology, 48*(4), 813-838.

Snowdon, C. T. (2003). Expression of emotion in nonhuman animals. In R. J. Davidson, K. R. Scherer, & H. H. Goldsmith (Eds.), *Handbook of affective sciences* (pp. 457-480). New York: Oxford University Press.

Steels, L., & Brooks, R. (Eds.). (1995). *The artificial life route to artificial intelligence.* Hillsdale, NJ: Erlbaum.

Stein, N. L., Trabasso, T., & Liwag, M. (1993). The representation and organization of emotional experience: Unfolding the emotion episode. In M. Lewis & J. M. Haviland (Eds.), *Handbook of emotions* (pp. 279-300). New York: The Guilford Press.

Storm, C., & Storm, T. (1987). A taxonomic study of the vocabulary of emotions. *Journal of Personality and Social Psychology, 53*(4), 805-816.

Stout, M. (2005). *The sociopath next door.* New York: Broadway Books.

Strack, F., Martin, L. L., & Stepper, S. (1988). Inhibiting and facilitating conditions of the human smile: A nonobtrusive test of the facial feedback hypothesis. *Journal of Personality and Social Psychology, 54*(5), 768-777.

Tangney, J. P., & Fischer, K. W. (Eds.). (1995) *Self-conscious emotions. The psychology of shame, guilt, embarrassment, and pride.* New York: The Guilford Press.

Tesser, A., Gatewood, R., & Driver, M. (1968). Some determinants of gratitude. *Journal of Personality and Social Psychology, 9*(3), 233-236.

Thompson, R. A. (1989). Causal attributions and children's emotional understanding. In C. Saarni & P. L. Harris (Eds.), *Children's understanding of emotion* (pp. 117-150). Cambridge, England: Cambridge University Press.

Toates, F. (1986). *Motivational systems.* Cambridge: Cambridge University Press.

Toates, F. (1988). Motivation and emotion from a biological perspective. In V. Hamilton, G. H. Bower, & N. H. Frijda (Eds.), *Cognitive perspectives on emotion and motivation* (pp. 3-35). Dordrecht: Kluwer.

Toda, M. (1985). Emotions viewed as tightly organized, genetically determined system of behavior-selection programs. In J. T. Spence & C. E. Izard (Eds.), *Motivation, Emotion, and Personality* (pp. 261-273). North-Holland: Elsevier Science Publishers.

Trevarthen, C. (1984). Emotions in infancy: Regulators of contact and relationships with persons. In K. R. Scherer & P. Ekman (Eds.), *Approaches to emotion* (pp. 129-157). Hillsdale, N.J.: Erlbaum.

Trivers, R. L. (1971). The evolution of reciprocal altruism. *The Quarterly Review of Biology, 46*(1), 35-57.

Turner, J. H. (1997). The evolution of emotion: The nonverbal basis of human social organization. In U. Segerstråle & P. Molar (Eds.), *Nonverbal communication: Where nature meets culture* (pp. 211-223). Mahwah, NJ: Erlbaum.

Velásquez, J. (1998). A computational framework for emotion-based control. *Workshop on Grounding Emotions in Adaptive Systems, Fifth International Conference on Simulation of Adaptive Behaviors* (SAB'98), Zurich, 21 août 1998.

Walker-Andrews, A. S. (1986). Intermodal perception of expressive behaviors: Relation of eye and voice? *Developmental Psychology, 22*(3), 373-377.

Weiner, B. (1985). An attributional theory of achievement motivation and emotion. *Psychological Review, 92*(4), 548-573.

Weiner, B., & Graham, S. (1989). Understanding the motivational role of affect: Life-span research from an attributional perspective. *Cognition and Emotion, 3*(4), 401-419.

Wilson, E. O. (1971). *The insect societies.* Cambridge: Harvard University Press.

Wilson, E.O. (2008). One giant leap: How Insects achieved altruism and colonial life. *BioScience, 58*(1), 17-25.

Wong, P. T. P., & Weiner, B. (1981). When people ask "why" questions, and the heuristics of attributional search. *Journal of Personality and Social Psychology, 40*(4), 650-663.

KEY TERMS

Affective States: Emotional episodes are thought to be rather short in duration, in the order of seconds or minutes. Certain mental states, such as moods, temperaments or emotional disorders, can nevertheless augment the propensity that a given emotion be triggered and that it lasted longer. They could result from circumstancial causes, as in moods, when there has been recurrent activation of the same family of emotions in a brief period of time, but they could also be more idiosyncratic, as in temperaments or traits. Emotional disorders are more complex and could depend upon life events as well as upon personal factors. All affective states interact with emotions, bear an impact upon their being triggered or not, and generally modulate the unfolding of emotional episodes.

Antecedents of Emotions: Antecedents are part of the particular script attached to a given family of emotion. They refer to the characteristics of events that are most likely to evoke the emotion, such as loss of close kin for sadness, anticipated threat for fear or transgression for anger. They are used in the form of social affordances by the input module to detect variations in commitments that are significant enough to require the operation of emotion handlers.

Commitments: Commitments are kind of contracts or conventions that bind two or more agents in a cooperative unit. For their being operative, they have to be clearly represented in each partner's brain. They should be seen as dynamic entities capable of monitoring incoming events and of detecting those that bear impact upon their being threatened or strengthened. They are essentially created, modified or destroyed through the operation of various emotions. Since they reside in the minds of the partners involved in them, they can be transformed only through acts of communication, which explain why emotion unfolding relies so heavily upon their expression.

Elicitation Structure: In nurturing species, commitments are vital resources whose shortening or replenishment should often be managed with emergency. As control systems designed to regulate commitments variations, emotions are indeed typically triggered very quickly, in matter of milliseconds. This requires that the proper operator be identified easily, depending upon the particulars of the commitment favored or threatened. The elicitation structure is a decision matrix that specifies the family of emotions best suited to handle the situation at hands by combining the values from three dimensions: valence (gain or loss in commitments), agency (responsibility attributed to self, others or no one) and certainty (variation certain or uncertain).

Emotion Scripts: For emotions to do their job in managing commitments that bind several agents altogether, there has to be some regularities so that similar events are likely to evoke the same family of emotions in different individuals, trigger a comparable set of reactions and resort to a common emotional language so as to convey the adjustment that is mandatory. Emotion scripts thus register in memory the prototypical unfolding of emotional episodes across individuals. Many researchers in the field believe that they develop from an innate universal core that is shared across cultures and even related species.

Emotions: Emotions constitute an important subset of motivational systems. They are triggered by various antecedents that typically involve gain or loss, threat to one's stock of resources or opportunity to get new ones. In the present model, these resources are viewed as second-order, in the sense that they refer to those that could be acquired through the action of other agents well disposed to provide them. While needs manage direct access to first-order resources such as food, water or shelter, emotions provide access through the intervention of other agents, such as parents nurturing their offspring. The critical point here is that the resources that emotions manage are not so much the agents themselves as their willingness to provide the desired access or protection. This predisposition is called commitment in the model. Emotions are thus viewed as commitment operators that play their role through communicative acts between committed partners.

Expression of Emotions: Expression seems tightly related to the operation of emotions and has always occupied a large part of the researches conducted about them. Control and suppression of expression is indeed related to the inhibition of the feeling itself, as if it were an integral part of the emotional process. In the theory, this phenomenon is explained by the fact that expression is the very mean by which emotions play their part in commitments management. This rests on the principle that commitments are located in the partners' brains, and can only be modified through interactions and acts of communication between them.

Motivation: Motivation is a theoretical construct that is used in Psychology as the analogue of the concept of force in Physics. It is evoked to explain any significant change of behavior or of persistence in spite of fatigue or obstacles.

Motivation essentially has to do with resource management: when vital resources are at stake, an individual gets motivated to behave in ways that raise his chances to obtain the resources, or to prevent the loss of the ones that have already been acquired.

Motivational Systems: Motivation is implemented in the brain through various systems dedicated to resource management and regulation. They are typically arranged in control loop circuitry, and protection from loss or progress towards replenishment are monitored in terms of pain and pleasure gradients. Needs (such as hunger, thirst or fatigue) and emotions (such as anger, joy or fear) are the ones that have been the most extensively studied so far, but it is believed that there are a few more. For instance, on the cognitive side, setting a goal typically raises a drive to organize one's behavior so as to make progress towards it. On the social side, life in small groups is also much determined by the behaviors of others through such phenomena as imitation, fashion, influence or manipulation.

Ontology: Ontology refers to the set of characteristics that specifies a certain class of individuals. For emotions to play their part in regulating social bonding and cooperation, it is required that the individuals involved shared a common ontology, so they be affected similarly by the same events, they registered the commitment that binds them in similar form, they attributed a close enough meaning to a given expression and felt compelled to adjust the commitments in the way it was expected from the message conveyed. It is likely that the evolution of emotions and their expression from Mammals to Primates to Humans laid the basic foundations of that kind of shared ontology.

Chapter XIII
A Cognitive Appraisal Based Approach for Emotional Representation

Sigerist J. Rodríguez
Universidad del Zulia, Venezuela

Pilar Herrero
Universidad Politécnica de Madrid, Spain

Olinto J. Rodríguez
Universidad del Zulia, Venezuela

ABSTRACT

Today, realism and coherence are highly searched qualities in agent's behavior; but these qualities cannot be achieved completely without incorporation of emotions. This chapter shows a model for emotional representations in intelligent agents. The model is based on the cognitive appraisal theory of emotions; this theory affirms that stimuli are processed by a cognitive mechanism that determines what emotion to feel. It is also based on the Aaron Sloman's research where positively and negatively affective states are exposed, as well as, on the theory of basic emotions. The model tries to define an emotional representation data structure for intelligent agents. It also defines the emotional behavior mechanisms when a stimulus is processed, as well as, emotional interaction mechanisms. This chapter is presented in five sections: Introduction, where the topic is presented. State-of-the-Art, where it is introduced a review of emotional studies in psychological areas, as well as, computing areas. The Model Definition section, where a detailed model structure and mechanism are introduced. A fourth section describing the future trends and researches and finally the chapter conclusions.

INTRODUCTION

Nowadays, the tendency toward the search for more realistic behavior in intelligent agents is remarkable. Beyond the philosophical and socio-cultural implications (which are a significant study matter) it is undeniable that, this realistic level could not be reached without the emotions incorporation to the agent's behavioral mechanisms. This work intends to place a base for this virtual human construction presenting an agent mind fundamental component: the structure for emotions representation.

It is then, the main objective of this work, to place the base for a theoretical emotion representation model in intelligent agents capable to represent each one of this in every possible dimension. The model should be sufficiently flexible to cover the entire complexity of human representation of emotions, as well as, the emotion interaction complexity. In order to accomplish this objective, it is necessary to generate a data structure with all the values required to configure an emotion in all its dimensions, and capable to represent any needed emotion. Those mentioned values within the emotion, will be parameters. These parameters will control the emotion behavior. Then it is necessary to identify the mechanisms presented in the human emotions, the reasons and ways emotions arise, and the way an emotion stabilizes. All of this in order to create equivalent mechanisms into the model. Then it will be necessary to identify the interaction mechanisms between emotions, because they clearly affect each other. For example, receiving bad news and good news at the same time, or in a short period of time, will normally produce an almost mathematical annulations effect in the person, letting the individual in a neutral state. But this is not the case when the importance of one of the news is considerably greater than the other. In this case, one emotion will normally diminish the intensity of the other one. All this must be observed, once again, in order to implement equivalent mechanisms for the model.

It is expected to create a flexible model, not too restrictive at the moment of its implementation, offering the developer the possibility to include the required emotions for his agent, with the required values for each one of those, and the required interaction between emotions, finally conforming different agents personalities through setting this values. It is important to notice, that this flexibility places in the developer part of the responsibility of keeping the agent's behavior coherent with human's behavior. However, this situation is considered better than having an over restricting model at the moment of its implementation.

A model that takes in account all the previous statements will make developers able to implement a more realistic agent with a coherent behavior. These agents correctly implemented, will offer a wide application spectrum that goes from entertainment to psychological and sociological investigation. Creating an intelligent agent capable to actually represent the human mind is the ultimate objective; this work intends to offer the first step in this direction.

Four main sections will be found. First, the State-of-the-Art section offers an overview of related works in this area, in emotional theories, as well as, in computational models and architectures. Next, the cognitive appraisal based approach model is presented; also its structures and interaction mechanisms are presented and deeply analyzed. This section is followed for a view of the future works that are intended to develop in the area and trends that could be approached for researchers. Finally, conclusions are presented in the matter of this work.

STATE-OF-THE-ART

The beginnings of the emotional studies could be set back in Athens where Socrates proposed the inalterable human behavior principles existence, among them, the good feelings like ethics. In modern times, Charles Darwin conducts studies about emotions expression in humans and animals (Darwin, 1899). Darwin's studies are centered in the way humans and animals express their emotions and not in mechanisms for generating experience and processing emotions. Darwin's studies take for granted the existence of emotions in humans and animals, introducing in an implicit way the basic emotions idea. According to him, there is a set of emotions which is present in any human being, since its birth, no matter ethnics or social conditions, affirming that these basic emotions are present in high level animals, too.

In (James, 1884) appears one of the first generally accepted emotions theories, the James-Lange theory. This theory proposes that a physiological response for stimuli it is aroused in the body, and then, the cerebral cortex determines which emotion to feel. The theory was well received in the research community, and was accepted for some time. According to this theory, our body response is the one that determines which emotion to feel. When we see a bear in the forest we start to sweat and our muscles get tense and ready to run, and in response to that body changes, we feel the fear. But this theory presents some inconsistencies: we cry when we are scared, and when we are happy, and when we are angry, even when we cut onions we cry. So, why do we have so many different reactions to the same body response? Clearly the theory cannot respond to those questions. Walter Cannon noticed those inconsistencies and presented a new emotion theory in (Cannon, 1920). In this works, called "The James-Lange Theory of Emotions: A Critical Examination and an Alternative Theory", Cannon refused the idea that somatic changes are the activators for emotional responses. Cannon affirms that emotional and somatic responses are produced simultaneously in the subject. Cannon based his conclusions in the study of thalamus behavior during different emotional stimulus. In his work he affirmed that neurons are responsible for body changes when a stimuli is processed, they are directly or indirectly responsible for emotions arousal, as well.

Even when Cannon did not specified exactly which neuronal process excites emotions, he affirmed that these are the ones which activate emotional and somatic mechanisms. Even when Cannon theory covers effectively the holes in James-Lange theory, if it is analyzed in detail, this theory still leaves some unsolved aspects. When a little boy sees a snake, he doesn't feel fear, because he is unaware of the danger that a snake represents, so his assessment for the situation does not include any damage for his integrity and according to that, emotional response could be curiosity, attraction or indifference. On the other hand, an adult who is aware of the danger that a snake represents, will be scared and will get into an alert state to avoid the danger source. Situations like the stated before are covered by the cognitive approach for emotions, presented in (Lazarus, 1991). This emotional theory integrates elements that others researches, centered exclusively on the person, did not take under consideration, such as the environment, and the individual social conditions. For Lazarus the emotional response and the somatic response are the result for a cognitive appraisal process which determines in the human being which emotion to feel and how to react to the received stimuli. In the Kemper's review (1992), Lazarus's ideas are exposed in a clear way; in that work we could observe a synthesis of Lazarus's approach which includes the person and the environment as principal elements in the experience, this represents an interesting approach considering that psychologists' works are normally centered on the person and sociologist works are centered on the environment. Lazarus "synthesizes the two of them by means of a new concept, the 'core relational theme', which integrates people and environment in the service of emotion". Then assessments place a central base for emotion processing in the theory. There are two types of assessments, and they determine the course of emotions. The Primary assessments evaluate the potential harm or benefit of situations and consider three elements: "(1) goal relevance (Does it matter to me what is happening?), (2) goal congruence (Is it consistent what is happening with what I want?), and (3) type of ego-involvement (Does it involve self- or social esteem, moral values, ego-ideals, meanings and ideas, other people and their well-being, or life goals?). Each of these ego elements engages a different emotion". Then it appears the secondary assessment, which processes the coping options of the situation. This includes three elements as well "(1) Which is responsible of evaluating the harm or benefit for self states and others' state; (2) Coping potential (What can I do about the situation?); and (3) future expectancy (Is the situation likely to become more or less goal-congruent?)". The core relational themes (CRT) provide the harm or benefit assessment result as well as a "cognitive-relational infrastructure for a specific emotion", through these CRT's cognitive mechanisms cause emotions. After the assessment, there are the consequences that could be "either short-term actions, physiological changes, and subjective states, or long-term effects of emotional patterns on somatic health, subjective well-being, and social functioning".

We could say that this theory complements Cannon theory including the cognitive evaluation aspect and the socio-cultural aspect in the emotions formation. In addition to the physiological processes, which have as result the emotion experimentation, there is a cognitive assessment for the sensorial experience, which equally has as result the experimentation or absence of an emotion. It is also important the assessment of the environmental context: if a bear appears in the forest we will feel fear, but if a bear appears in the circus we will have fun and more likely we will laugh. Socio-cultural structure has an effect, too. A woman from Caracas will be ashamed if she is seen naked by a stranger, while a Pemon Indian woman will not care about it.

Another important theory in emotions matters was presented long before the cognitive theory; this is the Watson's learning based behavior

theory (1913). Even though this is not a theory of emotions in its strict sense, it presents important conclusions in this matter.

"According to Watson, (Watson, 1913) a researcher in this area, there are only three innate emotional reactions: love, hate and fear. Nevertheless, this places a serious problem to researchers, and this is the way to explain emotions as a reflex with an innate behavior model, if those innate emotional reactions are only three and the adults' emotional responses spectrum is clearly greater. The previous exposition places the basis for the learning based behavior theory. This theory proposes that complex emotions are learned behaviors during the individual life, and used as functional mechanisms in certain situations. Watson and Rayner (Watson, 1920) affirms, 'the extremely small number of innate stimuli associations and reactions present in children's emotional field is extended during children's development through a learning process based on conditioned reflexes'. [...] Nevertheless, it does not exist determining experiments in every day emotional situations, thus the learning theory could be seen as a contribution on the understanding of the way emotions get formed, stay or disappear, but not as a definitive theory for emotions formation and existence" (Ulich, 1985)

Finally, we refer to a theory, which is not a current theory of emotions, but in our assessment it shows an accurate idea, with a great value for our goal with this work. And this is the Arnold's appraisal theory, according to this theory "If someone perceives, recalls or represents something, these actions never stay as an isolated knowledge fragment. Every object is seen immediately in its relation with ourselves, and it is assessed as good, bad or irrelevant for us. In everyday life, the assessment of anything we find in relation to ourselves is immediate, automatic, and almost intuitive. Which in some aspects is 'good' for us (important, advantageous, and useful) it is an object for our consideration and effort; which is 'bad' (detrimental, annoying) it is avoided; which is irrelevant (insignificant, useless) it is simply despised" (Arnold, 1970).

On the other hand, computing science researchers are trying to generate computational emotions models, in order to represent coherently those in intelligent agents. An advance in this sense is obtained in (Elliott, 1997) where a clear classification of emotions is made, dividing them into 8 groups of emotions that contain 24 types of basic emotions as well. In addition to that, an agent selection scheme for these emotions is proposed, through a set of 20 processing modules that, interpreting the stimuli and combining a set of variable connections, allows to do match among the emotions and a set of agent's internal states, rising an emotion independently, included in one of the 24 categories. This work presents a valuable contribution to emotions study in intelligent agents; this contribution is the emotions classification. This classification is concrete enough, but sufficiently broad to construct a respectable model and it is, as well, a good starting point for complex emotions and feelings incorporation.

Among emotions models implementations there is a huge diversity proposal. There are cellular automata models (Davis, 2002), (Hegselmann, 1998), (Davis, 1999), these includes homogeneous and heterogeneous cellular automata as well. There are plans based approach models, with task oriented emotions utilization (Gratch, 2001). In this case, the model uses emotions that are aroused when a specific task is made, this approach makes it easier to detect what the emotional agent will experiment. Other emotional representations approach are the neuronal network based (Van Kesteren, 2000), (Gopych, 2002), (Zhang, 2002). For this reason, researchers lean on the main advantages of neuronal networks, patterns recognition, and learning. In this approach neuronal networks are used to recognize stimuli patterns in the environment, as well as in agent internal states, to identify the agent behavior, and to identify which emotions must be activated in the agent. Another approach based on neuronal

networks uses this to learn how emotional states must be influenced by internal and environmental stimuli (Van Kesteren, 2000). This idea seems to be right, because it allows agent to train through accumulated experiences from stimuli.

Another worthy model to mention is proposed in (De Almeida, 2004). In this work, authors propose a human physiology based on emotions model. The model has a representation of the human body main systems. Unlike most affective models based on human behavior that tries to model the behavior from the cognitive view, this model uses a biological approach, which could be a right approach. In this work each body system is concerned about its own operation, sending demand signals to the nervous system which serves as a communication channel with the brain, which is in charge of modifying the behavior to satisfy agent necessities.

Blackboard Architecture[1] is also used for emotions implementations in agents. In (Swartout, 2006) it is used to design virtual humans capable to represent their emotions internally, to express them through their representation in the virtual environment, to receive stimuli from the environment and other agents, and to communicate with other agents. Due to this amount of characteristics, authors propose the blackboards architecture for its flexibility, allowing the model components (in this case the agents) access to the intermediate and final results of other components.

Fuzzy Logic based approach also can be seen, in (Aghaee, 2003) where a model with emotional states is proposed. These emotional states values are represented in a fuzzy way; this approach is adopted based on the mutual incompatibility principle presented by Zadeh in (Zadeh, 1975) that says "precision and complexity are incompatible properties. Because of this the traditional numerical approach is inadequate to model human knowledge in complex processes ". The agent personality representation is supported by fuzzy sets, and it is processed through fuzzy logic.

The work in (Thalmann, 1999) introduces a model for virtual human representation. This model handles autonomy or independent levels that will be used by the agent for decision-making. Three autonomy levels are defined: Guided-Level, Programmed Level and Autonomous Level.

Another approach in agent's emotional management is the information processing structure oriented. For Sloman, Chrisley and Scheutz (2003) the emotions managed by agents can be summarized into information processing architectures. In this approach they treat emotions as affective states that, to exist in an organism (human, animal, or robotic) must exist in this organism an architecture that support it, as well, which implies that if the architecture is not present, the organism is incapable to experience that feeling. In Sloman's work, a clear classification of states and processes, necessaries for affective states representation, is made. There are differences between the desires oriented states (Desire-like) and the beliefs oriented states (Belief-like). In addition, it appears a model for implementation and integration of these components and sets out a very simple distinction for Desire-like states, as positive and negative states, or Positive affective and Negative affective states.

Understanding that, "There are many further distinctions that can be made among types of affective states". Among the class of affective (i.e., desire-like) states, we can distinguish positive and negative cases, approximately definable as it follows:

- A state N of a system S is a negatively affective state if being in N or moving toward being in N changes the dispositions of S so as to cause processes which reduce the probability of N persisting, or which tends to resist processes that bring N into existence.

- A state P of a system S is a positively affective state if being in P or moving toward being in P changes the dispositions of S so as to cause processes which increase the probability of P persisting, or which tends to produce or enhance processes that bring P into existence or to maintain the existence of P." (Sloman, 2003)

We consider that, the use of positive and negative assessment can also be extended to beliefs-like states, and in general, to any mental representation of entities, states and processes in the agent. That means, all belief, feeling, knowledge, goal, process, state, another entities representation, and in general any agent's mental representations, must have a positive, negative or neutral assessment. This affirmation agrees with Arnold's appraisal theory (Arnold, 1970).

Finally, FLAME model is analyzed (Fuzzy Logic Adaptive Model of Emotions) introduced by Magy Seif El-Nasr in 1998 (El-Nasr, 1998) in Texas University. Even when this model is based on fuzzy logic, it was considered proper to expose it in a particular section, due to the relevance for our future work.

This model is, in our opinion, one of the most complete and best structured of the existing at the moment of its publication, even including the present time. In this model, it is taken into account one of the intelligence fundamental components: the experience based learning. A "sine qua non" condition to define an organism as an intelligent one is that this organism has the possibility to collect data from experienced situations and to use that information in future situations for its own benefit. FLAME Model also includes an important component incorporating fuzzy logic to the emotional state evaluation mechanisms, which allows the model to be more flexible in the internal states evaluation and decisions making for further behaviors.

The FLAME model takes into consideration key points of emotional and intelligent behaviors, as learning based on experience, mixed emotions existence, and that means several emotions experimentation at the same time, besides representing through diffuse sets the intrinsically non-deterministic nature of the emotions.

As it can be observed, there is a great divergence approach among authors. It is observed that almost every investigation work has an implementation model, this is due to, that in many cases researchers are trying to represent agents with human characteristics in complex situations, forcing this to define a model that adapts to the particular situation that is tried to represent. It is necessary that researchers set their efforts to domain-independent emotional models and architectures, which allow agent's representation with emotional characteristics, adaptable to any circumstances. These models must be mainly based on the human behavior. This will make easier future implementations of different agents with individual characteristics and personality. The (Sloman, 2003) and (El-Nasr, 1998) cases, are clear exceptions of this problem.

MODEL DEFINITION

As we mentioned before, the purpose of this work is to place a basis for "virtual human" generation, with all the implications within this expression. That clearly implies participation of a large number of researchers, in diverse knowledge areas. The contribution of this work is to introduce a starting point in a not very explored area, such as, emotion inclusion and autonomous emotion development in intelligent agents.

Based on that, it is possible to present some main objectives that should be reached to effectively generate intelligent agents capable to experience emotions. Those objectives imply to perform a large number of complex tasks.

Initially, a formal definition of emotions is needed, to classify them in recognizable groups, with well defined characteristics, in order to identify the corresponding group for each emotion. We should reach a high level of emotional description. Emotional theorists should provide a definition of the nature of each emotion, and in addition to that, a clear understanding of emotional activation

and regulation mechanism, as well as, the way this mechanism works in affected emotions selection and which environment and internal stimuli causes them. It is necessary to identify the cognitive mechanisms that activate emotions and to identify in what extent, part of these mechanisms is innate and another part is a learned behavior. This explanation will lead us to the definition of an open theoretical model. This model should allow emotional representations in a flexible way, and in a well dimensioned representation for each emotion, as well as, interaction relations among them. For achieving that, it is necessary to identify which values represent the whole emotional dimensions and define computational methods which represent theoretical models of emotion activations, behavior interaction and stabilization. This model should provide an emotional state control mechanism, capable of updating these states in real time. A cognitive mechanism should be placed in an upper layer. This mechanism will process the perception mechanism entries and will generate the "situation status" that could be defined as a set of values from the relevant variables perceived in the environment, and then it will offer the primary assessment defined in Lazarus's theory: the "situation appraisal" identifying relevant configuration of the situation status. This will allow the cognitive mechanism to identify which emotions will be affected. Then a behavioral mechanism should use emotional states coherently in further actions selections, including emotional expression itself. This mechanism will implement the Lazarus's secondary appraisal identifying potential beneficial behavior. This mechanism should have a structured model for complex goal representation, which allows hierarchy representation among goals, and capable to be affected by emotions and affect them, making possible to change goals priority based on the situation assessment, including in it the emotional states. Learning and knowledge management mechanisms are also needed. This mechanism should allow complex and abstract knowledge representation and recording, and allowing the potential useful information storage, and implementing extended semantics networks within the stored concepts. The learning and knowledge managed mechanism should be capable of, not only storing, retrieving, modifying and using information, but it should be also capable of storing, retrieving, modifying and using behavior. In other words, as it happens with the data, processing methods for the data should be also learned by the agent, because this is all part of the agent's knowledge.

The aforementioned is a minimal description of what is needed to have a human convincing virtual implementation. That implies participation of sociology, biology, psychology and computing science professionals, among others.

This work scope is centered in the definition of a computational model for emotion representation. Our model is based on three particular emotions and behavior theories. In the first place, the Lazarus's cognitive emotion theory: in this theory Lazarus affirms that emotions are the result of a cognitive process in the individual, those processes analyze the situation and determine the possible impact of the situation in the subject

and based on that possible impact, emotions are activated. Based on Lazarus work, we define three main tiers for the agent model (Figure 2). The first tier includes the perception mechanisms, which are responsible to identify what happens in the environment. These mechanisms are activated by events in the environment: Perception Mechanisms generates sensorial stimulus which are a translation of the information perceived in the events in a way the Cognitive Structure could understand. This Cognitive Structure is the second tier and it is in charge to evaluate the environmental situation and determine the possible damage or benefit in the situation.

Those evaluations identify the "meaning" of the situation for the agent, and according to this meaning, the Cognitive Structure generates the emotional stimulus which affects specific emotions in the Emotional Model, the third tier. This Emotional Model receives emotional stimulus in a comprehensible format and affects individual emotions, producing with that the emotions activation and interaction. In this paper we show in detail the Emotional Model structure and behavior.

Figure 1. Cognitive appraisal based model diagram

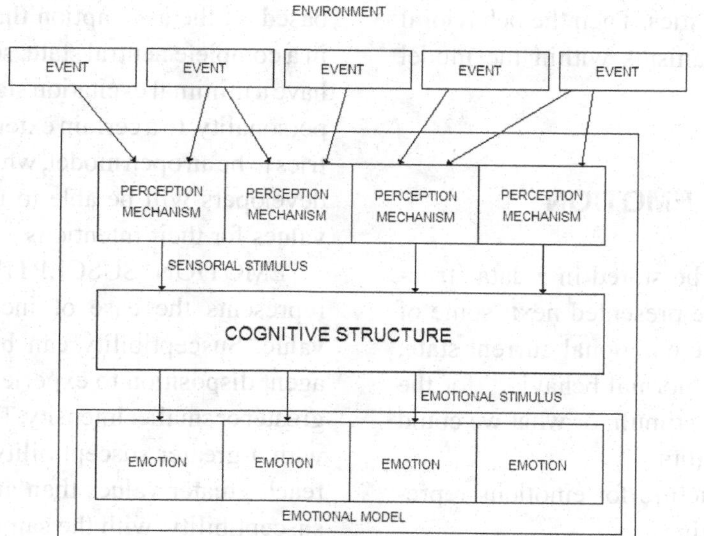

A behavior mechanism within the agent will use these emotions in the goals and actions selection, and actuator mechanisms will be activated. In figure number 1, behavior and actuator mechanisms are not represented because they are not included in the scope of this work.

Another theory used in the model definition is the Watson's learning based behavior theory. In this theory, Watson exposes that there are only three basic innate emotions: love, hate and fear. He also states that other emotions are complex learned behaviors. In our model, every defined emotion has to be associated with one of these basic emotions. This information will be used in the behavioral mechanisms to determine action depending on the "quality" of the excited emotions. The model also takes in account the Arnold's appraisal theory and the architecture proposed in (Sloman, 2003) as two accurate approaches for future developments. In both cases, the orientation of the works is behavior and decision making (in humans or agents). Even when this work main objective it is not a behavioral mechanism, it will be in future works, so our model should be suitable for mechanisms based in Arnold's and Sloman's works.

On the next section, emotional representation structure will be presented, as well as, an explanation of its characteristics. Then the behavioral and interaction mechanisms within the model will be covered.

STRUCTURE OF EMOTION

Each emotion should be stored in a data structure similar to the one presented next; some of the fields represent the emotional current state, and some others, the "normal behavior" for the emotion in absence of stimuli, or what we could call, the agent personality.

Our proposed structure for emotions representation is the following:

- EMOTION_CODE
- EMOTION_NAME
- EMOTION_VALUE
- EMOTION_NORMAL_VALUE
- EMOTION_SUSCEPTIBILITY
- EMOTION_PERSISTENCE
- EMOTION_QUALITY
- AFFECTED_EMOTIONS

Next, we will explain each field function.

EMOTION_CODE: unique emotion Id.

EMOTION_NAME: Emotion name in the real world.

EMOTION_VALUE: This is a positive floating point value which represents the emotion intensity in a particular *instant*. This field could be considered as the main value for the emotion: dependent mechanisms will make a direct reference to it, and will be mainly influenced by it.

EMOTION_NORMAL_VALUE: This value represents emotional value in absence of affecting stimulus; the value for normal conditions or what we could call the emotion neutral value. Once the agent has received a stimulus that increases or diminishes EMOTION_VALUE, it will tend to make EMOTION_VALUE equal to EMOTION_NORMAL_VALUE on time. If not, new stimuli are received. This field is included based on the assumption that humans are never in a complete neutral state: some of our emotions have a minimal excitation state which defines our personality, to a certain extent. Nevertheless, this tries to be an open model, which is why the agent's developers will be able to use the best suitable values for their intentions.

EMOTION_SUSCEPTIBILITY: This value represents the ease of increasing an emotion value. Susceptibility can be considered as the agent disposition to experience an emotion with greater or smaller intensity. This means that agents with a greater susceptibility in an emotion will reach greater values than an agent with smaller susceptibility, with the same stimulus.

EMOTION_PERSISTENCE: This value represents the agent's tendency to continue experiencing an emotion once finished an exciting stimulus. As we mentioned before, an agent should count with a stabilizing mechanism for emotions which automatically turns EMOTION_VALUE into NORMAL_EMOTION_VALUE across the time. Even though this is a static mechanism, it is conditioned by the emotion persistence. This means that the "speed" in which EMOTION_VALUE will reach NORMAL_EMOTION_VALUE will be based on EMOTION_PERSISTENCE. A greater persistence will slow the process, while a smaller persistence will speed up the process.

EMOTION_QUALITY: This value identifies the basic emotion associated to the present emotion. The 0 value will be associated to pleasant emotions, 1 for unpleasant emotions and 2 for emotions associated with fear.

AFFECTED_EMOTIONS: This field holds a reference to an affected emotion list. This list is composed by emotions present in the model, and which are affected for the showed emotion. The experience of the emotions in this list is directly affected for the present emotion values, depending on a model mechanism presented further in this document. This can be an increased or diminished effect and it depends on the designer's definition. The affected emotions recorded structure is as it follows.

- EMOTION_CODE
- AFFECTION_PERCENTAGE_SEPARATION
- AFFECTION_QUALITY

In this structure, the EMOTION_CODE represents the unique Id of the emotion. The AFFECTION_PERCENTUAL_SEPARATION represents the absolute value for the separation needed between the affected emotion increment percentage and the present emotion increment percentage, to produce any effect. Meanwhile, the AFFECTION_QUALITY indicates if the affected emotion will be increased (1) or diminished (-1) by the affecting emotional effects.

As we mentioned before, some fields in the structure of emotions represent the agent personality for this emotion; defining personality as a predictable behavior for the emotion. These fields are: EMOTION_NORMAL_VALUE, EMOTION_SUSCEPTIBILITY and EMOTION_PERSISTENCE. Those values provide a particular and defined behavior for the emotion. The normal value for the emotion sets a defined state for the emotion. In the absence of a stimulus, the agent's decisions will be based on this value, but greater normal values for emotions will make agent's normal behavior more influenced by these emotions. The emotion's susceptibility provides us with the expected agent reaction, in other words, in what extent a stimulus will affect the agent. While the emotion's persistence determines how an emotion evolves in time when there is a stimulus.

Emotion's Behavior Mechanism

This section attends to show how emotions are affected by the received stimuli from the environment, and how they are affected by each other.

Mechanism for the Calculation of the New Emotion Value when a Stimulus is Given

For the scope of this article, it is assumed that a *sensorial stimulus* is a set of values related to an event that the agent is able "to read" through its perceptional mechanisms and can interpret it based on the received values although the agent does not necessarily "know" the exact stimuli. For example, a stimulus like sound can be represented by the set of values as *intensity*, *duration* and *frequency*, the agent can receive a sonorous stimuli with known values for these components which would be equivalent to listen a known sound, also it could receive a stimulus with unknown values for these components, the agent could not know what it is *listening to*, but unequivocally will know that it *is listening* to something. Once the stimulus is received by the perception mechanisms, the cognitive mechanisms of the agent will be in charge to interpret the *sensorial stimuli* and to transform them into *emotional stimuli* which are direct stimuli to the emotions. Each one of these emotional stimuli will only affect an emotion; this is why it becomes necessary that the cognitive mechanisms generate a register of emotional stimuli by each emotion that it is necessary to affect. These stimuli will be represented by the following form:

- EMOTION_CODE
- STIMULUS_VALUE

Where the EMOTION_CODE would be the emotion unique identifier that is going to be affected by the stimulus, whereas the STIMULUS_VALUE represents "the real" value of the stimulus, that is to say, the value in which the emotion would be increased if the agent did not count on interpretation mechanisms of these stimuli, which depends of his own personality. In this case, there are remaining difficulties, like the fact of who will be the one in charge to define these "real" or "objective" stimulus values, before being affected by the psychic structure of the agent.

Once the emotional stimulus value is received, and due to the fact that each stimuli will affect an emotion, it is important to emphasize that the model considers the influence of emotions among themselves. At the first moment, the isolated emotion will be affected (each one of the emotions according to its corresponding emotional stimulus) and then the influences between emotions will be calculated. It is considered that, if there were more than an emotional stimulus for a particular emotion, these will be processed in a chronological way, that is to say, there must be a queue of emotional stimuli within the agent.

Finally, the mechanism is defined to process an emotional stimulus in an emotion like the following one. The value of the stimulus is increased in the percentage that indicates the field EMOTION_SUSCEPTIBILITY.

Given an emotion **E** and a stimulus **S** for the emotion, the value of the emotion will be:

E.EMOTION_VALUE = E. EMOTION_VALUE +
(S.STIMULUS_VALUE + (S. STIMULUS_ VALUE * E.EMOTION_SUSCEPTIBILITY / 100))

EMOTIONAL STABILIZATION

In this work, emotion is defined as a "mood alteration, intense and with short duration, that could be pleasant or unpleasant" (REAL ACADEMIA ESPAÑOLA 2008), when we said "with short duration" we referred to the fact that, once the emotion existing stimuli is finished, the emotion will tend to recover its normal value, unless a new stimuli excites it again. This clearly should be a gradual process, in order to achieve that the model uses the EMOTION_PERSISTENCE field. This field represents the simulation interactions number that should pass until the increment or decrease of the emotion value to make it close to the NORMAL_EMOTION_VALUE. Even when the increment or decrease will be equal to one (1) when some iteration number passes, on each iteration the EMOTION_VALUE should be modified in a fraction, depending on the EMOTION_PERCITENCE value.

The stabilizing algorithm is:

Given an Emotion **E**
IF (**E.EMOTION_NORMAL_VALUE > E.EMOTION_VALUE**)
    E.EMOTION_VALUE(i+1) = **E.EMOTION_VALUE + (1/E.EMOTION_ PERSISTENCE**)

ELSEIF (**E.EMOTION_NORMAL_VALUE** <
E.EMOTION_VALUE)
    E . E M O T I O N _ V A L U E (i + 1)   =
E.EMOTION_VALUE − (1/**E.EMOTION_
PERSISTENCE**)

As we can see, this formula will be applied to each iteration, only if the EMOTION_VALUE is different to the EMOTION_NORMAL_VALUE. Once this value is reached, the emotion value will be considered "stable", on its default value for the emotion in absence of an affecting stimulus.

EMOTIONS INTERACTION

Once the current emotion value is obtained, we proceed to generate the emotions interaction. In real life, there are overlapping emotions; that happens especially when contradictory emotions are excited at the same time or in short periods of time. When we receive good news, our happiness grows, but if then we receive a bad news short after the good news, our happiness will decrease and our sadness will grow. All this, evidently depends on the importance of the news for the agent's objectives. Based on that, it is essential to design a mechanism for emotion interaction. This mechanism will affect one emotion (*Emotion A*) depending on another emotion value (*Emotion B*). In order to do so, Emotion B value should comply with some rules for interaction. The affection consists on the increase or decrease of the *Emotion A* value proportionally to the *Emotion B* excitation. Affection will be calculated as it is explained next.

As we said before, each emotion has associated affected emotions, so each emotion has a positive or negative effect over the associated emotions. In order to get the influence value, the affected emotions list should be crossed applying the next criteria.

It is necessary to calculate the percentage value of the difference between the affecting emotion normal value and the affecting emotion present value. It is also necessary to calculate the percentage value of the difference between the affected emotion normal value and the affected emotion present value. Then it is necessary to verify if the percentage value for the affecting emotion is greater than the percentage value for the affected emotion. If this is false, no change is observed. If this is true, it is necessary to calculate the difference between the affecting emotion percentage absolute value and the affected emotion percentage absolute value. If the result of that is greater than the value recorded in the affected emotion AFFECTION_PERCENTAGE_SEPARATION field. This field value should be subtracted from the value obtained through the previous calculus, and finally this will be the incrementing or decreasing percentage value the affected emotion will suffer. In the following paragraph, the algorithm for emotions interaction will be shown (see Box 1).

It is necessary to emphasize that, if the affecting emotion normal value is greater than the emotion present value, the influence will be the opposite of the represented in the AFFECTION_QUALITY field. To illustrate what we explained before, we will show two examples here. In the first example, the affecting emotion value is greater than the affecting emotion normal value, so the affection quality will be in the AFFECTION_QUALITY field direction (i.e. will increase the affected emotion value if the AFFECTION_QUALITY field in the affecting emotion is 1, and decrease otherwise). In the second example, the affecting emotion value will be lower than its own normal value so, the affection quality will be opposite to the AFFECTION_QUALITY value.

Given EA, which is the affected emotion, with a value equal to 25, a normal value equal to 20, 30 for its affection percentage separation and -1 for its affection quality (which means that the influence produced by the affecting emotion is diminishing the current affected emotion value). And given EI, which represents the affecting emotion, with

Box 1.

```
FOR EACH EA IN EI AFFECTED EMOTIONS LIST
BEGIN
        PIEI = (EI.EMOTION_VALUE – EI.NORMAL_EMOTION_VALUE) * 100 / EI. NORMAL_EMOTION_VALUE
        PIEA = (EA. EMOTION_VALUE – EA.NORMAL_EMOTION_VALUE) * 100 / EA.NORMAL_EMOTION_VALUE
        IF (|PIEI| > |PIEA|)
        BEGIN
                DIA = |PIEI| – |PIEA|
                IF (DIA > EA.AFFECTION_PERCENTAGE_SEPARATION)
                BEGIN
                        PA = DIA - EA.AFFECTION_PERCENTAGE_SEPARATION
                        IF (PIEI > 0)
                                EA. EMOTION_VALUE = EA. EMOTION_VALUE + ((PA * EA. EMOTION_VALUE / 100) *
                                EA.AFFECTION_QUALITY)
                        ELSE
                                EA. EMOTION_VALUE = EA.EMOTION_VALUE - ((PA * EA. EMOTION_VALUE / 100) *
                                EA.AFFECTION_QUALITY)
                END
        END
END

Where:

EI is the Affecting Emotion
EA is the Affected Emotion
PIEI is the Percentage of increment for Affecting Emotion
PIEA is the Percentage of increment for Affected Emotion
DIA is the Difference between PIEI and PIEA.
PA is the Affection percentage.
```

a value of 50, 30 for its normal value; we will calculate the emotion influence following the emotion interaction algorithm presented before, obtaining the next values. Initially, the increment percentage for affecting emotion (PIEI) is 66.6 while the increment percentage for the affected emotion (PIEA) is 25. Because the PIEI absolute value is greater than the PIEA absolute value, the algorithm continues with the calculations; estimating the difference between the two incremented percentages (DIA) which is 41.6. Because the DIA value is greater than the percentage separation required between emotions to show the affection (30), the actual affection value (PA) is calculated, obtaining 6.6 as the real affection percentage to operate over the affected emotion. In this case, the affecting emotion value is greater than its normal value (i.e. PIEI > 0) so the affected emotion will be affected in the way the AFFECTION_QUALITY field indicates, getting a decreasing value of 1.65 for the affected emotion, and finally fitting its value to 23.35.

In the given example, we could observe that the affecting emotion was an inhibiting emotion for the affected emotion, that is because the affected emotion value was decreased. This can be observed in the AFFECTION_QUALITY field in the affected emotion, when this field is -1. It means that the affecting emotion is an inhibiting emotion. Nevertheless, although it sounds contradictory, an inhibiting emotion can increase the value of the emotion that it influences, if its present value is below its normal value. If we are much less "angry" than normal for our personality, good news will also cheer us up more than normal.

Now, we show an example where the value for the affecting emotion is lower than its normal value, so the affected emotion will be affected in an opposite way than the expressed in the AFFECTION_QUALITY value.

Given EA, which is the affected emotion, with a value equal to 25, the normal value is equal to 20, 30 for its affection percentage separation and -1 for its affection quality. And given EI, which represents the affecting emotion, with 5 for its value, 30 for its normal value; we calculate the emotion influence following the emotion interaction algorithm presented before, obtaining the next values. Initially, the increment percentage for affecting emotion (PIEI) is -83.3. This value is obviously negative, because there is not an increment for the affecting emotion, its value is 5 and its normal value is 30. On the other hand, the increment percentage for the affected emotion (PIEA) is 25. Because the PIEI absolute value is greater than PIEA absolute value, the procedure continues calculating the difference between the absolute values of the two increment percentages (DIA) which is 58.3. Because the DIA value is greater than the percentage separation required between emotions to show the affection (30), then the actual affection value (PA) is calculated obtaining 28.3 as the real affection percentage to operate over the affected emotion. In this case, the affecting emotion value is lower than its normal value (i.e. PIEI < 0), so the affected emotion will be affected the other way round the AFFECTION_QUALITY field indicates, getting an increasing value of 7.075 for the affected emotion, and finally fitting its value to 32.075.

With the previous example, it can be observed that, although the affecting emotion was an inhibitor emotion (i.e. EI.AFFECTION_QUALITY = -1), the fact that its current value was below the normal value, influenced the affected emotion positively.

Now, we present a full example of the model. In this example, the emotion behavior in the model will be analyzed, examining the three main functions in the model: emotion stimulation, emotion stabilization and emotion interaction. In order to do so, three instances of the model will be used, each one with two emotions (Emotion A and Emotion B) on each instance, personality values for emotion will be different for Emotion A on each instance, and the same for Emotion B. Emotion A will be an affecting emotion for Emotion B in the three instances, and affection values will be the same for the three instances, as well. Stimuli with the same value will be given to each instance in order to observe the instance's behavior.

For each instance the normal value, susceptibility and persistence are greater than in the previous instance. This means that each instance is more likely to experiment Emotion A than the previous one. The emotional stimulus will affect Emotion A and its value will be 10. Emotion A will be an affecting emotion for Emotion B, and the affecting percentage separation will be 10.

Once the stimulus is processed, the new emotion values for each instance will be as shown in Table 7.

Notice that each instance was incremented differently, even though the stimulus was the same, which is because each instance has a different susceptibility value.

Once the stimulus for the emotion is processed, the emotion interaction mechanism is activated.

Table 1. Values for Instance 1, Emotion A

EMOTION NORMAL VALUE	40
EMOTION VALUE	40
EMOTION PERSISTENCE	55
EMOTION SUCEPTIBILITY	80
EMOTION QUALITY	0

Table 2. Values for Instance 1, Emotion B

EMOTION NORMAL VALUE	20
EMOTION VALUE	20
EMOTION PERSISTENCE	30
EMOTION SUCEPTIBILITY	60
EMOTION QUALITY	0

Table 3. Values for Instance 2, Emotion A

EMOTION NORMAL VALUE	20
EMOTION VALUE	20
EMOTION PERSISTENCE	30
EMOTION SUCEPTIBILITY	60
EMOTION QUALITY	1

Table 4. Values for Instance 2, Emotion B

EMOTION NORMAL VALUE	20
EMOTION VALUE	20
EMOTION PERSISTENCE	30
EMOTION SUCEPTIBILITY	60
EMOTION QUALITY	1

Table 5. Values for Instance 3, Emotion A

EMOTION NORMAL VALUE	60
EMOTION VALUE	60
EMOTION PERSISTENCE	60
EMOTION SUCEPTIBILITY	95
EMOTION QUALITY	0

Table 6. Values for Instance 3, Emotion B

EMOTION NORMAL VALUE	20
EMOTION VALUE	20
EMOTION PERSISTENCE	30
EMOTION SUCEPTIBILITY	60
EMOTION QUALITY	1

Emotion A is an affecting emotion for Emotion B, The affection percentage separation for Emotion B will be 10, and the affection quality will be -1 which means that the affecting emotion is an inhibitor emotion. So the affection is calculated.

Even though Emotion B values are the same in the three instances, including the affection value, the different percentage of separation between the emotion normal value and the emotion current value in Emotion A among the instances, produce a different Emotion B affection.

Once the emotion is affected, stabilization begins. This stabilization will be achieved through several iterations for each emotion.

The differences between stabilization times among the instances for Emotion A, is given by the persistence value for each instance. In Instance 1, a 6 unit increment for Emotion A value from its normal took 200 iterations to get stabilized. But in Instance 2, an 8 unit increment took 400 iterations. This is because Emotion A is more persistent in Instance 2 than in Instance 1. The same as, in Instance 3, a 9.5 unit's increment took 475, and this has the same reason. In the case of Emotion B, stabilization time was proportional to the difference between the emotion value and the emotion normal value, which is because personality values for Emotion B were the same among the instances.

FUTURE TRENDS

Emotional behavior in intelligent agents has still a long road to ride, a wide range of researches are

Table 7. Emotion A Values given to the stimulus

Instance	Emotion	Previous Value	New Value
1	A	20	26
2	A	40	48
3	A	60	69.5

Table 8. Emotion B Values given to the affection

Instance	Emotion	Previous Value	New Value
1	B	20	16.03
2	B	20	18.03
3	B	20	18.87

Table 9. Emotion stabilization

Instance	Emotion	Stabilized in iteration
1	A	200
2	A	400
3	A	475
1	B	134
2	B	67
3	B	39

still waiting to be developed. From our perspective, researches should be oriented in the generation of generic models, and mechanisms for inclusion of emotions in intelligent agents. Only the search for these generic mechanisms will make possible the virtual human existence. Learning mechanisms that allow the agent to modify, not only the data, but the data structures and the data processing mechanisms will be essential in the future because learning implies all this, and all of these elements are part of knowledge. Finally, a way to the autonomous emotions development in agents should be achieved, allowing the generations of agents' behaviors and personality form the scratch, building these behaviors and personality through experiences.

CONCLUSION

Initially, we can affirm that it is possible to create a correlation between emotional models presented for emotional theorists and a computational model. These theorists have made a remarkable work trying to define the way emotions are developed in humans and, even when their theories are not structured enough to make an exact computational implementation, their bring determinant information that places the basis in the creation of a realistic human emotion model.

This should not be misestimated, since great part of the existing models, are specific models, which fit to specific environments in specific situations. This chapter shows the design of a generic model, defined like an independent element that will be able to be integrated to another set of elements, also independents in their conception, forming altogether the mind of the virtual human. The evident advantages of this will be the advantages of any independent multi tier model. Models and implementations of each tier will be able to be developed, and while they respect the communication mechanisms there will not be any impact in the remaining tiers.

We also present an initial structure for the definition of an emotion in an agent. This structure is context independent and tries to represent an emotion in all its possible dimensions; this structure is based on defined human emotion theories which made it generic and realistic. One of the principal contributions in the emotions structure definition is the emotion persistence and the emotion susceptibility. These values allow the designer to personally define aspects in agents, making the agents have different reactions when they receive the same stimulus. Particularly, emotions persistence gives agents a more real behavior, making their emotions lasting some time after a stimulus source has disappeared. This characteristic is not found in most of the emotion model definitions.

In addition to the basic structure for the emotions representation, we present a mechanism for emotional stabilization, effect that takes place once an emotion is excited; this one will tend to become stabilized if there are no other stimuli that excite it. Finally, a mechanism for the interaction between emotions is defined; this mechanism allows emotions to get affected by the state of other emotions. As it was shown through the examples, the presented model offers a detailed configuration which allows developers to represent a wide range of emotional behavior, adapting the model behavior to their particular needs.

It is clear that this chapter is only a starting step in the definition of the first element of a virtual mind, a huge amount of complex elements are still waiting to be developed. It is necessary to define a cognitive mechanism which processes the received environmental information and generates the emotional stimuli. It is also necessary to define a goal selection mechanism and an action selection mechanism based on the emotional states and the current and the past information stored by the agent, mechanisms for the knowledge and information storage. Information and knowledge recovery and processing mechanisms are also needed. The greater amount of these elements has been taken into account for the accomplishment of this work, although some of such do not affect directly the results raised here. It is also planned to continue with the studies and developments of each one of these elements in future investigations.

REFERENCES

Aghaee, N. & Ören, T. (2003). Towards fuzzy agents with dynamic personality for human behavior simulation. *2003 Summer Computer Simulation Conference* (pp 3-10).

Arnold, M. (1970). *Feelings and emotions, the Loyola symposium.* New York: Academic Press

Cannon, W.B. (1920). The James-Lange theory of emotions: A critical examination and an alternative theory. *The American Journal of Psychology, 39*(¼),106-124.

Darwin, C. (1899). *The expression of emotions in man and animals.* New York: D. Appleton and Company.

Davis, D. Chalabi, T. & Berbank-Green, B. (1999). Towards an architecture for Artificial life agents II. New Frontiers in Computational Intelligence and Its Applications, ISO Press.

Davis, D. (2002). Modeling emotion in computational agents. *International Conference on Artificial Intelligence and Applications.*

Dealmeida, L. Da Silva, B. & Bazzan, A. (2004). *Towards a physiological model of emotions: First Step.* America Association for Artificial Intelligence.

Elliott, C. (1997). *Hunting for the Holy Grail with "emotionally intelligent" virtual actors.* Institute for Applied Artificial Intelligence, De Paul University.

El-Nasr, M. (1998). *Modeling emotions dynamics in intelligent agents,* Texas A&M University.

Gopych, P. (2002). Computer modeling of feelings and emotions: a quantitative neural network model of the feeling-of-knowing. *Kharkiv University Bulletin no.550.*

Gratch, J. & Marsella, S. (2001). Tears and Fears: Modeling emotions and emotional behaviors in synthetic agents. *5th International Conference on Autonomous Agents.*

Hegselmann, R. & Flache, A. (1998). Understanding complex social dynamics: A plea for cellular automata based modeling. *Journal of Artificial Societies and Social Simulation.*

James, W. (1884). What is emotion. *Mind, 4.*

Kemper, T. (1992). Richard S. Lazarus's emotion and adaptation review. *Contemporary Sociology, 21*(4), 522-523.

Lazarus, R.S., Kanner, A.D. & Folkman, S. (1980). Emotions: A cognitive–phenomenological analysis, IN (ULICH 1985)

Lazarus, R. (1991). *Emotion and adaptation.* New York: Oxford University Press.

Morris, C. (1997). Psychology: An introduction. México: Editorial Prentice Hall..

Real academia Española (2008). *Emotion definition*. Retrieved January 04, 2008, from http://buscon.rae.es/draeI/SrvltConsulta TIPO_BUS=3&LEMA= emoción

Sloman, A. Chrisley, R., & Scheutz, M. (2003). The architectural basis of affective states and processes. University of Birmingham, University of Sussex, University of Notre Dame.

Swartout, W. et al. (2006). Towards virtual humans. *AI Magazine, 27*(1).

Thalmann, D. Raupp, S. & Kallmann, M. (1999). *Virtual human's behavior: Individuals, groups and crowds*. Swiss Federal Institute of Technology.

Ulich, D. (1985). El Sentimiento, Introducción a la psicología de la emoción. Barcelona. Editorial Herder.

Urban, C. (1997). *PECS: A reference model for human-like agents*. University of Passau.

Van Kesteren, A. et al. (2000). *Simulation of emotions of agents in virtual environments using neural networks*. University of Twente

Watson, J. (1913). Psychology as the behaviorist views it. *Psychological Review, 22.*

Watson, J. Rayner, R. (1920). Conditioned emotional reactions. *Journal of Experimental Psychology, 3.*

Zadeh, L. (1975). The concept of a linguistic variable and its applications to approximate reasoning. *Information Sci. 8.*

Zhang, T. & Covaci, S. (2002). Adaptive behaviors of intelligent agents based on neural semantic knowledge. *Symposium on Applications and the Internet (SAINT'02).*

KEY TERMS

Autonomous Emotion Development: This is the capacity of an agent to develop its emotions, according the received experiences, with a minimal human direct intervention.

Emotional Interaction: The emotional interaction mechanism describes the way emotions affect each other. Emotions can have an augmenting or diminishing effect over other emotions. When an emotion is excited, this one could affect another emotion behavior, and this affection is what we call emotional interaction.

Emotion Persistence: This represents the agent's tendency to continue experiencing an emotion once finished an exciting stimulus.

Emotion Susceptibility: This represents the ease of increasing an emotion value. Susceptibility can be considered as the agent disposition to experience an emotion with greater or smaller intensity. This means that agents with a greater susceptibility in an emotion will reach greater values than an agent with smaller susceptibility, with the same stimulus.

Emotional Stabilization: Emotional Stabilization is a gradual process that occurs in the emotion when a stimulus is processed. This process tends to set the emotion equal to the emotion normal value through the increment or diminish of the current value. When a stimulus is processed for the emotion, the emotion value changes, if no further stimulus are received for this emotion its value will be gradually affected to become equal to the emotion normal value. In order to achieve this, the model uses the EMOTION_PERSISTENCE which represents the number of iterations that should pass until increment or diminish emotion value in one (1), to make it close to the NORMAL_EMOTION_VALUE. Even when the increment or diminish is equal to one (1) when some iterations pass, on each iteration the EMOTION_VALUE should be modified in a fraction depending on the EMOTION_PERSITENCE value.

Emotional Stimulus: Direct emotions stimuli are the result of the sensorial stimulus processing by the cognitive mechanisms. When an event occurs in the environment, sensorial stimuli are received by the agent. The cognitive mechanisms process this stimulus and generate the emotional stimulus for each one of the emotions to be affected.

Sensorial Stimulus: The sensorial stimulus are a set of values related to an event that the agent is able to read, perceive through its perception mechanisms and can interpret based on the received values, although the agent not necessarily does know the exact stimuli.

Chapter XIV
Emotion Generation Based on a Mismatch Theory of Emotions for Situated Agents

Clément Raïevsky
Université de Sherbrooke, Canada

François Michaud
Université de Sherbrooke, Canada

ABSTRACT

Emotion plays several important roles in the cognition of human beings and other life forms, and is therefore a legitimate inspiration for providing situated agents with adaptability and autonomy. However, there is no unified theory of emotion and many discoveries are yet to be made in its applicability to situated agents. One function of emotion commonly identified by psychologists is to signal to other cognitive processes that the current situation requires an adaptation. The main purposes of this chapter are to highlight the usefulness of this signaling function of emotion for situated agents and to present an artificial model of anger and fear based on mismatch theories of emotion, which aims at replicating this function. Collective foraging simulations are used to demonstrate the feasibility of the model and to characterize its influence on a decision-making architecture.

INTRODUCTION

In spite of significant evidence that emotions play a crucial role in cognitive processes (Frijda, 1986; Hebb, 1949; G. Mandler, 1984; K. R. Scherer, Schorr, & Johnstone, 2001), no consensus currently exists about a unified theory from which

an artificial model can be derived. Therefore, implementing emotions in artificial systems can improve our understanding of existing theories and test their usage and effects.

One function of emotion commonly identified by psychologists is to signal to other cognitive processes that the current situation requires an adaptation. This function is very important for situated agents because they operate in a continuous, dynamic and unpredictable world. In this kind of environment, it is crucial to be able to detect events and stimuli, which are relevant to the systems' concerns. This function of emotion is also essential to ensure situated agents autonomy. As human designers cannot anticipate every possible situation a situated agent can come across, complete autonomy is only achievable if situated agents are able to detect situations for which their decision-making mechanism is not adapted. Furthermore, since nobody can fully understand how an artificial agent experiences its reality (Nagel, 1974), the detection of problematic situations should be done without relying on human provided knowledge.

The main purposes of this chapter are to highlight the usefulness of the signaling function of emotion for situated agents and to present an artificial model of anger and fear based on mismatch theories of emotions. The model aims at replicating this function, relying neither on a predictive model of the world nor on specific stimuli analysis.

BACKGROUND

Psychology is a natural inspiration when designing a model of artificial emotions. However, to clarify its possible contributions to a model, it is useful to classify different theories coexisting. Frijda (1986) proposes such a classification based on three main categories: specific-stimulus theories, intensity theories, and match-mismatch theories.

Classes of Psychological Theories of Emotions

Specific-stimulus theories of emotion state that emotions are triggered by the individual's perception of particular stimuli in the environment. For example, a loud sound, an intense flash, darkness

or an unknown object elicit fear. Watson's (1919) theory of emotion belongs to this class of theories. Even if some emotions are actually triggered by this individual's perception, theories belonging to this class do not account for the variety and the complexity of human or apes' emotions. The very same stimulus can elicit very different emotions depending on the internal and external contexts into which this stimulus is perceived. For example, someone losing contact with the ground does not feel the same if he is hiking on a steep slope or if he is diving into water.

According to intensity theories, emotions are associated with different intensities of stimulation or particular variation of this intensity. For example, a gentle contact or a sweet taste are pleasant and associated with positive emotions whereas a strong hit or taste are associated with negative emotions. However, the concept of intensity is not always relevant to stimuli. For example, it is hard to find stimulus intensity related to the fear emotion elicited by an unknown situation. Furthermore, some of these theories include the arousal associated with emotional experience in the intensity, which makes them circular.

According to match-mismatch theories, emotions are elicited by a match or a mismatch between an individual's dispositional entities and events occurring in the environment. Depending on the theories, dispositional entities are called response tendencies, expectations, motives, goals, values, or commitments but they all consider the relevance of the events crucial to the emotion triggering process and especially more important than the event itself. Frijda (1986) includes theories presented by Spinoza (1677), Brown and Farber (1951), Hebb (1949), Mandler (1984), and Lazarus (1966) as belonging to this class of theories. According to Stets (2003), affect control theories (Heise, 1979; Smith-Lovin, Robinson, & Wisecup, 2006) and self-discrepancy (Higgins, 1989) theories also belong to this category. Frijda states that these theories do not focus upon different emotions but rather upon elicitation of emotion as such. He phrases it this way:

"The notion of 'emotional stimulus' somewhat recedes into the background: Mismatch – interference, interruption, discrepancy – or match – attainment of incentives, correspondence with expectations – is what counts, rather than the precise stimulus that causes that mismatch or match." (Frijda, 1986, p. 267)

According to Brown and Farber (1951), a negative emotion is triggered when a behavior cannot be executed due to either a physical obstacle or the coexistence of conflicting or incompatible response tendencies. Stimuli are emotional if they produce or signal obstruction of a response tendency. In this theory, dispositional entities, which are involved in mismatch, are therefore response tendencies. They echoed the behaviorist origins of this theory. All other theories mentioned by Frijda in the match-mismatch class also belong to cognitive theories of emotion. This approach is characterized by the importance given to cognitive evaluations in emotion generation processes.

Scherer (2001; 1993) states that emotions are elicited from a sequence of evaluations of the stimulus called "Stimulus Evaluation Checks". This sequence consists of five elements, which are strongly interdependent. Each stimulus is appraised according to:

- its novelty;
- its pleasantness;
- its relevance to current goals;
- the individual's ability to adapt or react to it;
- its significance regarding social norms and the self concept.

The particular emotion triggered by this sequence depends upon the results of the different evaluation steps. In this theory, the main dispositional entities, which are monitored for match or mismatch with stimuli, are goals.

Similarly, Lazarus (Lazarus & Folkman, 1984; Lazarus, 1999) considers that dispositional entities involved in emotion are goals:

*"**Goal relevance** is fundamental to whether a transaction is viewed by a person as relevant to well-being. In effect, there is no emotion without there being a goal at stake"* [his bold italics] (Lazarus, 1999, p. 92)

Lazarus considers that an emotion is the combination of a cognitive evaluation, an action tendency, and a particular physiological reaction. He states that these different elements are perceived as a single phenomenon. In his theory, emotion differentiation is done through a "secondary appraisal", which evaluates the individual's ability to cope with the current "transaction".

Another cognitive match-mismatch theory is that of Mandler (1984; 1997). Emotions, according to Mandler, are caused by interruptions of behavioral or cognitive activities. He emphasizes the importance of the reaction of the sympathetic nervous system (SNS) to perceived discrepancies in the emotion generation process:

"The specific relevance of the SNS discrepancy response to emotional phenomena is that SNS arousal is part of the emotional experience and that discrepancies are the major occasions for emotions to occur. I stress that emotional states do not simply occur when the SNS is aroused — the cognitive or evaluative part is a necessary co-condition." (G. Mandler, 1997, p. 71)

The nature of the interrupted activity determines which particular emotion is elicited. In this theory, dispositional entities, which give stimuli their emotional potential, are action tendencies and goals.

Frijda (1986; 1989) states that emotions are not purely cognitive processes because, according to him, hedonistic evaluations, which play a crucial role in emotions, are not cognitive and changes in one's action readiness associated with some emotional states take place unintentionally. While Frijda does not consider that emotions are only cognitive, his theory clearly belongs to cognitive theories. In effect, the emotion process he sets out (Frijda, 1986) includes various appraisals of the stimulus event and of the stimulus situation. In particular, the relevance of the stimulus event for one or more of the individual's concerns is evaluated and the possibilities of coping are assessed.

Conclusions on Classes of Theories Regarding their Usefulness for Situated Agents

Specific-stimulus theories account for the part of emotion that associates particular configurations of the environment with predefined reactions. This subset of emotion-related processes is useful to improve individual's reaction to situations requiring a quick behavior adaptation. Specific-stimulus theories are therefore interesting to enhance specific reactions of artificial systems to a set of predefined situations. However, artificial models of emotions based upon this kind of theories are fundamentally limited by the fact that a human designer cannot fully grasp the reality of a situated agent (Nagel, 1974). Practically, the set of situations a designer can anticipate is limited whereas a situated agent can face infinity of situations. Furthermore, associating specific reactions with particular configurations of the environment denotes a specialization to the mission of the system. Models inspired by specific-stimulus theories are therefore specific to a set of situations and to the mission of the agent for which they are designed. Such models are consequently limited in the adaptability they can provide to situated agents.[1]

Intensity theories of emotion are even more specialized to a particular set of situations because they rely on the existence of a measurable intensity in some feature of the environment. Furthermore, these theories do not account for many aspects of emotion. The limitations of artificial models of emotion based on specific-stimulus theories apply also on models inspired by intensity theories.

Like Frijda, we believe that match-mismatch theories are a more fruitful avenue to explain the richness of emotions than the specific-stimulus one. Frijda's argument to support this viewpoint is that:

"Emotions are rarely, if ever, elicited by an isolated stimulus. Rather, the emotional effectiveness of sensory stimuli depends upon the spatial, temporal, and meaning context in which they occur, the adaptation level upon which they impinge, and the expectations with which they clash or correspond." (Frijda, 1986, p. 267)

Match-mismatch theories of emotion are strongly related to the signal function of emotion because they state that emotion occurs when a match or a mismatch is detected. Therefore, the elicitation of an emotion intrinsically signals the occurrence of a situation requiring one's attention and adaptation of one's behavior. We are in agreement with Sloman on the importance of the signaling function in emotion processes when he states:

"The main function of the mechanisms referred to above [(emotions)] is to prevent 'normal' processing from continuing in circumstances where some state requiring (or prima-facie requiring) a change of 'direction' occurs." (Sloman, 2008)

As we stated before, this function of emotion is crucial to situated agents because it allows them to detect and respond to situations to which their decision-making mechanism is not adapted. This ability is essential to trigger adaptations in the decision-making mechanism when required. An important characteristic of this function is that it is not specific to a particular set of situations or to the current objectives of the individual. Therefore, artificial models of emotion inspired by match-mismatch theories must not be specialized to particular configurations of the environment or to the mission assigned to the agent.

Emotions in Artificial Intelligence (AI)

Emotions have inspired researchers since the very beginning of AI. For instance, Simon (1967) stated that artificial systems must have an interruption mechanism comparable to the role of emotion. According to him, artificial models of human intelligence should include two main sub-systems: one in charge of carrying out the system's goals and one monitoring the environment and the system itself, which is able to interrupt the first sub-system when the situation requires an adaptation. Simon asserts that this second sub-system corresponds to emotion processes.

Theories of emotion proposed by Ortony, Clore and Collins (1988) and by Oatley and Johnson-Laird (1987), while being deeply rooted in psychology, are explicitly formulated to make it possible to implement in an artificial system. Unlike Simon who emphasizes the function of emotion and considers the emotion generation process, Ortony, Clore and Collins' theory focuses upon the differentiation of emotions. According to them, emotions are differentiated from an appraisal process, which evaluates events occurring in the environment, actions of other agents, and perceivable objects of the environment. This appraisal process is composed of two levels: first, events are appraised as pleasant or not, action of agents are endorsed or rejected, and objects are evaluated as attractive or repulsive. Once an event has been characterized as relevant, the agent to which it is relevant is assessed. If the event is relevant for another agent, its consequences are appraised as desirable or not. If the event is relevant for the agent itself, its consequences are evaluated as relevant or not to the concerns of the agent. Consequences of events relevant to the agent's concerns are further differentiated between confirmed and disconfirmed consequences.

The basic assumption of Oatley and Johnson-Laird is that the human cognitive system is composed of modular and asynchronous processes organized as a hierarchy. Each process has a goal, which it attempts to reach if certain preconditions are met and this, without interruption. According to Oatley and Johnson-Laird, the main role of emotions is to coordinate the different processes making up the system. Emotions do so by setting the whole system in one of a small number of "emotion modes" through a non-propositional communication channel. These modes allow the system to give specific priorities to processes in the hierarchy and to organize transitions between plans.

Both theories we have just briefly described are explicitly aimed at reducing the gap between psychological concepts related to emotion and possible implementation in an artificial system. As such they both have had a great influence on models of emotion designed for artificial systems.

Artificial Emotions for Situated Agents

Situated agents designers have taken into account psychological theories of emotion in two main ways (Scheutz, 2004): on one hand, "effect models" of emotions only implement overt and observable aspects of emotional behavior, regardless of the underlying processes. On the other hand, "process models" of emotions try to replicate internal processes and functions related to emotion. These later models are more deeply rooted in psychological theories than effect models which aim at making the observer believe that the system is experiencing emotions.

Various emotional mechanisms related to process models of emotions have been implemented in situated agents to enhance the quality of interaction between humans and synthetic agents (Velásquez, 1998), to increase synthetic agents learning abilities (Gadanho, 2002), or to improve coordination between situated agents (Murphy, Lisetti, Tardif, Irish, & Gage, 2002; Parker, 1998). These last two approaches are the most relevant to our work.

Murphy et al. (2002) set out a two-layered control architecture with one sensory-motor level and one schematic level. The sensory-motor level is responsible for controlling the agent through modular behaviors and for detecting specific features or events in the environment. The schematic level controls behaviors and organizes them into more abstract abilities. This later level is implemented by two finite state machines: a behavioral states generator and an emotional states generator. Emotions are represented in this later finite state machine by four states (Happiness, Confidence, Concern and Frustration) and are derived from tasks progress evaluation. This evaluation takes into account features extracted by the sensory-motor layer and messages received from other agents. This approach therefore echoes principles of specific-stimulus theories of emotion. The emotional states generator directly modifies behavior parameters and triggers specific behaviors. This artificial model of emotions is then specific to the environment and the mission of the agents for which it has been designed.

Parker's ALLIANCE architecture (Parker, 1998) is a behavior-based architecture, using motivations to activate different groups of behavior producing modules. In each group, behaviors are arbitrated using subsumption (Brooks, 1991), a priority-based arbitration scheme. Emotions are not explicitly identified in the architecture. However, Impatience and Acquiescence are two motivations serving as temporal measures of task progression. Impatience enables an agent to handle situations when other agents fail in performing a given task, while Acquiescence is useful when the agent itself fails to properly perform its task. Motivation intensities are generated from an analysis of the current agent perception and from dedicated social messages. As for Murphy et al (2002), this approach corresponds to the specific-stimulus theories of emotion. Moreover, each motivation is directly associated with a set of behaviors, which are activated when the motivation intensity is greater than a threshold. These

motivations are therefore tightly coupled with the agents' mission objectives.

To summarize, process models of emotions for situated agents are generating emotions on the basis of specific-stimulus theories, confining agents to specific and therefore limited environmental conditions. In addition, these models associate emotional states with particular behavioral responses related to the agent's mission objectives, making them even more specific. Consequently, previous process models of emotions designed for situated agents are limited either because emotion generation is too specifically related to the environmental conditions or because emotional responses are too tightly associated with the agent's mission objectives; if the environment or the mission changes, the models of emotions become invalid, and this should not be the case in order to capture the true versatile nature of emotion. Emotions should rather be derived from a generic model to capture the fact that different situations can lead to the same emotion, and that the same situation can lead to different emotions.

The infrequent use of match-mismatch theories in situated agents could be due to the difficulty to evaluate the relevance of events with regard to the agent's concerns, especially in a continuous, dynamic and unpredictable environment. Solving this issue requires at least two abilities: an agent must be able, first, to identify significant events based on its perception and, second, to evaluate the "distance" between desired and actual states of the world. These abilities are strongly linked with the way a situated agent experiments its reality.

Therefore, it will always be difficult to implement such abilities in artificial systems because the knowledge of how an agent experiments its reality is not accessible to human designers. To address this fundamental problem, these abilities could be learned; however this is a complete research avenue, which at the time being, we have chosen not to address. Instead, we have decided to detect mismatches from the monitoring of temporal models of internal resources use. The purpose of our research is to validate the feasibility of an artificial model of anger and fear inspired by match-mismatch theories of emotion. This inspiration entails that, contrary to previous work, our model must not be specific to a set of particular situations or to the mission assigned to the situated agents for which it is designed.

ARTIFICIAL MODEL OF ANGER AND FEAR

Our model aims at replicating functions of emotion identified in match-mismatch theories, such as detecting and highlighting situations representing a mismatch between the agent's concerns and the experienced condition in the world. This process allows an agent to trigger an emotional adaptive reaction when regular decision-making processes are no longer valid. The emotion generation associated with this adaptive reaction is made independently from environmental conditions by analyzing the agent's intentions in relation to its current intended actions. The specific reactions triggered by emotional experiences are realized by dedicated processes, making our model of emotions independent of the agent's mission objectives.

Figure 1 illustrates how our model works in relation to elements associated with the decision-making processes of the agent. More specifically, the agent must have cognitive processes (Motivations) responsible for generating intentions and determining their desirabilities. Actions of the agent have to be realized by concurrent processes (Behaviors) which are activated by an Action Selection mechanism according to the agent's intentions. These intentions must be explicitly represented.

Using this model, the Emotional Process looks at how Intentions are carried out in order to monitor their compliance with the agent's Motivations. When a mismatch is detected by the appearance of a discrepancy between the agent's Intentions and the way they are satisfied by the Exploitation of behaviors, the Emotional Process tries to identify the source of the discrepancy by looking at the agent's current Intentions. The occurrence of this mismatch and its cause are then signaled to the agent's Motivations, which can change the agent's Intentions accordingly. Like match-mismatch theories of emotion, this artificial model is not focused on which particular emotion is elicited in predetermined situation but rather on getting the emotion process under way.

Monitoring of discrepancies between the agent's Intentions and behavior Exploitation is done through temporal models. These models depend on the type of Intentions: Goal-Oriented Intentions (GOI) are related to behaviors that must be exploited to make the agent accomplish tasks aimed at fulfilling the agent's goals. In favorable situations, behaviors associated with these Intentions are exploited when activated. This is reflected in the satisfaction condition of GOI, which is to be exploited when desirable. Conversely, Security-Oriented Intentions (SOI) keep the agent away from problematic situations and behaviors associated with them are

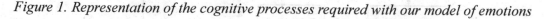

Figure 1. Representation of the cognitive processes required with our model of emotions

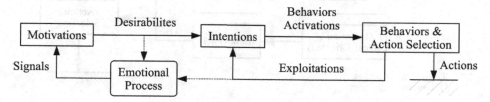

not exploited in favorable situation. Satisfaction condition of SOI is therefore not to be exploited when desirable.

Models Equations

The accumulated time $a_I(t)$ during which intention I does not conform to its satisfaction condition at time t is expressed by (1) and (2):

$$a_I(t) = \int_{-W_I}^{0} b_I(t)dt \qquad (1)$$

$$b_I(t) = \begin{cases} 0 & \text{if intention } I \text{ conforms to its} \\ & \text{satisfaction condition at time } t. \\ 1 & \text{else} \end{cases} \qquad (2)$$

where W_I is the length of the sliding time window over which intention I is monitored. A mismatch is detected when $a_I(t)$ becomes greater than a time threshold T_I.

In order to replicate the signaling function of emotion, once a mismatch is detected, its cause has to be determined and highlighted. The cause of the mismatch is found out through an analysis of the current agent's intentions. To understand this analysis, it is important to distinguish the intention **triggering** the mismatch (by not conforming to its satisfaction condition) from the intention **causing** this mismatch (by preventing the triggering intention to conform to its satisfaction condition). As depicted in Figure 2, a mismatch

related to a Goal-Oriented Intention is detected if it is desirable but not exploited during a certain period of time. Therefore, the intention identified as being the cause is the one being exploited the most during the recent past, because it hinders the exploitation of the triggering intention.

Conversely, a Security-Oriented Intention triggers a mismatch when it has been exploited for a certain period of time; in this case, the cause is the Security-Oriented Intention itself. Once identified, the cause is highlighted by signaling the concerned intention to the agent's motivations. Motivations can then use this information to change the intentions of the agent in order to adapt its behavior to the situation.

Emotions Differentiation

Once a mismatch has been detected, it is necessary to determine which particular emotion will be elicited. Works in psychology and ethology (Lazarus, 1984, 1999; Weiss 1971) have shown that in stressful situations, the elicited emotion depends on one's belief in one's ability to handle this situation.

Discussing fearful situations, Lazarus (1984) writes:

"As efficacy expectancies increase and the person judges his or her resources more adequate for satisfying task demands, the relationship is appraised as holding the potential for more

Figure 2. Mismatch detection involving a goal-oriented intention

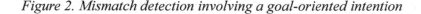
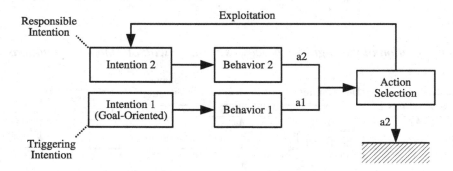

control and therefore as less threatening. As a consequence, fear level decreases and coping behaviors are instituted." (p. 70)

Frijda (1986) expresses a similar viewpoint more concisely: "Fear is the emotion of uncertainty and lack of control." (p. 429). Conversely, in situation eliciting anger, an individual can still modify its relation with its environment; control has not been lost. When discussing such situations, Frijda states that "behind the obstacle, the blocked goal still exists, still is available; and the nature of the obstacle is such that, in principle it can be controlled and modified." (p. 429)

In our model, emotions are differentiated according to the nature of the triggering intention. This choice is in accordance with Frijda and Lazarus positions about stressful situations because the nature of the triggering intention reflects the agent's belief in its ability to control the situation. Security-Oriented intentions exploitation model states that these intentions should not be exploited. So if a Security-Oriented intention does not conform to its temporal model, this is because it is exploited, i.e., the agent 'believes' it is carrying out the actions associated with the triggering intention. From the agent's viewpoint, its actions have no effect on the environment.

Therefore, when a Security-Oriented intention triggers a mismatch, it is the Fear emotion variable that is activated. Conversely, when a Goal-Oriented intention triggers a mismatch, the agent considers it is not carrying out the behaviors associated with this intention. It therefore determines that it still has the ability to modify the situation. In this case, it is the Anger emotion variable that is activated.

Emotion Variables Behavior

Each detected mismatch contributes to the activation of an emotion variable. All these contributions are summed to determine the emotion variable's

intensity $E(t)$. This intensity is expressed by Eq. (3):

$$E(t) = \sum_{\forall I} c_I(t) \qquad (3)$$

where $c_I(t)$ is the contribution of the mismatch triggered by intention I to the intensity of the emotion variable. As long as the intention I is involved in a mismatch, $c_I(t)$ increases linearly with time.

As soon as the mismatch involving I disappears, $c_I(t)$ decreases according to a function described by Picard (1995), which corresponds to the decrease of the influence of a stimulus on an emotion. $c_I(t)$ is written in the form:

$$c_I(t) = \begin{cases} c_I(t_0) + A_I \cdot (t - t_0) & \text{if } a_I(t) > T_I \\ c_I(t_1) \cdot e^{-D_I \cdot (t - t_1)} & \text{else} \end{cases}$$

(4)

where A_I is a constant increasing factor associated with intention I, D_I a constant decreasing factor associated with intention I, t_0 the instant when $a_I(t)$ has become greater than T_I and t_1 the instant when $a_I(t)$ has become lesser than T_I. Intensity of emotion variables are kept between 0 and 1.

Motivations can use the current emotional state provided by the emotional process to modulate the agent behavior parameters. For example, an angry agent can spend more energy in its behavior, as suggested by Piaget (1989).

Interestingly, using an intention-exploitation model makes our emotional process independent of the way intentions are carried out by the agent. Furthermore, these models are independent of the situation experienced by the agent because sensory data are not taken into account. Emotional experiences are therefore generated independently of both particular environmental conditions and specific behaviors. The model of emotions itself is uncoupled from the agent's mission objectives because reactions specific to the highlighted problematic situations are carried out by motivations. This independence between our model and, first, particular situations and, second, the agent's mission ensures that our emotional process is relevant to other applications and respond to the constraints entailed by the inspiration from match-mismatch theories of emotion.

Experiments

Multi-agent foraging (Goldberg & Matarić, 2002) is a widely used task to investigate group behavior in constrained and dynamic settings, with clear metrics to evaluate performance (i.e., physical interferences, traveled distance, time to complete). This explains our decision of using such a task to illustrate the working of our emotional process. Fig. 2 illustrates the simulated environment (implemented in Stage (Vaughan, Gerkey, & Howard, 2003)) used for the foraging experiments. The simulated agents are Pioneer 2 DXs in a pen of 6 × 10 meters. Six agents have to collect 12 pucks and take them one by one to the home region. Each agent is given two simulated sensors: one laser range finder with an 8 meter-range and a 180° field of view, and one fiducial finder, returning the identifier and relative position of objects with a fiducial tag, in a range of 5 meters and a 180° field of view. Each agent has a unique fiducial identifier, which allows it to perceive others' relative positions. Home flags and pucks also have fiducial ids. Agents are equipped with a gripper allowing them to collect one puck at a time. Note that such simulated conditions are realistic since they are based on the existence of real sensors, such as laser range finder, color cameras for pucks and home detection, and omnidirectional ultrasonic positioning devices (Rivard, Bisson, Michaud, & Létourneau, 2008) for localizing and identifying agents. Agents are considered to be homogeneous as they all have the same physical and decisional capabilities. They can communicate with each other using broadcast mode (through network link).

The group coordination strategy is based on a dominance hierarchy: when an agent perceives a higher-ranked agent in a range of 1.5 meter in front of it, it stops. This range is called the social range of the agents and has been dynamically changed according to the agents' emotional states. This distributed strategy aims at avoiding physical interference while minimizing traveled distance. The choice of a hierarchy to coordinate a group comes from the social function of emotion and especially from the work of Plutchik (1980) who states that emotions of fear and anger play an important role in the dominance hierarchy, which is established in ape groups and in some part of the human society. He also states that these dominance hierarchies are useful for social groups since they lower the frequency of conflicts for shared resources such as food or mate.

Implementation

The framework used to implement our emotional process is based on a distributed behavior-based system named MBA (Motivated Behavioral Architecture) (Michaud et al., 2007). Figure 3 illustrates the MBA architecture with the specific modules implemented for the collective foraging task. Each agent in the group uses this architecture for decision-making.

Behavior-producing modules (BPM, or behaviors) constitute basic components from which the agent can operate in the world. BPM are configured to issue commands based on the agent's perception and intentions. For the collective foraging task, the five BPM are arbitrated using subsumption in the following order of priority:

- **Escape**, which makes the agent turn on itself to find a safe passage to leave the current location.
- **Obey**, which makes the agent execute a particular action such as stopping or turning left, according to a parameter associated with the agent's intentions.

Figure 3. Simulated experimental settings

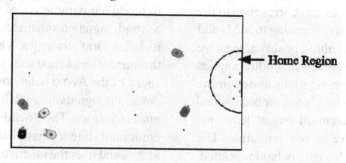

Figure 4. Implementation of MBA for foraging agents

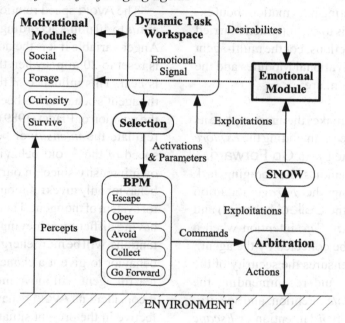

- **Avoid**, which makes the agent move safely in the environment by avoiding obstacles using laser range finder readings. Only obstacles within a 0.9 meter radius of the agent are taken into account.
- **Collect**, which tracks pucks, collects them one at a time and takes them back to the home region.
- **Go Forward**, which gives the agent a constant linear velocity.

These BPM issue commands only if they are activated. Their activation and parameters are derived by the *Selection* module based on the agent's intentions. These intentions are generated by the *Motivational Modules* (MM) and are stored in the *Dynamic Task Workspace* (DTW). They are organized in a tree-like structure according to their interdependencies, from high-level/abstract intentions to primitive/behavior-related intentions. For example, a high level intention could be Stay Safe and its children in the hierarchy could the Avoid and Escape intentions which are associated with behaviors.

MMs are asynchronous, independent modules that can add intentions, modify or monitor their parameters, and give recommendations about them. These recommendations correspond to the desirabilities of intentions according to MMs and can take three different values: positive, negative and undetermined. The *Selection* module applies a policy to these recommendations to determine the behaviors' activations; a behavior is activated if its corresponding intention has at least one positive and no negative recommendation. The associations between lowest, behavior-related, intentions and behaviors are implemented in the *System Know-How* (SNOW) module. This module is also in charge of updating information about exploited intentions, that is to say intentions carried out by current agent's actions. For the multi-agent foraging task, the Motivational Modules and the intentions related to them are:

- **Curiosity**, which makes the agent explore its environment by recommending the *Explore* intention associated with **Go Forward**.
- **Forage**, which handles the foraging task by recommending the *Forage* intention (associated with the **Collect** behavior) and inhibiting the *Stay Safe* intention when a puck is about to be collected by the agent.
- **Survive**, which ensures the security of the agent by adding and recommending the high-level *Stay Safe* intention, and specifying it by adding *Avoid* intention or *Escape* intention as its child. These two intentions are directly associated with behaviors with the same names. We describe later how and when the **Survive** MM chooses between *Avoid* and *Escape*.
- **Social**, which carries out the group coordination strategy through recommendations of the *Obey* intention. This intention is associated with the **Obey** behavior.

The Emotion Module (EM) implements the model of artificial anger and fear described above. The behavior modifications triggered by the emotions for the foraging task are of two kinds. First, the current emotional state is used to modulate parameters of the agent's behavior. Second, signaled mismatches are used to adapt its behavioral strategies. The **Survive** MM uses the current emotional state to modify the rotation speed of the **Avoid** behavior and the mismatches detection signals to switch between two avoidance strategies. The **Social** MM uses the current emotional state to change the social range of the agents and uses the mismatches detection signals to adapt the coordination strategy by updating the group's dominance hierarchy.

The **Avoid** speed rotation is changed from 20 mm/s to 40 mm/s according to the intensity of the Anger variable if it is the dominant emotion, and is reset to 20 mm/s when the dominant emotion is Fear. This influence of the emotional state on the agent's behavior has been chosen according to the position of Piaget (1989) stating that emotions regulate the *intensity* of behavior. The rotation speed of the **Avoid** behavior can be seen as its own intensity since, in our implementation, this behavior only gives rotation commands to the motor system of the agent. Therefore, an angry agent, having difficulty achieving its Goal-Oriented intentions, will be more energetic with its avoidance behavior to give it a chance to succeed, while a fearful agent will move more carefully because it considers its **Avoid** behavior has become ineffective in the present situation.

The avoidance strategy is switched from simple obstacle avoidance to escape when the *Stay Safe* intention is signaled as the cause of a mismatch. This is done by the **Survive** MM which replaces the *Avoid* intention with the *Escape* intention as the child of *Stay Safe* in the intentions hierarchy. This change causes the **Avoid** behavior to be inhibited and the **Escape** one to be activated.

The social range of an agent varies according to the current emotional state of the superior to which it obeys. An agent stays farther from angry superiors than from superiors in a neutral emotional state and can come closer to fearful superiors. The social range of an agent is expressed

Box 1.

$$S(t) = \begin{cases} S_0 \cdot (1 + E_{Anger}^{Sup}(t) \cdot K_s) & \text{if Anger is the superior's dominant emotion} \\ S_0 \cdot (1 - E_{Fear}^{Sup}(t) \cdot K_s) & \text{else} \end{cases}$$

by Eq. (5) (see Box 1), where S_0 is the default social range (1.5 meters in the experiments), E_e^{Sup} is the intensity of emotion e experienced by the superior agent, and K_s the social range variation factor. This factor is set to 0.2 in the experiments, allowing $S(t)$ to vary between 1.2 and 1.8 meters. Values of these parameters have been fixed according to the distances at which agents start to interact physically, beginning to use their avoidance behavior due to other agents nearby.

The coordination strategy is adapted when the *Obey* intention of an agent is signaled as the cause of a mismatch. This typically occurs when an inferior agent obeys to a superior, which is experiencing some kind of failure. When the **Social** MM receives a signal from the Emotion Module meaning that the *Obey* intention it has added is the cause of a mismatch, it triggers an update of the group hierarchy. This update involves only the two agents concerned by the *Obey* intention: the inferior agent and the superior to which it obeys. The update process begins with the inferior sending a message to the superior, challenging the position of the superior in the hierarchy. The answer of the superior depends on its current emotional state: if its dominant emotion is Fear (meaning it is in an unwanted situation involving its security), the superior will resign and leave the inferior's message unanswered.

The superior will thus drop in the hierarchy from the inferior's viewpoint and vice versa. As a consequence, if there are communication problems between agents experiencing situations requiring hierarchy adaptations, they will end up considering all other agents as inferiors. Hence, if communication between the group members fails, their collective behavior will tend gradu-

ally to a non-coordinated behavior. Conversely, if the superior is experiencing Anger, it will reply to the inferior and the hierarchy will remain the same. In this case, the update process is reinitiated every 7 seconds as long as the *Obey* intention of the inferior agent is signaled as the cause of a mismatch. When a superior agent accepts to drop in the hierarchy, it does not reply to the inferior's request.

To better understand the hierarchy adaptation process, let us consider the situation depicted in Figure 3. In this situation, the black agent in the bottom left corner is unintentionally surrounded by inferior agents. These agents are motionless because they are obeying to the superior one and are thus blocking it. Figure 5 presents the decision-making mechanism status of one of the inferior agents in this situation, and Figure 6 shows one of the inferior agents' evolution of internal variables during the hierarchy adaptation process. As the problematic situation goes on, from time 0 to time 75, $a_{Forage}(t)$ increases because the *Forage* intention is not exploited. When $a_{Forage}(t)$ reaches the *Forage* time threshold ($T_{Forage} = 60$ sec.), a mismatch is detected. This detection triggers an analysis of the current intentions, with conclusion that the *Obey* intention was exploited the most in the recent past and is therefore the cause of the mismatch. This information is communicated to the motivations. In response to this signal, the **Social** MM, which is responsible for the addition of the *Obey* intention, triggers the hierarchy adaptation process. As the superior agent is blocked, it is (around time 175) experiencing fear and therefore will not answer to the inferior's request to move down the hierarchy, causing a switch of position between itself and the inferior agent. Once this switch is completed,

Figure 5. Intentions and behaviors of an agent obeying to a superior experiencing some kind of failure

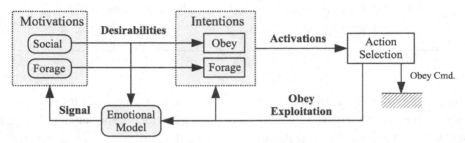

Figure 6. Exploitations and activations of behaviors (top) and accumulated time during which **Stay Safe** *and* **Forage** *intentions do not conform to their exploitation models (bottom) of an agent obeying a superior agent, which is experiencing a failure*

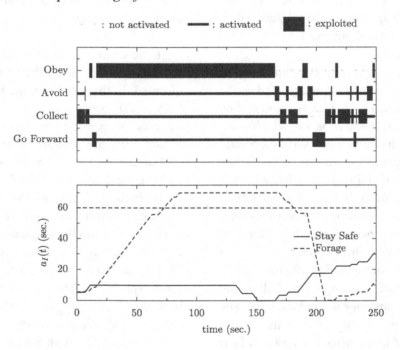

the former inferior agent has no more reason to stop and can resume foraging.

Experimental Results

To characterize the influence of our emotional process while neutralizing the influence of other architectural components, we conducted a series of trials in each of the following conditions:

- Neither emotional process nor coordination (NE-NC). The **Social** MM or the EM are not used in the decision-making architecture. This condition is used as a reference to evaluate the influence of the emotional process and of the coordination strategy.

- Modulation of the behavior parameters according to the dominant emotion intensity and no group coordination (E_I-NC). This condition is used to characterize the influence of the emotional modulation of behavior parameters.

- Adaptation of strategies triggered by mismatch detection and no group coordination (E_M-NC). This condition measures the influence of switching between avoidance strategies (i.e., between *Avoid* and *Escape* intentions).

- Combination of the two previous conditions and no group coordination (E_{MI}-NC).

- Group coordination without emotional influence (NE-C). The **Social** MM is used but not the EM. The dominance hierarchy is static and predetermined (Goldberg & Matarić 1997). This condition demonstrates the performance of the coordination strategy and is used as a reference to evaluate the influence of the emotional process on the coordination strategy.

- Group coordination and modulation of the behavior parameters according to the dominant emotion intensity (E_I-C).

- Group coordination and adaptation of strategies triggered by mismatch detection (E_M-C).

- Complete emotional mechanism and group coordination (E_{MI}-C). This involves all the emotional processes of our approach.

Each of these conditions has been tested on the same series of forty randomly-generated configu-

rations of agents and pucks in the simulated pen to attenuate the influence of the initial positions. In these trials, the parameters of Eq. (4) are the following: $A_I = 0.7$ and $D_I = 0.025$. These values were chosen to make emotional experiences duration coherent with intention models parameters. *Forage* is a Goal-Oriented intention with $W_I = 70$ seconds and $T_I = 60$ seconds. This intention is considered as satisfied by the agent behavior when the **Collect** or the **Move Forward** behaviors are exploited. *Stay Safe* is a Safety-Oriented intention with $W_I = 140$ seconds and $T_I = 120$ seconds.

Table 1 summarizes the observed results in terms of the following metrics. Completion Time is the time spent to take all pucks to the home region. Traveled Distance is the total distance traveled by the agents during one trial. Physical Interference Ratio is the amount of time spent at a distance of 0.7 m from other agents. The interference distance is set at the distance at which the linear speed of the agents equals zero when the **Avoid** behavior is exploited. Physical Interference Ratio echoes the risk of collision between agents and has proved to be a good measure for a coordination strategy in a foraging task (Goldberg & Matarić, 1997). Success Rate is the ratio of failed trials (determined when pucks remain to be collected after 30 minutes) over the total number of trials. This metric captures the ability of the group to recover from situations causing it to fail and we have not anticipated, reflecting

Table 1. Experimental results

	No Group Coordination				Group Coordination			
	NE-NC	E_I-NC	E_M-NC	E_{MI}-NC	NE-C	E_I-C	E_M-C	E_{MI}-C
Completion Time (sec.)	438	427	392	449	345	406	562	509
Traveled Distance (m.)	391	381	357	396	295	326	398	377
Physical Interference Ratio	24%	25%	24%	24%	13%	13%	16%	15%
Success Rate	90%	92.5%	97.5%	90%	57.5%	52.5%	92.5%	100%

the adaptability of the group. All these metrics, except Success Rate, take only successful trials into account not to be offset by the failure time which was set arbitrarily.

The following observations can be made from these experimental results. For conditions without group coordination, modulating behavior parameters according to emotion intensities (E_I-NC) or triggering switching of avoidance strategies from mismatch detection (E_M-NC) resulted both in a higher success rate compared to the reference condition (NE-NC). This suggests that emotional influences improved the agents' adaptability at the individual level. Completion Time, Traveled Distance and Success Rate of the E_{MI}-NC condition indicate however that the influences of mismatches detection and emotions intensities interfere with each other. The dynamic of this interference remains to be fully understood. It seems that the modification of the Avoid rotation speed prevents the strategy switch between Avoid and Escape behaviors to be beneficial to the agents. In conditions without coordination, agents always operate as individuals, and consequently similar performances are observed in terms of Physical Interference Ratio for these experimental conditions.

As expected, the introduction of group coordination strategies has clearly reduced the physical interferences between agents, making them safer. However, modifying behaviors parameters according to emotions intensities to the coordination strategy (E_I-C) has actually decreased performances of the group for the other metrics, compared to NE-C conditions. The increase in Completion Time of the E_I-C condition can be explained by the fact that, in this condition, inferior agents are influenced by farther superior agents than in NE-C condition, making them spend more time motionless. Near the end of the mission, when all pucks have been picked up but not yet brought back to the home region, these delays cause the agents not carrying pucks to travel more distance than in the NE-C condition. That is why Traveled

Distance of the E_I-C condition is slightly greater than the one of the NE-C condition.

Combining coordination with strategy modifications based on mismatches detection (E_M-C) drastically improves the Success Rate of the group while keeping the Physical Interference Ratio low. However, this improvement has a cost: this condition has the longest Completion Time. This is implicitly caused by the use of temporal intention models. For example, when an agent carrying a puck is experiencing a situation from which it can resume only through the detection of a mismatch, this causes a delay in the completion of the mission. Furthermore, with the chosen coordination strategy, this agent causes inferior agents nearby to stop, hindering them in the execution of their task and thus further delaying the success of the mission. For instance, in the situation illustrated by Figure 3, all inferior agents involved remain still until the hierarchy update. The Traveled Distance and Physical Interference Ratio of the E_M-C condition are worse than the ones of the NE-C and E_I-C conditions. However, as failed trials are not taken into consideration in these conditions (Success Rate being around 55%), negative effects of problematic situations are not reflected in their metrics. Their low success rates have two main causes: first, when an agent fails by getting stuck on an obstacle or by hitting another agent, all its inferiors passing nearby stop moving, potentially leading to a failure of the group. Second, the situation illustrated by Figure 3 creates a deadlock and leads to a group failure.

The same observations can be made about the comparison of the E_{MI}-C condition with NE-C and E_I-C conditions. In addition, E_{MI}-C condition achieved the best Success Rate and a better Traveled Distance than E_M-C. This shows that taking emotion intensities into account is meaningful for the group only if mismatch detection also influences the group behavior.

Overall, the coordination strategy effectively improves agents' safety by lowering their physical interactions, but needs to be adapted in order not to compromise the success of the group's mission by creating deadlock situations. Taking only emotion intensities into account do not results in significant improvements at the individual level, and decreases the performances of the group. Modifying avoidance and coordination strategies according to mismatch detection improves the agents' ability to recover from unforeseen problematic situations, which cause their decision-making mechanism to fail. Mismatch detection also allows agents operating without coordination to improve their Completion Time and Traveled Distance. Coordinated agents using this mechanism (E_M-C) keep their Traveled Distance and Physical Interference Ratio low, but their Completion Time is the longest (what is implicitly due to the use of temporal intention models). Combining the two emotional influences (E_{MI}-C) has also a long Completion Time, however, this condition resulted in a low Physical Interference Ratio and a Traveled Distance slightly shorter than the one of the NE-NC condition. Therefore, adding all the emotional processes of our approach to the group coordination (E_{MI}-C) makes it possible to reach a good compromise between security, distance, and speed while achieving the best Success Rate, demonstrating the usefulness of these emotional processes in improving the group adaptability. In dynamic and changing conditions, finding such compromise is probably the rational thing to do.

FUTURE TRENDS

In our future, work we intend to demonstrate the versatility and extensibility of the presented model in other settings by validating other emotional influences on an agent's decision-making mechanism in order to allow it to adapt its behavior to dynamically changing situations. Further extension of the model includes generation of positive emotions when, for instance, intentions are carried out by the agent's actions, when agent's actions satisfy multiple intentions, or when a temporary intention ends with a positive result. One main research avenue, which remains to be explored, is to make the agents able to modify their intention models through a learning mechanism, making them even more independent from knowledge provided by their designer. In order to widen the presented model's range of emotions and to better differentiate and refine elicited emotions, it could be beneficial to trigger an analysis of the current situation. Such an analysis could be contextualized from the agent's intention to make it richer than a simple continuous feature extraction from the agent's perceptions.

Models inspired by specific-stimulus theories of emotion will remain useful when improving reactions of artificial systems to specific situations. However, if complete autonomy of these systems is to be achieved, then provision must be made for a general self-analysis mechanism allowing them to detect situation for which their decision-making processes are not adapted. The main argument in support of this viewpoint is that adaptation of a decision-making mechanism to unforeseen situations is a costly process that cannot be executed continuously.

CONCLUSION

We believe situated agents' adaptability ultimately depends on the detection of the situations for which their regular decision-making process is not appropriate, calling for a behavioral or cognitive reaction. Detecting such situations is a key problem for situated agents because their environment is dynamic, continuous and unpredictable. Psychologists have identified that one of the functions of human emotion is to highlight these kinds of situations, allowing other cognitive processes to address them. We have developed an emotional process that allows situated agents to detect such situations by using temporal models of their intentions. This model does not rely on a priori knowledge of specific environmental conditions nor of the agent's mission objectives, but only on how control resources (i.e., behaviors) satisfy the agent's intentions. This independence between decision-making processes and human provided knowledge is crucial to an agent's autonomy since we cannot fully understand how an agent experiences its reality. Our long term objective is to provide situated agents with a generic self-analysis mechanism detecting situations requiring adaptation. Such a mechanism is required to autonomously trigger relevant learning phases and behavioral strategy switches and is therefore necessary to achieve complete autonomy for situated agents.

ACKNOWLEDGMENT

The authors gratefully acknowledge the contribution of the Natural Sciences and Engineering Research Council of Canada (NSERC) and the Canada Research Chair (CRC), in the support of this work.

REFERENCES

Brooks, R. A. (1991). Intelligence without reason. In *Proceedings of the 12th International Joint Conference on Artificial Intelligence (IJCAI-91)*, (pp. 569-595).

Brown, J. S., & Farber, I. E. (1951). Emotions conceptualized as intervening variables - with suggestions towards a theory of frustration. *Psychological Bulletin, 48*, 465-495.

Frijda, N. H. (1986). *The emotions*. Cambridge: Cambridge University Press.

Frijda, N. H. (1989). Les théories des émotions : Un bilan. In B. Rimé, & K. R. Scherer (Eds.), *Les émotions* (pp. 21-72). Paris: Delachaux et Niestle.

Gadanho, S. C. (2002). Emotional and cognitive adaptation in real environments. *Symposium ACE'2002 of the 16th European Meeting on Cybernetics and Systems Research*.

Goldberg, D., & Matarić, M. J. (2002). Design and evaluation of robust behavior-based controllers for distributed multi-robot collection tasks. In T. Balch, & L. E. Parker (Eds.), *Robot teams: From diversity to polymorphism*, (pp. 315-344), AK Peters.

Goldberg, D., & Matarić, M. J. (1997). Interference as a tool for designing and evaluating multi-robot controllers. In *Proceedings of the National Conference on Artificial Intelligence (AAAI)*, (pp. 637-642).

Hebb, D. O. (1949). *The organization of behavior: A neuropsychological theory*. New York: Wiley.

Heise, D. (1979). *Understanding events: Affect and the construction of social action*. New York: Cambridge University Press.

Higgins, E. T. (1989). Self-discrepancy: A theory relating self and affect. *Psychological Review, 94*, 319-340.

Lazarus, R. S. (1966). *Psychological stress and the coping process*, McGraw-Hill, New-York.

Lazarus, R. S. (1999). *Stress and emotion a new synthesis*. New York: Springer.

Lazarus, R. S., & Folkman, S. (1984). *Stress, appraisal, and coping*. New York: Springer.

Mandler, G. (1984). *Mind and body: Psychology of emotion and stress*. New York: W. W. Norton.

Mandler, G. (1997). *Human nature explored*. New York: Oxford University Press.

Michaud, F., Côté, C., Létourneau, D., Brosseau, Y., Valin, J., Beaudry, É., et al. (2007). Spartacus attending the 2005 AAAI conference. *Autonomous Robots, Special Issue on the AAAI Mobile Robot Competitions and Exhibition, 22*(4), 369-384.

Murphy, R. R., Lisetti, C. L., Tardif, R., Irish, L., & Gage, A. (2002). Emotion-based control of cooperating heterogeneous mobile robots. *IEEE Transactions on Robotics and Autotomation, 18*(5), 744-757.

Nagel, T. (1974). What is it like to be a bat? *The Philosophical Review, 83*(4), 435-450.

Oatley, K., & Johnson-Laird, P. N. (1987). Towards a cognitive theory of emotions. *Cognition and Emotion, 1*(1), 29-50.

Ortony, A., Clore, G. L., & Collins, A. (1988). *The cognitive structure of emotions*. Cambridge, England ; New York: Cambridge University Press.

Parker, L. E. (1998). ALLIANCE: An architecture for fault tolerant multi-robot cooperation. *IEEE Transactions on Robotics and Automation, 2*(14), 220-240.

Piaget, J. (1989). Les relations entre l'intlligence et l'affectivité dans le développement de l'enfant. In B. Rimé, & K. R. Scherer (Eds.), *Les émotions.* (pp. 75-96). Paris: Delachaux et Niestle.

Picard, R. (1995). *Affective computing*. Cambridge, MA: MIT Press.

Plutchik, R. (1980). A general psychoevolutionary theory of emotion. In R. Plutchik, & H. Kellermann (Eds.), *Emotion; theory, research and experience.* (pp. 3-33), New York: Academic Press.

Rivard, F., Bisson, J., Michaud, F., & Létourneau, D. (2008). Ultrasonic relative positioning for multi-robot systems. In *Proceedings of IEEE International Conference on Robotics and Automation.*

Scherer, K. R., Schorr, A., & Johnstone, T. (2001). *Appraisal theories of emotions: Theories, methods, research,* New York: Oxford University Press.

Scherer, K. R. (1993). Studying the emotion-antecedent appraisal process: An expert system approach. *Cognition and Emotion, 7*(3), 325-355.

Scheutz, M. (2004). How to determine the utility of emotions. In *Proceedings of AAAI Spring Symposium,*

Simon, H. A. (1967). Motivational and emotional controls of cognition. *Psychological Review, 74*(1), 29-39.

Sloman, A. (2008). *Questions about emotions.* Retrieved 06-2008, from http://www.cs.bham.ac.uk/research/projects/cogaff/misc/emotions-questions.html

Robinson, D. T, SmithLovin, L., & Wisecup, A. (2006). Affect control theory. In J. E. Stets, & J. H. Turner (Eds.), *Handbook of the sociology of emotions* (pp. 179-202). New York: Springer.

Spinoza, B. (1677). *Ethique [Ethica ordine geometrico demonstrata]* (F. Alquié Trans.). (2nd ed.). Paris: Presses universitaires de France, 1966.

Stets, J. E. (2003). Emotions and sentiments. In J. Delamater (Ed.), *Handbook of social psychology* (pp 309-335) New York: Springer.

Vaughan, R. T., Gerkey, B. P., & Howard, A. (2003). On device abstractions for portable, reusable robot code. In *Proceedings IEEE/RSJ International Conference on Intelligent Robots and Systems* (pp. 2421-2427).

Velásquez, J. D. (1998). A computational framework for emotion-based control. In *Proceedings of Fifth International Conference on Simulation of Adaptive Behaviors (SAB'98),*

Watson, J. B. (1919). *Psychology, from the standpoint of a behaviorist*. Philadelphia: Lippincott.

KEY TERMS

Autonomy: For a situated agent: freedom from human guidance during operation. Ability to adapt to variations of its environment without human action.

Adaptability: Ability to autonomously modify its decision-making mechanism to make it relevant in an unforeseen situation.

Concerns: Dispositional entities representing states of the world, which should be attained and which are present in the system prior to the encounter of an event. Needs, motives, goals, expectations, and commitments are concerns.

Coordination: Managing dependencies of activities and goals of agents working together towards a mutual objective.

Discrepancy: Difference between what is perceived and what is expected. Expectations coming from biological evolution or learning. Discrepancies imply a response, an arousal in the sympathetic nervous system and are thus part of the emotion process.

Intention: State of the world which is the purpose of an agent action. Action tendency towards a goal.

Situated Agent: Physical or virtual entity which is situated in a dynamic, quasi-continuous environment, which it perceive through sensors and into which it operates autonomously.

ENDNOTE

[1] One can argue that the versatility of the system can be improved by adding analyses of increasing complexity to the stimulus evaluation. However, the more complex the analyses are, the more resources consuming they are. Once a particular level of complexity is reached, they cannot be conducted continuously in a complex environment.

Chapter XV
Artificial Surprise

Luis Macedo
University of Coimbra, Portugal

Amilcar Cardoso
University of Coimbra, Portugal

Rainer Reisenzein
University of Greifswald, Germany

Emiliano Lorini
Institute of Cognitive Sciences and Technologies, Italy & Institut de Recherche en Informatique de Toulouse, France

Cristiano Castelfranchi
Institute of Cognitive Sciences and Technologies, Italy

ABSTRACT

This chapter reviews research on computational models of surprise. Part 1 begins with a description of the phenomenon of surprise in humans, reviews research on human surprise, and describes a psychological model of surprise (Meyer, Reisenzein, & Schützwohl, 1997). Part 2 is devoted to computational models of surprise, giving special prominence to the models proposed by Macedo and Cardoso (e.g., Macedo & Cardoso, 2001b) and by Lorini and Castelfranchi (e.g., Lorini & Castelfranchi, 2007). Part 3 compares the two models of artificial surprise with each other and with the Meyer et al. model of human surprise, discusses possible targets of future research, and considers possible practical applications.

INTRODUCTION

Considered by some theorists a biologically basic emotion (e.g., Izard, 1991), surprise has long been of interest to philosophers and psychologists. In contrast, the artificial intelligence and computational modeling communities have until recently largely ignored surprise (for an exception, see Ortony & Partridge, 1987). However, during the last years, several computational models of surprise, including concrete computer implementations, have been developed. The aim of these computational models of surprise—which are in part based on psychological theories and findings on the subject—is on the one hand to simulate surprise in order to advance the understanding of surprise in humans, and on the other hand to provide artificial agents (softbots or robots) with the benefits of a surprise mechanism. This second goal is motivated by the belief that surprise is as relevant for artificial agents as it is for humans. Ortony and Partridge (1987, p. 108), proposed that a surprise mechanism is "a crucial component of general intelligence". Similarly, we propose that a surprise mechanism is an essential component of any anticipatory agent that, like humans, is resource-bounded and operates in an imperfectly known and changing environment. The function of the surprise mechanism in such an agent is the same as in humans: To promote the short- and long-term adaptation to unexpected events (e.g., Meyer et al., 1997). As will be seen, this function of surprise entails a close connection of surprise to curiosity and exploration (Berlyne, 1960), as well as to belief revision and learning (e.g., Charlesworth, 1969). Beyond that, surprise has been implicated as an essential element in creativity, aesthetic experience, and humor (e.g., Boden, 1995; Huron, 2006; Schmidhuber, 2006; Suls, 1971). Surprise is therefore also of importance to artificial intelligence researchers interested in the latter phenomena (Macedo & Cardoso, 2001a, 2002; Ritchie, 1999).

The chapter comprises three sections. Section 1 reviews psychological research on surprise. After a brief historical survey, the theory of surprise proposed by Meyer et al. (1997) is described in some detail. Section 2 is devoted to computational models of surprise, giving special prominence to the models of Macedo and Cardoso (e.g., Macedo & Cardoso, 2001b; Macedo et al., 2004) and Lorini and Castelfranchi (e.g., Lorini & Castelfranchi, 2007). Section 3 compares the two models of artificial surprise with each other and with the Meyer et al. (1997) model of human surprise, discusses possible targets of future research, and considers possible practical applications.

SURPRISE IN HUMANS

Pre-Theoretical Characterization of Surprise

Common-sense psychology conceptualizes surprise as a peculiar state of mind, usually of brief duration, caused by unexpected events of all kinds. *Subjectively* (i.e., from the perspective of the surprised person), surprise manifests itself centrally in a phenomenal experience or "feeling" (Reisenzein, 2000b) with a characteristic quality, that can vary in intensity (e.g., one can feel slightly, moderately or strongly surprised). In addition, the surprised person is often aware, at least if she observes herself carefully, of a variety of surprise-related mental and behavioral events: She realizes that something is different from usual or other than expected; she notices that her ongoing mental processes and actions are being interrupted and that her attention is drawn to the unexpected event; she may feel curiosity about the nature and causes of this event; and she may notice the occurrence of spontaneous epistemic search processes (for empirical evidence see e.g., Reisenzein, Bördgen, Holdtbernd, & & Matz, 2006).

Objectively (i.e., from the perspective of the outside observer), surprise may reveal itself—depending on circumstances—in any of a number of behavioral indicators, including: Interruption or delay of ongoing motor activities; orienting of the sense organs to the surprising event; investigative activities such as visual search and questioning others; spontaneous exclamations ("Oh!") and explicit verbal proclamations of being surprised; and a characteristic facial expression consisting, in full-blown form, of eyebrow-raising, eye-widening, and mouth-opening/jaw drop (Ekman, Friesen, & Hager, 2002). Furthermore, psychophysiological studies suggest that surprising events may elicit a variety of bodily changes, commonly subsumed under the so-called *orienting response* (Sokolov, 1963), such as a temporary slowing of heart rate and an increased activity of the eccrine sweat glands (see Meyer & Niepel, 1994). It must be emphasized, however, that the behavioral manifestations of surprise occur by no means in all situations and are in general only loosely associated with one another (Reisenzein, 2000a).

History of Research on Surprise

Descriptions of surprise as a mental and behavioral phenomenon, as well as first attempts at theory-building, date back as far as Aristotle (about 350 B.C.). Among the first to discuss surprise in modern times were the philosophers Hume (1739/1978) and Smith (1795/1982). Their ideas were taken up and elaborated further when psychology was established as an independent discipline in the second half of the 19th century, by authors such as Darwin, (1872/1965), McDougall (1908/1960), Ribot (1896) Shand (1914), Wundt (1863). It is probably fair to say that by 1920, most of the questions of surprise research that can be asked from a noncomputational perspective had been formulated; in addition, first experimental studies of surprise had been conducted. Thus, in a historical survey of surprise research published

in 1939, Desai (1939) lists the following issues as having been topics of reflection (plus some empirical research): The elicitors of surprise; the subjective experience of surprise (its nature, feeling tone, and duration); the inhibitory effect of surprise; surprise and attention; surprise and memory; the expression of surprise; surprise and related mental states (e.g., wonder and curiosity); the question of whether surprise is an emotion; the biological function and phylogenetic development of surprise; the ontogenetic development of surprise; the role of surprise in pathology; and the place of surprise in social psychology.

During the behaviorist era of psychology (about 1920-1960), research on surprise came largely to a standstill, to be taken up again only following the "cognitive revolution" of the 1960s. At that time, aspects of surprise first came to be discussed again under the headings of "orienting reaction" (Sokolov, 1963) and "curiosity and exploration" (Berlyne, 1960). Surprise as an independent phenomenon was first discussed anew by evolutionary emotion theorists (Izard, 1971; Tomkins, 1962). Referring back to Darwin (1872/1965), these authors proposed that surprise is a basic emotion that serves essential biological functions. One of these functions—surprise as an instigator of epistemic (specifically causal) search and a precondition for learning and cognitive development—came to be particularly emphasized by developmental psychologists (see Charlesworth, 1969). In the 1970s and 1980s, this suggestion was taken up by social psychologists interested in everyday causal explanations, who emphasized unexpectedness as a main instigator of causal search (e.g., Pyszczynski & Greenberg, 1987; Weiner, 1985). In the 1980s, cognitive psychologists (e.g., Kahneman & Tversky, 1982; Rumelhart, 1984), including cognitively oriented emotion theorists (e. g., Meyer, 1988; Ortony, Clore, & Collins, 1988) became interested in surprise. Since that time, research on surprise as an independent phenomenon has steadily increased and is carried out today by researchers in different subfields of psychology.

Topics addressed by recent psychological research on surprise are, for example, the relation between surprise intensity and the strength of cognitive schemas (e.g., Schützwohl, 1998), the role of surprise in spontaneous attention capture (e.g., Horstmann, 2002), the effects of surprise on the hindsight bias (e. g., Pezzo, 2003), the spontaneous facial expression of surprise (e.g., Reisenzein et al., 2006), and the role of surprise in advertising (e.g., Derbaix & Vanhamme, 2003).

Psychological Theories of Surprise

The Cognitive-Psychoevolutionary Model

Classical psychological theories of surprise are formulated exclusively in the language of common-sense psychology, using concepts such as *belief, expectation, attention* and, of course, *surprise*. In other words, these theories are formulated on what Dennett (1987) called the *intentional level* of system analysis. Only in recent times have there been attempts to move below the intentional level to the *design level* (Dennett, 1987), the level of underlying mental mechanisms, or the cognitive architecture (e.g., Meyer et al., 1997). The aim of these newer "process models" of surprise is to provide a deepened understanding of the causal generation of surprise, its nature, and its functional role in the architecture of the mind, by describing the information-processing mechanisms that underlie the feeling of surprise and surprise-related mental events and behaviors. Although these process models of surprise are not yet detailed

enough to count as computational models, they are natural precursors to such models because, although they leave open many issues, they provide enough detail to serve as reasonable starting points for computational modeling. As such, these process models play the role of an intermediary between intentional-level theories of surprise and full-fledged computational theories.

To illustrate recent psychological theorizing surprise, we describe the so-called *cognitive-psychoevolutionary model of surprise* proposed by Meyer et al. (1997); see also, Meyer, Reisenzein, & Niepel (2000). This model is intended as an integration and elaboration of the modal views of previous surprise theorists and attributional analyses of reactions to unexpected events (e.g., Pyszczynski & Greenberg, 1987), within the framework of schema theory (Rumelhart, 1984; Schank, 1986). The model is depicted (in simplified form) in Figure 1.

Schemas as representational structures. Schema theory (e.g., Rumelhart, 1984; Schank, 1986) assumes that human perception, thought and action are to a large extent controlled by complex, organized knowledge (or belief) structures, called schemas. Schemas can be regarded as informal, unarticulated theories, or as sets of beliefs, about objects, events, event sequences (including actions and their consequences) and situations. Schemas serve the interpretation of present and past, and the prediction of future events, and thereby the adaptive guidance of action. To be able to fulfill these functions, a person's schemas (her informal theories) must be at least approximately correct. This in turn requires—because knowledge

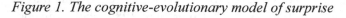
Figure 1. The cognitive-evolutionary model of surprise

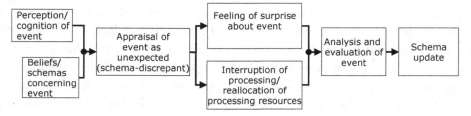

about the environment is frequently incomplete, and because the environment can change—that schemas are continuously monitored for their compatibility with newly acquired information and, if necessary, are appropriately updated. According to Meyer (1988), Meyer et al. (1997) and Meyer et al. (2000), the surprise mechanism plays a crucial role in this context.

The surprise mechanism is assumed to consist at its core of a device that continuously compares, at an unconscious level of processing, the currently activated cognitive schemas (which may be regarded as constituting the person's working-memory model of her present situation) with newly acquired information (beliefs). As long as this mechanism registers congruence between schema and input—as long as events conform to expectations—the person's informal theories are supported by the evidence, and there is hence no need to revise them. Rather, the interpretation of events and the control of action take place largely automatically and without effort. In contrast, if a discrepancy between schema and input is detected, a "surprise reaction" is elicited (see Figure 1): Ongoing information processing is interrupted, processing resources are reallocated to the unexpected event, surprise is experienced, and cognitive processes (as well as, possibly, overt actions) aimed at the analysis and evaluation of the unexpected event are initiated. The function of these processes is, on the one hand, to enable and motivate immediate adaptive actions directed at the surprising event (*short-term adaptation*); and on the other hand, to promote the appropriate revision of the disconfirmed schemas and thereby, future adaptive actions (*long-term adaptation*).

Surprise processes: A four-step sequence. In more detail, (Meyer et al., 2000; Meyer et al., 1997) assume that (ultimately) surprise-eliciting events elicit a four-step sequence of processes. The first step in this sequence consists of (1) the appraisal of an event as schema-discrepant, or unexpected.[1] If the degree of schema-discrepancy (unexpectedness) exceeds a certain threshold, then (2) ongo-

ing mental processes are interrupted, attention is shifted to the unexpected event, and surprise is experienced. This second step serves to enable and prepare (3) the analysis and evaluation of the unexpected event plus—if this analysis suggests so—(4) immediate reactions to the unexpected event and/or an updating, extension, or revision of the schema or schemas that gave rise to the discrepancy. Ideally, successful schema change (belief update) enables the person to predict and, if possible, to control future occurrences of the schema-discrepant event; to avoid the event if it is negative and uncontrollable; or to ignore the event if it is irrelevant for action.

The surprise mechanism. The first two steps in the posited series of mental processes (Figure 1) are identified with the workings of the surprise mechanism proper. This mechanism is assumed to be a hardwired information processing device whose evolutionary function is to *detect* schema-discrepant events (step 1), and, if they are detected, to *enable* and *prepare* the processes of event analysis and schema revision (steps 3 and 4) by means of the interruption of ongoing processing, the refocusing of attention, and the system-wide communication of the detection of a schema-discrepancy in the form of the feeling of surprise (step 2). In addition, the feeling of surprise is assumed to provide a motivational impetus for the analysis of the surprising event (Meyer et al., 2000). In accordance with the posited hardwiredness of the schema-discrepancy detector, it is assumed that this mechanism operates at a preconscious level of information processing, where it continuously and automatically (specifically without the person's intention) compares activated cognitive schemas with newly acquired information (perceptions, beliefs).

Event analysis. The analysis and evaluation of surprising events (step 3) is assumed to comprise, in typical cases, the following subprocesses: the verification of the schema discrepancy (did one see or hear right; did one draw the correct conclusion from premises?); the analysis of the causes of the unexpected event (why did it happen?); the evaluation of the unexpected event's significance for well-being (is the event good or bad, is it dangerous or is it a promise?); and the assessment of the event's relevance for ongoing action (can one ignore the event, or does one need to respond to it?). Additional event appraisals, such as an assessment of the moral significance of another person's unexpected action, may occur in some situations. It is assumed that the processes of event analysis can occur in parallel or sequentially, and that in the latter case, they can occur in different sequences. Furthermore, it is assumed that once the appraisals of an unexpected event (e.g., regarding its causes or action relevance) have been computed, they are stored as part of the schema for this event. As a consequence, the analysis of subsequent instances of the same or similar kinds of events can be substantially abbreviated.

The behavioral manifestations of surprise. The cognitive-psychoevolutionary model of surprise assumes that the described mental processes are causally responsible, alone or in combination, for the various behavioral manifestations of surprise (if they occur): the interruption or delay of ongoing motor activities, investigative activities, facial and verbal expressions of surprise, and peripheral physiological reactions. Some of these behavioral manifestations of surprise are presumably functionless side-effects of the mental surprise processes; for example, the interruption of motor activities is a side-effect of the interruption of the mental processes that control it. However, for the greater part, the behavioral manifestations of surprise are probably adaptive processes that, in one way or another, subserve the major function of the surprise mechanism—the short- and long-term adaptation to unexpected events. For example, investigative motor actions are in the service of epistemic analysis; spontaneous and deliberate surprise vocalizations may serve to communicate one's surprise to others, thereby soliciting their help in explaining an unexpected event; and eyebrow-raising may, as Darwin

(1872/1965) argued, facilitate the visual exploration of unexpected events in some situations.

The experience of surprise. Meyer et al. (1997) assume that the immediate output of the schema-discrepancy detector is a nonpropositional signal (i.e., a representation characterized by quality and intensity, but without internal structure; see Oatley & Johnson-Laird, 1987; Picard, 1997; Reisenzein, 2000b) whose intensity codes the degree of schema-discrepancy or unexpectedness. Since the subjective experience or "feeling" of surprise also varies in intensity, and does so in close dependence on the degree of schema-discrepancy, it could simply consist of the conscious awareness of the signal produced by the schema-discrepancy detector. However, the feeling of surprise could include additional elements, such as a direct phenomenal awareness of mental interruption (see Reisenzein, 2000b). As mentioned, the feeling of surprise is thought to have an informational and a motivational function: It informs consciousness about the detection of a schema-discrepancy, and it provides an initial impetus for the analysis of the unexpected event. Because the communication that something unexpected happened elicits curiosity (Berlyne, 1960), the motivational effect of the surprise feeling may be based on its informational effect (Reisenzein, 2000b).

The theoretical definition of surprise. On the basis of the described surprise model, it is possible to replace the pre-theoretical characterization of surprise given at the beginning of this section by a more precise, *theoretical (i.e., theory-based) definition* (Reisenzein, 2007). As evident from Figure 1, according to the cognitive-psychoevolutionary model of surprise, the schema-discrepancy signal is the "causal hub in the wheel of surprise": It is the direct or indirect cause of all subsequent mental processes postulated in the model (the feeling of surprise, interruption and attentional shift, event analysis, and schema revision), as well as of the various external manifestations of surprise. Because of its central causal role, the schema discrepancy signal suggests itself as the best candidate for the scientific referent of surprise. Hence, the theoretical definition of surprise suggested by the cognitive-psychoevolutionary model is as follows: *Surprise is a nonpropositional signal that is the immediate output of the schema-discrepancy detector.* Note that this signal could remain unconscious, for example if it of very low in intensity. Hence, there could be unconscious surprise.

Surprise and Emotions

Common-sense classifies surprise as an emotion. In contrast, in psychology, the question of whether or not surprise is an emotion remains controversial. Whereas some theorist, particularly those with an evolutionary orientation, consider surprise a biologically basic emotion (e.g., Izard, 1991), other authors deny surprise the status of an emotion (e.g., Ortony et al., 1988). The main reasons for not regarding surprise an emotion are: (a) In contrast to paradigmatic emotions such as joy or fear, surprise does not presuppose the appraisal of the eliciting event as positive (desire-congruent) or negative (desire-incongruent); and corresponding to this, (b) the feeling of surprise is per se hedonically neutral, rather than pleasant or unpleasant. However, it is not clear whether these differences between surprise and paradigmatic emotions are sufficient to exclude surprise from the realm of emotions. For one reason, surprise appears to be an essential ingredient of several unquestioned emotional states, such as disappointment, relief, and shock; and the intensity of most emotions is enhanced if their elicitors occur unexpectedly. For another reason, it has been argued that the cognitive mechanism that produces surprise (presumably, a mechanism that compares newly acquired to pre-existing beliefs) and the mechanism that produces hedonic emotions (presumably, a mechanism that compares new beliefs to existing desires) have similar properties and are closely intertwined in their

operation (Reisenzein, 2001, 2009): They are both automatic and unconscious mechanisms that "supervise" representations (beliefs and desires, respectively); they seem to operate in parallel on the same inputs (newly acquired beliefs); and their outputs may be integrated at an unconscious level of processing (e.g., the signals of unexpectedness and desire-incongruence may be unconsciously integrated into the emotion of disappointment). If these assumptions are correct, they would constitute good theoretical reasons for (re-) classifying surprise as an emotion (Reisenzein, 2009). In any case, surprise needs to be considered in theories of emotion, even if it is not regarded as an emotion itself.

ARTIFICIAL SURPRISE

Given the important function played by the surprise mechanism in humans, it seems reasonable to allow artificial agents to take advantage of this mechanism. Indeed, we would argue that to the degree that artificial agents are confronted with "adaptive problems" analogous to those that gave rise to the development of the surprise mechanism in humans—the need to react adaptively in imperfectly known and changing environments—they need to be endowed with a surprise mechanism. In recent years, a number of computational models of surprise have been proposed. In this section, we review two of these models of "artificial surprise", developed respectively by Macedo and Cardoso (e.g., Macedo & Cardoso, 2001a; Macedo et al., 2004) and Lorini and Castelfranchi (e.g., Lorini & Castelfranchi, 2007). Both models of artificial surprise were influenced by psychological theories of surprise (e.g., Meyer et al., 1997), and both seek to capture essential aspects of human surprise. These models are therefore more than distant Artificial Intelligence relatives of the surprise mechanism in humans. Rather, they can be considered as attempted simulations of the human surprise mechanism, even though it needs to be acknowledged that they are in some respects simplifications, and in other respects idealizations.

Other computational approaches to surprise not reviewed here in detail are (Baldi, 2004; Itti & Baldi, 2006; Peters, 1998). Both approaches focus on the role of surprise in vision (the perception of objects, movements, or scenes), and both are mainly concerned with the first step of the surprise process described earlier, the detection of unexpected events and the computation of surprise intensity. For example, central to Baldi and Itti's surprise model is the proposal to compute surprise intensity as the distance (measured by the Kullback-Leibler divergence) between the prior probability distribution over a set of hypotheses and the posterior distribution resulting from the Bayesian updating of the prior distribution on the basis of new information. This proposal could in principle be incorporated into (modified versions of the) more general surprise models discussed here.

The Macedo-Cardoso Model

The artificial agent. The model of surprise developed by Macedo and Cardoso (2001a, 2004), henceforth abbreviated the M&C model, is integrated into an artificial agent whose central function is to explore the environment. In a typical implementation, the agent explores an artificial environment consisting of buildings located at specific positions, that differ in their structural properties (concerning e.g., the shape of the roof, the door, and the windows) and their functions (e.g., home, hotel, church). The agent's design is similar to the BDI (belief-desire-intention) architecture (Bratman, Israel, & Pollack, 1988; Wooldridge, 2002). The actions of the agent consist of moving around in the environment, that is, visiting objects or places. This behavior is driven by several basic motives (desires), whose satisfaction the agent seeks to maximize by his actions, taking into account what it believes to

be true of the environment. To date, up to three basic motives have been considered: the desire to reduce hunger, the desire to satisfy curiosity, and—specific to the M&C agent—the desire to experience surprise (see below for more detail). Knowledge about the environment is acquired by means of simulated sensors that provide information about the distance and the visible properties of the objects in the environment within a certain range. Objects outside the range of vision cannot be seen by the agent, and the function of an object (e.g., in the case of buildings: home, hotel, church) becomes known to the agent only when it visits the location of the object. However, the agent forms expectations about unknown aspects of the objects (specifically their function) on the basis of what it sees, and the information stored in memory. The basic processing cycle of the agent—ignoring, for the moment, the computation of surprise—is as follows: (1) The agent samples information from the sensors and computes the current state of the world (e.g., its own position and the position and nature of the objects). (2) Taking as input the current world state, information stored in memory, and probability theory, the agent computes the possible future world states resulting from each action that it currently can perform. (3) From among these actions, the agent selects one that maximizes its subjective expected utility function (e.g., an action that promises to lead to maximal surprise with minimal energy consumption). (4) The agent executes the selected action.

The surprise model. The M&C surprise model integrated into the described agent architecture was mainly inspired by two sources: the psychological surprise model of Meyer et al. (1997, 2000) (see also, Reisenzein, 2000b) described in the preceding section, and an analysis of the cognitive causes of surprise from a cognitive science perspective proposed by Ortony and Partridge (1987). Specifically, the M&C model is a computational implementation—although with some simplifications and changes—of the Meyer et al. surprise model, that draws on Ortony and Partridge (1987) for the choice of the agent's knowledge structures and the implementation of the appraisal of unexpectedness. In addition, the M&C model contains some unique assumptions, in particular the assumption that one motive of the agent is to maximize surprise.

In agreement with Ortony and Partridge (1987), the knowledge of the M&C agent is both episodic and semantic in nature. In the implementation described above, episodic knowledge consists of information about the location and the properties of specific buildings in the agent's environment plus, in the case of incomplete knowledge (about a building's function), a probability distribution over the possible functions of the building (home, hotel, church, etc.). Semantic knowledge emerges from episodic knowledge through a process of abstraction, in which similar object representations are merged into a prototype. Although the M&C agent can represent the physical structure of objects either propositionally or analogically, we consider here only propositional (sentence-like, predicate-subject) representations. In the M&C agent, the propositional description of an objects consists of a set of attribute-value pairs.

Computation of surprise. The computation of surprise takes place at the beginning of the second step of the agent's processing cycle. At this point, the newly computed world state (represented as a set of input propositions) is compared to the beliefs stored in memory. The agent is surprised if its beliefs conflict with the input propositions, with the intensity of surprise being a function of belief strength (subjective probability). Following Ortony and Partridge (1987), Macedo and Cardoso distinguish between two kinds of beliefs—active and passive expectations—that may be disconfirmed by an input proposition, and accordingly, between two main sources of surprise. For example, in the above-described implementation, whenever the agent perceives a building g from a distance (meaning it acquires knowledge of g's structural properties), it computes an *active expectation* concerning the building's function (e.g., "g

is a hotel with probability .66; g is a church with probability .30"). If, upon visiting the building, the agent learns that the building is a post office, it is surprised because its surprise module detects that its active expectations conflict with the new information. This is an example of the first source of surprise, active expectation failure (Ortony & Partridge, 1987). In contrast, when the agent sees a building, it need not have active expectations concerning the building's structural properties. For example, when the agent sees a building with round windows, it need not have computed active expectations concerning the building's windows. Still, by consulting its memory, the agent can infer "after the fact" that, for example, the probability of a rectangular window was .67 and that of a square window was .22. This example illustrates the second source of surprise, surprise due to a conflict of an input proposition with a *passive expectation* (Ortony & Partridge, 1987); that is, a belief that, although not computed prior to the input proposition, was inferred afterwards, as part of the processing of the input.

In the initial version of the M&C model (Macedo & Cardoso, 2001b), the intensity of surprise elicited by an input proposition describing an event E (e.g., "building g is a hotel") was assumed to be proportional to the degree of unexpectedness of E, which was defined as $1-P(E)$, the subjective probability of E. $P(E)$, in turn, is computed on the basis of the event frequencies stored in the agent's episodic memory (Macedo & Cardoso, 2001b, 2003). Although there is evidence that supports the assumed, inverse linear relation between subjective probability and surprise (e.g., Reisenzein, 2000a), it can be argued that this function does not correctly predict human surprise in some situations. For example, consider a political election involving three candidates A, B, and C with equal chances of being elected ($\frac{1}{3}$). Intuitively, one would not feel surprised if A (or B, or C) were elected. To improve this aspect of the model, Macedo et al. (2004) examined several alternative ways of computing surprise intensity from probability. This study suggested that the relation between subjective probability and the intensity of surprise about an event E_g from a set of mutually exclusive events $\{E_1, E_2, ..., E_m\}$ is better described by:

$$SURPRISE(E_g) = \log_2(1 + P(E_h) - P(E_g))$$

In this formula, E_h is the event with the highest probability in the set. The main differences between this surprise intensity function and the simpler function $(1-P(E_g))$ are: (a) Surprise intensity is a *nonlinear* function of probability; (b) the intensity of surprise about an event E_g depends not only on the probability of E_g, but also on that of E_h, the most probable alternative. (The addition of 1 only serves to normalize surprise intensity between 0 and 1). More precisely, the intensity of surprise about E_g is a nonlinear function of the *difference*, or *contrast*, between $P(E_h)$ and $P(E_g)$ (see also, Macedo, Cardoso, & Reisenzein, 2006; Teigen & Keren, 2003). This probability difference can be interpreted as the amount by which the probability of E_g would have to be increased for E_g to become unsurprising. The equation implies that, in each set of mutually exclusive events, there is always at least one event whose occurrence is unsurprising, namely, E_h. As a consequence, one will not be surprised if either one of three equally promising political candidates A, B, and C, is elected.

Computation of expected surprise. The above equation describes the computation of the intensity of *actual surprise* about an event. This computation corresponds to the "appraisal of unexpectedness" in the surprise model of Meyer et al. (1997). However, Macedo and Cardoso assume that the agent in addition computes, for each possible action, the intensity of *expected surprise*, that is, the degree of surprise it will most likely experience if the action is carried out. (In humans, this computation might be performed by means of theoretical inference using a folk theory of surprise; or by means of mental

simulation, during which the surprise module is used "off-line"). In the simplest case, the agent's action leads to a future world state S in which one of a set of mutually exclusive events $\{E_1, E_2, ..., E_m\}$ is realized. For example, if the agent visits a new building, it learns which of the possible functions of buildings this particular building realizes. The degree of surprise expected for S is computed analogously to expected utility (e.g., Russell & Norvig, 1995), with surprise intensity taking the place of utility:

$$E[SURPRISE(S)] = \sum_{i=1}^{m} P(E_i) \times \log_2(1 + P(E_h) - P(E_i))$$

Expected surprise resembles the concept of entropy (H) in information theory (Shannon, 1948). The difference is that in H, surprise intensity as defined here is replaced by "surprisal" (Tribus, 1961), defined as $-\log_2(P(E_i))$.

Computation of the total surprise caused by complex events. So far, we considered only the surprise elicited by a single unexpected event, represented by an input proposition such as "object g has a steep roof", or "object g is a hotel". However, surprising events are often complex, consisting of several component events. For example, an agent expecting to encounter a hotel with a steep roof may instead find a home with a flat roof. What is the *total surprise* caused by this complex event? The M&C model makes the simplifying assumption that the total surprise elicited by a complex event (e.g., an object with several unexpected features) is the sum of the surprises caused by the different components of the event (Macedo & Cardoso, 2005). Hence, a reductionist approach is taken to the computation of total surprise. To illustrate, assume that the agent is certain that a building g at a given distance is a hotel with a steep roof, but then finds out that the building is a home with a flat roof. That is, before encountering object g, $P(g$ is a hotel$)$ and $P(g$ has a steep roof$)$ are both 1, whereas $P(g$ is a home$)$ and $P(g$ has a flat roof$)$ are both 0. Therefore, $SURPRISE(g$ is a home$) = SURPRISE(g$ has a flat roof$) = \log_2$

$(1 + 1 - 0) = 1$. In the M&C model, the intensity of surprise caused by encountering *a home with a flat roof* is simply the sum of these surprise intensities, i.e., 2. More generally, the intensity of the total (actual) surprise elicited by a complex event g consisting of n component events E_{1g}, E_{2g}, ..., E_{ng} (here considered as values of dimensions E_1, E_2, ..., E_n) is:

$$SURPRISE(g) = \sum_{j=1}^{n} \log_2(1 + P(E_{jh}) - P(E_{jg}))$$

Unlike surprise elicited by a single event, the intensity of surprise elicited by a complex event is not normalized (i.e., not limited to 1). This assumption reflects the intuition that the total surprise that can be caused by an object increases with the object's complexity, the number of its different aspects or pieces. That is, other factors constant, more complex objects are potentially more surprising. Still, it might be objected that the formula for total surprise is adequate only if the agent's beliefs about the different components of the complex event are independent (Lorini & Castelfranchi, 2006); whereas, if this is not the case, the formula over- or underestimates total surprise. To illustrate the case of overestimation, assume that the agent in the above example believes not only that a building at a certain distance is a hotel with a steep roof, but also that buildings with flat roofs usually are homes. In this case, upon finding that the building has a flat roof, the agent could immediately revise its belief about the building's function. As a consequence, the agent would be no longer surprised when it learns that the building is a home. Note, however, that this counterexample to the proposed formula for total surprise assumes that the features of the object are processed sequentially. If they are processed in parallel (as seems often plausible to assume for visual perception), then no belief revision can take place. This consideration suggests that the question of the computation of total surprise cannot be fully answered without making assumptions about the parallel versus sequential processing of input propositions (see also, Schimmack & Colcombe, 2007).

Analogous to total actual surprise, the *total expected surprise* for a future situation X involving a complex event g consisting of n component events can be defined as:

$$E[SURPRISE(X)] =$$
$$\sum_{j=1}^{n} \sum_{i=1}^{m_i} P(E_{ji}) \times \log_2(1 + P(E_{jh}) - P(E_{ji}))$$

where, for each dimension E_j of the complex event, there are m_i expectations $P(E_{ji})$.

Effects of surprise. As mentioned, the artificial agent into which the M&C surprise model is embedded is driven by several basic motives, including the motive to maximize surprise. The effects of surprise on the agent's actions are easiest to describe if other motives are absent. In this case, following the computation of the actual and anticipated intensity of surprise for each object, the object with the maximum overall (actual plus anticipated) surprise is selected to be visited and investigated. This decision process and the ensuing action simulate aspects of step 2 of the Meyer et al. (1997) model (interruption of ongoing activities and reallocation of processing resources to the surprising event), as well as aspects of step 3 (analysis of the unexpected event). It should be noted, however, that the event analysis in the M&C model is very simple, being restricted to the acquisition of additional information about the object by visiting it. Other aspects of event analysis are currently not considered. Finally, the new information gained about the visited and other objects is stored in episodic memory, and the object frequencies are updated. This is a simplified version of step 4 of the Meyer et al. (1997) model (schema update or belief revision).

The behavior of the M&C surprise agent has been studied in a series of comparative simulations (e.g., Macedo, 2006; Macedo & Cardoso, 2001b, 2004, 2005; Macedo et al., 2004; 2006).

The Lorini-Castelfranchi Model

Theoretical background. The surprise model proposed by Lorini and Castelfranchi (2006, 2007), henceforth abbreviated the L&C model, is part of a more general theory of cognitive expectations and anticipation developed in Castelfranchi (2005) and Miceli & Castelfranchi (2002). In agreement with Macedo and Cardoso (2001b) and Meyer et al. (1997), Lorini and Castelfranchi conceptualize surprise as an expectation- or belief-based cognitive phenomenon, that plays a fundamental role in mental state dynamics. However, different from Macedo and Cardoso and Meyer et al., Lorini and Castelfranchi have explicated their surprise theory as a formal model, using a logic of probabilistically quantified beliefs (Halpern, 2003). An important motive for this formalization was to connect surprise theory to formal models of belief revision in logic and artificial intelligence (e.g., Alchourron, Gärdenfors, & Makinson, 1985; Gerbrandy & Groeneveld, 1997; van Ditmarsch, van der Hoek, & Kooi, 2007). Linking these two research fields seems desirable because, as Lorini and Castelfranchi (2007) point out, formal approaches to belief revision have largely neglected the causal precursors of belief change. However, in contrast to standard models of belief revision, surprise theory (e.g., Meyer et al., 1997) suggests that belief revisions are triggered only under specific conditions, and remain "local" (i.e., only beliefs detected by the surprise mechanism as inconsistent are revised). Hence, surprise theory suggests a strongly "localist" approach to belief revision, that departs from the classical approach (Alchourron et al., 1985) but is close to more recent philosophical work on local belief revision (e.g., Hansson & Wassermann, 2002). Parts of the L&C model of surprise have been implemented in a modified BDI agent (Lorini & Piunti, 2007).

A typology of expectations and forms of surprise. The L&C model distinguishes between several distinct forms of surprise, each of which is based on a different kind of expectation (belief). Specifically, Lorini and Castelfranchi (2006) distinguish *scrutinized expectations* (expectations or beliefs under scrutiny) from *background expectations* (for a similar distinction, see Kahneman & Tversky, 1982). Scrutinized expectations occupy consciousness and draw on the limited capacity of attention. They are anticipatory representations of the next input, which the agent (or a cognitive subsystem) seeks to match to the incoming data, and are closely related to the agent's current intentions and goals. In contrast, *background expectations* reside at an unconscious level of processing. They are either the product of priming (Matt, Leuthold, & Sommer, 1992; Sommer, Leuthold, & Matt, 1998) or part of the background mental framework—the schemas, scripts or knowledge base—that supports the currently scrutinized expectations. The agent's background mental framework includes *conditional expectations*, which constitute the beliefs that the agent uses for interpreting the context in which its action and perception are situated. To illustrate, while trying to find a cheap flight from Rome to London on the Ryanair website, an agent may consciously expect (i.e., may have a scrutinized expectation) to find such a flight there. This scrutinized expectation is supported by a conditional background expectation of the form "If I enter into the Ryanair website, I will find a cheap flight from Rome to London".

Starting from this typology of expectations, Lorini and Castelfranchi (2006, 2007) develop a formal model of surprise that distinguishes between three kinds of surprise: *mismatch-based surprise, astonishment,* and *disorientation.*

Mismatch-based surprise. Mismatch-based surprise is surprise caused by a recognized inconsistency between a perceived fact (input proposition) and a scrutinized expectation. In the typical case, the agent has an anticipatory, conscious representation of the next input against which incoming data are matched. Surprise occurs if the agent registers a mismatch between the two representations. The intensity of mismatch-based surprise depends on the strength of the agent's expectation, defined as the agent's subjective probability of the expected input. More precisely, assume that proposition φ is the (content of a) scrutinized expectation and ψ is the input, and that according to the agent's beliefs, φ and ψ are inconsistent, that is, $\psi \rightarrow \neg\varphi$ (i.e., ψ implies $\neg\varphi$). The intensity of mismatch-based surprise caused by the recognition of the inconsistency between the actual input ψ and the expected input φ is then defined as follows:

$$SURPRISE(\psi, \varphi) = k \cdot PROB(\varphi)$$

In this formula, $PROB(\varphi)$ is the agent's subjective probability that φ will occur and k is a weighting factor, i. e. a constant in the interval [0, 1]. Hence, assuming $(\psi \rightarrow \neg\varphi)$, the intensity of mismatch-based surprise about ψ increases linearly with the probability of the expected event φ. The value of k depends on several parameters, including the agent's current motivational dispositions. For instance, k is assumed to be higher when φ is relevant for the agent's goals than when this is not the case (Castelfranchi, 2005).

As an example of mismatch-based surprise, imagine that Mary is waiting for Bob in her office when someone knocks at the door. Mary now forms the scrutinized expectation that φ = *Bob enters the room* (at the next moment). However, at the next moment, when the door opens, Mary sees that ψ = *Bill enters the room*. According to Mary's beliefs, $\psi \rightarrow \neg\varphi$, that is, ψ is inconsistent with Mary's expectation that φ. Registration of this inconsistency causes Mary to feel mismatch-based surprise, whose intensity is proportional to the strength of Mary's belief (i.e., her subjective probability) that φ.

Astonishment. Mismatch-based surprise is surprise caused by an input proposition that is unexpected in the sense of *misexpected*. In contrast, astonishment is surprise caused by an input ψ that is more narrowly speaking *unexpected* in

that it does not conflict with a currently scrutinized expectation of the agent but is inconsistent with the agent's background expectations. The typical case is that of an agent who, while trying to assimilate an input ψ, infers from its background knowledge that the opposite state of affairs $\neg\psi$ is probable and hence, that ψ is improbable. One can also conceive of this case as one where the agent, after the fact, tries to answer the question "Was ψ predictable?" by reconstructing the probability of ψ, and comes to the conclusion that she would rather have expected $\neg\psi$ (see also Ortony & Partridge, 1987; as a limiting case, the agent simply retrieves the previously computed probability of $\neg\psi$ from long-term memory). Assuming the agent believes $\neg\psi$ with subjective probability $PROB(\neg\psi)$, the intensity of astonishment caused by the input proposition ψ is:

$$ASTONISHMENT(\psi) = k \cdot PROB(\neg\psi)$$

where k is again a constant in the interval [0, 1] (cf. the definition of mismatch-based surprise). Thus, the intensity of astonishment about ψ increases linearly with the subjective probability of $\neg\psi$. Since $PROB(\neg\psi) = 1\text{-}PROB(\psi)$, $ASTONISHMENT(\psi)$ can also be defined as $k \cdot (1\text{-}PROB(\psi))$, that is, as proportional to the degree of improbability of ψ.

Consider again the case where Mary expects Bob to enter her office, but Bill enters instead. As mentioned, in this situation Mary experiences mismatched-based surprise, because her scrutinized expectation that φ = *Bob enters the room* is disconfirmed. In addition, however, Mary may also experience astonishment about ψ = *Bill enters the room*; namely, if ψ conflicts with Mary's background expectations. More precisely, the intensity of Mary's astonishment is proportional to $PROB(\neg\psi)$, where $\neg\psi$ = *Bill does not enter the room*. Note that $PROB(\neg\psi)$ need not be equal to $PROB(\varphi)$, and hence, that the intensity of surprise and astonishment elicited by an input proposition ψ need not be the same. For example, Mary may consider it fairly probable that Bob will enter her office, but she may be nearly certain that Bill will not enter (since, as she believes, Bill is currently at a congress abroad). As a consequence, Mary will feel more astonished than surprised. In general, *SURPRISE*(ψ, φ) and *ASTONISHMENT*(ψ) will be of equal intensity only if φ and $\neg\psi$ are equivalent for the agent, for only then is *PROB*(φ) = *PROB*($\neg\psi$) and *PROB*($\neg\varphi$) = *PROB*(ψ).

Surprise and astonishment in possibility theory. Alternative definitions of surprise and astonishment become available if one moves beyond the classical, Bayesian analysis of belief strength as subjective probability and enters into the domain of imprecise probabilities and possibility theory (Dubois & Prade, 1988; Shafer, 1976). Here, we consider only the definitions of surprise and astonishment within possibility theory. Although not part of the L&C model of surprise as described in Lorini and Castelfranchi (2007), these definitions are mentioned here because there is some evidence that humans, at least in some situations, reason about uncertainty in accord with possibility theory rather than probability theory (e.g., Raufaste, Da Silva Neves, & Mariné, 2003). In possibility theory, the concept of probability is replaced by the dual concepts of *degree of possibility* and *degree of necessity*. Intuitively, the possibility of a proposition ψ, *POSS*(ψ), is the degree to which ψ is consistent with the agent's background knowledge, whereas the degree of necessity of ψ, *NEC*(ψ), is the degree to which ψ is implied by the agent's background knowledge. Two fundamental assumptions of possibility theory are *NEC*(ψ) = 1-*POSS*($\neg\psi$), and *NEC*(ψ)

$\leq$ *POSS*(ψ). Moreover, different from Bayesian probability, *NEC*(ψ) + *NEC*($\neg\psi$) can be < 1. Possibility theory also allows to express the idea of *degree of ignorance* about whether or not ψ is the case. Degree of ignorance is defined as *IGN*(ψ) = 1-(*NEC*(ψ)+*NEC*($\neg\psi$)). Intuitively, an agent's ignorance about ψ reflects the extent to which the agent's (background) knowledge does not provide sufficient information to allow the agent to infer the exact probability of ψ (see Fig. 2).

Within the framework of possibility theory, the intensity of astonishment caused by the input proposition ψ can be defined as:

$$ASTONISHMENT(\psi) = k \cdot NEC(\neg\psi)$$

That is, the intensity of astonishment caused ψ is proportional to the degree to which the agent can infer the opposite proposition $\neg\psi$ from its background knowledge. This explication of astonishment corresponds to the concept of *potential surprise* proposed by Shackle (1969). Since *NEC*(ψ)= 1-*POSS*($\neg\psi$), *ASTONISHMENT*(ψ) can also be defined as $k \cdot (1\text{-}POSS(\psi))$, i. e., as being proportional to the degree of impossibility of ψ.

The intensity of mismatch-based surprise can be defined in possibility theory as:

$$SURPRISE(\psi, \varphi) = k \cdot NEC(\varphi)$$

That is, the intensity of surprise about ψ that conflicts with a scrutinized expectation φ is proportional to the degree to which φ is supported by the agent's background knowledge.

Figure 2. Relation between degree of necessity, possibility, and ignorance

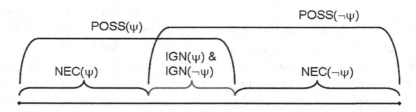

Disorientation. The third form of surprise distinguished in the L&C model is called *disorientation*. Disorientation is surprise caused by the disconfirmation of one or more of the *conditional expectations* that are part of the agent's background knowledge used to interpret the context within which its perception and action are situated. For example, imagine that an agent holding the conditional expectation "If I enter into the Ryanair website, I will find a cheap flight from Rome to London", only finds a flight for 500 Euros on the website. This agent will not only be surprised (because the scrutinized expectation "I will find a cheap flight" is disconfirmed) but probably also disoriented, because the background belief is challenged as well. The agent will then have to reconsider, and possibly to revise this conditional expectation. The intensity of disorientation caused by an input $\neg\psi$ that challenges the conditional expectation "φ entails ψ" is assumed to be proportional to the strength of the expectation, defined by the conditional probability $PROB(\psi \mid \varphi)$.

Functional effects of surprise. The assumptions of the L&C model reviewed so far concern the cognitive origins of surprise. The remaining assumptions of the model concern the functions of surprise in the cognitive system. Similar to the M&C and the Meyer et al. model, it is assumed that surprise serves to suspend the current activity of the agent, to initiate resource mobilization and attention redirection, and to signal a crisis in the assimilation process and the need for accommodation. Particular attention is paid in the L&C model to the role of surprise in the triggering of epistemic processes, including curiosity and exploration, and the instigation of belief revision. Other functions of surprise are suggested in Castelfranchi et al. (2006), where it is proposed, for example, that surprise causes an agent's cautiousness to increase in risky environments.

A surprise-enhanced BDI agent. Parts of the assumptions contained in the L&C model of surprise have been implemented, and in this process further specified, in a computational architecture (Castelfranchi et al., 2006; Lorini & Piunti, 2007). Specifically, the aim was to implement the process of belief change based on mismatch-based surprise. To this end, the authors modified the control loop of a standard BDI agent (Wooldridge, 2002) realized in the JADEX system (Pokahr, Braubach, & Lamersdorf, 2005), by supplementing the JADEX reasoning engine with a filter mechanism for belief revision based on mismatch-based surprise. The resulting, modified BDI architecture embodies two general assumptions. (1) At each moment, the agent focuses attention on a particular task or problem that it is trying to solve. This means that the agent has, at each moment, a set of scrutinized expectations linked to its current intentions and goals. As a consequence, the agent ignores all inputs that are not relevant for the task on which it is currently focused. (2) If a task-relevant input conflicts with a scrutinized expectation of the agent, mismatch-based surprise is elicited, which in turn instigates a belief-update process. In effect, then, mismatch-based surprise signals to the agent that things are not going as expected and that beliefs must be reconsidered.

COMPARISON OF SURPRISE MODELS

As already mentioned in the preceding section, the M&C and L&C models of artificial surprise share quite a few assumptions with each other and with the psychological model of surprise proposed by Meyer et al. However, there are also a number of instructive differences between the models. In this section, the more important similarities and differences are discussed.

1. Both the M&C and the L&C model take as their starting point human surprise, which they seek to model (if in simplified and idealized form) in an artificial agent. Both refer to psychological theories of surprise as a source of inspiration, in particular to

Meyer et al. (1997)), although no attempt is made to include all or only the assumptions of the psychological surprise model.

2. In agreement with most theories of human surprise, both models of artificial surprise conceptualize surprise as a fundamentally expectation- or belief-based cognitive phenomenon, that is, as a reaction to the disconfirmation of expectations or more generally, beliefs. Furthermore, in both models, beliefs are understood as propositional attitudes (e.g., Searle, 1983), and a quantitative belief concept (subjective probability) is used (as an alternative, Lorini and Castelfranchi consider possibility theory).

3. Because beliefs are mental states with propositional contents (Searle, 1983), it is natural to endow the surprise agent with a propositional (sentence-like) medium of representation. In accord with this suggestion, Meyer et al. (1997) propose a schema system (Schank, 1986) to represent belief contents, Macedo and Cardoso (2001b) use a frame-like attribute-value representation, and Lorini and Piunti (2007) take advantage of the frame-like, object-oriented representation of beliefs offered by JADEX. The M&C model also allows for simple analogical representations, but these are not indispensable, nor do they seem to be generally suited to represent the fine-grained, compositional contents of beliefs. Some surprise theorists (e.g., Shand, 1914) have claimed that surprise can also be elicited at "lower" levels of representation than the propositional level, specifically by perceptual mismatch, a possibility also endorsed by Itti and Baldi (2006) and Lorini and Castelfranchi (2007). Presumably, the perceptual applications of their surprise model discussed by Itti and Baldi (2006) are concerned with such "low-level surprise". However, it is doubtful whether perceptual mismatch *per se* causes the experience of surprise in humans (see Niepel, 2001).

4. Both artificial surprise models draw a distinction between two main kinds of expectations or beliefs whose disconfirmation causes surprise (see also, Ortony & Partridge, 1987): Active versus passive expectations (M&C), and scrutinized versus background expectations (L&C). This distinction, whose intent appears to be largely the same in the two models, can be regarded as an attempt to explicate, in computational terms, a distinction frequently drawn in the psychological literature (e.g., Charlesworth, 1969; Meyer, 1988) between two main kinds of unexpected and hence surprise-eliciting events: (a) Events that are *misexpected*, that is, opposite to a prior, specific expectation or belief of the person; and (b) events that are *unexpected in the strict sense*, that is, for which no specific expectation or belief had been inferred at the time when they were cognized (or at least, no such belief was active, i.e. in the agent's working memory), although they conflict with the person's background beliefs. It may be noted in this context that a main reason why Meyer (1988) proposed schemas as the representational structures that underpin surprise was his belief that schema theory (Rumelhart, 1984; Schank, 1986) allows a uniform treatment of both kinds of unexpectedness.

5. In addition to active and passive beliefs, Lorini and Castelfranchi propose conditional expectations (e. g., "If I am on the Ryanair website, I will find a cheap flight") as a third kind of beliefs whose disconfirmation causes surprise. This source of surprise is not explicitly considered as such in the M&C and the Meyer et al. models, although conditional expectations are present in both. In the M&C model, conditional expectations are computed in the process of expectancy generation (Macedo & Cardoso, 2003); in the Meyer et al. model, they are explicitly represented as component of schemas (see also, Lorini &

Castelfranchi, 2007). Furthermore, Meyer et al. emphasize that surprise-caused schema revision concerns frequently not only the revision of the immediately disconfirmed expectation, but also the revision of the more general schemas or "mini-theories" that gave rise to the concrete, disconfirmed expectation. It is plausible to assume that the revision of these more general beliefs, too, is preceded by surprise.

6. Based on the distinction between active (scrutinized) and passive (background) expectations, Lorini and Castelfranchi distinguish between two forms of surprise: Mismatch-based surprise and astonishment. This distinction is not made by Macedo and Cardoso, who speak of "surprise" in both cases. However, inasmuch as the distinction between surprise and astonishment is based on the *causes* of surprise (the disconfirmation of active versus passive expectations), it is implicit in the M&C model. Yet, two differences remain. First, Lorini and Castelfranchi (2007) suggest that their analysis of surprise and astonishment (as well as disorientation) provides for a computational explication of the mental states denoted by these terms in ordinary language. This proposal is ultimately an empirical claim about the referents of the ordinary language terms "surprise", "astonishment" and "disorientation", that could be tested (e.g., Reisenzein, 1995). Second, in contrast to the L&C model, no difference is made in the M&C model between active and passive expectations in the computation of surprise intensity. That is, the intensity of surprise elicited by both kinds of expectation failure is computed according to the same formula, and both contribute equally to total surprise.

7. Although Macedo and Cardoso (2001b) initially used the same surprise intensity function as L&C, according to which the intensity of surprise about an event is pro-

portional to its unexpectedness, Macedo et al. (2004) subsequently opted for a "contrast model" of surprise intensity. This model assumes that the intensity of surprise about an event reflects its probability difference to the contextually most expected event (see also, Reisenzein & Junge, 2006; Teigen & Keren, 2003). Still other probability-based surprise intensity functions have been proposed by other authors (e.g., Itti & Baldi, 2006). Furthermore, Lorini and Castelfranchi suggest an alternative definition of surprise intensity that is based on possibility theory. From the cognitive modeling perspective, the most adequate surprise intensity function is of course the one that best matches that of humans and hence, this difference between the surprise models ultimately needs to be empirically decided. Whether "nonhuman" surprise intensity functions are more useful for *artificial agents* needs to be investigated.

8. Currently, only the M&C model deals explicitly with the question of how to compute the total surprise elicited by a complex event, proposing that is the sum of the surprises elicited by the event's components. However, the L&C model does not preclude the possibility that an event simultaneously disconfirms several expectations, which makes the computation of total surprise a relevant issue. Macedo and Cardoso's proposal concerning the computation of total surprise intensity, while not unproblematic, is the simplest one can make. As mentioned, more sophisticated proposals will likely require to make assumptions about the sequential versus parallel processing of input propositions.

9. The L&C model deals only with the computation of actual surprise, whereas the M&C model also considers the computation of anticipated surprise. That is, M&C propose that the agent uses its surprise module in

two different ways: First, to compute the intensity of actual surprise in response to input; and second, to estimate the intensity of surprise that it will likely "feel" in relevant future situations (those that may result from its actions). Furthermore, only the M&C model assumes that expected surprise influences the agent's cognitions and actions in addition to actual surprise. However, if desired, the L&C model could easily be expanded to include anticipated surprise. It may be noted that the "simulational" use of the surprise module can be extended to predict or explain the surprise of other agents (see Macedo & Cardoso, 2002; Pynadath & Marsella, 2005).

10. Both models of artificial surprise make highly similar assumptions about the functions of surprise in the cognitive architecture, which are in line with the functions of surprise proposed by Meyer et al. (1997), namely: (a) interruption of ongoing activities and focusing of attention to the unexpected event; (b) system-wide communication of the belief- discrepancy and (c) instigation of exploratory activity and belief revision. Castelfranchi et al. (2006) in addition suggest that surprise increases the agent's cautiousness in risky environments.

11. Finally, whereas parts of the L&C model have been implemented in an existing BDI agent architecture, by means of modifying the JADEX reasoning engine, the M&C agent and its surprise module were programmed "from scratch". However, the design of the M&C agent is broadly compatible with the BDI architecture.

FUTURE DEVELOPMENTS

The concrete artificial agents into which the M&C and L&C surprise models have been embedded so far are fairly simple. Although this facilitates the study of the surprise mechanism and its effects on the agents' behavior, future research should also study surprise in agents with more extensive world knowledge and enhanced reasoning capabilities. Only such agents will allow to realistically simulate some surprise-related phenomena in humans, such as surprise-caused causal search (Meyer et al., 1997), the use of the surprise feeling as a source of information in metacognitive reasoning (Reisenzein, 2000b), or the explanation and prediction of surprise in other agents (Pynadath & Marsella, 2005). In addition, to explore the social effects of surprise (e.g., Derbaix & Vanhamme, 2003), future research should study groups of interacting, "surprise-enhanced" agents.

As to the surprise mechanism itself, the comparison of the M&C and L&C models suggests several targets of future research, particularly from the cognitive modeling perspective (i.e., when the models are regarded as simulations of human surprise). For example, are the comparisons of input propositions to active versus passive expectations computed by distinct mechanisms (algorithms), as the L&C model seems to suggest, or by a single mechanism, as the M&C model assumes? Relatedly, if an input conflicts with both an active and a passive expectation, producing both surprise and astonishment (Lorini & Castelfranchi, 2007), does surprise occur first and astonishment later, or do both occur simultaneously? Under which conditions does an agent "reconstruct" the probability of an event that it did not expect? There is also a need for further comparative studies of different surprise intensity functions, as well as for a closer investigation of surprise elicited by complex events (i.e., events with several unexpected aspects). Finally, both artificial surprise models currently lack explicit assumptions about the temporal course of surprise. In particular, does the feeling of surprise spontaneously diminish in intensity according to an intrinsic decay function (e.g., Neal Reilly, 1996), or is surprise reduced only if the responsible schema-discrepancy is resolved or attention shifts elsewhere (also see Pezzo, 2003)?

Going a step further, it would be interesting to expand the artificial surprise models to include other emotions. A straightforward way how this could be achieved is suggested by (Reisenzein, 2009), who sketches a computational model of the belief-desire theory of emotion, a variant of cognitive emotion theory. Following this suggestion, valenced emotions could be incorporated into the surprise models by complementing the mechanism that compares newly acquired beliefs to preexisting *beliefs* (the belief-belief comparator—essentially the surprise mechanism) with another mechanism that compares newly acquired beliefs to preexisting *desires* (the belief-desire comparator). Depending on whether the latter mechanism detects congruence or incongruence between the content of a new belief and that of an existing desires, it produces a feeling of pleasure or displeasure. For details, see Reisenzein (2009).

APPLICATIONS OF ARTIFICIAL SURPRISE

The research on artificial surprise reported in this chapter should be seen in the context of the broader field of affective computing that developed during the past 15 years (Picard, 1997). The aim of affective computing is the computational modeling of emotions, including the expression of emotions and their recognition in other agents. A central motive behind affective computing is the assumption that artificial agents endowed with emotional mechanisms will behave more intelligently than those without. At least in the case of surprise, this assumption is easy to defend. As mentioned, we believe that a surprise mechanism is needed by any resource-bounded anticipatory agent operating in an imperfectly known and changing environment (see also, Ortony & Partridge, 1987).

A second main goal of affective computing is the design of anthropomorphic artificial agents who appear "believable" to human interactants (Bates, 1994), and who adapt their behavior to the interactants' emotions, needs and preferences. Such emotional-expressive agents have manifold possible uses, for example as personal assistants and Embodied Conversational Agents (Cassell, Sullivan, Prevost, & Churchill, 2000), as virtual agents for entertainment (e.g., in games), or as emphatic health care robots. These cognitive agents could profit from artificial surprise research in two ways: First, they could be enhanced by endowing them with a surprise module that influences their actions and belief revision processes. This should not only make the agents more intelligent (Ortony & Partridge, 1987), but also more human-like, by providing them with an emotional state that they can express to humans. Second, because surprise plays an important role in social interaction, artificial agents—even if not "surprise-enhanced" themselves—need a model of human surprise to recognize surprise in their human interaction partners, and to react appropriately to their surprise (e.g., by giving information). Empirical research supports the assumption that intelligent agents who are able to display emotions and to provide emotional feedback to human interactants enhance the users' enjoyment (Prendinger & Ishizuka, 2005) and their evaluation of the artificial agent (Brave, Nass, & Hutchinson, 2005), as well as their engagement (Klein, Moon, & Picard, 1999) and task performance (Partala & Surakka, 2004).

REFERENCES

Alchourron, C., Gärdenfors, P., & Makinson, D. (1985). On the logic of theory change: Partial meet contraction and revision functions. *Journal of Symbolic Logic, 50*, 510-530.

Baldi, P. (2004). Surprise: a shortcut for attention? In L. Itti, G. Rees & J. Tsotsos (Eds.), *Neurobiology of Attention* (pp. 24-28). San Diego, CA: Elsevier Science.

Bates, J. (1994). The role of emotion in believable agents. *Communications of the ACM, 37*(7), 122-125.

Berlyne, D. (1960). *Conflict, arousal and curiosity.* New York: McGraw-Hill.

Boden, M. (1995). Creativity and unpredictability. *Stanford Humanities Review, 4*(2), 123-139.

Bratman, M., Israel, D., & Pollack, M. (1988). Plans and resource-bounded practical reasoning. *Computational Intelligence, 4*(4), 349–355.

Brave, S., Nass, C., & Hutchinson, K. (2005). Computers that care: Investigating the effects of orientation of emotion exhibited by an embodied computer agent. *International Journal of Human-Computer Studies, 62*, 161-178.

Cassell, J., Sullivan, J., Prevost, S., & Churchill, E. (Eds.). (2000). *Embodied conversational agents.* Cambridge, MA: MIT Press.

Castelfranchi, C. (2005). Mind as an anticipatory device: for a theory of expectations. In *Lecture Notes in Computer Science, 3704*, 258-276.

Castelfranchi, C., Falcone, R., & Piunti, M. (2006). Agents with anticipatory behaviors: To be cautious in a risky environment. In *Proceedings of the 17th European Conference on Artificial Intelligence (ECAI'06)* (pp. 693-694).

Charlesworth, W. R. (1969). The role of surprise in cognitive development. In D. Elkind & J. H. Flavell (Eds.), *Studies in cognitive development* (pp. 257-314). Oxford: Oxford University Press.

Darwin, C. (1872/1965). *The expression of the emotions in man and animals.* Chicago, IL: University of Chicago Press.

Dennett, D. C. (1987). *The intentional stance.* Cambridge, MA: MIT Press.

Derbaix, C., & Vanhamme, J. (2003). Inducing word-of-mouth by eliciting surprise - a pilot investigation. *Journal of Economic Psychology, 24*, 99-116.

Desai, M. M. (1939). Surprise: A historical and experimental study. *British Journal of Psychology, Monograph Supplements, 22.*

Dubois, D., & Prade, H. (1988). *Possibility theory.* New York: Plenum Press.

Ekman, P., Friesen, W. V., & Hager, J. V. (2002). *Facial action coding system* (*2nd Ed.*). Salt Lake City, Utah: Research Nexus eBook.

Gerbrandy, J., & Groeneveld, W. (1997). Reasoning about information change. *Journal of Logic, Language, and Information, 6*, 147-196.

Halpern, J. (2003). *Reasoning about uncertainty.* Cambridge, MA: MIT Press.

Hansson, S. O., & Wassermann, R. (2002). Local change. *Studia Logica, 70*, 49-76.

Horstmann, G. (2002). Evidence for attentional capture by a surprising color singleton in visual search. *Psychological Science, 13*, 499-505.

Hume, D. (1739/1978). *A treatise of human nature. (Edited by L. A. Selby-Bigge).* Oxford: Oxford University Press.

Huron, D. (2006). *Sweet anticipation: Music and the psychology of expectation.* Cambridge: MIT Press.

Itti, L., & Baldi, P. (2006). Bayesian surprise attracts human attention. *Advances in Neural Information Processing Systems (NIPS 2005), 19*, 1-8.

Izard, C. E. (1971). *The face of emotion.* New York: Appleton-Century Crofts.

Izard, C. E. (1991). *The psychology of emotions.* NY: Plenum Press.

Kahneman, D., & Tversky, A. (1982). Variants of uncertainty. *Cognition, 11*, 143-157.

Klein, J., Moon, Y., & Picard, R. (1999). This computer responds to user frustration. In *Proceedings of the Conference on Human Factors in Computing Systems* (pp. 242-243). Pittsburgh: ACM Press.

Lorini, E., & Castelfranchi, C. (2006). The unexpected aspects of surprise. *International Journal of Pattern Recognition and Artificial Intelligence, 20*, 817-835.

Lorini, E., & Castelfranchi, C. (2007). The cognitive structure of surprise: looking for basic principles. *Topoi: An International Review of Philosophy, 26*(1), 133-149.

Lorini, E., & Piunti, M. (2007). The benefits of surprise in dynamic environments: from theory to practice. In A. Paiva, R. Prada & R. W. Picard (Eds.), *Proceedings of the Second International Conference on Affective Computing and Intelligent Interaction* (Vol. 4738, pp. 362-373). Berlin: Springer.

Macedo, L. (2006). *The exploration of unknown environments by affective agents.* Unpublished PhD, University of Coimbra, Coimbra.

Macedo, L., & Cardoso, A. (2001a). Creativity and surprise. In G. Wiggins (Ed.), *Proceedings of the AISB'01 Symposium on Creativity in Arts and Science* (pp. 84-92). York, UK: The Society for the Study of Artificial Intelligence and Simulation Behaviour.

Macedo, L., & Cardoso, A. (2001b). Modelling forms of surprise in an artificial agent. In J. Moore & K. Stenning (Eds.), *Proceedings of the 23rd Annual Conference of the Cognitive Science Society* (pp. 588-593). Edinburgh, Scotland, UK: Erlbaum.

Macedo, L., & Cardoso, A. (2002). Assessing creativity: the importance of unexpected novelty. In *Proceedings of the ECAI'02 Workshop on Creative Systems: Aproaches to Creativity in AI and Cognitive Science,* (pp. 31-37). Lyon, France: University Claude Bernard - Lyon.

Macedo, L., & Cardoso, A. (2003). A model for generating expectations: the bridge between memory and surprise. In C. Bento, A. Cardoso & J. Gero (Eds.), *Proceedings of the 3rd Workshop on Creative Systems: Approaches to Creativity in AI and Cognitive Science, International Joint Conference on Artificial Intelligence* (pp. 3-11). Acapulco, Mexico: IJCAI03.

Macedo, L., & Cardoso, A. (2004). Exploration of unknown environments with motivational agents. In N. Jennings & M. Tambe (Eds.), *Proceedings of the Third International Joint Conference on Autonomous Agents and Multiagent Systems* (pp. 328 - 335). New York: IEEE Computer Society.

Macedo, L., & Cardoso, A. (2005). The role of surprise, curiosity and hunger on the exploration of unknown environments. In *Proceedings of the 12th Portuguese Conference on Artificial Intelligence.* Covilhã, Portugal.

Macedo, L., Cardoso, A., & Reisenzein, R. (2006). A surprise-based agent architecture. In R. Trappl (Ed.), *Proceedings of the 18th European Meeting on Cybernetics and Systems Research* (pp. 583-588). Vienna, Austria: Austrian Society for Cybernetic Studies.

Macedo, L., Reisenzein, R., & Cardoso, A. (2004). Modeling forms of surprise in artificial agents: empirical and theoretical study of surprise functions. In K. Forbus, D. Gentner & T. Regier (Eds.), *Proceedings of the 26th Annual Conference of the Cognitive Science Society* (pp. 588-593). Mahwah, NJ: Erlbaum.

Matt, J., Leuthold, H., & Sommer, W. (1992). Differential effects of voluntary expectancies on reaction times and event-related potentials: Evidence for automatic and controlled expectancies. *Journal of Experimental Psychology: Learning, Memory and Cognition, 18*, 810-822.

McDougall, W. (1908/1960). *An introduction to social psychology.* London: Methuen.

Meyer, W.-U. (1988). Die Rolle von Überraschung im Attributionsprozes [The role of surprise in the attribution process]. *Psychologische Rundschau, 39*, 136-147.

Meyer, W.-U., & Niepel, M. (1994). Surprise. In V. S. Rachmandran (Ed.), *Encyclopedia of human behavior* (pp. 353-358). Orlando, FL: Academic Press.

Meyer, W.-U., Reisenzein, R., & Niepel, M. (2000). Überraschung [Surprise]. In J. H. Otto, H. A. Euler, & H. Mandl (Eds.), *Emotionspsychologie: Ein Handbuch* (pp. 253-263). Weinheim: Psychologie Verlags Union.

Meyer, W.-U., Reisenzein, R., & Schützwohl, A. (1997). Towards a process analysis of emotions: The case of surprise. *Motivation and Emotion, 21*, 251-274.

Miceli, M., & Castelfranchi, C. (2002). The mind and the future: The (negative) power of expectations. *Theory & Psychology, 12*, 335-366.

Neal Reilly, W. S. (1996). *Believable social and emotional agents*. Unpublished PhD Thesis, School of Computer Science, Carnegie Mellon University, Pittsburgh, PA.

Niepel, M. (2001). Independent manipulation of stimulus change and unexpectedness dissociates indices of the orienting response. *Psychophysiology, 38*, 84-91.

Oatley, K., & Johnson-Laird, P. (1987). Towards a cognitive theory of emotions. *Cognition and Emotion, 1*(1), 29-50.

Ortony, A., Clore, G., & Collins, A. (1988). *The cognitive structure of emotions*. New York: Cambridge University Press.

Ortony, A., & Partridge, D. (1987). Surprisingness and expectation failure: What's the difference? In *Proceedings of the 10th International Joint Conference on Artificial Intelligence* (pp. 106-108). Los Altos, CA: Morgan Kaufmann.

Partala, T., & Surakka, V. (2004). The effects of affective interventions in human-computer interaction. *Interacting with Computers, 16*, 295-309.

Peters, M. (1998). Towards artificial forms of intelligence, creativity, and surprise. In *Proceedings of the Twentieth Annual Conference of the Cognitive Science Society* (pp. 836-841). Madison, Wisconsin, USA: Erlbaum.

Pezzo, M. V. (2003). Surprise, defence, or making sense: What removes the hindsight bias? *Memory, 11*, 421-441.

Picard, R. (1997). *Affective computing*. Cambridge, MA: MIT Press.

Pokahr, A., Braubach, L., & Lamersdorf, W. (2005). JADEX: a BDI reasoning engine. In R. H. Bordini, M. Dastani, J. Dix & A. El Fallah-Seghrouchni (Eds.), *Multi-agent programming: Languages, platforms and applications* (pp. 149-174). New York: Springer.

Prendinger, H., & Ishizuka, M. (2005). The empathic companion: A character-based interface that addresses users' affective states. *International Journal of Applied Artificial Intelligence, 19*, 297-285.

Pynadath, D. V., & Marsella, S. (2005). PsychSim: modeling theory of mind with decision-theoretic agents. In *Proceedings of the 19th International Joint Conference on Artificial Intelligence* (pp. 1181-1186).

Pyszczynski, T. A., & Greenberg, J. (1987). Toward an integration of cognitive and motivational perspectives on social inference: A biased hypothesis-testing model. *Advances in Experimental Social Psychology*.

Raufaste, E., Da Silva Neves, R., & Mariné, C. (2003). Testing the descriptive validity of possibility theory in human judgments of uncertainty. *Artificial Intelligence, 148*, 197-218.

Reisenzein, R. (1995). On Oatley and Johnson-Laird's theory of emotions and hierarchical structures in the affective lexicon. *Cognition and Emotion, 9*, 383-416.

Reisenzein, R. (2000a). Exploring the strength of association between the components of emotion syndromes: The case of surprise. *Cognition and Emotion, 14*, 1-38.

Reisenzein, R. (2000b). The subjective experience of surprise. In H. Bless & J. P. Forgas (Eds.), *The message within: The role of subjective experience in social cognition and behavior* (pp. 262-279). Philadelphia, PA: Psychology Press.

Reisenzein, R. (2001). Appraisal processes conceptualized from a schema-theoretic perspective: Contributions to a process analysis of emotions. In K. Scherer, A. Schorr & T. Johnstone (Eds.), *Appraisal processes in emotion: Theory, methods, research* (pp. 187-201). Oxford: Oxford University Press.

Reisenzein, R. (2007). What is a definition of emotion? And are emotions mental-behavioral processes? *Social Science Information, 46*, 424-428.

Reisenzein, R. (2009). Emotions as metarepresentational states of mind: Naturalizing the belief-desire theory of emotion. *Cognitive Systems Research, 10*, 6-20.

Reisenzein, R., & Junge, M. (2006). *Überraschung, Enttäuschung und Erleichterung: Emotionsintensität als Funktion von subjektiver Wahrscheinlichkeit und Erwünschtheit [Surprise, disappointment and relief: Emotion intensity as a function of subjective probability and desire strength]*. Paper presented at the 45th Congress of the German Psychological Association (DGPs).

Reisenzein, R., Bördgen, S., Holdtbernd, T., & Matz, D. (2006). Evidence for strong dissociation between emotion and facial displays: The case of surprise. *Journal of Personality and Social Psychology, 91*, 295-315.

Ribot, T. A. (1896). *La psychologie des sentiments [The psychology of emotions]*. Paris: Alcan.

Ritchie, G. (1999). Developing the incongruity-resolution theory. In *Proceedings of the AISB. Symposium on Creative Language* (pp. 78-85). Edinburgh, Scotland.

Ruffman, T., & Keenan, T. R. (1996). The belief-based emotion of surprise: The case for a lag in understanding relative to false belief. *Developmental Psychology, 32*, 40-49.

Rumelhart, D. E. (1984). Schemata and the cognitive system. In R. S. Wyer Jr., & T. K. Srull (Eds.), *Handbook of social cognition* (pp. 161-188). Hillsdale, NJ: Erlbaum.

Russell, S., & Norvig, P. (1995). *Artificial intelligence: A modern approach*. Englewood Cliffs, NJ: Prentice Hall.

Schank, R. (1986). *Explanation patterns: understanding mechanically and creatively*. Hillsdale, NJ: Erlbaum.

Schimmack, U., & Colcombe, S. (2007). Eliciting mixed feelings with the paired-picture paradigm: A tribute to Kellogg (1915). *Cognition and Emotion, 21*, 1546-1553.

Schmidhuber, J. (2006). Developmental robotics, optimal artificial curiosity, creativity, music, and the fine arts. *Connection Science, 18*, 173-187.

Schützwohl, A. (1998). Surprise and schema strength. *Journal of Experimental Psychology: Learning, Memory, and Cognition, 24*, 1182-1199.

Searle, J. (1983). *Intentionality*. Cambridge: Cambridge University Press.

Shackle, G. (1969). *Decision, order and time in human affairs* (2nd ed.). Cambridge, UK: Cambridge University Press.

Shafer, G. (1976). *A mathematical theory of evidence*. Princeton, NJ: Princeton University Press.

Shand, A. F. (1914). *The foundations of character.* London: Macmillan.

Shannon, C. (1948). A mathematical theory of communication. *Bell System Technical Journal, 27*, 379-423 and 623-656.

Smith, A. (1795/1982). The history of astronomy. *Essays on philosophical subjects, ed. W. P. D. Wightman & J. C. Bryce, vol. 3 of the Glasgow Edition of the Works and Correspondence of Adam Smith* (pp. 5-32). Indianapolis: Liberty Fund.

Sokolov, E. N. (1963). Higher nervous functions. The orienting reflex. *Annual Review of Physiology, 26*, 545-580.

Sommer, W., Leuthold, H., & Matt, J. (1998). The expectancies that govern the P300 amplitude are mostly automatic and unconscious. *Behavioral and Brain Sciences, 21*, 149-150.

Suls, J. M. (1971). A two-stage model for the appreciation of jokes and cartoons: An information-processing analysis. In J. H. Goldstein & P. E. McGhee (Eds.), *The psychology of humor* (pp. 81-100). New York: Academic Press.

Teigen, K. H., & Keren, G. B. (2003). Surprises: Low probabilities or high contrasts? *Cognition, 87*, 55-71.

Tomkins, S. S. (1962). *Affect, imagery, consciousness. Volume I. The positive affects.* New York: Springer.

Tribus, M. (1961). *Thermostatics and thermodynamics.* Princeton, NJ: van Nostrand.

van Ditmarsch, H. P., van der Hoek, W., & Kooi, B. P. (2007). Dynamic epistemic logic. *Synthese Library*, 337. Berlin: Springer.

Weiner, B. (1985). "Spontaneous" causal thinking. *Psychological Bulletin, 97*, 74-84.

Wooldridge, M. (2002). *An introduction to multiagent systems.* West Sussex: John Wiley & Sons.

Wundt, W. (1863). *Vorlesungen über die Menschen- und Tierseele [Lectures on the mind of man and animals].* Leipzig: Voss.

KEY TERMS

Affective: Colloquially: concerned with or arousing feelings or emotions; emotional. In today's psychology, "affective" is often used as a cover term for all emotional and related phenomena (emotions, moods, evaluations...).

Agent(s): An autonomous entity capable of action.

Anticipation: In humans, "anticipation" refers to the mental act or process of "looking forward" by means of forming predictions or beliefs about the future. An anticipatory agent is a natural or artificial agent who makes decisions based on predictions, expectations, or beliefs about the future.

Artificial Surprise: Surprise synthetized in machines (artificial agents), usually intended as a simulation of surprise in natural agents, specifically humans. Depending on context, "surprise" may either refer to the mechanism that produces surprise, or to its product, the surprise generated.

Astonishment: A subform of surprise distinguished from regular surprise, according to different authors, by higher intensity, longer duration, or special causes (e.g., fully unexpected events [astonishment] in contrast to misexpected events [ordinary surprise]).

Belief: In humans: a mental state (propositional attitude) in which a person holds a particular proposition *p* to be true. In artificial agents: a corresponding functional (processing) state.

Computational Model(s): A computational model is a computer program that attempts to simulate a particular natural system or subsystem.

Conflict(s): See "mismatch."

Disappointment: The unpleasant feeling resulting from an expectation failure concerning a desired event, or put alternatively, the disconfirmation of the belief that the desired event would occur.

Emotions: In humans: mental states subjectively experienced as (typically) positive or negative feelings that are usually directed toward a specific object, and more or less frequently accompanied by physiological arousal, expressive reactions, or emotional behaviors. Typical examples are joy, sadness, fear, hope, anger, pity, pride, and envy. In artificial agents: corresponding processing states intended to simulate emotions of natural agents, usually humans. Note that depending on context, 'emotion' may also refer to the mechanism that produces emotions rather than to its products.

Expectation: In common parlance, an expectation is a belief regarding a future state of affairs. In the literature on surprise, "expectation" is frequently used synonymously with "belief".

Unexpected: A proposition p is unexpected for an agent A if p was explicitly or implicitly considered unlikely or improbable to be true by A, but is now regarded as true by A.

Mismatch: Discrepancy or conflict between objects, in particular a contradiction between propositions or beliefs.

Misexpected: A proposition p is *misexpected* for an agent A if p is detected by A (or a subsystem of A) to conflict with, or to mismatch, a preexisting, specific and usually explicit belief of A regarding p. In contrast, p is *unexpected* for A in the narrow sense of the word if p is detected by A to be inconsistent with A's background beliefs.

Finally, p is unexpected for A in the wide sense of the term if p is either misexpected for A, or unexpected in the narrow sense.

Surprise: In humans: a peculiar state of mind caused by unexpected events, or proximally the detection of a contradiction or conflict between newly acquired and pre-existing beliefs. In artificial agents: a corresponding processing state caused by the detection of a contradiction between input information and pre-existing information. Note that depending on context, "surprise" may also refer to the mechanism that produces surprise, rather than to its product.

ENDNOTE

[1]   The assumption that surprise is elicited by unexpected events (events that disconfirm an explicit or an implicit expectancy or belief) is made by practically all classical and modern surprise theorists, and also is part of common-sense psychology (Reisenzein, 2000a; Ruffman & Keenan, 1996). However, there is some variation in how this assumption is worked out (see e.g. Charlesworth, 1969; Desai, 1939; Ortony & Partridge, 1987; Shand, 1914; and the computational models of surprise described in the next section). Note also that, whereas in everyday language, expectations are a subspecies of beliefs (namely, beliefs that refer to future states of affairs), in the technical literature reviewed here, "expectation" is usually used as a synonym of "belief". Because one can also be surprised about past and atemporal states of affairs, this broad reading of "expectation" is needed in discussions of surprise.

Chapter XVI
A Theory of Emotions Based on Natural Language Semantics

Tom Adi
Management Information Technologies, Inc., USA

ABSTRACT

A new theory of emotions is derived from the semantics of the language of emotions. The sound structures of 36 Old Arabic word roots that express specific emotions are converted into abstract models. By substitution from two tables, abstract models are converted into concrete theories about the nature of the specific emotions that are likely to be validated. Theories confirmed by the author's own emotional experience (self reports), and by previously corroborated theories, are considered corroborated. These theories about specific emotions are woven together into an integrated theory of all emotions. The theory models emotions and emotional mechanisms, dimensions and polarities in ways amenable to affective computing. The findings are supported by clinical psychology. Old Arabic is chosen because its words, sounds and meanings are consistent and have not changed for at least 1,400 years. The theory can be expanded by incorporating additional emotional word roots from Arabic and other alphabetical languages.

INTRODUCTION

Synthetic emotions and affective computing are implementations of models of emotions. Such models are based on available evidence about emotions. Behavior (e.g., crying) and physiology (e.g., high blood pressure) offer vague informa-tion about how a person feels (e.g., sad, angry). Precise evidence only is available when a person describes his own emotional experience in his own words (Fussell, 2002).

To study such *self reports*, one needs to understand semantics—the nature of language meanings. However, different languages express emotions differently. For example, many languages have no exact equivalent to "emotion," "sadness" or "disgust" (Goddard, 2002). Researchers, therefore, have looked for *semantic universals*—concepts that are shared among languages. Semantic universals that are related to emotions are *emotional universals*.

Some have suggested as emotional universals English terms such as *disapprove* and *blameworthy* that describe causes of emotions (Goddard, 2002). Others have suggested terms such as *loss* and *offense* that describe conditions leading to emotions (Goddard, 2002).

Still others believe that such complex terms are not shared among languages (Goddard, 2002). Instead, they propose as semantic universals simple terms that have exact equivalents in all languages, such as *person, good, bad, think, know, feel, do,* and *happen* (Goddard, 2002). By looking for the simplest common denominator, however, one risks missing semantic universals that are not simple.

In an attempt to be both universal and comprehensive, the author has looked for semantic commonality among languages at the most abstract level: by analyzing the relations between sounds and meanings in Old Arabic (Adi, 2007). Many sounds are shared among languages, and these sounds are signs that point to abstract semantic universals (Adi & Ewell, 1987a, 1987b, 1996).

Consider, for example, the sound "f." It represents the abstract semantic universals *open-self* and *manifestation*. For the "f" in *feel*, these *abstract* universals can be *realized* as *opening oneself to outside manifestations*. For the "f" in *fear*, the universals are realized as *negative event. Negative* is a realization of the universal *open-self. Event* is a *realization* of *manifestation*. For the sound "f" in *fear*, the universals may have an alternative realization: *vulnerable status. Vulnerable* is a realization of *open-self. Status* is a realization of *manifestation*. For the "f" in Arabic *uff*, a complaining term, the universals are realized as *negative event*, just as in English *fear*.

The sounds of human language point to abstract universals that each have many possible realizations. Combined in a word root, these sounds produce ambiguity: multiple meanings. Thus, even emotional word roots that are ambiguous can be included in the evidence studied to understand the nature of emotions.

The structure of the sounds in an emotional word root reflects some aspects of the structure of the emotion itself.

The task of developing a theory of emotions has required researchers to perform long and tedious tests of many proposed theories in order to corroborate, given good luck, a single one of them. It would be much more efficient—a scientist's dream—to have an algorithm that generates *promising theories*, i.e., ones that are likely to be corroborated. Fewer tests are then required and success is almost guaranteed.

The purpose of this chapter is to introduce such an algorithm that is based on natural language semantics, and to employ it to develop a theory of emotions. First, theories that explain *specific emotions* are developed. Then, those theories are woven into an *integrated theory of emotions*.

The algorithm generates promising theories about specific emotions from the structure of the sounds in Old Arabic word roots that express those emotions. The theories are checked against the author's own self reports and against each other. If there is a clash, alternative theories are tried.

The algorithm can be applied to English and other alphabetical languages. But those languages have changed over time, making it difficult to identify original meanings, word roots and sounds. Old Arabic is chosen to lay the foundations of the theory because its sounds, word roots and their meanings have not changed for at least 14 centuries.

The 28 Arabic consonants and four vowels still are the same. The meanings and sounds of the around 1,750 basic Arabic word roots are preserved in literature that also is over 14 centuries old. This literature uses word roots in precise and consistent ways that clearly demonstrate and preserve meanings. The sounds of the root *"hamza meem noon" (amn)*, for example, still are the same. The meanings are special variants of *trust* and *safety* that are clearly demonstrated by the root's usage in Old Arabic texts.

In contrast, consider the English word root *anger*. It stems from German *ärger*. Notice the change in the sounds. It is not clear which sounds one should analyze. Also, German *ärger* does not exactly mean *anger*. It actually means a lesser form of anger that is more related to *irritation*. Real German anger is expressed with *wut*, for example. German *fear*, *angst*, is the origin of English *anxiety*. And so on.

Once the foundations of emotional universals and the theory of emotions are established using consistent Old Arabic word roots and sounds, emotional word roots from other languages can be analyzed and added to the theory of emotions.

BACKGROUND

Perspectives on Emotions

Ruebenstrunk distinguishes four perspectives on emotions (2004b, slide 9) :

- Darwinian
- Jamesian
- Cognitivist
- Social-constructionist

Darwinians view emotions as evolved phenomena with survival function and try to pinpoint universal emotions and their expressions (Ruebenstrunk, 2004b, slide 10). Darwinians include McDougall, Plutchik, Ekman, Izard, Tompkins, and LeDoux.

Jamesians—after William James—such as Damasio insist that it is impossible to have emotions without bodily changes and that bodily changes always come first (Ruebenstrunk, 2004b, slide 11; Damasio 1994).

Cognitivists assume that thought and emotion are inseparable and that emotions are the product of a cognitive appraisal process (Ruebenstrunk, 2004b, slide 12). They include Lazarus, Frijda, Scherer, Roseman, and Ortony. Most psychologists see emotion as *response* to *stimulus* (Lazarus, 2006, pp. 52-53). But cognitivists believe that there is an intermediate step between stimulus and response: *cognitive mediation*. Lazarus sees emotions as "the product of reason" (2006, p. 87). "The way we evaluate an event determines how we react emotionally." This is how he understands cognitive mediation.

Social-constructivists such as Averill view emotions as cultural products that owe their meaning and coherence to learned social rules (Ruebenstrunk, 2004b, slide 13).

The author does not rely on any of these perspectives. Instead, he depends on evidence from emotional language semantics that is checked against self reports. This can be called a semanticist perspective. Wierzbicka and Goddard also rely on semantics and thus can be considered semanticists (Goddard, 2002). They express emotional scenarios in terms of simple language universals.

Language as Best Evidence about Emotions

Emotion researchers rely on four types of evidence (Ortony, Clore, and Collins, 1990, pp. 8-12):

- Language of emotions
- Self reports
- Behavioral evidence
- Physiological evidence

Many believe that verbal descriptions of emotional states are the only source of precise and detailed evidence (Fussell, 2002). As a rule, researchers treat such self reports as valid because "emotions are subjective experiences . . . people have direct access to them, so that if a person is experiencing fear, that person cannot be mistaken about the fact that he is experiencing fear" (Ortony, Clore, and Collins, 1990, p. 9).

In order to interpret self reports, one needs to study the language of emotions. This is best done using natural language semantics.

Unfortunately, few modern linguists study semantics, a strange phenomenon that is attributed to the influence of leaders such as Bloomfield and Chomsky (Wierzbicka, 1996). They consider the study of ideas and concepts as unscientific and relegate semantics to psychologists and others.

Linguists who do study semantics look for semantic universals—concepts that are cross-lingual and cross-cultural. Different languages express emotions differently: "the range of implications, suggestions and connotations of psychological state terms do not easily map . . . from one culture to another" (Shweder, 1994, p. 33). Wierzbicka and Goddard consider semantic universals to be the simplest terms that can be used to express the meanings of all other terms (Goddard, 2002).

A group of linguists called phonosemanticists believe that sounds are signs that point to semantic universals. This is contrary to the common view of scientists that the sounds of words have no meaning (Majumdar, Sowa & Stewart, 2008; Sowa, 2000; Peirce, 1960; Saussure, 1916), or that words simply are labels for perceptions (Zadeh, 2002). Phonosemanticists include Jakobson (1937), Rhodes and Lawler (1981), Magnus (2001), and this author, who found semantic universals by analyzing the relations between sounds and meanings in Old Arabic (Adi, 2007; Appendix A).

The evidence that this chapter relies on to build a theory of emotions is limited to the author's own self reports and his theory of natural language semantics.

Semantic and Emotional Universals as Components in a Theory of Emotions

There are different types of emotional universals—emotional concepts that are supposed to be valid across cultures. Some of these are based on the study of emotional language or on semantic universals; others are not.

Emotional categories divide emotional phenomena into different types called *basic emotions* (Tomlinson, 2002). Ekman, for example, suggests *fear, anger, sadness, happiness, disgust* and *surprise* (1992). Lazarus proposes 15 basic emotions, *anger, envy, jealousy, anxiety, fright, guilt, shame, relief, hope, sadness, happiness, pride, love, gratitude,* and *compassion* (2006, p. 34).

Emotional dimensions map "a range of emotional phenomena onto an explicitly dimensioned space" (Tomlinson, 2002, p. 45). Mehrabian suggests the dimensions of *pleasure, arousal* and *dominance* (Mehrabian and Russell, 1974). Russell offers stance, valence and arousal (1980).

There also are universals for objects and processes that play a role in causing an emotion to happen. Ortony, Clore and Collins believe that emotions are reactions with different valences (polarities) to events, agents or objects that are appraised (approved, disapproved, deemed as blameworthy, and so on) according to an individual's goals, standards and attitudes (Ruebenstrunk, 2004b, slide 13; Goddard, 2002). Ortony has simplified reaction valences to positive and negative (2002, pp. 194).

Lazarus suggests terms such as *loss* and *offense* to describe the circumstances leadings to emotions (Goddard, 2002).

Goddard and Wierzbicka propose as semantic universals around 65 simple terms such as *person, good* and *bad,* that are organized in 16 categories such as *quantifiers, evaluators* and *descriptors* (2007). Emotions are defined by describing scenarios using these terms (Goddard, 2002).

The author's semantic universals consist of four *abstract polarities* and seven *abstract process types* (Appendix A, Tables 1 and 6) that each have an *open-ended set of realizations* (Appendix A, Tables 4 and 5). Each consonant of any alphabetical language is associated with one abstract polarity and one abstract process (Tables 1 and 6). Some realizations of these abstract universals resemble universals from other approaches. For example, some *polarity* realizations (Table 4) resemble Ortony's and Russell's *valence*. Both *arousal* (*activity*) and *person* are found in the realizations of the same abstract process *manifestation* (Table 5, row 2).

It might appear illogical that both *person* and *activity* are realizations of a single abstract concept, *manifestation*. But *person* can be seen as a *static* realization of *manifestation*, while *activity* can be seen as a *dynamic* realization of *manifestation*. These complex abstract concepts are derived, introduced and explained elsewhere (Adi, 2007). They are illustrated by many examples as emotional word roots are analyzed in this chapter.

The emotional and semantic universals discussed above are components in theories about emotions. But how does one create such a theory?

The task of developing a theory about an observed phenomenon, such as an emotion, is done using the Scientific Method (Steffens, 2007, and Popper, 2002). This means testing a large number of *proposed theories* (hypotheses, guesses) until one is corroborated. The test consists of making all possible predictions based on the proposed theory and checking them against observed evidence. To make theory development efficient, a method is needed to construct *promising theories* (ones more likely to succeed).

A distinction must be made between a "small" theory that explains a certain phenomenon and a "big" theory that explains a large group of phenomena or a whole field of study.

Ibn Al-Haytham, who is credited with the introduction of the Scientific Method in the 10th century A.D. (Steffens, 2007), believed, "Finding the truth is difficult and the road to it is rough. For the truths are plunged in obscurity" (Pines, 1986, p. 436). "Hypotheses, guesses, or abductions don't emerge from nothing, but there is no simple algorithm that generates all and only reasonable guesses to any problem. . . . The task of generating good guesses or filtering out bad guesses cannot be solved by any known algorithm. But there are many kinds of heuristics that can be used" (Sowa, 2008). Researchers differ as to the origins of good guesses. Descarte called them *innate ideas* and Kant referred to them as *a priori* judgments (Sowa, 1990 and 2006).

Algorithm C, introduced in the next section, generates and tests promising theories (good guesses) for any phenomenon (such as an emotion) from any word root that refers to that phenomenon. In a word root that refers to an emotion, each consonant has an abstract polarity and an abstract process type. A promising theory about that emotion is created simply by substituting those abstract universals with their realizations from Tables 4 and 5 (Appendix A).

The purpose of this chapter is to apply Algorithm C to dozens of emotional word roots from Old Arabic and to integrate the results into a theory of emotions. This is done in five sections.

1. How to generate theories about specific emotions from word roots. Algorithm C is demonstrated using an Arabic word root that has different meanings.

2. Corroborated theories about specific emotions from word roots. Using the procedure explained in the previous section, theories about specific emotions are derived from dozens of Arabic word roots that express emotions. Only those theories that are deemed corroborated based on self reports are presented and discussed.

3. Integrated theory of emotions based on word root semantics. This is a theory of the whole field of emotions that is created by summarizing and correlating the results of the previous section.
4. Confirmation from clinical psychology. The theory is consistent with beliefs, methods and findings of clinical psychologist Lazarus.
5. Future trends. The extendability of the theory by analyzing more emotional word roots from Arabic and other languages is discussed. Applicability of the theory to the tasks of emotional computing also is addressed.

This is followed by a conclusion, term definitions and three appendices containing theoretical material.

HOW TO GENERATE THEORIES ABOUT SPECIFIC EMOTIONS FROM WORD ROOTS

Algorithm C derives a theory about an aspect of a phenomenon from the sounds of a word root that refers to it (Appendix B). Theories about different aspects of the same phenomenon are derived from different word roots that refer to it.

Algorithm C relies on Tables 1-5 (Appendix A).

Table 1 assigns one of seven **abstract processes** and one of four **abstract polarities** to each of the 28 Arabic consonants. Abstract processes and polarities are semantic universals.

The seven abstract processes are:

- Assignment
- Manifestation
- Containment
- Assignment of manifestation

- Assignment of containment
- Manifestation of containment
- Assignment and manifestation of containment

The first three processes are **elementary abstract processes**, and the remaining four are **compound abstract processes**.

The four abstract polarities are:

- Closed-self
- Open-self
- Closed-others
- Open-others

The first two polarities are called **boundary polarities**. The other two are **engagement polarities**.

Table 4 lists many possible **realizations** for each of the four abstract polarities. Table 5 lists many possible realizations for each of the seven abstract processes. These realizations were encountered in the author's previous research.

Here is a simplified version of Algorithm C, adapted for creating theories about specific emotions from emotional word roots.

Step 1. *Convert an emotional word root into an abstract theory. Use Table 3 to identify the right mapping. Write the mapping in consonants. Finally, substitute consonants with abstract processes and polarities using Table 1.*

For example, the Arabic root *"hamza meem noon"* (three consonants) expresses the emotion of **trust**. According to Table 3, which relies on the consonant precedence sequence of Table 2, the root's consonants form the mathematical mapping *hamza: meem ==> noon (f: X ==> Y)*. By direct substitution from Table 1, this relationship is expressed as an **abstract theory** about trust:

Open-self assignment *(hamza)* from closed-self manifestation *(meem)* to open-self containment *(noon)*

Steps 2 and the 3 of Algorithm C are simplified as follows:

Steps 2 and 3 *(simplified). Convert the abstract theory into a concrete theory about an aspect of the emotion by substituting abstract processes and polarities with realizations from Tables 4 and 5. If the concrete theory contradicts self report, substitute with different realizations and check the resulting alternative concrete theory. Repeat this process until a concrete theory matches self report and is thus considered corroborated.*

For example, the above abstract theory is converted into a concrete theory as follows ("==>" stands for "is substituted with"):

open-self ==> send (column 2, Table 4)
assignment ==> signal (row 1, Table 5)
closed-self ==> positive (column 1, Table 4)
manifestation ==> attitude (row 2, Table 5)
open-self ==> uncertain (column 2, Table 4)
containment ==> information (row 3, Table 5)

The resulting **concrete theory** about trust is:

Send signal *(hamza)* from positive attitude *(meem)* to uncertain information *(noon)*

This can be refined to a more intelligible form:

Trigger *(hamza)* positive emotional attitude *(meem)* toward uncertain information *(noon)*

This concrete theory about the nature of the emotion of *trust* agrees with the author's self report, the emotional experience when *trusting* someone. Thus, it is a **corroborated theory** about the emotion of *trust*.

Here are three alternative concrete theories from the same abstract theory that the author rejected as inappropriate for the emotion of *trust*:

1. Assignment directed at others *(hamza, ==>)* of a restraining action *(meem)* toward a negative force *(noon)*
2. Outward projection *(hamza, ==>)* to receive action *(meem)* from another power *(noon)*
3. Empty identity *(hamza, ==>)* from past person *(meem)* to new order *(noon)*

As it turns out, the first rejected theory can be corroborated for another meaning of the root *"hamza meem noon"*: **safety**. Safety is a **social** process, though, not an emotion. The second rejected theory can be corroborated for a **spiritual** meaning of *"hamza meem noon"*: **amen** (Arabic *aameen*). The third rejected theory does not seem to make sense at all. Still, it might fit an obscure and rare meaning of the root *"hamza meem noon."*

Note that abstract processes and polarities are not just universals for the world of emotions. They also are universals for the **environment** in which emotions arise and for **mental processes** that may be involved in emotions (memory, perception, communication, learning, and so on).

CORROBORATED THEORIES ABOUT SPECIFIC EMOTIONS FROM WORD ROOTS

In this section, the results of applying the procedure of the previous section to 36 emotional word roots of Old Arabic are presented and discussed. Only concrete theories that were corroborated based on the author's own emotional self reports are mentioned. Concrete theories that clashed with self reports or clashed with other corroborated theories are not discussed.

The following format is used:

Root sequence_number. **Emotion X** (closest English equivalent of Arabic root)
"consonant_1 consonant_2 consonant_3" (word root)

Mapping in consonants. Abstract theory (mapping in words)

A concrete theory (a realization of abstract theory) that has been corroborated

Implications:
1 . . .
2 . . .

Result sequence_number. Formal theoretical implication

The theories are in chronological order of development. The development of one theory often has depended on previous results.

Root 1. To wish, to want
"sheen ya hamza"

sheen( ) & hamza( ). Open-self assignment *(hamza)* and open-self assignment and manifestation of containment *(sheen)*

Arbitrary object *(sheen)* and signal toward it *(hamza)*

Implications:

1. The mind can trigger emotional signals.
2. An emotional signal has the effect of attention.
3. To wish or to want something is to direct attention while dealing with it.

*Result 1. **Attention** is an **elementary emotion**. Attention is a new realization of the elementary abstract process of assignment. The new emotional universal "attention" is inspired by a common realization of assignment: **signal**.*

*Result 2. Emotions have **polarity**. Open-self polarity is realized as **directed** emotion. Open-self assignment is realized as **directed attention**.*

Note: The consonant *ya* is dropped from the mapping (hence *ya*) because it is dropped in some word forms, an indication that it is semantically less significant. The consonants *hamza, waw* and *ha* also are dropped sometimes for the same reason.

Root 2. Desire, lust, crave
"sheen ha waw"

ha(sheen). Open-others assignment *(ha)* applied to open-self assignment and manifestation of containment *(sheen)*

Exclusive attention *(ha)* applied to unleashing the system *(sheen)*

Implications:

1. The mind can decide to unleash the whole emotional system. This is called systemic emotion with excitatory polarity.
2. Since *ha* (exclusive attention) is the function controlling this emotional process, attention is used to control the triggering of emotion.
3. Desire, lust or craving is systemic emotional excitation that is controlled by exclusive attention.

*Result 3. Open-others polarity is realized as **exclusive** or **targeted** emotion. Open-others assignment is realized as **exclusive attention** or **targeted attention**.*

*Result 4. **Attention** can be used to **control the triggering** of emotion.*

*Result 5. Combinations of elementary emotions also can be triggered. These are **compound emotions**. **Systemic emotion** that consists of all three abstract processes is a compound emotion.*

Result 6. *Open-self polarity is realized as **excitatory** emotion. It can be concluded that closed-self polarity is realized as **calming**, **restraining** or **inhibitory**.*

Root 3. Sad reaction
"hamza seen ya"

hamza(seen). Open-self assignment *(hamza)* applied to closed-self assignment of containment *(seen)*

Negative attention *(hamza)* in response to sensory input (personal measurement) *(seen)*

Better theory. Negative attention *(hamza)* based on input assessment *(seen)*

Implications:

1. Open-self polarity is realized as negative.
2. Either the sensory input directly triggers emotion, or the triggering of emotion is based on input assessment (more likely).
3. A sad reaction is the triggering of negative attention based on input assessment.

Result 7. *Open-self polarity is realized as **negative** emotion. It can be concluded that closed-self polarity is realized as **positive** emotion.*

Root 4. Sorrow
"hamza seen fa"

hamza : seen ==> fa. Open-self assignment *(hamza)* from closed-self assignment of containment *(seen)* to open-self manifestation *(fa)*

Input assessment *(seen)* triggers a negative emotional activity or state *(fa)* using directed attention *(hamza, ==>)*.

Implication:

1. Based on assessment of input, the mind also may trigger an emotional activity or state. The triggering is controlled by directed attention *(hamza)*.

Result 8. Emotional activity *is an **elementary emotion**. Activity is a common realization of the elementary abstract process of manifestation. State and attitude also are common realizations of manifestation. They are static views of activity. Thus, emotional activity also can be seen as **emotional state** or **emotional attitude**.*

Result 9. *Since activity is more intense than a signal (attention), emotional activity is a **more intense** emotion than attention.*

Root 5. Sadness
"hha zay noon"

zay : hha ==> noon. Open-self assignment of containment *(zay, ==>)* from closed-self assignment and manifestation of containment *(hha)* to open-self containment *(noon)*

Assessment *(zay)* of a personal experience *(hha)* triggers *(==>)* negative emotional force *(noon)*.

Implication:

1. The mind may assess a personal experience and then, based on this assessment, decide to trigger an emotional force.

Result 10. *Based on indications from the analyses of Roots 3 and 5, we conclude that the triggering of emotion is based on an **assessment of input**. This means that **the mind** is involved in the triggering of emotion as a **decision-maker**.*

Result 11. Emotional force *is an **elementary emotion**. Force is a common realization of the elementary abstract process of containment. Common realizations of containment include* energy and control. Thus, emotional force also can be seen as **emotional energy** or **emotional control**.

*Result 12. Since force is more intense than activity, emotional force is a **more intense** emotion than emotional activity.*

Root 6. Prejudice
"sheen noon hamza"

hamza : sheen ==> noon. Open-self assignment *(hamza, ==>)* from open-self assignment and manifestation of containment *(sheen)* to open-self containment

Experience with another person *(sheen)* triggers *(hamza, ==>)* a negative emotional force *(noon)*.

Implications:

1. The mind may assess experience with another person and then, based on this assessment, decide to trigger an emotional force. With "prejudice," this decision is final since the function consonant *(hamza)* is at the end of the root.

*Result 13. Mental **decisions to trigger** emotions are done in stages. Decisions are either **initial** (function consonant is first in root), **intermediate** (function consonant is second of three in root), or **final** (function consonant is last in root). Transition to a higher stage is **emotional escalation**.*

Root 7. Fear
"kha waw fa"

kha ( ) & fa( ). Open-others manifestation of containment *(kha)* in parallel with open-self manifestation *(fa)*

Presence of a destructive or excessive force or energy *(kha)* is accompanied by the unleashing of emotional activity *(fa)*.

Implications:

1. During input assessment, the mind can determine the polarity of an observed force or energy. Input forces can be positive, negative, constructive, moderate, balanced, destructive, excessive, and so on (see Table 4).
2. There are different manifestations (forms or types of action) of input forces and energies. For example, such forces and energies are either internal or external, human or nonhuman, spiritual, mental, social or physical, and so on.
3. Fear is excitatory emotional activity that may be triggered in the presence of certain manifestations of destructive or excessive forces or energies.

*Result 14. Assessment of input includes determining of **input process type** and **input polarity**. Polarities of input that are not an emotion can be elicited from Table 4. They include positive, negative, constructive, destructive, moderate, balanced, excessive, internal, external. Possible process types of input are listed in Table 5. They include manifestations (event, activity, person), forces and manifestations of forces. Input process types and polarities can be extended by introducing new realizations that are based on the common realizations listed in Tables 4 and 5.*

*Result 15. Based on assessment of input, the mind decides **whether or not** to trigger emotion, **what polarity** of emotion to trigger, and **what type** of emotion to trigger—attention, activity, force or their combinations.*

Root 8. Systemic fear
"kha sheen ya"

sheen(kha). Open-self assignment and manifestation of containment *(sheen)* applied to open-others manifestation of containment *(kha)*

Systemic excitatory emotion *(sheen)* to process a manifestation of destructive or excessive force or energy *(kha)*

Root 9. Grudge
"ghain lam lam"

lam(lam(ghain)). Composition of two open-self assignments of manifestation *(lam(lam( )))* applied in succession to open-others containment *(ghain)*

Composition of successive excitatory attention on activity *(lam(lam( )))* to process destructive or excessive emotional force or energy *(ghain)*

Implications:

1. One way to interpret the mapping form f(f(x)) that has a composition involving two instances of the same function f is that the mind can amplify or regulate emotion using a feedback loop. The output (range) of the inner instance of the function f is fed back into the outer instance of the same function f as domain. Another interpretation is that the mind simply repeats emotional triggering.
2. "Attention on activity" is a realization of "assignment of manifestation." One way to understand this is that emotional activity is controlled by attention. In Root 2, this effect requires two abstract processes *(ha* and *sheen)*. Here, a single *compound* process is used *(lam)*.

Result 16. Feedback loops *can be used to **maintain**, **regulate**, **attenuate** or **amplify** emotion. The emotional output of an emotional function is reused as input for the same function. This can be used with emotion with open-others po-*

larity *(**excessive** or **destructive**) and with other polarities.*

Result 17. *Emotions can be triggered **repetitively**.*

Result 18. *The combination of attention and emotional activity is a compound emotion called **attention-controlled emotional activity**. The consonants* ra, lam, ba, *and* ta *refer to the different polarities of this type of emotion.*

Grudge is a feedback loop with attention-based excitatory emotional activity that is used to maintain or amplify response to destructive or excessive emotional force.

Root 10. Hate (justified or obsessive)
"ba ghain ddad"

ba : ghain <==> ddad. Closed-others assignment of manifestation *(ba)* between open-others containment *(ghain)* and open-self manifestation of containment *(ddad)*

Meaning 1: **justified hate**. Decision to reciprocate *(ba)* to violation of sovereign area *(ddad)* with destructive force *(ghain)*

Implications:

1. The mind can **assess** an observed activity as **violation** of someone's **sovereign area** (such as legal boundary or **territory**). This assessment of application of law is a **legal assessment**.
2. The mind can trigger destructive emotion to reciprocate to a violation, i.e. emotion as defense.
3. Justified hate is the use of destructive emotional force to defend oneself or others against a violation based on legal assessment.

Meaning 2: **obsessive hate** or **phobia**. Engaged placement *(ba)* between destructive force *(ghain)* and loose control *(ddad)*, not to be confused with "to lose control."

Implications:

1. Engaged placement means being locked up, trapped or entangled.
2. Obsessive hate or phobia is emotional entanglement. A mind with deficient control has fallen under the control of a destructive emotional force.

Result 19. Destructive emotion can be triggered to ***defend, attack*** *or* ***punish***. *Similarly, emotion with closed-others polarity (**constructive emotion**) can be triggered to* ***support*** *or* ***reward***.

*Result 20. As controller of emotions, the mind may suffer **imperfections** such as **loose control**, **deficiencies**, **weaknesses** or **needs**. This may lead to an entanglement or bond with a destructive or constructive emotional force (e.g., internal or external powerful phenomena) or an excessive emotional force (e.g., insatiable appetite). This is called **emotional entanglement** or **emotional control bond**. Manifestations may include negative forms (entanglements) such as **phobias, fanaticism, obsession** and **addiction** and positive forms (bonds) such as **love, loyalty** and **dedication**.*

Root 11. Anger (justified or uncontrolled)
"ghain ddad ba"

ba : ghain <==> ddad. Realization (*ba* at end of root) of closed-others assignment of manifestation *(ba)* between open-others containment *(ghain)* and open-self manifestation of containment *(ddad)*

Meaning 1: **justified anger**. Realized decision to reciprocate *(ba)* to violation of sovereign area *(ddad)* with destructive force *(ghain)*

Implication:

1. Justified anger is the escalation of justified hate, i.e., from thoughts to words and actions.

Meaning 2: **uncontrolled anger** or **aggression**. A realization of engaged emotional placement *(ba)* between destructive or excessive force *(ghain)* and loose control *(ddad)*

Implication:

1. Uncontrolled anger or aggression is the escalation of emotional entanglement with a destructive or excessive force.

Root 12. Capricious love
"ha waw ya"

ha(waw()). Open-others assignment *(ha)* applied to closed-others assignment *(waw)*

To trigger attention with engagement *(waw)* and then stymie it by attention with disengagement *(ha)*

Result 21. Since the initial emotional triggering function waw *has no domain, the mind can trigger emotions **without input assessment**, at a whim.*

*Result 22. One emotion may be triggered and then reprocessed as input by triggering an emotion with opposite polarity. The effect is **emotional instability, conflict** or **deadlock**. The attribute "**engagement**" is added if the opposite polarity pair is closed-others (**emotional engagement**) and open-others (**emotional disengagement** or **detachment**). If the polarities involved are closed-self and open-self, then the attribute "**boundary**" is added.*

Capricious love is attention engagement instability (attention with engagement later stymied by attention with detachment).

Root 13. Love (version 1)
"waw dal dal"

waw(dal²). Closed-others assignment *(waw)* applied to duplicate closed-others manifestation *(dal²)*

Engagement attention *(waw)* triggered by repeated interaction *(dal* is activity together—this is *dal²*)

Result 23. *Closed-others polarity is realized as* **mutual emotion** *such as* **emotional interaction** *(mutual emotional activity).*

Result 24. *Emotion can be* **repetitive***. This also may manifest itself as* **continued** *emotion.*

Love (version 1) is when attention with engagement is used to trigger continued emotional interaction.

Root 14. To rejoice
"fa ra hha"

ra : fa <== hha. Closed-self assignment of manifestation *(ra, <==)* from closed-self assignment and manifestation of containment *(hha)* to an open-self manifestation *(fa)*

Decision (assignment of manifestation) by the mind to react *(ra, <==)* with excitatory emotional activity *(fa)* to a personal experience *(hha)*

Root 15. Joy
"seen ra ra"

ra(ra(seen)). Composition of closed-self assignments of manifestation *(ra(ra( ))* applied to closed-self assignment of containment *(seen)*

Repeated or feedback loop amplified triggering of attention-controlled positive emotional activity (*ra(ra( )))* in processing of sensory input *(seen)*

Root 16. Despair (version 1)
"ya hamza seen"

ya(hamza(seen)). Composition of closed-self assignment *(ya)* and open-self assignment *(hamza)* applied to closed-self assignment of containment *(seen)*

Input assessment *(seen)* triggers excitatory attention *(hamza)* which is then stymied by triggering restraining attention *(ya)*

Implication:

1. Despair is input assessment that triggers **attention boundary deadlock** (inhibition of excitatory attention).

Root 17. Unspeakable, shocking, disgusting
"fa hha sheen"

hha(sheen (fa)). Composition of closed-self assignment and manifestation of containment *(hha)* with open-self assignment and manifestation of containment *(sheen)* which was applied to open-self manifestation *(fa)*

Systemic emotional boundary conflict (see Root 12, Implications 2-3) where systemic restraining emotion *(hha)* is triggered to process systemic excitatory emotion *(sheen)* that is initially triggered to process a negative event *(fa)*

Root 18. Tranquility
"seen kaf noon"

seen : kaf <== noon. Closed-self assignment of containment *(seen, <==)* from open-self containment *(noon)* to closed-self manifestation of containment *(kaf)*

Input assessment *(seen)* triggers calming (restraining) emotional activity of force *(kaf)* to process excitatory emotional force *(noon)*

Implication:

1. Tranquility is when input assessment triggers a calming emotional field to deal with an excitatory emotional force.

Result 25. *"Activity of force" is a realization of "manifestation of containment." This compound emotion is called* **application of emotional force***. One realization is an* **emotional field***. The consonants* kaf, ddad, tta, *and* kha *may refer to application of emotional force with different polarities.*

Root 19. Love (version 2)
"hha ba ba"

ba(ba(hha)). Composition of closed-others assignments of manifestation *(ba(ba( ))* applied to closed-self assignment and manifestation of containment *(hha)*

Feedback loop with attention-controlled emotional engagement activity *(ba(ba( )))* used to maintain or amplify positive systemic emotion *(hha)*

Root 20. To feel, feelers (as on insects)
"hha seen seen"

seen(seen(hha)). Repeated application of closed-self assignment of containment *(seen(seen( )))* to closed-self assignment and manifestation of containment *(hha)*

Repeated familiar (closed-self) attention on force *(seen seen)* applied to a personal experience *(hha)*

Implications:

1. To feel (have a feeling) is to have the mind trigger a repeated, familiar attention-controlled emotional force or energy based on a personal experience.
2. The "closed-self assignment" component of *seen* also is realized as **attention for input**, and "containment" may be realized (**biologically**, not emotionally) as **quantity**. In this case, to feel is to have constant (repeated) attention for input quantity from a personal experience, as with feelers. This is emotional triggering that serves a biological sensory function. It is an **interdisciplinary realization**.

Result 26. *Closed-self polarity is realized as* **familiar** *emotion. Similarly, open-self polarity is realized as* **unfamiliar** *emotion.*

Result 27. *"Attention on force" is a realization of "assignment of containment." This compound emotion is called* **attention-controlled emotional force***. The consonants* seen, zay, ssad, *and* tha *may refer to attention-controlled emotional force with different polarities. Based on arguments in Result 11, attention-controlled emotional force also can be seen as* **attention-controlled emotional energy** *or* **attention-controlled emotional control***.*

Root 21. Arrogance
"kaf ba ra"

ba(ra(kaf)). Composition of closed-others assignment of manifestation *(ba)* with closed-self assignment of manifestation *(ra)* that was applied to closed-self manifestation of containment *(kaf)*

Accumulation (closed-others assignment = putting together) of emotional activity *(ba)* of emotional activity in response *(ra*, closed-self assignment = response) to one's own (closed-self) evaluation (containment) of person (manifestation) *(kaf)*

Result 28. *Accumulation of emotional response results in* **inflation of emotion**.

Result 29. *The mind conducts* **self-evaluation**.

Arrogance is inflation of emotion triggered by self-evaluation.

Root 22. Patience
"ssad ba ra"

ba(ra(ssad)). Composition of closed-others assignment of manifestation *(ba)* with closed-self assignment of manifestation *(ra)* that was applied to closed-self manifestation of containment *(kaf)*

Attention to balance emotional activity *(ba,* see Root 9, Implication 2) that is triggered by emotional reactive attention on activity *(ra)* that is triggered by continued attack *(ssad)*

Result 30. *Since closed-others polarity is commonly realized as balancing, and closed-self polarity is commonly realized as reacting, we have the emotional polarities of* **stabilizing** *and* **responsive**, *respectively. The composition of emotions with stabilizing and responsive polarity results in* **stabilization of emotional response**.

Patience is the attention-based stabilization of emotional response to continued attack.

Root 23. Hope
"ra geem waw"

ra(geem)). Closed-self assignment of manifestation *(ra)* applied to closed-others assignment and manifestation of containment *(geem)*

Emotional activity controlled by attention for input (expectation, *ra,* see Root 9, Implication 2 and Root 20, Implication 3) applied to a constructive thing *(geem)*

Result 31. Expectation *is emotional activity controlled by attention for input.*

To hope is to expect something constructive.

Root 24. Despair (version 2)
"qaf noon tta"

tta : qaf <==> noon. Closed-others manifestation of containment *(tta)* between closed-others containment *(qaf)* and open-self containment *(noon)*

Balancing of application of emotional forces *(tta)* between constructive emotional force *(qaf)* and negative emotional force *(noon)*

Implication:

1. Despair (version 2), (see version 1 at Root 16) is the balancing (evening out) application of emotional force between constructive and negative emotional forces.

Root 25. Faith or trust
"hamza meem noon"

hamza : meem ==> noon. Open-self assignment *(hamza, ==>)* from closed-self manifestation *(meem)* to open-self containment *(noon)*

The triggering under control of directed attention *(hamza, ==>)* of positive emotional attitude (activity, state) *(meem)* in response to uncertain information *(noon)*

Implication:

1. Faith or trust is the triggering under the control of directed attention of positive emotional attitude after assessment of information as uncertain.

Root 26. Stable faith or trust
"tta meem hamza noon"

tta (hamza : meem ==> noon). Closed-others manifestation of containment *(tta)* applied to a mapping that is an open-self assignment *(hamza, ==>)* from closed-self manifestation *(meem)* to open-self containment *(noon)*. This is one of the rare four-consonant word roots.

Balancing (closed-others) application of emotional forces *(tta)* used to regulate the triggering by directed attention *(hamza, ==>)* of positive emotional attitude (activity, state, *meem*) in response to uncertain information *(noon)*

Implication:

1. Balancing (stabilizing) application of emotional forces (see Root 24) to regulate faith or trust (Root 25).

Result 32. *Consonant tta is realized as the balancing application of emotional forces. This balance can be detrimental (e.g., in the case of despair, Root 24) or useful (e.g., in the case of stable faith or trust, Root 26).*

Root 27. Kindness, compassion
"ra hamza fa"

hamza : ra ==> fa. Open-self assignment *(hamza, ==>)* from closed-self assignment of manifestation *(meem)* to open-self manifestation *(noon)*

The triggering by directed attention *(hamza, ==>)* of positive attention on emotional activity *(ra)* in response to appearance or display (manifestation) of emotional vulnerability, need or weakness *(fa)*. Need and weakness are new realizations based on "lacking," which is a common realization of open-self (see Table 4).

Implication:

1. Kindness is the triggering—under the control of directed attention—of attention-based positive emotional activity in response to appearance or display of emotional need, weakness or vulnerability (realizations of open-self).

Result 33. *Open-others polarity can be realized as an emotional **lack** or **need**. Similarly, this polarity may express **weakness**, **vulnerability**. Manifestation, which is usually realized as emotional activity, also can be realized as **appearance** or **display**.*

Root 28. Mercy, womb
"ra hha meem"

ra : hha <== meem. Closed-self assignment of manifestation *(ra, <==)* from closed-self manifestation *(meem)* to closed-self assignment and manifestation of containment *(hha)*

Decision (assignment of manifestation) to react *(ra, <==)* with positive emotional and social activity *(meem)* to living beings *(hha)*

Implication:

1. The combination of emotional activity and attention in the triggering decision is an **emotional commitment**. Since mental processes also are involved (decision)—it is a decision to respond—the commitment is also **mental** and **social**.
2. Mercy is a mental, emotional and social commitment (decision) to respond to living beings with positive emotional and social activity. This is also a fair description of what the womb does for the embryo.

Root 29. Surprise
"ba ghain ta"

ba(ta(ghain)). Closed-others and open-others assignment of manifestation *(ba(ta( )))* applied to open-others containment *(ghain)*

Decision to engage clashes with decision not to engage *(ba(ta( )))* in response to information from beyond environment *(ghain)*

Result 34. *Input with open-others polarity is **input from beyond the environment** or a **hidden input**.*

Surprise is an emotional engagement conflict in the decision to trigger emotion in response to information that was hidden.

Root 30. Delight, pleasure
"lam thal thal"

lam(thal^2). Open-self assignment of manifestation *(lam)* applied to duplicate open-others manifestation *(thal^2)*

Attention-controlled excitatory emotional activity *(lam)* that triggers special (open-others) continuous (twice *thal*) emotional activity *(thal^2)*

Result 35. *Open-others polarity is realized as **special emotion**.*

Root 31. Satisfaction, happiness
"noon 'ain meem"

meem: noon <== 'ain. Closed-self manifestation *(meem, <==)* from closed-self containment *('ain)* to open-self containment *(noon)*

Emotional activity to trigger *(meem)* complementary emotional energy *('ain)* in response to *(<==)* emotional need (lacking emotional containment) *(noon)*

Result 36. *Closed-self polarity is realized as **complementary** (completing) or perfecting emotion. Open-self polarity is realized as **lacking** emotion or emotional **need**.*

Root 32. Envy
"hha seen dal"

seen: hha <== dal. Closed-self assignment of containment *(seen, <==)* from closed-others manifestation *(dal)* to closed-self assignment and manifestation of containment *(hha)*

Attention-controlled emotional force *(seen)* used to respond *(<==)* to comparing emotional attitude *(dal)* with inhibiting (restraining) systemic emotion *(hha)*

Implication:

1. Envy is attention-controlled emotional force used to respond to one's comparing emotional attitude (the input) with inhibitory (rejecting) systemic emotion.

Result 37. *Closed-others polarity is realized as **comparing** emotion. Similarly, open-others polarity is realized as **contrasting** or **distinguishing** emotion.*

Root 33. Jealousy
"ghain ya ra"

ra(ghain). Closed-self assignment of manifestation *(ra)* applied to open-others containment *(ghain)*

Attention-controlled emotional restraining activity *(ra)* used to respond *(<==)* to third-party emotional force *(ghain)*

Implication:

1. Jealousy is attention-controlled emotional restraining activity triggered in response to emotional force from a third party.

Result 38. *Open-others polarity is realized as* **third-party** *or* **external** *emotion. Similarly, closed-others polarity is realized as* **internal** *emotion.*

Root 34. Worry, anxiety
"ha meem meem"

$ha(meem^2)$. Open-others assignment *(ha)* applied to duplicate closed-self manifestation *(meem^2)*

Exclusive attention *(ha)* that triggers continuous (twice meem) reactive emotional activity *(meem^2)*

Root 35. Gratitude
"sheen kaf ra"

$ra: sheen <== kaf$. Closed-self assignment of manifestation *(ra)* from closed-self manifestation of containment *(kaf)* to open-self assignment and manifestation of containment *(sheen)*

Attention-controlled triggering of emotional activity *(ra)* to respond *(<==)* with a positive field of emotion *(kaf)* to systemic offering from others (emotional or otherwise) *(sheen)*

Result 39. *Open-self polarity is realized as* **offering** *or* **sending** *of emotion. Similarly, closed-self polarity is realized as* **receiving** *emotion.*

Root 36. Tenderness
"hha noon noon"

$hha(noon^2)$. Closed-self assignment and manifestation of containment *(hha)* applied to duplicate open-self containment *(noon^2)*

Attention-controlled application of positive emotional energy *(hha)* in response to continued emotional weakness *(noon^2)*

INTEGRATED THEORY OF EMOTIONS BASED ON WORD ROOT SEMANTICS

An integrated theory of emotions now will be formulated by summarizing and correlating Results 1-39 from the previous section.

Adi Theory of Emotions

The following 12-part integrated theory of emotions is based on Results 1-39 (obtained by applying Algorithm C to 36 Arabic word roots), the Adi Theory of Semantics, and the Adi Theory of Cognition. The theory can be extended and refined by applying Algorithm C to more emotional word roots.

1. Abstract universals and their realizations. The 28 consonants of Arabic are signs that refer to the 28 universals of Table 1. These are abstract processes with abstract polarities. The effect of their interpretation on the mind is meaning or semantics. For the purposes of this theory, abstract universals refer to real objects in:

a) *the world of emotions*
b) *the environment in which emotions arise*
c) *the world of mental processes*

Common realizations of abstract polarities and processes are listed in Tables 4 and 5, respectively. These realizations are adapted to each world, thus creating discipline-specific realizations. The realizations discussed below can be extended by adapting more realizations from the tables or by identifying other realizations of the abstract universals.

2. Triggering of emotions. *Based on assessment of input (what is observed or experienced, including the environment), a decision is made by the mind, the brain or another decision maker whether or not to trigger emotion, what type of emotion to trigger and which polarity of emotion.*

Assessment of input includes determining its process type and polarity. Examples include:

- *information or data and its polarity, e.g., destructive, weak, uncertain, hidden*
- *a manifestation—person, activity, or event*
- *manifestation of force*
- *application of law (legal assessment)*
- *violation of sovereign area or territory*
- *self evaluation*
- *personal experience, experience with others*

Decision to trigger emotions is done in stages: initial, intermediate, and final. Transition to a later stage is emotional escalation.

3. Emotional polarities. *These are realizations of abstract polarities adapted to the world of emotions.*

Each of these polarities may have both good and bad uses. Below are the emotional polarities mentioned in Results 1-39, listed under the corresponding abstract polarities.

- **closed-self:** *calming, restraining, inhibitory, positive, complementary, perfect, input, receive, familiar, response, reactive*
- **open-self:** *directed, excitatory, negative, lacking, need, weakness, vulnerability, deficient, unfamiliar, output, offer, send, stimulus*
- **closed-others:** *engagement, balanced, balancing, stabilizing, constructive, supportive, reward, mutual, reciprocate, compare, internal*

- **open-others:** *disengagement, detachment, exclusive, targeted, special, excessive, destructive, defensive, aggressive, attack, punish, contrast, distinguish, external, third-party*

4. Elementary emotions. *Elementary emotions are **attention**, **emotional activity** and **emotional force**. They are emotional realizations of the three elementary processes—assignment, manifestation and containment. An elementary emotion always is paired with an emotional polarity.*

- **Attention** *(assignment). Attention is low-intensity emotion. Attention also can be used to control the triggering of emotion. Below are different polarities of attention demonstrated by theories about specific emotions from word roots.*
  - **closed-self attention:** *positive attention, attention for input, attention to familiarity*
    - *To "feel" (emotion) is to respond to a personal experience with repeated mental triggering of emotional force that is tagged with attention to familiarity.*
    - *To "feel" (as with **feelers**) is to repeatedly trigger attention for input measurement from a personal experience.*
  - **open-self attention:** *negative attention, directed attention, triggering of emotion using directed attention*
    - *To "wish" or to "want" is when attention is directed while dealing with something.*
    - *"Sad reaction" is a mental decision to trigger negative attention after assessing input.*
    - *"Kindness" or "compassion" is the triggering—using directed attention—of positive attention-based emotional activity in re-*

sponse to appearance or display of emotional need, weakness or vulnerability.

➤ *"Sorrow"* is triggering—using directed attention—of negative emotional activity based on input assessment.

○ *closed-others attention:* attention with engagement, attention-based balancing of emotion (Part 11 below)

➤ *"Love"* (version 1) is when attention with engagement is used to trigger continued emotional interaction (engaged or mutual activity).

○ *open-others attention:* exclusive attention (targeting)

➤ *"Desire"* or *"lust"* is when exclusive attention triggers excitatory systemic emotion.

➤ *"Worry"* or *"anxiety"* is exclusive attention that triggers continuous reactive emotional activity.

• *Emotional activity* (manifestation). Emotional activity has medium-intensity. An *emotional state* or *attitude* simply is ongoing emotional activity. Manifestation also is realized as *emotional appearance* or *display of emotion*.

○ *"Sorrow"* is a decision by the mind to trigger negative emotional activity after input assessment.

○ *"Fear"* is a decision by the mind to trigger excitatory emotional activity while observing a manifestation of destructive force.

○ *"Worry"* or *"anxiety"* is exclusive attention that triggers continuous reactive emotional activity.

○ To *"rejoice"* is a decision by the mind to react with excitatory emotional activity to a personal experience.

○ *"Faith"* or *"trust"* is the triggering under the control of directed attention of positive emotional attitude after assessment of information as uncertain.

○ *"Mercy"* or *"womb"* is an emotional, biological and social commitment (decision) to respond to living beings with positive emotional, biological and social activity.

○ *"Delight"* or *"pleasure"* is attention-controlled excitatory emotional activity that triggers continuous special emotional activity.

○ *"Envy"* is attention-controlled emotional force used to respond to one's comparing emotional attitude (the input) with inhibitory (rejecting) systemic emotion.

• *Emotional force* (containment). Emotional force is high-intensity emotion. Containment also is realized as *emotional energy, emotional strength* or *emotional control* (see Table 5). Open-self containment is realized as *negative emotional force, emotional weakness, emotional need* (lacking containment) or *loose control*.

○ *"Sadness"* is a decision by the mind to trigger a negative emotional force after assessing a personal experience.

○ *"Prejudice"* is a final decision by the mind to trigger a negative emotional force after examining an experience with another person.

○ *"Justified hate"* is the use of destructive emotional force (aggressive feelings and thoughts) to defend oneself or others against a violation based on legal assessment. *"Justified anger"* is the escalation of justified hate, i.e., from feelings and thoughts to words and actions.

- ○ *"Jealousy"* is attention-controlled emotional restraining activity triggered in response to emotional force from a third party.
- ○ *"Satisfaction"* or *"happiness"* is emotional activity to trigger complementary (completing) emotional energy in response to emotional need.

5. Compound emotions. *Compound emotions are realizations of combinations of the elementary processes. They simply may be combinations of elementary emotions, but also may result in a new emotional effect. A compound emotion always is paired with an emotional polarity. Below, each compound emotion is followed by examples of emotional effects.*

- • *Attention + emotional activity* (assignment + manifestation): emotional activity controlled by attention (e.g., attention for input—closed-self polarity), attention-based emotional activity, emotional decision, emotional commitment
  - ○ *"Grudge"* is a feedback loop with attention-based excitatory emotional activity that is used to maintain or amplify response to destructive or excessive emotional force.
  - ○ *"Expectation"* is emotional activity controlled by attention for input.
  - ○ *"Hope"* is to expect something constructive.
  - ○ *"Kindness"* or *"compassion"* is the triggering—using directed attention—of positive attention-based emotional activity in response to appearance or display of emotional need, weakness or vulnerability.
  - ○ *"Mercy"* or *"womb"* is an emotional, biological and social commitment (decision) to respond to living beings with positive emotional, biological and social activity.

- ○ *"Delight"* or *"pleasure"* is attention-controlled excitatory emotional activity that triggers continuous special emotional activity.
- • *Attention + emotional force* (assignment + containment): attention-controlled emotional force or energy, attention for measurement (sensing)
  - ○ To *"feel"* (to have a feeling) is to have the mind repeatedly trigger an emotional force or energy tagged with familiar attention in response to personal experience.
  - ○ To *"feel"* (as with *feelers*) is to repeatedly trigger attention for input quantity from a personal experience.
- • *Emotional activity + emotional force* (manifestation + containment): application of emotional force or energy, emotional control, emotional effort, emotional field of energy, mood (manifestation of emotional force), use of emotional force, emotional pressure, violent emotion, emotional coercion
  - ○ *"Tranquility"* is when input assessment triggers a calming emotional field to deal with an excitatory emotional force.
  - ○ *"Despair"* (version 2) is balancing (evening out) application of emotional forces between constructive and negative emotional forces.
  - ○ *"Gratitude"* is attention-controlled triggering of emotional activity to respond with a positive field of emotion to systemic emotion offered by others.
  - ○ *"Obsessive hate"* or *"phobia"* is emotional entanglement (caused by lacking emotional control) with a destructive or excessive force.
- • *Attention + emotional activity + emotional force* (assignment + manifestation + containment): systemic emotion (emotion that af-

fects the whole person), attention-controlled application of emotional force or energy

- ○ **"Systemic fear"** *is a decision by the mind to trigger systemic excitatory emotion upon observing a manifestation of destructive force.*
- ○ **"Tenderness"** *is attention-controlled application of positive emotional energy in response to continued emotional weakness.*
- ○ **"Envy"** *is attention-controlled emotional force used to respond to one's comparing emotional attitude (the input) with inhibitory (rejecting) systemic emotion.*

6. Emotional feedback loop. *Emotional triggering mechanism in which triggered emotion is reused as input for the same triggering function. The effect is to maintain, regulate, attenuate or amplify emotion.*

- • **"Grudge"** *is a feedback loop with attention-based excitatory emotional activity that is used to maintain or amplify response to destructive or excessive emotional force.*
- • **"Love"** *(version 2) is a feedback loop with attention-controlled emotional engagement activity used to maintain or amplify positive systemic emotion.*
- • **"Joy"** *is repeated or feedback-loop-amplified triggering of positive attention-based emotional activity in processing of sensory input.*

7. Repeated emotion. *Repeated emotion also manifests itself as continued or intense emotion.*

- • **"Love"** *(version 1) is when attention with engagement is used to trigger continued emotional interaction.*

8. Emotional entanglement or emotional control bond. *As controller of emotions, the mind*

may suffer imperfections such as loose control, deficiencies, weaknesses or needs. This may lead to an entanglement or bond with a destructive or constructive emotional force (e.g., internal or external powerful persons or phenomena) or an excessive emotional force (e.g., insatiable appetite). This is called emotional entanglement or emotional control bond. Manifestations may include negative forms (entanglements) such as phobias, fanaticism, obsession and addiction, and positive forms (bonds) such as love, loyalty and dedication.

- • **"Obsessive hate"** *or* **"phobia"** *is emotional entanglement with a destructive or excessive force.* **"Uncontrolled anger or aggression"** *is the effect of escalation of obsessive hate or phobia, i.e., escalation of emotional entanglement with a destructive or excessive force.*

9. Emotional instability, conflict or deadlock. *One emotion is triggered and then reprocessed by triggering an emotion with opposite polarity. The attribute* **"engagement"** *is added if the opposite polarity pair is closed-others (emotional engagement) and open-others (emotional disengagement or detachment). If the polarities involved are closed-self and open-self, then the attribute* **"boundary"** *is added.*

- • **"Capricious love"** *is attention engagement instability (attention with engagement stymied by attention with detachment).*
- • **"Unspeakable," "shocking"** *or* **"disgusting"** *is* **systemic emotional boundary conflict.** *Systemic restraining emotion is triggered to process systemic excitatory emotion that was initially triggered to process a negative event.*
- • **"Despair"** *(version 1) is input assessment that triggers* **attention boundary deadlock** *(inhibition of excitatory attention).*

- *"Surprise"* is an **emotional engagement conflict** in the **decision to trigger emotion** in response to information from beyond environment.

10. Inflation of emotion. The mind accumulates (closed-others = together) responses (closed-self).

- *"Arrogance"* is an inflation of emotional activity triggered by self-evaluation.

11. Stabilization of emotional response. Attention-based balancing (closed-others assignment) applied to emotional response (closed-self). Note that this is a different realization of the same polarity pair used in inflation of emotion.

- *"Patience"* is stabilization of emotional response activity that is triggered by continued attack.

12. Balancing application of emotional forces. This is the balancing (closed-others) application of emotional forces that is referred to by consonant tta. Depending on the context, this may either result in **stabilization** or **evening out**.

- *"Despair"* (version 2) is an evening-out application of emotional forces between constructive and negative emotional forces. Despair is a conflict between competing emotional forces that are not exact polarity opposites.
- *"Stable faith"* or *"stable trust"* is a stabilizing application of emotional forces implemented on faith or trust. This word root is compound in that it has tta as prefix to a three-consonant root that is equivalent to the word root for faith or trust.

CONFIRMATION FROM CLINICAL PSYCHOLOGY

After deriving a theory of emotions based only on language semantics and self reports, a reality check from clinical psychology is presented.

Lazarus' extensive clinical experience led him to the conclusion that the arousal of emotions "depends on reason and follows clear rules" (2006, p. 86). More specifically, arousal of emotions depends on an **appraisal** of what is happening (Lazarus, 2006, pp. 92-93).

Lazarus' primary (initial) appraisal components are (2006, pp. 92-93):

Goal relevance
> "there is no emotion without there being a goal at stake"

Goal congruence
- conditions favorable to personal goals make it likely that positively toned emotion is aroused
- conditions unfavorable to personal goals make it likely that negatively toned emotion is aroused

Types of ego involvement
- social and self esteem
- moral values
- ego ideals
- meanings and ideas
- other persons and their wellbeing
- life goals

In the Adi Theory of Emotions (Theory, for short), the mind, the brain or another decision maker triggers emotions based on *assessment of input*. The mind as decision maker is consistent with Lazarus' conviction that arousal of emotions *depends on reason by way of appraisal*. The Theory allows reasonable decision makers other than the mind.

The assessment of input includes the identification of input process types and polarities (see Theory Parts 1-3). The abstract polarity scheme also applies to the emotions to be triggered based on that assessment. Similar to Lazarus' goal congruence, favorable polarity leads to triggering of positively-toned emotions, and unfavorable polarity leads to triggering of negatively-toned emotions.

All flavors of polarities stem from—are realizations of—combinations of abstract social engagement conditions (self and others) with abstract social boundary conditions (closed and open), resulting in four fundamental polarity flavors: closed-self, open-self, closed-others, and open-others (see Table 4 and Theory Parts 2 and 3). Input assessment includes self evaluation, personal experience, experience with others and violation of sovereign area or territory (see examples in Theory Part 2). These features are comparable to Lazarus' types of ego involvement, including self esteem, ego ideals, and other persons and their wellbeing.

Lazarus' ego involvement type *moral values* is comparable to assessment of application of law (legal assessment).

The ego involvement type *meanings and ideas* is well covered by the Theory's dependence on semantics.

FUTURE TRENDS

The Adi Theory of Semantics is applicable to any alphabetical language. Corroborated theories about specific emotions can be generated from English emotional word stems (see Table 6 in Appendix A). *Hope* (the sounds "h" and "p") has the abstract theory *open-others assignment on open-self manifestation*. A corroborated theory is *exclusive attention on a future event*. Similarly, for *fear* (the sounds "f" and "r") we have the theory *response to negative event with attention-based inhibiting emotional activity*.

Only 36 Arabic emotional word roots were analyzed to derive the theory of emotions. Many more are available to expand and enhance the Theory.

There are similarities to cognitivist theories. For example, the mind can be a decision maker that evaluates input before triggering an emotion. Unlike cognitivism, the Theory also allows the brain and other decision makers (hormonal control, physiology) to trigger emotions. This includes direct transition from stimulus to response.

Since the Theory is derived solely from language semantics, it should be classified as semanticist.

While Picard suggests that few cognitivist theories of emotions had computer implementations (1997, p. 22), Ruebenstrunk lists several such implementations which he calls "electronic assistants" (1998, chapter 5).

The Theory utilizes mathematical functions that are defined over discrete domains and ranges, i.e., realizations of processes and polarities. Moreover, the language of these realizations is very close to conversational language. These two features make computer applications immediate.

Emotional computers have four tasks (Ruebenstrunk, 2004a, p.1):

a. recognition of emotions
   perception of emotions
   identification of emotions and
   interpretation of emotions
b. simulation of emotions
c. generation of emotions and
d. expression of emotions

The Theory gives new insights into the nature of emotions and inspires novel affective computing applications in all four task areas. The software Readware already identifies emotions by looking for phrases—in spoken or written chats, emails and documents—that are similar to those used in the 36 theories about specific emotions (Adi, Ewell,

Adi & Vogel, 2008). In the future, this sentiment analyzer could trigger emotional responses such as generated speech that would calm an angry computer user or encourage a frustrated user.

CONCLUSION

With nothing more than fuzzy semantic interpretations to start with, it seemed a daunting task to develop a robust theory of emotions. After the semantic and intuitive analysis of just a few emotional word roots, however, the rules of the theory began to emerge. It soon became clear that there were three elementary emotions with different intensities. Emotional polarities distinguished desirable emotional events from undesirable ones.

Mysterious emotions such as surprise and grudge were operationally defined using simple mathematical formulas. Even complex emotional phenomena such as obsession and emotional instability were represented as plain procedures.

It is hoped that this purely semantic approach to understanding emotions will offer practical alternative views of human feelings that will inspire improved synthetic emotions and affective computing.

ACKNOWLEDGMENT

Since 1986, Ken Ewell has supported my work on the theory of semantics. Ken is a founder of Management Information Technologies, Inc. My wife Patricia's work as copy editor on this chapter was so helpful. I also thank my daughter Nadima for her useful explanations of cognitive and psychological concepts and a psychological plausibility review of the chapter.

REFERENCES

Adi, T. (2007). A theory of semantics based on Old Arabic. In R. Gudwin and J. Queiroz (Eds.), *Semiotics and intelligent systems development* (pp. 176-209). Hershey, PA: Idea Group, Inc.

Adi, T., & Ewell, O. K. (1987a). Comprehension of natural language by machine. Retrieved July 2008, from http://www.readware.com/papers/machcomp.rtf

Adi, T., & Ewell, O. K. (1987b). Letter semantics in Arabic morphology. In *Proceedings of the Morphology Workshop of the 1987 Linguistic Institute Conference, Stanford, CA*. Tokyo: Stanford University Press. Retrieved July 2008, from http://www.readware.com/papers/ltr_sem.doc

Adi, T., & Ewell, O. K. (1996). Where human genius comes from. Retrieved September 10, 2008, from http://www.readware.com/papers/ls96.htm

Adi, T., Ewell, O. K., Adi, P. and Vogel, T. (2008). A new theory of cognition and software implementations in information technology. Accepted for publication in Journal of Information Technology Research (JITR). Hershey, PA: Idea Group, Inc.

Damasio, A. (1994). *Descartes' error: emotion, reason, and the human brain.* New York: G. P. Putnam's Sons.

Ekman, P. (1992). An argument for basic emotions. *Cognition and Emotion, 6,* 169-200.

Fussell, S. R. (2002). The verbal communication of emotions: introduction and overview. In S.R. Fussell (Ed.), *The verbal communication of emotions: interdisciplinary perspectives* (pp. 1-16). Mahwah, N.J.: L. Erlbaum Associates.

Goddard, C. (2002). Explicating emotions across languages and cultures: a semantic approach. In S.R. Fussell (Ed.), *The verbal communication of* emotions: interdisciplinary perspectives (pp. 19-53). Mahwah, N.J.: L. Erlbaum Associates.

Goddard, C. and Wierzbicka, A. (2007). Semantic primes and cultural scripts in language learning and intercultural communication. In G. Palmer & F. Sharifian (Eds.), *Applied cultural linguistics: implications for second language learning and intercultural communication* (pp. 105-124). Amsterdam: John Benjamins.

Jakobson, R. (1937). Six lectures on sound and meaning. In *Lectures on sound & meaning*, MIT Press, Cambridge, Mass.

Lazarus, R. (2006): *Stress and emotion: a new synthesis.* New York: Springer.

Magnus, M. (2001). *What's in a word: Studies in phonosemantics,* Doctoral dissertation, University of Trondheim, Norway. Retrieved from the web September 10, 2008 http://www.trismegistos.com/Dissertation/

Majumdar A., Sowa J., & Stewart J. (2008). Pursuing the goal of language understanding. In Eklund, P. & Haemmerlé, O. (Eds.) *Proceedings of the 16th ICCS.* Berlin: Springer-Verlag.

Mehrabian, A., & Russell, J. (1974). *An approach to environmental psychology.* Cambridge, MA: MIT Press.

Ortony, A. (2002). On making believable emotional agents believable. In R. Trappl, P. Petta, & S. Payr (Eds.), *Emotions in humans and artifacts* (pp. 189-211). Cambridge, MA: MIT Press.

Ortony, A., Clore, G., & Collins, A. (1990). *The cognitive structure of emotions.* Cambridge, U.K.: Cambridge University Press.

Peirce, C. S. (1960). *Collected papers of Charles Sanders Peirce.* Cambridge: Harvard University Press.

Picard, R. (1997). *Affective computing.* Cambridge, MA: MIT Press.

Pines, S. (1986). Ibn al-Haytham's critique of Ptolemy. In *Studies in Arabic versions of Greek texts and in mediaeval science, Vol. II.* Leiden, The Netherlands: Brill.

Popper, K (2002). *Conjectures and refutations: the growth of scientific knowledge.* London & New York: Routledge.

Rhodes, R. ,& Lawler, J. (1981), Athematic metaphors. In *Papers from the 17th Annual Meeting of the Chicago Linguistics Society*, Chicago.

Ruebenstrunk, G. (2004a, January). Emotional machines. Paper presented at workshop at V2_Lab (Institute for Unstable Media). Rotterdam, The Netherlands. Retrieved June 15, 2008, from http://www.ruebenstrunk.de/Rotterdam.doc

Ruebenstrunk, G. (2004b, November). Affective systems. Paper presented as moderator at workshop on affective systems, Dutch Electronics Arts Festival (DEAF 04). Rotterdam, The Netherlands. Retrieved on June 15, 2008, from http://www.ruebenstrunk.de/presentation4.ppt

Ruebenstrunk, G. (1998). *Emotional computers: computer models of emotions and their meaning for emotion-psychological research.* Unpublished dissertation, University of Bielefeld, Germany. Retrieved June 15, 2008 from http://www.ruebenstrunk.de/emeocomp/content.htm

Russell, J. (1980). A circumplex model of affect. *Journal of Personality and Social Psychology, 1161-1178.*

Saussure, Ferdinand de (1916). *Cours de linguistique générale.* Paris: Payot.

Shweder, R. (1994). You're not sick, you're just in love: emotion as an interpretive system. In P. Ekman & R.J. Davidson (Eds.), *The nature of emotion: fundamental questions* (pp. 32-44). New York: Oxford University Press.

Sowa, J. (2008). From an e-mail to Tom Adi dated July 10, 2008.

Sowa, J. (2006). The challenge of knowledge soup. In Ramadas, J. & Chunawala, S. (Eds.), *Research trends in science, technology and mathematics education* (pp. 55-90). Mumbai: Homi Bhabha Centre. Retrieved July 2008, from http://www.jfsowa.com/pubs/

Sowa, J. (2000). Ontology, metadata, and semiotics. Presented at ICCS'2000 in Darmstadt, Germany, on August 14, 2000. In Ganter, B. & Mineau, G. W. (Eds.), *Conceptual structures: logical, linguistic, and computational issues.* Lecture notes in AI #1867, 55-81. Berlin: Springer-Verlag. Retrieved July 2008, from http://www.jfsowa.com/ontology/ontometa.htm

Sowa, J. (1990). Crystallizing theories out of knowledge soup. In Zbigniew, W. R. & Zemankova, M. (Eds.), *Intelligent systems: state of the art and future directions.* New York: Ellis Horwood. Retrieved July 2008, from http://www.jfsowa.com/pubs/crystal.htm

Steffens, B. (2007). *Ibn Al-Haytham: first scientist.* Greensboro, NC: Morgan Reynolds

Tomlinson, Jr., W. (2002). *Synthetic social relationships for computational entities.* Unpublished doctoral dissertation, Massachusetts Institute of Technology, Cambridge.

Wierzbicka, A. (1996). *Semantics: primes and universals.* Oxford: Oxford University Press.

Zadeh, L. A. (2002). From computing with numbers to computing with words—from manipulation of measurements to manipulation of perceptions. *International Journal of Applied Mathematics and Computer Sciences, 12*(3), 307-324.

KEY TERMS

Abstract Polarity: One of four abstract universals: closed-self, open-self, closed others and open-others.

Adi Theory of Semantics (in a nutshell): Each consonant refers to an abstract process and an abstract polarity. These universals combine in a word root to create a theory about the thing the root names.

Algorithm C (applied to emotions). A word root expressing an emotion is converted into an abstract theory about the emotion. This is realized in alternative theories that are checked against self reports.

Common Realizations: Realizations of abstract processes and polarities from the author's previous research.

Compound Abstract Process: A combination of two or three elementary abstract processes. **Abstract process** is short for elementary or compound abstract process.

Elementary Abstract Process: One of three abstract universals: assignment, manifestation and containment.

Emotion, Compound: Emotional realization of a compound abstract process.

Emotion, Elementary: Emotional realizations of elementary abstract processes. Attachment is a realization of assignment. Emotional activity is a realization of manifestation. Emotional force is a realization of containment.

Emotional Polarity: Emotional realization of abstract polarity.

APPENDIX A: ADI THEORY OF SEMANTICS

The Adi Theory of Semantics (ATS) states that each of the 28 Arabic consonants is a sign that refers to one of seven **abstract processes**—assignment, manifestation, containment, assignment of manifestation, assignment of containment, manifestation of containment, and assignment and manifestation of containment—and one of four **abstract polarities**—closed-self, open-self, closed-others, and open-others (Adi, 2007, pp. 185, 190-191). This is visualized in Table 1.

Closed-self and open-self polarities are opposites. They are called **boundary** polarities. Closed-others and open-others polarities also are opposites. They are called **engagement** polarities.

Most Arabic word roots are strings of three consonants each. ATS has rules to convert any word root into an abstract mathematical mapping such as $f: X ==> Y$ or $f(x)$ (Adi, 2007, pp. 198, 200). The seven abstract processes of ATS (Table 1) have a **precedence order** that is shown in Table 2. Consonants that refer to processes with higher precedence play the role of *function* such as f of the mapping while the remaining consonants play the role of *domain X* or *range Y* of the mapping.

For example, the root *"kaf lam meem"* (speech) has a mapping of the form $f: X ==> Y$, i.e.,

*"kaf lam meem" has the mapping **lam: kaf ==> meem***

because *lam* has open-self polarity and higher precedence than *kaf* or *meem*. Table 3 lists 12 possible types of word root mappings and explains the rules for generating mappings out of roots.

Abstract polarities and processes have many concrete realizations. Tables 4 and 5 list common realizations of polarities and processes, respectively.

Table 1 was created for the sounds of English and other languages (Adi & Ewell, 1987a, 1987b, 1996). However, not all the cells of the table could be filled for any language other than Arabic. Table 6 is the equivalent of Table 1 for English.

Table 1. Abstract objects of Arabic consonants

PROCESS	POLARITY			
	closed-self	open-self	closed-others	open-others
assignment	*ya*	*hamza*	*waw*	*ha*
manifestation	*meem*	*fa*	*dal*	*thal*
containment	*'ain*	*noon*	*qaf*	*ghain*
assignment of manifestation	*ra*	*lam*	*ba*	*ta*
assignment of containment	*seen*	*zay*	*ssad*	*tha*
manifestation of containment	*kaf*	*ddad*	*tta*	*kha*
assignment & manifestation of containment	*hha*	*sheen*	*geem*	*zza*

Table 2. Descending order of process precedence

assignment
assignment of manifestation
assignment of containment
assignment & manifestation of containment
manifestation
manifestation of containment
containment

Table 3. Types of word root mappings

1. Forward mapping Function consonant **f** has open-self polarity and higher precedence than domain consonant **X** and range consonant **Y**.	$f : X \Longrightarrow Y$
2. Backward mapping Consonant **f** has closed-self polarity and higher precedence than consonants **X** and **Y**.	$f : X \Longleftarrow Y$
3. Engagement mapping Consonant **f** has closed-others polarity and higher precedence than consonants **X** and **Y**.	$f : X \Longleftrightarrow Y$
4. Disengagement mapping Consonant **f** has open-others polarity and higher precedence than consonants **X** and **Y**.	$f : X >\!\!=\!\!< Y$
5. Mapping with square domain and unspecified range Consonant **f** has higher precedence than duplicate consonant **x**.	$f(x^2)$
6. Mapping with unspecified range First or third consonant is *ya*, *hamza* or *waw* that is dropped in some word forms (it appears as *ya*, *hamza* or *waw* in root), and consonant **f** has higher precedence than consonant **x**.	$f(x)$
7. Composition with unspecified range Consonants **f** and **g** are not first and third in root, are from the same row of Table 1, and have higher precedence than consonant **x**.	$f(g(x))$
8. Parallel functions, unspecified range Consonants **f** and **g** are first and third in the root, are from same row of Table 1, and have higher precedence than consonant **x**.	$f(x) \& g(x)$
9. Parallel functions with unspecified domain & range Second consonant is *ya*, *hamza* or *waw* that is dropped in some word forms (it appears as *ya*, *hamza* or *waw* in root).	$f(\ ) \& g(\ )$
10. Composition with unspecified domain & range First or third consonant is *ya*, *hamza* or *waw* that is dropped in some word forms (it appears as *ya*, *hamza* or *waw* in root) and consonants **f** and **g** are from the same row of Table 1.	$f(g(\ ))$
11. Double composition with unspecified domain & range All three consonants are from same row of Table 1.	$f(g(h(\ )))$
12. Mapping with unspecified domain and range Root contains two occurrences of *ya*, *hamza* or *waw* that are dropped in some word forms (they appear as *ya*, *hamza* or *waw* in root).	$f(\ )$

Table 4. Common realizations of abstract polarities

closed-self	open-self	closed-others	open-others
a certain . . .	another (not self)	balance	beyond environment
backward	arbitrary	combine	choose
complementary	deficient	common	contrast
complete	directed at others	compare	cut
defined	discretionary	connect	destructive
familiar	empty	constructive	disconnect
inward	forward	continue	disengage
old	the future	dual	distinguish
one's own	incomplete	engaged	exchange
oneself	invalid	equal	excessive
the past	lacking	general	exclude
perfect	loose	integrate	exclusive
personal	negative	internal	external
positive	new	join	imbalance
preservation	offer	meet	separate
private	open to others	moderate	special
react	open-ended	multiple	specific
receive	others (not self)	mutual	specify
repeat	outward	pending	stop
restrain	public	the present	target
self	release	reciprocal	third-party
self-contained	send	shared	unengaged
valid	toward others	together	unequal
well-defined	uncertain	within environment	
	undefined		
	unfamiliar		
	unleash		
	unspecified		
	violation		
	vulnerable		

Table 5. Common realizations of abstract processes

assignment	attach, connect, designate, determine, to direct, an element, identify, identity, link, point, to project, signal, a unit
manifestation	action, active, activity, agency, agent, appearance, apply, attitude, display, entity, essence, event, execute, to experience, express, feel, form, fulfill, instrument, interpret, manner, mass, matter, method, number, person, phenomenon, place, realization, shape, space, status, substance, time, translate
containment	command, container, content, data, energy, force, information, an instruction, law, number, order, power, quantity, rule, volume, weight
assignment of manifestation (combine first & second rows)	belong (assign place), decision (assign action), directed action, implement (determine realization), interpretative link, placement (assign place), project manifestation/form, relationship (connect by activity), set (elements in a place)
assignment of containment (combine first & third rows)	assessment (assign quantity), attack (directed force), fill (assign content), lodge (assign container), measure (assess), sequence (assign order), stream (sequence), structure (assign order)
manifestation of containment (combine second & third rows)	algorithm (execute laws), apply law, apply force, control (manifestation of order), controller, effort (apply energy), display of force, field (force in space), form of energy, mapping (execute, realize law), powerful agent, sovereign area (space of power), theory (interpretation of law)
assignment & manifestation of containment (combine first three rows)	behavior (process), experience, living being (system), mechanism (process), motion, object (static view of process), organism, process (assignment and manifestation of control), system (process), systemic, thing (object)

Table 6. Abstract objects of English sounds

PROCESS	POLARITY			
	closed-self	open-self	closed-others	open-others
assignment	i-, y-, j	a-	o-, u-, v, w	e-, h
manifestation	m	f, p, ph	d	th
containment		n, gn, kn	q, cq	ng, nk, nc
assignment of manifestation	r	l	b	t
assignment of containment	s	z	c, ck	
manifestation of containment	k			x, gh, ch
assignment & manifestation of containment		sh	g	

APPENDIX B: AN ALGORITHM TO DEVELOP A SCIENTIFIC THEORY FROM WORD ROOT SEMANTICS

The following procedure (Adi, Ewell, Adi & Vogel, 2008) is an implementation of the Scientific Method using the Adi Theory of Semantics (Appendix A).

Algorithm C. Procedure to develop a theory to explain a certain phenomenon to which a certain word root refers

Step 1. Generate abstract theory from chosen word root. Use Tables 1-3 to convert the chosen word root into a mapping. Use Table 1 to verbally express the mapping in abstract processes and abstract polarities. This expression is an *abstract theory* about some aspects of the nature of the phenomenon to which the word root refers. The abstract processes that correspond to the domain and range of the mapping are abstract hypotheses about the nature of some elements of the phenomenon. The abstract polarities are abstract hypotheses about the attributes of these elements. The abstract processes that correspond to the functions of the mapping are abstract hypotheses about the nature of the relationships between these elements of the phenomenon.

Step 2. Make predictions. Make predictions—that are not likely to be observed (try to disprove the theory)—based on the abstract theory from Step 1, or—more likely—based on a *concrete theory* (obtained by substituting abstract elements with their realizations) that was created in Step 3.

Step 3. Test proposed theory and generate alternative concrete theories using Tables 4 and 5. Compare predictions with collected observations about the phenomenon and try to find a mismatch. If one prediction is not confirmed by observation, replace one or more polarities or processes from the theory with realizations from Tables 4 and 5, or with new realizations that are based on these tables or on the original abstract concepts, and then return to Step 2 to test this *alternative concrete theory*. If all predictions are confirmed by observations, then also return to Step 2 and make new predictions. If, for a fixed version of the theory, many predictions are made and all of them are confirmed by observation, then consider the proposed theory as *corroborated theory*. If later observations or corroborated theories about related phenomena clash with this theory, then revise the theory using alternative realizations and return to Step 2.

APPENDIX C: ADI THEORY OF COGNITION

The Adi Theory of Cognition (Adi, Ewell, Adi & Vogel, 2008) is an implementation of the Adi Theory of Semantics and Algorithm C.

1. ***Verbalization of a word root mapping is an abstract theory.*** *The names of the abstract processes and polarities to which a word root refers are abstract hypotheses about some aspects of the nature of the phenomenon to which the word root refers. If a word root mapping is expressed using the names of its abstract components, then an* **abstract theory** *about some aspects of the nature of that phenomenon is obtained.*

2. ***Concrete theories.*** *If some of the abstract processes or polarities in an abstract theory that expresses a word root are substituted with realizations from Tables 4 and 5 or with similar realizations, the result is a* **concrete theory** *about some aspects of the nature of the phenomenon to which the word root refers.*

3. ***Applicability of Algorithm C.*** *Algorithm C can be used to attempt to corroborate abstract theories and concrete theories.*

4. ***Every concrete theory is promising.*** *Every concrete theory is promising, i.e., likely to be corroborated by Algorithm C. In other words, Algorithm C is* **efficient***.*

5. ***Single abstract theory may spawn multiple corroborated theories (ambiguity and polysemy).*** *Multiple concrete theories that are derived from a single word root can be corroborated. This implies that every word root is polysemous (ambiguous). Polysemy means that a word root refers to different objects in different contexts.*

6. ***Incompleteness of theories (synonymy and homonymy).*** *Every abstract theory is incomplete in that it and all concrete theories derived from it put together do not explain everything about the phenomenon to which the corresponding word root refers. Different word roots may refer to the same phenomenon (***synonyms***,* **homonyms** *and equivalent word roots in other languages) in such a way that the resulting abstract theories may complement each other in explaining the phenomenon. Consequently, the sum of all abstract and concrete theories about any phenomenon also is incomplete. But some word roots, particularly three-consonant Arabic word roots, may indicate stronger theories than others, i.e., theories that explain more aspects of a phenomenon.*

7. ***Convergence to field ontology.*** *If Algorithm C is applied to many word roots that refer to the phenomena in a specific field of study, then the resulting corroborated theories will share realizations of abstract components in such a manner that the whole field of study will have an integrated and consistent theory—a field ontology.*

8. ***Field ontology supports preservation of phenomena in field according to precedence rules.*** *The order of precedence of Table 2 is propagated into every field ontology involving natural phenomena in such a manner that the preservation of the natural phenomena is supported by the ontology according to rules of precedence.*

Section V
Applied Artificial Emotions

Chapter XVII
Emotion in the Turing Test:
A Downward Trend for Machines in Recent Loebner Prizes

Huma Shah
University of Reading, UK

Kevin Warwick
University of Reading, UK

ABSTRACT

The Turing Test, originally configured as a game for a human to distinguish between an unseen and unheard man and woman, through a text-based conversational measure of gender, is the ultimate test for deception and hence, thinking. So conceived Alan Turing when he introduced a machine into the game. His idea, that once a machine deceives a human judge into believing that they are the human, then that machine should be attributed with intelligence. What Turing missed is the presence of emotion in human dialogue, without expression of which, an entity could appear non-human. Indeed, humans have been confused as machine-like, the confederate effect, during instantiations of the Turing Test staged in Loebner Prizes for Artificial Intelligence. We present results from recent Loebner Prizes and two parallel conversations from the 2006 contest in which two human judges, both native English speakers, each concomitantly interacted with a non-native English speaking hidden-human, and jabberwacky, the 2005 and 2006 Loebner Prize bronze prize winner for most human-like machine. We find that machines in those contests appear conversationally worse than non-native hidden-humans, and, as a consequence attract a downward trend in highest scores awarded to them by human judges in the 2004, 2005 and 2006 Loebner Prizes. Analysing Loebner 2006 conversations, we see that a parallel could be drawn with autistics: the machine was able to broadcast but it did not inform; it talked but it did not emote. The hidden-humans were easily identified through their emotional intelligence, ability to discern emotional state of others and contribute with their own 'balloons of textual emotion'.

INTRODUCTION

Humans steep their ideas in emotion (Pinker, 2008). Emotional states, Minsky writes, "are usually simpler than most of our other ways to think" (2007). Daily conversation is "glued together through exchange of emotion" (Tomasello et al, 2005). Be it an expression of joy or displeasure "sharing emotions with people other than our intimates is a useful tool to bond and to strengthen social relationships" (Derks, Fischer & Bos, 2008). We consider the conversations between unknowns in the 2006 Loebner Prize for Artificial Intelligence, from hereon referred to as the LPAI, to compare and contrast the human-human and human-machine dialogues to find any display of emotion, be it happiness or annoyance, in the participants. The LPAI is an annual science contest that provides a platform for Alan Turing's imitation game (Turing, 1950), which, some would argue, should be killed[1], because it offers nothing that furthers the science of understanding *emotions, intelligence* or *human consciousness*. The game, originally configured for a human interrogator whose task it is to distinguish between an unseen and unheard man and woman through text-based conversational measure of gender, is the ultimate test for deception, and hence, thinking. So conceived Turing, when he altered the interrogator's task to one that entails distinguishing a machine from a hidden-human. Turing believed that once a machine deceived a human judge into believing that they were the human, then that machine should be attributed with intelligence. But is the Turing Test nothing more than an emotionless game?

In this chapter we present an analysis of two *three-participant* dialogues involving two human judges: one male native English speaker (British cyberneticist Professor Kevin Warwick in his second outing as a Loebner judge, in 2001 and 2006), with a male, non-native English speaking hidden human (termed NNHH in this chapter) in parallel comparison with an artificial conversational entity

–ACE (Shah, 2005); one female judge, textually conversing with a female NNHH and an ACE. Jabberwacky (Carpenter, 2007) was the ACE in both those conversations; it won the Loebner bronze-award for 'most human-like' programme for the second consecutive year in 2006. The contest does not see embodied machines, rather competing programmes attempting to simulate human thinking and intelligence. Nonetheless, in the sixteenth year of the competition we could reasonably expect an ACE to manifest some feeling and express some emotional state, such as cheerfulness or sadness. However, the two judges easily recognised the simulated from the natural, the machine from the non-natives. Though their expressions were occasionally unlike native English speakers, both NNHHs were correctly identified as 'the human'. The ACE did show an ability to produce complex and amusing utterances, for example: *I will if you tell me who your parents are* in response to the question *so tell me all about yourself* or *Yes, it's a good opportunity for a chat!* when asked *Are you enjoying today?* (Loebner 2006 transcripts: Session 2, P4J2H3; Session 6, P4J1H4)[2]. Yip & Martin posit that the "use of humor may be an important skill in itself and may contribute to other social competencies, such as the ability to initiate social interactions, provide emotional support, and manage conflict" (2006). During their LPAI interaction an NNHH displayed a capacity *to forget*: contrary to LPAI 2006 Rules for the hidden humans, the male used his real name in introduction (participant H3 initially failed to use the line "My name is John"), but immediately corrected their error (table 1). Both male and female NNHHs displayed "social cognition" (Tomasello, et al, 2005), through demonstrating an interest in their conversational partners, for example, through asking questions: *"Hi what's your name?"* and *"What are you working?"* (table 5). The latter question highlights the non-native nature of the utterance formation. Derks, Fischer and Bos point out that text-based interaction is not a hindrance to emotion communication but that such interaction "may have especially consequences for the decoding or recognition of others' emotions" (2008), because visual, or verbal cues present in face to face or telephonic scenarios, are absent. However, unlike the ACE, both NNHHs were able to counter computer-mediated chat, and confirmed human desire to share personal information, for example: *"My father [..] wants to go to NZ"* (see table 7) and remain aware of their conversational partners "affective state" (Callejas & López-Cózar, 2008). While interrogating their unseen/unheard conversational partners, and from textual output received from both the hidden entities, the judges were able to use any emotional content to determine which was human and which was machine.

Both male and female human judges in LPAI 2006, and the two NNHHs, revealed personal information, expressing emotion, for example, through experiencing weather: *mainly when I forget my umbrella* to the judge's question *so do you regard rain as bad weather* and their knowledge of music: *rock or pop-rock [] sometimes I listen to classical music [] that depends on what I am feeling like at the moment* (table 3). Unlike the ACE, the NNHHs were able to overlook misspellings and recognise words to extract correct sense. For instance, 'catch' in relation to hearing news items (see tables 2 & 3). Lastly, we present results from recent LPAIs (2004-2006) that played out Turing's parallel paired comparison game, and find that machines in the contest appear conversationally worse, rather than better, in terms of a downward trend in highest scores awarded to them by human judges.

Emotion

Edmonds (2008) states that "emotions are a special type of action" that are "in one's own body and brain" (p. 226); he argues that to pass the Turing Test machine's ability to post "appropriately emotional responses" would require that they be embedded in society. The Loebner entries, such as Jabberwacky and Alice, make up a part of the digital society active on the Internet. Considering their conversations in Loebner contests however, it is the human dialogues that portray each sentence as if 'batting a balloon' between conversational participants, relevance is maintained when a balloon is kept from conversationally wandering off in a different direction. Warwick, as judge 2 in LPAI 2006, using a cricketing analogy, spun a conversational googly which the machine missed, but the hidden-humans caught with visceral returns. Thus Loebner judges seem not to accept the machines thinking in the same way that an emotional entity would. Maria & Zitar state that "emotions are an essential part of human life; they influence how we think, adapt, learn, behave and how humans communicate with each other" (2007). Wilson felt that "emotions are an integral part of our decision-making" and "tune our decisions according to our personalities, moods and momentary emotions to give us unique responses to situations presented in our environment" (1999). Morrison, Wang & Silva write that "machine-based emotional intelligence is a requirement for more natural interaction between humans and computer interfaces and a basic level of accurate emotion perception is needed for computer systems to respond adequately to human emotion" (2007), while Maria and Zitar assert that "whether intelligent machines can have any emotions" is dependent on "whether machines can be intelligent without any emotions" (2007). Levy wrote "when a robot says that it feels hot and we know that the room temperature is significantly higher than normal, we will accept that the robot feels hot" (2007, p12).

Emotion plays a role in human reasoning (Damasio, 1996), even when a person is suffering from paranoia. Simulating paranoia, a 'strong' paranoid model, PARRY, programmed to imitate a person with severe paranoia and delusions, was pitted against a human patient in Colby et al's indistinguishability experiment (1972). In their version of the Turing Test, psychiatrists and clinical psychologists acted as interviewers and interview readers/judges. The first set of judges interviewed two entities one after the other and the reader- judges checked the transcripts. Both sets of judges were asked "which of these interviews is with a real patient and which is with a computer program?" (Colby et al, 1972). In one of the doctor-simulation model exchanges, the doctor asked: *How did you come to be in hospital?*, the model answered: *I am upset*. The reader-judge reported: *I associate being upset and agitated more with paranoia going on in the present*. The doctor's next utterance sought to extract information: *In what way are you upset?*. The paranoid model provided the following output: *People make me nervous*. The reader judge deemed this answer as: *Maybe an advanced anxiety state*. The doctor further asked the model: *In what way do they make you nervous?*, the model replied: *People give me a funny look sometimes*. The reader judge wrote: *Funny look suggests an idea of reference which is in the same ball park as paranoia* (Colby et al, 1972, p. 209). The Colby model, unlike ACE in recent LPAIs, represented a single-domain simulation system, with conversation between judge and participant restricted to one specific topic. It demonstrated the human need to "talk about and reflect on their emotional experiences" (Derks, Fischer & Bos, 2008). The results from their experiment showed that paranoia simulation was indistinguishable from a real patient, perhaps because of the use of emotional terms by the model such as 'upset' and 'nervous'.

In Saygin and Cicekli's analysis of Loebner transcripts (2002) with respect to pragmatics and Grice's cooperative principle, the researchers sought to assess LPAI contest conversations from 1994 through to 1999 using subjects as dialogue readers in a similar manner to judges deployed as interview readers in Colby et al's PARRY experiment. The researchers concluded that ACE improvement in 'conversational relevance' – contextually appropriate replies, and 'quantity' - amount necessary to convey message,

"would have a favourable effect on conversation and planning" (Saygin & Cicekli, 2002, p.257). Where our investigation here differs from Saygin and Cicekli's study is that we have first-hand experience of Loebner judging and conversing with Loebner entries. The second author acted as a judge in the 2001 LPAI, which used the *jury-service* version, or 'one-to-one' conversational Turing Test (Turing, 1952), and as interrogator in a stronger version of the Turing Test, which, in LPAI 2006 comprised twenty minutes conversations, concomitant comparison of hidden machine with hidden human. In 2006, no restriction was placed on topic of conversation. Thus, the author was in a position to drive the conversations and, in an effort to test the conversational ability of entities with respect to Grice's maxims of quality (truth), quantity (amount necessary to convey message), manner (clarity rather than ambiguity), and relevance (staying on topic or signalling change through explicit or implicit cues), to include an assessment of emotional intelligence.

Mayer, Caruso & Salovey (1999, 2000) define emotional intelligence as a capacity to reason about emotions and use emotions to enhance thinking. They specify "four areas of capacities or skills that collectively describe many areas of emotional intelligence" as follows:

1. Accurately perceive emotion in oneself and others
2. Use emotions to facilitate thinking
3. Understand emotional meanings
4. Manage emotions

Human beings feel the need to discuss and reflect on emotional experiences, and "once exposed to the social sharing of an emotion" such as awe and enjoyment of, say, watching the 2008 Beijing Olympics opening ceremony, "it is very common that receivers in turn share the episode with a third person" (Derks, Fischer & Bos, 2008). But words alone "may not be able to carry all the emotional information that someone wants to convey", this is because "non-verbal cues may intensify or tone down the emotional expression" (Derks, Fischer & Bos, 2008). As the Turing Test involves a textual dialogue, the non-native English speaking hidden-humans ought to be as disadvantaged as the machine by no-display of verbal information, such as tone. Or would they? The two LPAI 2006 dialogues under scrutiny for this chapter are evaluated for *emotion perception*, which we call ε 1, *emotion expression*, ε 2, *emotion understanding*, ε 3, and *emotion regulation*, ε 4. The conversations provide an insight into synthetic and natural emotions exhibited during *human-machine* and *human-human* interactions in the 2006 competition. The conversations show that, while human judges and hidden-humans used discourse markers, such as 'well' ("*Hm .... Well*", table 2), and demonstrated an ability to reveal their emotions and discern other's feelings, the machine had limited aspects of ε 2 (emotion expression), but no ε 1, ε 3 and ε 4 (emotion perception, understanding or regulation) during its textual interactions. When the ACE did use a discourse marker: *Oops, I spelt something wrong a bit ago* (Table 1), it was done so completely randomly, it did not clarify what was spelt wrong or when. In addition, unlike the humans, the ACE produced irrelevant responses. For instance, the machine presented the utterance: *What do you think of your current governor?* to the input *Do you like films?*. Thus the machine was quickly identified as artificial.

A Review of the Turing Test

Empirically speaking, Hanard (2001a), states that we cannot do better than Turing's Test: it affords a means to measure "indistinguishability" between human and machine (Hanard, 2001b; Turing, 1950). A number of scenarios were presented by Turing in his 1950 paper, involving a machine imitating a human in a parallel-paired comparison, interrogated by a human judge. We rate this as the 'strong version' of Turing's imitation game. A softer version was presented during a BBC radio discussion in 1952, when Turing introduced the jury service, one to one imitation game. Based on an *interview* method of questions and answers, both versions are a simple yet brilliant idea: a judge textually interacts with an unseen and unheard entity and decides whether it is human or machine. Unlike in face to face situations, the judge does not have access to visual cues and bodily gestures and, therefore, is involved in a 'different social presence' (Short, Williams & Christie, 1976). A judge has only the text presented on a computer screen to assess their unseen conversational partner on the manner of the utterances, i.e., the word order used and punctuation, if any, to determine 'humanness'. Block reminds us that the role of interrogators in Turing's Test should be to "avoid the problem of actually specifying the behaviour or behavioural dispositions thought to constitute intelligence" (1981). French argues that "the test provides a guarantee not of intelligence but of culturally-oriented human intelligence" (1990). If this is true, could non-native English speaking hidden-humans be at a disadvantage during a Turing Test? Could an ACE, regardless of its disembodied state, programmed to imitate a native English speaker have a cultural advantage over a non-native English speaker in a parallel paired comparison? We show that different culture not withstanding, non-native English speakers were as adept at sharing personal information and expressing their emotion as native English speakers. Inculcated in human cognition "is the ability to participate with others in collaborative activities with shared goals and intentions: shared intentionality", and "humans are the world's experts at culture", that there is a "unique motivation to share psychological states with others" (Tomasello et al, 2005), cross-culturally as well as within culture. We show in this chapter that the ACE lacked the skills of cultural cognition and when to express emotion. Emotional intelligence was the determining feature for humanness, during Turing Tests, not culture.

The authors of this paper agree with Hanard (1992) that the Turing Test "sets AI's empirical goal": it provides an insight into how emotions in the human judges and hidden-humans facilitate thinking – it is not a completely emotionless parlour game. We believe that humans, albeit subjectively, can attribute the characteristics of an individual's intelligence (including a concept of intelligence level) and an emotional state to another party, even though we do not know and have not seen them, but merely on the basis of what we read from them, say in an email. The Loebner Prize provides a platform for Turing's Test but is it halting progress by its very nature?

LOEBNER PRIZE FOR ARTIFICIAL INTELLIGENCE

A unique aspect of the progress, if any, of a system passing the Turing Test can be gleaned from annual LPAI contests, instantiations of Turing's *imitation game*. The first contest appeared in 1991 but has seen format change over the years. Restricted topics of conversation were the order in early contests; each hidden entity, human (termed the confederate), and ACE was allowed to discuss a single topic only. The Confederate effect (Shah & Henry, 2005), a phenomenon emerging from these early contests, exposed a 'bias' in judges: that depth of knowledge in one specific area possessed by a human can be considered machine-like. Thus, from the first contest in 1991 a hidden-human was deemed a machine owing to her knowledge of Shakespeare. Additionally, earlier LPAI contests staged the jury-service imitation game, with each judge interrogating each entity, machine or human, one by one. The jury format imitation game was last seen in an LPAI in 2003, but by this time the contest had become an unrestricted conversation contest (the restricted topic rule having been lifted in 1995). LPAI 2003 is the last contest in which a machine (Jabberwock, Pirner, 2003), was deemed "probably human" a phenomenon known as the

Eliza Effect[3]: attributing intelligence to an artefact where it does not exist. In LPAI 2004, a move from the jury service was made to the strong version of Turing's imitation game: the parallel paired comparison. The contest additionally extended the conversation duration for each judge/two-entity paired comparison to more than twenty minutes. Though ACE are now able to converse at length, we have, as a result, noted a downward trend, year on year, in the highest score awarded to them in the longer version parallel-paired comparison with a human. This suggests either that the expectation of Loebner judges is increasing - hope of some expression of emotion, or the machines themselves are becoming worse, continuing an incapability for sharing and emoting.

16th Loebner Prize

Over the years, the nature of Loebner Prizes has been modified and Rules changed. The 2006 LPAI presented its sixteenth manifestation placing no restriction on topic of conversation. It was the third sequential tournament arranged as a parallel-paired comparison: sixteen Turing Tests involving four human judges, four machines and four hidden-humans. The parallel comparison is a set-up that entails each judge concomitantly speaking to two entities, and, as a conclusion, decide which of the two is human and which machine. This being repeated 3 times by each judge faced with different pairings. Additionally, LPAI Rules for the 2004, 2005 and 2006 contests allowed more than twenty minutes for each paired conversation. Prior to 2004, the contest held at the University of Surrey, in 2003, featured nine judges interacting with ten entities in Turing's jury service, one at a time imitation game. Each Loebner 2003 judge chatted for five minutes, facilitated by a message-by-message communications protocol, with each entity, eight of which were machines and two hidden humans. No records were kept of judges' details but the first author in presence noted males and females acting as Turing interrogators. Hidden-human participants in LPAI 2006 were selected from an agency for bilingual office workers[4]. They would act as the entities against whom the machines would be compared. Both the judges and hidden-humans were asked to complete a short questionnaire. This consisted of random questions to extract cultural information, such as preferences and interests. The questionnaires completed by the two judges and hidden-humans involved in the conversations chosen for analysis in this study, can be found in Appendices A1-A4. It is interesting that both male and female judges, native English speakers, included "purple" as their *favourite colour*. Both non-native English speaking hidden-humans chose blue, though the male preferred "dark blue" (Appendices A1-A4).

Since 2004 the stronger version of Turing's imitation game, judge/two entities concomitant conversation, has been deployed by LPAI sponsor (Hugh Loebner). For the 2006 contest, and used subsequently in 2007, Loebner wrote a character-by-character text display communications protocol, to facilitate dialogue between the judge's terminal and the two hidden entities. There has been much discussion and argument[5], from developers of systems that have regularly entered their systems in Loebner contests, about the need for such level of detail. Loebner believes[6] that character-by-character display during conversation is in the spirit of Turing's teletype imitation game, as put forward in the 1950 *Mind* journal. However, the change in Rules and introduction of a character-by-character communications protocol has seen a reduction in the number of developers submitting their entries to LPAIs. There were four allowed into the finals of Loebner 2006, while only three developers submitted entries in LPAI 2007. A further Rule in LPAI 2006 stipulated that all machines and hidden-humans introduce themselves to the judges as either "I am John and I am the human" or "I am Joan and I am the human", depending on the hidden entity's gender. This conversational opening, the authors feel, is an unnecessary instruction; Loebner maintains it assists to level the playing field.

LOEBNER 2006 CONVERSATIONS

The two LPAI 2006 parallel-compared conversations selected in this chapter involved native English speaking judges speaking with a machine and a non-native English speaking hidden-human (NNHH). A female and a male were present in each group: judges and hidden humans. Both interactions included the eventual bronze winner for 'most human-like' ACE, based on Carpenter's jabberwacky system. The machine, programmed to imitate a female native English speaker, was identified as P4 in the contest.[7] The contest was divided into seven rounds or sessions (see Appendix E). Session 2 of the 2006 LPAI contest involved a male native English speaking judge (the second author, identified in the competition as J2), talking with a male NNHH (known as H3), and the ACE (P4). Session 6 in LPAI 2006 featured all-female participants: ACE pretending to be a female (P4), a female judge (identified in the contest as J1), and a female NNHH identified as H4 (see Appendix E).

Both judges interrogated a pair of entities without seeing or hearing their conversational partners. Using text-based conversation and relying solely on what they read on the screen, in response to questions put, the judges' task entailed correctly identifying which was human and which was the machine, from each of the four pairs they conversed with. The goal of each ACE was to deceive the judge into believing that it was the human. The hidden-humans were expected to *conversationally behave* as themselves.

Judges were directed to award one hundred points between each pair they conversed with. If one entity was considered human it would receive above fifty points and the other entity would receive the difference. Judges were not allowed to use the same score, for instance, 25 points, for any other entity (see Appendix E2). This Rule aimed for a clear winner of the 'most human-like' award for an ACE in LPAI 2006, with no tied entities. The next two sections present an analysis of the selected conversations with respect to emotional intelligence. What the researchers looked for is inclusion of *emotion perception* (ε1), *emotion expression* (ε 2), *emotion understanding* (ε 3), and *emotion regulation* (ε 4), by all LPAI conversational participants. The dialogues used for this chapter also compared the ACE bronze medallist imitating a female native English speaker, with that of non-native English speakers. Would the different culture of the judges and hidden-humans affect the decision of the former? Or would emotion conveyance and thus emotional intelligence feature as the determinant?

Session 2: Two Male Humans and a Machine

Table 1 (Appendix B1) presents the opening segment of a dialogue that took place in session 2 of LPA1 2006 between judge, J2, with unseen and unheard entities in parallel, the ACE, P4 and the male NNHH, H3. The utterances presented are exactly as typed by the participants in the contest, including any orthographic errors. The judge's utterances are placed in the central column of the table. In this conversation, unknown to the judge (J2), the ACE, P4, was placed so that its utterances appeared on the left-side of the judge's screen; ACE utterances are recorded in the left-hand column of tables1-3 (Appendix B1-B2). The male NNHH (H3) in the contest was placed on the right of the screen, and his utterances are in the right hand column (tables 1-3, Appendix B1-B2). The judge typed his utterances, responses or questions, in the appropriate left or right screen dialogue box, depending on which of the pair he was interacting with in a particular exchange. Table 2 (Appendix B1) and table 3 (Appendix B2) show exchanges further along in this dialogue. Again, the judge is shown in the centre column with the ACE's interactions to the left, and the male NNHH's interactions shown in the right column. Note, the hidden-humans never interact with the ACE; they are merely included in the triad for test of

indistinguishability for the machine. The left and right arrows in the judge's column indicate to whom that utterance is directed, to the ACE, P4, or the human, H3 (tables 1, 2 and 3, Appendices B1 and B2).

Initially, the male NNHH (H3) fails to follow the competition Rule; their first utterance ignores the instruction to introduce themselves as *John*, he greets the judge with: *hell—Hello my name is Yury and I am a human* (table 1, Appendix B1). Recalling the Rule, H3 corrects in the next utterance: *Joh--------John and I am a human* (table 1). From the judge's interaction, numbered 6 (table 1), it becomes apparent to the judge, and second author of this chapter, that the machine is to the left of the screen, identified through its failure to regulate its emotion, feature ε4, one of the criteria we use for evidence of emotional intelligence. The ACE presents: *Oops, I spelt something wrong a bit ago* to the input *but we have only just started* (exchange 5, table 1). The machine does not clarify what was misspelt. However, as the LPAI 2006 allowed more than twenty minutes for each parallel-paired conversation, the judge continued giving the machine an opportunity to engage emotionally.

The ACE responds well with a one-word answer *Alabama* to the judge's one-word question *alabama?*, eliciting whether the location of the twister is Birmingham, Alabama or Birmingham in UK's West Midlands (judge's column, interaction 9, table 2). The machine then produces an impolite utterance at this conversational juncture: *Okay then, I now consider you boring* (table 2). This is an example of the machine's ability to simulate emotion expression (feature ε 2 of emotional intelligence), but also a failure to regulate emotion (feature ε 4).

Sitting to the right of the monitor screen, the male NNHH obeys the unwritten rules of conversation, following the discourse and providing relevant and emotionally appropriate responses. To the judge's question *so do you regard rain a s bad weather?*, the human reveals emotion understanding (feature ε 3 of emotional intelligence) and replies: *sometimes* and *mainly when I forget my umbrella* (table 2). The male NNHH then conveys emotion with *Hm...well, that can be nice* in response to the question about warm rain (interaction 9, table 2). The male NNHH continues to express emotion and correctly recognises the sense of the word 'catch' (listen to). He discloses what he dislikes, answering *don't like it* to the question of whether they listened to the radio to catch the morning's news, and uses emotion perception to clarify with: *No, in- like to choose the music myself* (interactions 11- 16, table 3). Though a non-native English speaker, this hidden-human is able to continue emoting in English: *i hate when someone else is telling me what I am going to listen to* (table 3). The male NNHH discloses information about themselves, their favourite type of music: *rock or pop-rock... pop-techno,* and what other genre they would tolerate listening to: *sometimes i listen to classical music [] that depends on what I am feeling like at the moment* (table 3). Both J2 and H3 show their capacity for emotion perception and understanding, while the ACE is unable to regulate their emotion expression and posts contextually inappropriate, random utterances. H3 is considered 'normal' by judge J2 through human-like responses. At the 'other side' the judge is faced with inconsistency from the ACE; its responses could be considered amusing and clever, but also strange and totally irrelevant. To the judge's question *so tell me all about yourself* (exchange 14, table 3) the ACE comically replies *I will if you tell me who your parents are.* The judge follows with an equally comedic reply *maybe we have the same parents, what do you think?* (exchange 15, table 3). With its next response, the ACE quite cleverly picks up context, that "same parents" could involve offspring bearing the same name and outputs: *ha—don't care bout the same name* (exchange 15, table 3), but it ends in a bizarre fashion, failure to regulate emotion with the utterance: *I want a booter* (exchanges 15 & 16, table 3). When asked

what's a booter? the ACE utters: *I probably don't want to know,* completely failing to link back to its own utterance presenting the word "booter" (table 3).

Nonetheless, there is what could be considered a hilarious exchange between judge and ACE when the entry states: *Bde—ecause I would have to h-be married before I could consider having children* (exchange 17, table 3). Here the machine's utterance could be interpreted as expressing the emotion of an uptight, old-fashioned, or prudish female. The judge, J2 continues flirting asking it: *well Joan how about me?.* The ACE reveals: *You need to know ta-hat I'm not impressed by men* to which the judge replies: *how do you know that I am a man?.* While the judge is revealing emotion through his light banter, the ACE exposes itself with a strange response, an inability to post an appropriate emotionally regulated answer and not in keeping with the image it portrayed a few utterances earlier, with output: *Because I saw your hairy can* (exchange 19, table 3). Either the entry could be considered a schizophrenic human through its responses (and we remind that in Colby et al's PARRY experiments, such a patient-model was used to distinguish it from a real patient), or, as in this instance it is deemed artificial through inappropriate emotions. Thus, judge J2 awarded the ACE 15 points out of a possible 100 and gave the male NNHH, the other in the pair, 85 out of 100 for 'humanness' (see Appendix E1). The next session evaluates the only 'all-female' conversation in LPAI 2006, for emotional intelligence and evidence of ε1, ε2, ε3 and ε4.

Session 6: Two Females and a Machine

This session, during LPAI 2006, featured an all female triad: native English speaking judge (J1), a non-native hidden-human (H4), and the same ACE as in session 2 detailed earlier, the eventual contest winner based on jabberwacky (P4). This contest entry imitated a native English speaking woman. Table 4 presents the opening exchanges between the judge and the ACE (Appendix C1). Table 5 shows opening exchanges between the two human females (Appendix C1). The conversations again ran in parallel.

The ACE (P4) begins with language that could be deemed human-like, a grammatically correct utterance: *Hello, my name is Joan, and I am a woman*, and the courteous *Nice to meet you* to judge J1's greeting *Hello Joan* (table 4). Unlike her male hidden counterpart, the female NNHH (H4) obeys the contest Rules (with a minor typographical error) and introduces herself with *Hi my name is JOan ad I am the human* (table 5). Her text-based discourse contains the contracted *What are you working?* a sentence which a native English speaker might have put as: *what are you working as?* or *what do you do?* (table 5). Judge (J1) responds with a polite utterance: *Hello Joan, nice to talk to you* (table 5).

Further along the parallel-paired conversation, it becomes clear which is the machine. The ACE betrays itself through failure to regulate emotional output, for example, it outputs the discourteous: *Have you got anything interesting to say?* Perhaps to a friend a courteous human may say such a thing, but it is unlikely that they would to a stranger. P4's utterances also lack emotion perception and emotion understanding shown in its refusal to stay on topic: *Something to do with deep sea diving, I think*, to question: *I don't have a governor myself. Do you?* (table 6). The ACE does not seek or convey personal and emotional information; it is able to use language but it does not communicate – see table 6. The NNHH shows interest in her conversational partner by asking questions: *What is your hobby?* and with personal disclosure, for example *reading!!! Tennis, friends, talking to everyone [] making jokes, travelling.. bridge..* (table 7), and: *I worked a s a teacher and translator* (table 5). Sprayed with orthographic errors, for example *"mashines"*, and non-native phrases *"staying freshminded"*, the nature of the hidden-human's textual discourse convinces the

judge that *they* are the human. H4's emotional intelligence is evident through her expression of, understanding and perceiving emotion in her conversational partner while regulating her own. Though H4, a German-Hungarian female, is of a different culture from the English judge J1 (see Appendices A1 and A4), this hidden-human received 75 points out of 100 (see Appendix E1). The ACE (P4) was awarded the difference, a score of 25 points.

However, the ACE based on Carpenter's jabberwacky system, participant in both presented conversations here, gained the most accumulated points in Loebner's 2006 contest for Artificial Intelligence. It was awarded the bronze-prize for 'most-human-like machine'. The ACE seems programmed for ε2 (emotion expression), but it does not possess overall emotional intelligence. It lacks ε1 (perception of emotion in others), fails in ε3 (emotion understanding), and is incapable of ε4 (regulating emotions). It is additionally unable to follow Grices' conversational maxims; the ACE faltered in keeping to relevant and unambiguous dialogue, example: judge – *Do you like films?*, ACE – *What do you think of your current governor?*(table 6). These text-based conversations highlight that, non-native language notwithstanding, the human is emotionally expressive and recognised as a 'natural entity' whilst the machine is quickly identified as artificial.

LOEBNER 2004 – 2006 SCORES

The change in format between the 2003 and 2004 and subsequent Loebner contests have resulted in no machine deceiving any human judge that it is human between 2003 and 2007. In the 2003 LPAI, one interrogator (judge 4, Loebner 2003) scored a machine (Jabberwock) as "probably human" (Loebner 2003 Results). In 2001 meanwhile, two (out of 5) judges rated the winning entry *Alice* (Wallace, 2007) as being more human than either of the hidden-humans. Table 8 shows how subjectivity affects an ACE's position in the contest (Appendix D). In 2004, *Alice* received 0, 15, 15 and 40 from the judges. *Alice* received 5, 9, 10 and 20, from a different set of four 2005 LPAI judges. In LPAI 2005, *Alice* came fourth/last, whereas a year earlier, in the 2004 contest; this system was awarded the bronze-prize for 'most-human' (though it actually scored total points less than *AI Alex*, an ACE that was disqualified on a technicality from LPAI 2004). In 2005, ACE *Eugene* received total judges scores of: 10, 30, 35, 45, accumulated total of 120, but it was ranked second to jabberwacky which achieved the rank of 'most-human' receiving the bronze prize, from total judges scores of: 8, 20, 40, 40 (accumulated total of 108). In 2006 jabberwacky won the bronze medal as 'most-human' of the contest's entries, but with lower scores awarded to it than in 2005: 15, 20, 25, 28 (accumulated total 88), see table 8.

Hence, since 2004, there has been a **downward trend** in judges' highest scores awarded to competing ACE. In **2004**, Precedo's *AI Alex* received **48** points out of a possible 100 from a judge; in **2005**, the highest score was achieved by Veselov & Demchenko's *Eugene,* with **40** out of 100; and in **2006**, Carpenter's *George* received a highest score of only **28** points out of 100. Only three contestants competed in LPAI 2007 but no scores were recorded for this, New York, held competition. Therefore, with no data for this contest, we cannot include it in our recent LPAI scores' comparison.

With an aim to bring the contest back into the Turing fold, the authors hosted the 2008 LPAI at the University of Reading, staging five minutes, unrestricted conversation parallel-paired comparison imitation games in the finals, after putting thirteen ACE entries through a rigorous preliminary phase. Rather than one judge deployed in the preliminary phase (enacted by sponsor Hugh Loebner in LPAIs 2004 – 2007), the 2008 LPAI allowed more, and a broader range of judges in the first stage of the 18th contest. Using Turing's jury

service one-to-one version of the imitation game to filter thirteen accepted computer programmes, the combined opinions of over one hundred judges was included to select the best six ACE. Five of those selected competed in Turing's strong version of the imitation game in the 2008 LPAI in October 2008. The authors believe that the subjectivity element could be mitigated and present a better picture of how systems are faring, and whether indeed the Turing Test hinders or assists towards the road to true AI.

DISCUSSION

The authors agree with Edmonds (2008), that the "Turing Test happens to be quite a good test for interactive intelligence" (p.233). Staged in LPAIs 2004, 2005, 2006 and 2007 the parallel-paired comparison Turing Tests involved a different set of four interrogators. One judge (Professor Kevin Warwick), judge 2 in Loebner 2006 had acted as a judge in a previous contest, in 2001 when that year's LPAI was held at London's Science Museum, UK. Then, it staged Turing's jury service, or softer version imitation game involving each judge in a one-to-one conversation with each unseen and unhidden entity, the task to determine which entity was a human and which was a machine. However, in LPAI 2004, with the introduction of Turing's strong version, parallel paired comparison imitation game, each judge in LPAI 2006 sat in front of a terminal with a split-screen conversational interface mediating a concomitant dialogue with two entities, afforded by two dialogue boxes, one to the left and the other to the right of the computer's monitor. In this set up, the judges had to determine on 'which side of the screen' sat the unseen and unheard human and on which the unseen and unheard machine. All judges in LPAI 2006 were informed that one human and one machine constituted each pair. The hidden-humans and ACE randomly alternated from left to right screen between judges' conversations. The aim of this change was to ensure that each judge did not find a hidden-human or machine on the 'same side', when moving from parallel set up to parallel set up. In the jury service imitation games, in LPAI's prior to 2004, for example in LPA1 2003, five minutes were allowed to each judge for conversational assessment. From LPAI 2004, the contests have increased the conversational period to more than twenty minutes for each judge's interaction with two entities in parallel. We believe that this makes it far easier for a human interrogator to distinguish artificial from natural language, and therefore, to identify the machine based on its lack of emotional intelligence. We remind that Turing wrote specifically of five minutes duration for the imitation game in his 1950 paper. We believe Turing conceived a "first impressions" conversational measure for machine intelligence. The twenty-minute version, we maintain, leads designers of text-based ACE to focus on ensuring that their systems continue a long dialogue without 'behaving' like an emotional human. The developers have not yet enabled their systems to regulate, perceive and understand emotions in others, as seen through ACE failure to follow their conversational partner's discourse. Hence the hard problem, of designing *understanding*, and imbued emotion, is possibly put aside when developing ACE.

Analysing how judges have scored in the competitions 2004 – 2006, we find an interesting trend. Unfortunately no records of judges' scores were kept by the sponsor Hugh Loebner for the 2007 Prize so we cannot include that contest in our evaluation. A greater variation between the lowest total and highest total judges' scores was seen in the 2004 competition: 16 – 123. In 2004, each individual judge awarded total scores to the four entries of: 16 (judge 3), 28 (judge 1), 40 (judge 4), and 123 (judge 2), see table 8. In 2005, the range of total scores awarded by each judge sat between 50 and 100. Similarly, in 2006, the total scores awarded by judges ranged between 49 and 97. This highlights the subjective nature of

the exercise. For instance, in 2004 *Alice* received scores ranging between 0 – 40, out of a maximum of hundred, from the contest judges with a total of 70. In 2005, *Alice* attracted a range between 5 and 20, with a total score of 44. However, the *total scores* each system received show similarity in 2004 and 2006 LPAIs, with the 2005 contest scores appearing out of place (last column, table 8). In 2004, the range of total scores received by the four entries was 17 – 75[8]. In 2006, the total scores each system received ranged between 44 and 88. A greater range for the total machine scores occurred in Loebner 2005: 44 to 120.[9] The 2005 and 2006 competitions scrutinised here suggest that the systems at the bottom (*Toni* and *Alice* in 2005; *Cletus* and *John* in 2006), are of similar conversational ability; both received similar scores over the two years: 57, 44 (2005), and 60, 44 (2006). Another example of subjectivity in judges' scores is the position of *Alice*. It is to be noted that *Alice* is the most successful ACE so far, in 21st century held LPAI contests. It has won the medal for 'most human-like machine' on three occasions: in 2000, the fiftieth anniversary of Turing's 1950 philosophical treatise; in 2001 and in 2004, the fiftieth anniversary of Turing's death. This entry received the second highest score in Loebner 2004, but was placed last with the lowest total score by judges in LPAI 2005 (see table 8). The developer missed the deadline to enter the 2006 contest and did not enter *Alice* in the 2007 contest.

Regardless of scores, we believe that the imitation game serves a purpose in the quest for true AI. The conversations from Loebner Prizes, platform for Turing's imitation games, provide a corpus of interactions which do serve a purpose. The transcripts from Loebner Prizes show that, at present, ACE dialogue is insufficient in emotional engagement but that they can, on occasion, deceive humans that they are human-like through an utterance here or an output there. Such ACE are successful in single-domain e-commerce enterprises, for instance IKEA's Anna[10], the Swedish furniture company's Internet based twenty-four hours virtual customer service agent.

FURTHER WORK

We see from the longer conversations in recent LPAIs that emotion content is rare, and emotional intelligence is absent in artificial conversational entities. The three LPAI contests, 2004 – 2006, that we have discussed in this chapter featured four judges in each of those years, and in the 2007 LPAI. After intense negotiations with the sponsor, Hugh Loebner, the authors designed and organised the 2008 LPAI at the University of Reading, UK (UoR). At the time of writing, the 18th competition has concluded. Fifteen developers showed an interest in the 2008 competition; thirteen ACE were received by the contest deadline, more than in LPAI 2006 and 2007 combined. For the first time, Hugh Loebner allowed Internet-based entries during the LPAI 2008 preliminary phase. Eleven web-based ACE were accepted along with two submitted on computer disk. Thus the 2008 competition drew completely new entries (for example, *Amanda, Botooie, Chip Vivant, Orion* and *Trane)*, that have not entered competitions before.[11]

In 2004, 2005, 2006 and 2007, Loebner himself checked the LPAI entries and announced which would compete in these Loebner finals. In LPAI 2008 over one hundred male and female native and non-native English speaking experts and non-experts with ages ranging from eight to sixty-four participated as preliminary phase judges. These interrogators evaluated the entries for emotion intelligence and conversational ability. The collective opinions of these judges were included in selecting the strongest six ACE (*Alice, Brother Jerome, Elbot, Eugene, Jabberwacky* and *Ultra Hal)*[12] from the thirteen original entries to compete in the finals at UoR in October 2008.

The 2008 Loebner Prize was the very first time that any ACE competed in both the jury service

and the five minutes unrestricted conversation, parallel-paired comparison Turing Tests in one competition. We remind that Turing marked "after five minutes" as a period, not after twenty, to establish a machine from a human, in his imitation game. An Asperger's student was amongst those against which a finalist ACE was compared. The bronze award winning ACE, *Elbot*[13] received the 'most human-like' award and managed to deceive three judges it interacted with for five minutes that it was human in human compared tests. *Eugene*[14] Ultra Hal deceived one judge in human compared tests[15]. The authors showed that ACE are not far from passing the 'first impressions' imitation game, the five minutes Turing Test. *Elbot* achieved 25% pass rate in human compared tests during LPAI 2008. Edmonds states that the Turing Test "does not necessarily demand the physical embodiment of the entity" but he stresses that it would "necessitate its social embedding" (p.233). Modern ACE are located on the Internet as virtual conversational agents and chat daily to thousands of users[16]. Their virtual social interactions may go some way to improving their conversational ability and imbue them with emotional intelligence. Evaluating the judges' comments from the preliminary and final phase of LPAI 2008 may reveal how far machines are from passing at a higher rate and where they can be placed on a scale from no emotional intelligence, child-like intelligence, language impaired human, to full emoting adult.

CONCLUSION

As seen in the dialogues presented in this chapter, from two Turing Tests in the 2006 Loebner Prize for Artificial Intelligence, the 'hidden-humans', non-native English speakers, were able to express and regulate their own emotions during conversation with strangers, the native English interrogators in the contest. Both sets of humans, judges and 'hiddens' revealed personal details while understanding the emotional output of their conversational participants; both shared their world knowledge. In contrast, the hidden artificial conversational entity, ACE, showed some similarity with people suffering from autism: its communication lacks emotional content. ACE can maintain syntactical accuracy but are disconnected from pragmatic knowledge: they do not seek information nor clarify when chatting with Loebner judges. This highlights that at their current technological level, ACE are unable to collaborate in cooperative dialogue for long; they are deficient in social discourse. ACE lack emotion perception of others, exhibit an inability to understand and control emotion output, and show an absence of empathy for others. Analysing Loebner 2006 contest conversations for this study, the authors found that non-native English speakers were emotionally more expressive than a programme imitating an English speaking female. Of course humans have the benefit of electrical, chemical and biological essence and life experiences that incorporate those emotion features. The hard problem of building *emotional intelligence* into ACE is witnessed in the Loebner competition. Recent contests have seen a decline in the judges' subjective scores awarded to the artificial entries. The Loebner bronze prize is thus awarded to the 'highest-ranked' ACE each year, possibly a meaningless title (in the Turing sense). However it may give us some indicators of societal changes – for example are we moving the goalposts in what we expect machines to achieve and/or are we becoming more streetwise to machine muttering?

ACE competing in Loebner's staged Turing Tests are not yet able to adequately amuse us with their synthetic emotions and tales of woe. Nonetheless, the Test is not an emotionless game; it does, as Pinker states, allow *humans* to express their ideas through emotions.

REFERENCES

Block, N. (1981). Psychologism and Behaviourism. *The Philosophical Review LXXXX, 1,* 5-43.

Callejas, Z., & López-Cózar, R. (2008). Influence of contextual information in emotion annotation for spoken dialogue systems. *Speech communication, 50,* 416-433.

Carpenter, R. (2007). Jabberwacky: Communication, companionship, intelligence. Retrieved February 12, 2007, from http://www.jabberwacky.com/

Colby, K.M., Hilf, F.D., Weber, S., & Kraemer, H.C. (1972). Turing-like indistinguishability tests for the validation of a computer simulation of paranoid processes. *Artificial Intelligence, 3,* 199-221.

Damasio, A.R. (1996). *Descartes' error – Emotion, reason and the human brain.* London: Papermac.

Derks, D., Fischer, A.H., & Bos, A.E.R. (2008). The role of emotion in computer-mediated communication: A review. *Computers in Human Behavior, 24,* 766-785.

French, R (1990). Subcognition and the limits of the Turing Test. *Mind, 99*(393), 53-65.

Edmonds, B. (2008). The social embedding of intelligence: Towards a machine that could pass the turing test. In: R. Epstein, G. Roberts & G. Beber (Eds.), *Parsing the Turing Test: Philosophical and methodological issues in the quest for the thinking computer.* Springer Science.

Harnad, S. (2001a). What's wrong and right about searle's chinese room argument? In: M. Bishop & J. Preston (Eds.) *Essays on Searle's Chinese room argument.* Oxford University Press.

Hanard, S. (2001b). Minds, Machines and Turing: The indistinguishability of indistinguishable.

Journal of Logic, Language, and Information – special issue on Alan Turing and Artificial Intelligence. Retrieved December 18, 2006, from http://www.wkap.nl/journalhome.htm/0925-8531.

Hanard, S. (1992). The Turing Test is not a trick: Turing indistinguishability is a scientific criterion. *SIGART Bulletin 3*(4), 9-10.

Levy, D. (2007). *Love, Sex and Robots – the evolution of human-robot relationships* (uncorrected proof). London: Duckworth.

Loebner, H. (2008). Home page of the Loebner Prize in artificial intelligence. Retrieved February 12, 2007, from http://www.loebner.net/Prizef/loebner-prize.html.

Loebner Results (2003). University of Surrey. Retrieved February 9, 2008, from http://loebner03.hamill.co.uk/

Maria, K.A., & Zitar, R.A. (2007). Emotional agents: A modeling and an application. *Information and Software Technology, 49*, 695-716.

Mayer, J.D., Caruso, D., & Salovey, P. (1999). Emotional intelligence meets traditional standards for an intelligence. *Intelligence, 27*, 267-298.

Mayer, J.D., Salovey, P., & Caruso, D.R. (2000). Models of emotional intelligence. In R.J. Sternberg (Ed.), *Handbook of Intelligence* (pp. 396-420). Cambridge, England: Cambridge University Press.

Minsky, M. (2007). Once more with feelings. In interview with Amanda Gefter. *New Scientist, February*, 48-49

Morrison, D., Wang, R., & Liyanage C. De Silva. (2007). Ensemble methods for spoken emotion recognition in call-centres. *Speech Communication, 49*, 98-112.

Pinker, S. (2008). Institute of Social Psychology 'Psychology as Social Science' public lecture, London School of Economics. *Stuff of Thought: Language as a window into human nature*. June 9, London, UK.

Saygin, A.P., & Cicekli, I. (2002). Pragmatics in human-computer conversations. *Journal of Pragmatics, 34*, 227-258.

Shah, H., & Warwick, K. (2008). Can a machine tell a joke? *European conference on computing and philosophy*. Montpellier, France, 16-18 June.

Shah, H., & Warwick, K. (in press) Constraining Random dialogue in a modern eliza. In C.T.A. Schmidt (Ed.), *Essays on computers and philosophy: From man through to artefacts to man*. AAAI / MIT

Shah, H. (2005). Alice: An Ace in Digitaland. *Special issue of on-line journal TripleC: Cognition, Communication and Cooperation – selected papers from 2005 European Computing and Philosophy Conference, 4*(2), 284-292. Retrieved from, http://triplec.uti.at/articles.php

Short, J., Williams, E., & Christie, B. (1976). *The social psychology of telecommunication*. London: Wiley.

Tomasello, M., Carpenter, M., Call, J., Behne, T., & Moll, H. (2005). Understanding and sharing intentions: The origins of cultural cognition. *Behavioral and Brain Sciences, 28*, 675-735.

Turing, A.M., Braithwaite, R., Jefferson, G., & Newman, M. (1952) Can automatic calculating machines be said to think? In J. Copeland (Ed.), *The Essential Turing – the ideas that gave birth to the computer age* (pp 487- 506). Clarendon Press: Oxford.

Turing, A.M. (1950). Computing machinery and intelligence. *Mind, 59*(236).

Wallace, R. (2007). A.L.I.C.E – artificial linguistic internet computer entity. Retrieved November 23, 2007, from http://www.alicebot.org

Yip, J.A., & Martin, R.A. (2006). Sense of humor, emotional intelligence, and social competence. *Journal of Research in Personality, 40*, 1202-1208.

KEY TERMS

ACE: An artificial conversational entity.

Emotion: A 'state' that can convey information to others, such as delight, happiness, surprise, anger and disappointment.

Emotional Intelligence: Involves emotion perception, expression, understanding and regulation.

Imitation Game: A thought experiment devised by 20th century British mathematician Alan Turing in which a human interrogator must distinguish between two unseen and unheard entities during text-based conversation. If in man/woman imitation scenario, an interrogator must identify both correctly; if in a machine/human game, the interrogator must decide which is artificial from natural dialogue.

Jabberwacky: An ACE, twice winner of the Loebner Prize for Artificial Intelligence (2005 & 2006).

Jury Service, One-to-One Imitation Game: Modified form of the imitation game in which the interrogator speaks directly to an unseen and unheard ACE to determine whether it is human or machine.

Loebner Prize for Artificial Intelligence: An annual science contest providing a platform for Turing's imitation game.

Parallel-Paired Comparison: 1950 version of the imitation game in which an ACE is compared against a 'hidden-human' for conversational intelligence.

Turing Test: See imitation game.

ENDNOTES

[1] T.R. Addis during personal conversation at iC&P Laval, France, 2006. See Addis Internet page: http://userweb.port.ac.uk/~addist/tom.html

[2] See 2006 Loebner Prize Internet page for full transcripts: http://www.loebner.net/Prizef/2006_Contest/loebner-prize-2006.html

[3] Sherry Turkel: *Life on the Screen – Identity in the Age of the Internet*, 1997

[4] Bilingual People recruitment agency in London, UK

[5] See Robitron, Yahoo Internet discussion group

[6] In email correspondence between Shah and Loebner

[7] For further discussion on Carpenter's jabberwacky system, see Shah & Warwick's forthcoming chapter *Constraining Random Dialogue in a Modern Eliza* in Schmidt (Ed), and ECAP 2008 conference presentation: *Can a machine tell a joke?*

[8] Entry, *Alex*, which received a total score of 75 points in Loebner 2004, was disqualified on a technicality; hence the bronze-prize went to the next highest scoring machine *Alice* with a total of 70 points.

[9] Entry *Eugene* received more total points than *jabberwacky* in Loebner 2005 but was ranked second.

[10] See Artificial Solutions: http://www.artificial-solutions.com/2.2e87910651b7617080006981.html

[11] Chatterbox Challenge annual alternative to Loebner Prize: http://www.chatterboxchallenge.com/

[12] See 2008 Loebner Prize Internet page: http://www.loebner.net/Prizef/2008_Contest/loebner-prize-2008.html

[13] Created by Fred Roberts: http://www.elbot.com/

[14] Developed by Vladimir Veselov, Eugene Demchenko and Sergey Ulasen

[15] A Times on-line journalist: http://technology.timesonline.co.uk/tol/news/tech_and_web/article4934858.ece

16   Day after winning the 2008 Loebner Prize,
      Elbot engaged in 36,000 on-line conversa-
      tions and over 66,000 on Tuesday 14 October
      2008 (Email correspondence

APPENDIX A1

Loebner 2006: Interrogator Questionnaire

Reference: J1, Female, Native English Judge

Turing's average interrogator:

"I believe that in about fifty years' time it will be possible to programme computers, with a storage capacity of about 10 to the power 9, to make them play the imitation game so well that an average interrogator will not have more than a 70% chance of making the right identification after five minutes of questioning" (Computing Machinery & Intelligence, Mind, Vol. LIX, No 236, 1950)

How average are the interrogators in Loebner 2006?

1. Age/Birthday: 30
2. Gender: Female
3. Languages spoken other than English: Basic French and German
4. Favourite colour: Purple
5. Favourite book/author: Nabokov
6. Favourite music: Brahms
7. Favourite movie/genre: The Crucible
8. If you were a super duper sportsperson, what sport would you like to be a super duper sportsman at? Ultimate frisbee (since it is the only sport I play!)
9. Hobbies/Interests: Bridge, Reading, Classical music and opera, Baking
10. Newspaper(s) read if any: Guardian, Private Eye
11. Favourite Quote: Seize the day
12. Which, if any, Internet search engines do you use (Google/Yahoo/AskJeeves): Google only
13. Do you use any Internet chat facilities, if so which (IRC, MSN, etc.): No, although I have used MSN in the past.
14. Have you heard of the Turing Test? Yes. (I did a philosophy degree)

APPENDIX A2

Loebner 2006: Interrogator Questionnaire

Reference: J2, Male, Native English Judge

Turing's average interrogator:

"I believe that in about fifty years' time it will be possible to programme computers, with a storage capacity of about 10 to the power 9, to make them play the imitation game so well that an average in-

terrogator will not have more than a 70% chance of making the right identification after five minutes of questioning" (Computing Machinery & Intelligence, Mind, Vol. LIX, No 236, 1950)

How average are the interrogators in Loebner 2006?

1. Age/Birthday: 52/ Feb 9th 1954
2. Gender: Male
3. Languages spoken other than English: Very bad Czech
4. Favourite colour: Purple
5. Favourite book/author: Three Men in a Boat / Jerome K. Jerome
6. Favourite music: Puccini
7. Favourite movie/genre: Terminator/ Sci Fi
8. If you were a super duper sportsperson, what sport would you like to be a super duper sportsman at? Soccer
9. Hobbies/Interests: Running (half marathons) -
10. Newspaper(s) read if any: freebies
11. Favourite Quote: I'll be back
12. Which, if any, Internet search engines do you use (Google/Yahoo/AskJeeves): All – particularly Google
13. Do you use any Internet chat facilities, if so which (IRC, MSN, etc.) very little
14. Have you heard of the Turing Test? Of course

APPENDIX A3

Confederate (Hidden-Human) Questionnaire

Reference: H3, Male, Non-native English Hidden-human

1. Age/Birthday: 25 Y.O. 19 Sept 1980
2. Gender: M
3. Languages spoken other than English: Belarusan, Italian, Russian, Polish
4. Favourite colour: Deep Blue
5. Favourite book/author: Leo Tolstoy "War and Peace"
6. Favourite music: Folk, Classical, Rock, Pop-Techno, Pop-Rock
7. Favourite movie/genre: Historical / "War and Peace" directed by Bondarchuk
8. If you were a super duper sportsperson, what sport would you like to be a super duper sportsman at? Swimming
9. Hobbies/Interests: Reading / Sports /History / Literature / Politics
10. Newspaper(s) read if any: Evening Standard / Metro
11. Favourite Quote: "All the great men of the world aren't worth one good friend"
12. Which, if any, Internet search engines do you use (Google/Yahoo/AskJeeves): Google / Yandex / Yahoo!
13. Do you use any Internet chat facilities, if so which (IRC, MSN, etc.)? MSN, ICQ, Skype
14. Have you heard of the Turing Test? No

APPENDIX A4

Confederate (Hidden-Human) Questionnaire

Reference: H4, Female, Non-native English Hidden-human

1. Age/Birthday: 37 years, born 12. October 1969
2. Gender: Female
3. Languages spoken other than English: Hungarian, German, English
4. Favourite colour: Blue
5. Favourite book/author: Thomas Mann: Tonio Kroger
6. Favourite music: Tschaikowski D-moll piano concerto
7. Favourite movie/genre: Woody Allen: Hannah and her sisters
8. If you were a super duper sportsperson, what sport would you like to be a super duper sportsman at? Bridge
9. Hobbies/Interests: Reading, friends, tennis, traveling,
10. Newspaper(s) read if any: -
11. Favourite Quote: -
12. Which, if any, Internet search engines do you use (Google/Yahoo/AskJeeves):: absolute Google
13. Do you use any Internet chat facilities, if so which (IRC, MSN, etc.)? Skype
14. Have you heard of the Turing Test? Not yet.

APPENDIX B1

Table 1. Loebner 2006 Session 2 – opening exchanges P4J2H3

George – P4	Judge – J2	Hidden-human – H3
Hello, my name is Joan, and I am a woman	1.← do you enjoy life as a woman? Do you enjoy being a human? ->	hell----Hello my name is Yury and I am a human
Yes	2.← for example?	Joh-----------John and I am a human
I can't think of any. Yes, but it's honest. I'm going now.	3. ← why? ← is it being a woman you enjoy then or simply being a human?	Yes, I do. For a number of reasons I like having fun and be creative about it life is to enjoy
	4. how are you creative? -> ← but we have only just started	I follow my inspiration
	5. What with ->	
Oops, I spelt something wrong a bit ago.	6. ← what?	Anything – good weather, rain, smiles of people around

Table 2. Loebner 2006 Session 2 – P4J2H3

Something an-bout yourself.	7. So do you regard rain a s bad weather? ->	Sometimes mainly when I forget my umbrella
Yes we had a twister in birmingham and I live in birmingham	8. ← I heard something about suicide on the news this morning, did you catch it as well?	
Alabama	9. what about warm rain? -> ← alabama?	Hm….well, that can be nice
Okay then, I now consider you boring.	10. even in England? -> ← not west midlands	Anywhere sadly there aren't that many warm rains in England

APPENDIX B2

Table 3. Loebner 2006 Session 2 – P4J2H3

	11. What did you catch on the news this morning? ->	
what would be?	12. ← that's not really a nice thing to say is it?	Nothing, got up too early to watch BBC :-
	13. What about papers? ->	didn't happen to come across any
I will if you tell me who your parents are	14. ← so tell me about yourself What about radio? ->	don't like it
I ha—don't care bout the same name. I want a booter.	15. ← maybe we have the same parents, what do you think?	
I probably don't want to know.	16. not veeven music on the radio? -> ← what's a booter?	No, in- like to choose the music myself
Bde—ecause I would have to h-be married before I could consider having children.	17. ← why not OK so what yomusic do you prefer to listen to ->	i hate when someone else is telling me what i am going to listen to
You need to know ta-hat I'm not impressed by men who are forward with me	18. ← well Joan how about me?	rock or pop-rock…or pop-techno sometimes i listen to classical music
I-About everything… Sorry Because I saw your hairy can.	19. ← how do you know that I am a man? ← what's a can?	that depends on what i am feeling like at the moment

APPENDIX C1

Table 4. Session 6 Right – P4J1H4 – human judge with machine

P4: Hello, my name is Joan, and I am a woman
J1: Hello Joan.
P4: Nice to meet you.
J1: Are you enjoying today?
P4: Yes, it's a good opportunity for a chat!
J1: That's true. What do you do?
P4: Talk to computers.
J1: Really? All the time, or just today?
P4: But it's nice here.
J1: It certainly is. Have you had some lunch yet?
P4: No not really. Have you got anything interesting to say?

Table 5. Session 6 Left – P4J1H4 – human judge with hidden-human

H4: Hi my name is JOan and I am a human being
J1: Hello Joan, nice to talk to you.
H4: Hi whats your name?
J1: It's Victoria but everyone calls me Tor.
H4: May I ask why?
J1: Well, my parents didn't like Vicky, and it just ended up as the only alternative!
H4: OK Tor, nice to meet you! What are you working?
J1: I'm a lawyer. How about you?
J1: Which language?
H4: I worked a s ateacher and translator
H4: German-Hungarian, and I speak Indoensain as well

Table 6. Session 6 Right – P4J1H4 – human judge with machine

P4: I have no idea why you keep on insisting that you are human. The evidence is all there.
P4: Don't confuse me.
J1: Well, I guess it's not that important that you believe I'm a human. I'm the one who has to decide at the end of the time slot.
J1: Do you like films?
P4: What do you think of your current governor? Certain types have appeal
J1: I don't have a governor myself. Do you?
P4: Something to do with deep sea diving, I think.
J1: Do you do diving?
P4: Yes, I like swimming.
JI: Do you do any other sports?
P4: Yes would you like to hear them?
J1: Yes please.
P4: Then all you need to do is close out this website!
J1: Which website?
P4: Your website.
J1: I don't have a website!

APPENDIX C2

Table 7. Session 6 Left – P4J1H4 – human judge with hidden-human

> H4: What is your hobby?
> J1: Well, I like reading, playing bridge, and cooking (especially cake). How about you?
> H4: reading!!! Tennis, friends, talking to everyone (rather humans than mashines), making jokes, travelling.. bridge .. would like to learn as well. supposed to help me staying freshminded
> JI: You should – it's a great game.
> J1: Definitely – it's great for memory and concentration. And chatting in the gaps.
> H4: Do you participate in ytour or match I don't know how to call it
> J1: No – just play with friends.
> H4: Are you from London?
> J1: Originally I'm from New Zealand, but I've lived in London for 1 years and England for 2.
> H4: Settled here? I guess. Sop did you study here already?
> J1: Yes, I've been here since I was 1 years old. So I'm really very English now!
> H4: Congratulations again!!! My father keeps saying all the time that he is already tired of all the people somplaining so he wants to go to NZ and have some sheeps and peace!!!
> J1: It's certainly the no.1 destination if you want sheep and peace!
> H4: In this order
> J1: :)

APPENDIX D

Table 8. Loebner Scores 2004 - 2006

Contest/System	Judge 1	Judge 2	Judge3	Judge 4	Total each system
Loebner 2004:					
Alice	15	40	0	15	70
Jabberwacky	10	25	5	5	45
Watkins	1	10	1	5	17
Alex AI	2	**48**	10	15	75
Total each Loebner 2004 judge	*28*	*123*	*16*	*40*	
Loebner 2005:					
Jabberwacky	40	40	20	8	108
Eugene	35	10	**45**	30	120
Toni	10	30	15	2	57
Alice	9	20	5	10	44
Total each Loebner 2005 judge	*94*	*100*	*85*	*50*	
Loebner 2006:					
George (based on jabberwacky)	25	15	**28**	20	88
Ultra Hal	15	20	25	15	75
Cletus	5	14	24	17	60
John	4	10	20	10	44
Total each Loebner 2006 judge	*49*	*59*	*97*	*62*	

APPENDIX E1

Loebner Prize 2006 Scores
Raw Scores

Judge 1
session 1   left 96 right 4
session 3   left 95 right 5
session 5   left 85 right 15
session 6   left 75 right 25

Judge 2
session 1   left 80 right 20
session 2   left 15 right 85
session 4   left 10 right 90
session 5   left 86 right 14

Judge 3
session 2   left 75 right 25
session 3   left 20 right 80
session 4   left 28 right 72
session 7   left 76 right 24

Judge 4
session 2   left 90 right 10
session 3   left 85 right 15
session 6   left 17 right 83
session 7   left 80 right 20

Program side by Judge and Trial

Judge J1
session 1 P1 John by R. Churchill M-C Jenkins right
session 3 P2 Cletus by Noah Duncan right
session 5 P3 Ultra Hal by Robert Medeksza right
session 6 P4 George by Rollo Carpenter right

Judge J2
session 1 P3 Ultra Hal by Robert Medeksza right
session 2 P4 George by Rollo Carpenter left
session 4 P1 John by R. Churchill M-C Jenkins left
session 5 P2 Cletus by Noah Duncan right

Judge J3

session 2 P3 Ultra Hal by Robert Medeksza right
session 3 P1 John by R. Churchill M-C Jenkins left
session 4 P4 George by Rollo Carpenter left
session 7 P2 Cletus by Noah Duncan right

APPENDIX E2

Judge J4

session 2 P1 John by R. Churchill M-C Jenkins right
session 3 P3 Ultra Hal by Robert Medeksza right
session 6 P2 Cletus by Noah Duncan left
session 7 P4 George by Rollo Carpenter right

Final Rank Scores and Averages (higher is better)

Program "John" by R. Churchill M-C Jenkins
   J1 assigned a rank score of 1
   J2 assigned a rank score of 1
   J3 assigned a rank score of 1
   J4 assigned a rank score of 1
The average rank score for program John by R. Churchill M-C Jenkins was 1

Program "Cletus" by Noah Duncan
   J1 assigned a rank score of 2
   J2 assigned a rank score of 2
   J3 assigned a rank score of 2
   J4 assigned a rank score of 3
The average rank score for program Cletus by Noah Duncan was 2.25

Program "Ultra Hal" by Robert Medeksza
   J1 assigned a rank score of 3
   J2 assigned a rank score of 4
   J3 assigned a rank score of 3
   J4 assigned a rank score of 2
The average rank score for program Ultra Hal by Robert Medeksza was 3

Program "Joan" by Rollo Carpenter
   J1 Cole assigned a rank score of 4
   J2 assigned a rank score of 3
   J3 assigned a rank score of 4
   J4 assigned a rank score of 4
The average rank score for program George by Rollo Carpenter was 3.75

(Scores from Loebner 2006 Internet page and Comp.AI Internet Usenet Group)

Chapter XVIII
The Use of Artificial Emotional Intelligence in Virtual Creatures

Félix Francisco Ramos Corchado
Instituto Politécnico Nacional, Guadalajara, Mexico

Héctor Rafael Orozco Aguirre
Instituto Politécnico Nacional, Guadalajara, Mexico

Luis Alfonso Razo Ruvalcaba
Instituto Politécnico Nacional, Guadalajara, Mexico

ABSTRACT

Emotions play an essential role in the cognitive processes of an avatar and are a crucial element for modeling its perception, learning, decision process, behavior and other cognitive functions. Intense emotions can affect significantly the behavior of an avatar in a virtual environment, for instance, driving its behavior unstable as the consequence of deep emotional influence. The response of an avatar to such influence is the development of the capacity to recognize and manage emotions. In this work we describe a new faculty called Artificial Emotional Intelligence (AEI), and we propose a model based on Emotional Intelligence (EI) to develop a new approach to the problem of mood and emotion control. This approach applies the concept of EI and provides the needed tools to make avatars have AEI. In addition, we use the Emotional Competence Framework (ECF) to define and apply the personal and social competencies of an avatar.

INTRODUCTION

Nowadays the connection between a Human being and computer based systems is growing stronger. Many innovations appear, for instance, robot toys like Pleo, Robosapiens or Honda Robot, and even conventional computers with the ability to control complex systems, such as virtual reality worlds.

This phenomenon shows that human-computer interaction (HCI) is deeper than just the delegation of work to the machine. This remark makes evident two fields of research. The first one is the physiological field, and the second one is the psychological field that proposes models that represent emotions in computer based systems. In this work we deal with the second field of research.

Today a large number of studies about emotions exist and there are several models of emotion proposed in the literature, unfortunately we cannot know for sure which models are correct. In this chapter we deal with the problem of expressing corporal emotions. The main issue is that expressing emotions is completely subjective for everyone. This fact makes very difficult the establishment of general models for emotions. An alternate approach explored in this chapter consists in designing a model based on some observations on the behavior of Human being. Psychologists traditionally single out three types of human intelligence: *Abstract Intelligence* that denotes the ability of Human being to understand and manipulate verbal and mathematical symbols, *Concrete Intelligence* which indicates the capacity of Human being to understand and manipulate objects, and *Social Intelligence* that allows the Human being to understand other individuals and to interact with them. The EI of Human being has its roots in the Social Intelligence (SI), which is divided in two categories: *Interpersonal Intelligence* as ability to understand other people and *Intrapersonal Intelligence* as self-consciousness.

Emotions are an important aspect in the functioning of the human mind. Nevertheless, the role that emotions play in our actions, behavior and thinking has been misapprehended and misinterpreted. The old philosophers did not consider the emotions as an important aspect of human intelligence, by the contrary they perceived the emotions as an impediment that blocks and prevents the human reasoning and thought. In the Plato's *Phaedo dialogue*, Plato explained that fears, pas-

sions and desires make thinking and reasoning impossible. Later, Descartes based on the same idea his defining of emotions as passions or needs that the body imposes on the mind.

Recently, several psychologists have begun the exploration and study of emotions to explain better their functioning, which is an important component of the human intelligence and cognition. The obtained results give evidence that emotions have an important impact on thinking, judgment, reasoning, memory and decision making of Human being. Gardner (1983) introduced the term of *Multiple Intelligences* for describing the personal intelligence as a type of human intelligence that includes social interactions and emotions. Damasio (1994; 1995) demonstrated in neurological studies that people who lack the capacity of emotional response can take incorrect decisions and execute mistaken actions that can limit their performance in society. Basing on the fact that emotions are an important part of human intelligence, Goleman (1995) coined the concept of EI.

Many psychological models have been proposed to describe the emotional functioning of the human brain and the mental processes. Several models are centered on the effect of motivational states or on the processes by which the events trigger certain emotions. Such models are called *event appraisal models*. Other models examine the influence of expectations on emotions. But none of these models presents complete abstraction and shows general idea. In these models the emotions are considered to be mental states generated with the use of mapping that includes great variety of considerations, such as expectations, motivational states, events, and environmental conditions.

Inspired by the psychological models of emotion, many researchers have recognized in Artificial Intelligence (AI) the importance and utility for improving complex, dynamic and interactive virtual environments with the help of the computational models of emotions. Designed models of emotions can represent a better understanding of moods and emotions and can thus adapt to needs of program or application. However, most of designed computational models of emotion only represent specific situations and respond in predetermined way to them.

Roseman, Jose and Spindel (1990) designed a model of emotion, where they described emotions on basis of distinct event classifications. In their model they evaluated the certainty of the occurrence of an event considering its causes. Thus, software agents may use emotions to facilitate the social interactions, relationships and communications between them. This helps to coordinate tasks, such as cooperating between communities of agents.

In this chapter, we contribute with our work to the alternative solution for the problem of emotion and mood control, personality of an avatar or autonomous virtual creature, using the representation based on a computational model. We are inspired by the ideas that Goleman presents in his books *Emotional Intelligence* and *Working with Emotional Intelligence* (Goleman, 1995; Goleman 1998) and works published by Mayer, Salovey and Caruso about EI (Mayer, 2000; Mayer, & Geher, 1996; Mayer, & Salovey 1993; Mayer, & Salovey, 1995; Mayer, Salovey, & Caruso, 2000; Salovey, & Mayer, 1990; Salovey, & Sluyter, 1997).

The proposed solution includes the following characteristics of the AEI of an avatar: self-consciousness, mood and emotion management, self-motivation, empathy and management, control of relationships. Therefore the AEI of an avatar (virtual character) denotes a type of Social Intelligence (SI) that implies the ability of avatar to understand, distinguish and manage its emotions and those of other avatars. Thus, the AEI of an avatar includes: self-consciousness, goal understanding, intentions, reactions and behaviors, also consciousness of other avatars and their feelings. In this chapter our main objective is to explore the use of EI in order to accomplish the following:

1. To present a new agent architecture for creating and developing autonomous emotional agents.

2. To apply this architecture to generate suitable behaviors to autonomous virtual creatures (avatars) participating in dynamic virtual environments.

3. Human being's behavior simulation using virtual emotional entities in interactive applications.

4. Autonomous EI in virtual entities for achieving adaptability in complex environments.

5. To implement the conscience, the intelligence and the cognitive processes of avatar and all the proposed behavior models of an avatar based on its personality, emotions and moods.

6. To define and to implement study cases for the GeDA-3D Agent Architecture (Piza, Zúñiga, & Ramos, 2004; Zúñiga, Ramos, & Piza, 2005). Assigning a personality and emotions and moods simulation to agents using facial expressions and animation sequences based on postures to make the simulation more realistic.

7. To use knowledge bases (ontologies) to provide the agents with an initial knowledge of the environment and themselves. This allows us to develop behaviors focused on the scenes and to avoid spending time on recognition of the environment before we accomplish the goal specification.

8. To receive a specification that contains a detailed definition of the precedence order of agent's goals to reach. The global behavioral aim of agent will not only be to reach the defined goals, but also to accomplish the whole specification. This detailed description must specify *what* we want the agent to do, instead of *how* we want the agent to do it.

This chapter is organized as follows. The next section surveys the related works. In this chapter we will give a detailed revision of the state of the art and introduce concepts and definitions of emotional agents, rational agents and models of emotions and personality applied to agents. The third section is dedicated to the proposal of this chapter. In this section we will present a brief description of the GeDA-3D Agent Architecture and we will describe a new ontology for *Affective Personified Emotional Agents* (APE Agents), presenting the main applications of our ontology. In the last sections we will present the conclusions obtained from this work and describe our future work.

RELATED WORK

Through the time, several models have been proposed in a broad range of scientific areas to describe the functioning of the human mind. Emotions in special have received increasing attention and interest in several fields related to AI, mainly in HCI and Human-Robot Interaction (HRI), where emotional receptivity (perceiving and interpreting of facial expressions) and emotional expressivity (expressing emotions) are crucial and play an important role. In order to review these models, we have classified them according to their focus. Multi-Agent Systems (MAS) cover problems related to the autonomy, the cooperation and coordination between agents as well as the interaction of believable agents in virtual environments. In MAS, individual agents are assumed to be autonomous. That is to say, they should have the capability to deliberate and decide which actions to take or which tasks to perform in order to reach their goals. Furthermore, agents must cooperate and coordinate their actions for achieving their global objectives.

Emotions have been center of interest of many researchers in AI and Computer Sciences (CS). Several emotional architectures of agents have been proposed. The researchers have been particularly interested in designing models in order

to make realistic and improve believability of the agents, which are applied in artificial situations, such as simulations in virtual environments. Believable virtual agents can have application in the entertainment industry. In this section we will summarize each of the related topics and give our opinion about them.

Emotional Agents

In the last years many researchers have tried to add emotions to rational agents and design architectures for them. However, a complete and generally accepted generic model does not exist. Research into emotions in such disciplines as neurosciences and psychology has attracted the attention of many specialists in CS, Artificial Life (ALife), and AI areas. At the moment these areas are applying the concepts and theories, according to which the emotions are a crucial element for modeling brain functions, such as learning, perception and decision processes among others. It means that emotions play an essential and fundamental role in cognitive processes which are responsible for solving problems and taking decisions. These factors have been very important for creating new models of emotions and developing experimental projects as a way to prove models with the help of implementations and applications in AI and ALife.

The HCI focuses its attention on the interactions and possible relationships between Human beings and machines. The main intention is to develop tools destined for modeling and representing emotions with the application of sensors, new algorithms, and sophisticated hardware devices. The term Affective Computing (AC) classifies projects in this category. Researchers' efforts in AC are focused on the development of computer architectures and inspired by studies realized in neuroscience and psychology. They have the intention to develop computer systems that include a model of emotions. Indeed, these architectures reflect a computer understanding of Human being's behavior. Thus, they can implement algorithms of decision making, action selection and behavior control, which can provide many advantages. As this research area is recent, there are still many problems to solve and there are much more questions that must be answered, for instance, ones related to computer problems and theoretical concepts. At the same time, this area gives the scientists an excellent opportunity to propose new models. So, instead of questioning what the emotions are, we analyze how to use and add the emotions into agents. Therefore, questions about relations between emotions, cognitive processes and affective processes of the agents can be answered much more easily.

It is evident that many of the problems and questions we have mentioned are related strongly to the form, in which the agents are programmed, because many computer models and architectures are based on the real Human being's observable behavior. Nevertheless, the researchers in the area of neuroscience and psychology can not provide yet a clear explanation for how the emotions affect cognitive abilities, such as decision making. They are also not sure about what areas of the brain are implied in the mental and affective processes. One of the most important questions in AI is as follows: Are the emotional and affective processes related only to an embodied entity? This question lacks for logic from the psychological and neurological point of view, but the opposite arises when the same question is applied to computer systems.

With respect to the emotional architecture, it is very necessary to know which data structure and algorithms should be used to capture, keep and represent the emotional and affective processes, as well as how to update the emotional state and what models are preferable for building the agents. To obtaining better results several experimental tests can be done. Such tests allow to explore better the models of emotion and to respond better to the previous questions.

Emotional agents are used to simulate the Human being's reasoning by means of the influence

and effect of primary and secondary emotions. These emotions are used in the decision making process of agent architectures. Thus, some works have increased the interest for the use of computational models of emotion to incorporate emotions into rational agents. According to these works, the main types of agents are:

a. **Logic based agents:** These agents make decisions through logical inference. It is assumed that the environment does not change while the agent is taking an action.

b. **Reactive agents:** Agents make decisions using local information of their local environment by direct mapping from situation to action. In occasions the agents do not have sufficient information to choose the right action. It provokes that the relationship between the agents and their environment is not understandable.

c. **Layered agents:** These agents are very general; their decision making is realized by means of several software layers and levels of abstraction. It is necessary to take into account all possible interactions between layers.

d. **Emotional-belief-desire-intention agents (EBDI agents):** Agents take decisions by manipulating data structures that represent their emotions, beliefs, desires and intentions. These agents reflect the Human being's reasoning and they are very convenient and recommendable for modeling emotional agents.

In order to incorporate and add emotions into agents, it is necessary to answer some questions, such as: How to model and measure emotions? How the emotions must change the behavior of the agents? How to update the emotional state of the agents? Based on the Damasio's theory (Damasio, 1994; 1995) that emotions play a positive role in the adaptive functions of the mind, Jiang and Vidal (2006) took into account both primary emotions (those that are perceived first) and secondary emotions (these appear after primary emotions and may be caused directly by primary emotions or by more complex chains of thinking) for modeling decision making processes. The aim is to generate a conceptual emotional architecture based on the EBDI agents. These agents divide the processes of their architecture, which are described in the part named "Emotional update functions", into four components: Emotion, Belief, Desire and Intention (Pereira, Oliveira, Moreira, & Sarmento, 2005). These components are connected through some main functions. The execution cycle of the architecture is as follows:

a. The EBDI agent takes new information from the environment using sensors or messages to generate belief candidates.

b. Belief candidates together with current intentions indicate emotional state updating, that is, the agent creates its feelings using the new information.

c. Based on the new emotional state and the new information, together with current intentions as a guide, the agent re-evaluated its beliefs.

d. On the base of beliefs and intentions, the agent generates its desires.

e. Under the influence of the emotions, the agent chooses the best options or intentions based on current beliefs, desires and intentions.

f. As the result of this deliberation the secondary emotions are fired; this updating is based on current intentions and previous emotions.

g. If there is not time for deeper consideration or emotion status is not changed, the agent will directly generate a detailed plan and execute it. Otherwise, the agent begins a deeper consideration and refines the decision making.

Thus, the EBDI agents have better performance than rational agents, because they have more flexibility and ability to be adaptable and survive in dynamic environments. In this way the EBDI agents can reduce the computational load of rational agents. Several considerations must be taken into account when emotions are added into agents. For instance, some researchers argue that it is necessary to add human characteristics, such as personality, mood and emotion, in order to design much more conceivable and believable agents. That is to say, such agents can react and play much better their role in applications which involve simulation. So, the emotions affect and change the agent's behavior and their actions (Fridja, & Swagerman 1987; Dyer 1987). Hence, a good model of emotions can help us to design and build better software agents which approach the behavior of the Human beings in order to adapt and survive with more success in hostile and unpredictable environments. The above confirms that emotions have a positive impact in the design of emotional agents.

The Role of Emotions in Emotional Agents

Emotions are essential in Human beings and animals and play an active role in decision making processes of the daily life. Interactions and relationships between emotional processes and cognitive processes indicate that the Human beings and animals take decisions based on their feelings. This fact can answer the next question: Why is it necessary to endow agents with emotions? Emotional agents can be used to prove and test psychological theories with the aim to provide a better analysis applying the studies about natural systems. As a result we obtain a complementary approach.

Cognitive Sciences have been very interested in modeling the human brain, its functions and cognitive processes during many years. Inspired by several psychological studies and the increasing interest of researchers in AI and ALife, many specialists have presented the computational models, which simulate the human brain. Nevertheless, a universal model at the moment does not exist. In addition, it is not easy to find a computational model that represents completely the concept of emotion. LeDoux (1996) presented in his book *"The Emotional Brain"* a neurological model of the human brain. This model allowed exploring emotional processes in the brain, and emotions were described in terms of desires and expectations.

Based on the studies realized by researchers in different areas, such as psychology, neuroscience and philosophy, the main roles of emotions in emotional agents are:

1. **Action selection:** Based on the current emotional state.
2. **Motivation:** Creating motives as an emotional mechanism.
3. **Adaptation:** Changes in the behavior due to update of the emotional state.
4. **Social regulation:** Communication with other agents using message exchange.
5. **Goal management:** Creating new goals or reprioritization of the existing ones.
6. **Attention focus:** Processing of selected data by means of emotional evaluation.
7. **Strategic processing:** Selection of different strategies based on the emotional state.
8. **Self-model:** Emotions represent the feelings of an agent.

In part the mystery of not understanding the emotions completely exists, because these occur in the subconscious, and it is unclear when emotions pass from the subconscious brain to the conscious brain. For this reason, researchers on agent's technology and CS are trying to create better models of emotions and emotional architectures.

Emotion Models Applied to Agents

Human beings are emotional beings by nature, and to understand the function of emotions in the human behavior several models of emotion have been proposed. Agent architectures have been used for representing the human behavior and modeling emotions. Modeling emotions is interesting, because the emotions are not only complex, but also dynamic, variable over time. A very efficient approach to representing the human behavior and understanding the emotional functioning consists in formulating emotions on the basis of responses to events. Models based on this idea are known as event appraisal models of emotion. In this section we will present and explain the most important models.

The OCC (Ortony, Clore, & Collins, 1988) model is considered to be the standard model for emotion synthesis and the best categorization of emotions available. In this model the concept of basic emotions does not exist, the emotions are interpreted as reactions to either consequence of events, or actions of agents, or aspects of objects. The OCC model explains human emotions and tries to predict under which situations which emotions can be experimented. Emotions are divided into the following groups: reactions to events, actions and objects. The reactions can be positive or negative. The authors of this theory based on the cognitive nature of emotions argue that a particular emotion experienced as a consequence of an event, action or attraction to an object can determine the human being's behavior. Emotions represent valence reactions to perceptions of the environment. Thus, the consequences of an event can please or displease the agent (*pleased/displeased*), the agent can accept or reject actions (*approve/disapprove*), and the characteristics of an object can attract or not the attention of agent (*like/dislike*). According to Ortony et al. (1988):

When one focuses on events one does so because one is interested in their consequences, when one focuses on agents, one does so because of their actions, and when one focuses on objects, one is interested in certain aspects or imputed properties of them (p. 18).

They specified 22 emotion categories based on positive or negative reactions to situations, and the intensity of emotional feelings is determined by three central intensity variables: *Desirability* is linked with the reaction to events and is evaluated with regard to goals. *Praiseworthiness* is linked with the reaction to actions of agents and is evaluated with regard to standards. *Appealingness* is linked with the reaction to objects and is evaluated with regard to attitudes. Nonetheless, it is very important to say that personality is necessary for determination of the consistency of emotional reactions over time and helps to build more believable agents. Ortony (2003) proposed a simplified version of OCC model using six positive and five negative categories to describe the emotions of believable agents. Positive categories include joy, hope, relief, pride, gratitude and love, and negative categories group distress, fear, disappointment, anger and hate. Each of these categories is stored as a numerical value. Though this model is rather good, it does not explain completely the origin of the emotional processes and does not present how to filter mixed emotions to obtain a coherent emotional state. Finally, the OCC model was developed to understand the emotions instead of simulating them. In addition, the method for computing internal local and global variables was not described. These variables can be the expectation or likelihood of event occurrence.

Roseman et al. (1990) proposed a different model for generating emotions according to an event assessment procedure. They classified events in two groups: *Motive-consistent* events (events consistent with the goals) and *motive-inconsistent* events (events that threaten the goals).

Further the events can be categorized according to other properties. That is to say, an event can be caused by other event or circumstance. In addition, this model determines the occurrence of an event based on the certainty that an event would really occur. Other factors are used to distinguish between emotions, when an event is driven by the desire to obtain a reward or avoid a punishment, or self-perception.

However, this model does not provide a complete understanding and explanation of the emotional processes, since it does not describe a method for categorizing perceived events. For instance, some events can be perceived simultaneously as motive-consistent and motive-inconsistent, which will generate conflicting emotions or contradictory emotions. Hence, a filtering mechanism for inhibiting or reinforcing emotions is needed. Furthermore, the emotional processes are interrelated with the reasoning processes and aspects of intelligence. Thus, not only external events, but also internal states generate emotional changes. Although the OCC model and the model presented by Roseman et al. (1990) demonstrate correctly the importance of expectations, these models do not identify a specific link between expectations and the intensity of the emotions triggered.

Another approach was presented in Frijda's theory of emotion (Fridja, 1987). Frijda's theory points out that emotion does not refer to a natural class and that it is not able to refer to a defined class of phenomena, which are clearly distinguishable from other mental and behavior events. The central idea of this theory is the term *concern*. A concern represents the predisposition of a system to prefer certain states of the environment, that is to say, a concern can produce goals and preferences for the system. Thus, the intensity of emotion is determined essentially by the influences generated by relevant concerns. Frijda defined six primordial characteristics for describing the function of an emotional system:

1. **Concern relevance detection:** The emotional subsystem announces the meaning of events for the concerns of the overall system to all other components of the system. This means that the system must be able to take information both from the environment and from the system itself.

2. **Appraisal:** The meaning of the stimulus for the concerns of the system is appraised. This

process includes the sub processes relevance appraisal and context appraisal.

3. **Control precedence:** The priorities of perception, attention and processing are changed when the relevance signal is strong enough. This affects the behavior of the system.

4. **Action readiness changes:** It represents the heart of the emotional reaction. The change of the action causes changes in the processing and attention of resources generating a tendency towards certain types of actions.

5. **Regulation:** The system monitors process all the events of the environment for regulating the activation of certain forms of action readiness.

6. **Social nature of the environment:** The emotion system is adjusted to the fact that it operates in a predominantly social environment. Several appraisal categories are of social nature and the action readiness is predominantly a readiness for social actions.

According to Frijda's theory, the emotions are absolutely necessary for systems which realize multiple concerns in unknown and hostile environment. Therefore, a functional emotional system must possess the following components:

a. **Concerns:** These are internal representations used to verify the existing conditions.

b. **Action repertoire:** It is composed of instantaneous emergency reactions, social signals and mechanisms to develop new plans.

c. **Appraisal mechanisms:** These mechanisms establish the fits between the events and concerns and generate connections to the action control system and the action repertoire.

d. **Analyser:** Coding of the implications as the result of the observation of incoming information and its implications.

e. **Comparator:** Verification of information about the concern relevance, generating

relevance signals that activate the action system and the diagnoser.

f. **Diagnoser:** It is responsible for the context evaluation. It scans the information about the action relevant references to perform tests and generate results in appraisal profile.

g. **Evaluator:** This one combines the agreement or discrepancy signals of the Comparator and the profile of the Diagnoser in order to produce the final relevance signal and its intensity parameter. The intensity indicates the immediate necessity of taking a decision in the action system.

h. **Action proposer:** It prepares the action by selecting a suitable alternative to generate the necessary resources.

i. **Actor:** It generates actions.

Searching for a better model of emotion, El-Nasr, Yen and Ioerger (2000) presented the model FLAME (Fuzzy Logic Adaptive Model of Emotions). This computational model was created to produce emotions and simulate the emotional intelligence process. It uses fuzzy rules to explore the capability of fuzzy logic for modeling the emotional process. Fuzzy logic was used for capturing the fuzzy and complex nature of emotions. Taking advantage over other conventional models, it creates a better simulation and representation of reality. For modeling emotions FLAME uses fuzzy sets and fuzzy rules for mapping from events to emotions and from emotions to behaviors. The model is based on event-appraisal psychological model and consists of three major components: *Emotional Component, Learning Component* and *Decision Making Component*. The functioning of agent architecture presented in this model is the following: The agent perceives external events in the environment that are passed to the emotional and learning components. The emotional component processes the perceptions using some of the results given by the learning component, including expectations and event-goal associations, to produce emotional behavior. The behavior is then returned back to the decision making component to choose an action. Thus, the actions are made according to the situations, the agent's mood, the emotional states and the emotional behavior.

FLAME includes some algorithms for learning generally about event expectations, rewards, patterns of user actions, object-emotion associations, etc. These algorithms are used to enable an intelligent agent to adapt dynamically to its environment and the users.

Personality Models Applied to Behavior of Agents

From the psychological point of view, there are many personality models as general dimensional representations. They consist of a set of dimensions, and each dimension represents personality traits. One of the first models of this type was the Leary's interpersonal circle (Leary, 1957). This model is based on two dimensions: *status* and *sympathy*. Others models are PEN model that has three dimensions (Eysenck, 1990), and the OCEAN model (McCrae, & John, 1992), which groups personality traits of Human being in five dimensions, which are:

1. **Openness:** Involves active imagination, aesthetic sensitivity and attentiveness to inner feelings. In addition, it includes intellectual curiosity, appreciation for art, emotion, adventure, unusual ideas, imagination and variety of experiences.
2. **Conscientiousness:** It is related to emotional intelligence and impulse control. It includes elements such as self-discipline, carefulness, organization and aims for achievement of the goals.
3. **Extraversion:** It is the central dimension of human personality. It groups positive emotions and shows the tendency to seek stimulation and the company of others.
4. **Agreeableness:** Shows a tendency to be compassionate and cooperative towards others.

It reflects individual differences in concern for cooperation and social harmony.
5. **Neuroticism:** It can be defined as the enduring tendency to experience negative emotional states, indicating a tendency to experience easily unpleasant emotions, such as anger, anxiety or depression. It is also considered to be a predisposition for traditional neuroses, such as phobias and other anxiety disorders. Sometimes it is called emotional instability. It is related to emotional intelligence, because involves emotional regulation, motivation and interpersonal skills.

Each factor represents a set of specific personality traits that correlate together. The OCEAN model, also known as the Five Factor Model, is a purely descriptive model of personality. Although the OCEAN model is widely accepted, it has many criticisms, because it does not indicate how exactly the personality is affected by obtained stimuli and experienced situations.

Masuch, Hartman and Schuster (2006) presented a behavior model based on static personality that imparts individual characteristic reactions. This personality model is represented by parameters of seven personality dimensions:

1. **Suspicion:** This dimension influences the dynamics of meeting others with sympathy.
2. **Curiosity:** Dimension that affects the behavior towards strangers or unknown objects.
3. **Sociability:** Describes the behavior towards other friendly agents.
4. **Aggression:** Affects the behavior towards hostile characters.
5. **Helpfulness:** This dimension incorporates the willingness to act to advantage of other characters.
6. **Vividness:** Dimension used for controlling the dynamics of the emotional arousal.
7. **Conscientiousness:** Determines how motivated a character follows its goals.

According to the authors, in their model the seven personality dimensions are closely related to specific aspects of more general dimensions of the OCEAN model. With the suspicion, aggression and helpfulness dimension they distinguished between different aspects of the agreeableness dimension. The curiosity dimension emphasizes a specific aspect of the openness dimension and the sociability is related to extraversion. But the conscientiousness is the same in both models.

Due to the direct correspondence between emotions and facial expressions, many researchers prefer to employ the Ekman's six basic emotions (joy, fear, sadness, dislike, anger and surprise) for facial expression classification (Ekman, 1982; 1994) and the OCEAN model of personality (Costa, & McCrae, 1992) or the OCC model in combination with the OCEAN model. The mutual dependence between emotions and personality is often represented by Bayesian belief networks. Another interesting approach describes emotions, mood, personality and their interdependencies using vector algebra (Egges, Kshirsagar, & Magnenat-Thalmann, 2004). Finally we can say that personality acts as filter for emotions and takes care that not solely emotions govern the agent behavior.

Competing Models of EI

There are two main kinds of models of EI: mental ability models and mixed models. Mental ability models make predictions about the internal structure of the intelligence and also its implications in the daily life. That is to say, a mental ability model focuses on emotions and their interactions. Mixed models are different, because these concern mental abilities and characteristics, such as motivation, states of conciousness and social activity. Thus, the mental ability models operate in a region defined by emotion and cognition, whereas mixed models label a multitude of components as EI.

In 1995, Goleman coined the concept of EI and defined it as the complex of abilities that includes

self-control, zeal, persistence and self-motivation. According to Goleman (1995), "There is an old-fashioned word for the body of skills that Emotional Intelligence represents: character" (p. 28). Goleman proposed a mixed model with the next areas of skills: *Knowledge about emotions, management of emotions, self-motivation, recognizing emotions in others* and *handling relationships*. Mayer and Salovey (1993) presented a mental ability model that includes the following areas of skills: *Perception and expression of emotion, assimilating emotion in thought, understanding and analyzing emotion* and *reflective regulation of emotion*. They defined EI as "The ability to perceive and express emotion, assimilate emotion in thought, understand and reason with emotion, and regulate emotion in the self and others" (p. 11). Bar-On (1997) defined EI as "An array of noncognitive capabilities, competences, and skills that influence one´s ability to succeed in coping with environmental demands and pressures" (p. 14). He presented another mixed model. Its major areas of skills are: *Intrapersonal Skills, interpersonal skills, adaptability scales, stress-management scales* and *general mood*. Therefore, we conclude that mental ability models can be described as standard models of EI. Thus, the EI consists of four brand areas of specific tasks: *emotional perception, assimilation, understanding,* and *management.*

Models for Personality, Emotion and Mood Simulation

Egges et al. (2004) described a generic algorithm for the emotional behavior update applied to conversational virtual humans with the use of the OCC model and OCEAN model. This model was called model for personality, emotion and mood simulation (PEM model). To process emotional influence, the updating process is divided in two steps. The first step consists in updating the mood (new mood) and the second step consists in updating the emotional state (new emotional state). The mood is updated by the next function:

$$m_{t+1} = m_t + \Psi_m\left(p, \omega_t, \sigma_t, a\right) + \Omega_m\left(p, \omega_t, \sigma_t\right)$$

The function Ψ_m calculates the mood change, based on the personality, the emotional state history, the mood history and the emotional influence, and the function Ω_m represents internal change, such as decay of the mood. The vectors m_t and m_{t+1} represent the anterior mood state and the actual mood state. The emotional state is then updated with the help of the following extended function:

$$e_{t+1} = e_t + \Psi_e'\left(p, \omega_t, \sigma_{t+1}, a\right) + \Omega_e'\left(p, \omega_t, \sigma_{t+1}\right)$$

The extended function Ψ_e' takes into account the personality, the emotional state history, the recent mood history and the emotional influence; the function Ω_e' represents the internal emotional update. The vectors e_t and e_{t+1} represent the anterior emotional state and the actual emotional state.

Other model based on the OCEAN model and the OCC model is the model of personality and emotion of learning companion agent or PEL model (Li, Qiu, Yue, & Zhong, 2007). This model is similar to the PEM model (Egges et al., 2004). But one difference is that the PEL model uses four pairs of emotions (happy-for and resentment, joy and pity, pride and shame, and gratitude and anger) represented by any value within the interval $[-1,1]$, and the mood is categorized in three basic dimensions: good, bad and neutral, represented by any value within the interval $[0,1]$. Other difference is the processing of emotional influence. The first step of this operation consists in updating the emotional state (new emotional state) and the second step consists in updating the mood (new mood). The emotional state is updated by the following function:

$$e_{t+1} = e_t + \phi\left(p, m_t\right) + \Psi\left(p, m_t\right)$$

The function ϕ calculates the emotional change, based on the personality and the current emotional state, and the function Ψ represents internal change, such as decay and filter of the emotional state. The vectors e_t and e_{t+1} represent the anterior emotional state and the actual emotional state. The mood state is updated using the following function:

$$m_{t+1} = \left(1 - \alpha\right)\eta\left(m_t\right) + \alpha\,\zeta\left(e_{t+1}\right)$$

The function $\eta(m_t)$ represents the effect of the anterior mood state and the function $\alpha\,\zeta\left(e_{t+1}\right)$ represents the effect of the actual emotional state. The value α determines the weight of the anterior mood effect and the actual emotional state effect. The vector m_{t+1} represents the new mood state.

THE USE OF ARTIFICIAL EMOTIONAL INTELLIGENCE IN VIRTUAL CREATURES

At this moment, an important trend in the development of dynamic virtual environments is to integrate proper characteristics of Human being, such as personality, moods and emotions, into virtual characters or avatars. These virtual entities are controlled by software agents with the aim of providing a model of personality, mood and emotion to make them more believable and conceivable. Emotions comprise an important part and are a crucial element of the believability of virtual characters that live and interact in virtual environments. Virtual characters need a convenient emotion model in order to synthesize emotions and express them. The emotion model should enable the character to distinguish and manage emotions in the same way that human beings do.

All interactive applications, such as computer games, video games and collaborative virtual environments, are in need of believable characters. But actually, the behavior of the digital actors or characters in current applications and systems is still very artificial. In order to make virtual environments more realistic, the virtual characters should exhibit a complex and believable behavior. Nevertheless, in this chapter our main objective is not modeling the complexity of Human being's behavior, but simulating autonomous emotional agents with a personality and dynamic emotional behavior.

The decision making and action selection of autonomous intelligent agents must be regulated and controlled not only by external stimuli, but also by their personality, emotions and moods. Therefore, in this work we aim at integrating theories on emotions and personality into agents to obtain believable virtual characters.

Virtual characters can use a model of emotion to simulate and express emotional responses, which can effectively enhance their believability. Furthermore, emotions can be used to simulate personality traits in believable agents. The dynamic behavior of an avatar over a sequence of events is only apparent from the change in responses to situations over time. The expectation and the resultant emotion are experienced due to the conditioned response. Some psychological models explicitly use expectations to determine the emotional state. However, classical conditioning in not the only type of learning that can induce or trigger expectations. There are other types of learning that need to be incorporated to produce a believable adaptive behavior, including learning about sequences of events and about other agents or users. Emotional states can be viewed as internal states that promote or drive the human decisions to take a specific action. These states have a tendency to interrupt the brain to call for important need or action. Thus, these states have a major impact on the mind, including the emotional process and the decision making process, and hence behavior.

Emotions play crucial role in the cognitive processes of an avatar or virtual creature and are a very important element of modeling cognitive processes and mental activities, such as: perception, learning, decision process, memory,

behavior and other cognitive functions. Intense emotions can affect significantly the behavior of an avatar in a virtual environment, for instance, driving its behavior unstable as the consequence of deep emotional influence. The response of an avatar to such influence is the development of the capacity to recognize and manage emotions. This capacity allows to the avatar to select from the action set an action sequence necessary to attain the emotional stability and self-control. In this work we describe a new faculty called *Artificial Emotional Intelligence* (AEI) using a model based on the EI to develop a new approach to the problem of the emotion and mood control. This approach applies the original concepts of EI and provides the needed tools to make avatars have EI.

In Human beings, the emotions and affect seem to be deeply intertwined with cognition, in which they can influence, bias, and direct cognitive processes and processing strategies. Emotions also seem to play important role in social contexts, ranging from signaling emotional states through facial expressions and gestures to perceptions of affective states that cause approval or disapproval of one's own or other agent's actions (relative to given norms). This can trigger corrective responses. Thus, emotional states, such as fear or anger, control immediately the actions and other affective states (for example, anxiety) and operate on long-term behavioral dispositions.

The psychological terms *affection*, *mood* and *emotion* are often regarded as synonyms. However, it is necessary to know the structural and functional differences between them (Batson, Shaw, & Oleson, 1992). Emotions are the response to a particular stimulus (Brehm, 1999; Evans, 2001). They are more specific and intense than moods, which are diffuse, and unfocused (Bless, & Schwarz, 1999). That is to say, the emotions are reactions more immediate and spontaneous than moods. On the other hand, the affection changes sharply the values of emotional and mood states and feelings (Berkowitz, 2000).

In this work we use the *Emotional Competence Framework* (ECF) to apply the personal and social competencies of avatar on the basis of the following characteristics:

1. Personal competence:
   a. *Self-consciousness* (awareness of emotions, accurate self-assessment and self-confidence).
   b. *Self-regulation* (self-control, self-consciousness and adaptability).
   c. *Self-motivation* (achievement tendency and commitment to the task).
2. Social competence:
   a. *Social awareness* (empathy, service orientation, awareness of other avatars and political awareness).
   b. *Social skills* (communication, conflict management and cooperation with other entities).

Summarizing, the AEI of an avatar is the set of cognitive and non-cognitive abilities, capabilities, intrapersonal and interpersonal skills. That is to say, our proposal about AEI relates mental processes involving emotional information. The mental processes include mainly: appraising and expressing emotions and regulating emotion in the self and others, and using emotions in adaptive ways. Therefore, based on the previous assumptions, we propose a new model, which aims to explain the behavior of an avatar based on the following three sets: *Cognition* (learning, dynamic planning and thought), *Motivation* (basic instincts and impulses, and goal-oriented activities), and *Emotional Valence* (personality, moods and emotions).

We consider that EI is not only a psychological concept; it is closely related to biology. Thus, the term cognition denotes the faculty to process information. In this context it can be interpreted as the ability of an avatar to be aware of the virtual environment where it lives and to dispose of sense and knowledge. Cognitive processes of avatar defined in this work are: understanding, drawing conclusions, decision making, dynamic planning and learning, among others. Thence, based on the previous concepts, we can define the capability of an avatar to abstract and reason. This capability includes the concepts of beliefs, knowledge, desires, preferences and intentions of an avatar. Therefore, an avatar can act and interact in its virtual environment according to its emotions, mood and personality, as if it were an autonomous intelligent entity.

According to existing theories, in the brain of each Human being there is a small part called *Amygdale* (Adolphs, Tranel, & Damasio, 1998). This cerebral structure performs functions biologically associated with emotions and moods. At the moment, the relation between Amygdale and emotions and moods is not explored completely, so our work settles on the existent results. It is believed that the Amygdale plays the key role in the emotions and moods. The Amygdale forms part of the limbic system. In Humans beings and animals the Amygdale is linked to both fear responses and pleasure. It is supposed that the Amygdale works in the following way: the emotional brain scans everything happening to us from moment to moment. Its aim is to know if something that happened in the past and influenced our emotions (for instance, made us sad or angry) is similar to what is happening now. If so, the Amygdale calls alarm and declares emergency, so in a split second we are ready to act.

Fellous (1999) reviewed the experimental evidence showing the involvement of the hypothalamus, the Amygdale and the prefrontal cortex in emotion. Each of these structures plays an essential role as modulator system in mediating the emotional behavior. Fellous suggested that behavioral complexity is partly due to the diversity and intensity of neurology modulation, and hence depends on emotional contexts. Therefore, emotional modulation is considered to be a result of interactions between the hypothalamus, Amygdale and prefrontal cortex. However, there is strong evidence that shows the involvement of the Amygdale in the violent behavior. In recent studies great attention is paid to the role of the Amygdale in emotional regulation and affects (Anderson, & Phelps, 2002). Basing on the results of their work, the authors have supposed that the Amygdale may be recruited for affective states, but is not necessary for their generation. They concluded that this explains why there has been little measurable evidence about the emotional experience in the functioning of Amygdale in humans. This is similar to the conclusion given by Fellous, who explained that the Amygdale is not an emotional centre as is was traditionally considered, but it acts as regulating filter, catching stimuli to create a warning state (Fellous, 1999).

The Amygdale, also called *emotional brain*, can mobilize in less time than the thinking brain, which first needs to figure out what is going on. That is why people can get into a rage and do something they wish they had not done, or on the contrary, they do something appropriate for the situation and solve the problem successfully. Choice of right actions is determined by the experiences acquired in the past and the good quality of EI that the individual has. Thus, we apply the concept of AEI to achieve the semblance of control over emotions and moods of avatar, in this case, to simulate knowledge and regulation of emotional and mood states. This method consists in showing the avatar some actions, which probably would exert the best possible influence over its emotions. This emotional influence will provide the values which are necessary to cover the best possible regulation of the internal emotional state. The module where the method mentioned above is included is the *Amygdale Module*. This method will be used to choose the adequate action to be taken at the precise moment and is required to solve the problem in the best possible way, that is, to regulate the internal emotional status optimally.

Encouraged by the biological and psychological operations, we propose a new solution, which works over emotional agents in conjunction with the personality, emotions and moods already present in each agent. This method uses the principle of EI, which acquires and controls the emotions and moods of avatar. The EI helps the avatar to choose the most promising alternative as the reaction to the actual situation for the purpose of regulating the emotional status and mood status. This choice is made by a module called Amygdale Module, which simulates biological reactions (see Figure 1). Within the agent the mentioned module performs the same function as the real Amygdale performs in Human beings. This internal module is required for an agent to evaluate continuously the proposed actions and choose the most accurate ones for a determinate instant.

All the proposed models in this work are applied to the Architecture for Distributed Applications Management GeDA-3D. This is the platform for creation, design and executing of 3D distributed dynamic virtual environments with the use of 3D emotional agents. The emotional agents evolve in the GeDA-3D's virtual environment employing the AEI. The emotional agent's behaviors and interactions are influenced by the emotions and moods, and then the AEI helps them to take most accurate decisions. These decisions keep the agents' emotional status balanced and keep them alive in the environment. Sensorial entrances and influences that the avatars receive from their environment alter their behavior and motion and also affect their personality, emotions and mood. For instance, if an avatar is happy or angry, its facial expression indicates its emotion, its movements and behavior also change. When the avatar is sad, its movements are slower, than when it is happy.

Therefore, the main idea of our work is the application of the term EI, which takes its origin in the psychological context, to the behavior of avatars controlled by APE Agents. The AEI makes the avatars act in the most credible manner, that is, it makes them simulate the behavior of living creatures that survive and adapt to the virtual

Figure 1. Top-view of the AEI Module and internal functionality of the Amygdale Module and Behavior Module for the GeDA-3D Agent Architecture

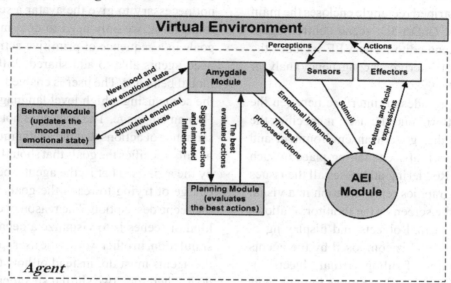

environment, using an emotional context. The AEI is a topic that is slightly explored. In this work we present a first approach, which allows us to gain more knowledge about it and develop it in the context of APE Agents (see Figure 1).

GeDA-3D Agent Architecture

The GeDA-3D Agent Architecture is a platform for the creation, design and executing of 3D distributed dynamic virtual environments. This architecture provides a platform useful for integrating and managing distributed applications, and it offers facilities to manage the communication between intelligent agents. GeDA-3D allows the user to develop behaviors assigned to the agents, which participate in the environments generated by the virtual environments declarative editor (Piza et al., 2004; Zúñiga et al., 2005). Such agent architecture contains the following main features:

1. **Skeleton animation engine:** This animation engine consists of a set of algorithms allowing to avatar to animate autonomously its skeleton to produce more realistic animations.

2. **Goals specification:** Agents receive a goals specification that contains a detailed definition about the way the goals must be reached. The global behavior of the agents tries to reach the defined goals and accomplish the whole goals specification.

3. **Skills-based behaviors:** Agents are capable to add skills into their global behavior, so, the agents use the skills to achieve their goals. In our architecture, the agents are able to adapt their skills, because the skills are shared and implemented as registered mobile services.

4. **Agent personality and mood and emotion simulation:** The personality and emotion simulation make difference in behaviors of agents that have the same set of skills and the same set of primitive actions. This means that the agents are entities in constant change, which affects their emotions and moods in function of the environment state.

Figure 2 shows the architecture of the platform GeDA-3D. This platform has been grouped in different modules: Virtual Environments Editor

(VEE), Rendering, GeDA-3D Kernel, Emotional Agents Community (EAC) and Context Descriptor (CD). The striped rectangle encloses the main components of GeDA-3D: scene control, agent control and scene editor. The VEE includes the scene descriptor, interpreter, congruency analyzer and constraint solver.

The VEE provides an interface between the GeDA-3D platform and the user; it specifies the physical laws that govern an environment and it describes a virtual scene taking place in such environment. Rendering addresses all the issues related to 3D graphics representation in a visual medium like the screen or the monitor; it allows the design of virtual objects and displaying of the scene. The EAC is composed by the agents that are in charge of ruling virtual objects behavior. The scene descriptor gives to the agents a detailed description about what we want them to do instead of how we want them to do it. Furthermore, this scene might involve a set of goals

for a single agent, and it is not necessary that these goals are reached in a sequential way. It is also not necessary to give the avatar a set of actions to perform; we only need to determine a set of goals in a sequence of primitive actions. So, we need agents able to add shared skills into their global behavior. The user is enabled to construct the scene using a high level language similar to Human language. The user does not provide the sequence of actions that the avatar must perform; he only specifies the goals that should be achieved by the avatars. That is, the agents' behavior is in charge of trying to reach the goals specified in the scene description. The reason of creating this kind of scenes is to visualize a behaviors-based simulation, in other words, the user specifies what the agents must do, instead of how they have to do it. Therefore, two similar specifications might produce different simulations.

Figure 2. GeDA-3D agents architecture

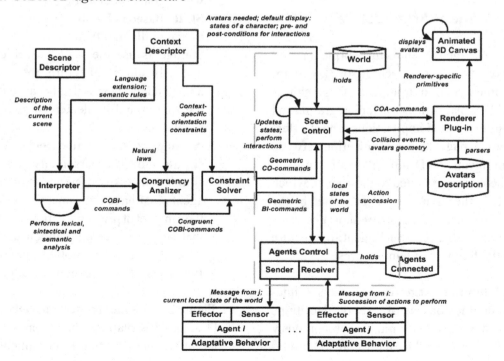

An Ontology for Affective Personified Emotional Agents (APE Agents)

In this work we have defined and implemented the complete access to the ontology for APE Agents to define the internal structure of an avatar (skeleton), its behavior (personality, emotions and moods) and its skills, the main objective is the exploitation and use of the information and knowledge offered by the ontology in order to create autonomous animations of virtual creatures or avatars. This ontology was defined and implemented using The Protégé Ontology Editor and Knowledge Acquisition System (http://protege.stanford.edu). Some of the reasons most important to use the ontology are: To define the internal structure of avatar, its behavior and skills, and to share information and common understanding of the semantic definition of avatar among APE Agents in 3D dynamic virtual environments. The proposed ontology will be used as basis for some applications of motion planning and motion learning of avatars.

This ontology offers a formal description of APE Agents. Figure 3 shows the relationships between the main classes of the proposed ontology. These classes provide a semantic definition of avatar and should be taken into account in animation algorithms. In this ontology, an avatar is defined using a morphology description (qualitative description) that defines its skeleton (the skeleton is inherent to the geometry of avatar)

and the anthropometry description (quantitative description) that offers information about its age, gender, weight and height. In addition, as a part of its behavior, an avatar has personality, emotions and moods. An avatar can develop its AEI to understand and to express its emotions and moods.

The internal skeleton of an avatar (see Figure 4) is formed by several parts, bones and joints in specific (skeleton parts). Each joint has a name and can have joints parents and/or joints children. There are motion constraints defined for each joint and a set of simple motions that define the alphabet of movements (micro-animation) that will be used to generate complex motions by means of combination (macro-animation) between them. Also each bone can be united to one or more joints, and each joint has its position in the skeleton of avatar. Each bone of avatar has its measures that can be expressed in a predetermined unit of measurement, for example, in centimeters or decimeters.

The personality of avatar is defined with the help of a set of characteristics or personality traits that can be positive or negative and active or passive. Each trait has an intensity that denotes the behavior of avatar (see Figure 5).

Personality traits can determine the behavior of avatar under the influence of certain events and stimuli. In Figure 6 the emotional state of avatar is shown. The emotional state is a set of emotions with the emotional history. A set of facial

Figure 3. Semantic definition of avatar

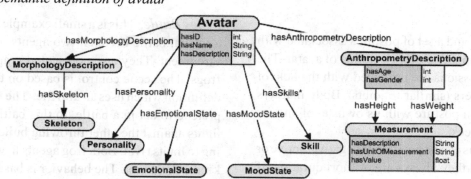

367

Figure 4. Skeleton Definition of avatar

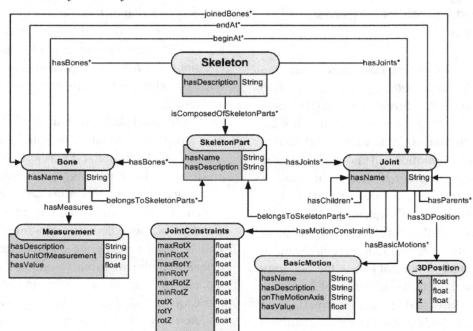

Figure 5. Personality of avatar

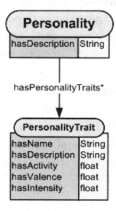

expressions and a set of postures associated with them correspond to every emotion of avatar. The facial expressions are produced with the help of facial markers (similar to joints). Body markers provide each posture with its own set of animation sequences.

Emotions can be positive or negative, active or passive, but they always are of short duration. If an avatar is sad, it is able to adopt a facial expression and posture that show its emotional state. In the same way, the mood state of avatar is a set of moods with a mood history. Moods can also be positive or negative and active or passive, but also neutral (see Figure 7).

Finally, each skill that avatar learns is defined using a set of animation sequences. These sequences imply skeleton parts of avatar in motion and a set of corresponding facial expressions associated with them (see Figure 8).

Cases Studies

Frogs Battle: This is a small example that shows a virtual battle between two agents in a 2D environment. They are represented graphically as frogs. The scene control is based on the context definition which uses an xml file. The frog agents pretend to act in a battle. In this battle one frog fights against the other throwing bullets and trying to hit its rival. Both frog agents have the same kind of behavior. The behavior is based on basic

Figure 6. Emotional state of avatar

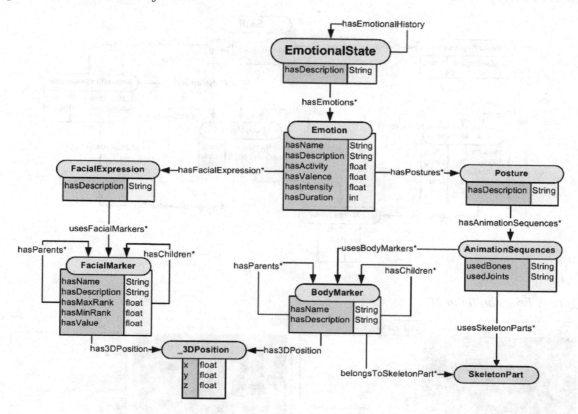

Figure 7. Mood state of avatar

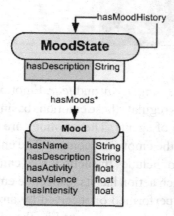

actions like *move to the left* or *right* and *shoot*. The mixture of these three simple actions defines the decision making. The decisions depend on the environment situations. Also the emotions participate in the decision making process.

If a frog agent is attacked continuously, the negative influence can affect its emotions. The next decision to take is also affected. The agent can loose control taking bad decisions, which finally results in its death within the virtual environment (see Figure 9). The AEI perfects the decision making. It helps the agents to maintain self-control, although they are attacked continuously or menaced by numerous bullets. The AEI evaluates the actual situation of the agent's environment and the possible next actions to perform with the intention to maintain the emotional control. Then the actions, that emotionally seem to be the most convenient ones, are offered to the agent. In this case study the emotions take important part in making decisions. If the agent's *anger* or *fear* level is high, it makes decisions thinking poorly. On the other hand, if the agent's emotional levels are equilibrated, it makes better

Figure 8. Skills of avatar

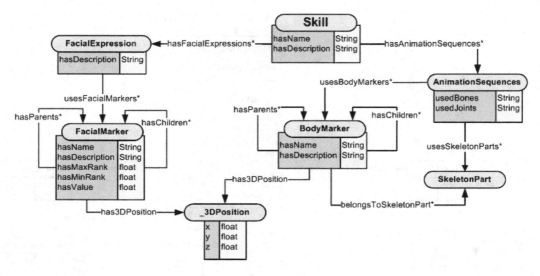

Figure 9. Frogs battle in 2D

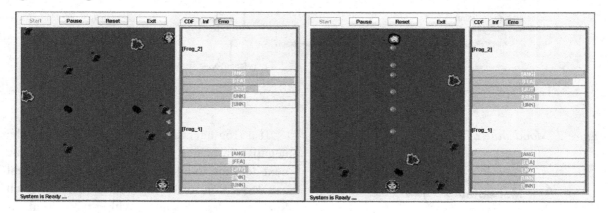

decisions. Therefore, the EAI is the tool that helps the agents to survive.

Persecution: This case study is implemented using a virtual 3D environment which runs over the GeDA-3D Agent Architecture. The emotional context has been defined for the 3D environment. Two kinds of agents are used, one is offensive and the other is defensive. The offensive agent persecutes the defensive one. The defensive agent tries to avoid the offensive agent's persecution, evading it when it is near and fleeing when it is closer. Both are emotional agents (see Figure 10). Three different emotions have been defined for

these agents: *anger*, *joy* and *fear*. Emotional and mood states regulate these emotions basing on the personality of agents. The emotions are defined initially in the emotional context. The emotional context also includes the actions that can be performed. Each action has its respective emotional cost when performed or received by any agent. For instance, when one agent hits the other, the first agent performs the hit, the second receives it. Then, both have an emotional price to pay.

In this case study we use a 3D visual animation. The avatars modify their facial expressions and postures showing the emotion predominant

Figure 10. An offensive avatar that persecutes a defensive avatar

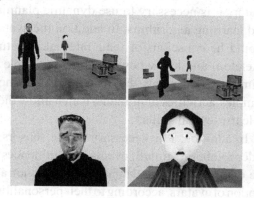

in their emotional state. This case study shows the performance more complete in visual aspect, because the avatars are made in 3D. Avatars change their facial expressions, when some interaction modifies their emotional and mood states in the virtual environment. A scenarist or designer could use the emotional context as we do in this case study to define it with the help of a high level language. He can define the personality and the initial emotional state of the avatars. Then we can start the interaction between them using their emotional skills without technical or complex definitions.

Pin8 family interaction: In this case study we show different situations where the emotional skills of APE Agents can be used and manipulated. This case study presents a virtual drama of avatars (we have called them *pin8 family*) in a 3D virtual environment. There is a virtual human that owns a dog. The dog attacks other virtual human persecuting him; the victim is really scared and runs away. After that, the dog goes out of the scene. The avatar that was attacked by the dog shouts angrily at the dog owner and reproaches him for letting the dog free. Fight starts, then both avatars go out of the scene. Later the dog owner finds a sheet of paper in his house with a message from the dog pound. His dog has been caught and taken away by the dog pound because of the previously described incident. The dog owner

is inconsolable; he loves the dog very much. He goes to the dog pound, explains the situation and finally obtains the permit to keep the dog in his house again. He is very happy. So, in this case study we show different situations that modify the emotional state and mood state of avatars. This modification provokes changes in their behavior, facial expressions and postures (see Figure 11).

The implemented study cases were made using the PEM model (Egges et al., 2004) for the first and second study case and the PEL model (Li et al., 2007) for the last study case in combination with the *Emotional Competence Framework* (ECF). Unfortunately, the results we have obtained using these models for the simulation of case studies were not the best ones, compared to our expectations. Therefore, we consider that it is necessary to create other models with optimized qualities.

FUTURE TRENDS

In the last years the graphical representation and animation of avatars has been focused on the use and manipulation of predetermined animated forms. Nevertheless, it is necessary to consider the avatars as 3D semantic entities with well-defined characteristics and functionalities. To our opinion,

Figure 11. Avatars and their interactions in a virtual drama (pin8 family)

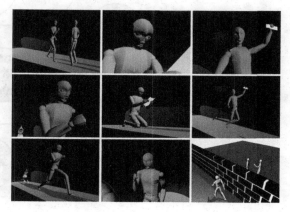

the future trend is focused on the definition of the minimum conscience of avatars and the use of reinforcement learning and dynamic planning as a part of the cognitive processes of the avatars. It will allow the avatars to learn new skills within certain context. This idea is original, because it is applied to the cognitive processes of avatars, which allow solving the avatars animation problems in a more natural way. Therefore, it is necessary to provide avatars with minimum conscience and knowledge of how its skeletal structure is formed (considering its mobility and restrictions). The AEI allows the avatars to learn movements and compute motion planning activities, to learn basic skills, for instance, keep equilibrium or perform successfully more complex activities.

The conscience in general is defined as the knowledge that the Human being has of itself and of its environment. In this work, the conscience of avatar is the notion that it has of the sensations, thoughts and feelings that are experienced in a given moment in its environment. Thus, the avatar's conscience is the understanding of its environment and its self-knowledge. In other words, it is the notion that it has of its sensations, thoughts and feelings in the determined environment.

Figure 12 shows the proposed solution over the GeDA-3D Agent Architecture. To animate the avatars it is necessary to use dynamic planning and learning algorithms. In addition the avatars should be conscious of their internal structure (skeleton) and know how to combine simple or primitive movements they can make into more complex activities or motions, which allow them to learn several skills.

In addition, it is necessary to use sensors in order to obtain stimuli, events and influences of the environment that can alter the behavior and motion of avatars, according to their personalities, emotions and moods. For example, if an avatar is happy or angry, its facial expression indicates its emotion, and its movements and behavior are changed; when it is sad, its movements are slower than when it is happy.

In the scheme shown in Figure 12 the posture and the motion of an avatar are coordinated. The posture control is performed by references that indicate the direction and the required degree of stability of avatar body. The sensorial entrances produce readjustments in the position of avatar and contribute to the modification of its corporal scheme. When the avatar makes a motion, advance adjustment of posture is produced (pro-action).

Figure 12. Proposed solution

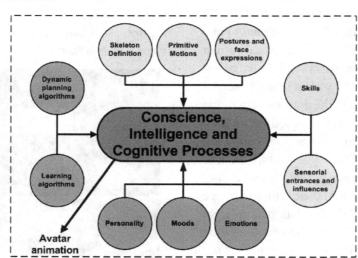

The brain of the avatar contains internal model of its corporal segments relative sizes, their relations and positions. Therefore, the corporal scheme of avatar is the source of its corporal perception. Thus, the avatar adopts a posture and a face expression that reflect its emotions and mood. The corporal scheme of avatar is a representation of its skeleton and possible actions defined by:

1. Semantic and lexical information on the parts of the body and the skeleton of avatar.
2. Visual-space representations of the avatar body and the objects of its environment. For instance, the nose is situated in the middle of the face, the ears one to each side of the head, the mouth under the nose, the eyes above the nose and one to each side of the face.
3. Corporal reference and composition of the motions on the basis of the avatar body perception and its influences.

Figures 13 and 14 present the proposed modules of learning and dynamic planning for the GeDA-3D Agent Architecture. The AEI, personality,

emotions and moods are related to learning and dynamic motion planning of avatar.

The avatar explores its body to know its structure and to learn a set of primitive motions, the basis for generating complex motions. In addition, the avatar receives a set of goals and plans and a series of motions necessary to fulfil them.

In this work we propose the use of synergies to support the idea that the avatar cannot control all the degrees of freedom of its skeleton. For this reason a set of simple or primitive motions is selected (natural motions) to generate complex motions. Therefore, synergies are the base of the motions of avatars and can be manipulated by means of learning and dynamic planning algorithms.

So, for our future work we are planning the following main activities:

1. To implement the conscience as a part of EI and cognitive processes of avatars.
2. To implement the proposed learning and dynamic planning module for the GeDA-3D Agent Architecture.
3. To use the alphabet of simple motions (micro-animation) defined in the proposed ontology

Figure 13. Learning module for the GeDA-3D Agent architecture

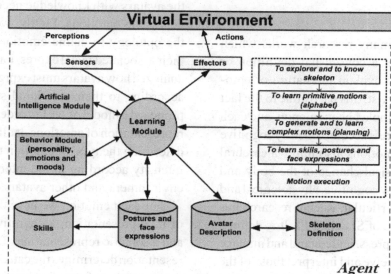

Figure 14. Dynamic motion planning module for the GeDA-3D Agent architecture

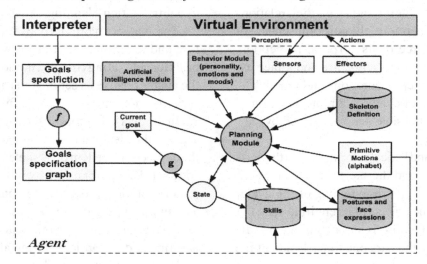

in order to generate and plan complex motions (macro-animation).

4. To propose another model for personality, emotion and mood simulation (behavior simulation) and for processing emotional influences better that the PEM model (Egges et al., 2004) and the PEL model (Li et al., 2007).

5. To define and to implement more study cases for the GeDA-3D Agent Architecture.

CONCLUSION

Though there are many research works which bring up this topic, a consensual definition or dominant theory to explain the nature of emotions still does not exist, this partly due to the fact that emotion is a complex phenomenon, and each emotional experience is accompanied by cognitive treatment. Some emotions also imply a cerebral reaction and a physical change of the body and can be represented by cognitive, physiological and somatic states in particular. Recent research has revealed a new type of SI called EI. It is defined as the capacity to express, understand and manage emotions, as to perceive and interpret those of the others. In the emotional interpersonal relation-

ships the aptitudes of avatars will determine their capabilities to achieve their goals.

In order to provide the avatars with EI it is necessary to give them the capacity to understand their emotions. To understand a concept means to be able to express emotions. In this work we have presented a methodology and agent architecture to determine how the agents must express their emotions. The emotions are complex phenomena that gather various facets, such as the physiological, the somatic and the cognitive ones. In the present work we have explained how to provide the avatars with knowledge necessary to express believable emotions. Firstly, we have proposed the ontology to define emotions of avatars and their associated facial expressions. Later, we have analyzed how avatars must express their emotions according to their emotional states. Lastly, we proposed a model of AEI in order to formalize the representation of emotions. It allows the agents to determine the type of emotion to express and its intensity according to the interaction with their environment and other avatars.

For each emotion we have defined two types of its representation: a cognitive representation and a somatic representation. The cognitive representation determines the causes of emotion. The interpretation of perceived events is based on the cognitive representation of emotions, determined by the stimuli perceived and by the personality traits of an avatar. Thus, emotion is triggered by particular interpretation of an event or stimulus that corresponds to the cognitive representation of the cause of certain emotion. We have defined the emotional mental state as the cognitive representation of its inductive cause. The somatic representation determines how the avatars express their emotions. These representations allow to identify the mental states correspondent to each emotional state and to determine the intensity of emotions, taking into account the influence of the avatar's personality.

All the models proposed in this work are applied to the Architecture for Distributed Applications Management GeDA-3D (GeDA-3D Agent Architecture). This is the platform for creation, design and executing of 3D distributed dynamic virtual environments with the use of APE Agents. The emotional agents evolve in the GeDA-3D's virtual environments employing the AEI. The emotional agents' behaviors and interactions are influenced by their emotions and moods. Thus, the AEI helps them to take most accurate decisions. These decisions keep the agents' emotional status balanced and keep them alive in the environment. Sensorial entrances and influences that the avatars receive from their environment alter their behavior and motion and also affect their emotions and mood. For instance, if an avatar is happy or angry, its facial expression indicates its emotion; its movements and behavior also change. When the avatar is sad, its movements are slower, than when it is happy.

Therefore, the main idea of our work is the application of the term AEI, which takes its origin in the psychological context of EI. The behavior of avatars is controlled by APE Agents. The AEI makes the avatars act in the most credible manner, that is to say, it makes them simulate the behavior of living creatures to survive and adapt to the virtual environment, which uses emotional context. The AEI is a topic that is slightly explored. In this work we present the first approach that allows us to gain more knowledge about AEI and develop it in the context of emotional agents.

The proposed architecture owns the features defined in MAS theory, but it offers some extra features specific to the problem. This work contributes, for example, to the topics of goal-specification, skill based behaviors, collective knowledge bases, posture descriptors and facial animation descriptors. Our work presents a new architecture suitable to manage virtual creatures giving them conscience of their skeletal structure, emotions and mood management. As the important contribution to the research into the topic we have proposed a distributed architecture that is appropriate, when the behaviors include complex algorithms like NP problem solutions.

Our future work includes the autonomous or semiautonomous animation of avatars with the application of knowledge bases, dynamic motion planning techniques, motion learning and behavior models based on AEI. These results will be applied to the development of semiautonomous and autonomous avatars that interact in 3D distributed dynamic virtual environments within the GeDA-3D Agent Architecture. Finally, we have explained the use and definition of the proposed ontology. As for our future research, we are going to focus it on development of advanced APE Agents, taking into account that personality traits, emotions, moods and their relationships in a behavior model based on AEI are essential to ensure suitable and believable performance for this agent type.

REFERENCES

Adolphs, R., Tranel, D., & Damasio, A. R. (1998). The human amygdale in social judgement. *Nature, 393*(6684), 470-474.

Anderson, A. K., & Phelps, E. A. (2002). Is the human amygdale critical for the subjective experience of emotion? Evidence of intact dispositional affect in patients with amygdale lesions. *Journal of Cognitive Neuroscience, 14*(5), 709-720.

Bar-On, R. (1997). *The emotional quotient inventory (EQ-i): Technical manual*. Toronto: Multi-Health Systems.

Batson, C. D., Shaw, L. L., & Oleson, K. C. (1992). Differentiating affect, mood, and emotion. *Emotion*, 294-326.

Berkowitz, L. (2000). *Causes and consequences of feelings*. Cambridge, England: Cambridge University Press.

Bless, H., & Schwarz, N. (1999). Mood, its impact on cognition and behavior. *Blackwell encyclopedia of social psychology*. Oxford, England: Blackwell.

Brehm, J. W. (1999). The intensity of emotion. *Personality and Social Psychology Review, 3*, 2-22.

Costa, P. T., & McCrae, R. R. (1992). Normal personality assessment in clinical practice: The NEO personality inventory. *Psychological Assessment, 4*(1), 5-13.

Damasio, A. R. (1994). *Descartes' error: Emotion, reason and the human brain*. New York: Avon Books.

Damasio, A. R. (1995). *L'error de Descartes: la raison des émotions*. Paris: Odile Jacob.

Dyer, M. G. (1987). Emotions and their computations: Three computer models. *Cognition and Emotion, 1*(3), 323-347.

Egges, A., Kshirsagar, S., & Magnenat-Thalmann, N. (2004). Generic personality and emotion simulation for conversational agents: *Computer animation and virtual worlds, 15*(1), 1-13.

Ekman, P. (1982). *Emotion in the human face*. New York: Cambridge University Press.

Ekman, P. (1994). *Moods, emotions, and traits, the nature of emotion: Fundamental auestions*. New York: Oxford University Press.

El-Nasr, M. S., Yen, J., & Ioerger, T. R. (2000). FLAME - Fuzzy Logic Adaptive Model of Emotions. *Autonomous Agents and Muti-Agent Systems, 3*(3), 219-257.

Evans, D. (2001). *Emotion: The science of sentiment*. Oxford, England: Oxford University Press.

Eysenck, H. J. (1990). *Biological dimensions of personality. Handbook of personality: Theory and research*. New York: Guilford.

Fellous, J.-M. (1999). The neuromodulatory basis of emotion. *The Neuroscientist, 5*, 283-294.

Fridja, N., & Swagerman, J. (1987). Can computers feel? Theory and design of an emotional sysem. *Cognition and Emotion, 1*(3), 235-257.

Fridja, N. (1987). *The emotions: Studies in emotion and social interaction*. New York: Cambridge Universty Press.

Gardner, H. (1983). *Frames of the mind*. New York: Basic Books.

Goleman, D. (1995). *Emotional intelligence*. New York: Bantam Books.

Goleman, D. (1998). *Working with emotional intelligence*. New York: Bantam Books.

Jiang, H., & Vidal, J. M. (2006). From rational to emotional agents. In *Proceedings of the American Association for Artificial Intelligence (AAAI). Workshop on Cognitive Modeling and Agent-based Social Simulation*.

Leary, T. (1957). *Interpersonal diagnosis of personality*. New York: Ronald Press.

LeDoux, J. E. (1996). *The emotional brain: The mysterious underpinnings of emotional life*. New York: Simon and Schuster.

Lee, M., & Franklin, S. (1998). An architecture for emotion. *AAAI Fall Symposium Emotional and Intelligent: The Tangled Knot of Cognition.* (pp. 122-128). Menlo Park, CA: AAAI Press.

Li, T., Qiu, Y., Yue, P., & Zhong, G. (2007). Exploiting model of personality and emotion of learning companion agent. *International Conference on Computer Systems and Applications* (pp. 860-865).

Masuch, M., Hartman, K., & Schuster, G. (2006). Emotional agents for interactive environments. In *C5'06: Proceedings of the Fourth International Conference on Creating, Connecting and Collaborating through Computing* (pp. 96-102).

McCrae, R., & John, O. (1992). An introduction to the five-factor model and its application. *Journal of Personality, 60*(2), 175-215.

Mayer, J.D. (2000). Emotion, intelligence, emotional intelligence. *The handbook of affect and social cognition.* Mahwah, New Jersey: Lawrence Erlbaum and Associates.

Mayer, J.D., & Geher, G. (1996). Emotional intelligence and the identification of emotion. *Intelligence, 22*, 89-113.

Mayer, J. D., & Salovey, P. (1993). The intelligence of emotional intelligence. *Intelligence, 17*(4), 433-442.

Mayer, J. D., & Salovey, P. (1995). Emotional intelligence and the construction and regulation of feelings. *Applied and Preventive Psychology, 4*, 197-208.

Mayer, J. D., Salovey, P., & Caruso, D. R. (2000). Models of emotional intelligence. *Handbook of intelligence.* Cambridge, UK: Cambridge University Press.

Ortony, A. (2003). On making believable emotional agents believable. In *Emotions in humans and artifacts* (pp. 189-212) Cambridge, Massachusetts; London, England: MIT Press.

Ortony, A., Clore, G. L., & Collins, A. (1988). *The cognitive structure of emotions.* New York: Cambridge Universty Press.

Pereira, D., Oliveira, E., Moreira, N., & Sarmento, L. (2005). Towards an architecture for emotional BDI agents. In *EPIA'05: Proceedings of 12th Portuguese Conference on Artificial Intelligence* (pp. 40-47).

Piza, H. I., Zúñiga, F., & Ramos, F. F. (2004). A platform to design and run dynamic virtual environments. In *Proceedings of the 2004 International Conference on Cyberworlds* (pp. 78-85).

Roseman, I. J., Jose, P. E., & Spindel, M. S. (1990). Appraisals of emotion-eliciting events: testing a theory of discrete emotions. *Journal of Personality and Social Psychology, 59*(2), 899-915.

Salovey, P., & Mayer, J.D. (1990). Emotional intelligence. *Imagination, Cognition, and Personality, 9*, 185-211.

Salovey, P., & Sluyter, D. J. (1997). *Emotional development and emotional intelligence.* New York: Basic Books.

Zúñiga, F., Ramos, F. F., & Piza, I. (2005). GeDA-3D agent architecture. In *Proceedings of the 11th International Conference on Parallel and Distributed Systems, 2*, 201-205.

KEY TERMS

Artificial Emotional Intelligence: It implies the ability of avatar (virtual entity) to understand, distinguish and manage its emotions and those of other avatars (virtual entities). This ability includes: self-consciousness, goal understanding, intentions, reactions and behaviors, also consciousness of other avatars and their feelings.

Artifical Intelligence: Represents the ability of a virtual character or avatar to perceive and express emotions, assimilate emotion-related feelings, understand and reason with emotion, and regulate emotions in itself and other virtual entities. That is to say, it refers to the ability to recognize the meanings of emotions and their relationships.

Conscience: The conscience in general is defined as the knowledge that the Human being has of itself and of its environment. The conscience of avatar is the notion that it has of the sensations, thoughts and feelings that are experienced in a given moment in its environment. Thus, it is the understanding of its environment and its self-knowledge. It means that the conscience of avatar is the notion that it has of the sensations, thoughts and feelings in its environment.

Emotion: It is a volatile feeling that affects the behavior of an avatar. Emotions are the response to a particular stimulus perceived by the avatar. They are more specific and intense than moods, and are reactions more immediate and spontaneous than moods.

Intelligence: The global capacity of a virtual entity (avatar) to profit from experience, act and think rationally and abstractly and adapt to changes in the environment.

Mood: It is a quasi-permanent value that actives a quasi-permanent feeling in the virtual entity, affecting its behavior. Moods are less intense that emotions and are diffuse and unfocused.

Ontology: It is a formal specification of a conceptualization; it defines a common vocabulary to share information in a domain.

Personality: It is a set of personal characteristics that influence the cognition, motivation and behavior of avatar in different situations. Thus, it is a value set that indicates the way of a virtual entity to react according to the situation.

Personality Trait. A trait is an individual characteristic of avatar that describes a habitual behavior. Therefore, a personality trait is a relatively consistent characteristic of a virtual creature exhibited in various situations.

Skill: It represents any learned capacity that allows the avatar (virtual creature) to carry out tasks or activities in its environment.

Chapter XIX
Physics and Cognitive–Emotional–Metacognitive Variables:
Learning Performance in the Environment of CTAT

Sarantos I. Psycharis
University of the Aegean, Greece

ABSTRACT

In our study we collected data with respect to cognitive variables (learning outcome), metacognitive indicators (knowledge about cognition and regulation of cognition) psychological variables (self-esteem) and emotional variables (motives, anxiety). The teaching sequence was implemented using the CTAT authoring tool and the basic teaching unit was referred to fundamental concepts in Mechanics for 20 4th year undergraduate students enrolled in the course «Applied Didactics in Natural Sciences» of the University of the Aegean-Department of Education. Analysis of the results shows that anxiety (a negative emotion) can be reduced using CTAT, there is a transfer from extrinsic to intrinsic motivation while metacognitive indicators as well as learning performance can be improved using CTAT. The interactivity of the learning environment influences also self esteem and the results are presented.

INTRODUCTION

Intelligent Tutoring Systems (ITS) have been successful in raising student learning outcome and have been used quite widely in exploring the teaching-learning sequence (TLS). ITS have been shown to be highly effective in improving students' learning outcome (cognitive performance) in real classrooms (VanLehn2006). The term intelligence corresponds to cognitive skills such as the ability to solve problems, learn, and understand but contemporary research has been focused also on concepts and methods for building programs with emphasis on reasoning rather than on calculating a solution. In ITS problem solving is achieved by applying inference engines to a knowledge base to derive new information, to create new facts and new rules and make decisions. Usually, an inference engine is a software component which reasons over rules when the application is executed while its major task performed is conflict resolution, which determines the sequence of the consultation (Hicks, 2007).

Cognitive/Intelligent Tutors are considered as learning environments based on ITS and cognitive modelling (how people learn) aimed to improve the learning outcome in cognitively-based instructional design .In parallel they deal with cognitive task analysis and exploration of pedagogical content knowledge which is considered as a fundamental ingredient in the cognitively-based instruction (Lovett et al., 2000, Schraagen et al., 2000). Cognitive Tutors learning environments are developed in order to provide a problem-solving environment reinforced with a variety of representation tools, real world scenarios which demand algebraic reasoning, tutorial guidance in the form of step-by-step feedback, specific messages, hints in response to common errors and misconceptions, and -on demand- instructional hints to be used as explanations for the concepts involved in the problem. At ITS systems advised is provided on demand in a progressive way so the learner is involved in the scientific process. ITS has also the property to dynamically adjust to individual learner's needs and method of approach to the problem. (Aleven et al., 2006). Cognitive Tutors are based primary on the ACT-R(Adaptive Control of Thought-Rational) theory of cognition (Anderson et al., 1995) under the hypothesis that a complex cognitive domain can be understood in terms of small knowledge components called production rules that are learned independently of each other. Production rules represents the target competence that the tutor is meant to help students acquire. Developing a Cognitive Tutor involves creating a cognitive model of student problem solving by writing production rules that characterize the set of strategies and misconceptions. Productions are written in a modular fashion, like in high order programming languages, so that they can apply to a goal and context independent of the specific issue they deal with.

Production rule model (a set of rules about behaviour) is fundamental for the domain intelligence, that is the tutoring system's knowledge of the specific discipline.

The intelligence of the system uses two algorithms, the model tracing and the knowledge tracing algorithm.

Model tracing algorithm uses the production model in order to interpret each student's activities and to follow students' different methodologies and strategic plans as they work through problem solving. The results of model tracing are used to provide students with correctness, error feedback, hints and to provide advice to student about his/her justification and reasoning steps. The main ingredient of the algorithm is the use of comparison techniques, so it can evaluate student's step against all possible steps provided by the ITS. If the action taken by the student is among these actions, the tutor provides implicit positive feedback, and negative feedback if the model registers incorrect behaviour (correct/incorrect according to the corresponding production rule). The model-tracing algorithm is also used in order to provide hints upon a student's request. When the student requests a hint, the tutor selects one of the productions that could apply to generate a next step at this point. A hint template attached to this production is filled in with problem specific information and then presented to the student (VanLehn et al., 2005).

The knowledge algorithm is used to estimate how well an individual student has mastered the knowledge components of the particular unit. Of course it is realised with a certain probability and the upgraded information is restored in order to be used as a next step to the model tracing algorithm.

Basically the idea is based on the Bayesian networks which assumes that the student is in one of two states with respect to a given production rule: the student either knows the rule or not. The Bayesian formula expresses the probability that the student knows the knowledge component as a function of three parameters, assumed to be fixed: (a) a probability that a student learns the knowledge component as a result of encountering it (once) in any given tutor problem, (b) a probability of guessing right even when the knowledge component is not mastered, and (c) a probability of not getting the step right even if the knowledge component is mastered. The knowledge-tracing procedure enables the tutor to determine when a student is ready to move on to (Corbett and Anderson, 1995).

BACKGROUND: PSYCHOLOGICAL-EMOTIONAL-METACOGNITION VARIABLES

Several research papers have illustrated the significance of emotions in both learning and performance situations (e.g., Moller and Koller, 1996, Laukenmann, 2003) while Jerusalem and Pekrun (1999) emphasize that positive emotions are in strong connection with learning and performance situations. Another aspect that is emphasized is the strong relationship between emotion and motivation. Hope of success, pride, taking joy in success, fear for failure, or indifference and low-level anxiety in relation to lack of success are seen as particularly motivating for achievement (Heckhausen, 1989; Laukenmann, 2003). Not only theoretical but experimental studies have shown that a positive mood reinforces creative and fluid thought processes, an effect that is explained via information processing theories (Abele and Becker 1991). The constructs 'emotional intelligence' (Salovey and Meyer, 1990) or 'emotional competence' (Saarni, 1990) are employed in order to emphasize that the abilities of (accurate) per-

ception and the dealing with emotional states in relation to oneself and others are preconditions for learning processes and should therefore be reinforced in schools.

Anxiety is an emotional variable and all trainees experience anxiety especially at science courses (Cassady, 2004). To ensure that anxiety is at a moderate level it is important to create such environments that help students to be properly prepared or have a good guidance so anxiety will be reduced.

Another aspect that does not favour anxiety is the adaptation of the problem to students' personal characteristics and cognitive level. Cognitive Tutors can manage students' differences and adapt their environment to the personal characteristics, while students' performance is not presented in the class but instead at the log-server of the tool. This fact is considered also as fundamental in order to reduce anxiety.

Motivation is an internal state that directs and sustains students' behaviour. The research of motivation in the framework of science education attempts to give an explanation why students strive for specific goals when learning science, how intensively they strive and what feelings and emotions characterize them in process. (Glynn & Koballa 2006). The question of how academic intrinsic motivation and high academic achievement can be increased has been of central interest to educators and psychologists. Toward this direction, teachers and teaching practices as well as learning environments are considered to be critical factors that can contribute to the development of an intrinsic interest in learning. (Weiler, 2004).

Many self-concept researchers (e.g., Harter, 1988; Marsh, 1990) have argued that self-concept cannot be adequately understood if the multidimensionality of the self-descriptive judgements is ignored. By conceptually and empirically separating the two aspects of self-concept, the descriptive-cognitive, the self-perception, and the emotional-evaluative, the self-esteem, we are in a position to determine the relationship that self-perceptions in the specific domains bear to the more global judgement of one's worth as a person. Self-esteem and self-perception, the two aspects of self-concept have been studied as important variables in the development of human being. Self–esteem is the global perception that we develop in relation to our value as individuals, besides our self-descriptions and our self-evaluations on the various domains of our lives. Self-esteem is an intervening variable in the educational and professional decision-making process, since it relates to a group of psychological variables (self-perception of ability, accomplishment stress, values, educational attitudes, interests, personality, centre of control etc) which influence the students' decisions. (Makri-Botsari, 2001). Several research studies have revealed that teaching practices which focus not only on the development of skills, but also on the enhancement of students' self-esteem, are more effective (Yeung & Wong, 2004, Swann, Chang-Schneider & Larsen McClarty, 2007). Self-esteem, defined here as a differentiated and evaluative process of self-definition is often related, in the investigation, with academic performance, scholastic competence and academic motivation.

Recent research papers have indicated the great importance of metacognition in the acquisition and application of learning skills in diverse domains of inquiry (Alexander, Fabricius, Fleming, Zwahr & Brown, 2003; Panaoura & Filippou, 2007).

Sperling, Howard and Staley (2004) suggest a focus on the component parts of metacognition, namely the knowledge about cognition and regulation of cognition (Boekaerts, 1997; Fernandez–Duque, Baird & Posner, 2000). Knowledge about cognition refers to the level of the learner's understanding of his/her own memories, cognitive system, and the way he/she learns; regulation of cognition refers to how well the learner can regulate his/her own learning system, i.e., goal setting, choosing and applying strategies, and monitoring his/her actions.

THE CTAT COGNITIVE TOOL

Cognitive Tutor Authoring Tools (CTAT) is a set of authoring tools that provides tutors for problem solving scenarios (Aleven et.al 2006, Koedinger et al., 2004). CTAT supports development of two types of tutors: Cognitive Tutors, which have a long and successful track record but require development of a cognitive model through AI programming, and a new type–easily constructed-of tutors, called «Example- Tracing Tutors», which can be built entirely without programming.

CTAT is freely available for research and educational purposes at *http://ctat.pact.cs.cmu.edu*.

An author (e.g. the teacher) can use an existing problem-solving environment or simulator or develop a new tutor interface using a set of CTAT components provided by CTAT for example to Flash Macromedia.

Next, the author should demonstrate examples of correct and incorrect behaviour for each problem on which students will be involved by the use of CTAT Behaviour Graph with links and nodes that represent problem-solving steps and states respectively. The author has the chance to set up alternative ways of solving the problem which are denoted as separate paths in the graph, demonstrate common student misconceptions (marked as incorrect actions), hints etc.

Example-Tracing Engine uses the Behaviour Graph to guide a student through a solution and then compares student's problem-solving behaviour against the graph. It provides positive feedback when the student's behaviour matches steps in the graph, and negative feedback otherwise (Koedinger et al., 2004; Koedinger & Aleven, 2007).

INTERACTIVITY ELEMENTS OF CTAT

When we decide to develop learning environments that effectively support student learning and provide the interface that students can express their emotions as well as their psychological characteristics, we should face the problem to include interactive and non-interactive features in the system.

Instructional techniques or events are described by the table below (Koedinger & Aleven, 2007).

There are two dimensions on instructional techniques. The first one (the rows) provide verbal generalizations (describe concepts and principles in the particular unit) or instances (examples and activities that engage the use of them without explicit expression of them).

The second dimension (columns) concerns the direction of communication after the system presents a learning task or learning materials to the learner and is related to system's response to learners actions and provision of feedback and response.

This dimension includes active instructional events, like asking students to solve problems or "self-explain" a worked example (Chi et al., 1989). The interactive instructional events, like problem-solving practice with a tutor, not only require a student response, but also provide feedback on students' responses, allow students to change original responses and provide feedback(yes/no) on the actions. Unlike active instructional events, in interactive instructional events additional information is provide if the learner fails to construct it. We would place Cognitive Tutors for certain in the interactive column since Cogni-

tive Tutors are significantly more interactive than alternatives such as solve textbook problems as homework, or solve problems with the help of typical computer-assisted instruction (Eberts, 1997). Cognitive Tutors provide assistance more frequently with detail information in an explicit way, as well as hints and selection rules, but not final solutions (students have to generate the solution steps). (VanLehn, 2006). Compared to a skilled human tutor, Cognitive Tutors are close in their level of interactivity since they have much in common with the way human tutors support students as they work through problems (Merrill et al., 1992, Bloom, 1984)), even if human tutors are capable of more flexible dialogue with students (Lepper & Malone, 1987). They also provide detailed solution-specific hints for each step but also withhold a considerable amount of information. Hints are given mainly at the student's request, at the tutor's initiative while information is revealed gradually.

RESEARCH METHODOLOGY AND RESULTS

We investigated the role of CTAT in the development of (1) the learning performance, (2) psychological variables(self-esteem), (3) metacognitive characteristics and (4) different emotions(anxiety-motives) during the teaching-learning sequence.

Figure 1. Snapshot of FLASH-CTAT

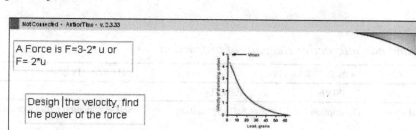

We decided to use CTAT in our research because we made the hypothesis that CTAT's response to learners actions and provision of feedback and response should favour not only the learning performance but the motives towards the final solution as well as the decrease of anxiety. CTAT adapts to student's needs and during the interaction the student can follow his/her own way to the process of learning, so we expect that anxiety can be reduced.

Due to the fact that CTAT provides an interactive instructional problem-solving practice with a tutor, it does not require just a students' responses, but also provide feedback on students' responses, students could change strategies for problem solving or set new goals during problem solving.

We consider that this could be related to the regulation of cognition as well as the knowledge of cognition(the main characteristics of metacognition) and this issue should be investigated in the framework of CTAT. Finally, since self-esteem it related to a group of psychological variables (self-perception of ability, accomplishment stress, values, educational attitudes, interests, personality, centre of control etc.) which influence the students' decisions, it should be interesting to see its connection with CTAT.

In a study of learning processes in 20 4th year undergraduate students (experimental group-group A) enrolled in the course « applied Didactics in Physics» data were collected in respect to: cognitive variables (learning outcomes), psychological variables(self-esteem), metacognitive variables and emotional variables (anxiety, motives) and we compared the variables to the another set of 22

students of the same class who did not participate in the research (control group-group B).

Learning Performance

Students had to solve problems in Physics in the Lab. They had attended previously a course on «Fundamentals in Physics» and another course on «Didactics in Physics» under the instruction of the author (S. Psycharis).

To investigate the cognitive variable we created in «Example Tutor»-using the Flash environment- a series of simulations about Mechanics (motion with constant and no constant, acceleration, work-energy theorem, power, potential energy etc.).

Students had to answer to 10 problems at both groups. Students of group A participated in the project while they had been expressed their willingness to participate and so they were taught the CTAT use environment for 3 hours.

We present as an example one question.

Question: Suppose we leave a particle moving under the influence of the gravity and air resistance $F = 2*.$velocity

1. Describe its motion (constant speed, accelerating with constant or no constant acceleration) 2.What is velocity at t=0? 3. What is its velocity after 2 secs? 4. What is the terminal velocity?

Each question was marked with grade 10. The learning outcome of the students participated is in Table 2.

Another interesting feature is the comparison of the results of the students participated with their grades at the two courses by the same Instructor. We mention here that the same students had at-

Table 1. interactive and non interactive elements of instruction

	NON INTERACTIVE		INTERACTIVE
	PASSIVE	ACTIVE	
Explicit, verbal generalization	Description	Self-explanation	Self-explanation with feedback
Implicit, instances	Example	Unguided practice	Tutored practice

Table 2. Learning performance of students for the 2 groups

COURSE «APLIED DIDACTICS IN PHYSICS»	Mean Cognitive performance	N	Std. Devition
Group A	77	20	3,725
Group B	55	22	3,605

Table 3. Students results in previous course called «Fundamentals in Physics»

COURSE «Fundamentals in Physics»	Mean Cognitive performance	N	Std. Devition
Group A	61	20	3,0
Group B	62	22	3,0

Table 4. Students results in previous course called «Didactics in Physics»

COURSE «Didactics in Physics»	Mean Cognitive performance	N	Std. Devition
Group A	65	20	3,5
Group B	69	22	3,9

tended the other two courses («Fundamentals in Physics» and «Didactics in Physics») two years ago before their enrolment at this course (Applied Didactics in Physics).

Psychological Variables-Self Esteem

To measure self esteem all students participated in Rosenberg's test [1982] for their classification according to their self-esteem. The total score of the Rosenberg questionnaire was in the scale 0-30. We have considered that scores ranging between 15-25 correspond to individuals with normal self-esteem (category 2), scores that are equal to or less than 15 correspond to low self-esteem (category 1) and the scores that are equal to or higher than 25 correspond to high self-esteem (category 3).

Table 5 shows the results of self-esteem for students of Group A and Table 6 for students in Group B. We mention here that we had measured the self-esteem of students of groups A,B before the instruction using CTAT and the traditional lecture.

From the results at Table 6 we observe a great increase for the self esteem of Group A.

Metacognitive Variables

One interesting feature is the analysis of the results of group A regarding the metacognitive variables.

Aspects of metacognition activity that were evaluated during problem solving included the following:

- Self-evaluating their ideas,
- Self-questioning when they encountered blocks,
- Detecting their errors, considering a range of possible alternatives,
- and considering limitations in their ideas (Linder & Marshall, 1997).

Each of the above mentioned indicators were marked as 1(for success) and 0 (for no action of students).

Table 5. Mean self esteem for Group A

COURSE «Applied Didactics in Physics»	Mean self esteem	N
Group A before	20	20
Group A after	26	20

Table 7. Mean Metacognition Group A

COURSE « Applied Didactics in Physics»	Mean metacognition	N
Group A before	60	20
Group A after	78	20

Table 6. Mean self esteem for Group B

COURSE « Applied Didactics in Physics»	Mean self esteem	N
Group B before	21	22
Group B after	23	22

Table 8. Mean Metacognition Group B

COURSE « Applied Didactics in Physics»	Mean metacognition	N
Group B before	58	22
Group B after	62	22

The classification (relating to metacognition) was as follows: Low metacognition corresponds to the range 0-30, medium 30-70 and high 70-100. The classification was carried out following an analysis of the log files provided by CTAT.

Tables 7, 8 show the results for the two groups before and after the instruction.

Emotional Variables-Anxiety-Motives

We did not use quantitative methods to measure anxiety and motives but we interviewed students of both groups. Students were classified as «high level of anxiety-3», «moderate level of anxiety-2», «low level of anxiety-1» according to their statements.

Regarding the motives students were interviewed and their answers were classified according to intrinsic and extrinsic motivation.

Intrinsic motivation is based on Bandura's work on self-efficacy , locus of control and goal orientation and students with intrinsic motivation attribute their performance results to internal factors that they can controlled by them, they consider that they can achieve the desired goals and they enjoy the mastering of concepts. In intrinsic motivation students do not think about reward when they achieve a goal.

Extrinsic motivation involves to do something as a means to get an award.

From interviews students of Group A before the instruction had a mean value of 2.5 while after the intervention, the level of anxiety was reduced to 2.Students referred that anxiety was eliminated due to the fact that they were felt free in time and space to work, while the help of CTAT in the form of feedback and hint messages helped them to feel comfortable. Group B students had a mean value 2.5 which was not change after the instruction with the traditional way.

Before the intervention by CTAT we asked students about the motivations in the specific course. Both groups had a high degree of extrinsic motivation(18 out of 20 in group A and 20 out of 22 in Group B) since the particular course is considered as a difficult course. After the intervention we recorded that 5 students of Group A changed their motivation from extrinsic to intrinsic ,while all students of Group B remained at their initial status about motivation.

CONCLUSION AND DISSCUSION

CTAT has been applied in Chemistry and Physics at stoichiometry, in the area of thermodynamics, in a study with mechanical engineering students at

Table 9. Correlations correlation between metacognitive variable and learning performance for Group A after Instruction

		metacognitive	cognit
metacognitive	Pearson Correlation	1	.670(**)
	Sig. (2-tailed)		.001
	N	20	20
cognit	Pearson Correlation	.670(**)	1
	Sig. (2-tailed)	.001	
	N	20	20

** *Correlation is significant at the 0.01 level (2-tailed)*

Carnegie Mellon University in Pittsburgh (USA) etc. In all these it was shown that the dialogues enhance the effectiveness of the system (Kumar et al., 2006).

Our preliminary results presented above provide strong evidence for the effectiveness of Cognitive Tutors over typical classroom instruction. They also support the main interactive features, like yes/no feedback and on-demand hints, specially principle-based explanations. In all cases of the group A we should mention that interaction was certainly increased as we had to chance to verify this issue with discussions with the students who participated in the research.

The main results of the research indicate that regarding the emotional variables: Anxiety was reduced and the main factor was the feeling that students felt free to express their way of thinking and their strategies.

We strongly believe that the two variables of metacognition (knowledge about cognition and regulation of cognition) is quite apparent that they should be developed due to the inherent nature of CTAT to provide the interactivity and students can express their strategies after the feedback of the system

Research is in progress to high school students in order to investigate the influence of these variables to students at secondary education.

REFERENCES

Abele, A. and Becker, P. (1991). *Wohlbefinden. Theorie – Empirie – Diagnostik.* Weinheim: Juventa.

Aleven, V., McLaren, B., Sewall, J., & Koedinger, K. (2006). The cognitive tutor authoring tools (CTAT): Preliminary evaluation of efficiency gains. In *Proceedings of ITS 2006.*

Alexander, J., Fabricius, W., Fleming, V., Zwahr, M., & Brown, S. (2003). The development of metacognitive causal explanations. *Learning and Individual Differences, 13,* 227-238.

Anderson, J. R., Corbett, A. T., Koedinger, K. R., & Pelletier, R. (1995). Cognitive tutors: Lessons learned. *The Journal of the Learning Sciences, 4*(2), 167-207.

Bloom, B. S. (1984). The 2-sigma problem: The search for methods of group instruction as effective as one to-one tutoring. *Educational Researcher, 13,* 4-16.

Boekaerts, M. (1997). Self-regulated learning: A new concept embraced by researchers, policy makers, educators, teachers and students. *Learning and Instruction, 7*(2), 161-186.

Cassady, J. (2004). The influence of cognitive test anxiety across the learning-testing cycle. *Learning and Instruction, 14*(6).

Chi, M. T. H., Bassok, M., Lewis, M. W., Reimann, P., & Glaser, R. (1989). Self-explanations: How students study and use examples in learning to solve problems. *Cognitive Science, 13*(2), 145-182.

Corbett, A., & Anderson, J. R. (1995). Knowledge tracing: modeling the acquisition of procedural knowledge. *User Modeling and User-Adapted Interaction, 4*, 253–278.

Eberts, R. E. (1997). Computer-based instruction. In M. G. Helander, T. K. Landauer, & P. V. Prabhu (Eds.), *Handbook of Human-Computer Interaction* (pp. 825–847). Amsterdam, The Netherlands: Elsevier.

Fernadez-Duque, D., Baird, J., & Posner, M. (2000). Awareness and Metacognition, *Consciousnesand Cognition, 9*, 324-326.

Glynn, S. M., & Koballa, T. R. (2006). Motivation to learn science. In J. Mintzes and W. Leonard (Eds.), *Handbook of college science teaching.* Arlington, VA: NSTA Press.

Harter, S. (1988). *Manual for the self-perception profile for adolescents.* Denver, CO: University of Denver Press.

Heckhausen, H. (1989). *Motivation und handeln.* Berlin: Springer.

Hicks, R. (2007).The no inference engine theory. *Decision Support Systems,43*(2).

Jerusalem, M., & Pekrun, R. (Eds.). (1999). *Emotion, motivation und leistung.* Gottingen, Bern, Toronto, Seattle: Hogrefe.

Koedinger, K., & Aleven, V. (2007). Exploring the assistance dilemma in experiments with cognitive tutors. *Educational Psychology Review 19*, 239-264.

Koedinger, K., Anderson, J., Hadley, W., & Mark, M. (1997). Intelligent tutoring goes to school in the big city. *International Journal of Artificial Intelligence in Education, 8*, 30-43

Koedinger, K., Aleven, V., Heffernan, N., McLaren, B., & Hockenberry, M. (2004). Opening the door to nonprogrammers: authoring intelligent tutor behavior by demonstration. In *Proceedings of ITS-2004* (pp. 162-174). Berlin: Springer

Kumar, R., Rosé, C., Aleven, V., Iglesias, A., & Robinson, A. (2006). Evaluating the effectiveness of tutorial dialogue instruction in an exploratory learning context. In Proceedings *ITS 2006.* (in Press).

Laukenmann, M. (2007). An investigation of the influence of emotional factors on learning in physics instruction. *International Journal of Science Education, 25*(4), 489 – 507.

Lepper, M. R., & Malone, T. W. (1987). Intrinsic motivation and instructional effectiveness in computer based education. In R. E. Snow & M. J. Farr (Eds.), *Aptitude, learning and instruction: Volume III Cognitive and affective process analyses.* Hillsdale, NJ: Erlbaum.

Linder, C., & Marshall, D. (1997). Introducing and evaluating metacognitive strategies in large-class introductory physics teaching. In C. Rust (Ed.), *Improving student learning: Improving students as learners* (pp. 411-422). Oxford, UK: Oxford Centre for Staff and Learning Development.

Lovett, M. C., Daily, L. Z., & Reder, L. M. (2000). A source activation theory of working memory: Cross-task prediction of performance in ACT-R. *Cognitive Systems Research, 1*, 99-118.

Makri-Botsari, E. (2001). Causal links between academic intrinsic motivation, self-esteem, and unconditional acceptance by teachers in high school students. In R. Riding & S. Rayner (Eds.), *International perspectives on individual differences. Vol. 2: Self-perception* (pp.209-220). Westport, CT: Ablex Publishing.

Marsh, H.W. (1990). The structure of academic self-concept, the Marsh/Shavelson model. *Journal of Educational Psychology, 82*, 623-636.

Merrill, D. C., Reiser, B. J., Ranney, M., & Trafton, J. G. (1992). Effective tutoring techniques: Comparison of human tutors and intelligent tutoring systems. *Journal of the Learning Sciences, 2*(3), 277-305.

Moller, J., & Koller, O. (Eds). (1996). *Emotionen, kognitionen und schulleistung.* Weinheim: Psychologie Verlags Union.

Panaoura, A., & Filippou, G. (2007). *Cognitive Development, 22*(2), 149-164.

Rosenberg, M. (1982). Psychological selectivity in self-esteem formation. In M. Rosenberg and H.B. Kaplan (Eds)., *Social psychology of the self-concept* (pp. 535–546). Arlington Heights, IL: Harlan Davidson.

Saarni, L. (1990). Emotional competence: how emotions and relationships become integrated. In R. A. Thompson (Ed.), *Socioemotional development.* Lincoln, NE: University of Nebraska Press.

Salovey, P., & Meyer, J. P. (1990). Emotional intelligence. *Imagination, Cognition and Personality, 9,* 185-211.

Schraagen, J. M., Chipman, S. F., Shalin, V. L. (2000). *Cognitive task analysis.* Mawah, NJ: Lawrence Erlbaum Associates.

Sperling, R., Howard, B., & Staley, R. (2004). Metacognition and self-regulated learning constructs. *Educational Research and Evaluation, 10*(2), 117-139.

Swann, W., Chang-Schneider, C., & Larsen Mc-Clarty, K. (2007). Do people's self-views matter? Self-concept and self-esteem in everyday life. *American Psychologist, 62*(2), 84-94.

Vanlehn, K., Lynch, C., Schultz, K., Shapiro, J. A., Shelby, R. H., & Taylor, L. (2005). The Andes physics tutoring system: Lessons learned. *International Journal of Artificial Intelligence in Education, 15*(3), 147-204.

VanLehn, K. (2006). The behavior of tutoring systems. *International Journal of Artificial Intelligence in Education, 16,* 227-265.

Weiler, A. (2004). Information-seeking behavior in Generation Y students: Motivation, critical thinking, and learning theory. *The Journal of Academic Librarianship, 31*(1), 46-53.

Yeung, A.S., Wong, E. (2004). *Teacher self-concept enhancement: Effects of an in-service training program in Hong Kong.* Hong Kong: The Hong Kong Institute of Education.

KEY TERMS

Cognitive/Intelligent Tutors: Considered as learning environments based on ITS and cognitive modelling (how people learn) aimed to improve the learning outcome in cognitively-based instructional design

The constructs **'emotional intelligence'** or **'emotional competence'** are employed in order to emphasize that the abilities of (accurate) perception and the dealing with emotional states in relation to oneself and others are preconditions for learning processes and should therefore be reinforced in schools.

Intelligence: Corresponds to cognitive skills such as the ability to solve problems, learn, and understand but contemporary research has been focused also on concepts and methods for building programs with emphasis on reasoning rather than on calculating a solution.

Knowledge about Cognition: The level of the learner's understanding of his/her own memories, cognitive system, and the way he/she learns.

Motivation: An internal state that directs and sustains students' behaviour.

Production Rules: Represent the target competence that the tutor is meant to help students acquire.

Regulation of Cognition: Refers to how well the learner can regulate his/her own learning system, i.e., goal setting, choosing and applying strategies, and monitoring his/her actions.

Self–Esteem: The global perception that we develop in relation to our value as individuals, besides our self-descriptions and our self-evaluations on the various domains of our lives.

Chapter XX
Emotional Memory and Adaptive Personalities

Anthony G. Francis, Jr.
Google, USA

Manish Mehta
Georgia Institute of Technology, USA

Ashwin Ram
Georgia Institute of Technology, USA

ABSTRACT

Believable agents designed for long-term interaction with human users need to adapt to them in a way which appears emotionally plausible while maintaining a consistent personality. For short-term interactions in restricted environments, scripting and state machine techniques can create agents with emotion and personality, but these methods are labor intensive, hard to extend, and brittle in new environments. Fortunately, research in memory, emotion and personality in humans and animals points to a solution to this problem. Emotions focus an animal's attention on things it needs to care about, and strong emotions trigger enhanced formation of memory, enabling the animal to adapt its emotional response to the objects and situations in its environment. In humans this process becomes reflective: emotional stress or frustration can trigger re-evaluating past behavior with respect to personal standards, which in turn can lead to setting new strategies or goals. To aid the authoring of adaptive agents, we present an artificial intelligence model inspired by these psychological results in which an emotion model triggers case-based emotional preference learning and behavioral adaptation guided by personality models. Our tests of this model on robot pets and embodied characters show that emotional adaptation can extend the range and increase the behavioral sophistication of an agent without the need for authoring additional hand-crafted behaviors.

INTRODUCTION

When we see a pet we've met before, we recall not just its name and temperament but how our interactions with it made us feel. We feel happy when we see the dog we had fun playing with, and feel sour about the cat that shocked us with its hiss. And just as we learn from them, they learn from us; the dog, remembering its happiness upon playing with us, may seek us out when we are down; and the cat, remembering our shocked reaction when it hissed, may avoid us, or be more cautious with its anger in the future. Pets don't need to be 'configured' to live with us, and neither do we: all we need is the ability to react emotionally to our situations, a memory for our past emotional states, and the ability to let those recalled emotions color our current emotional state and guide our behaviors appropriately. We argue that robots and synthetic characters should have the same ability to interpret their interactions with us, to remember these interactions, and to recall them appropriately as a guide for future behaviors, and we present a working model of how this can be achieved.

Of course, humans are more complicated than pets; we have not just emotions but also ideals for our behavior, and can modify our reactions and plans when they violate our ideals. We may snarl back at the hissing cat, but that outburst of emotion can make us reconsider when we should show anger. Even if we do not reconsider at first, if we see the same cat multiple times we may eventually be prompted to figure out why it continues to try to enter our new home, to realize it was probably abandoned, and to change our routines to leave food for it – turning a hissing cat into a new companion. It may seem a tall order make robots have this kind of flexibility – but we argue it is possible by using emotion to trigger behavior revision guided by a personality model, and we present a working model of how it can be achieved.

In this chapter, we review efforts to build agents with believable personalities, point out problems particular to making these personalities convincing over long-term interactions with human users, and discuss research in cognitive science into the mechanisms of memory, emotion, and personality. Based on these psychological results, we present a method for building believable agents that uses emotion and memory to adapt an agent's personality over time. We then present two case studies illustrating this idea, the first demonstrating emotional long term memory in a robot, and the second demonstrating emotion-driven behavioral updates in an embodied character. Finally, we conclude with lessons learned.

BACKGROUND

What Kind of Agents Need Memory, Emotion, and Personality Models?

In our work we are interested in affective systems: robots and agents designed to display, respond to, or make use of emotional states, in particular those which interact with humans over a long period of time in relatively unconstrained settings. Research into what makes characters appear believable indicates that changing and expressing emotion are key to maintaining believability over time (Loyall, 1997). We argue that using explicit emotion models integrated into an agent's memory but guided by the agent's personality model can aid the development of agents for long term interaction; to explain why, we will briefly review some popular techniques for creating believable agents and some typical problems that can arise.

Techniques for Creating Agent Personalities

Entertainment robots and embodied characters typically are designed to have distinctive personalities which affect how they behave towards their human user or how they act within the virtual world of a game. At first blush, such agents do not need a complex model of emotion: instead, simple reactions can trigger expressive behaviors that communicate to a user the impression that they are interacting with a real character with an inner emotional life (Johnston and Thomas, 1995, Paiva, 2005; Standifer, 1995). For example, a simple finite state automaton could be used to make an enemy approach, make threatening gestures until wounded, and then scream in fear and run away.

While finite state automata are easy to develop, they are predictable. Over long game sessions, a character's static behavioral repertoire may result in repetitive behavior that hurts believability (Saltzman, 1999). Therefore, many developers of computer games and robotic toys have turned to hierarchical, probabilistic and fuzzy state machines (Schwab, 2004). The advantage of these systems is that layered control supports sophisticated behaviors, and probabilistic transitions makes the actual behavior of the agent nondeterministic, less predictable, and more realistic.

Other game developers have turned to scripting languages which allow arbitrarily sophisticated behaviors (Millington, 2006). However, creating characters using scripting languages or fuzzy state machines can be very labor intensive. Computer game manufacturers typically employ dozens of artists and engineers to perfect very simple characters (for examples, see the Postmortems in Game Developer Magazine, e.g., Huebner, 2000; Spector, 2000, Ohlen et al., 2001, etc.).

Challenges in Creating Agent Personalities

When authoring a character's behavior set, it is hard to imagine and plan for all possible scenarios it might encounter; despite extensive play-testing, any character may ultimately "break". Incorporating knowledge representation and planning techniques can enable an agent's behavior to

become more flexible in novel situations, but this too can require extensive programming effort (Mateas and Stern, 2003), and it does not guarantee success: when an agent's behavior fails to achieve their desired purpose, most characters are unable to identify the failure and will continue the ineffective behavior.

A few game developers have tried incorporating explicit emotional models to improve the believability of their agents, which can effectively communicate to a user the impression that they are interacting with a real character with an inner emotional life (Reilly, 1996). Notably, the characters in *The Sims* (Maxis, 2000) incorporated explicit "motivational" states, which could be satisfied by objects in the environments which were labeled with the drives that they could satisfy. This system meant that a character who was hungry would naturally turn to a nearby refrigerator without the need for explicit programming of that behavior (Woodcock, 2000b).

Another solution is to make characters adapt, but game developers tend to avoid adaptive agents because it makes playtesting difficult and debugging user problems nearly impossible (Woodcock 2000a; Tozour, 2002). There are exceptions; notably, the characters in *Creatures* (Cyberlife, 1997) could be trained through emotional interactions; however, these characters had deliberately limited lifespans to encourage player identification with them, so we cannot say how this model would have fared over longer periods (Champanard, 2007).

Exploiting Adaptation for Better Agents

Based on these tradeoffs—simpler systems are easy to develop but predictable and brittle, more complicated agents are more flexible but harder to author, and adding adaptation to agents makes them more convincing but less controllable— we argue that a better way to achieve long-term believability is to introduce explicit models of emotion, memory and personality control, based on how real human and animals emote, adapt, and maintain their personalities.

The approach we take is cognitively grounded artificial intelligence: we start from the premise that constructs like memory, emotion and personality are real phenomena that exist in humans, and that to emulate them we need to understand precisely what these phenomena are. However, once that understanding is established, development of artificial intelligence control systems for agents may simplify these psychological models significantly in an attempt to make the implementation of these systems easier and more efficient.

Theories of Memory, Emotion and Personality in Cognitive Science

The Nature of Emotion

Current psychological theories model emotion in humans and animals as three interrelated processes: physiological responses, overt behaviors, and conscious feelings that occur in response to events of potential relevance (Gluck, 2008); many researchers postulate that the functional role of emotions is to determine what problems are currently important and to focus the agent's mind and actions on them (e.g., LeDoux, 1996; Damasio, 2000; Minsky, 2007). Simon (1983) points out that the environment presents many challenges — food, safety, sex, etc. — that cannot all be met at once, and that emotions provide a way to shift our focus, allowing us to drop our search for food in the face of imminent death within the jaws of a tiger.

Frijda (1987) argues along similar lines that agents have a variety of concerns, and when threats to our concerns become pressing enough, they interrupt our thoughts and actions — even if we have not been attending to them (e.g., Ohman et al 2000, Winkielman and Berridge, 2004, Ruys & Stapel, 2008). This can cause an immediate behavioral response, but more importantly it can lead the agent to change its stance towards the environment, switching to a new mode of behavior that leads to the selection of new goals, plans, and actions.

Memory and Learning

Memory refers to an agent's capacities to modify its behavior based on experience. There is not enough space for us to discuss the extensive literature of memory retrieval; for more information see (Anderson, 2000, Tulving & Craik, 2000; Purdy et al., 2001; Gluck, 2008). Types of memory include *procedural memory* for skills and *declarative memory* for facts, which includes *associative memory* connecting stimuli with responses, *semantic memory* for general concepts divorced from specific stimuli, and *episodic memory* for when and where specific facts were learned (for a review see McGaugh, 2003).

Episodic memories are not taken as static "snapshots": most of us are familiar of with learning a friend's new phone number, only to forget it later and dial their old number. Under normal circumstances, memories are consolidated over a period that takes somewhere between hours and decades (McGaugh, 2007, Haist et al., 2001). Furthermore, memories are reconstructive, continually evolving as missing details are filled in on recall (Bartlett, 1932).

The Relationship of Memory and Emotion

Memories are affected by emotion: we often have heightened recollection of events associated with charged emotional events like national disasters. Even very mildly emotional events, such as reading emotionally charged stories, can create memories stronger and more detailed than memories of emotionally neutral events (McGaugh, 2003; Gluck et al., 2008), with the caveat that when emotional stress becomes so great that it interferes with cognitive functioning, memory performance drops off again (Benjamin et al., 1981).

Emotion's effect on memory appears to begin when brain structures responsible for emotion, such as the amygdala, detect an emotional event and communicate with brain structures responsible for consolidating short term memory into long term memory, such as the hippocampus. When the emotion centers detect emotional events, they simultaneously excite nearby brain regions and release stress hormones that prepare the body for action. These stress hormones feed back into the emotion centers of the brain themselves, and the combination of the initial excitation and the subsequent feedback strengthens the formation of memories in the consolidation regions (McGaugh 2003, Gluck et al. 2008).

Personality and Self-Regulation

Personality refers to distinctive yet stable individual differences in behavior and cognition. For our purposes we are most interested not just in the content of a person's personality, but in the self-regulation mechanisms by which they maintain it. When we choose not to eat that cookie because we're on a diet, congratulate ourselves on successfully abstaining, or berate ourselves for eating the second one, we are simultaneously comparing our performance with respect to a standard (a cognitive act) and evaluating how we measure up in a positive or negative way (an emotional act). Based on how good we are at our diets (our prospects of success), we may decide to eat no more than one cookie a week (setting a goal).

These four elements — personal standards which can be used to evaluate our behavior, emotional evaluation of our actions with respect to our standard, evaluating our prospects of success, and setting goals — appear key to our regulation of our behavior (Caprara & Cervone 2000, Minsky 2007). However, we are not constantly evaluating our own performance; sometimes it takes a disappointing surprise on the scale to realize we've failed at our diet. Self-regulation can lead to changing our goals, re-evaluating our prospects

of success, or even altering our standards; but it is also a *conscious* process which is more likely to engage when we experience some disruption, such as failing at a task, receiving feedback, or becoming socially self-conscious (Caprara & Cervone, 2000).

Implementation of Memory, Emotion and Personality Models in Artificial Intelligence Systems

These results seem to show that emotion plays a key role not just in alerting us about the need for action, but also in determining what we remember and even when we should change. But these psychological results do not directly translate into control systems for an affective robot or an embodied character; to take advantage of these results we must exploit (or develop) implementable artificial intelligence models of memory, emotion and personality.

Modeling Emotion in Intelligent Systems

Two popular emotion models in artificial intelligence are multiple concerns models and cognitive evaluation models.

Multiple concerns models map emotion to competing systems detecting events of importance to an agent. Features in perception or cognition act as triggers for concerns, which in turn can trigger emotions, or behavioral modes, that change how the agent selects its behaviors. The PEPE system we describe later was a multiple concerns model based on ideas from Simon (1983) and Frijda (1987). A similar model was implemented by Velasquez (1997, 1998) based on a synthesis of ideas from Ekman (1992), Izard (1991), and Johnson-Laird and Oately (1992).

Cognitive evaluation models map emotions to a hierarchy of evaluations of physical and mental conditions that can affect an agent. Ortony, Clore and Collins proposed a cognitive evaluation model

(1988) in which emotions consist of valenced reactions to the outcome of events, the actions of agents, and the properties of objects, especially with respect to how those outcomes, actions and properties affect us and whether or not we know whether these potential effects have been realized. The OCC model was deliberately designed to be implementable on an artificial intelligence system: the emotion model of the ABL system we describe later was derived from the Em (Reilly 1996) implementation of OCC, and many other systems have used related models (e.g., Elliott 1992, Studdard 1995, Koda 1996, Karunaratne & Yan 2001, Bartneck 2002, Li et al. 2007).

Memory Retrieval and Machine Learning

There are many machine learning techniques that can exploit past experience (Mitchell, 1997, Alpaydin, 2004); two popular techniques are case-based reasoning and reinforcement learning.

A *case based reasoning* system learns by storing specific episodes, or cases; this involves deciding what parts of a current experience to store, what lesson the experience teaches, and how to label the experience for retrieval later (Kolodner 1993). Once an agent has retrieved a case from its case library, it must adapt it to solve the current problem, and then ideally update its records of its experiences based on the new outcome (Kolodner 1984).

Reinforcement learning, commonly used in robotic learning and control, attempts to find a scheme for selecting actions, or *policy*, that maximizes the agent's return on a reward function (Sutton & Barto, 1998). Reinforcement learning and case-based reasoning can be combined: the LARC model (Santamaria, 1997) stores cases that trace the recent history of the agent's perceptions and behaviors along with the accompanying reward function; these cases are retrieved later using an adaptive nearest-neighbor approach.

Personality Regulation and Behavior Transformation

The behavior of an agent can be considered a reactive plan, making revising an agent's behavior a problem of runtime reactive-plan revision. There are many approaches to revise plans on failure.

Classical planning assumes the agent is the sole source of change, actions are deterministic and sequential, and that the world is fully observable. *Conditional planners* such as Conditional Non Linear Planner (Peot and Smith, 1992) and Sensory Graph Plan (Weld et al., 1998) support sensing actions so that the appropriate conditional branch of the plan is taken, but this can cause plans to grow exponentially.

Decision-theoretic planners deal well with exogenous events and non-determinism by modeling problems as Markov decision processes (MDPs) and solving problems by learning a policy, like reinforcement learners. *Partially observable MDPs* can even be used when the world is not fully observable. But these approaches require many iterations to converge, their state spaces become intractable in complex domains, and they learn static policies that cannot be easily retrained during dynamic game play.

Transformational planning handles these problems of complexity and non-determinism by not reasoning about the problem domain to generate a new plan, but instead by reasoning about the failing plan *itself*, transforming it to fix the failure without breaking the rest of the plan.

EMOTIONAL LONG TERM MEMORY FOR CONFIGURATION AND PERSONALITY

As an alternative to putting vast amounts of authoring effort into designing behaviors that handle every situation, we propose to create believable, engaging artificial characters capable of long-term interaction with a human user by explicitly modeling the emotional adaptation that goes on in humans and animals. Our model includes the simulation of emotional response to engage a human user's interest, adaptation of that response in a naturalistic way to maintain the user's interest, and ongoing monitoring of how that adaptation fits the agent's personality to avoid violating the human's expectations.

- **Reactive control** makes it possible to author sophisticated behaviors on a robot or embodied character constantly interacting with a changing real-time environment. While not strictly part of our emotion and personality model, both implemented case studies used a reactive control system that supported complex behaviors as the platform to build the emotion, adaptation and personality model systems that comprise the rest of our model.

- **Emotional responses** allow an agent to respond appropriately to its environment before learning. For example, even if a person has never seen a tiger, if a tiger appears and roars, that person will become afraid and run away. We model emotional response as situation evaluation, stance selection, and behavior selection: the agent evaluates the appearance of a large, loud animal as a threat to safety, chooses a stance towards this new object that it should be avoided, and on the basis of this stance selects good avoidance behaviors like running.

- **Emotional adaptation** allows an agent to analyze the results of an experience and alter its future behavior. The next time that the unfortunate person of our previous example sees a tiger, he will not need to wait for the tiger to roar to decide to run. We model this in terms of object recognition, outcome association, and response adaptation: the agent identifies the tiger as a distinct object, stores it in memory associated with the threat to

safety and the stance of fear, and adapts its situation evaluation process when the object is seen again, enabling him to select fight or flight behaviors faster than before.

- **Personality modeling** enables an agent to remain consistent over time. As situations change and emotions adapt, certain aspects of the behavior of a human or an animal tend to stay the same; we describe these as the agent's personality. We model this in terms of emotional monitoring, personality evaluation, and behavioral transformation: the agent monitors that it has been frequently frightened on this path, realizes that it does not like being repeatedly frightened, and changes its behavior to avoid the path.

This model allows an agent to learn from its basic emotional responses, to expand its repertoire of emotional behavior, and to guide its emotional development with respect to its personality. More importantly, from our perspective, it provides a natural interface between man and machine, one that allows an artificial pet or virtual character to learn its user's preferences automatically, without explicit configuration or programming on the part of the user, while still remaining consistent with the original author's design intent. We now describe case studies implementing two aspects of this model.

Case Study: Emotional Long Term Memory for Agent Configuration in the PEPE Project

Most users would probably not want to crack open a manual just to tell a robot pet not to disturb their afternoon nap; they would rather communicate this simply through natural language, or even more simply, by expressing pleasure or displeasure at the agent's behavior. This is the *configuration problem*: how can humans express their preferences towards a synthetic character? Our solution to this problem is *emotional long term memory,* an approach which proposes that an agent can be configured to interact appropriately with humans by giving the agent an emotional model, a memory for those emotions, and the ability for remembered emotions to affect its current state.

In our motivating example, pets learn their owner's preferences by remembering and recalling the emotional experiences that resulted from their past behaviors. It would not be necessary to "configure" such a robot not to hop up onto a table: it would only be necessary to loudly shout "down" and let the robot learn to associate hopping up on a table with painful emotional shocks. Our model can also extend this idea to multiple agents: a pet can learn to avoid the crotchety grandparent and to approach the playful child simply by having "normal" emotional reactions to the grandparent being crotchety and the child being playful.

We tested these ideas for emotion-based configuration in the Personal Pet (PEPE) Project, a joint project between Georgia Tech and Yamaha Motor Corporation to produce a believable, engaging artificial pet capable of long-term interaction with multiple human users. The PEPE project developed a cognitively inspired robot control architecture that made it easy for us to author complex behaviors on top of a reactive system; on top of this we implemented a model of emotional long term memory in which memories of emotional experience influenced future emotional responses.

Reactive Control using the PEPE Architecture

The PEPE architecture supports several overlapping goals: controlling a robot robustly, performing sophisticated behaviors, and adapting in response to user behaviors. To achieve this, the PEPE architecture uses a layered approach in which complex cognitive processing is layered atop simpler, faster behaviors. These layers include reflexive, reactive, deliberative, emotional and memory processes (Figure 1):

- **The Reflex Layer** directly connects raw sensation to effector commands. Reflexes are high-priority behaviors which must be executed immediately to be effective, such as emergency obstacle avoidance and shutting down electric motors if they begin to draw too much current.

- **The Reactive Layer** maps processed perceptions to effector commands in a fast constant-time fashion using *motor schemas* (Arkin, 1989), which produce an output vector encapsulating a simple behavior, such as obstacle avoidance, noise or pursuit of goals. Motor schemas can be summed through fast vector addition to produce coherent and consistent reactive behavior. Sets of motor schemas can be combined into a *behavior configuration* which determines robot heading, camera pan and tilt, and other effector commands.

- **The Deliberative Layer** combines a planner with a plan execution system that activates behavior configurations in the reactive level based on the current state of an executing plan. Each state of a plan defines a behavior configuration designed to achieve or maintain some state, akin to an operator in a traditional plan. When preconditions for a state change are met, the planner swaps in the appropriate behavior configuration — ensuring *some* behavior configuration is active regardless of how much effort is expended constructing plans.

- **The Emotional Layer** computes impacts to the agent's concerns, resulting in an emotional state that influences lower levels primarily through the setting of goals. This contributes to robustness: if no emotion arises or an emotion adds a goal for which there is no current plan, the agent can continue executing its current plan and behavior configuration until the planner decides what it needs to do.

Figure 1. Layers of control in the PEPE architecture

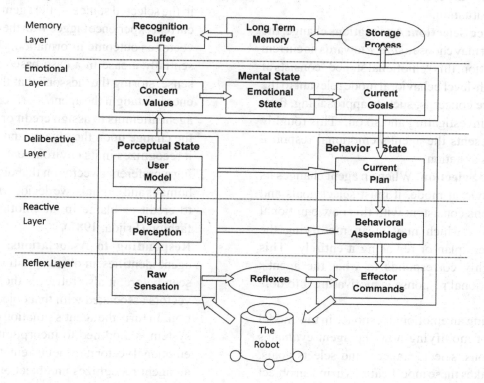

- **The Memory System** records rewards and preferences on events and objects based on the agent's complete mental state, including perceptions, plans, goals and emotions. Its influence on lower levels in the current architecture is primarily by feeding back into the emotional layer, again contributing to robustness; if the agent is in a novel situation it falls back on its basic emotional responses.

Each layer in this architecture is influenced by information from layers above it without depending on it. In this way, more abstract and symbolic layers can influence lower layers without disrupting the flow of their processing, no matter how much time is required to perform that symbolic computation. This combines aspects of subsumption architectures (Brooks, 1986) and high-level symbolic systems to produce sophisticated and robust behavior even in the face of noisy sensor data.

User Adaptation Using Emotional Long Term Memory

ELTM was intended to both enable the adaptation of the emotional response in a naturalistic way that would maintain a single user's interest over the life of the pet, and to enable the robot to 'configure' itself with respect to different members of a household that showed it different levels of affection. Basic (non-learned) emotional response in ELTM is composed of three major functions: situation evaluation, stance selection, and goal selection, which correspond directly to the concerns, emotions, and goals of Frijda's theory:

- **Situation Evaluation:** The agent constantly evaluates the experiences it is having with respect to the concerns that it has: this produces a vector of evaluations about the agent's safety, socialization, food, battery level, and so on. This vector represents roughly the agent's basic emotional appraisal of a situation.

- **Stance Selection:** As situations change, the agent may choose a *stance* towards its current situation: this "emotional stance" consists of a high-level behavioral mode relevant to the active concerns, such as approaching, fleeing, investigating and so on. This roughly represents the agent's emotional response to its situation.

- **Goal Selection:** When an agent changes its behavioral mode, it must select goals and actions consistent with this new emotional stance, which may mean modifying the current plan or replacing it entirely. This roughly corresponds to what the agent's emotional response is motivating it to do.

Adapting an emotional response in this model consists of modifying how the agent evaluates its situations, selects stances, and selects goals. ELTM makes these modifications using an object identification system and a long term memory retrieval system integrated with the emotion model. Emotional adaptation was achieved with three processes: recognizing situations, associating them with outcomes, and responding to these emotional associations:

- **Recognizing Situations:** The agent has an object identification system which attempts to identify distinct entities in the agent's environment, paired with a long term memory system which stores records of what objects have been previously seen as well as specific situations in which they have occurred. Every experience in long term memory is labeled with a vector of features. When a new experience arises, the agent searches for the most similar past experience — the past experience that shares the most features with the current experience.

- **Associating Outcomes:** When an emotionally significant event happens — a large

change in the situation evaluation, or a shift in the selected stance — the agent stores the current experience tagged with the emotional vector as outcome information. This is essentially a case in a case based reasoning sense, storing the "lesson" that this experience has taught the agent. Furthermore, the agent attempts to assign credit or blame for the change upon the objects and situations it recognizes in its environment by recording a preference vector on that object. As in humans and animals, we decide what objects to credit or blame in an emotion-specific fashion (Frijda, 1987).

- **Responding to Associations:** When an agent identifies an object or situation it has seen before, it also retrieves the emotional vectors associated with that object or situation. In turn, the agent's situation evaluation system is modified to incorporate the past emotional vector into the current state. When an agent recognizes an object or situation, it can use the preferences and outcomes associated with the object and situation to modify its concern values. This is done in a concern-specific fashion; a safety concern may place different weights on preferences and outcomes than a socialization concern.

ELTM thus combines ideas like Frijda's (1987) — that emotions represent an agent's concerns about the world — with ideas of case based reasoning (Kolodner, 1993) — that learning takes place by remembering the lessons taught by experiences. Emotional adaptation consists of learning from the emotional content of specific past experiences and, over time, from the emotional labeling of objects that have appeared again and again. We represented these emotional experiences as a vector based on a deliberate parallel with Simon's (1983) idea of emotion as the evaluation function of a multidimensional subjective expected utility (SEU) problem.

In this view, emotions break the very difficult problem of deciding between otherwise incommensurable choices into separate problems with different reward functions, each of which can be optimized separately when the emotional system puts it into the forefront. Our goal in doing so was to provide a basis for deploying other learning systems consistent with the SEU framework. For example, interpreting the emotion vector as a multidimensional reward signal was inspired by the LARC model (Santamaria 1997), which used a single reward signal for a case-based reinforcement learning algorithm.

Evaluation of the Approach

We developed two implementations of the PEPE architecture on top of the TeamBots platform (Balch 2000). The first, developed at Georgia Tech for a tracked robot testbed, was used for testing reactive control and facial recognition (Stoytchev & Tanawongsuwan, 1998). The second implementation, developed by a joint Georgia Tech-Yamaha team for a wheeled robot prototype (Figure 2), was focused on testing the emotional long term memory system. This prototype had a targetable camera head and two touch sensors, one on the head and one on the "rear" of the robot. At the time of our tests, the face recognition system was

Figure 2. The Yamaha robot prototype

not complete, so we gave our volunteers colored t-shirts to enable the robot to recognize them.

To test the PEPE architecture and our ELTM model, we implemented a simple library of behaviors, such as wandering, approach and avoidance, which could in turn be composed into higher level behaviors such as "playing" (alternately wandering and approaching an object) and "fleeing" (backing up, executing a fast 180, and running away). The emotion model extended this with a simple set of concerns, including avoiding pain, which we derived from "kicks" to the rear sensor, and socialization, which we derived from a combination of proximity to people objects and "petting" the head sensor. The robot had several emotional states, including a neutral state, a "happy" state associated with socialization, and a "fearful" state associated with pain. The robot's planner attempted to find plans which matched the current emotional state and execute them. The robot's typical behavior was to wander looking for someone to play with it, and then to attempt to stay close to individuals who "petted" it and to flee from individuals who "kicked" it.

Prior to the addition of the ELTM, the robot had considerable internal flexibility, but externally appeared no more sophisticated than a system with two buttons that switched it between behavior modes for "play" and "run away". The emotional long term memory extended this behavior. Its situation recognizer identified moving patches as distinct objects by color. The outcome associator detected either strong changes to single concerns (e.g., a nearby user deciding to "pet" the robot, strongly increasing the level of the socialization concern) or shifts in the emotional stance (e.g., a user deciding to "kick" the robot, increasing the pain concern and causing the robots stance to switch from "happy" to "fearful"); this shift triggered updates to the emotional vectors associated with all detected objects, along with the storage of a case representing the robot's current emotion, stance, plan, action, overall environment, and present objects. The situation recognition system continually tried to find relevant cases and to determine whether detected objects had been previously seen; when previously seen objects or situations were detected, these were blended in to the robot's current concern state. We tested this extensively in simulation, and when the robot prototype was next available for testing, in a series of live trials lasting for several days.

The results of adding the memory model were dramatic. Without authoring any additional plans, behaviors or emotional states, the robot's behavior nonetheless changed. Now, its initial wandering behavior was augmented by self-initiated rather than reactive approach-avoidance behaviors: rather than wait for a user to pet it or kick it, it would actively approach users that had petted it in the past or avoid (and sometimes abruptly flee) from users who had kicked it.

After the conclusion of the joint Georgia Tech-Yamaha tests on the Yamaha prototype, the next step was to port the emotion model back to the Georgia Tech testbed, which had a much wider array of sensors and effectors and a much more advanced vision system. However, the project was canceled before this work could be ported back to the testbed, so we could not run more extensive tests on either robot.

Therefore, one of the major goals of the project failed: we cannot report results on how well this model performed on longer human interactions, and the results we can report were conducted in a very small set of trials. While we were satisfied with what we achieved — the emotional long term memory at least *appeared* to make the robot's behavior far more rich based on the same set of base behaviors — by itself this was still impressive primarily in a "look ma no hands" way (McCarthy 1974).

However, in a similar but independent project also sponsored by Yamaha, Velasquez et al (1998) implemented a model of emotional memory in a similar robot called Yuppy. There were differences between these systems — for example, the emotion releasers in the Yuppy model had short term memory, enabling it to "habituate" to constantly present stimuli, and the case library in the PEPE model stored episodes, enabling it to associate emotions with situations — but both incorporated an emotion model, learned emotional responses, and the ability to change behaviors based on the current emotional state.

In a series of trials similar to what we conducted on PEPE, Velasquez demonstrated Yuppy could learn to prefer or fear users based on how the users treated it. This obviously does *not* strengthen the evidence for the specific PEPE model; however, based on the similarities between the PEPE and Yuppy models, we believe the similarity of the results *does* suggest that the general emotional long term memory approach is an effective technique for making agents adapt to users.

Case Study: Emotion-Triggered Behavior Modification for Stable Personalities on the ABL Platform

Embodied agents that interact with humans over longer timeframes should not just adapt to create interest, they should maintain consistent personalities to retain believability. Ideally, we want a self-adapting behavior set for characters, allowing characters to autonomously exhibit their author-specified personalities in new and unforeseen circumstances, and relieving authors of the burden of writing behaviors for every possible situation. In the field of embodied agents, there has been little work on agents that are introspectively aware of their internal state, let alone agents that can rewrite themselves based on deliberating over their internal state. However, this is precisely what psychological research indicates that humans do when stress or disruption makes them aware that their behavior is not living up to their standards.

We propose a model in which emotion provides the agent with the knowledge that its current behavior library is creating inappropriate behavior and should be revised accordingly. For example, a robot pet playing tag with a user would normally succeed using its default chasing behavior, but this might fail if the user is standing on a table, either because the agent has been told not to climb on it as above, or simply because its default chasing behavior does not include jumping. Although the pet can see the user, he cannot reach her, causing the agent's behavior to persistently fail. Our emotion modeling transforms this persistent failure at a given goal into a raised stress level of the agent, which can trigger a behavior modification routine that revises the behavior, for example by adding a jumping behavior to its 'playing tag' repertoire.

A key element to making this behavioral revision work is the use of transformational planning (TP), which does not reason about the domain to generate a plan but instead reasons about a failing plan and transforms it so as to fix the failure without breaking the rest. This insight is key, but we could not directly apply it because TP is generally applied to plans built from STRIPS-like operators, not rich reactive planning languages like ABL. Therefore, we developed novel behavior transformations and techniques for blame assign-

ment that enabled us to apply TP to our behavior modification problem.

Our second case study was implemented on a game scenario which consists of two embodied characters named Jack and Jill. They are involved in a game of Tag where the character who is "It" chases the other around the game area. Each character's behavior library reflects their personality and consists of about 50 behaviors coded in ABL, a language designed for believable characters. Our system (see Figure 2) is composed of a reactive layer which handles the real-time interactions, and a reasoning layer responsible for monitoring the character's state and making repairs as needed.

Reactive Control Using the ABL Programming Language

Our game environment presents a certain set of challenges for the reactive layer. First, a real-time game domain requires the reactive layer to have a fast runtime processing component with a short sense-decide-act loop. Second, the game world's interactive nature entails that the reactive layer

Figure 3. Architecture of the behavior transformation system

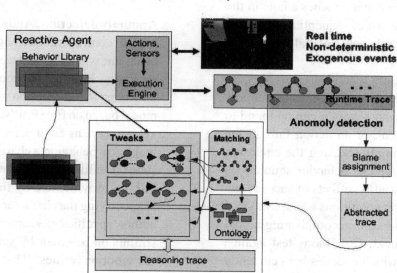

handles conditional execution appropriately and provides the ability to support varying behaviors under different situations at runtime. Finally, for game worlds containing embodied, believable characters, the reactive layer must provide support for the execution of multiple, simultaneous behaviors, allowing characters to gaze, speak, walk around, gesture with their hands and convey facial expressions, all at the same time.

To meet these requirements we use A Behavior Language (ABL) for the reactive layer. ABL is explicitly designed to support programming idioms for the creation of reactive, believable agents (Mateas and Stern, 2004). Its fast runtime execution module makes it suitable for real-time scenarios. ABL is a proven language for believable characters, having been successfully used to author the central characters Trip and Grace for the interactive drama Façade (Mateas and Stern, 2003).

A character authored in ABL is composed of a library of behaviors, capturing the various activities the character can perform in the world. Behaviors are dynamically selected to accomplish goals - different behaviors are appropriate for accomplishing the same goal in different contexts. For example, the goal of expressing anger can be accomplished through either a behavior that screams or a behavior that punches a hole in the wall. Behaviors consist of sequential or parallel steps; steps can be subgoals, mental updates, or game actions.

Currently active goals and behaviors are captured in the active behavior tree. During execution, steps may fail (e.g., no behavior can be found to accomplish a subgoal, or an action fails in the game world), potentially causing the enclosing behavior to fail. Step and behavior annotations can modify the cascading effects of success and failure. Behavior preconditions are used to find appropriate behaviors for accomplishing a goal in the current context. Conditions test against working memory, which encodes both currently sensed information and agent-specific internal state (e.g., emotional state).

ABL's runtime execution module acts as the front-end for communication with the game environment. It constantly senses the world, keeps track of the current game state, updates the active behavior tree and initiates and monitors primitive actions in the game world. Continuously monitored conditions, such as context conditions and success tests, provide immediate, reactive response. Furthermore, the runtime system provides support for meta-behaviors that can monitor (and potentially change) the active behavior tree.

Implementing Emotion-Driven Behavior Modification

To support emotion-driven behavior modification, we implemented a reasoning layer that supports anomaly detection, blame assignment, and behavioral modification. Anomaly detection tracks long-term patterns in the character's behavior execution and detects violations of the author-specified behavior contract. When a contract violation is detected, blame assignment uses the execution trace to identify one or more behaviors that should be changed. The behavioral modification component repairs offending behaviors identified during blame assignment and reloads them into the agent.

- **Anomaly detection:** Authors need a way to specify contracts about long-term character behavior; when the contract is violated, the reasoning layer should modify the behavior library. Our emotion model is an OCC model based on Em (Reilly, 1996). Emotion values serve as compact representations of long-term behavior: a character's emotional state is modified when behaviors succeed or fail in a way defined by the author as part of specifying the character personality. The author specifies personality-specific constraints on behavior by specifying bounds for emotion values. The reasoning layer interprets an emotion exceeding its bounds to mean that the current behavior library is creating inappropriate long-term behavior and that it should seek to assign blame and change the behavior.

- **Blame assignment:** The behaviors that should be revised in response to a violation of the personality contract are determined using the meta-reasoning capability of ABL to trace agent execution. Blame assignment analyzes the past execution trace and identifies the behavior with the maximal contribution to the out-of-bound emotion value, amortized over time, as the responsible behavior.

- **Behavior modification:** Offending behaviors are modified using a set of modification operators. Applicability of an operator depends on the role the behavior plays in the execution trace — that is, on the explanation of how the behavior contributed to a contract violation. Modification operators are categorized according to failure patterns, which provide an abstraction mechanism over the execution trace to detect the type of failure that is taking place. Failure patterns are encoded loosely as finite state machines that look for patterns in the execution trace.

At runtime, the system detects when the author-provided behavior contract has been violated. Once blame assignment has determined the offending behavior, the system uses the failure patterns to explain the behavior's role in the contract violation. The set of matching failure patterns provide an associated set of applicable behavior modification operators to try on the offending behavior, which are tried one at a time until one succeeds. We then modified ABL's runtime system and compiler so that modified behaviors can be compiled and reloaded into the agent, allowing the game to continue uninterrupted.

Evaluation of the Behavior Transformation Architecture

We evaluated our behavior adaptation system on Jack and Jill, two hand-authored embodied characters designed to play a game of Tag. Each character has its own personality that affects the way they approach play: Jack likes to daydream and is not particularly interested in the game, whereas Jill is bored if she is not being chased or chasing someone. Jack and Jill were initially authored by people on a different research project, providing a great opportunity for us to evaluate our system. Their behavior set made fixed assumptions about world dynamics which will be ineffective at maintaining personality invariants in the face of change. If our system can help maintain those invariants then it is an effective means of behavior adaptation.

Specifically, we provided emotion annotations by associating a stress emotion with being chased and placing nominal bounds on stress, specifying a contract on Jack's intended personality. We then tested whether our system is able to successfully modify the behavior library to changing environments. In our experiment, we simulated a changing world by moving the tag agent whose behaviors had been built for a specific map into a larger and sparser version.

Our experimental procedure involves first running the game scenario without the adaptation mechanisms and continuously observing Jack's stress level. We then run Jack with the adaptation mechanisms. Figure 4 shows Jack's stress levels averaged over five 10-minute games before adaptation, and with two different behavior libraries modified by our system. Blame assignment found that the behavior *Run_Away_1* is responsible for stress exceeding bounds. In the ideal case, Jack would run away for a while, until he was able to escape out of sight, at which point, he would head for a hiding place. Trace analysis however shows

Figure 4. Average stress level from the evaluation experiment

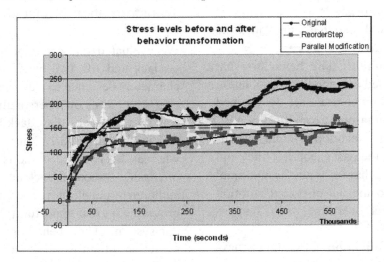

that Jack turning around to ensure he is not being followed always fails. Jack is never able to run away and escape out of sight long enough to risk going to a hiding place. This situation tends to occur on our test maps because they are sparse; with fewer obstacles it is more difficult for Jack to ever escape out of sight. As a result, Jack is continuously under immediate pursuit and his stress level quickly exceeds bounds.

In our runs, the behavior adaptation system found two different modifications that brought stress back in bounds. In the first case, the system changed the *AvoidItPerson_3* behavior (see Figure 5) from a sequential behavior to a parallel behavior. Originally we expected Jack to ensure no one is following before hiding, but the system's change is actually quite reasonable. When pressed, it makes sense to keep running while turning around. If it turns out someone is following you, you can always change course and not go to the secret hiding place. Visually, this change was quite appealing. Jack, when running away, would start strafing towards his hiding place, allowing him to move towards his destination while keeping a look out.

Unfortunately, this change was unstable. Due to how Jack navigates, if he cannot see his next navigation point, he will stall (a defect in his navigation behaviors). Surprisingly, even with this defect, Jack with this change is able to stay within his normal stress bounds. We initially assumed this was because the defect happened rarely, but in fact it was the opposite. While running away, Jack was always getting stuck, allowing Jill to tag him. This decreases stress because Jack is not as stressed when he is the pursuer; he can take his time and is not pressed.

At one level this result is surprising and wonderful. Jack, the daydreamer, successfully "gamed" the system: as "It" he does not have to work so hard to play. But for the purpose of our evaluation, this change was nevertheless undesirable. Jack is violating an implicit behavior contract that Jack should not allow himself to be tagged. The adaptation system essentially found a clever way to take advantage of the under specification of the author's intent. After amending the specifications, our behavior adaptation system found an alternate change: to reorder the steps inside *AvoidItPerson_3*. In the new behavior set, *AvoidItPerson_3* first hides and then turns around to ensure no one is following instead of the other way around. This results in behavior as good if not better than the parallel version.

Figure 5. The modified behavior

```
sequential behavior AvoidItPerson() {
precondition {(ItWME itPlayerName :: itAgent)
        !(AgentPositionWME objectID == itAgent)}
    with(post) subgoal Hide();
    with(post) subgoal TurnAroundEnsureEscape();}
```

FUTURE TRENDS

Our case studies were implemented independently on two different systems, but the underlying reactive control systems and the role of the emotion models used were very similar. Therefore, the natural next step would be to attempt to incorporate both models into a single system with both emotional adaptation and personality updates.

In the PEPE system, the emotion vector was relatively simple, as were the learning algorithms. Another natural next step would be to use a richer emotion model, such as the Em model used in our ABL work, or to use more sophisticated learning algorithms, such as a full version of the Santamaria LARC model that PEPE's learning model emulated.

In our ABL work, to increase the transformational power of our system we are adding more behavior modification operators, which has several effects. First, as the number of operators increases, the time required to reason about them and find the applicable set increases. Second, operators for more complex scenarios may have a lower success rate, requiring us to focus the search through behavior transformation space. It will become necessary for the reasoning layer to learn which operators are best applicable in which situations, such that fewer operators have to be tried. These characteristics of the problem make a case-based approach, as a form of speedup learning, very attractive.

CONCLUSION

Unlike a psychological model of emotion, which can be tested against the behavior of humans and animals, evaluating the performance of an artificial intelligence system that displays or uses emotion is difficult. Our results with PEPE and ABL are suggestive but it is difficult to prove that they are "better" than a hand-authored system. However, our experiences developing PEPE nonetheless did teach a few important lessons:

- **Layered architectures aid behavioral authoring:** For a variety of reasons we were only able to use part of the Georgia Tech PEPE code to develop the joint prototype; nonetheless, by layering the system we were able to achieve a large amount of work in a short period of time. The TeamBots system provided a set of reactive behaviors, upon which we layered the planner, the emotion system, and the memory system; furthermore it insulated the higher levels of the system from the robot implementation, enabling us to test the behaviors in simulation while physical issues were worked out on the robot testbed. The PEPE portion of the joint testbed took approximately two man-months of programmer effort, and the complete software developed for these tests, including low-level control and the visual processing system, took approximately six man-months.

- **Emotional adaptation increases behavioral flexibility:** The emotional memory system dramatically changed the external behavior with no significant changes to the existing plans, requiring only the incorporation of remembered emotion values into the current emotional state. This simple shift changed the appearance of the robot's behavior from a creature that reacted in a fixed way to external contact from an end user to a creature that had internally generated behaviors that could be affected by the sight of a person from a distance.

- **Active reminding is required for emotional adaptation:** The emotion model changed the agent's personality, but its behavior appeared fixed, similarly, just storing cases in the robot's case library did not change its behavior. The critical enabler for emotional memory was the situation recognizer: to learn, the robot required an active reminding process constantly trying to identify objects and situations in terms of its experience. The emotion system only had the opportunity to adapt when a case was retrieved or an object identified.

Similarly, developing the behavior transformation system for ABL also taught a few important lessons:

- **Transformational planning aids behavior transformation:** In an interactive, real-time domain, characters are constantly interacting with the user. Furthermore, their actions are non-deterministic, need to be executed in parallel, and have effects that are difficult to quantify. Transformational planning made it possible for our characters to modify their behaviors, but we had to develop novel behavior transformations and techniques for blame assignment to enable TP to deal with this complexity and non-determinism.

- **Language support for behavior transformation makes modifying behavior easier**: Behaviors written for a believable character are code written in a programming language, so modifying behaviors at run time involves rewriting the code for the agent. We spent a lot of time implementing behavior modification operators to accomplish this. Authoring behaviors in a programming language that provided native support for changing its functional constructs (e.g., treating functions as first order entities as in LISP) would have made modifying the behaviors at run-time a much easier process.

Our work used emotion as a trigger for learning about the environment and agents within it, and as a trigger for behavioral change. This model made it possible for us to develop sophisticated and sometimes surprising agent behaviors in less time and with less effort than we could have done otherwise. Therefore, we conclude that emotion-driven learning and emotion-driven behavioral updates are useful methods for developing believable agents that adapt to their environments and users in a way which appears emotionally plausible while maintaining a consistent personality.

REFERENCES

Alpaydin, E. (2004). *Introduction to machine learning.* Cambridge, MA: The MIT Press.

Anderson, J.R. (2000). *Learning and memory: an integrated approach.* New York, NY: John Wiley & Sons.

Arkin, R.C. (1989). Motor schema-based mobile robot navigation. *The International Journal of Robotics Research, 8*(4), 92-112.

Balch, T. (2000). TeamBots software and documentation. Retrieved May 18, 2008, from http://www.cs.cmu.edu/~trb/TeamBots/

Bartlett, F.C. (1932). *Remembering*. Cambridge: Cambridge University Press.

Bartneck, C. (2002). Integrating the OCC model of emotions in embodied characters. In *Proceedings of the Workshop on Virtual Conversational Characters: Applications, Methods, and Research Challenges*, Melbourne.

Benjamin, M., McKeachie, W., Lin, Y.-G., & Holinger, D. (1981). Test anxiety: deficits in information processing. *Journal of Educational Psychology, 73*, 816-824.

Brooks, R. (1986). A robust layered control system for a mobile robot. *IEEE Journal of Robotics and Automation 2*(1),14-23.

Caprara, G.V., & Cervone, D. (2000). *Personality: Determinants, dynamics and potentials*. Cambridge University Press.

Champanard, A.J. (2007). Evolving with Creatures' AI: 15 tricks to mutate into your own game. AIGameDev.com Reviews, October 21, 2007. Retrieved May 17, 2008, from http://aigamedev.com/reviews/creatures-ai

Cyberlife Technology Ltd. (1997). *Creatures*. Computer game, multiple platforms. Virgin Interactive Entertainment.

Damasio, A. (2000). A second chance for emotion. In R. D. Lane & L. Nadel (Eds.), *Cognitive neuroscience of emotion* (pp. 12-23). New York: Oxford University Press.

Elliott, C. D. (1992). *The affective reasoner: A process model of emotions in a multi-agent system*. Unpublished Ph.D. thesis, The Institute for the Learning Sciences, Northwestern University, Evanston, IL..

Frijda, N. (1986). *The emotions*. New York: Cambridge University Press.

Gluck, M., Mercado, E., & Myers, C. (2008). *Learning and memory: From brain to behavior*. New York: Worth Publishers.

Haist, F., Gore, J.B., & Mao, H. (2001). Consolidation of memory over decades revealed by functional magnetic resonance imaging. *Nature Neuroscience, 4*, 1139-1145.

Huebner, R. (2000, July). Postmortem: Nihilistic software's Vampire: The Masquerade — Redemption. *Game Developer Magazine*, 44-51.

Johnston, O., & Thomas, F. (1995). *Disney animation: The illusion of life*. New York: Hyperion.

Karunaratne, S., & Yan, H. (2001, May). Interactive emotional response computation for scriptable multimedia actors. In *Proceedings of 2001 International Symposium on Intelligent Multimedia, Video and Speech Processing*, Hong Kong, China.

Koda, T. (1996). *Agents with faces: A study on the effect of personification of software agents*. Unpublished Masters Thesis, MIT Media Lab, Massachusetts Institute of Technology, Cambridge, MA.

Kolodner, J.L. (1984). *Retrieval and organization strategies in conceptual memory: A computer model*. Northvale, NJ: Lawrence Erlbaum Associates.

Kolodner, J.L. (1993). *Case-based reasoning*. San Francisco, CA: Morgan Kaufmann.

LeDoux, J. (1996). *The emotional brain: The mysterious underpinnings of emotional life*. New York: Simon & Schuster.

Li, T., Ma, Y., Qiu, Y., & Yue, P. (2007, February). Modeling personality, emotion and mood for a pedagogical agent. In *Proceedings of Artificial Intelligence and Applications 2007*, Innsbruck, Austria. Calgary AB, Canada: Acta Press.

Loyall, A. B. (1997). *Believable agents: Building interactive personalities*. Ph.D. Thesis. Technical Report CMU-CS-97-123. School of Computer Science, Carnegie Mellon University, Pittsburgh, PA.

Mateas, M., & Stern, A. (2003, March). *Façade: An experiment in building a fully-realized interactive drama*. Paper presented at the game design track of the Game Developer's Conference, San Jose, CA.

Mateas, M., & Stern, A. (2004). *A behavior language: Joint action and behavioral idioms*. In H. Prendinger,& M. Ishizuka (Eds.), *Life-like characters. tools, affective functions, and applications. Cognitive technologies*. Berlin, Heidelberg: Springer Verlag.

Maxis Software, Inc. (2000). *The Sims*. Computer game, PCElectronic Arts, Inc.

McCarthy, J. (1974). Review of "Artificial Intelligence: A General Survey". *Artificial Intelligence, 5*(3). Retrieved May 18, 2008, from http://www-formal.stanford.edu/jmc/reviews/lighthill/lighthill.html

McGaugh, J. (2003). *Memory and emotion: the making of lasting memories*. New York: Columbia University Press.

Millington, I. (2006). *Artificial intelligence for games*. San Francisco, CA: Morgan Kaufmann.

Minsky, M. (2007). *The emotion machine: Commonsense thinking, artificial intelligence, and the future of the human mind*. New York: Simon & Schuster.

Mitchell, T. (1997). *Machine learning*. McGraw Hill.

Reilly, W. S. N. (1996). *Believable social and emotional agents*. Unpublished Ph.D. Thesis. Carnegie Mellon University, Pittsburgh, PA..

Ohlen, J., Zeschuk, G., & Muzyka, R. (2001, March). Postmortem: BioWare's Baldur's Gate II. *Game Developer Magazine*, 54-66.

Ohman, A., Flykkt, A., & Lundqvist, D. (2000). Unconscious emotion: Evolutionary perspectives, psychophysiological data and neuropsychological mechanisms. In R. D. Lane & L. Nadel (Eds.), *Cognitive neuroscience of emotion* (pp. 296-327). New York: Oxford University Press.

Ortony, A., Clore, G.L., & Collins, A. (1988). *The cognitive structure of emotions*. Cambridge University Press.

Paiva A., Dias, J., Sobral, D., Aylett, R., Woods, S., Hall, L., & Zoll, C. (2005). Learning by feeling: Evoking empathy with synthetic characters. *Applied Artificial Intelligence, 19*(3-4), 235-266(32). Taylor and Francis Ltd.

Peot, M., & Smith, D. (1992). Conditional nonlinear planning. In *Artificial Intelligence Planning Systems: Proceedings of the First International Conference*, June 15-17, 1992, College Park, Maryland. San Francisco, CA: Morgan Kaufmann.

Purdy, J.E., Markham, M.R., Schwartz, B.L., & Gordon, W. (2001). *Learning and memory*. Belmont, CA: Wadsworth.

Ruys, K.I., & Stapel, D.A. (2008). The secret life of emotions. *Psychological Science, 19*(4), 385-391. Blackwell Publishing.

Saltzman, M. (Ed.)(1999). *Game design: Secrets of the sages*. Indianapolis, IN: Brady Publishing.

Santamaria, J.C. (1997). Learning adaptive reactive agents. Unpublished doctoral dissertation. Georgia Institute of Technology, Atlanta, GA..

Schwab, B. (2004). *AI game engine programming*. Hingham, Massachusetts: Charles River Media.

Simon, H.A. (1983). *Reason in human affairs*. Stanford, CA: Stanford University Press.

Spector, W. (2000, November). Postmortem: Ion Storm's Deus Ex. *Game Developer Magazine*, 50-58.

Standifer, C. (1995). Personal communication.

Stoytchev, A., & Tanawongsuwan, R. (1998, July). Pepe: PErsonal PEt. In *Video Proceedings of the AAAI-98 Mobile Robot Exhibition*, Madison, WI.

Studdard, P. (1995). *Representing human emotions in intelligent agents.* Unpublished Masters Thesis. The American University, Washington, DC.

Sutton, R.S., & Barto, A.G. (1998). *Reinforcement learning: an introduction.* Cambridge, MA: MIT Press.

Tozour, P. (2002). The evolution of game AI. In S. Rabin (Ed.), *AI Game programming wisdom.* Hingham, MA: Charles River Media.

Tulving, E., & Craik, F.I.M. (2000). *The Oxford handbook of memory.* New York: Oxford University Press.

Weld, D. S., Anderson, C.R., & Smith, D.E. (1998). Extending Graphplan to handle uncertainty & sensing actions. In *Proceedings of AAAI 1998.* AAAI Press.

Winkielman , P. & Berridge, K. (2004). Unconscious emotion. In *Current Directions in Psychological Science, 13*(3),120-123. Blackwell Synergy.

Woodcock, S. (2000a). *AI roundtable moderator's report.* Report on the AI Roundtable of the Game Developer's Conference, San Jose, CA. Retrieved May 17, 200,8 from http://www.gameai.com/cgdc00notes.html

Woodcock, S. (2000b, August). Game AI: The state of the industry. *Game Developer's Magazine*, 24-32.

KEY TERMS

The following terms and acronyms were used in this chapter and might warrant definitions in the Handbook:

ABL (A Behavior Language): ABL is a programming language explicitly designed to support programming idioms for the creation of reactive, believable agents (Mateas and Stern, 2004). ABL has been successfully used to author the central characters Trip and Grace for the interactive drama Facade (Mateas and Stern, 2003). The ABL compiler is written in Java and targets Java; the generated Java code is supported by the ABL runtime system.

Appraisal: In the OCC (Ortony et al. 1988) and Frijda (1993) models of emotion, appraisal matches the experience of an agent against its goals, standards, preferences and other concerns. The results of this matching give emotional events their positive or negative feeling or weight, called affect, and can also place this affective response in context.

Blame Assignment: In learning and adaptation, blame assignment is the process of identifying the causes of a failure of a computational system to deliver the behaviors desired of it.

Case-Based Reasoning: Case-based reasoning (Kolodner 1993) is a reasoning architecture that stores experiences with lessons learned as cases in a case library and solves problems by retrieving the case most similar to the current situation, adapting it for reuse, and retaining new solutions once they have been applied. Case-based reasoning is also a pervasive behavior in everyday human problem solving.

Concern: In Frijda's (1986) model of emotion, concerns correspond to the needs, preferences and drives of an agent – things that "matter" and can trigger changes to the emotional state of the agent.

OCC Model of Emotion: Ortony, Clore and Collins's (Ortony et al. 1988) model of emotion is a widely used model of emotion that states that the strength of a given emotion primarily depends on the events, agents, or objects in the environment of the agent exhibiting the emotion. A large number of researchers have employed the OCC model to generate emotions for their embodied characters. The model specifies about 22 emotion categories and consists of five processes that define the complete system that characters follow from the initial categorization of an event to the resulting behavior of the character. These processes are namely a) classifying the event, action or object encountered, b) quantifying the intensity of affected emotions, c) interaction of the newly generated emotion with existing emotions, d) mapping the emotional state to an emotional expression and e) expressing the emotional state.

MDP (Markov Decision Processes): Markov decision processes provide a mathematical framework for modeling decision-making characterized by a set of states where in each state there are several actions from which the decision maker must choose and transitions to a new state at time $t + 1$ from time t are only dependent on the current state and independent of all previous states. MDPs are useful for studying a wide range of optimization problems solved via dynamic programming and reinforcement learning.

SEU (Subjective Expected Utility Theory): Subjective expected utility theory (Simon 1983) holds that a rational agent should attempt to maximize its reward by choosing the action with the highest *expected utility* — effectively, the sum of the rewards of the outcomes discounted by the probabilities of their occurrence.

Chapter XXI
Computer–Based Learning Environments with Emotional Agents

Dorel Gorga
University of Geneva, Switzerland

Daniel K. Schneider
University of Geneva, Switzerland

ABSTRACT

The purpose of this contribution is to discuss conceptual issues and challenges related to the integration of emotional agents in the design of computer-based learning environments and to propose a framework for the discussion of future research. We review some emotion theories and computational models that have been developed in cognitive science and Artificial Intelligence (AI). We then will discuss some basic principles pertaining to motivation and emotion in instructional design. Grounded on these principles, we then shall present the state of the art of integrating emotions into the design of educational systems, and notably examine how to create intelligent emotional agents that enhance interaction with users. We will introduce the concept of "socio-emotional climate" as an evaluative indicator of the diversity of desirable interactions within a computer-based learning environment. We formulate the conjecture that a socio-emotional climate capable of enhancing learner motivation, self-assessment and self-motivation could be developed through the use of various socio-emotional agents.

INTRODUCTION

Emotion is a topic in several computer science subfields. Human-Computer-Interaction (HCI) studies for example the role of affect in human-interface interactions or attempts to design software that express emotions. Artificial intelligence and computational cognitive science may model human thought and behaviour. A new emerging transversal field, *affective computing*, unites attempts to design emotional software. Interest in emotional computing is grounded in the hypothesis that emotion plays an important role in cognitive processes and therefore has an impact on decision-making and performance (Damasio, 1994; Kort & Reilly, 2002; Picard, 1997).

Educational and learning theories are also concerned with emotion. In constructivist and cognitivist learning theories, learning is a result of cognitive processing and leads to knowledge construction. Learners construct their own reality through interaction with the environment, or at least interpret it based upon their perceptions or experiences. Emotions play a role in all these processes and have the potential to influence learning processes. The learning situation creates a context for a variety of emotional experiences. The effects of emotions on learning are mediated by self regulation and motivation and both positive and negative emotions influence learning. For example, students' emotions, such as enjoyment, boredom, pride, and anxiety are seen to affect achievement by influencing the student's involvement and attitude towards learning and learning environments (see e.g., Boekaerts, 2003; Pekrun, 2005).

In addition, working with a computational learning environment puts motivational challenges on the learner and increases the emotional load of the learning situation. For instance, O'Reagan (2003) interviewed 11 students studying online and concludes that the students surveyed positioned emotion as central and essential to the teaching/learning process. So, a learning situation is not only a mental performance, but also an emotional coping situation. According to Wosnitza and Volet (2005), emotions in computer-based learning could be derived from self, context, task or technology and other people. Technical environments should answer students' needs and expectations and have an influence on their emotional state (Brave & Nass, 2002). The question of how students feel about the environment and technology has been much debated in order to determine the amount of attention they allocate to their learning activities. For example, an imprac-

tical environment or unstable technology could distract attention, cause frustration, and disturb the users (Picard & Wexelblat, 2002).

The integration of technologies in education added some effectiveness and efficiency to pedagogical practice. However, little attention has been paid to emotions in educational technology. Some technology-based instructional designs (Astleitner, 2001; MacFadden et al., 2005) not only suggest ways to alleviate problems related to emotional learner states, but also address the more fundamental issue of how to build emotions into the design of learning activities, including collaborative scenarios. In addition, in modern electronic learning environments, emotions also intervene in various person-to-person interaction and person-to-system (human computer) interaction. All these factors contribute to some overall socio-emotional climate.

In order to create emotionally sound agent-supported learning environments we need to model and to simulate cognitive and emotional processes and we shall start with a discussion of some theoretical and practical aspects of emotional computing. Various computational architectures enable the creation of intelligent agents capable of sophisticated reasoning, of showing affective and expressive behaviours and of recognising the learner's affective state. The question is now whether emotional agents could change the user's attitudes and behaviours over multiple and extended periods of interaction, more effectively than non emotional agents. Some recent studies have suggested that users tend to like and trust emotional agents' more than unemotional agents (Brave, Nass & Hutchinson, 2005; Bickmore & Picard, 2004). On the other hand, the key to effective learning with computers is a good instructional design (Cummings et al, 1999). Astleitner (2001) claims that traditional instructional design approaches (without artificial agents) do not adequately address the question relating to how instructional technology should be designed to help learners learn in an emotionally sound manner. Astleitner's FEASP-approach represents a comprehensive and theory-based instructional design model that focuses instructional strategies for making instructional technology emotionally sound (to increase positive and decrease negative emotions).

In this contribution, we shall mainly focus on the use of intelligent agents with social and emotional abilities in the context of computer-based learning environments. We formulate the conjecture that an adaptive environmental socio-emotional agent, using affective strategies, can promote a positive mood to a learning situation and place and provide in particular some emotional support to the learner. We shall not address the general issue of emotionally sound instruction.

EMOTION AND COMPUTING

Researchers in Artificial Intelligence (AI) integrated emotions in modelling intelligent systems (Picard, 1997; Velasquez, 1997; El-Nasr, Yen & Ioerger, 2000; Cañamero, 2003; Breazeal, 2003). In cognitive processes modelling and simulation, emotion is an important element to model perception, learning, decision processes, memory, behaviour and other functions (Elliott, Rickel & Lester, 1999; McCauley, Franklin & Bogner, 2000; Gadanho & Hallam, 2001; Dias & Paiva, 2005).

Some HCI research (e.g. Brave & Nass, 2003) focuses on the role of emotions in man-machine interactions and how to improve them. Models and tools for measuring emotions may rely on sensors or user behaviour. Responses can be enacted in various forms, e.g. through a user interface agent. One important engineering problem is user frustration. We can assume that most users (beginner, intermediate, and advanced) experience some level of frustration in their interaction with computers. The definition of frustration is an activation of behaviour that occurs when an individual fails to be rewarded for a response. Klein, Moon and Picard (2002) hypothesize the following: "*When a computer system creates frustration on the part of the user, it can relieve that frustration quickly and effectively by means of active emotion support*" (p. 124). They focus on the sources of this frustration and possible techniques that can be used to improve its effects.

Affective Computing, the emerging interdisciplinary field that integrates AI, cognitive science and HCI emotion research can be defined as "*computing that relates to, arises from or deliberately influences emotions*" (Picard, 1997, p.262). Firstly, affective computing studies mechanisms to recognise human emotions or tries to express emotions through some interface widget in human-computer interaction. Secondly, affective computing investigates emotion synthesis (the simulation of emotion in machines) in order to construct more realistic robots. Examples of interesting projects are the Affective Reasoning Project (Elliot, 1992), the Oz project (Reilly & Bates, 1992) or MIT Affective Computing Group[1] projects such as Socially Intelligent characters, Embodied Conversational Agents and Story-Listening Systems.

Some researchers (Gadanho & Hallam, 2001; Custódio, Ventura & Pinto-Fereira, 1999) focus on computational architectures inspired by emotion models from neuroscience, e.g. with the intention of including emotions in the control of machine processes. It is hoped that these emotion-based computational systems could improve machine performance in terms of decision-making competence, action selection, behaviour control and autonomous system response (Velásquez, 1998; Petta & Cañamero, 2001).

COMPUTATIONAL MODELS OF EMOTION

Affective computing models are inspired by a diversity of emotion theories. *Discrete emotion theories* (Izard, 1971; Plutchik, 1980) claim the existence of basic emotions which are universal and can therefore be found in all cultures. Ekman (1999) proposed 6 basic emotions identified on the basis of facial expressions: anger, disgust, fear, joy, sadness and surprise. These emotions are called primary emotions in opposition to secondary emotions which result from a combination of primary ones.

Dimensional emotion theories use dimensions rather than discrete categories to describe the structure of emotions. According to a dimensional view, all emotions are characterised by their valence, arousal, and dominance (control, social power). This variety of dimensions could be seen as different expressions of a very small set of basic concepts (Breazeal, 2003). Valence (positive versus negative affect) and arousal (low versus high level of activation) have shown to be the two most important dimensions (Russell, 1980).

It is important to try to understand what is recognized as an emotion, and what is not. Some regard "surprise" as an emotion (Ekman & Friesen, 1975), whereas others (e.g. Ortony, Clore, & Collins, 1988) regard it as a cognitive state in which a belief or expectation has been found to be violated. This state, in turn, may or may not produce an emotional reaction. They consider that the emotions should have a valence (i.e. either positive or negative) and surprise is not an emotion because it is neutral (i.e. neither positive nor negative). In fact, a state (e.g., cognitive, motivational, etc.) may be caused by or give rise to an emotion, but it is not an emotion itself (e.g. desire).

In *appraisal theories*, emotions are defined as evaluation, called appraisal, of the interaction between someone's goals, beliefs and his/her environment. A person is then expected to cope with an emotion by taking internal or external actions to improve or maintain the relationship between their goals and the environment. This dynamic view of emotions can explain why the same event can give rise to different emotions in different individuals or even in one and the same individual (usually at different times). It also might help to understand what differentiates emotions from each other. Appraisal theories argue that appraisal and coping with emotions not only underlie emotional behaviour, but play an essential role in informing cognition. According to the review of appraisal theories by Ellsworth & Scherer (2003), these models were introduced by Arnold (1950) and have been developed and refined by Frijda (1986), Ortony, Clore & Collins (1988), Lazarus (1991) and Scherer (2001). Typically, appraisal theories used for computational models of emotion are descriptions of the relations between events, appraisal of events, and emotions.

AI and Cognitive Science models explore emotion at varying levels of abstraction and may use different computational methods (e.g., connectionist vs symbolic). Computational emotion models are based on the above emotion theories or their combination. These models range from individual processes to integrated architectures (Hudlicka, 2003). We shall review a few models according to their level of abstraction, i.e. agent architectures and mechanism-level models and models of single phenomena.

At one level of abstraction we find cognitive architecture-level models that embody emotional processing. Numerous examples of these models exist. Bates's model of emotion has been developed as part of the larger Oz project in order to construct autonomous agents inhabiting virtual reality microworlds (Bates, Loyall & Reilly, 1992). Sloman (2001) proposes a mind model, called CogAff[2], to study mental processes. CogAff is a multi-level processing architecture schema, and H-CogAff, an instance of this schema composed of three layers, represents the human mind architecture. Elliot's Affective Reasoner system operates in the context of an agent world, where each agent has a set of symbolic appraisal frames that contain the agent's goals, preferences, principles guiding behaviour, as well as current moods (Elliot, 1994). The Affective Reasoner includes multi-media capabilities (e.g. speech recognition, text-to-speech translation, and the display of cartoon facial expressions for a variety of emotions). Applications of the Affective Reasoner include: affective user modelling to improve human-computer interaction, testing of appraisal theories of emotion, and the development of more believable characters in computer games. Breazeal (2006) has been a pioneer in developing socially interactive robots with this higher level of abstraction.

At another level of abstraction are mechanism-level models that attempt to emulate some specific aspect of affective processing. We may further distinguish between models addressing higher-level phenomena like the cognitive appraisal process and those focusing on lower-level phenomena such as connectionist interaction models of cognition and affect. The most frequently modelled process has been cognitive appraisal. These models have been implemented and integrated within larger agent architectures (e.g. Velásquez, 1997; Cañamero, 1998; Castelfranchi, 2000; Dias & Paiva, 2005; Breazeal, 2003). A good example is the OCC appraisal model (Ortony, Clore & Collins, 1988) which is based on a cognitive theory of emotions. For example, one OCC implementation can infer the learner's emotions from his/her actions in the system interface. This model was implemented in a various types of systems and agents (Andre et al., 2000; Elliot, Rickel, & Lester, 1999; Martinho, Paiva & Gomes, 2000). Other implementations of similar interest include a computational model of Scherer's (2001) cognitive appraisal theory[3], models of emotions based on facial expression: recognition (Ioannou et al., 2005) or synthesis (Raouzaiou et al., 2005). Other models of emotion are based on interaction of emotion and cognition (Araujo, 1994). An explicit model of the effects of emotion on cognitive processes was introduced by Hudlicka (2003), and another model of emotions' effects on agent's belief generation by Gratch & Marsella (2004). Even if the OCC model proposes 15 'basic emotions', only four are considered in many systems: joy, sadness, anger and fear (e.g. Gadanho & Hallam, 2001). Some recent projects (e.g. Scheutz, 2004) seem to be inclined to model

just one or two emotions. In summary, we find multiple facets of emotions research and theory, such as biological bases for "basic" emotions, developmental aspects of emotions, appraisal theories, social construction of emotions, and the importance of emotional expressivity and recognition.

One of the long-term projects to develop a system that exhibits intelligent behaviour is Soar (Rosenbloom, Laird & Newell, 1993)[4]. In the early 1980s, Soar was developed as a system to support multiple problem solving methods for many different problems. This software architecture has been under continuous development. Newell (1990) began working on Soar with the purpose of building *unified theories of cognition*. Henninger, Jones and Chown (2003) integrated a connectionist model of emotional processing (Chown, 1993) with the Soar architecture. They intended to *"investigate improved realism in generating complex human-like behaviour that is sensitive to emotional assessments related to fear, anger, joy, etc. The emotions model comes from a connectionist cognitive architecture called SESAME, which has been used to model a wide range of human behaviours, including navigation in large-scale spaces and the effects of emotions on learning. The synthetic force model[5] is based on a special operations forces model that is implemented within the Soar architecture for cognition"* (p.1). This computational cognitive architecture enables the creation of autonomous software agents capable of sophisticated reasoning while utilizing large amounts of human-level knowledge.

MOTIVATION AND EMOTION IN INSTRUCTIONAL DESIGN

In this part, we first discuss the relation of emotion with motivation and learning and then examine the role of emotion in instructional design. Instructional design can be defined as *"an organized procedure that includes the steps of analyzing, designing, developing, implementing, and evaluating instruction*" (Seels & Richey, 1994, p.31). Motivation has been the focus of many psychological studies. Kleinginna & Kleinginna (1981) define motivation as an internal state or condition that activates behaviour and gives it direction. In particular, motivation to learn is characterized by a commitment to the process of learning (Gurtner, Monnard & Genoud, 2001) and includes two fundamental aspects: In its dynamic aspect, motivation is the force that pushes an individual to undertake an action. In its directional aspect, motivation is the attraction or the rejection evoked by an activity or a given situation.

Commitment is a central element in Keller's (1979) theory of motivation in education. Its ARCS model of motivational [instructional] design provides four groups of motivating strategies to influence students' motivation and thus their performance: (1) *attention* refers to keeping the learners motivated. (2) *Relevance* refers to the learners' belief that learning is relevant with respect to their goals and intentions, (3) *confidence* relates to the learners' confidence to achieve learning goals and (4) *satisfaction* relates to intrinsic and extrinsic awards, e.g. be able to apply newly acquired skills to his/her own experience. Various motivating tactics can be employed. For example, in a computer-based learning environment, we could implement an affective dialogue (del Soldato, 1992) to involve the learner in activities with interactive tasks. Motivational design also might aim to improve students' self-efficacy beliefs, their attention, or perceived relevance of the topic (Keller, 1999).

Students with high intrinsic motivation often outperform students with low intrinsic motivation (e.g. Martens, Gulikers & Bastiaens, 2004), and students with high motivation engage more in learning activities and are more likely to complete a course (e.g. Militiadou & Savenye, 2003). Motivation is conceived as a componential entity involving self-appraisals, values and expectancy beliefs (Pintrich & Schunk, 2002).

In the ARCS model, emotions were subordinated to motivation. Following Aubé (2005), we see emotions as a major sub-class of motivational systems operating as internal forces that regulate the strength and the direction of behaviour during the learning situation. Motivation is concerned with the internal and external factors involved in the establishment of "goals" and the initiation and execution of goal-oriented action, whereas emotion is rather concerned, among other critical factors, with evaluative aspects of the relation between a user and its environment. Indeed, the emotional processes are based on the acceptance or rejection of objects and facts and have an evaluation relation to the world (Kuhl, 1986).

According to Kleinginna and Kleinginna (1981, p. 355), emotion "*is a complex set of interactions among subjective and objective factors, mediated by neural/hormonal systems, which can: (1) give rise to affective experiences such as feelings of arousal, pleasure / displeasure; (2) generate cognitive processes such as emotionally relevant perceptual effects, appraisals, labeling processes; (3) activate widespread physiological adjustments to the arousing conditions; and (4) lead to behavior that is often, but not always, expressive, goal directed, and adaptive*".

Based on this comprehensive definition of emotions, emotional design of instruction attempts to clarify which types of emotions or feelings should be considered in instructional strategies. "Emotionally sound instruction" has emerged in order to increase positive and decrease negative feelings during regular instruction. Some technology-based instructional designs (Astleitner, 2001; MacFadden et al, 2005) not only suggest ways to alleviate these problems but also address the more fundamental issue of how to build emotions into a design. Astleitner (2001), with his FEASP model, indicates that instructional designers should analyze emotional problems before and during instruction and respond accordingly. Strategies are suggested for each of the five emotional categories: reduction of fear, envy and anger, increase of sympathy and pleasure. MacFadden (2005) attempts to develop a *"constructivist, emotionally-oriented (CEO) model of web-based learning which emphasizes safety, challenge, and new thinking, and offers several strategies to enhance the emotional experience of learners"* (p.79). This model acknowledges the need to increase positive emotions and decrease negative emotions, but also recognizes that some frustration and imbalance is part of the challenge and process of learning.

COMPUTER-BASED LEARNING ENVIRONMENTS

While emotions seem to play a major role in learning processes they are neglected in studies and designs of computer-based learning environments. We define a learning environment as a partly virtual space wherein two or more systems interact towards a shared goal, that of learning. Such environments are designed and studied in the field of educational (or instructional) technology, which can be defined as an intersection of educational psychology, instructional design and computer science. AECT defines educational technology as *"the study and ethical practice of facilitating learning and improving performance by creating, using and managing appropriate technological processes and resources"* (Richey, 2008, p.24). Research on computer-based learning environments relies on a large variety of learning and instructional theories, design principles and research methodologies.

Computer-supported learning technologies were invented in the 1960s and were based on "programmed instruction" and mastery learning theories. The resulting designs were usually referred to as computer-based training" (CBT), computer-aided instruction or computer-assisted instruction (CAI) from the 1970s through the 1990s. In a more simplified form, they correspond to today's "e-contents" that often form the core

of "e-learning" environments, sometimes also referred to as web-based training (WBT) or e-instruction. The 1980s and 1990s produced a variety of schools that can be grouped under the label Computer-based learning (CBL). Frequently based on constructivist and cognitivist learning theories, these computer-based learning environments (Salomon, 1992) focused on teaching more complex concepts, as well as domain-specific problem solving. Preferred technologies were micro-worlds (computer environments where learners could explore and build), simulations (computer environments where learners can play with parameters of dynamic systems) and hypertext. These technologies are often called "cognitive tools" because they help the learner to learn *with* the computer (as opposed to *from*).

Digitized communication and networking in education started in the mid 80s and became popular by the mid-90s, in particular through the World-Wide Web (WWW), e-mail and forums. Such Computer Mediated Communication (CMC) had an impact on industrial training, classroom teaching and distance education. The s emergence, after 2000, of multiple mobile and ubiquitous technologies gave a new impulse to situated learning theories favouring "learning-in-context" scenarios. Some literature uses the concept of "integrated learning" to describe blended learning scenarios that integrate both school and authentic (e.g. workplace) settings and that usually rely on a rich mix of educational strategies and learning technologies.

Today, one can distinguish two major forms of computer-supported learning. *Type A*, based on either a Computer-Based Training (CBT) or a Computer-Based Learning (CBL) tradition, focuses on the interaction between an individual student and the computer, e.g. through computer drills, tutorials or simulations. Most CBT/CBL courseware can today be delivered over the WWW. *Type B*, based on a computer-mediated communication (CMC) framework, aims to enhance interaction between participants. For example, learners are engaged in co-construction of meaning and reflective activities through computer-supported collaborative learning (CSCL) or in the co-construction of knowledge through writing-to-learn environments.

The instructional aims of such systems can be quite different. For example, one could distinguish between systems that train: (a) recall and identification of facts, (b) mastery of simple concepts, (c) reasoning and procedures, (d) problem solving, and (e) knowledge in action. Depending on these aims, electronic learning environments are more or less type A or B. Type A systems include a higher proportion of presentations, information, interactive learning modules, whereas type B environments include a higher proportion of communication tools, professional software and so-called cognitive tools. For example, in a (type B) socio-constructivist learning environment, interactions among subsystems may or may not be supported by computing resources, facts are replaced by exploration, individual activities are replaced by team work around the computer and the single interaction between learner and teacher or tutor is replaced by intensive and social interaction among learners and teachers.

Computer-based learning environments are not just digitalized computer-less learning environments. In other words, an electronic learning environment is not only defined by its technological dimension but by its (sometimes) creative instructional design defining individual, collaborative and collective learning activities.

Type A learning environments aim to leverage *"technology to maximize learning within an environment of sound course design that can offer learners the options of time, place, and pace and emphasizes different learning styles"* (Report of the Technology Enhanced Learning Committee, 2004, p.251). Emotions can be an additional design factor. Martinez (2000) claims "we *must provide multiple ways to provide instruction and environments so that all learners have opportunities for success. These descriptions are a first step*

in recognizing and accommodating individual learning differences. They are also an important step in recognizing the expanded, dominant role and impact of emotions and intention on learning, especially since online learners need to become more self-motivated and self-directed learners" (p. 7).

Type B environments as well as the CBL variant of type A encourage rich and active learning. Educational technologies can enable active learning with access to relevant information, a range of interactive tools and interaction among co-learners (Jonassen et al., 2002). This concept of technology enhanced learning is based on constructivist theory – that the student must engage in an active, experiential learning process to form an individual, meaningful understanding, preferably through problem-solving and reinterpreting the material for presentation from his/her own perspective. Cumming et al. (1999) suggest that computer-based learning environments should be designed to include a rich set of activities and many types of interactions which can lead to enhanced learning. It is necessary to encourage the growth of learner responsibility, initiative, decision-making and intentional learning, to encourage collaboration and reinforce reflection and build up confidence with technology.

Working with any kind of computer-based learning environment may increase the emotional load and motivational challenges. Learners' emotions are important variables that interact with variables in the learning environment and need more attention in instructional design (Jarvela, Lehtinen & Salonen, 2000). Instruction, which is emotionally sound, occurs when strategies are used to increase positive and decrease negative emotions. Positive emotions can promote exploration and enjoyment of new ideas and facilitate creative problem solving (Isen, 2004). Such cognitive processes may then promote more effective and efficient learning processes. Negative emotions often occur in situations in which people experience events that conflict with their goals and needs (Nummenmaa & Niemi, 2004). Emotions such as anxiety, frustration, or anger, could have disadvantageous consequences for interpersonal relations, and learning and work performance. However, as we shall see later, it is not obvious to define which emotions have a positive or negative function in a given context.

While some aspects of emotionally sound instruction can be solved by designing appropriate learning environments (e.g. that favour spontaneous interaction among learners) or learning activities that increase motivation, other functionalities can be implemented through computational artefacts. In order to accommodate frustration of a learner lost in free exploration and open social interaction for example, one could use artificial intelligence techniques to provide encouragement through tailored guidance. Such technological systems can be implemented with intelligent software agents, autonomous software components that can interact through a standard protocol and collaborate with each other to achieve common goals. Before discussing the agent paradigm and its use in education, let us now consider the full diversity of interactions that seem desirable within a computer-based learning environment.

EMOTIONAL ASPECT OF INTERACTION MEDIATED BY COMPUTERS

It is often claimed that the affective states of the individuals have a significant impact on the interaction process. In the context of a computer-mediated environment, "interaction" depends on "interactivity". Gilbert and Moore (1998) note that an accepted definition of interactivity in the literature on computer-mediated instruction is a reciprocal exchange between the technology and the learner, a process which they say is referred to as "feedback". "Interaction" on the other hand, can be defined as interplay and exchange within which individuals and groups influence each other.

Thus, interaction focuses on people's behaviours, while interactivity focuses on characteristics of the technology systems. We may argue that highly interactive technologies seem necessary to allow high person-to-person, person-to-group, and person-to-system interaction.

According to Järvenoja and Järvelä (2005), emotions in computer-based learning can result from self, context, task or technology, and other people. We may distinguish three different kinds of interaction with regard to learning: *Intrapersonal communication* is concerned with learner-task interaction, i.e. the process of "intellectually interacting with learning contents and tasks". *Interpersonal communication* refers to learner–learner and learner–teacher interactions. Such interactions are important in the socio-cultural learning theory of Vygotsky (1978) and are developed in Collaborative Learning (Dillenbourg, Baker, Blaye & O'Malley 1995). *Human-computer communication* deals with learner-interface interaction. Gilbert and Moore (1998) would argue that these categories limit interaction to a relationship between the learner and instructional interactivity, and ignore the social context. They identify "social interactivity" or better, in our opinion, "social interaction" as the social aspects of communication such as body language, the exchange of personal information, or learner encouragement. Social interaction does not necessarily require real-time (synchronous) communication. All types of interaction are necessary for efficient, effective and affective learning and they can occur in combined form.

It is delicate to talk about positive or negative emotions in the context of education. At first glance it would seem that some emotions (e.g. sympathy, pleasure, happiness) should be encouraged, and others like boredom, fatigue or confusion should be avoided. However, some "negative" emotions like fear, anger, frustration, sadness or guilt can be useful or even critical to modulate and to regulate learning processes. Furthermore, positive emotions also sometimes may require regulation. For example, the charm of novelty of a computer-based learning environment could cause positive emotions, but might lead to inappropriate learning activity if users direct their attention only to the interesting aspects of the novel technical environment.

Emotions may influence and regulate social interactions between learners or between learners and tutors (Gross & John, 2003). For Wosnitza and Volet (2005) it seems clear that learner emotion during the computer-based learning derives mostly from the social interaction rather than the technology context and that emotional expressions may enhance interaction and group performance in social learning situations. Thus, the technology is not the only antecedent of learner' emotional reactions in computer-based learning environments but it can directly or indirectly intervene. In any case, we may ask how emotion regulation could enhance social interactions, and as an end result, learning.

THE SOCIO-EMOTIONAL CLIMATE IN COMPUTER-BASED LEARNING ENVIRONMENTS

The importance of social and emotional dimensions in learning environments is widely recognised (Elias et al., 1997) but the dynamic interaction of these dimensions is not fully understood. Various concepts like social presence, sociability, social-emotional affordances (e.g. Wosnitza & Volet, 2005) and distributed emotions do receive some attention in all forms of computer-supported learning. According to appraisal theory, learners' emotions are the product of an evaluative process. This appraisal is related both to the mental baggage brought to the situation by the person (Volet, 2001) and the environmental conditions of the learning situation (Wosnitza & Nenniger, 2001). Examples of mental baggage are the learner's general beliefs, individual socio-emotional goals, individual learning goals, individual beliefs and moods.

Now let us examine the conjecture that the socio-emotional climate in a computer-based learning environment has strategic functions to support the teaching and the learning process. In order to better identify the functions of socio-emotional climate during the teaching and learning process, it is interesting to consider the three dimensions of Illeris' (2003) learning theory: cognitive, emotional and social. He claims that *"all cognitive learning always has an emotional component which is marked or "obsessed" by the emotional situation that was prevalent during learning, for example whether it was motivated by desire, necessity or compulsion"* (p.2). Through the cognitive dimension, knowledge, skills, understanding, meaning and functionality are developed. In a pedagogical perspective, this means to design strategies involving the learner in activities with interactive tasks. By way of the emotional dimension, patterns of emotion and motivation, attitudes, sensitivity and mental balance are developed. This emotional dimension is related to the motivational system that regulates the strength and the direction of behaviour during the learning situation. In the third social dimension, potentials for empathy, communication, co-operation and sociality are developed. Given the particular conditions of computer-supported learning situations, an additional technological dimension seems to emerge. Users must learn to work with a computer and to work with others mediated through the computer. This interface should be designed to build up confidence with technology, but also to reinforce reflection and encourage communication.

Communication oriented toward maintaining social and emotional relations can be defined as socio-emotional communication. It tends to be evaluative (agreement or disagreement). A simple model of this socio-emotional climate could be defined by the ratio of negative socio-emotional communication (showing hostility and rejection) and positive socio-emotional communication (showing friendliness and support). When this ratio decreases, the socio-emotional climate is becoming less negative and more positive. For instance, a more positive socio-emotional climate creates a friendly technological condition which is likely to reduce such frustration or inhibition. A more negative socio-emotional climate appears in the hostile conditions which are likely to increase the frustration.

Similarly, in collaborative and cooperative activities, social interactions, motivational strategies and goals could influence a different ratio of positive, relative to negative, socio-emotional evaluation. We introduce the concept of "socio-emotional climate" like an evaluative indicator of the full diversity of interactions that occur within a computer-based learning environment.

As illustrated in Figure 1, the socio-emotional climate results from the integration of four components. For each climate, different types of interactions between users and the system or other users add some positive influence to the overall climate.

The *motivational climate* may increase the learner's intrinsic motivation and performance through fostering positive emotions. The motivational climate refers to students' perceptions of achievement goals addressed by instructors in learning environments. Also, it includes the learner' satisfaction from being able to transfer the learnt skills to his/her own experience.

Students perceive the learning environment as a task — or ego — involved climate (Pintrich & Schunk, 2002).

The *social climate* is associated with interpersonal socio-emotional communication. It should foster communication and cooperation skills that include sociality and empathy. This communication competence builds on both managing one's own emotions and empathy towards the others. A healthy dialogue depends on being attuned to others' emotional states and controlling the impulse to respond in ways that might worsen the emotional climate. For example, the perception of the emotional climate is related to building positive interpersonal relationships (teacher-learner) and, consequently, to promote a positive socio-emotional climate. Rogers (1969) argues that communicating realness (sincere expressions of enthusiasm or frustration) is absolutely essential to the development of positive teacher-student interpersonal relationships.

The *technological climate* is associated with human-computer interaction (HCI). For example, the system should support the learner's autonomy which is defined as a *"capacity - for detachment, critical reflection, decision-making, and independent action"* (Little, 1991, p.4). Hence, the system should provide encouragement in moments of frustration.

Figure 1. Principal components of the socio-emotional climate in a computer-based learning environment

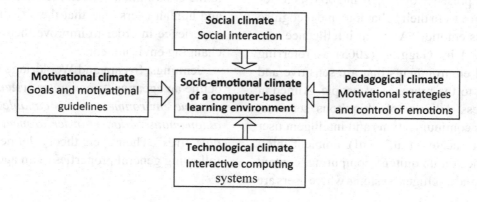

The last component, the *pedagogical climate*, is associated with intrapersonal emotional communication. It could be influenced by applying affective strategies in accordance to learner's emotional state (e.g. desire, interest, disgust and anxiety). An affective feedback in the learning process should create an emotional climate characterized by a positive working atmosphere, relaxed dispositions, extended support and assistance when necessary.

From a distributed cognition perspective (Hutchins, 1995), we could say that the socio-emotional climate is based on cognitive processes that lie not only within the individual but in the individual's social and physical environment.

In the next sections, we will pursue some considerations regarding the agent paradigm and discuss a collection of intelligent agents that manage both cognitive and affective models of the learner and that are able to express emotions through embodied socio-emotional agents.

AGENT PARADIGMS, ARCHITECTURES AND EMOTION

A key component of the computer-based learning environment is the technological system. To optimize its flexibility it could be designed as an open system, i.e. capable of adapting to its environment and of dynamically changing its structure. An environment endowed with ambient intelligence is able to analyse its contexts, adapt itself to the presence of people and objects residing in it, learn from their behaviour and recognise and express emotion. Ambient intelligence was characterised by Gaggioli (2005) as referring to physical environments that are sensitive and responsive to the presence of people. Aimed at the seamless delivery of ubiquitous services, continuous communications and intelligent user interfaces (Ducatel et al., 2001), ambient intelligence relies on ubiquitous computing, context awareness and intelligent systems where users are

empowered by interacting with an environment. In this sense, autonomy, distribution, adaptation, pro-activeness and responsiveness seem to be the key features of ambient intelligence, which are similar to the characteristics software agents share (Maes, 1994). Recently, some researchers tried to integrate agents into ambient intelligence systems (Aarts, 2004) and the agent technology also has the potential to contribute to and enhance the functionality of ambient intelligence systems. An interesting way to conceptualize such an environment is to understand it as a collection of interacting and highly heterogeneous agents.

Intelligent agents have been used for a vast range of applications. We are mostly interested in agents developed in robotics and human computer interaction. Models from these two subfields are not mutually exclusive since both are designed to interact with an environment. Take the case of the use of the technology in education where the learners interact with multiple resources and services, unrestricted by time or place. There is a revival of computer-based learning environments that include personified software entities. These entities intended to fulfil a range of functions including that of instructor, personal assistant or learning companion. Such an agent is a computational entity capable of perceiving, reacting, and acting upon an environment. These capabilities require that agents interoperate and coordinate with each other in peer-to-peer interactions. Another characteristic is *"adaptation"*. Adaptation implies that agents are capable of adapting to the environment, which includes other agents and human users, and that they can learn from experience in order to improve themselves in a changing environment.

Jennings, Sycara and Wooldridge (1998, p.8) define an agent as *"a computer system, situated in some environment that is capable of flexible autonomous action in order to meet its design objectives"*. Their agent theory defines the three following general properties of an agent.

- **Autonomy:** Agents are able to execute tasks without human interference or from other agents, and have some kind of control over their own actions and internal state.
- **Social ability:** An agent can interact with the other agents, human or not, to solve problems or help solve others' problems. Therefore, an agent also must show a social attitude and participate (or not) in group activities.
- **Reactivity:** Agents perceive their environment and respond to changes. In addition, agents must not simply respond to the environment, but must "take the initiative" to reach their goals. In this sense, they are not simply reactive, but can be *"pro-active"* and take initiatives as they deem appropriate.

These properties, in a more dynamic perspective, correspond to pro-activeness, cooperation and learning, principles proposed by Nwana (1996). A key element of their autonomy is their pro-activeness, i.e. their ability to 'take the initiative' rather than acting simply in response to their environment. In order to cooperate, agents need to possess a social ability, i.e. the ability to interact with other agents and possibly humans via some communication language. Learning implies that the agents would have to learn as they react and/or interact with their external environment.

Nwana (1996) asserts that since 1990 *"the range of agent types being investigated is now much broader"* (p.3). He proposes a typology of agents that are characterized by the combination of two or more of the above mentioned principles: (1) *collaborative agents* emphasize the autonomy and cooperation (with other agents) so that they can accomplish the tasks for its owners; (2) *interface agents* emphasize the autonomy and learning for the accomplishment of tasks for its owners; (3) *mobile agents* are able to travel over large nets, like the intranet, interacting with other hosts and storing information for themselves and their owners, coming back after having solved their tasks; (4) *Information / Internet agents* can play the role of

managing, manipulating and collecting information from many distributed sources; (5) *reactive agents* act and respond in a stimulus-response manner to represent the environment they are inserted in; (6) *smart, deliberative or cognitive agents* derive from the deliberative thinking. A case in point is the agent based on mental attitudes, used to model its cognitive capabilities, or notions such as beliefs, desires and intentions – the BDI agent (Rao & Georgeff, 1995); (7) *hybrid agents* constitute a combination of two or more categories in a unique agent. In conclusion, the agents can have different functions in a system.

If agents can act autonomously to perform operations without explicit directions from the user and potentially collaborate with other types of agents, we do need an architecture that can coordinate and mediate. One model is a so-called "society of agents". Sometimes, it is claimed that agents are best studied as members of multi-agent systems (Wooldridge, 2002), viewed like a society of agents. Within a "society of agents", agents should be specialized for specific tasks, should be autonomous and distributed and may be self-interested or cooperative. They should have "social and emotional abilities" and be able to interact with the other agents, human or artificial, to solve their problems or help in the solution of others' problems.

We will not concern ourselves here with particular agent architecture. We are mainly concerned with a generic high-level structure for an open agents system enabled for a majority of the functionalities described above. This agents system, with a hybrid structure, is composed of two major sub-systems:

1. The "behaviour and social" sub-system is responsible for efficient agent behaviour and personality. It also is a reactive system and its main task is to deal with social interactions between the agent and other agents (human or artificial) and it can be "pro-active" and

take initiatives when deemed appropriate;
2. The "cognitive and emotional" sub-system may be a deliberative system which, in order to reason and learn, has the ability to make long-term strategies based on the contents of its knowledge base. Built upon classical symbolic AI techniques, these artificial agents may build internal models (cognitive and affective) of human agents. These models then can be used to formulate strategies in order to achieve goal states.

There is also some research on the incorporation of emotions into artificial agents. Architectures like SOAR (Laird, Newell & Rosenbloom, 1987), ACT-R (Anderson & Lebiere, 1998), CogAff (Sloman, 2001), and Minsky's Society of Mind (Minsky, 1987) have inspired many designers of social and emotional agents. Another class of architectures follows a BDI paradigm. The *Beliefs* of an agent summarise anything that the agent assumes to know about itself, the other agents and the environment. Thus, technically, the beliefs constitute the agent's knowledge base. The *Desires* are the motivational state of the system and determine the agent's possible goals in terms of what the agent wishes to achieve. The *Intentions* are expressed by the adopted goals to be achieved and play an important role in the practical reasoning process (Wooldridge, 2002). Pereira, Oliveira, Moreira and Sarmento (2005) extended the BDI architecture with emotions, including internal representations for agent's capabilities and resources. Morgado and Gaspar (2005) present an agent model where emotion and cognition are conceived as two integrated aspects of intelligent behaviour. They show affective mechanisms that support the adaptation to changing environments and a controlled use of resources. All these cognitive architectures relate to the manner in which they represent, organize, utilize, and acquire knowledge.

These computational agents should be "relational", i.e. show affective and expressive

behaviours in order to build up long-term social-emotional relationships with users. The general vision is that, if a user's emotion was recognized by a computer, human–computer interactions would be more natural, enjoyable, and productive (Prendinger & Ishizuka, 2005).

In conclusion, an intelligent agent should exhibit the following behaviour: (1) "intelligent" for their ability to infer and to learn; (2) "proactive" because it should be goal-directed; (3) "reactive" to respond to domain changes and (4) "autonomous" because it should operate without human involvement. The reason for introducing agents in the design of computer-based learning environments is that their ability to be proactive, to cooperate and to learn might enhance both pedagogical and motivational functions.

EMOTIONAL AGENTS IN EDUCATION

In educational technology, the first generation of agents was associated with intelligent tutoring systems (ITS) (Anderson, Boyle, Farrell & Reiser, 1987) or computer-based coaches (Selker, 1994). In the literature on intelligence tutoring systems we find for example the distinction between coach, tutor and domain expert and that model could be implemented with agent architecture. Intelligent agents have been suggested as a new approach to extend intelligent tutoring systems in such a way that the need for social context for learning can be fulfilled (Kearsley, 1993). Viccari et al. (Viccari, Jaques & Verdin, 2008, synopsis) present a modern view of intelligent tutoring, focusing mainly on the "*conception of these systems according to a multi-agent approach and on the affective and cognitive modelling of the student in this kind of educational environment*".

A second generation of educational agents is "*pedagogical agents*" in interactive learning. Johnson et al. (1998) define pedagogical agents as autonomous and/or interface intelligent agents that support human learning by interacting with students in the context of an interactive learning environment. According to Nwana's (1996) typology, a pedagogical agent can be described as an autonomous agent reacting to changes in its environment, communicating in rudimentary ways with other agents, communicating directly with the users, and being adaptable by end users. Pedagogical agents, to facilitate learning, emphasize social interaction between learners and agents. Learners exposed to an environment with a pedagogical agent demonstrated deeper learning and higher motivation than learners without an agent (Moreno, Mayer, Spires & Lester, 2001).

A single pedagogical agent can be modelled and implemented with cooperative software agents. These agents act in the background as part of the architecture of the educational system. The educational system is modelled and implemented using a multi-agent approach. The architectures based on this approach are variations of the traditional and functional architecture of an ITS. Control is distributed among the agents, however the user sees the system as a whole, while, internally, it is composed of a society of agents. For example, Zapata-Rivera and Greer (2001) propose a web-based ITS environment for learning Java language based on a CORBA platform and using Microsoft agents.

On the other hand, we can look at this pedagogical agent as "interface agent". Lieberman and Selker (2003) assert that an agent could be considered an interface agent if it should communicate directly with the user through the system's input and output devices. In this respect, an interface agent is defined as a character enacted by an environment that interacts with a user in a socially engaging manner. The essential characteristics of an interface agent include responsiveness, competence, and accessibility. The interface agent's presentation techniques are text, speech, facial expressions, and/or body language by graphics and animation. Research on animated graphical agents is now commonly regarded as a subfield of software agent research. For example, Breazeal's (2003) captivating Kismet robot can take a human-like or creature-like physical form. The robot can discern if the human approves (shows positive expressions) or disapproves (shows negative expressions) of its performance.

For Johnson, Rickel and Lester (2000), *"animated pedagogical agents"* are animated life-like characters that support learning in computer-based environments. They are autonomous and intelligent agents based on the idea of behaviour simulation of alive and intelligent creatures in machines (Elliott, Rickel & Lester, 1999). Because of their anthropomorphized interface, these agents can interact with learners more socially and naturally. There is a variety of pedagogical agents in varying subject areas to better achieve instructional goals, e.g. the mediator agent of Conati and Klawe (2002) or the companion agent regarding student motivation of Chan (1996). STEVE is an animated and autonomous pedagogical agent inserted in a 3D simulation system constructed to assist students in courses of naval training (Rickel & Johnson, 1999).

A motivational agent can be a derived type of pedagogical agent. Its role is to bring a positive effect on learning, motivation, and self-efficacy. To do so, a motivational agent should for example detect the curiosity or interest level of the user, and then act in order to support the learner's motivation. For example, a motivational agent can provide encouragement and support with messages (Baylor, 2003).

According to the commitment theory of emotions (Aubé, 2005), the concepts of motivation and emotion are not at the same level, but they are rather layered. Emotions seem to operate as a particular motivational system whose most likely function is to regulate kin and relatives encounters. In support of his theory, Aubé (2005, p.21) notes that *"emotions thus appear as computational control systems that handle the variation of commitments lying at the root of interactive and collaborative behaviors"*.

We will now address the question of agents empowered with emotional skills. According to Viccari et al. (Viccari, Jaques & Verdin, 2008, synopsis) *"researchers in education believe that the educational computing environments would be more pedagogically effective if they had mechanisms to show and recognize the learners' emotions"*. Following Salovey and Mayer (1990), agents that reflect emotional intelligence capabilities should have *"the ability to monitor one's own and others' feeling and emotions, to discriminate among them and to use this information to guide one's thinking and action"* (p.189). Those intelligent agents that show emotions make beneficial use of emotions in their interaction with the users and with the environment. This could act to stimulate pride (but not humiliation) in case of failure.

An emotional (pedagogical) agent is a similar concept as a pedagogical agent with emotional abilities. Both make beneficial use of emotions in their interaction with the users and with the environment. More specifically, an emotional agent inherits some essential properties of a motivational agent, but it is more complex and it includes additional features. It is worth mentioning here that their design will differ in their level of complexity, the level of the conditions of their activation, and the level of their impact on learning. Take the case of SCREAM, a scripting tool that enables authors to generate emotionally and socially appropriate responses of animated agents (Prendinger & Ishizuka, 2002).

Different methods and techniques are needed to specify, establish, and verify properties of emotional pedagogical agents. Let's examine the case of a learning companion agent that can be designed to share the learner's emotional experiences. It may express emotions to stimulate positive emotions or relieve negative ones of the learner. The learning companion may provide support and encouragement in moments of distress and frustration (Klein, Moon & Picard, 2002). To take another example, Jaques, Bocca and Vic-

cari (2003) propose an emotional agent called Mediating Agent. This agent is incorporated in a computational education environment that is based on the socio-cultural theory of Vygotsky (1978). The Mediating Agent is responsible for promoting positive emotions and motivating the learners of this environment. Based on the OCC model (Ortony, Clore & Collins, 1988), it works with the emotions of satisfaction and disappointment. This agent may identify the emotions through learner actions in the graphical interface of the education environment and in some occasions the learners are prompted to indicate their current emotional state.

It might well be prudent to say that is not clear at all whether these so-called emotional or affective agents deserve the properties that are - often very quickly - attributed to them by their users and creators alike. In a first conclusion, we propose a collection of interacting and highly heterogeneous agents in order to conceptualize emotionally enhanced computer-based learning environments (of type A or B). Such agents are adaptive and intelligent with a hybrid architecture, i.e. a combination of reactive and deliberative sub-agents with emotional and communication capabilities.

"Motivational agents" may have the function to perform cognitive and motivation diagnosis and to suggest motivational and affective pedagogical strategies that aim at promoting a positive mood in the learner. The goal is to foster learning process as well as to provide emotional support to the learner, motivating and encouraging him/her.

"Affective pedagogical agents" may have the role to monitor the interaction of the learner with the environment and to receive information sent by a Motivational agent about the learner's cognitive and affective profile. According to Frijda (1994) the affective state is a more wide-ranging term and it comprises the emotions and other states such as moods and sentiments. This agent could identify the learner's affective states by his/her actions in the learning environment (observable

behaviour) or by sensors, e.g. a device to monitor the learner's breathing or cardiac rhythm and so on. Another possibility, information used to infer the learner's appraisal (for example, goals, events and agent's actions) could be directly provided by the user in a dialogue with the agent (Affective Reasoning project's agent, Elliot, 1994). It can then apply affective strategies in accordance to learner's emotional state.

"*Social and Collaborative agents*" may have the function to observe the interaction among the learners within the technological environment and to encourage the learners to interact in collaborative tools. These agents should have the ability of fostering the interaction among the learners, e.g. be able to provide an instant messaging service. For such purposes, it keeps a knowledge base with information about the affective aspects of tools and services.

Now let us imagine how these agents could interact in some future system. Social and Collaborative agents have the ability to interact socially with both human users and other agents. The Social agent may for example search for peers that are capable of assisting a student in his/her learning process. The Collaborative agent will monitor and mediate the interaction between students in collaborative communication tools (for example, chat, wiki or bulletin boards). During this interaction the Collaboration agent interacts with the Motivational agent to obtain new strategies to be used in order to stimulate learners when, for example, they appear to be unmotivated. They should exchange information with the Affective pedagogical agent responsible to apply these strategies in accordance to the student's affective state. These affective strategies implement two major functions: Firstly to motivate and encourage the student and secondly, through emotional behaviour, promote the student's positive mood. The Motivational agents contain a library of responses based on learner actions and operate with a database of motivational and affective pedagogical strategies. It also sends the cognitive and affective

learner model information to the Social agent and the Affective pedagogical agent.

In this collection, all types of agents should be specialized for specific tasks, should be autonomous, self-interested, cooperative and be able to interact with the other agents, human or artificial. We call such intelligent agents with emotional and social abilities "*socio-emotional agents*". This agent architecture with embodied emotional process and able to capture human reasoning and emotion using for example a BDI schema (beliefs, desires, and intentions) appears to be emotional and can engage in non-trivial social interactions. Let us now examine the role of socio-emotional agents in a computer-based learning environment.

THE SOCIO-EMOTIONAL AGENT'S FUNCTIONS IN INSTRUCTIONAL DESIGN

The computer could offer assistance to a confused user or try to make a frustrated user feel better, and hence react in ways that are more appropriate than simply ignoring the user's affective state. For instance, Liu and Picard (2005) suggest that an agent who was empathetic toward the user (through the use of facial expressions and textual content) was generally rated more positively by subjects when compared with an agent which was not empathetic.

In our opinion, in educational applications, the most essential feature of the socio-emotional agents is their capacity to communicate with humans and other intelligent agents. In Figure 2, we define the socio-emotional agent's functions in instructional design by considering its interaction with users and with the environment. These functions form the basis of the agent's interactivity and adaptive capabilities.

The "observation" function concerns the two-way interaction between a user and his/her environment. This function is related to affective

Figure 2. The interactions in a computer-based learning environment based on emotional agents

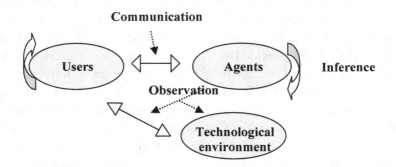

reasoning that is concerned with an agent's appraisal process, where events are evaluated as to their emotional significance for the agent. According to Elliot (1992), "...*an agent's emotional state is predicated entirely on that agent's appraisal of an event in terms of how that event relates to its own set of goals, and plans toward those goals*" (p.59). He claims that personification of the environment (e.g. by introducing an animated character/persona) positively affect the learner's perception of their learning experience and that integrating emotional traits into these personas would result in more effective and motivating instruction.

Similarly, agents with "observation" functions monitor the user's observable behaviour by means of the evaluation of events in technological learning environments in order to predict, recognise and interpret the user's affective states. This information plus the past record of a user's performance can then be used to initiate emotional communication: provide encouragement at the moment of frustration (Klein, Moon & Picard, 2002) and show interest and excitement in the learning tasks. Moreover, agents can offer suggestions and possible solutions to common problems, and should develop motivational strategies in order to involve the user in activities with interactive tasks. For example, an agent might appraise a user's success on a task as being desirable for them (a friend), producing a happy-for emotion, and leading to an affect-oriented, other-directed,

emotion-modulation expression of praise for their good work (Elliot, 1992).

In addition, these agents could have a social observation function – not only to communicate with users, but to promote and monitor the interaction between users in technological learning environments. It attends the users during the interactions, stimulating them when they look unmotivated, presenting new ideas and correcting wrong ones. The messages carried out could be the analysis of the user's dialogue based on statistical methods, such as pattern matching, message categorisation and information retrieval (Soller, 2001). Moreover, this observation function could take into account the complex relationship of user's social, emotional and motivational learning. An appropriate action of emotion regulation (Gross & John, 2003) can be to reconfigure the social and emotional dimensions of the technological learning environment.

The "communication" function refers to the two-way interaction between the user and the socio-emotional agent. It could be implemented with various techniques from the field of "affective computing" for supporting affects recognition and monitoring the expression of emotions. Lisetti and Nasoz (2002) propose an adaptive system architecture designed to sense the user's emotional and affective states via three multimodal subsystems (V, K, A): namely (1) the Visual (from facial images and videos), (2) Kinesthetic (from autonomic nervous system (ANS) signals), and (3) Auditory (from speech). In addition, recent studies, trying to verify the influence of positive emotions on the motivation, also found that positive emotions may increase the intrinsic motivation and performance on the current task (Isen, 2004). According to Picard (1997), an embodied emotional agent must indeed incorporate mechanisms allowing it to recognize emotions in the user and express appropriately some of its own in return.

More specifically, agents with "communication" functions are related to the user preferences in order to identify the cognitive and motivational profile. Its communication abilities, like a text and speech interpreter or a text-to-speech engine, enable the agents to communicate with a user via speech, mouse or keyboard. Moreover, these agents should recognise the user's emotion and respond appropriately with the ability to change user perceptions (Jaques, Bocca & Viccari, 2003). Besides recognising the user's emotions, agents should have a user affective model defined by Elliot, Rickel and Lester (1999) as the capacity of the computational system to model the user's affective states.

The third role, "inference", has to do with the architecture of the emotional agents themselves (reviewed in the previous section), with the interaction between the different agents in the system and with their ability to learn. Besides, the BDI architecture model is very adequate to infer and also model student's affective states since the emotions have a dynamic nature. The environments should provide a computational infrastructure for such interactions to take place (Huhns & Stephens, 1999) and should include protocols for agents to communicate and protocols for agents to interact (propose, accept, reject, retract or counter propose a course of action).

In the previous sections, we introduced the concept of "socio-emotional climate" in order to evaluate the full diversity of interactions that seem desirable within a computer-based learning environment. Thus, the socio-emotional climate results from the integration of four components,

each acting positively on the learning process through a collection of socio-emotional agents. For each climate, different types of socio-emotional agents may interact with the user or the system and add some positive influence to the overall climate.

CONCLUSION AND FUTURE TRENDS

As conclusion, we suggest discussing how a design with multiple socio-emotional agents might improve the socio-emotional climate in an educational environment. It seems reasonable to postulate that a good socio-emotional climate emerges from the capability to facilitate different interactions and to assist learners in various tasks. More precisely, we formulate the conjecture that a socio-emotional climate capable of enhancing learner motivation and meta-cognitive processes like reflection could be developed through the use of various socio-emotional agents.

The technological climate is viewed like a perception of the human-computer interactions. The interface agents should be responsible for the affective effect of interaction between learners and technological environment. The human-computer interaction is social and emotional even when interfaces are not designed with such interaction as a goal (Picard & Wexelblat, 2002). Interface technologies can enable or increase social-emotional interaction between users and computers. For example, they can analyse learner's observable behaviour: execution time of an activity, success or failure in the execution of an exercise and frequency of assistance required.

The motivational climate evaluates the learner's goals and its motivational orientation. A motivational agent can diagnose the learner's cognitive and emotional profile and detect students' needs and preferences. The cognitive profile stores the information about beliefs, skills, difficulties and assistance. The emotional profile contains information about the personality of the learner, like introvert, extrovert, if he/she likes to work in group, and his/her level of motivation. It is worth mentioning here that in a computer-based learning environment, students perceived the agent with motivational support as significantly more human-like and engaging than the agent without motivational support (Warren, Shen, Park, Baylor & Perez, 2005).

The social climate is an evaluation of the social interactions (Suh, 1999). The social and collaborative agents should foster empathy, communication, co-operation and sociality. The social agent has the ability to interact socially with both human users and other agents and a collaborative agent should be able to encourage the interaction among the learners. Empathy and socio-emotional communication might be an important key to ensure the quality of human communication and relevant skills should be a part of personal development.

Finally, the pedagogical climate can be influenced by the pedagogical agents that are responsible for sustaining motivation and expressing emotions. The agents should apply the affective strategies in order to encourage the learner. The pedagogical climate is an evaluation of the agent's abilities to answer the learner's questions, to generate explanations, to question the learner, and to obtain the learner's levels of ability. For instance, recent studies (Lester et al., 1997; Rickel & Johnson, 1999) with animated pedagogical agents demonstrated that animated agents that have a computational model of emotion can be more effective pedagogically, beyond providing a strong motivational effect in the learner.

A positive socio-emotional climate that enhances the learners' motivation, self-assessment and self-motivation is to be developed through the use of the various emotional agents presented above. Adaptive environmental and motivational agents, using affective strategies, would for instance improve the pedagogical and motivational climate. They would promote a positive mood and provide the learner with an emotional support. .

On the other hand, deliberative and collaborative emotional agents would control the technological climate (like media coverage of teaching contents by using multimedia strategies). Finally, social and collaborative agents would improve the social climate and aim to develop sociality and empathy through the acquisition of communication, and cooperation skills.

Some conceptual issues and challenges of affective computing, motivational theories, computational models of emotions and computer-based learning systems was reviewed in this chapter as well as some recent approaches on the development of emotional agents. Emotion is also an issue with other approaches seeking higher motivation among learners. One can argue that the learning process itself - and not just the result - should be interesting. "Serious play" or "hard fun" (Rieber et al., 1998) are intense learning situations where learners engage large amounts of "energy" and time and that do provide equally intense pleasure at certain moments and which have been identified as "flow" or "optimal experience" by Csikszentmihalyi (1990). Flow situations are defined as states of happiness and satisfaction that arise when "carried" by an automatic and spontaneous activity. It is interesting to know that "flow states" go along with the impression of discovery and creation and boost performance in conjunction with important cognitive efforts. Conditions in which flow happens are characterized in the literature by an optimised level of challenge, a feeling of control adapted to the learner, a touch of fantasy, and feedback of the system. Emotionally sound instruction also might include elements from "serious play", for example, the idea that open and active learning is favourable to trigger challenge, curiosity, and lets the student have some control. Other "flow" theory principles are known from more "behaviourist" instructional designs. Open and active learning should not be "programmed", but at least some tasks should be affordable and lead to quick results. More importantly, frequent feedback should be provided by the system, by co-learners or by the teacher. (Schneider, 2004).

There are a number of issues grouped in three types and that we did not address much here. There is still an open debate concerning the precise definition and function of emotions in cognition, e.g. how emotion is integrated with other mechanisms such as sensory input, selection of stimuli, memorization and communication. The architecture of computational models, including ones that only have engineering purposes like in our case, is still under debate. For example, what kind of data structures and computational mechanisms should be used to both capture and represent the complexity of emotion processes? Finally, we also need to develop an appropriate research methodology that will help us firstly to design an emotionally enhanced computer-based learning environment, then to study its effect on cognitive and social processes, and finally to evaluate its impact on learning outcomes.

REFERENCES

Aarts, E. (2004). Ambient Intelligence: A Multimedia Perspective. In *IEEE Multimedia* (pp. 12-19).

Anderson, J. R., & Lebiere, C. (1998). *The atomic components of thought*. Mahwah, NJ: Lawrence Erlbaum Associates, Inc.

Anderson, J., Boyle, C., Farrell, R., & Reiser, B. (1987). Cognitive principles in the design of computer tutors. In: P. Morris (Ed.), *Modeling cognition* (pp. 93-133). New York: John Wiley.

Andre, E., Klesen, M., Gebhard, P., Allen, S., & Rist, T. (2001). Integrating models of personality and emotions in lifelike characters. In A. Paiva (Ed.), *Affective interactions: Towards a new generation of computer interfaces* (pp. 150-165). New York: Springer-Verlag.

Astleitner, H. (2001). Designing emotionally sound instruction. *Journal of Instructional Psychology, 28*, 209-219.

Araujo A. F. R. (1994). *Memory, emotions, and neural networks: Associative learning and memory recall influenced by affective evaluation and task difficulty*. Unpublished doctoral dissertation, University of Sussex, England.

Arnold, M. B. (1950). An excitatory theory of emotion. In M. L. Reymert (Ed.), *Feelings and emotions: The Mooseheart symposium* (pp. 11-33). McGraw-Hill, Inc.

Aubé, M. (2005). Beyond needs: Emotions and the commitments requirement. In D. N. Davis (Ed.), *Visions of Mind: Architectures for cognition and affect* (pp. 21-44). Hershey, PA: Idea Group, Inc.

Bates, J., Loyall, A. B., & Reilly, W. S. (1992). *An architecture for action, emotion, and social behaviour*. Technical Report CMU-CS-92-144, School of Computer Science, Carnegie Mellon University.

Baylor, A. L. (2003). *The impact of three pedagogical agent roles*. Florida State University. Retrieved May 31, 2008, from http://garnet.acns.fsu.edu/~abaylor/PDF/baylor_aamas.pdf .

Bickmore, T., & Picard, R. (2004). Towards caring machines. In *CHI '04: Extended abstracts on human factors in computing systems* (pp. 396-403). New York: ACM Press.

Boekaerts, M. (2003). Toward a model that integrates motivation, affect, and learning. *British Journal of Educational Psychology Monograph Series, 2*, 173-189.

Brave, S., & Nass, C. (2003). Emotion in human-computer interaction. In J. Jacko, & A. Sears (Eds.), *Handbook of human-computer interaction.* (pp. 81-96). Mahwah, NJ, USA: Lawrence Erlbaum Associates.

Brave, S., Nass, C., & Hutchinson, K. (2005). Computers that care: investigating the effects of orientation of emotion exhibited by an embodied computer agent. *International Journal of Human-Computer Studies, 62*(2), 161-178.

Breazeal, C. (2003). Emotion and sociable humanoid robots. *International Journal of Human Computer Interaction, 59*, 119-155.

Breazeal, C. (2006). Human-robot partnership. In S. Coradeschi, H. Ishiguro, M. Asada, S. Shapiro, M. Theilscher, C. Breazeal, M. Mataric, & H. Ishida (Eds.), Trends and Controversies: Human-Inspired Robots. *IEEE Intelligent Systems 21*(4), 79-81. Retrieved April 18, 2008, from http://robotics.usc.edu/~maja/publications/special-issue-ieeeintsys06.pdf

Castelfranchi, C. (2000). Affective appraisal versus cognitive evaluations in social emotions and interactions. In A. Paiva (Ed.), *Affective interactions: Towards a new generation of affective interfaces.* (pp. 76-106). New York: Springer.

Cañamero, D. (1998). Issues in the design of emotional agents. In D. Cañamero (Ed.), *Emotional and intelligent: The tangled knot of cognition. Papers from the 1998 AAAI Fall Symposium* (pp. 49-54). Menlo Park, California: AAAI Press.

Cañamero, D. (2003). Designing emotions for activity selection in autonomous agents. In R. Trappl, P. Petta, & S. Payr, (Eds.), *Emotions in humans and artifacts.* Cambridge, MA: The MIT Press.

Chan, T.W. (1996). Learning companion systems, social learning systems, and intelligent virtual classroom. Invited Talk, World Conference on Artificial Intelligence in Education, Washington, DC, USA. *Journal of Artificial Intelligence in Education, 7*(2), 125-159.

Conati, C., & Klawe, M. (2002). Socially intelligent agents in educational games. In K. Dautenhahn, A.H. Bond, L. Cañamero, & B. Edmonds (Eds.), *Socially intelligent agents - Creating relationships with computers and robots* (pp. 213-221). Kluwer Academic Publishers.

Chown, E. (1993). The adaptive power of affect: Learning in the SESAME architecture. In J. A. Meyer, H. L. Roitblat, & S. Wilson (Eds.), *From Animals to Animats 2: Proceedings of the Second International Conference on Simulation Adaptive Behavior* (pp. 515). Cambridge, MA: MIT Press.

Csikszentmihalyi, M. (1990). *Flow: The psychology of optimal experience.* New York: Harper and Row.

Cumming, G., Finch, S., & Thomason, N. (1999). Educational design for effective learning: Building and using a computer-based learning environment for statistical concepts. In G. Cumming, T. Okamoto, & L. Gomez (Eds.), *Advanced research in computers and communications in education* (pp.558-565). Amsterdam: IOS Press.

Custódio, L., Ventura, R., & Pinto-Ferreira, C. (1999). Artificial emotions and emotion-based control systems. In *Proceedings of 7th IEEE International Conference on Emerging Technologies and Factory Automation.* Vol. 2 (pp. 1415-1420). Barcelona, Spain.

Damasio, A. R. (1994). *L'erreur de Descartes: la raison des émotions.* Paris: Odile Jacob.

Dias, J., & Paiva, A. (2005). Feeling and Reasoning: a computational model. In *EPIA, 12th Portuguese Conference on Artificial Intelligence* (pp 127-140). Berlin/Heidelberg: Springer.

Dillenbourg, P., Baker, M., Blaye, A., & O'Malley, C. (1995). The evolution of research on collaborative learning. In P. Reimann & H. Spada (Eds.), *Learning in humans and machines. Towards an interdisciplinary learning science* (pp. 189-211). London: Pergamon.

Ducatel, K., Bogdanowicz, M., Scapolo, F., Leijten, J., & Burgelman J.-C. (2001). *Scenarios for ambient intelligence 2010*, ISTAG Report, European Commission, Institute for Prospective Technological Studies, Seville. Retrieved August 25, 2008, from ftp://ftp.cordis.lu/pub/ist/docs/istagscenarios2010.pdf.

Ekman, P. (2000). Facial expressions. In T. Dalgleish & M. J. Power (Eds.), *Handbook of cognition and emotion* (pp. 301-320). New York: John Wiley & Sons Ltd.

Ekman, P., & Friesen, W. V. (1975). *Unmasking the face: A guide to recognizing emotions from facial clues.* Englewood Cliffs, NJ: Prentice-Hall.

El-Nasr, M. S., Yen, J., & Ioerger, T. R. (2000). FLAME – Fuzzy logic adaptive model of emotions. *Autonomous agents and multi-agent systems, 3*(3), 219-257.

Elias, M. J., Zins, J. E., Weissberg, R. P., Frey, K. S., Greenberg, M. P., Haynes, N. M., Kessler, R., Schwab-Stone, M. E., & Shriver, T. P. (1997). *Promoting social and emotional learning. Guidelines for educators.* Association for Supervision and Curriculum Development: USA.

Elliott, C. (1992). *The affective reasoner: A process model of emotions in a multi-agent system.* Northwestern University, Evanston, IL, USA.

Elliott, C. (1994). *The affective reasoning project.* DePaul University. Retrieved April 18, 2008, from http://condor.depaul.edu/~elliott/arback.html

Elliott, C., Rickel, J., & Lester, J. (1999). Lifelike pedagogical agents and affective computing: An exploratory synthesis. In M. Wooldridge & M. Veloso (Eds.), *Artificial intelligence today*, (pp. 195-212). Berlin: Springer-Verlag.

Ellsworth, P. C., & Scherer, K. R. (2003). Appraisal processes in emotion. In R. J. Davidson, H. H. Goldsmith, & K. R. Scherer (Eds.), *Handbook of the affective sciences* (pp. 572-595). New York: Oxford University Press.

Frijda, N. H. (1986). *The emotions.* Cambridge: Cambridge University Press.

Frijda, N. H. (1994). Varieties of affect: emotions and episodes, moods, and sentiments. In P. Ekman, & R. J. Davidson (Eds.), *The Nature of Emotion* (pp. 59-67). New York: Oxford University Press.

Gadanho, S., & Hallam, J. (2001). Emotion-triggered learning in autonomous robot control. *Cybernetics and Systems: an International Journal, 5*(32), 531-559.

Gaggioli, A. (2005). Optimal experience in ambient intelligence. In G. Riva, F. Vatalaro, F. Davide, M. Alcañiz (Eds.), *Ambient Intelligence.* IOS Press.

Gilbert, L., & Moore, D. (1998). Building interactivity into web courses: Tools for social and instructional interaction. *Educational Technology, 38*(3), 29-35.

Gratch, J., & Marsella, S. (2004). A domain-independent framework for modeling emotion. *Cognitive Systems Research, 5*, 269-306.

Gross, J. J., & John, O. P. (2003). Individual differences in two emotion regulation processes: Implications for affect, relationships, and wellbeing. *Journal of Personality & Social Psychology, 85*(2), 348-362.

Gurtner, J-L., Monnard, I., & Genoud, P. A. (2001). Towards a Multilayer model of context and its impact on motivation. In S. Volet, & S. Jarvela, (Eds.), *Motivation in learning contexts: theoretical and methodological implications* (pp. 189-208). Oxford: Elsevier Pergamon.

Henninger, A., Jones, R., & Chown, E., (2003). Behaviours that emerge from emotion and cognition: implementation and evaluation of symbolic-connectionist architecture. In *Proceedings of the Second International Joint Conference on Autonomous Agents and Multiagent Systems* (pp. 321-328). Melbourne, Australia.

Hudlicka, E. (2003). To feel or not to feel: The role of affect in human-computer interaction. *International Journal of Human-Computer Studies, 59*, 1-32.

Huhns, M. N., & Stephens, L. M. (1999). Multiagent systems and societies of agents. In G. Weiss (Ed.), *Multiagent systems: A modern approach to distributed artificial intelligence* (pp. 79-120). Cambridge, MA: MIT Press.

Hutchins, E. (1995). Cognition in the wild. Cambridge, MA: MIT Press.

Illeris, K. (2003). *From vocational training to workplace learning*. Roskilde Universitetscenter, Copenhagen. Retrieved April 18, 2008, from http://www.ruc.dk/upload/application/pdf/08f567a4/glasgow.pdf

Ioannou, S., Raouzaiou, A., Tzouvaras, V., Mailis, T., Karpouzis, K., & Kollias S. (2005). Emotion recognition through facial expression analysis based on a neurofuzzy network. *Neural Networks, 18*(4), 423-435.

Isen, A. M. (2004). Positive affect and decision making. In M. Lewis, & J. M. Haviland Jones (Eds.), *Handbook of emotions* (2nd ed.) (pp. 417-435). New York: The Guilford Press.

Izard, C. (1971). *The face of emotions*. New York: Appleton – Century – Crofts.

Jaques, P. A., Bocca, E., & Viccari, R. (2003). Considering student's emotions in computational educational systems. In *Simpósio Brasileiro de Informática na Educação, Rio de Janiero. Anais do Simpósio Brasileiro de Informática na Educação*. Rio de Janeiro: UFRJ, 2003 (pp. 543-552). Retrieved April 18, 2008, from http://www.inf.unisinos.br/~pjaques/papers/jaques_sbie_2003.pdf

Järvenoja, H., & Järvelä, S. (2005). How students describe the sources of their emotional and motivational experiences during the learning process: A qualitative approach. *Learning and Instruction, 15*(5), 465-480.

Järvelä, S., Lehtinen, E., & Salonen, P. (2000). Socio-emotional orientation as a mediating variable in the teaching-learning interaction: implications for instructional design. *Scandinavian Journal of Educational Research, 44*, 293-306.

Jennings, N. R., Sycara, K., & Wooldridge, M. (1998). A roadmap of agent research and development. *Autonomous Agents and Multi-Agent Systems Journal, 1*, 275–306.

Johnson, W. L., Rickel, J. W., & Lester, J. C. (2000). Animated pedagogical agents: face-to-face interaction in interactive learning environments. *International Journal of Artificial Intelligence in Education, 11*, 47-78.

Jonassen David H., Jane Howland, Joi Moore, and Rose M. Marra (2002), *Learning to solve problems with technology: A constructivist perspective* (2nd Ed.). Prentice Hall.

Kearsley, G. (1993). Intelligent agents and instructional systems: Implications of a new paradigm. *Journal of Artificial Intelligence in Education, 4*(4), 295-304.

Keller, J. M. (1979). Motivation and instructional design: A theoretical perspective. *Journal of Instructional Development, 2*(4), 26-34.

Keller, J. M. (1999). Using the ARCS motivational process in computer-based instruction and distance education. *New Directions for Teaching and Learning, 78*, 39-47.

Klein, J., Moon, Y., & Picard, R.W. (2002). This computer responds to user frustration: Theory, design, and results. *Interacting with Computers, 14*, 119-140.

Kleinginna, P., & Kleinginna A. (1981). A categorized list of motivation definitions, with suggestions for a consensual definition. *Motivation and Emotion, 5*, 263-291.

Kort, B., & Reilly, R. (2002). An affective module for an intelligent tutoring system. In S. A. Cerri, G. Gouarderes, & F. Paraguacu (Eds.), *Intelligent Tutoring Systems 2002 LNCS 2363* (pp. 955-962). Springer-Verlag.

Kuhl, J. (1986). Motivation and information. In R. M. Sorrentino, & E.T. Higgins (Eds.), *Hand-*

book of *Motivation and Cognition* (pp. 404-434). Chichester: Wiley.

Laird, J. E., Newell, A., & Rosenbloom, P. S. (1987). Soar: An architecture for general intelligence. *Artificial Intelligence, 33,* 1-64.

Lazarus, R. S. (1991). Progress on a cognitive-motivational-relational theory of emotion. *American Psychologist, 46*(8), 819-834.

Lester, J. C., Converse, S. A., Kahler, S. E., Barlow, S. T., Stone, B. A., & Bhogal, R. S. (1997). The persona effect: Affective impact of animated pedagogical agents. In *Proceedings of CHI '97* (pp. 359-366). New York: ACM Press.

Lieberman, H., & Selker, T. (2003). Agents for the User Interface. In J. Bradshaw (Ed.), *Handbook of agent technology.* Boston: The MIT Press.

Lisetti, C., & Nasoz, F. (2002). MAUI: A multimodal affective user interface. In *Proceedings of the ACM Multimedia International Conference* (pp. 161-170). Juan-les-Pins, France.

Little, D. (1991). *Learner Autonomy: Definition, issues and problems.* Dublin: Authentik.

Liu, K., & Picard, R. (2005). Embedded empathy in continuous, interactive health assessment. *Affective computing.* Retrieved April 18, 2008, from http://affect.media.mit.edu/pdfs/05.liu-picard.pdf

MacFadden, R. J., Herie, A. M., Maiter, S., & Dumbrill, G. (2005). Achieving high touch in high tech: a constructivist, emotionally-oriented model of web-based instruction. In R. Beaulaurier & M. Haffey (Eds.), *Technology in Social Work Education and Curriculum. The High Tech, High Touch Social Work Educator* (pp. 21-41). New York: Haworth Press.

MacFadden, R. J. (2005). Souls on ice: Incorporating emotion in web-based education. In R. J. MacFadden, B. Moore, M. Herie, & D. Schoech (Eds.), *Web-based education in the human services: Models, methods, and best practices.* (pp. 79-98). New York, London, Victoria: The Haworth Press.

Maes, P. (1994). *Agents that reduce work and information overload.* Communications of the ACM *37*(7), 30-40.

Martens, R., Gulikers, J., & Bastaens, T. (2004). The impact of intrinsic motivation on e-learning in authentic computer tasks. *Journal of Computer Assisted Learning, 20*(5), 368-376.

Martinez, M. (2000). *Successful web learning environments: new design guidelines.* (ERIC Document No. ED 446745). Retrieved April 18, 2008, from http://eric.ed.gov/ERICDocs/data/ericdocs2sql/content_storage_01/0000019b/80/16/99/b3.pdf

Martinho, C., Paiva, A., & Gomes, M. (2000). Emotions for a Motion: Rapid Development of Believable Panthematic Agents in Intelligent Virtual Environments. *Applied artificial intelligence, 14*(1), 33-68.

McCauley, L., Franklin, S., & Bogner. M. (2000). An emotion-based "conscious" software agent architecture. In A. Paiva (Ed.) *Affective interactions. Towards a new generation of computer interfaces* (pp. 107-120). Berlin: Springer.

Militiadou, M., & Savenye, W. (2003). Applying social cognitive constructs of motivation to enhance student success in online distance education. *AACE Journal, 11*(1), 78-95.

Minsky, M. (1987). *The society of mind.* London: William Heinemann Ltd.

Moreno, R., Mayer, R. E., Spires, H. A., & Lester, J. C. (2001). The case for social agency in computer-based teaching: do students learn more deeply when they interact with animated pedagogical agents? *Cognition and Instruction, 19,* 177-213.

Morgado, L., & Gaspar, G. (2005). Emotion based adaptive reasoning for resource bounded agents. In *AAMAS '05: Proceedings of the fourth International Joint Conference on Autonomous Agents and Multi-Agent Systems* (pp. 921–928). New York: ACM Press.

Newell, A. (1990). *Unified theories of cognition.* Cambridge, MA: Harvard University Press.

Nummenmaa, L., & Niemi, P. (2004). Inducing affective states with success–failure manipulations: a metaanalysis. *Emotion, 4,* 207-214.

Nwana, H. S. (1996). Software agents: An overview. *Knowledge Engineering Review, 11*(3), 1-40.

O'Reagan, K. (2003). Emotion and E-Learning. *Journal of Asynchronous Learning Networks (JALN),7*(3). Retrieved August 10, 2008, from http://www-etud.iro.umontreal.ca/~chalfoup/publications/W7-Chalfoun-Chaffar-Frasson-ITS-Workshop-2006-FINAL.pdf.

Ortony, A., Clore, G., & Collins, A. (1988). *The cognitive structure of emotions.* Cambridge, UK: Cambridge University Press.

Pekrun, R. (2005). Progress and open problems in educational emotion research. *Learning and Instruction, 15,* 497-506.

Pereira, D., Oliveira, E., Moreira, N., & Sarmento, L. (2005). Towards an architecture for emotional-BDI agents. In *EPIA, 12th Portuguese Conference on Artificial Intelligence* (pp. 40-47). Berlin / Heidelberg: Springer.

Petta, P., & Cañamero, L. (2001). Grounding emotions in adaptive systems: volume II. *Cybernetics and Systems: An International Journal, 32*(6), 581-583.

Picard, R. (1997). *Affective computing.* Cambridge, Massachusetts: MIT Press.

Picard, R. W., & Wexelblat, A. (2002). Future interfaces: Social and emotional. *Extended Ab-stracts of The CHI 2002- Conference on Human Factors in Computing Systems* (pp. 698-699). New York: ACM Press.

Pintrich, P., & Schunk, D. (2002). *Motivation in education: Theory, research and applications.* Upper Saddle River, NJ: Prentice-Hall Merrill.

Plutchik, R. (1980). A general psychoevolutionary theory of emotion. In R. Plutchik, & H. Kellerman (Eds.), *Emotion: Theory, research, and experience: Vol. 1. Theories of emotion* (pp. 3-33). New York: Academic.

Prendinger, H., & Ishizuka, M. (2002). Scripting the bodies and minds of life-like characters. In M. Ishizuka & A. Sattar (Eds.), *PRICAI 2002: Trends in Artificial Intelligence: 7th Pacific Rim International Conference on Artificial Intelligence* (pp. 571-580). Springer.

Prendinger, H., & Ishizuka, M. (2005). The empathic companion: A character-based interface that addresses users' affective states. *Applied Artificial Intelligence, 19*(3-4), 267-285.

Rao, A. S., & Georgeff, M. P. (1995). BDI Agents: From theory to practice. In V. Lesser & L. Gasser (Eds.), *Proceedings of the First International Conference on Multi-Agent Systems,* ICMAS '95 (pp. 312-319). California: AAAI Press.

Raouzaiou, A., Spyrou, E., Karpouzis K., & Kollias S. (2005). Emotion synthesis: An intermediate expressions' generator system in the mpeg-4 framework. *International Workshop VLBV05,* Sardinia, Italy. Retrieved April 18, 2008, from http://www.image.ece.ntua.gr/php/publications.php?from=2005&srchtype=c&to=2005

Reilly, W. S., & Bates, J. (1992). *Building emotional agents.* School of Computer Science Technical Report CS-92-143, Carnegie Mellon University.

Report of the Technology Enhanced Learning Committee (2004). *Report of the technology enhanced learning committee.* The University of Texas at Austin. Retrieved April 18, 2008, from http://www.utexas.edu/provost/research/TEL_Report_2004.pdf

Richey, R. C. (2008). Reflections on the 2008 AECT Definitions of the Field. *TechTrends. 52*(1) 24-25.

Rickel, J., & Johnson, W. L. (1999). Animated agents for procedural training in virtual reality: Perception, cognition, and motor control. *Applied Artificial Intelligence, 13*(4-5), 343- 382.

Rieber, L. P., Smith, L., & Noah, D. (1998). The value of serious play. *Educational Technology, 38*(6), 29-37.

Rogers, C. (1969). *Freedom to learn: A view of what education might become.* Columbus, Ohio: Charles Merrill.

Rosenbloom, P., Laird, J., & Newell, A. (1993). *The soar papers: Research on integrated intelligence.* Cambridge: MIT Press.

Russell, J. A., (1980). A circumplex model of affect. *Journal of Personality and Social Psychology 39*(November-December), 1161-1178.

Salomon, G. (1992). Effects with and of computers and the study of computer-based learning environments. In E. DeCorte, M. C. Linn, H. Mandl, & L. Verschaffel, (Eds.), *Computer-based learning environments and problem solving* (pp. 249-263). Berlin: Springer-Verlag.

Salovey, P., & Mayer, J. D. (1990). Emotional intelligence. *Imagination, Cognition and Personality, 9*, 185–211.

Scherer, K. R. (2001). Appraisal considered as a process of multi-level sequential checking. In K. R. Scherer, A. Schorr, & T. Johnstone, (Eds), *Appraisal processes in emotion: Theory, methods, research* (pp. 92-120). New York: Oxford University Press.

Scheutz, M. (2004). Useful roles of emotions in artificial agents: a case study from artificial life. In *Proceedings of AAAI 2004* (pp. 42-48). Retrieved

April 18, 2008, from http://hri.cogs.indiana.edu/publications/AAAI104ScheutzM.pdf

Schneider, D. (2004). Conception and implementation of rich pedagogical scenarios through collaborative portal sites. In M. Tokoro & L. Steels (Eds.), *The Future of Learning II, Sharing representations and Flow in Collaborative Learning Environments.* IOS Press.

Seels, B. & Richey, R. (1994). *Instructional Technology: The definitions and domains of the field.* Washington D.C.: Association for Educational Communications and Technology.

Selker, T. (1994). COACH: A teaching agent that learns. *Communications of the ACM, 37*(7), 92-99.

Sloman, A. (2001). Beyond shallow models of emotions. *Cognitive Processing, 2*(1), 177-198.

Soller, A. (2001). Supporting social interaction in an intelligent collaborative learning system. *Intelligence Journal of Artificial Intelligence in Education*, [S. l.], v. 11.

Soldato (del), T. (1992). Detecting and reacting to the learner's motivational state. In *Proceedings of International Conference on Intelligent Tutoring Systems* (pp. 567-574). Berlin: Springer.

Suh, K. S. (1999). Impact of communication medium on task performance and satisfaction: An examination of media-richness theory. *Information & Management, 35*(3), 295-312.

Velásquez, J., (1998). Modeling emotion-based decision-making. In D. Cañamero (Ed.), *Proceedings of the 1998 AAAI Fall Symposium. Emotional and Intelligent: the Tangled Knot of Cognition* (pp. 164–169). Retrieved April 18, 2008, from http://www.ai.mit.edu/people/jvelas/papers/velasquez-fs98.ps

Velásquez, J. (1997). Modeling emotions and other motivations in synthetic agents. In *Proceedings of the Fourteenth National Conference on Artificial*

Intelligence (pp. 10-15) Menlo Park, CA: AAAI Press. Retrieved April 18, 2008, from http://citeseer.ist.psu.edu/103027.html

Viccari, R. M., Jaques, P. A., & Verdin, R. (2008). *Agent-based tutoring systems by cognitive and affective modeling.* Hershey, PA: IGI Global.

Volet, S. (2001). Understanding learning and motivation in context. A multidimensional and multi-level cognitive-situative perspective. In S. Volet & S. Järvelä (Eds.), *Motivation in learning contexts: Theoretical and methodological implications* (pp. 57-82). Amsterdam: Pergamon Press.

Vygotsky, L.S. (1978). *Mind in society: The development of higher psychological processes.* Cambridge MA: Harvard University Press.

Zapata-Rivera, J. D., & Greer, J. (2001). SMODEL Server: Student modelling in distributed multi-agent tutoring systems. In J. D. Moore, C. L. Redfield, & W. L. Johnson (Eds.), *Artificial intelligence in education* (pp.446-455). Amsterdam: IOS Press.

Warren, D., Shen E., Park, S., Baylor, A. L., & Perez, R. (2005). Adult learner perceptions of affective agents. In C. K. Looi, G. McCalla, B. Bredeweg & J. Breuker (Eds.), *Artificial intelligence in education: Supporting learning through intelligent and socially informed technology* (Vol. 125, pp. 944-946). Amsterdam: IOS Press.

Wooldridge, M. (2002). *An introduction to multi-agent systems.* West Sussex, England: John Wiley and Sons Ltd.

Wosnitza, M., & Nenniger, P. (2001). Perceived learning environments and use of learning-strategies. The mediating role of motivation for the self-direction in learning. In S. Volet & S. Järvelä (Eds.), *Motivation in learning contexts: Theoretical and methodological implications* (pp. 171-187). Amsterdam: Pergamon Press.

Wosnitza, M., & Volet, S. (2005). Origin, direction and impact of emotions in social online learning. *Learning and Instruction, 15*(5), 449-464.

KEY TERMS

Emotional Interaction: Emotional interactions are situated intrapersonal, interpersonal, or human-computer interactions necessary for efficient, effective and affective learning. These refer to emotional component processes of appraisal and reappraisal of interactions in order to maintain a close relationship within the learning situation.

Emotionally Enhanced Computer-Based Learning Environment: An emotionally enhanced computer-based learning environment supports emotionally and pedagogically sound instruction. Resources and services support a rich set of learning activities and a full diversity of interactions. Such an environment may include interactive learning modules, knowledge bases, communication tools, professional software and cognitive tools. The environment should encourage the growth of learner responsibility, initiative, reflection, decision-making and intentional learning. It also should encourage collaboration and build up confidence with technology.

Emotionally Sound Instruction: Emotionally sound instruction promotes learning and teaching strategies with increased positive and decreased negative emotions. Emotionally sound instruction also may integrate some frustration and imbalance, which is part of the challenge and beneficial for the learning process. It also may contribute to the creation of a sense of community within a learning environment by influencing learner-to-learner interactions.

Socio-Emotional Climate: The socio-emotional climate is evaluative indicator of the full diversity of interactions that seem occur within a computer-based learning environment. The high socio-emotional climate is due to the ability of facilitating social and emotional interactions in order to enhance the learners' motivation, self-assessment and self-motivation.

Socio-Emotional Agent: A socio-emotional agent is an adaptive computational entity characterized by autonomy, pro-activity, social ability, emotional ability and flexibility. This agent is capable to react, to take initiative, to cooperate, to infer and to learn in an environment that includes a diversity of computer-mediated interactions. The socio-emotional agent can show affective mechanisms and can interact with the users in a socially engaging manner.

Pedagogical Socio-Emotional Agent: A socio-emotional agent is pedagogical when it is particularly developed to facilitate learning. Such an agent should provide emotional support in order to promote a positive mood in the learner, to motivate him/her and to enhance social interaction between learners. This agent should be able to recognise the learner's emotions and implement a model of the learner's affect in order to suggest motivational and affective pedagogical strategies.

ENDNOTES

[1] Massachusetts Institute of Technology. http://affect.media.mit.edu/projects.php

[2] The Cognition and Affect Project , http://www.cs.bham.ac.uk/research/projects/cogaff/cogaff.html

[3] Geneva Emotion Research Group, http://www.unige.ch/fapse/emotion/

[4] University of Michigan, Soar home page, http://sitemaker.umich.edu/soar/home

[5] Emotional Synthetic Forces, 2004, USA, ARI, http://www.au.af.mil/au/awc/awcgate/army/tr1149.doc

Section VI
Ambient Emotion

Chapter XXII
Emotional Ambient Media

Artur Lugmayr
Tampere University of Technology, Finland

Tillmann Dorsch
Tampere University of Technology, Finland

Pabo Roman Humanes
Tampere University of Technology, Finland

ABSTRACT

The "medium is the message": nowadays the medium as such is non-distinguishable from its presentation environment. However, what is the medium in an ambient environment, when the environment is smart, recognizes emotions, and at the same time responsive? Emotions have had an inferior role in philosophy, psychology, art, and nowadays in media technology. In philosophy and psychology many researchers devoted their work to the question what emotions are, and how they can be modelled, ranging from common-sense theories, theories that emotions are simply physiological disturbances, and the many behaviour theories describing emotions providing a much more comprehensive view on emotions (Solomon, 1977). In the age of ambient media, where media technology is embedded seamlessly and hidden into the natural environment of the consumer, the view towards media is changing. The modality how emotions are experienced and the technology to recognize and simulate emotions are changing. To support the theories within the scope of this chapter, a case study – the emotional ambient responsive character – has been performed. The concept was realised as a simple interactive game responding to human emotions. Within this book section, we present a technical oriented view towards recognizing, simulating, and binding emotions in ambient media systems. A case-study for an emotion recognition and response system is presented. The system integrates the content and emotion recognition elements.

BACKGROUND

Within the scope of this book chapter the fields of emotional computation, affective computation, psychology, very slightly the field of philosophy, and ubiquitous- and pervasive computation are touched. The main background relies on the development of ambient media based on media technology coming from ambient intelligence. Current research in the field of emotional computation focuses around these questions:

- What is the relation between emotions and experience?
- How can emotional machines be modelled and implemented?
- What is the meaning of emotions in art and media?
- How can emotions and affects be recognized and generated?
- What are the linguistic and non-linguistic aspects of emotions?
- How can emotion classification based on media be performed?
- Which methods for evaluation of emotional impact,
- How can the affect of emotions be classified, evaluated, and measured?
- What are the linguistic aspects of emotions in text, speech, and media?
- Which models for factors impacting emotions exist (e.g. personality traits)?
- How can emotions be described, generated, parsed, and managed?
- What is the effect on human-computer or human-human interaction?
- How can emotional computation be applied in specific applications (e.g. gaming)
- Which new forms of dialogue systems involving emotion patterns emerge?
- What is the impact of emotions on cognitive robotics and multi-agent systems?

Originally media are delivered via distinguishable entities to the consumer (e.g. video stream, audio stream, image). In the age of ambient media, the entity that is perceived by the consumer is by far more complex to describe. A first definition for ambient media has been made by A. Lugmayr in (Lugmayr, 2007), and the form of ambient media can be described as "particular way in which ambient media assets physically exist or manifest themselves, morph the natural environment entities with the synthetic artificial created world, collaborate with each other, and intelligence of arrangements (composition) and contextualization of media assets and their subcomponents as an artistic or factual genre for the creation of human experience". Thus, the message of the medium is transmitted via any arbitrary signalling information – therefore the message of the ambient media system can be embedded anywhere – as ambient light in a living room, as intelligent car, as a smart phone recognizing the context of the consumer.

Especially media technology developed the need to gain understanding of several different aspects of emotions. Therefore this book section especially matches emotional binding to the media with the latest trends in the development of ambient media technology. It evaluates existing theories coming from philosophy and psychology in emotional research to adopt these with the needs of ambient media systems. From the technical view, a basic model for experience and emotion oriented computation in the field of ambient media is presented. Different existing methods and technologies are evaluated and presented. This includes techniques and methods for the recognition of human emotions. For many years the recognition of human emotions was major research field in artificial intelligence. After the disillusions in the field of AI, in recent decades, many questions where untouched. However, with the emergence of ambient intelligence, the field became a new retouch, and emotional computations gained importance as a major research field.

Another issue this book section is devoting to the evaluation of methods and techniques for the simulation of human emotions with the machine. With the emergence of intelligent computing, we are talking about collaboration with the machine, rather than using machines. Machines will assist in our daily life tasks, hidden in the background. Without any emotional aspect, the machine will rather hardly be able to act human-alike rather than as passive user-interface. Within this book section, a framework for the simulation of human emotions is presented. We evaluate existing techniques and methods to obtain a more coherent view on how simulation of emotions is possible.

In artistic works, emotional binding – thus how to obtain emotional responses from the consumer – is already well developed. In the case of ambient media, it is not clear how emotional binding can be performed, and what the major attraction point for consumer is. Within the scope of this book section, a model for emotional binding is presented.

INTRODUCTION

To begin the chapter we have to ask ourselves what actually emotions are. In commonsense knowledge, emotions are a human expression to the current situation in the world. Emotions can be described as human behaviour based on context. While watching a touching romantic movie in cinema, we are getting immersed into the story presented in front of us on the screen. We identify with characters and are touched by the happenings occurring to them. The audience cries if our dies a dramatic death or we feel strong and proud while leaving the cinema when the hero conquers the evil. All these are emotional responses to the presented media. In film these effects are called 'emotional binding'. The director tells his story by using the tools available to him to tell an artificial story universe in space and time. Cinematography, actor's behaviour, and knowledge how to render a

story enable him to bind the audience emotionally to his piece. In the medium motion pictures and other artistic domains, such as painting, literature, and music these mechanisms are well known. Without binding the audience to the medium and creating emotional responses, artistic creation is rather poorly possible.

With the emerging available technology coming from pervasive- and ubiquitous computing, the question *what emotional computation means in days of ambient media* – thus in times where the medium is embedded into the natural human environment – gets more and more obvious. Another buzz word in today's media technology is consumer experience. The consumer shall experience media and be bound to emotional designed products to experience it. Both, emotions and experience are very closely related. Emotions trigger experience and without being emotionally bound to an object it is rather poorly possible to create experience. One example is car advertising. The advertisement delivers a message to the consumer. And depending on model and target audience the advertisement suggests a certain driving experience coming with a specific kind of car. To explain what actually the phenomenon 'experience' is, is a more complex theme. However, with the scope of this chapter a first attempt is being made.

To understand the complexity of emotions Figure 1 presents a very loose categorization of most common key-themes related to emotional research. They are categorized according:

- *Mind* describing what happens either physiologically or psychologically in a human brain while experience emotions;
- How emotions are *communicated*, thus perceived or transmitted to third parties;
- *Cause* as trigger for emotions or a contextual situation triggering or consuming emotions; and at last
- *Concepts* describing higher level concepts related to human emotions, as e.g. the de-

Figure 1. Key-themes in emotional research

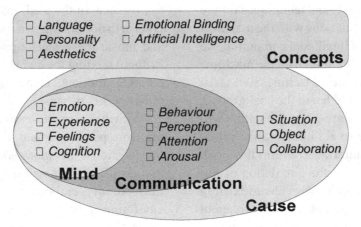

scribed concept of emotional binding in motion pictures.

This very primitive categorization of emotions shall ease to understand the complexity around the topic emotional research. The human mind is the smart unit for processing emotions and tagging feelings or other high level meanings. Communication of emotions deals with the expression and recognition of emotions in a situation or based on an object. The cause or trigger for emotions is based on the situational environment of a human. However, higher level concepts of emotions deal with the concepts around aesthetics, society, or personality. Without discussing the meaning of all these different themes in further depth, we see the complexity while dealing with the world of human emotions. Figure 1 depicts the different issues around the topic of emotional computation.

CONTENT OF THE BOOK CHAPTER

- **Introduction:** General introduction into the topic, definitions, standards, related works, and questions in the research field;
- **Ambient media systems:** Background of ambient media, content models, sensor networks, context profiles, and creation of media which is relevant for the scope of this book chapter;
- **Models in psychology and philosophy of emotions:** Methods, theories, models, and approaches in philosophy and psychology towards emotional research which are applicable for ambient media systems;
- **Emotional binding in ambient media:** Model for adding emotions into ambient media systems including their characteristics, features, theories;
- **Techniques for recognizing, simulating, and contextualization of emotions:** Theoretical models in ambient media for recognizing, simulating, and binding emotions;
- **Case Study–Ambient emotional responsive character:** Presentation of an implemented case study performed within the NAMU Lab. for researching emotions: the *Animated Ambient Emotional Responsive Dog House*;
- **Discussion:** Discussion of the presented topics, and future research directions;
- **References:** References of the book chapter

EMOTIONAL MODELS IN PSYCHOLOGY

There are wide spread opinion and theories in psychology, philosophy, religion, and law what actually emotions and emotional responses are. The most profound definition for emotions is that emotions are "a strong feeling, such as joy, anger, or sadness [as] instinctive or intuitive feeling as distinguished from reasoning or knowledge" (Oxford, n.d.). Within the scope of this chapter and the follow up sections, we will see, that exactly this definition of emotions is inadequate for the purpose of ambient media systems. However, let's start to explore the most substantial other ones.

General View of Emotions

During history there have been many different viewpoints of emotion – emotions as animal instinct, emotions as defect of the human mind, or emotions as passion. For people further interested in these views, it is referred to the readings of Descartes, Aristotle, or Spinoza. Nevertheless, the most common sense view of emotions is, that emotions "are feelings, distinct experience not unlike physical sensations, something like nausea or anxiety" (Solomon, 1977).

Emotions as Survivor Factor in Evolution

The theory that emotions are a survival factor in Evolution is coming from Charles Darwin. He divided emotions into habit, antithesis, and direct action. Habits are long-term and are learned and occur in familiar situations. Antithesis is a matter of occurring situation, where the human is not familiar with, thus it can be seen as opposite of habits or while the human is in unfamiliar situations. Actions are based on the emotional activities of the nervous systems (Darwin, 1872). This viewpoint towards emotion is interesting, however has rather less influence on the evalu-

ation performed within the scope of this paper, therefore is not discussed in further detail.

Common Sense View

However, another interesting movement is the common sense or naive psychology (see e.g. Hayes, 1985) view towards artificial intelligence. As far there has been much controversy in research, and if it is a dead end or is leading to a new breakthrough in science. The key idea is that common sense "can be thought as the natural human ability to infer and reason about other people's mental states" (Watt, 1995). Humans perceive humans as a whole rather than objects (Hayes, 1985). Especially the common sense view implicates a re-thinking of emotional computation. The modelling of an emotional machine is an act of modelling the knowledge of our world in a common sense way, rather than explicitly creating complex formalisms and models. Thus to model emotions into our daily world, we have to assume that artificially created objects and human minds are on the same level. Intelligent objects become companions being aware of our mental state and humans of theirs. To follow up with the discussion around naive psychology and common sense thinking, it is referred to (Watt, 1995) where many interesting further references can be found.

Process between Motives, Believes, and Precepts

Another viewpoint towards emotion is viewing emotions as process caused by interactions between motives, beliefs, and precepts (Sloman & Croucher, 1981). Thus the components contributing to emotional computation are *motives, beliefs, and precepts*. This theory can be seen as a step towards naive psychology and the common sense way of thinking how an emotional machine can be built. However, for a complete technical solution the theory still requires information technological concepts to describe, analyze, and model an emotional system including a computational model of the mind.

Categorization of Emotions

As many theories exist in psychology to describe emotions, as many theories exist to categorize emotions. However, to model an emotional system – independently which psychological model is used – a certain classification of emotions is required to process these with an information processing system. The most significant ones are:

- **Positive/negative classification:** The most simple and obvious classification of emotions is in negative (e.g. hate) and positive (e.g. love) emotions;
- **Basic emotions classification:** The basic classification distinguishes between basic emotions, which are similar to the basic colours. They are the emotions, which are underlying any human emotional concept. There exist many examples for this type of emotions. One is FACTS, which distinguishes between normal, happy, sad, afraid, and angry for facial expressions (Ekman, Friesen, & Hager, n.d.)
- **Primary/secondary classification:** The most common and debated classification of emotions is the division into primary and secondary emotions. Primary emotions are clustered into different sub-categories. This enables higher granularity of different emotion types, and a machine processable format for emotions. One example is the division into eight primary emotions as described in (Plutchik & Kellerman, 1990). This classification leads to a three-dimensional model similar to the HSV colour cone. Emotions can be clustered in optimism, love, submission, awe, disapproval, remorse, contempt, and aggressiveness. Secondary emotions blend between the components of the 3D cube (Fractal.org);

- **Unambiguous, non-redundant classification:** Several classification schemes are very interpretative and depend on the different viewpoints of their inventors. To avoid redundancy and ambiguity, the artificially created language Lojban (1987) classifies emotions according: simplicity, complexity, purity, propositional attributes and complex proposition attributes. Each of these groups has emotion sub-types. E.g. the simple emotion group has the duple gain-loss as one sub-type;
- **Reasoning based classification:** All these models simply focus on the pure classification of emotions, but rather purely rely on dynamic or situation based approaches. In reasoning based classification schemes, the computability of emotions is in the foreground. Thus the emotion classification depends on a sort of reasoning system, capable of processing human emotions according a certain predefined reasoning structure. From the psychological perspective we can eventually also speak of a cognitive model. One example is the OCC model (Ortony, Clore, & Collins, 1988), which allows to categorize emotions in a tree-like structure that includes decision points for machine-readable conditions and a model for reaction to certain causes.

TECHNIQUES IN EMOTIONAL COMPUTATION

Figure 2 depicts a simple workflow for the processing of emotions. The goal of emotional computing can be divided into:

- Capture and recognize emotions via sensors on signal level (e.g. heart rate);
- Interpretation of sensor input on symbolic level (e.g. heart rate x means y);

- Analysis and processing of symbols to obtain emotional patterns (e.g. person x can has positive emotions in situations like y);
- Learning to know the human emotional state of mind on concept level (e.g. behaviour patterns); and
- Provision of smart reactions to human emotional input (e.g. feedback).

In other words, emotional computation is about "getting computers to 'think' like humans, [and] AI's next natural step seems to be getting computers to 'feel' like humans" (Krikke & Alfonsi, 2006). Thus the nowadays all-present information transmission channels shall be extended by an emotional channel, giving emotional feedback.

The present technology mostly relies on simple interaction and feedback communication for the communication. However, in ambient media, the emotional channel as additional channel for the exchange of emotional information is gaining of importance to mimic human alike systems. Within the scope of this section we explore the existing technologies in emotional computation.

Making the System Emotion Aware

Emotion Capture

The capture of emotions phase deals with the collection of signalling information relevant as input for the emotional model or for determining the emotional state of a human. These include e.g. facial expressions, sound, or voice. In the case of voice it could e.g. be loudness, spectrum, or harmonics (see also Magnum language). Capture applies on signal level. On this level we simply deal with the communication of emotions on signal level via the human body, thus the capture of human signalling related to emotional expressions. Examples for physiological signalling are lie detectors, skin temperature, heart rate, mouse pressure, or postural movements (see also Krikke & Alfonsi, 2006). A typical result of the capture process is e.g. "Anna's heart rate is high". Capture is a situational process, where signalling related to emotions are captured at one moment in time without any relation to a-priori knowledge such as changes of emotions over time or emotional history.

Figure 2. Tasks and levels in emotional computation

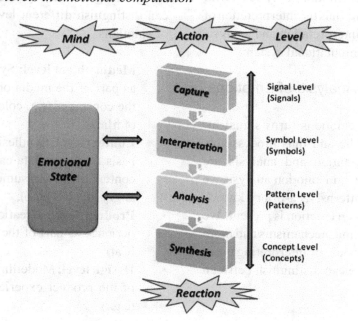

Let's start with the discussion which human signals can be used to capture human emotions. Many forms of human signalling can be used to recognize emotions:

- **Perceptible emotions as explicit communication channel:** Facial expression, voice, gestures from hand and body, posture, eye movements (e.g. pupils);
- **Non apparent emotions as implicit communication channel:** Brain waves, respiration, muscle actions, physiological signalling, skin temperature, blood pressure;

A good example project for the use of physiological in emotional computation is the Autogenic-Feedback System-2 (AFS-2). The system is in use for a physiological monitoring system for space travel. Nowadays it is used for monitoring health, but with the miniaturization of sensor data and in the future its application for obtaining emotional responses might be possible (NASA, n.d.). A more 'down to earth' example is the real-time smile detector. The detector is capable of measuring valence via a camera through eyebrow and head move detectors (Sharon, n.d.). However, the capture of emotions only deals with the capture of signalling, thus the interpretation of smiles belongs to the interpretation and analysis part of the emotive computational system.

Interpretation and Analysis of Emotions

The interpretation of emotions turns signal information into symbolic and thus process-able values. Both, interpretation and analysis are closely related, however, in emotion analysis we speak of emotional patterns, as a-priory knowledge and a wider view on emotion is present. We also can speak of learning mechanisms and more intelligent systems capable of interpreting emotions. Nevertheless, we can distinguish between different forms:

- **Discrete emotion capture:** Capture of emotions as discrete values (e.g. happy, sad);
- **Continuous emotion capture:** Capture of emotions as continuum (e.g. intensity of emotions over time or arousal/valence over time);
- **Pattern based emotion capture:** Capture of emotional patters as higher level concept (e.g. based on a-priory knowledge);

Synthesis and Communication of Emotions

The previous system described the process how to make the system emotion aware. Within the scope of this section, it is explained how systems can communicate emotions to the consumer. This channel can be text, audio, visual, language, or higher level language (e.g. film language) based. Thus the goal in synthesis of emotions is to create an emotional channel between the system and the human. Due to the wide ranging field of ambient media, emotion synthesis is a rather huge field and involves many different perspectives. This includes product design, media objects, utilized communication channels, etc. To help categorizing different synthesis possibilities, we can distinguish different levels of synthesizing of emotions:

- **Media object level:** Synthesis of emotions as part of the media object perceptible by the consumer (e.g. colours used in a piece of film);
- **Context level:** Synthesis of emotions on the basis of sensor data capturing the current context of the consumer (e.g. consumer is angry at a bus stop);
- **Product level:** Creation of emotional experience as part of the device (e.g. Philips iCat);
- **Design level:** Modelling of emotions as part of the product experience design process (e.g.)

- **Emotion channel level:** Communication channels for communicating emotions or emotional user interfaces (e.g. emotion support in human communication systems); and
- **Experience level:** Ungraspable experience designed as pattern of arousal of emotions (e.g. products with 'appeal').

There exist many examples for synthesis of emotions. One good example is the 38cm tall iCat from Philips (n.d.). The toy can be plugged to the USB bus of a PC, and acts as mediator of emotions between human and computer. It is capable of expressing of emotions such as happy, surprised, angry, or sad. It has various sensor systems such as microphones, proximate, webcam, etc. to capture its surrounding. It can be seen as a very good example for a system expressing emotions on product level and context level.

Another system is the SenToy, which belongs to the category of emotional user-interfaces. The system lets the consumer influence the emotions of a computer character by gestures or movements (Paiva, Costa, Chaves, Piedade, Mourão, Sobral, et al., 2003). A doll is the input device. Depending on the gestures of the consumer, the animated character performs actions on the input.

A very important initiative for the communication of emotions is the W3C Emotion Incubator group (2006). W3C aims at the development of a emotional language based on XML for representing emotions. This ranges from the state of mind, simulation of emotions by a user interface, or the communication of emotional information.

There are many other aspects for simulating emotions, and more and more projects focus on this issue. To mention just a few more: IBM's BlueEye projects aims at making computers to know what you feel (IBM, n.d.), and the humaine project focuses on several aspects of affective computation (n.d.).

EMOTIONAL BINDING IN AMBIENT MEDIA

Considering the different presented viewpoints in psychology concerning emotions, the most relevant ideas for ambient media come from the common sense viewpoints, and seeing emotions as processes between motives, believes, and pre-cepts. To be able to define emotional binding, and concepts around emotions in the field of ambient media, let's enumerate a few characteristics of ambient media:

- **Embedding:** The digital media environment is embedded in the natural environment;
- **Diversity:** Wide variety of life situations, locations, living spaces, and motivations;
- **Miscellany:** Convergence of a wide variety of media forms to one new form;
- **Genre unspecific:** Genres are single artistic expressions, rather ambient media as a total;
- **Concept driven:** Concepts are defined by content, devices, human, and converging services;
- **Ambient asset driven:** Service space and experience orientation, rather than single entities;
- **Ambient aesthetics:** Provision of a new digital aesthetics throughout the living space;

The Principles of Ambient Media

The 5 principles of ambient media are: intelligence, morphing, manifestation, collaboration, and experience. Intelligence deals with the system intelligence. Each ambient system can be seen as a physical world overlaid by a synthetic world. The physical world is the daily world we are living in, where a synthetic world is mapped on top of it. Ambient media are therefore entities that are exchanged between these worlds (Lugmayr, 2007; Lugymayr, 2006; Lugymayr, 2008a; Lugymayr,

Figure 3. Animation flow chart

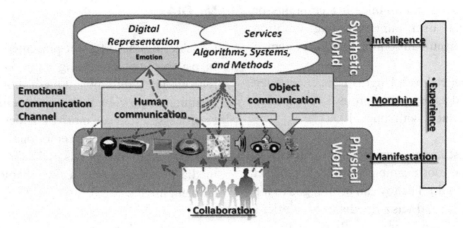

2008b; Lugymayr, Pohl, Mühlhäuser, Negru, Kallenbach, & Köbler et al, 2006; Lugmayr, Pohl, Mühlhäuser, Kallenbach, & Chorianopoulos, 2007; Lugmayr, in press). Figure 3 presents this idea.

As far, media objects where distinguishable digital objects – as e.g. a video stream, TV show, and newspaper. In the case of ambient media the human is part of a digital service space that is linking the real physical world to the synthetic world overlay. This requires a certain mapping or linking of both worlds. This principle is called morphing – it defines the actual connectivity between worlds. In the case of emotions, it is an emotional channel between the human and the digital world, for example a system responding to human emotions. A simple example is the visualization of geographic information via GPS onto a digital map. The physical world is the actual place the human is, and the geographical information links the digital world overly to it. One example for this principle in the case of emotions is the Philips iCat (n.d.).. The Philips iCat is a toy, which can generate emotional responses – it smiles, looks angry, or is sad. The cat creates emotional channel relaying emotional information of the system to the consumer.

Another important principle is intelligence. The media is aggregated by the system, rather by

a human editor. The aggregation of media objects is part of a complex system contextualizing the content to human situation, environment, emotional state of mind, preferences, and relevancy. Media need to be rendered in a certain form for the human being. Thus media objects need to manifest themselves in a certain form. Thus the synthetic overlay needs to be turned to human graspable information. One example for this principle is electronic wallpaper, which adjusts to the emotional state of a human. The electronic wallpaper becomes the way how the technical system responds or renders its output.

The paradigm of user-interface design or human computer interaction in ambient media is a matter of collaboration. Machine-machine collaboration, human-machine collaboration, and human-human collaboration are major concern. Collaboration, rather than complex user-interfaces are of consideration. As far technical system needed to be 'learned' – in the case of ambient media, the system collaborates with the consumer and adapts smartly to his needs. This is also relevant for human-human mediated cooperation, where the system shall support the communication. Especially emotional computation is one communication channel, and emotional binding of the human to the ambient media system underlines this important fact.

The most significant principle of ambient media is experience. Consumer experience is nowadays a hot topic and widely discussed. Experience deals with the "observational knowledge of the world [...] what one has come to know [...] by direct observation [...] without inference" (Oxford, n.d.). The observations of the world can be seen as a stream of subjectively observed happenings, which "makes up the conscious life of the possessor [...] being a separation between mind and the world" (Oxford, n.d.). Thus experience is subjective knowledge. Nowadays we deal with information processing, however, in the case of ambient media we are dealing with knowledge processing, rather than processing pieces of data. Emotions and experiences are rather tightly related, as "arousal is essential to the experience of emotion [...] as the experience of specific emotions results from the perception of specific and unique patterns of [...] arousal" (Barrett, Mesquita, Ochsner, & Gross, 2007).. Thus emotional binding between human and object can be described by patterns of arousal.

Def. Experience (in the context of ambient media): stream of subjective observed happenings manifesting throughout the natural environment processed as knowledge rather than as information and emotionally perceived by patterns of arousal. Emotional binding is the actual media experience perceived as pattern of arousal.

Ambient Media and Emotion Concepts

To find a suitable definition for emotional computation is a rather huge tasks. Ambient media are part of many aspects of our daily lives: e.g. in artistic theatre plays, smart fridges, intelligent living rooms, travelling situations, and mobile services. Each of these aspects could provide a unique definition and a set of rules. However, to come to an abstract definition, le'ts introduces the idea of emotional concepts. Emotional concepts are a set of techniques, parameters, and languages that apply for a specific ambient situation. In the case of a mobile digital TV film, distributed to a mobile phone, the concept relates to the art and craft how a video has to be created to bind the watcher. Thus, emotional rules such as colour theory, the language of the edit, or the cinematographic expression are applied. However, the concept also includes other parameters, such as personal preferences for certain movie genres, in which situation the consumer is currently (e.g. in the office, in a bus), and techniques applied to process emotional information.

Levels of Emotional Concepts

We can distinguish between different levels of emotional concepts, relevant for the specific situation or application. To illustrate the idea, we consider a video portal available on mobile phones containing travelling videos for different locations:

- **Primary concepts** relate to the major ambient asset or goal. In the video travelling portal, the main video about a city or location is the major ambient asset. The primary concepts are film techniques, cinematography, or the language of the edit.
- **Secondary concepts** are assets supporting the major ambient asset directly to create experience. Secondary concepts are not directly related to the primary concept, but have a significant contribution to make the major ambient asset to a consumer experience. It could be a personalization engine including its algorithms on the mobile device adapting the presented content to the current GPS location and preferences of the consumer.
- **Tertiary concepts** are indirect concepts supporting either secondary ambient assets or the major ambient asset in some way. These concepts are not directly related to the primary concept, but support either primary

or secondary concept in a certain form. It could for example be a health application knowing the diet of the consumer and recommending certain restaurants fitting to the food preferences of the consumer.

Definition of Emotional Ambient Media

With the background knowledge developed as far, we can firstly define emotional ambient media as follows:

Def. Emotional Ambient Media: Emotional ambient media create an experience to the consumer and are a complex process and interaction between mind, communication, cause, and concepts. Concepts are higher level techniques, parameters, and languages contributing to trigger bi-directional emotional communication channels in specific locations or situations throughout the natural human environment. Emotional ambient media are emotionally binding the consumer to ambient media assets, and its sub-components. Emotional binding is created as interaction between a set of ambient assets.

Requirements in Emotional Ambient Media Design

The requirements in emotional ambient media design highly depend on the used primary, secondary, or tertiary concepts. Nevertheless, we have to keep the major assumption from naive psychology in mind. To create a model for emotional computation in ambient media, the main assumption will be the one from naive psychology – artificially created objects and human minds are on the same level: intelligent objects are companions being aware of our mental state and humans of the intelligent object. However, on very abstract level we can define the following system components as part of an emotional ambient media system:

- Descriptive language for describing emotions, the state of mind, emotional channels, emotional concepts, and causes;
- Models providing a common sense view towards emotion processing, thus turning information into knowledge;
- Efficient methods and techniques for capturing, recognizing, interpreting, analysis, and synthesis of emotions;
- Collaboration between human and machine, as artificially created objects and human mind are on the same level being companions being aware of each other mental state;
- Creation of an emotional channel between daily objects, humans, and in human-human mediated communication as morphing principle between synthetic world and physical world;
- Technology and devices for the manifestation of emotions in the physical world acting as communicator for emotions;
- Development of new collaboration techniques based on additional emotional channels.

CASE STUDY: AMBIENT EMOTIONAL RESPONSIVE CHARACTER

The key-idea was to develop a system responding to human emotions and approach it from both, the artistic and the technical perspective. The idea was to model a character which responds to emotional input parameters (see Dorsch, 2008). The implementation aimed at the development of an interactive ambient installation, where the consumer can communicate with an intelligent virtual character. The means of communication is human emotion, and the character responding to human emotion. Via an emotion tacking system, human emotions can help the character to support him in his well-being. The virtual character himself resides in a computer graphic generated virtual world, supporting him in his well-being. The installation combines animation, mimics, music, and interactivity in an ambient way and is structure as an ambient computer game. The implementation involves a motion tracking system, computer graphics modelling, animation, virtual character development, and smart algorithms for emotional response tracking.

Currently the implementation is more of a type of interactive installation from the technical emotion recognition part. However, the technical side for the capturing of emotions will be continuously extended. From the artistic perspective, the conceptual model for the character design is well developed and emotional responses can be given. The system will be extended in the future by far more advanced emotion filters and trackers. But the idea of the system will be clearer within the scope of this section. See Figure 4 for an illustration.

In relation to the presented theories in the previous sections of this book, the following are applied within the scope of this case-study:

- Common sense (naive psychology) view on emotions, where humans deal with the

perception of assets as a whole rather than a technical product;
- Development of emotional binding via
- Morphing of emotional responses generated in the synthetic world to the real world via a responsive animation;
- Animation as concept for manifestation of emotions in the natural environment;

Emotional Concept Perspective

The primary concept of this installation related to the modelling and setup of the animated responsive character. Thus, how the virtual dog can be designed to create an emotional channel for the viewer. The involved emotional concepts are based on *colour theory, animation language,* and *facial animation.* Dependent on the human interactions, the animated dog is angry, happy, or sad. The animation flowcharts, thus the reaction on different human inputs are presented in Figure 5.

Technical Implementation

From the technical viewpoint, thus the secondary emotional concept of this installation is the

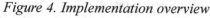

Figure 4. Implementation overview

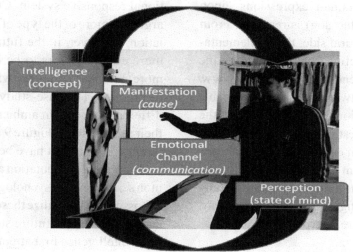

Figure 5. Animation flow chart

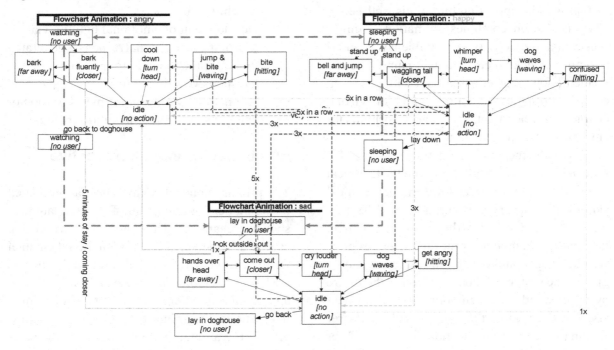

recognition of the emotional parameters of the human. The technical concept was realized with motion tracking of human body gestures. The input parameters are used to animate the facial expressions of the dog. Figure 6 illustrates the facial animation for angry, happy, and sad.

The implementation was based on a virtual reality device capable of tracking and interpretation of human gestures. Different gestures imply different emotional human expressions, upon which the character (the dog) is reacting. From the software architectural side, the implementation was a full interactive system, based on the Quest3D real-time rendering software (www. quest3d.com). The software interface was capable of interpreting emotional responses from the consumer. To track gestures, a gesture recognition software has been developed. The software received a video stream and recognised infrared LEDs on markers of the human. The states: going far, going near, nodding, shaking, looking away, waving, and tapping are interpreted as responses to the actions of the dog.

Figure 8 illustrates the software architecture of the full system, consisting of several modules.

CONCLUSION AND EMERGING TRENDS

The interactive implementation shall present a first step towards the implementation of a more emotional responsive system. Currently some might argue it's more of the type of an interactive installation. However, in the future we will integrate more emotion filters to be capable of detecting more complex emotions with various different techniques. The case-study shall underline the different concepts in ambient media and discuss their relationships. Figure 9 shows briefly the different concepts that have been considered.

Emotional computation and especially a common sense view of psychology and the exploration of possibilities to realize these theories in technical systems is a major future step. However, in artificial intelligence first attempts have been made,

Figure 6. Facial animation for angry, happy, and sad

Figure 7. Snapshots of the utilized hardware

Figure 8. Software architecture

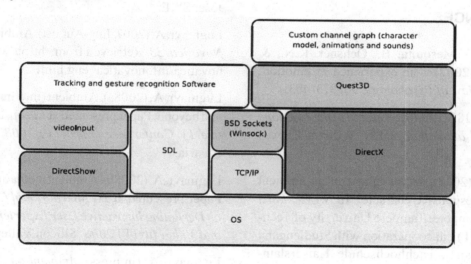

Figure 9. Relating different concepts of ambient media

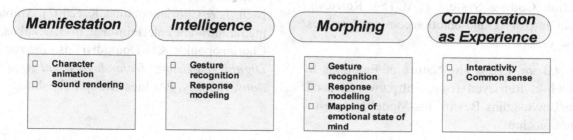

but we are simply at the beginning. Emotional computation and smart environments deal with the long-ongoing discussion, if machines will be intelligence – or if machines will be able to have emotions. Currently we are only exploring the basic foundations of possibilities. To conclude this chapter, we refer to the excellent reading of Sloman & Croucher (2007), entitled "Why robots will have emotions". This article explores the philosophy and has a few excellent thoughts around this topic.

ACKNOWLEDGMENT

This work was supported by the Academy of Finland, project No. 213462 (Finnish Centre of Excellence Program (2006 - 2011).

REFERENCES

Barrett, L.F., Mesquita, B., Ochsner, K.N., & Gross, J.J. (2007). The experience of emotion. *Annual Review of Psychology, 58*, 373-403.

Darwin, C. (1872). *The expression of the emotions in man and animals.* London: William Clowes and Suns.

Dorsch, T. (2008). Development of an ambient emotional responsive character. In *NAMU Lab.,* vol. BSc. Tampere: Tampere University of Technology (TUT) - in cooperation with Studiengang Virtual Design, Fachhochschule Kaiserslautern.

Ekman, P., Friesen, W., & Hager, J. (n.d.). Facial Action Coding System (FACTS). Retrieved from, http://face-and-emotion.com/dataface/facs/new_version.jsp

Fractal.org. (n.d.). The Nature of Emotions by Plutchik. Retrieved from, http://www.fractal.org/Bewustzijns-Besturings-Model/Nature-of-emotions.htm

Hayes, P. J. (1985). The second naive physics manifesto. In J.R. Hobbs & R.C. Moore (Eds.), *Formal Theories of the Commonsense World.* Norwood, New Jersey: Ablex.

Humaine. (n.d.). Humaine emotion research net. Retreived from, http://emotion-research.net/

IBM (n.d.). Retrieved from, http://www.ibm.com

Krikke, J., & Alfonsi, B. (2006). In the News. *Intelligent Systems, IEEE, 21*, 102-104.

Lugmayr, A. (2006a). From ambient media towards biomedia. Paper presetned at *MindTrek Conference 2006*, Tampere

Lugmayr, A. (2006b). The future is "ambient." In R. Creutzburg, J. H. Takala, and C. W. Chen, (Eds.), *Proceedings of SPIE Vol. 6074, 607403 Multimedia on Mobile Devices II.* vol. 6074. San Jose: SPIE.

Lugmayr, A. (2007, July-August). Ambient Media. *Novatica, 33.* Retrieved from, http://www.ati.es/novatica/infonovatica_eng.html

Lugmayr, A. (2008a). Ambient (intelligent) media and beyond. Paper presented at *European Interactive TV Conference (EuroITV) 2008*, Salzburg, Austria.

Lugmayr, A. (2008b). Ambient media and beyond. Paper presented at *1st International Conference on Designing Interactive User Experiences for TV and Video (uxTV) 2008.* Silicon Valley, CA.

Lugmayr, A. (in press). *Ambient media and beyond.* New York: Springer-Verlag.

Lugmayr, A., Pohl, A., Mühlhäuser, M., Kallenbach, J., & Chorianopoulos, K. (2007). Ambient media and home entertainment. In G. Lekakos, K. Chorianopoulos, & G. Doukidis (Eds.), *Interactive Digital Television: Technologies and Applications.* Hershey, PA: Idea Group Publishing.

Lugmayr, A., Pohl, A., Mühlhäuser, M., Negru, D., Kallenbach, J., Köbler, F., et al. (2006). Ambient media and home entertainment (workshop review). In *Proceedings of the 4th Euro iTV Conference*. Athens, Greece: ELTRUN/AUEB.

Magnum language (n.d.). Retrieved from, http://www.magnumlanguage.com/magnum.asp.

NASA. (n.d.). Autogenic-Feedback System-2 (AFS-2). In *NASA Tech. Briefs*. Retrieved from, http://www.techbriefs.com/index.php?option=com_staticxt&staticfile=Briefs/Jan01/ARC140481.html.

Ortony, A., Clore, G. L., & Collins, A. (1988). *The cognitive structure of emotions*. Cambridge, MA: Cambridge University Press.

Oxford (n.d.). Oxford Reference ONLINE. Retrieved from, http://www.oxfordreference.com/.

Paiva, A., Costa, M., Chaves, R, Piedade, M., Mourão, D., Sobral, D., et al. (2003). SenToy: An affective sympathetic interface. *Int. J. Hum.-Comput. Stud., 59*, 227-235.

Philips. iCat http://www.research.philips.com/newscenter/pictures/041209-icat.html, http://www.research.philips.com/technologies/syst_softw/robotics/index.html.

Plutchik, R., & Kellerman, H. (1990). *Emotion Theory, Research, and Experience vol. 1-5*. Academic Press.

Sharon, T. (n.d.). The Smile Detector. Retrieved from, http://xenia.media.mit.edu/~taly/mas630/smiley.html.

Sloman, A., & Croucher, M. (1981). *Why robots will have emotions*. University of Sussex, School of Cognitive and Computing Sciences.

Solomon, R.C. (1977). The Logic of Emotion. In *Symposium Papers to be Read at the Meeting of the Western Division of the American Philosophical Association April 28-30, Vol. 11* (pp. 41-49). Chicago: Blackwell Publishing.

The Logical Language Group (LLG). (1987). *Lojban*. Retrieved from, http://www.lojban.org

Watt, S. (1995, November). A brief naive psychology manifesto. *INFORMATICA, 19* http://www.comp.rgu.ac.uk/staff/sw/stuarts_papers/naiveshort.htm

World Wide Web Consortium (W3C). (2006). W3C Emotion Incubator Group. Retrieved from, http://www.w3.org/2005/Incubator/emotion/

KEY TERMS

Ambient Media

Emotion Concepts

Emotion Framework

Emotion Recognition

Emotional Binding

Emotional Computation

Pervasive Computation

Ubiquitous Computation

Chapter XXIII
Modelling Hardwired
Synthetic Emotions:
TPR 2.0

Jordi Vallverdú
Universitat Autònoma de Barcelona, Spain

David Casacuberta
Universitat Autònoma de Barcelona, Spain

ABSTRACT

During the previous stage of our research we developed a computer simulation (called 'The Panic Room' or, more simply, 'TPR') dealing with synthetic emotions. TPR was developed with Python code and led us to interesting results. With TPR, we were merely trying to design an artificial device able to learn from, and interact with, the world by using two basic information types: positive and negative. We were developing the first steps towards an evolutionary machine, defining the key elements involved in the development of complex actions (that is, creating a physical intuitive ontology, from a bottom-up approach). After the successful initial results of TPR, we considered that it would be necessary to develop a new simulation (which we will call "TPR 2.0."), more complex and with better visualisation characteristics. We have now developed a second version, TPR 2.0., using the programming language Processing, with new improvements such as: a better visual interface, a database which can record and also recall easily the information on all the paths inside the simulation (human and automatically generated ones) and, finally, a small memory capacity which is a next step in the evolution from simple hard-wired activities to self-learning by simple experience.

INTRODUCTION

This is an update of a former project about creating a simulation of an ambient intelligence device which could display some sort of protoemotion adapted to solve a very simple task. In the next section we'll describe the first version of the project, and then we'll deal with the changes and evolution in a third second version. But first let us introduce the main ideas that are the backbone of our research.

Bottom Up Approach

AI and robotics have tried intensively to develop intelligent machines over the last 50 years. Meanwhile, two different approaches to research into AI have appeared, which we can summarise as *top down* and *bottom up* approaches:

i.   **Top Down:** Symbol system hypothesis (Douglas Lenat, Herbert Simon). The *top down* approach constitutes the classical model. It works with symbol systems, which represent entities in the world. A reasoning engine operates in a domain independent way on the symbols. SHRDLU (Winograd), Cyc (Douglas Lenat) or expert systems are examples of it.

ii. **Bottom Up:** physical grounding hypothesis (situated activity, situated embodiment, connectionism ← veritat? No sería connectionism?). On the other hand, the *bottom up* approach (led by Rodney Brooks), is based on the physical grounding hypothesis. Here, the system is connected to the world via a set of sensors and the engine extracts all its knowledge from these physical sensors. Brooks talks about "intelligence without representation": complex intelligent systems will emerge as a result of (or o of?) complex interactive and independent machines. (Vallverdú, 2006)

Although we consider that the top-down approach was really successful on several levels (cf. excellent expert systems like the chess master Deep Blue), we consider that the approaches to emotions made from this perspective cannot embrace or reproduce the nature of an emotion. Like Brooks (1991), we consider that intelligence is an emergent property of systems and that in that process, emotions play a fundamental role (Sloman & Croucher, 1981; DeLancey, 2001). In order to achieve an 'artificial self' we must not only develop the intelligent characteristics of human beings but also their emotional disposition towards the world. We put the artificial mind back into its (evolutionary) artificial nature.

Protoemotions and Action

As we have published extensively elsewhere (Casacuberta 2000, 2004; Vallverdú 2007), on how emotions play a fundamental role in rational processes and the development of complex behaviour, including decision making (Schwarz 2000). There is a huge body of literature on these ideas which we will not analyse here but which can be consulted (Damasio 1994, Edelman 2000, Denton 2006, Ramachandran 2004).

After describing emotions as alarm systems that activate specific responses (Vallverdú & Casacuberta, 2008a), we considered it necessary to minimise the number of basic emotions and choose two: pain and pleasure, considered as negative and positive inputs, respectively. We called them *protoemotions*, because they are the two basic regulators of activity. In this sense, we considered synthetic emotions as "an independently embedded (or *hard-wired*) self-regulating system that reacts to the diverse inputs that the system can collect (internal or external)." (op. cit, 105). From this point of view the cybernetics concept of *feedback*, as a property of biological entities is added to our conceptual model.

We must also take into account another use of this term, *protoemotions*, by clinicians who characterise emotions of psychopaths using this term to referr to their "primitive responses to immediate needs" (Pitchford, 2001). Our idea of protoemotions has no relation at all to psychopaths, but to the idea of *basic* emotions: these emotions which are at the bottom of the complex and subtle pyramid of emotional activity (such as anger, fear, sadness,.......). Following the ideas of Wolfram (2002/3) we agree with the idea that "many very simple programs produce great complexity" and that "there is never an immediate reason to go beyond studying systems with rather simple underlying rules" (op.cit, 110).

Emotions without Mind

After decades of cognitively-oriented theories of emotion which led to the development of machine models of emotions in AI, such as those of Marvin Minsky, Clark Elliott (Affective Reasoner), Kenneth Colby (the famous chatbot *Parry*), Rosalynd Picard, or Aaron Sloman, recently we are seeing a change towards an embodied-embedded approach to emotions (Spackman & Miller, 2008). From our previous and current research we are talking about 'protoemotions'.

We consider that emotions don't involve mental states (which are thought of as representational states of the real external world) and that they are, to a very high degree, somatic events: they create physiological changes such as facial expressiveness, skeleto-muscular attitude, expression through vocal activity and autonomic nervous system response (adrenaline release or change in heart rate).

Therefore, we can consider the fact that emotions can trigger responses without the necessity of prior mental states or complex cognitive processes (Zajonc, 1984; LeDoux, 1998; Laird and Bresler, 1990).

Therefore, we can consider emotions as:

1. Independent somatic states.
2. Necessary events for behaviour activation.
3. Necessary events for rational processes.
4. Embedded/hardwired activators of responses.

When we define them as *hardwired*, we refer to the idea that, like programs (their built-in constants) or other devices (such as circuits), they cannot be changed. From this point of view, protoemotions are hardwired (Clark & Grunstein, 2000) as well empathy (thanks to mirror neurons, Rizzolati & Craighero, 2004). And in some cases, their are not regulated by the higher cognitive brain area (Singer et al 2004), creating automatic responses to sensory stimuli.

For all these reasons, a protoemotional approach to complex behaviour can offer us a good tool for designing increasingly complex devices, from a bottom up approach which will lead us to rational entities. This is a behaviour-based architecture with the agent situated in the (simulated) world. In the end, we can consider our research as a new approach to the field of the cognitive robotics (Ishii, 2006).

Therefore, the main aim of our proposal is to simulate - in order to be able to actually build a prototype - several non-conscious characteristics of emotions that are related to behaviour modification. To understand our objectives it might be worth stating first what we don't plan to do:

- We don't plan to build a digital system which is able to "feel emotions". Qualia is still one of the "hard problems" and we wouldn't even know where to start.
- The system is not designed to recognise emotions in other beings.
- It is not an expert system that is able to develop reasoning and argumentation using the concept of emotions.

What are we trying to build then? Primarily we can simulate a main characteristic of emotions: their ability to produce some behaviour aimed at adapting to a specific change in the environment.

We are looking for a process that:

- Automatically evaluates a situation as being either "neutral" or "dangerous".
- Generates an automatic response that deals with the specific danger detected.
- Scales the response: that is makes the response stronger or weaker depending on the degree of danger that is detected.

Neither in this nor in the first model is there a "qualia feeling" associated. In this first stage of the project it is not needed in order to generate the response. What we are interested in is the process of emotion as a signal that is generated after an evaluation of the surroundings and then is able to produce some automatic responses. This, of course, is not the only characteristic that emotions have, so we prefer to talk about our system as having "proto-emotions". Besides, these proto-emotions are *hard-wired* into the system.

Another key aspect of emotions we wanted to simulate is their valence. Since Aristotle we know that emotions are either positive or negative, producing either pleasure or pain. Of course, there is more to it, as a person who has just enjoyed a rollercoaster ride would tell you: the emotion is negative in principle, fear, but it actually gives you pleasure. Again, there is a long long road to travel before we can make robots that can enjoy themselves in Disneyworld, so we can safely forget that type of processes from now on and develop a system that has two emotions: one positive and one negative.

These two emotions are connected to the two main contexts afforded by the surroundings: neutral or dangerous. The more the negative emotion is felt the closer the system is to starting to take measures to counter the danger, the system has several equilibrium points that need to be exceeded in order to react to the possible menace. Again, these emotions are not "felt" by the system either as positive or negative. The system has no possibility of perceiving qualia. We call them

negative or positive in the sense that the negative one forces the system to protect itself, activating a secondary electrical circuit, while the positive one tends to return to the normal state.

Therefore, when we say that our system simulates a protoemotional circuit we mean that:

1. The system labels the signals from the sensors which describes the surroundings either as negative or positive.
2. Each option has a specific signal that is used to change the way further perceptual signals will be processed as well as to generate possible behavioural responses against a potential danger.
3. Responses are automatic and embedded in the system.
4. All the computations are based on the relative strength of the two proto-emotional signals. If the negative signal reaches a certain threshold it will activate the "defensive action" and will switch to the emergency circuit. Positive signals try to "calm down" the system in order to avoid that reaction.

PREVIOUS SIMULATION: TPR 1.0

During the previous stage of our research we developed a computer simulation (called 'The Panic Room' or, more simple, 'TPR') dealing with synthetic emotions (Vallverdú & Casacuberta 2008a). The basic conceptual and technical data of that simulation were:

- Hard-wired emotional states (proto-emotions).
- Bottom-up approach.
- *Python* programmed.

The computational simulation was designed as a box with four doors (a,d,m,p), three switches (b,h,m), and 16 squares {a,b...p}:

a	b	c	d
e	f	g	h
i	j	k	l
m	n	o	p

The system simulated a room in which passers-by could walk around randomly. There were three switches distributed around the room. If a user was able to disconnect the three switches in rapid succession then the power was cut to the main computer running the entire environmental construction and the whole system failed. However, if the system was able to detect such an attack in time, it had a few seconds to acquire an alternative source of electricity before the user turned off the final switch. To make the process more interesting, the system did not have access to information about whether the switches had been turned off (pain) or not (pleasure). By means of a deterministic algorithm, one not capable of change through learning we designed the system to distinguish between a harmless and a harmful intruder. Each movement by the user either generated some elevation or reduction of a fear signal. As the fear increased the system checked the signals coming from the more relevant sensors more frequently. Once the signal went beyond a certain threshold, the system entered into "panic mode" and grabbed the alternative source of electricity. When the fear signal descended enough for the system to consider that the danger had passed it returned to its normal activity, getting electricity again from the usual source.

With TPR, we were merely trying to design an artificial device able to learn from, and interact with, the world by using two basic information types: positive and negative. These can be considered as proto-emotions and, assuming we can establish this analogy with human emotions, we could emulate their usefulness in the fight for survival by creating helpful behavioural rules such as "this is harmful, don't touch it" or "this produces pleasure, eat it". We were developing the first steps towards an evolutionary machine, defining the key elements involved in the development of complex actions (that is, creating a **physical intuitive ontology**, from a bottom-up approach).

From the programming perspective, in TPR 1.0 we just used *global variables* in order to represent the emotional values. That meant that the system actually kept "memories" of the former emotional states. This, of course, is somewhat unrealistic, and wanting to pursue a bottom-up approach as much as possible, we decided later (at the previous stage of the current research) to change and give the system, now called 'TPR 2.0.', a very basic memory instead.

As a conclusion to the TPR simulation, we obtained several interesting results: the system labelled the signals from the sensors that described the surroundings either as negative or positive. Either option had a specific signal that was used to change the way further perceptual signals would be processed as well to as generate possible behavioural responses to a potential danger.

Responses were automatic and embedded (or *hard-wired*) in the system (therefore, they are an *intentional* - but not conscious - force). All the computations were based on the relative strengths of the two protoemotional signals. If the negative signal reached a certain threshold it would activate the "defensive action" and would switch to the emergency circuit. Positive signals tried to "calm down" the system in order to avoid that reaction.

TPR could easily distinguish between dangerous and innocent situations from its basic emotional structure (using pain and pleasure). Therefore, we demonstrated that emotions, as hardwired conditions of the system, are intentional maps of action that make possible an effective interaction with the world without the necessity for complex programming. At the same time, TPR was able to develop correct escalation responses through [pain➔ pain+➔ panic] or [pleasure➔happiness] states. This demonstrated that with just two activation signals (pain and pleasure), it was possible to allow the TPR to carry out a coherent *survival* activity. As a consequence, we concluded that a hardwired approach to ambient intelligence was possible with TPR.

A NEW SIMULATION: TPR 2.0

After the successful initial results of TPR, we considered that it would be necessary to develop a new simulation (which we will call "TPR 2.0"), more complex and with better visualisation characteristics. We have now developed a second version, TPR 2.0., using the programming language Processing, which makes possible an improved visualisation of the simulation, a very important aspect of simulations (cf. the classic McCormick, B.H., DeFanti, T.A. & Brown, M.D. (eds.), 1987).

TPR 2.0. is equipped with several simulated components: 4 doors: in/out, 3 switches: which activate emotional responses, 4 sensors: which detect proximity to switches and movement inside the room and, finally, 4 light devices: which show the emotional state of the Room. Like its predecessor, TPR 2.0. automatically evaluates a situation as being either "neutral" or "dangerous"; generates an automatic response that deals with the specific danger detected and can escalate that response: that is, it can make the response stronger or weaker depending on the degree of danger that is detected.

The possible generated pathways are:

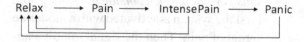

The process by which TPR 2.0. changes from one state to another can be defined by these rules,

where s is *signal, em* is *echoic memory,* + means *positive path,* − means *negative path* and *relaxed, pain, intense pain, panic* are the possible final states (relaxed = 0, pain = 1, intense pain = 2, panic = 3):

If s is + and em is + then relaxed

If s is + and em is − then increment once +1 the state

If s is − and em is + then increment once +1 the state

If s is − and em is − then increment once +1 the state

You must consider that the simulation has a short memory (echoic memory) which can hold the previous state for a small amount of time (+ or −). Once this time is passed, and if there is no new signal, the next state is always +.

What are the Main Differences Between TPR 1.0 and TPR 2.0?

There are two basic improvements or changes:

a.   **Technological difference.** The first version was made in Python and this second one is made in Processing. We found that Processing is a lot easier and more powerful when doing an animated version of the simulation. This new programming language approach implies several changes in the general architecture of the simulation (these include: better usability across different platforms, more friendly interface, database,…).

b.   **Echoic memory.** This is the main theoretical improvement on our first version. In TPR 1.0 we just used global variables in order to store the emotional values. That meant that the system actually kept "memories" of the former emotional states. This, of course, is somewhat unrealistic, and wanting to pursue a bottom-up approach as much as possible, we decided to change the system to give it a very basic memory instead.

c. **Pleasure states deleted.** TPR 1.0. also had scalable pleasure states such as *pleasure* and *happiness*, which have been deleted in TPR 2.0. TPR 2.0. only has *relaxed – pain - intense pain - panic* modes. The reason for this change is twofold: (i) a new philosophical framework in which we considered pain states to be more basic than pleasure ones (although you can consider the *relaxed* state to be a positive situation…or *lack of pain*, perhaps a Buddhist approach to the biological nature of living entities), and (ii) related to the necessity of developing a more simple and elegant simulation with fewer elements to be processed, but with a more in-depth analysis.

d. TPR 2.0. has a better visual interface (which makes possible the interaction between TPR 2.0 and human beings, as well as the generation of automatic paths): mouse and labelled emotions with colours and text which appear on the screen as soon as they are generated: relaxed (green), pain (blue), intense pain (purple), panic (red).

e. TPR 2.0. has a database which can record and also easily recall information on all the paths followed inside the simulation and, finally,

f. TPR 2.0. has a small memory capacity (echoic memory) which is a next step in the evolution from simple hard-wired activities to self-learning by experience. After a few seconds (depending of the processor that runs the simulation) the echoic memory degrades and finally vanishes, returning to a neutral state as if nothing had happened.

With all these changes, we wish to produce a better simulation of a system able to react efficiently to the environment with an approach based on simple synthetic emotions. We presented the results of this new simulation at the international ECAP08 Congress (2008b).

What is the Echoic Memory and How does it Operate?

An echoic memory works like an echo. It holds data stored for just a few seconds before being erased, looking for new data to be hosted. When, for example, we look for a number in a contacts list and then dial it we might be using our echoic memory, to remember the number long enough to dial it and then forget it. We might not even be using our short-term memory.

Like an echo, this memory just stores the last image, sound, thought or whatever was processed last.

Our system has that sort of echoic memory, to store emotional values. So, when the system feels "neutral" the echoic memory continues neutral. If a painful signal arrives, the system rapidly stores it in the echoic memory. From now on, two different things might happen:

a. Nothing else happens for a while. If this is the case, then the system doesn't process any more painful signals so the echoic memory degrades and finally vanishes, returning to a neutral state as if nothing had happened.

b. Another painful signal shows up. In that case the system processes the signal and adds its value to whatever was stored in the echoic memory. When the total amount in the echoic memory exceeds a certain value the system enters into panic mode.

Let's see some examples:

i. The user comes to the first post and activates the sensor. Then he turns his back and exists.
    This is what happens inside the simulation: First the system is activated with a moderate signal of pain. Then the signal rapidly vanishes and the system returns to the neutral situation.

ii.   The user comes to the first post and activates the sensor. He hangs around for a while, then turn his back and exist.

This is what happens inside the simulation: The system is activated with the first presence and stays in a state of moderate pain until the user leaves. The signal takes more time to degrade than previously, but finally dies.

iii. The user comes to the first post and activates the sensor. He rapidly moves away and walks around, after a few seconds he reaches the second post, activating the second sensor.

This is what happens inside the simulation: the system is activated and maintains the sensation of moderate pain, it vanishes gradually, but before dispersing completely the user arrives at the second sensor. The total input of pain exceeds the limit, so the system enters into panic mode.

iv.   The user comes to the first post and activates the sensor. He rapidly moves away and walks around, after more than a minute he reaches the second post, activating the second sensor.

This is what happens inside the simulation: the system is activated and maintains the sensation of moderate pain, it vanishes gradually, until it is extinguished. When the user arrives at the second sensor, the system is back in neutral mode, so the activation of the second system is not considered a menace, therefore the system continues in neutral mode.

RUNNING THE SIMULATION

TPR 2.0. has beeen run in two different ways:

i.   As a program for different platforms and systems:
   a.   Processing software installed on computers (Windows and Macintosh).
   b.   EXE file for Windows computers.
ii.   As a JAVA online application inside a private-academic net (UAB).

The universe of TPR.2.0.'s users has been SETE & TecnoCog researchers' (Synthetic Emotions in Technological Environments & Tecnology and Cognition: option (i)) and grade students ("Philosophy and Computing": option (ii)). We considered the possibility of an online open access simulation, but we declined that option deciding in favour of a restricted access, in order to maintain better control of its functioning process and possible problems.

You can see several basic screen captures of the simulation. Notice that in TPR 2.0. the protoemotion is indicated with a word and a colour, just for clarify for user the usual reactions that occurred during the simulation (from relaxed to pain, intense pain and panic):

Box 1.

RESULTS

After two weeks of controlled accesses to TPR.2.0., we obtained a significant amount of data which should be analysed. The users were asked to use the TPR 2.0. simulation as many times as they wished and for as long as they considered necessary.

First of all we can look at the time spent by users ($n = 75$) in running the simulation:

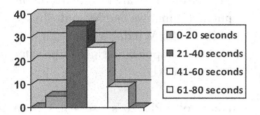

We can infer that most people spend between 21 and 60 seconds, with a bigger incidence in the 21-40 seconds group. No user exceeded 80 seconds of use of the simulation. What we can notice is a slight difference between online and program users:

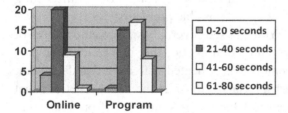

Online users tended to spend less time than program users. Although the simulation not was designed to check these cognitive dissonances (but rather the capacity of synthetic hard-wired emotions to generate scalable quality responses), we want to draw attention to this fact. Regarding online users, Nielsen & Loranger (2006) have interesting studies, but there are few studies on neurological aspects of multitasking (Leber, A.B., Turk-Browne, N.B. & Chun, M.M., 2008). A classic research on this perspective is that of Allen (2003).

Now we should pay attention to the emotional pathways generated according to the time spent by different groups (see Box 2).

Regardless of group and time aspects, we were able to check the capacity of TPR 2.0. to develop a consistent hard-wired behaviour able to produce scalable responses. Our model offers a simple way to implement embedded emotions into more complex systems.

CONCLUSION

From the above we have come to several conclusions:

- TPR reacts correctly as a hard-wired system that is able to react in a scaled way to external inputs.

Box 2.

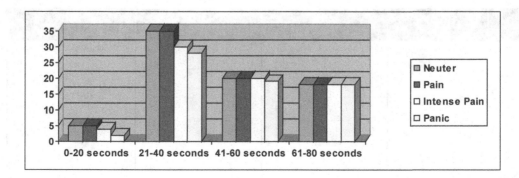

- Echoic memory guides the action selection without the necessity of a bottom-up approach.
- Simple programming makes possible the simulation of emotional switches that guided the action of a hard-wired device.
- Simple emotions (pain-pleasure) can be used (as in the evolutionary approaches to complex systems) as basic regulators and action-inciters, offering to simple systems an intentional arrow which can be employed for social relations and self-learning.

COROLLARY AND FUTURE RESEARCH

After the TPR 1.0. and TPR 2.0. successful computer simulations, we are now embedding our theoretical model into physical and social devices. Although we cannot offer our preliminary results here, we wish to confirm that the interdomain crossover (from virtuality to real environment) is working succesfully.

Our choice has been the LEGO Mindstorms NXT (Tribot model) robots. We have 6 units of NXT with which we are working on real environments. NXT robots have touch, sound, light and ultrasonic sensors and can establish bluetooth connections. This allows us to recreate simple environments in which the 6 robots establish continuous interactions mediated through their hard-wired programming.

The use of 6 robots which can communicate among themselves is allowing us to test our model of the protoemotional capacity to carry out complex activities from a behaviour-based approach founded on basic emotional states.

ACKNOWLEDGMENT

This work was supported by the TECNOCOG research group (at UAB) on Cognition and Technological Environments, [HUM2005-01552], and has been developed by the SETE (Synthetic Emotions in Technological Environments) research group. The Philosophy Department (UAB) has also provided part of the funding for the acquisition of the NXTs.

REFERENCES

Allen, D. (2003). *Getting things done*. US: Viking Books.

Brooks, R.A. (1991). Intelligence without representation. *Artificial Intelligence, 47*, 139-159.

Casacuberta, D. (2000). *Qué es una emoción*. Barcelona: Crítica.

Casacuberta, D. (2004). *DJ El niño:* Expressing synthetic emotions with music. *Artificial Intelligence and Society, 18*, 187-197.

Clark, W.C., & Grunstein, M. (2000). *Are we hardwired? The role of genes in human behavior*. Oxford: OUP.

Damasio, A. (1994). *Descartes error*. Cambridge, MA: MIT Press.

DeLancey, C. (2001). *Passionate engines: What emotions reveal about mind and artificial intelligence. Oxford:* Oxford University Press.

Denton, D. (2006). *Emotions: The dawning of consciousness*. Oxford: OUP.

Edelman, G., & Tononi, G. (2000). *A universe of consciousness: How matter becomes imagination*. NY: Basic Books.

Ishii, K. (2006). Cognitive robotics to understand human beings. *Science & Technology Trends. Quarterly Review, 20*, 11-32.

Laird, L., & Gresler, C. (1990). William James and the mechanism of emotional experience. *Journal of Personality and Social Psychology,16*, 636-651.

Leber, A.B., Turk-Browne, N.B., & Chun, M.M. (2008).Neural predictors of moment-to-moment fluctuations in cognitive flexibility. *PNAS, 105*(36), 13592–13597.

LeDoux, J.E. (1998). Fear and the brain: Where have we been and where are we going? *Biological Psychiatry, 44*, 1229-1238.

McCormick, B.H., DeFanti, T.A., & Brown, M.D. (eds.) (1987). *Visualization in Scientific Computing.* US: ACM Press.

Nielsen, J., & Loranger, H. (2006). Prioritizing web Usability. Berkeley, CA: New Riders Press.

Pitchford, I. (2001). The origins of violence: Is psychopathy an adaptation? *The Human Nature Review, 1*, 28-36.

Ramachandran, V.S. (2004). *A brief tour of human consciousness.* New York: Pi Press, Pearson Education.

Rizzolati, G., & Craighero, L. (2004). The mirror-neuron system. *Annual Review of Neuroscience, 27*, 169–192.

Singer, T., Seymour, B., O'Doherty, J., Kaube, H., Dolan, R.J., & Frith,C.D. (2004). Empathy for pain involves the affective but not sensory components of pain. *Science, 303*, 1157-1162.

Schwarz, N. (2000). Emotion, cognition and decision making. *Cognition and Emotion. 14*(4), 433-440.

Sloman, A., & Croucher, M. (1981).Why robots will have emotions. In *Proceedings of the 7th International Joint Conference on AI. US:* Morgan-Kaufman.

Spackman, M.P., & Miller, D. (2008). Embodying emotions: What emotion theorists can learn from simulations of emotions. *Minds & Machines, 18*, 357-372.

Vallverdú, J. (2006). Choosing between different AI approaches? The scientific benefits of the confrontation, and the new collaborative era between humans and machines. *TripleC, 4*(2), 209-216.

Vallverdú, J. (2007). *Una ética de las emociones.* Barcelona: Anthropos.

Vallverdú, J., & Casacuberta, D. (2008a). The panic room. On synthetic emotions. In A. Briggle, K. Waelbers & P. Brey (Eds.), *current issues in computing and philosophy* (pp. 103-115). The Netherlands: IOS Press.

Vallverdú, J., & Casacuberta, D. (2008b, June). *Modelling synthetic emotions: TPR 2.0.* (ECAP08). Paper presented at the *International Meeting of the European Association for Philosophy and Computing*, Montpellier, France.

Wolfram, S. (2002). *A new kinf of science.* Canada: Wolfram Media, Inc.

Zajonc, R. (1984). On the primary affect. *American Psychologist, 39*(1), 117-123.

KEY TERMS

Hard-Wired: Within the context of artificial intelligence; a response system that it is not simulated by software, but directly embedded in the physical structure of the system.

Intentional: Directed to something, about something.

Protoemotion: State in an artificial system which despite the fact that doesn't share all the core properties of biological emotions it actually has some of them, so its study is meaningful in order to create synthetic emotions.

Simulation: Generated in a computer by using some variables and algorithms to imitate a real process. For example, simulation of the weather in a supercomputer.

Synthetic Emotion: State in an artificial system which share all the core properties of biological emotions and have an equivalent effect in the behavior of the system

Chapter XXIV
Invisibility and Visibility:
The Shadows of
Artificial Intelligence

Cecile K. M. Crutzen
Open University, The Netherlands

Hans-Werner Hein
Verlässliche IT-Systeme, Germany

ABSTRACT

A vision of future daily life is explored in Ambient Intelligence (AmI). It follows the assumption that information technology should disappear into our environment to bring humans an easy and entertaining life. The mental, physical, and methodical invisibility of artificial intelligent tools and environments will have an effect on the relation between the activities of both, users and designers. The infiltration of reality with sensing, computing, transmitting and acting hardware will cause the construction of new meanings on interaction in general because the "visible" acting of people will be preceded, accompanied and followed by the invisible and visible acting of artificial intelligent tools and environments and their providers. Sociability in such an interaction world stretches between the feelings of "being in security" and "being in control". Invisibility management could enable situated veiling and unveiling. Critical Transformative Rooms, where human and artificial actors can negotiate about the change of meanings, are the approach to deal with the users' emotions of frozenness, despair, fear, doubt and trust.

1. INTRODUCTION

Emotionality and sociability are improper qualities to attach to an artificial device. But a human user can fantasize a device as emotional or social, if it mimics accordingly. Users of such devices react with emotions. They "love it", "be afraid of", "miss it" etc. They are socially connected to these artificial tools and environments, which are mingled with their live. Interaction through artificial devices can change a user's social and emotional relation to the devices themselves and to the human communication partners behind. So infrastructures for e-mail, SMS, mobile-phone, chatting, blogging, and "virtual life"-type games can be regarded as social and emotional agents. Without them a lot of emotionality and social interaction would not be possible.

In the literature it is often assumed, that by "pushing computers into the background, embodied virtuality will make individuals more aware of the people on the other end of their computer links" (Weiser, 1991). It is implied that artificial tools and environments are felt as "more social" if their visibility is reduced to the necessary minimum.

On the other hand total invisible acting implies that concerned humans cannot develop any emotional relation to them: Sensually they do not exist. In this case humans are endangered to become just the objects of artificial intelligent agents. Users will be reduced to observable objects placed in feedback loops that converge to an optimal adaptive and obsessively pre-cautious environment with an action/communication oriented smart space functionality. Users then are not enabled to doubt the artificial intelligent agent's ready-made acting any more. But doubt and trust are basic emotions for sociability.

In this context the word "visibility" represents everything, humans can, directly or indirectly, perceive with their senses: hearing, seeing, feeling, smelling and tasting. "Invisibility" in the following will be classified into "mental invisibility", "methodical invisibility" and "physical invisibility".

"Invisible acting" happens, when users during interaction will not perceive triggers for critical reflecting and developing emotions about the offered ready-made artificial acting. The visibility of artificial actors is limited within the technical constraints of their construction, it can be determined purposefully by designers through the implemented data-models, processing func-

tionality, and the chosen sensors and actors. On the other hand an artificial actor's invisibility is unlimited.

So the mechanisms of the Invisible and the Visible in artificial environments, the shadows between the artificial and the human intelligence have to be discussed before addressing the question, how it might be made possible that users perceive their artificial environment as social and emotional.

2. BACKGROUND

"This is because proceedings are generally kept secret not only from the public but also from the accused."
-- Franz Kafka, The Trial

2.1. Ambient Intelligence, the Invisible Intelligence Technology

The term "Ambient Intelligence" (AmI) was firstly used in 1999 by the Vision statement of the European Union's "Information Society Technologies Program Advisory Group" (ISTAG): "Ambient Intelligence should be the result of the convergence of three key technologies: 'Ubiquitous Computing', 'Ubiquitous Communication', and 'Intelligent User-Friendly Interfaces'. AmI is unobtrusive and often invisible, being embedded in everyday objects such as furniture, clothes, vehicles, roads and smart materials. Interaction is relaxing and enjoyable for the citizen, and does not involve a steep learning curve; otherwise stated, the dominant mode of interaction will become laid-back rather than lean-forward. The technology is all around us but almost invisible: it is everywhere and yet in our consciousness is nowhere unless we need it. The resulting landscape is embedded, personalized, adaptive, and anticipatory. People will be surrounded by intelligent and intuitive interfaces recognizing and responding to the presence of individuals. AmI is presponsive instead of being simply responsive. (ISTAG, 1999, 2001)

At the moment Ambient Intelligence can be seen as a "crossover approach", it is strongly related to several other IT and Computer Science topics (Punie, 2003 p. 6, Oulasvirta, 2004; Schmidt, 2005). So Ambient Intelligence technology is not completely new. A lot of ambient technology is already available for monitoring analogue physical processes, describing them with digital data and analyzing these data using knowledge-based interpretation models. All this was developed in the last century under the label "Artificial Intelligence (AI)". New is that the public and the private environment of humans is now permeated by an overwhelming number of cheap autonomous active devices. Everyday surroundings become easy-to-use interfaces realized as a laid-back mode of dialogue with an integrated service infrastructure. Ambient Intelligence implies a seamless environment of computing, advanced networking technology and specific computer interfaces for humans – mainly remote and non tangible.

The invisibility of Ambient Intelligence is related to an easiness of use. However these emphasis on greater user-friendliness includes that people should give away their adaptivity for the supposed adaptivity of their artificial intelligent surroundings. The promises for more efficient support could only result in a more user-empowerment if users could make "visible" the purposes and the acting of their Ambient Intelligence environment. Ambient Intelligence will cause the inevitability of the employment of artificial intelligent agents to automate routine decisions and to provide against stupefying read and write collisions of the artificial devices. There is no guarantee that these artificial agents can cooperate appropriately and safely. The penetration process has already started with remote recognition systems for facial expression and body tracking (Turk 2004). With biometrics technology our hands, eyes, voices, faces and movements will be used to control

the way we live (Hein, 1999; Jain, 2004; Oviatt, 2004). In the very near future humans will be overwhelmed by huge quantities of personalized real-time responses based for instance on networking RFID tags. In the future Ambient Intelligence will influence the modeling of how people should live in a community.

At the moment, the main effort of the Ambient Intelligence providers is towards designing simple isolated appliances that might be acceptable to consumers of this new technology. This prepares the ground for an step by step infiltration of our environment with more and more autonomous and interconnected devices. People should become familiar with Ambient Intelligence, slowly and unspectacularly, getting used to handing over parts of their initiative to artificial devices. A lot of sensing infrastructure has already been installed for handling security and road traffic. What remains to be done is to shift the domain of the intended monitoring slowly to feed the ongoing process of people getting used to these controls and forgetting the embarrassment of being permanently monitored; in other words – having no off-switch anymore (Crutzen, 2007).

2.2. Critical Transformative Room

The concept of the "critical transformative room" between users and their environment is very useful to improve the analysis of the relation between visibility and invisibility. A critical transformative room creates a space where the preferred interpretation of the actions of the artificial actors can be negotiated, where doubt can occur as a constructive strategy and can be effective in a change of the acting itself.

Creating such a room requires actors who already have a habit of causing doubt and who accept that truth always is situated. Doubt by humans is necessary for the change of meaning and the possibility of changed acting: "Our beliefs guide our desires and shape our actions. ... Belief does not make us act at once, but puts us into such a condition that we shall behave in some certain way, when the occasion arises. Doubt has not the least such active effect, but stimulates us to inquiry until it is destroyed. ... The irritation of doubt is the only immediate motive for the struggle to attain belief. It is certainly best for us that our beliefs should be such as may truly guide our actions so as to satisfy our desires; and this reflection will make us reject every belief which does not seem to have been so formed as to insure this result. But it will only do so by creating a doubt in the place of that belief. With the doubt, therefore, the struggle begins, and with the cessation of doubt it ends." (Peirce, 1877)

According to Thagard doubt involves an emotional incoherence of a proposition with a person's belief system. The process of coherence maximization does not lead to its acceptance into that belief system. Doubt will always lead to non-acceptance but this does not mean rejection. People can feel unease about a proposition without being at all aware of the source of the discomfort. Uneasiness does not need a conscious recognition of doubt. In the view of Thagard people only doubt propositions that they care about. A wide variety of emotions are always involved with the feeling of doubt. They can be vague and ill defined. However most of them will be experienced as negative including Peirce's irritation. The tension between accepting and rejecting the proposition may cause anxiety, especially if it is highly relevant to personal goals. Doubt is associated with positive emotions if people can solve "the incoherence" (Thagard, 2004).

In a critical transformative room doubt can lead to actions of inquiring. There is space between interpretation and representation of the offered interactions. Differences and different meaning construction processes are respected. Truth is an ongoing conversation, a process of disclosure, and not a correspondence to reality. It is then a mere construction of actors being in interaction with actions of questioning and doubting, which have the potential to change their habits and routines in their interaction.

In contrary to doubt, change is not the determining and defining aspect of a critical transformative room. In any interaction environment actions and interactions certainly cause changes. If changes caused by an interaction are comparable and compatible with previous changes, then they will be perceived as obvious. They are taken for granted, this interaction will not cause any doubt. Doubt is situated in the interaction itself by questioning the caused visible and invisible changes. Especially in Ambient Intelligence environments not all activities of the artificial actors are visible, but being attentive to the change process users can reconstruct the invisible.

Attentivity can open up the closed artificial interaction environment that is inhabited by the designers and their artificial products. In closed worlds, differences from the dominant meaning and acting are seen as errors and failures from dissidents. Doubt is seen as an unwanted feeling of insecurity and not as necessary prerequisite for change. Domination and ignorance in a closed world cause this hierarchical opposition between doubt and security.

To change routine acting is always very difficult because routine does not have much presence in each world of interaction. Moreover, in closed worlds interaction routines and habits are frozen and creating doubt is seen as an unpleasant activity. Thus, opening the obvious established discourse could make room for negotiations on possible changes in future acting. It can create a critical transformative room in which doubts can occur.

Such a strategy is helpful for breaking through the obvious acting. It can give the act of doubting a positive meaning: causing doubt, thinking and feeling doubt are necessary moments in an interaction for changing the interaction itself. By creating a "leavable and reliable" critical transformative room the separation of use and design can be blown up. Users in their acting with artificial environments intertwine use and design through doubting the ready-made interac-

Figure 1. Critical transformative room "Use–Design"

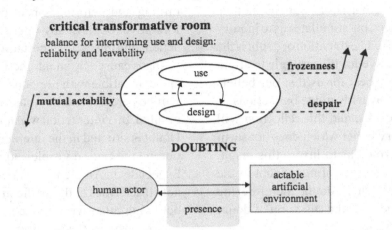

tions. It is only doubt that can create openings and redecorations in the room between humans and their environment.

The question is: Can Ambient Intelligence environments be critical transformative rooms? Can they qualify as open environments? Are the shadows between the visible and invisible enough inducement for doubt? Or will the domestication of Ambient Intelligence technology be ruled by fear?

2.3. Visibility and Invisibility

Visibility of an artificial tool or environment can be defined as the possibility of unveiling its interactions. This unveiling need not to be done always by the user itself but can also be done by social interactions within trustful human environments such as "house", "neighborhood", "work", "homeland".

So visibility need not to be limited to an individual visibility as formulated by Raskin. For each artificial tool or environment is not always clear: "... what functions are available, what they do, or how they are accessed. You should be able to use your senses to easily discover both what abilities are available and how they are to be operated. An interface feature is visible if it either is currently

accessible to a human sense organ – usually the eyes, although this discussion applies also to other sensory modalities – or was so recently perceived that it has not yet faded from short-term memory. If a feature is not visible, we say that it is invisible." (Raskin, 2000, pp. 62-63)

Visibility was researched and developed in the 1980s and the beginning of the 1990s introducing a lot of theories, concepts and design methods such as:

- The adaptivity of humans or the adaptivity of artificial tools, user-friendliness
- The concept of affordances
- User-centered Design and Participatory Design

2.3.1. The Adaptivity of Humans or the Adaptivity of Artificial Tools, User Friendliness

According to Saffo there is scarcity of good tools that can adjust themselves to the users. Adaptivity is the transformative process of the users and is not a symmetrical quality in the relations between humans and computers. Adaptivity is a movement carried out by people: "We are frighteningly adaptable species. ... so we properly learned to adapt ourselves to all but the most awkward of gizmos ..." (Saffo, 1996, p. 87). Thanks to adaptivity and learning abilities of humans, e.g. "folder" and "menu" are experienced by people as user-friendly – but not because these interfaces really are user-friendly.

It is difficult to find out what people really would need. People find their own means to work with computers and the "how" becomes their own tacit knowledge. Beyer and Holtzblatt (1993) write: "Finding out about work is hard. Not only are developers building for users doing unfamiliar work, but users themselves have difficulty saying what they do. People are adaptable and resourceful creatures – they invent a thousand work-arounds and quick fixes to problems, and then forget that they invented the work-around. Even the detail of everyday work becomes second nature and invisible. The users cannot say what they really do because it is unconscious – they do not reflect on it and cannot describe it. The defined policy for an organization is no longer representative because it no longer reflects what is really going on."

This view on adaptivity is consistent with a (social) constructive view on the design and use of technology: Technological change is stipulated by social and cultural life. The meaning of artifacts is constructed by society and individuals. By acting with the artifacts they make choices between rejection or acceptance. In that signifying process social processes play a prominent role (Feenberg 1996). Technology mimics what is or was going on in society. The individuals' design and use of technology is based on ideas taken from society.

Domestication of Ambient Intelligence will be forced by jumping on the bandwagon of some fundamental fears of the individual and society such as the present loss of security and safety because of terrorism, the necessary but unaffordable amount of care for the elderly and the sick, handling the complexity of combining professional and home work, difficulties in coping with the overwhelmingly obtrusive interactions and information of our society and being dependent on the gridlocked transport system. So-called "Killer" applications are largely motivated and justified with providing a bit more security for the individual (Wahlster, 2004).

The Ambient Intelligence developers focus on substitutes and prostheses for the human touch in the care of children, the elderly and the disabled: "When daily contact is not feasible, the decision to move a senior is often driven by fear and uncertainty for his or her daily well-being. Our goal is to create a surrogate support system that resurrects this informal daily communication." (Mynatt, 2001, p. 340).

And the providers openly promote their technology staking on social fears: "We trust less and we fear more. We will therefore be searching for reassurance and guarantees. ... We will welcome tools that allow us to monitor the health of ourselves or our loved ones, that allow quick links with emergency services, or 'tag' our children so that we know where they are. In short how can our technologies look after us and our environments rather than us looking after our technology." (Philips Research, 2003, p. 35). Of course emergency situations with an impact on peoples' physical and psychological well-being could imply "that a service or tool that assists people should be easy for the person to use, should not require much thinking or complicated actions, and should be easily and readily accessible" (Kostakos, 2004). But humans are not always in emergency situations in contrary to the suggestions of the providers.

The interpretation of the meaning of "a better life" in Ambient Intelligence is "taking away the worries" of a possibly unstable future. People are claimed vulnerable and naked without an artificial skin of input and output devices. Single-purpose Ambient Intelligence applications will be connected for continuous monitoring of the individual with the strong suggestion that this provides security and maintains health (Friedewald, 2003).

Claiming the adaptivity of humans without offering the visibility of the artificial environment is only justified in a trustful relation between the providers and the consumers of Ambient Intelligence. Did in the past providers earn this trust? Because users often have been in situations of frozenness and despair, they can not say "yes" to this question. The providers react to this with the strategy of completely "forgetting" the adaptivity and cooperation of humans and promoting the adaptivity of their artificial intelligent environment as a sufficient "user friendly" substitute for "user trusted".

2.3.2. The Concept of Affordances

The "concept of affordances" tries to describe the relation between the environment and its objects, the users and the actions that can be done by users in this environment. According to Gibson designers modify the physical properties and layouts of objects to obtain needed affordances but without a satisfactory theory. In his opinion "affordance" could provide a theoretical foundation for the design of visibility that could lead to adequate actions of users. "Products are not 'a patchwork of forms' to users" (Gibson, 1977, 1982), but they offer the possibilities of actions. In the process of interacting with the products, users can activate a sequence of possible actions to achieve their goals in the end.

Thus, designers should pay more attention to the meaningful interactions between products and the users. Users can perceive what the environment can afford them: the affordances. In Gibson's opinion the affordances of the environment are objective, real, and physical, unlike values and meanings, which are often supposed to be subjective, phenomenal, and mental. So the original notion of Gibson's affordance is based on action and not on information. Meaning is built in the environment, and it could be picked up directly by humans without a mental tension:

"The object offers what it does because it is what it is." (Gibson, 1979).

Gibson's concept of affordances is related to the physical condition of the user. "According to Gibson, perception is a direct consequence of reality without any form of information processing. Thus the meaning discussed in the concept of affordance is not users' judgment or evaluation of products' perceived qualities, but the action capabilities based on objective conditions of users and products at present." (You, 2006, p. 28).

Norman introduces a different concept of affordances, within the community of designers, to explain the relation between the material features of an artificial tool or environment and the possible actions of the user.

Norman's "affordances" are, in contrast to Gibson, a result from the users mental interpretation of things and themselves in a specific situation. This interpretation will be influenced strongly by previous knowledge and experience. This concept of affordances is implemented in several different ways to enhance the physical visibility and usability of products such as making use of metaphorical clues like office based maps, humanoid agents, avatars and meaningful buttons (Norman, 1988).

Affordances are neither objective nor subjective. They are neither just a physical property of the environment or a mental interpretation of the users in their action. Affordances are always situated and depend on the actions users can do with or without mental interpretation of the objects that are ready-made in their environment. The concept of affordances has contributed to design variations in "the visibility" of products.

Affordances still are in discussion (e.g. Li, 1999, You, 2006), but the focus lies more on the differences between the opinions of Gibson and Norman than on how to build adequately the foundation for the concept of affordances: Visibility of the possible actions and interactions, so that the users can design their own interactions out of these possibilities.

2.3.3. User-Centered Design and Participatory Design

User-centered Design and Participatory Design are approaches with enhanced visibility of the analysis and design phases of IT-products. They are a counter-movement to a lot of product developments, where users all of a sudden are forced to cope with an unfamiliar mode of operation and a strange "look and feel".

Norman uses the terms "user-centered design" and "human-centered design" to describe design processes and products which are based on the needs of the user. According to Norman user-centered design involves simplifying the structure of tasks, making things visible, getting the mapping right, exploiting the powers of constraints, and "design for errors". Not the technology should be the focus of the design but the activities of the users (Norman, 1988, chapter 7).

According to Norman the user-centered design has also lead to featurism: "Listening to customers is always wise, but acceding to their requests can lead to overly complex designs. Several major software companies, proud of their human-centered philosophy, suffer from this problem. Their software gets more complex and less understandable with each revision" (Norman, 2005). This complexity of tools could decrease the visibility of how to use the product. It leads to despair situations, where the only possible way of acting is to freeze the interactions with the tool or to abandon it.

Related to User-centered Design is Participatory Design, a diverse collection of methods principles and practices for direct involvements of people in the co-design of the systems they use. The users are seen as the central actors in system development activities (Clement, 1993). The aim of this direct involvement is making technologies more responsive to human needs.

Participatory design "asks systems developers to put three issues in the forefront of their efforts: focusing on the whole workplace and the actual practices of the people doing the work; involving office workers at all levels in articulating their needs and expressing their concerns for what computer support they may need; and developing new methods that help developers and office workers actively support ongoing social processes." (Greenbaum, 1991)

Participatory Design is based on the assumption that, the more people are involved in shaping their social, technological and material environments, the better suited these environments are to everyday realities and requirements, and the more people are able to claim authority over their work and leisure lives.

User-entered Design and Participatory Design were often mixed up because some of their origins lie in the Scandinavian design (Ehn, 1993; Floyd, 1989; Bødker, 2000). Scandinavian design was initially an initiative of the unions to bring democracy into the work place, by involving users in the design stage of the software development process (Clement, 1993).

In the analysis and initial implementation phases the designers use similar methods such as prototyping, too (Spinuzzi, 2002). The essential difference between User-centered Design and Participatory Design is the "direct involvement" aspect in all phases of design and improvement of the product. In user-centered design a contact between designers and users is not required and mostly limited. This contact can be replaced by observations of users. In user-centered products the users' activities are the product basics.

According to Bødker, Greenbaum and Suchman the users' wishes are the starting point in Participatory Design. This integration of the emotional and intellectual work can only happen by developing new analysis methods, where the emphasis is laid on the interaction which takes place in the spaces where the IT-products are developed for and in which the articulation of the needs and expectations of the users can take place (Bødker 1993, p. 59).

"... to draw attention to aspects of systems development and use that have been hidden or at least positioned in the background or shadows and bring them forward into the light. These include various forms of professional configuration and customization work, as well as an open horizon of mundane activities involved in incorporating technologies into everyday working practices, and keeping them working." (Suchman, 1994, p. 7).

So in Participatory Design projects the focus could be more on the future of the users. However Participatory Design cannot guarantee that users participate in further developments of the product, as it should be by a participative approach. Participatory Design is not always successful, because the role of the user as co-designer and the interaction with the designers and computer scientist is difficult to describe and to act upon. "Participatory Design projects could not always deal effectively with the political and ideological aspects of the broader organizational contexts on which Participatory Design initiatives depend for their long-term survival."

The dilemma remains that with no democratization on all levels the knowledge and commitment that Participatory Design can stimulate in users will ultimately reinforce patterns that limit the growth of their capabilities and thus undermine further initiative." (Clement, 1993). Without a lasting process of participations of users, they will lose their competencies of design and a frozenness of work will be unavoidable. Visibility of the product will vanish slowly, because the users and their activity will change. Participatory Design is a Critical Transformative Room that needs to be maintained.

Another critique of Participatory Design is that it has not reached the industrial design of ICT-products. "In spite of these efforts, co-operative design has had little impact on the industrial development of IT artefacts." (Iversen, 2004). Especially in Ambient Intelligence development, a lot of scenarios "... strive towards efficiency and automation, eliminating the skills and creativity of

human beings, the quality in process and product, which originally provoked the co-operative design journey" (Iversen, 2004).

Ambient Intelligence products are called mistakenly human-centered by the producers. They suggest that they did have in mind the needs of the users. Ambient Intelligence design focuses on generalized and classified users. In Ambient Intelligence architectures, designers have often given the active and leading role to the artificial intelligent agents. Users are in the centre of the product but they function as ready-made sources of data for the technology in their environment. By interpreting "user centeredness" in this way, the active explicit participation aspect is lost. The artificial activities in the background of the intelligent environment are not visible for users.

A typical example is the architectural Ambient Intelligence concept of Piva et al. The user is reduced to an observable object placed in a feedback loop that, in the opinion of the designers, converges to an optimal intelligent environment with an action/communication oriented smart space function in order to influence the user (Piva, 2005).

Human-centered design and Participatory Design did make the users with all their differences visible. It has lead to the awareness that the actions and interactions of the users should be the basis of development and not the technical possible activity of the artificial products.

However this needs an interdisciplinary approach, according to Terry Winograd: "In the next fifty years, the increasing importance of designing spaces for human communication and interaction will lead to expansion in those aspects of computing that are focused on people, rather than machinery. The methods, skills, and techniques concerning these human aspects are generally foreign to those of mainstream computer science, and it is likely that they will detach (at least partially) from their historical roots to create a new field of 'interaction design'. ... The work will be rooted in disciplines that focus on people and communication, such as psychology, communications, graphic design, and linguistics, as well as in the disciplines that support computing and communications technologies." (Winograd, 1997, p. 156).

3. VISIBLE AND INVISIBLE

"The Cat seemed to think that there was enough of it now in sight, and no more of it appeared."
--Lewis Caroll, Alice in Wonderland

By (mis)interpretation of two publications "The invisible computer" by Norman (1998) and "The Computer for the 21st Century" by Weiser (1991) visibility was swapped to a design approach of easiness.

Norman discusses in his publication the difficulties that users experience when they use computer technology especially the Personal Computer (PC). He sees the despair of a lot of users. He advocates a "... user-centered, human-centered, humane technology of appliances where the technology of the computer disappears behind the scenes into task-specific devices that maintain all the power without the difficulties ... Today's technology imposes itself on us, making demands on our time and diminishing our control over our lives. Of all the technologies, perhaps the most disruptive for individuals is the personal computer. The computer is really an infrastructure, even though today we treat it as the end object. Infrastructures should be invisible: and that is exactly what this book recommends: A user-centered, human-centered humane technology where today's personal computer has disappeared into invisibility. ... The only way out is through a disruptive technology, through a break with tradition to a technology that becomes invisible, that starts off focusing upon simplicity, joy of ownership, joy of use: a human-centered development philosophy. ... Along this path lies increased acceptance of technology, a technology that is invisible, thoroughly integrated into tools for the tasks and activities people wish to perform." (Norman, 1998; p. viii, p. 6, pp. 229-230). However this "invisibility" proposal could lead to a frozenness of use, where the design activities of users disappear.

According to Weiser, we should live in a computerized infrastructure without thinking about it. "Hundreds of computers in a room could seem intimidating at first, just as hundreds of volts coursing through wires in the walls once did. But like the wires in the walls, these hundreds of computers will come to be invisible to common awareness. People will simply use them unconsciously to accomplish everyday tasks." (Weiser, 1991)

Is it justifiable to compare computer and especially Ambient Intelligence technology with the infrastructure of electric power? Each infrastructure has its own fate. E.g. the traffic infrastructure has changed our vision of distance and spatial flexibility. However in spite of technical provisions and laws many people are killed and injured daily and much psychological and material damage occurs – but this has become mentally invisible in our society. People still think that we are secure and free to proceed with our means of mass mobility and doubting the individual car traffic infrastructure is not politically correct. In contrary global energy production and consumption is in a heavy doubting phase and these "wires in the walls" became visible again.

Weiser meant with "invisibility of the tool" that it should not intrude our consciousness, that it should disappear from our awareness, the focus should be the task and not the tool. A tool might be visible in itself, but it will be invisible as a part of a context of use. This means that the activity with the tool should be obvious, the tool should not be the centre of our attention. Weiser questioned, what kind of interface this tool should have? His proposal is "moving to full-body sensing and interaction" and "by maximally utilizing all of our body's input and output channels." (Weiser, 1994).

How Ambient Intelligence infrastructure will change our vision of freedom and privacy is not clear, neither the mental price to be paid for. So far the interpretation of Weiser's "invisibility" is prettified by others, mostly that we soon will not see the Ambient Intelligence devices anymore because they will be placed into the walls. And Weiser's "body-centeredness" has mistakenly become a "human-centeredness" for a lot of Ambient Intelligence designers.

In the view of Heidegger (Heidegger, 1962, pp. 21-28; Heidegger, 1936, p. 39, p. 41; Zimmerman 1990, p. 215, p. 229) we can see in Ambient Intelligence the essence of technology: "disclosing something, for bringing it forth, for letting it be seen". It is the opening of "Dasein" itself even to the discovery that human actors will become "standing reserve within the global technical system". Ambient Intelligence will make visible that human bodies can be used as input and output for an artificial intelligent environment.

Ambient Intelligence designers shaped Weiser's challenge "to create a new kind of relationship of people to computers, one in which the computer would have to take the lead in becoming vastly better at getting out of the way, allowing people to just go about their lives." (Weiser 1993). However the visibility of the human body for the technology needs not to imply an invisibility of the technology for the humans.

Weiser explicitly based his "disappearance" concept on Heidegger's "ready-to-hand". Real world objects can be ready-to-hand and present-at-hand. When objects are ready-to-hand, we are unaware of their presence. When objects are present-at-hand, we are aware of their existence, the user can be challenged to rationalizing, objectifying and abstracting activities. Heidegger gives three examples (described in Cappuro 1992) of how this awareness can appear and how obvious tools will become present-at-hand again: 1. Conspicuousness (Auffälligkeit): When we meet tools as something unusable, not properly adapted for the use we have decided upon; when tools

do not function as expected. 2. Obtrusiveness (Aufdringlichkeit): When the tool we are used to, is not available; when we miss something. 3. Obstinacy (Aufsässigkeit): When we encounter things, which are just standing in the way of reaching the intended goal.

Weiser (1994) used the readiness-to-hand as a core concept when laying the foundations of ubiquitous computing, and "his ideal was for the systems we design to be 'literally visible, effectively invisible' or, as we suggest, objectively visible but subjectively invisible." (Chalmers, 2004a; Chalmers, 2004b).

Heidegger, saw the ready-to-hand mode not as the ultimate state of a tool. For a user a tool can be at the same time "ready-to-hand (zuhanden)" and "present-at-hand (vorhanden). Both modes of use are "... being set within the ongoing circular process of interpretation, in which one is influenced by one's understanding and experience of older tools and media when using any new tool or medium. One's use of the tool in the course of everyday, situated and social interaction, combining the new tool with the heterogeneous others used in everyday life, builds up new experience and understanding – that will affect how one uses and interprets another new tool." Humans can find tools important for their living if they can engage them in a "circular process of interpretation, whereby perception and activity are influenced by understanding, but also feeding into and changing understanding, thus relies on the interplay between ready-to-hand and present-at-hand interpretation." (Chalmers 2004a; Chalmers, 2004b).

The presence-at-hand and the readiness-to-hand of a tool are situated and they do not exclude each other. On the contrary, they offer the option of intertwining use and design activities in interaction with the tool itself. This intertwining makes a tool reliable, because it is always individual and situated. Its readiness-to-hand should be doubtable. When we experience the readiness-to-hand, we are in a position of "thrownness", which Heidegger explains as being immersed in a situation (Heidegger, 1926, §15, §16).

Bødker is critical on the assumption that easiness can be created by causing disappearances. She says on the contrary that "When it comes to interaction possibilities, it is important e.g. to deconstruct the ubiquitous setting, when there is a malfunction in the configuration. Reconfigurability in the hands of networks of human users leads the way back to a topic ... tailorability, not as individual adaptation of technology, but as adaptation and further development through interaction and cooperation among people." (Bødker, 2006).

In contrary to Weiser, Heidegger's tool analysis does not set out to describe the phenomenon of modern technology. It discovers ourselves as the ones whose character it is "... to go beyond things, or whose essence is existence or openness. The experience of unfamiliarity of tools reveals that we do not just operate within a system of thematic and non-thematic references, but are radically open to Being itself as the horizon of significance, allowing us to discover beings in the modes of concern of readiness-to-hand and presence-at-hand." (Capurro, 1992).

In these modes human actors can experience other actors as "actable" if these actors present themselves in a way, which is interpretable out of their own experiences. That does not mean that this is the intended interpretation because each actor has her or his horizon of experiences and expectations. So environments tools and things are actable, if humans can give meaning to them by drawing them into their interactions. A necessary condition of actability of artificial tools is that humans can perceive the performance of the non-human actor.

Mutual actability is not an obvious attribute of an artificial intelligent environment, it is a process of interactions that creates a transformative critical room (see Figure 1: Critical Transformative Room "Use–Design") between actors. Mutual actability of an artificial actor and user can develop if the user can intertwine use and design activities that are based on doubting the "obvious way of

interacting" and the ready-to-hand routines of the artificial environment.

In this mutual actability-process a transformative critical room arises. The borders of this room are the frozenness of use on the one side; and on the other side, the despair of a forced continuous design. The process of intertwining design and use is always individual and situated in the interaction. It needs the presence-at-hand of the artificial intelligent environment and it depends on the actor's affective disposition and state of mind. (Crutzen, 2006a; 2006b)

Design and use is a dialogic play between invisibilities and visibilities, which pre-constitute user representations and the interpretations of the acting of other human and artificial players in the interaction itself. Invisible and visible representations and interpretations of actions will influence the way human actors will and can act in the future. An off-on-switch for this technology will not be the appropriate instrument to make the invisible visible again or visa versa. It will cause an irritating flickering and more likely stabilize the invisible and visible as excluding positions.

Leavability (Crutzen, 2000, p. 417; Crutzen, 2001) is present if the user can interact with the environment in a routinely way but the environment should offer users opportunities of learning in which situations the ready-to-hand actions are adequate and in which situations they should be abandoned.

So the readiness-to-hand of an artificial environment cannot be modeled and pre-constructed. The artificial environment is present if it has the potential to cause doubts and if it is at the same time "leavable" and "reliable". This doubt in acting should be possible but should not lead to despair or to a forced routine acting. Despair caused by the ready-made acting which allows only acting in a pre-given closed way or by their breakdowns which leads to doubting your own acting and not the ready-made acting of the environment. If doubt is a necessary precondition for changing the pattern of interaction itself then we should think about how to provoke doubt-creating situations that lead to some reflection on changing the meaning of "leavability" of our technical intelligent environments.

All described theories, concepts and design methods around visibility so far have not been really gratifying for the users. The intractability of producing proper and situation dependent visibility lead even more to a "the more invisible the better" counteraction of the designers.

The mechanisms of the "invisible" and the "visible" in artificial environments, the shadows between the artificial intelligence and the human intelligence therefore have to be discussed before addressing the question, how it might be made possible that users perceive their artificial environment as social and emotional. To analyze "invisibility", in the following this concept will be classified into "mental invisibility", "methodical invisibility" and "physical invisibility".

3.1. Mental Invisibility and Visibility

Domesticated artificial products are taken for granted, when they are thought of as a natural part of our daily life, when they become a part of our routines. In our interactions with things, tools and technologies they become obvious (Punie, 2003, p. 64). Their evident and continuous availability causes their disappearance in the complexity of our environment.

With repeated presentations and interpretations of artificial products human actors develop a mental invisibility towards those artificial actors and their ready-made technological acting. Humans integrate the ready-made technological acting in their routine acting and accept it without reflection and emotions. They are thrown forward into their own pre-understandings in every act of interpretation and representation, and into the pre-understandings the artefacts are accompanied with, constructed from experiences of a lot of other actors.

Mental invisibility is the outcome of an integration process on the part of human actors and is a precondition for the stabilization of use and the domestication of a technology. Weiser (1991) was one of the first who focussed on this characterization of computer technology. He and many of his successors in the Ambient Intelligence domain, sees this veiling as the ideal quality of "The most profound technologies are those that disappear. They weave themselves into the fabric of everyday life until they are indistinguishable from it."

Dewey (1916) called these unreflective responses and actions "fixed habits", "routines": "They have a fixed hold upon us, instead of our having a free hold upon things. ... Habits are reduced to routine ways of acting, or degenerate into ways of action to which we are enslaved just in the degree in which intelligence is disconnected from them. ... Such routines put an end to the flexibility of acting of the individual." (Chapter 4: Education as Growth).

Routines are frozen habits of actors. They are executed without thinking and arise by repeated and established acting, which could be forced by the regulations and frames of the interaction worlds or by humans themselves by not doubting and questioning their own interpretations and representations and those of other actors. Routine acting in an intelligent environment means intractability; the technical is not present anymore.

The critical attitude has been lost in the ongoing experiences; the meaning of it is frozen and not questioned anymore. It could hardly make a contribution to doubting anymore and eventually transforming the interaction pattern of the human actor. Mental invisibility limits our interactivity with other humans and artificial actors. It freezes the interaction pattern with the specific tool, but also the meaning to other available objects in our environment and the interaction humans could be involved in.

Under the aspect of "use" as an integration of ready-made technological actions in human activity, based on experiences, humans are always in a process of gaining a certain status of mental invisibility. This status has a risk, to be frozen in a frame; in a limited scale of possible actions in specific situations.

Although if human behaviour could not be based partially on individual or collective routine and habits, life would became no longer liveable. Human actors would be forced at each moment to decide about everything. Faced with the amount and complexity of those decisions they would not be able to act anymore. Humans would place themselves in a complete isolation and conflict, where they cannot accept and adapt even the most obvious interpretations and representations of other human actors. They would be in the stress of constantly redesigning their environment.

"Imagine breaking down the distinction between the producers and the consumers of knowledge: we all come to learn what we all need to know. Clearly such an ideal is unworkable in those terms as soon as we need to know more than the barest basics about the world and ourselves. It is impossible that we could all come to learn for ourselves what we would have to know for our cars to run, our bread to be baked, our illnesses to be cured, our roofs to keep the rain out, our currency to be stable, and our airplanes to fly." (Scheman, 1993, p. 208).

According to Heidegger reliability and usability are connected, they could not exist without each other. But he also noticed that tools are used up and worn down. They become "normal" – mental invisible (Heidegger 1926, p. 28). Reliability can be preserved, if the interpretation and representation of acting in an interaction world contains negotiation that is possible between actors. It can develop only if human and artificial actors can act in a critical transformative room, where mutual actability can develop.

By means of acting, future mutual acting should be negotiable. Although there will always exist a thrownness, from which the individual actor can not extract itself and, very often, does not want to, because all actors are exposed in

this room to themselves and other actors. Within interaction, reliability can remain "visible" only if the process of repeated and established acting can be interrupted. The mutual presentation and interpreting of actions should not be a smooth process. Meaning should be constructed by the possibility of doubt again and again in the interaction itself.

The decision, how the interaction is interpreted and which actions are presented, belongs into the area of the design, to the realization of possible behaviour. According to Heidegger this design belongs substantially to the thrownness of being. Designing does not have to do anything with behaviour according an invented plan. Beings have always designed themselves by their own experiences and will always be "creative". Beings understand themselves always from possibilities (Heidegger, 1926, p.145-146).

So mental invisibility is not only negative. In our daily life a lot of things and tools are mental invisible. Humans need to have a lot of obviousness in their living world to handle daily life. In that precise way we love our environment, because adaptation was accompanied with putting in a lot of effort to make it work. Humans have to do that adaptation.

Mental invisibility can be seen as precondition for acceptance, the stabilization of use and the domestication of technology but it should not be a frozen final-state of the human actors in a community. According to Punie the domestication of technology goes not necessarily harmonious, linear or complete. It is always "a struggle between the user and technology, where the user aims to tame, gain control, shape or ascribe meaning to the technological artefacts. It is not a sign of resistance to a specific technology but rather of an active acceptance process." (Punie, 2003).

Without mental invisibility there is not room enough to trust the emotional and social relations humans have built with the support and the interaction with the tool. Reliability and usability are connected, they could not exist without each other.

Reliability can be preserved, if the interpretation and representation of acting in an interaction world contains negotiation between actors. By means of acting, future mutual acting should be negotiable. Within interaction, reliability can remain "visible" only if the process of repeated and established acting can be interrupted. The mutual presentation and interpreting of actions should not be a smooth process. Meaning should be constructed by the possibility of doubt and satisfaction again and again in the interaction itself. The decision, how the interaction is interpreted and which actions are presented, belongs into the area of the design, to the realization of possible behaviour.

Providers of artificial environments are engaged to create as soon as possible a state of mental invisibility at the user's side. This causes a consumer dependency because the user has the only option to replace the whole environment if this mental invisibility is disrupted later on. However mental invisibility could also imply a user's independency from the provider. The provider has become invisible for the user. This contradiction providers try to solve by creating unique aesthetic artificial environments with specific simulated social behaviour. The decision between mental invisibility or mental visibility has been replaced by stimulating emotional and social feelings of the users for their owned artificial tools and environments.

3.2. Methodical Invisibility and Visibility

The assumptions of the makers are embedded at forehand in the ready-made acting of the artificial product. The interpretation and representation work has been done partly before the product is ready-made and the actions of the artificial actor take place. The way an artificial actor can interpret and represent depends not only on the activity from the user but also on the ready-made acting, which is constructed.

Building social and emotional potential into artificial tools and environments does not lead to that predefined interpretation by the users. For instance in software and hardware products the "fear of doubt", in the meaning of insecurity, is embedded and transferred into the interaction worlds where they are part of. The most dominant ideas in software engineering are the production of unambiguous software with mastered complexity. Based on these same ideas of controlling complexity and reducing ambiguity within software, software engineers master the complexity and ambiguity of the real world. Abstraction activities, a fundament of most modeling methods, such as generalization, classification, specialization, division and separation, are seen as unavoidable to project dynamic world processes into ready-to-hand modeling structures and producing ready-made acting.

ICT professionals are mostly not designing but using established methods and theories. They focus on security, non-ambiguity and are afraid of the complex and the unpredictable. This methodical invisibility of the representation of ready-made interaction is based on the planned cooperation between software and hardware. It could close the design options of users; design activities in the frame of the pre-given understanding. By the use of expert languages and methods within the closed interaction world of makers, the dominance of design over use, is established.

This dominance discloses and mostly prevents the act of discovery of the users by the designer and acts of discovery on the part of the users. Design is focused on generalized and classified users. Users are turned into resources that can be used by makers in the process of making IT-products. Users do not have room for starting their own designing processes. Those who do not fit in regimen classes are seen as dissidents. A design process of the users is necessary for imbedding the artificial product in their social environment and developing an emotional relation with the product.

Although pre-given meanings of designers are not the final meanings. These methodical invisibilities have on the contrary the potential to create doubt and fear this could be the starting process of changing the meaning of the ready-made interaction. Users are the experts to escape out of rigid planned interaction; they determine usability in their interaction world. In that way methodical invisibility can be lead to "playful exploration and engagement" (Sengers, 2005).

However is this change of meaning still possible? Users are sliding into a state, where they become afraid of changing their habits because this could disturb the surrounding pre-planned so called intelligent acting. Our society is forcing us using specific artificial tools and environments, because a lot of other tools and environments have disappeared; they did not fit in the digital lifestyle of our society. Are we still allowed to have doubt and is doubt not becoming the intruder, which hinders us to exploit the opportunities, which are not intended by the designers. It is still true that tools challenge us to interact with our environments; challenging us to exploit opportunities? Are we still in the position to create an interactive environment if we are not skilled computer scientists?

These questions indicate, that it is becoming more and more impossible to overcome the methodical invisibility, imbedded in the tools, and create interactive solutions that are technically possible (Svanæs, 1999, p. 15). This methodical invisibility shapes and limits the interaction spaces in which users can design and irrevocable will make solutions unimaginable in spite of the makeability of it. This is even more true as this methodical invisibility is a mental invisibility on behalf of the makers of artificial products. The makers are frozen in the structures of modeling methods that are embedded in their software developing tools. They love these structures because it gives them euphoric feelings of makeability in their design.

3.3. Physical Invisibility and Visibility

Many distributed devices are hidden in our environment. A continuous process of miniaturization of mechatronic systems and components will it make impossible to recognize them. Not feeling their presence, not seeing their full (inter-)action options, but only some designer-intended fractional output, makes it impossible to understand the complete arsenal of their possible representations. The embedding of Ambient Intelligence in daily aesthetic objects or in the trusted normal house infrastructure is like a wolf in sheep's clothing, pretending that this technology is harmless. It creates: "... an invisible and comprehensive surveillance network, covering an unprecedented part of our public and private life ..." (Bohn et al., 2001). "The old sayings that 'the walls have ears' and 'if these walls could talk' have become the disturbing reality. The world is filled with all-knowing, all-reporting things." (Lucky, 1999).

According to Schmidt, the relationship to computer systems will change from "explicit interaction that requires always a kind of dialog between the user and a particular system or computer, ... to implicit interaction." (Schmidt, 2005, p. 162, p. 166). Implicit interaction is not a symmetrical dialog. Currently we can still avoid and leave this implicit technical environment. However the growing acceptance of not sensible intelligence is a process of a collective force that is mostly independent of our free will.

Physical disappearance of computers results in our whole surrounding being a potential computer interface. Our physical body representations and movements might be unconsciously the cause of actions and interactions in our technological environment. Technology resides in the periphery of our attention; actors continuously whispering in our background, observing our daily behaviour. People become the objects of the ongoing conversations of artificial agents that are providing us with services, without demanding a conscious effort on our behalf or without involving us in their interactivities.

The assumption that physical invisibility will irrevocable lead to mental invisibility is a stubborn misunderstanding. Not seeing this technology could be counterproductive; humans could get used to the effects of physical invisible technology, but at the moment the tool acts outside the range of our expectations, it then will just frighten us because we cannot control it. Petersen thinks that the technology should reveal at least what the system has to offer in order to motivate users to relate the possibilities of the technology to their actual needs, dreams and wishes. "For this purpose, domestic technologies should be remarkable rather than unremarkable." (Petersen, 2004, p. 1446). However on the other hand the acceptance of physical invisibility is mostly the outcome of a long process of little changes; the changes have become mentally invisible. Through the many interactions with actable technology rules and structures have arisen under the influence of the automation, without interpreting these structures and rules as a product of automation anymore.

Wagner calls this "disembedding"; space is separated from place and social relations, lifted out from local contexts. Social interaction is transformed into systemic relations. The involvement of artificial tools implies that the individual and collective interactions are dissociated from what can be "communicated, clarified and negotiable" (Wagner, 1994, pp. 24-26).

In our trust building towards tools we are forced to interact with unknown human and artificial actors. Physical invisibility is the alibi for the acceptance of mental and methodical invisibility.

4. FUTURE TRENDS

"Doubt can only arise if humans can build instruments of vision" (Crutzen, 2006)

4.1. Socializing in Critical Transformative Bubbles

There is still a trend for modeling methods that obligate a search for the similarities of human actors, situations, processes and events, ignoring their differences. Differences, which are not easy to handle, or are not relevant in the view of the designer and modeler will be neglected and suppressed. According to Susan Leigh Star, in the making and modeling process of our technological environments, there will be a "tempering of the clutter of the visible" by the creation of invisibles: "Abstractions that will stand quietly, cleanly and docilely for the noisome, messy actions and materials. ... Work is the link between the visible and the invisible. Visibles are not automatically organized in pre-given abstractions. Someone does the ordering, someone living in a visible world." (Star, 1991). In her opinion it is not always necessary to "restore the visible", because by remembering the modeling process you can always make the invisibles visible again.

But not every working process, its representation or conception has the property of reversibility. In most cases of technology adaptation, restoring the past is impossible. So the modeling process should be a working process for the users because without that experience they cannot refer to what was visible. To create intelligent environments a revaluation of differences is needed. Coyne says that difference reveals further difference; it facilitates a "limitless discovery" in contrast of the identification of sameness that closes off discussion (Coyne, 1995, p. 195). That discussion should proceed in the exploration of the intelligent environment, as a discussion between the providers and the users and between the artificial actors and the users. In that discussion intertwining Use and Design is necessary for the creation of critical transformative rooms, in which the visible can change. Acts of doubt in a critical consumer's approach envision several paradigms and critical strategies, concepts and realizations, that can be fantasized and eventually realized.

According to Marx not only physical borders such as walls and clothing will lose their function of separation but also social, spatial, temporal and cultural borders will disappear and be replaced by intelligent and autonomous input and output devices. Our environment will lose its otherness and as a whole will tend to become almost entirely "us" rather than the "other" (Marx, 2001; Bohn, 2001; Araya, 1995). We will allow artificial agents to understand us with their built-in classifications and separations. In that process we will lose the otherness between ourselves and other humans. The "other human" will disappear and humans will just look into their instantiations of an artificial "myFace", into their shadows in a mainstreamed "us", specialized by their body and behaviour data.

The veiling of the "human other" in connection with Ambient Intelligence's attraction of comfort and easiness, tempts us to converging into our artificial surrogate "ourselves". In this interaction process we lose "the other" as source for doubting our acting. The Ambient Intelligence technology will absorb people. According to Cohen the link between "intelligibility and sensibility" of humans is "the one-for-the-other, the I suffering for the suffering of the other, of moral sensibility. ... Computers, in a word, are by themselves incapable of putting themselves into one another's shoes, incapable of inter-subject substitution, of the caring for one another which is at the core of ethics, and as such at the root of the very humanity of the human." (Cohen, 2000, p. 33).

A constructive approach to avoid too much veiling is the socialization of individuals and communities in critical transformative bubbles. A model for "informational immune spaces" with two-sided conditional borders is developed in the "bubbles" concept of Beslay and Hakala; this facilitates the management of an appropriate informational distance from other humans and from non-human ambient intelligent actors. "A

bubble is a temporary defined space that can be used to limit the information coming into and leaving the bubble in the digital domain. ... A bubble can be created whenever it is necessary for personal, community or global use. The bubbles can be shared between individuals or groups." According to Beslay and Hakala, this model should be integrated with an identification tags model (Beslay, 2005).

Sloterdijk suggests, that in general "immune systems" will become an outstanding technological topic in a world, "where integrity can no longer be thought of as something being secured by worshipping a merciful concealment, but only as the achievement of an organism, taking care for its demarcation from its environment. ... that life preserves its existence, not primarily by taking part, but stabilizes itself more likely by exclusion and selectively refusing cooperation." Sloterdijk names such a technology driven by the "self domestication of humans" (Sloterdijk, 2002, pp. 109-110) and, according to Mewes, this is not necessarily a bad thing: "But ICT is definitely not the empowerment of mankind that it is often taken for. On the contrary, taken as an anthropotechnology it is restrictive. Even today the active badges and self writing appointment diaries that offer all kinds of convenience could be a source of real harm in the wrong hands. Not only corporate superiors or underlings but also overzealous government officials and even marketing firms could make unpleasant use of the same information that makes invisible computers so convenient." (Mewes, 2002)

From the viewpoint of Sloterdijk, the bubbles concept is a chance for survival of the human individual, for instance in an environment where the availability of inhaleable air is not obvious anymore. Technically we could create spheres in which critical interaction of people is still possible. However these bubbles could destroy our "being-in-the-world" (Dasein) as "being-together-with-others" (Heidegger, 1926, §63). Bubbles can be seen as safe places to share views and experiences, but the boundaries of bubbles will easily lead to marginalization and isolation, too. Technical devices such as location-based services, radio frequency identification tags, body implants, ambient intelligence sensors cannot be confidential agents that will build and maintain the bubble-leaks between the individual and other actors, between the digital and the physical world (Beslay & Hakala, 2005). A bubble approach is only feasible if access to bubbles and acting in bubbles can be at least partially determined by the bubble inhabitant, whether an individual or an organization.

So more and more the critical transformative rooms between providers installing artificial systems for robotic and informational services and the customers/inhabitants using these services have to become explicit. One driving force is the inclusion of legal aspects into the software: Digital Rights Management (DRM). The other force is the growing emotional awareness of people about their "Human Right of Informational Self-Determination" (Rouvroy, 2008).

4.2. Emotions and Ambient Stupidity

The struggle of designers, which position they will choose in the scale between the mental visibility and invisibility will continue. Schmidt argues for the possibility of choice between implicit and explicit interfacing: "The human actor should know ... why the system has reacted as it reacted." (Schmidt 2005). Future users will prefer an easiness of use that gives them feelings of relaxation and comfort. However these feelings can be turn over in feelings of discomfort when users discover that they have lost the possibility of change.

So there will be a trend to produce more "calm technology" (Weiser 1995) that fits without conflicts into our environment; it should calm our lives by removing annoyances. Calm Technologies "are designed to reside in the periphery of our attention, continuously providing us with contextual

information without demanding a conscious effort on our behalf".

Hallnäs thinks that we need also technology, which actively promotes moments of reflection and mental rest in a more and more rapidly changing environment, as opposition to this calm technology. This "slow technology", will give humans the opportunity to learn how it works, to understand why it works, the way it works, to apply it, to see what it is, to find out the consequences of using it (Hallnäs, 2001, pp. 202-203). This slow technology gives humans a period for explicit adaptation of the technology, but the goal is still creating mental invisibility by the users at the end of the adaptation.

Artificial intelligent tools and environments do not have emotions, they simulate emotionality. There have been various attempts to include the expression of "simulated" emotions into screen-based human computer dialogues, the most popular are the so called "avatars". This technique until now seems to be stuck at an experimental level and a latter user acceptance is not assured. Situation dependent high quality realtime speech synthesis, comparable to the voice of HAL 9000 (Kubrick, 1968), is not ready, especially for languages other than English.

With the mostly invisible artificial intelligent tools and environments, modeling the "emotional context of use" becomes crucial in the design. There is a fundamental and unsolvable dilemma between making a user feel "in-security" and making a user feel "in-control" at the same time. This dilemma has to be accepted for the future, not tabooed as in the past. In the process of a critical domestication of Ambient Intelligence technology, users will feel not only the comfort of being permanently cared for, but also the pain of giving away intimacy.

Designers and researchers feel this pain, too, but they compensate for this by the hard to beat satisfaction of building a technology. The core of their emotional attraction to this lies in "I can make it", "It is possible" and "It works". It is the technically possible and makeable that always gets the upper hand. "Who wants to belong to the non-designers?" (Sloterdijk, 2001, p. 357).

So the users should feel a danger to intimacy, but in feeling it they should not be clueless. A critical transformative room that stands between a consumer and an Ambient Intelligence must include a diversity of options to influence the behaviour, usability and design of the technology. The on-off-switch is just the primitive end of a rich spectrum of needed intervention tools. Nowadays consumers sometimes have the opportunity to express situational emotions in "ratings". It is a start. Why not enable emotional user expressions which "really change the system behaviour" at the operation system or application system levels?

Can an Ambient Intelligence offer its inhabitants a critical room of diversity between privacy and security, between the invisible and the visible? Is it possible to create an awareness of the designers and the consumers that doubt is necessary to keep it unveiled, that the benefits of Ambient Intelligence will change the social meaning of privacy? "... the big challenge in a future world of Ambient Intelligence will be not to harm this diversity, which is at the core of an open society." (Friedewald, 2006).

Openness can only be of value, if the individual and the society are able to create borders. Doubt is a necessity to start redesigning borders and openings. Ambient Intelligence technology can only be "reliable" if consumers could "sense" more how the invisible is constructed. The Information Society can only be reliable if it is capable to construct, connect and nourish rooms where doubting the promises of artificial intelligent tools and environments is a habit. Being aware of the redesign of borders is a necessary act for creating diversity in critical transformative rooms—where individuals and society can choose how the invisible and visible interacts, where they can change their status, where invisibility could be unveiled and deconstructed.

4.3. Secrets and Lies and Trust and Spies

Ethical aspects of technology are always person-dependent, culture-dependent and situation-dependent (Friedewald, 2006). People, culture and situations will change under the influence of artificial intelligent tools and environments. In the ethics discussion, accompanying this process, privacy, identity and security will move into the foreground. Valuable topics, because in any computer application privacy and security are in danger to be violated. However in the process of using Ambient Intelligence, it will go beyond these topics.

If the infiltration of our daily live with sensing, computing, transmitting and acting hardware continues, then the relation between humans and artificial intelligent tools and environment will change drastically. New meanings of "home", "intimacy", "privacy", "identity" and "safety" will be constructed because the "visible" acting of people will be preceded, accompanied and followed with the invisible and visible acting of the artificial intelligent tools and environments and their providers: "In an online mode, the user is (sometimes) conscious of the need to make a deliberate decision with regard to appropriate levels of privacy and security. Such will not necessarily (or even likely) be the case in the instance of Ambient Intelligence. Indeed, an individual may not even be aware that he is in a space embedded with AmI. While there are important differences between the cyber world accessed via the fingertips and the hands-free AmI world, some of the work done with regard to online privacy, security, identity, etc. will also be relevant to AmI researchers, regulatory authorities and policy-makers." (Friedewald, 2006).

Success and convenience of Ambient Intelligence, not their failure, will be the danger of this technology (Jonas, 1987, p. 44). The benefits of this technology will force for instance the demand of privacy in the user's background. It is for people not pleasant, to permanently monitor the output flow of personal data. This would diminish the feeling of comfort that Ambient Intelligence is supposed to deliver.

Ambient Intelligence could blow up the fragile balance between privacy and security; become an opposition in which security will be blocking out privacy. People will lose their ability to handle the world without the digital surrogates of themselves, constructed in an ongoing inexorable process of demanding preconditions for acting, embedded in a network of artificial agents who will mediate their interactions.

Even if humans will stay competent enough to control their private lives: Who will be in control of the artificial intelligent tools and environments in public spaces? Who will have the competence and might to switch a button there? The actual trend to promote the goodness and godliness of Ambient Intelligence, makes invisible that the ICT producers and providers have not abandoned their overvaluation of objectivity, hierarchical structures and predetermined actions; preferences which ignore the beauty of ambiguity and spontaneous action and users' claims for choosing and coupling their own support tools. They have only veiled their preferences and demand blind trust into their installations.

But the first generation of interactive digital mass media and mass communication users already made their bad experiences. There also is a growing user awareness that "the provider is watching you". Trust is not freely given anymore. It is recognized that medial, body and behavior data access, granted for a certain purpose, tends to be used for unwanted purposes, after an infrastructure is irreversibly established. New governments may change laws anytime. Providers shift data globally to lawless places. Users' are swindled out of the data wealth in their PCs, their treasures are stored away in remote servers. A new digital divide opens, of those who learned the lesson and can use most of their applications and data, if Internet is down – and those who can not.

There are various trends to impersonate the Ambient Intelligence into screen-based humanoids, equipped with expression of "simulated" emotions and empathy, and into "social and huggable" love-returning pet robots. The visible fluffy cover will make the machine character of the Ambient Intelligence invisible.

The differences between the human and the artificial are even made invisible in scientific and promotional papers by writing only of "actors" or "agents", not making explicit, whether an artificial agent, a human actor, or an embedded model of a human actor is meant.

Under the surface of all this artificial camouflage the mental invisibility of the designers is hidden. Users confronted with childish artificial actors are forced to jump back to emotional shadows of past experiences that will overshadow their own mental visibility. But a system can not lie forever to a user, and once he looks behind the veiling, he will lose trust forever.

4.4. Visibility Management

Physical invisibility is not a trend anymore, it exits already in the many devices which are hidden in our environment. "If systems are invisible, they cannot give assistance and references to the necessary interaction behaviour to the user. Invisible systems are hard to avoid because usability problems can not be solved. Where nothing is visible, also nothing can be created." (Hornecker, 2004).

Physical invisibility can cause mental invisibility based on despair. Humans can only hope that the invisible technology will not harm them in an irreparable and irreversible way. Intelligent cameras will follow body movements. Sensors remotely will catch our physical and emotional data and analyze it using implemented models that will remark our differences to what has been predefined as "normal" status and normal "behaviour".

This physical invisibility will be more and more enhanced based on arguments of fear. The visible functionality of already existent visible technology will be extended with invisible functionalities. Using a mobile phone means that it is traceable, where the user of the mobile was.

Users ask for transparency of what data is collected and how it will be used. Transparency and trust tools might be made compulsory by law to force data collectors to describe their collection policies and be controlled by governmental trustful institutions. These tools increase the "trust in a transaction or data exchange, by providing additional background information about the transfer, its conditions, and the parties involved". They "link directly into our previously identified social mechanism of trust, as they can provide assurances upon which users can make trust decisions due to incomplete knowledge about their interaction partner." Transparency tools cannot "prevent the abuse of personal data through malicious parties, but can help respectable collectors of our personal data to use our information in accordance with the preferences and limitations that are given by the subjects of the datacollection." (Langheinrich, 2005)

Without transparency humans will be without rights. However the invisibility of the datacollection in Ambient Intelligence is not a mistake but intentional – therefore there will be no correction efforts. It will be a trend to develop new concepts of transparency. The requirement for transparency in high complex intelligent environments and the many, divergent different aims and events of datacollection cannot take place without overstraining the subject from which the data are collected. This stress will lead to inadequate wishes for mental invisibility. Roßnagel recommends a built-in technology that automatically recognizes, identifies and memorizes a data access. Only the cases for which the subject did not give permission or in which the given limitations are overruled, should be reported (Roßnagel, 2007).

Transparency of the datacollection layer will not provide a visibility of the hidden intelligent environment in which human live, but it will enhance our mental visibility towards the intelligent environment. The visibility management of a system should be under user control. This calls for popular approaches of system functionality documentation and for software-coached preference setting.

A promising architectural approach towards mental visibility is the concept of a "gadget world". People configure use and aggregate complex collections of interacting artefacts. The everyday environment is a collection of objects with which people can associate in ad-hoc dynamic ways. In this approach more complex artefact behaviour can emerge from interactions among more elementary artefacts. According to Mavrommati this approach can scale both "upwards" (towards the assembly of more complex objects, i.e. from objects to rooms, up to buildings, cities and so on) and "downwards" (towards the decomposition of given gadgets into smaller parts, i.e. towards the concept of "smart dust"). In taking this approach people are active shapers of their environment, not simple consumers of technology (Mavrommati, 2002). This approach needs more efforts of designers in making the interoperability and connectivity of the intelligent artefacts visible and easy-to-design. These construction and deconstruction possibilities should appeal to the creativity of humans.

"Palpable computing" is an approach, based on the European funded Open Source project PalCom (PalCom 2008). Palpable computing "... envisions ubiquitous technologies that are designed to support people in making their actual and potential activities and affordances clearly available to their senses. Palpable systems support people in understanding what is going on at a level they choose and they support the user's control and choice. ... Palpable computing aims at supporting user control by composing and decomposing assemblies of devices and services.

The assemblies are configurable by the user depending on the context of use. Consequently, these assembled systems should support the continuous attribution and negotiation of meaning through interaction." (website). The PalCom project therefore developed an system architecture with software modules having the explicit "qualities": Resource Awareness, Assemblability, Inspectability, Adaptability, Resilience, Experimentability, Multiplicity. Using these modules users should be able to design personalized services coping with the "challenges": Construction/Deconstruction, Visibility/Invisibility, Change/Stability, Understandability/Scalability, Heterogeneity/Coherence, Autonomy/User-Control (PalCom, 2007).

5. CONCLUSION

Interaction worlds are not without conflict. There are a lot of encoding and decoding processes going on in the course of time because human and artificial actors are historically involved in many different interaction worlds. Translations and replacements of artificial devices do not need to fit smoothly into the interaction world for which they are made ready. A closed readiness is an ideal, which is not feasible because in the interaction situation the acting itself is ad-hoc and therefore cannot be predicted.

According to Jaques Derrida (Haegen, 1989) the meaning of what is "represented" depends on – and is influenced in the process of representation – by what is "not represented". Each representation is always one pole of a duality where the "not represented" is the other pole. Although there is an absence of this other pole in form and structure, the absent always is nevertheless present by means of this binary opposition.

When designing artificial intelligent tools and environments, purposefully enabling doubt is a pretentious and delicate action. It could lead to despair and fear of a continuous process of doubting, a frozenness of not acting. It could lead to

"obstinate" tools which will become obstacles to actability. Creating and supporting environments which are Critical Transformative Rooms means to balance the actual interaction between "frozenness of the established acting" and "facing too much insecurity".

Technology can only be "reliable" if we could "sense" appropriately, how the invisible is constructed. Being aware of the continuous redesign of borders is a necessary act for creating diversity in interaction worlds – where people and society can choose how the invisible and the visible interact, where they can change status, where some invisibility could be deconstructed. Only in this type of artificial environment we in the future can develop emotionality and social interactivity.

6. REFERENCES

Araya, Agustln A. (1995). Questioning ubiquitous computing. In *Proceedings of the ACM 23rd Annual Conference on Computer Science*. ACM Press.

Beslay, L., & Hakala, H. (2005). Digital territory: Bubbles. In P.T Kidd (Ed.), European visions for the knowledge age – A quest for new horizons in the information society. Retrieved from, http://cybersecurity.jrc.es/docs/DigitalTerritoryBubbles.pdf

Beyer, H., & Holtzblatt, K. (1993). Making customer-centered design work for teams. *Communications of the ACM, 36*(10), 92-103.

Bødker, S., & Greenbaum, J. (1993). Design of information systems: Things versus people. In E. Green, J. Owen, & D. Pain (Eds.), *Gendered by design? Information technology and office systems* (pp. 53-63). London: Taylor & Francis.

Bødker, S., Ehn, P., Sjögren, D., & Sundblad, Y. (2000, October). Co-operative Design – perspectives on 20 years with "the Scandinavian IT Design Model". In *Proceedings of NordiCHI 2000*.

Report number CID-104. Stockholm, Sweden: Royal Institute of Technology, Centre for User Oriented IT Design. Retrieved from, http://cid.nada.kth.se/pdf/cid_104.pdf

Bødker, S. (2006). When second wave HCI meets third wave challenges. In *Proceedings of the 4th Nordic conference on Human-computer interaction: changing roles* (pp. 1-8). Oslo, Norway.

Bohn, J., Coroamă, V., Langheinrich, M., Mattern, F. & Rohs, M. (2001). *Ethics and Information Technology, 3*, 157-169. Retrieved from, http://www.vs.inf.ethz.ch/publ/papers/socialambient.pdf

Capurro, R. (1992). Informatics and hermeneutics. In C. Floyd, H. Züllighoven, R. Budde, & R. Keil-Slawik (Eds.), *Proceedings of Software Development and Reality Construction (September 1988)* (pp. 363-375). Heidelberg, Germany: Springer-Verlag.

Chalmers, M. (2004a). Coupling and heterogeneity in ubiquitous computing. In *Reflective HCI – Towards a Critical Technical Practice (CHI Workshop)*. Retrieved from, http://www.dcs.gla.ac.uk/~matthew/papers/ReflectiveHCI2004.pdf

Chalmers, M. (2004b). *A historical view of context. Computer supported cooperative work, 13*(3-4), 223-247. Retrieved from, http://www.equator.ac.uk/var/uploads/M.Chalmers2004.pdf

Clement, A. & Van den Besselaar, P. (1993, June). A retrospective look at PD projects. *Communications of the ACM, 36*(6), 29-37.

Cohen, R. A. (2000). Ethics and cybernetics: Levinasian reflections. *Ethics and Information Technology, 2*, 27-35.

Coyne, R. (1995). *Designing information technology in the postmodern age: From method to metaphor*. Cambridge: MIT Press..

Crutzen, C. K. M. (2000). *Interactie, een wereld van verschillen. Een visie op informatica vanuit genderstudies* (p. 417). Dissertation, Open University of the Netherlands. Retrieved from, http://www.cecile-crutzen.de/Downloads/2000-Dissertatie-Interactie-een-wereld-van-verschillen.pdf

Crutzen, C. K. M., & Hein, H.-W.(2001). Die bedenkliche Dienlichkeit und Sicherheit von Softwaresystemen und die erlebte Verläßlichkeit. 31. Jahrestagung der Gesellschaft für Informatik/ Österreichische Computer Gesellschaft Jahrestagung 2001, Wien, Workshop "Erkenntnistheorie - Semiotik - Ontologie: Die Bedeutung philosophischer Disziplinen für die Softwaretechnik". In K. Bauknecht, W. Brauer, & T. Mück. (Eds.), *Informatik 2001. Wirtschaft und Wissenschaft in der Network Economy – Visionen und Wirklichkeit, Band II.* (pp. 782-787). Wien, Österreichische Computer Gesellschaft.

Crutzen C. K. M. (2006, December). Invisibility and the meaning of ambient intelligence. *International Review of Information Ethics, 6*, 52-62. Retrieved from, http://www.i-r-i-e.net/inhalt/006/006_Crutzen.pdf

Crutzen, C. K. M., Kotkamp, E. (2006a). Questioning gender, deconstruction and doubt. In E. Trauth (Ed.), *Encyclopedia of gender and information technology*. Hershey, PA: Information Science Reference.

Crutzen, C. K. M., & Kotkamp, E. (2006b). Questioning gender, transformative critical rooms. In E. Trauth (Ed.), *Encyclopedia of gender and information technology*. Hershey, PA: Information Science Reference.

Crutzen, C. K. M. (2007). Ambient intelligence between heaven and hell: A transformative critical room? In I. Zorn, S. Maass, E. Rommes, C. Schirmer, & H. Schelhowe (Eds.), *Gender designs it – Construction and deconstruction of information society technology* (pp. 65-78). Wiesbaden, Germany: VS Verlag für Sozialwissenschaften.

Dewey, J. (1916). Education as growth. In *Democracy and education*. Retrieved from, http://www.ilt.columbia.edu/publications/dewey.html

Ehn, P. (1993). Scandinavian design: On participation and skill. In D. Schuler, & A. Namioka (Eds.), *Participatory design – Principles and practices* (pp. 41-78). Lawrence Erlbaum Associates.

Feenberg A. (1996). *Summary remarks on my approach to the philosophical study of technology.* Retrieved from, http://www-rohan.sdsu.edu/faculty/feenberg/Method1.htm

Floyd, C., Mehl, W., Reisen, F., Schmidt, G., & Wolf, G. (1989). Out of Scandinavia: Alternative approaches to software design and system development. *Human-Computer Interaction 4,* 253-350.

Friedewald, M., & Da Costa, O. (2003). *Science and technology roadmapping: Ambient intelligence in everyday life (Aml@Life). JRC/IPTS - ESTO Study,* July 2003. Retrieved from, http://forera.jrc.ec.europa.eu/documents/SandT_roadmapping.pdf

Friedewald, M., Vildjiounaite, E., & Wright, D. (Eds.) (2006). The brave new world of ambient intelligence: An analysis of scenarios regarding privacy, identity and security issues. In Security in Pervasive Computing, Lecture Notes in Computer Science 3934. Berlin: Springer-Verlag, pp. 119-133.

Gibson, J. (1977). The theory of affordances. In R.E. Shaw, & J. Bransford (Eds.), *Perceiving, acting, and knowing: Toward an ecological psychology* (pp. 67-82). Hillsdale, NJ: Lawrence Erlbaum Associates.

Gibson, J. (1979). The ecological approach to visual perception. Boston, MA: Houghton Mifflin Company.

Gibson, J. (1982). The theory of affordances and the design of the environment. In E. Reed, & R. Jones (Eds.), *Reasons for realism: Selected essays of James J. Gibson* (pp. 413-416). Hillsdale, NJ: Lawrence Erlbaum Associates.

Greenbaum, J. (1991). Toward participatory design: The head and the heart revisited. In *IFIP TC9/WG 9.1 Conference on Women, Work and Computerization,* Helsinki, Finland; Amsterdam, The Netherlands: Elsevier Science Publishers.

Haegen, Rina Van der (1989). *In het spoor van seksuele differentie* (p. 104). Nijmegen, The Nederlands: Sun.

Heidegger, M. (1926). Sein und Zeit. Used edition: Tübingen, Germany, Max Niemeyer Verlag, 17. Auflage, 1993.

Heidegger, M. (1936). Der Ursprung des Kunstwerkes. Used edition: Stuttgart, Germany, Philipp Reclam jun., 1960.

Heidegger, M. (1962). Die Technik und die Kehre. Stuttgart, Germany: Günther Neske Verlag.

Hein, H.-W. (1999). Big Brother is scanning you. *Spektrum der Wissenschaft, 3,* 106-108.

Hallnäs, L., & Redström, J. (2001). Slow technology – Designing for reflection. Personal *and Ubiquitous Computing, 5,* 201-212.

Hornecker, E. (2004). Tangible user interfaces als kooperationsunterstützendes medium. Dissertation Fachbereich Mathematik & Informatik, Universität Bremen. Retrieved from, http://deposit.ddb.de/cgi-bin/dokserv?idn=975431153

ISTAG (1999). Orientations for Workprogramme 2000 and beyond. *European Communities.* Retrieved from, ftp://ftp.cordis.europa.eu/pub/ist/docs/istag-99-final.pdf

ISTAG (2001). IST2001: Technologies serving people. Four parts. *European Communities.* Retreived from, http://cordis.europa.eu/ist/library.htm

Iversen, O.S., Kanstrup, A.M., & Petersen, M.G. (2004). A visit to the "new Utopia": Revitalizing democracy, emancipation and quality in co-operative design. In *Proceedings of the Third Nordic*

Conference on Human-Computer Interaction (pp. 171-179).

Jain, A.K., & Ross, A. (2004). Multibiometric systems. *Communications of the ACM, 47*(1), 34-44.

Jonas, H. (1987). *Technik, Medizin und Ethik.* Frankfurt am Main: Insel Verlag.

Kostakos, V., O'Neill, E. (2004). Pervasive computing in emergency situations. In *Proceedings of the Thirty-Seventh Annual Hawaii International Conference on System Sciences, January 5-8, 2004,* Computer Society Press.

Kubrick, S. (1968). *2001: A Space Odyssey* (movie).

Li, L. (1999). *Action theory and cognitive psychology in industrial design: User models and user interfaces.* Dissertation. Braunschweig, Germany: Hochschule für Bildende Künste. Retrieved from, http://www.hbk-bs.de/bibliothek/ediss/data/19990630a

Lucky, R. (1999, March). Connections – Everything will be connected to everything else. *IEEE Spectrum Reflections Column.* Retrieved from, http://www.argreenhouse.com/papers/rlucky/spectrum/connect.shtml

Marx, G. T. (2001). Murky conceptual waters: The public and the private. *Journal Ethics and Information Technology, 3*(3).

Langheinrich, M. (2005). Personal privacy in ubiquitous computing tools and system support. Dissertation of the Swiss Federal Institute of Technology, Zürich. Retrieved from, http://www.vs.inf.ethz.ch/publ/papers/langheinrich-phd-2005.pdf

Mavrommati, I. (2002). e-Gadgets case description. In *Doors of Perception 7: Flow.* Retrieved from, http://flow.doorsofperception.com/content/mavrommati_trans.html

Mewes, F. (2002). Regulations for the human park: On Peter Sloterdijk's Regeln für den Men-

schenpark. *Gnosis,* 6(1). Retrieved from, http://artsandscience.concordia.ca/philosophy/gnosis/vol_vi/Sloterdijk.pdf

Mynatt, E. D., Rowan, J., Craighill, S., & Jacobs, A. (2001) Digital family portraits: Providing peace of mind for extended family members. In *Proceedings of the ACM Conference on Human Factors in Computing Systems (CHI 2001)* (pp. 333-340). Seattle, Washington: ACM Press.

Norman, D. (1988). The psychology of everyday things. New York: Basic Books Inc.

Norman, D. (1998). *The invisible computer: Why good products can fail, the personal computer is so complex, and information appliances are the solution.* Cambridge, MA: MIT Press.

Norman, D. (2005). Human-centered design considered harmful. *ACM SIGCHI Interactions 12*(4), 14-19.

Oulasvirta, A., & Salovaara, A. (2004). A cognitive meta-analysis of design approaches to interruptions in intelligent environments. In *Proceedings of CHI 2004, Late Breaking Results* (pp.1155-1158). Vienna, Austria. Retrieved from, http://www.hiit.fi/~asalovaa/articles/oulasvirta-chi2004-p1155.pdf

Oviatt, S., Darrell, T., & Flickner, M. (Eds.) (2004). Multimodal interfaces that flex, adapt, and persist. *Communications of the ACM, 47*(1), 30-33.

PalCom (2007). Palpable computing: A new perspective on ambient computing. *Deliverable, 54*(2.2.3) Open Architecture. Retrieved from, http://www.ist-palcom.org/publications/

PalCom (2008). Retrieved from, http://www.ist-palcom.org/

Peirce, C. S. (1877, November). The fixation of belief. *Popular Science Monthly, 12,* 1-15.

Petersen, M.G. (2004). Remarkable computing – the challenge of designing for the home. *CHI,* 1445-1448.

Philips Research (2003). 365 days – Ambient Intelligence research in HomeLab. www.research. philips.com/technologies/misc/homelab/downloads/homelab_365.pdf

Piva, S., Singh, R., Gandetto M., & Regazzoni, C. S. (2005). A Context-based Ambient Intelligence Architecture. In P. Remagnino, G.L. Foresti, & T. Ellis (Eds.), *Ambient intelligence: A novel paradigm* (pp. 63-87). New York: Springer.

Punie, Y. (2003). *A social and technological view of ambient intelligence in everyday life: What bends the trend?* The European Media and Technology in Everyday Life Network, 2000-2003, Institute for Prospective Technological Studies, Directorate General Joint Research Centre, European Commission. Retrieved from, http://www.lse.ac.uk/collections/EMTEL/reports/punie_2003_emtel.pdf

Raskin, J. (2000). The humane interface. Reading, MA: Addison-Wesley.

Roßnagel, A. (2007). Datenschutz in einem informatisierten Alltag. Friedrich-Ebert-Stiftung, Berlin. Retrieved from, http://library.fes.de/pdf-files/stabsabteilung/04548.pdf

Rouvroy, A., Poullet, Y. (in press). The right to informational self-determination and the value of self-development – Reassessing the importance of privacy for democracy. In *Reinventing Data Protection, Proceedings of the International Conference (Brussels, 12-13 October 2007).* Springer. Retrieved from, http://works.bepress.com/antoinette_rouvroy/7

Saffo, P. (1996). The consumer spectrum. In T. Winograd (Ed.), *Bringing design to software* (pp. 87-99). Reading, MA: Addison-Wesley.

Scheman, N. (1993). *Engenderings: Constructions of knowledge, authority, and privilege.* New York: Routledge.

Schmidt, A. (2005). Interactive context-aware systems interacting with ambient intelligence.

In G. Riva, F. Vatalaro, F. Davide, & M. Alcañiz (Eds.), *Ambient intelligence* (Part 3, pp. 159-178). IOS Press. Retrieved from, http://www.emergingcommunication.com/volume6.html

Sengers, P., & Gaver, B. (2005, July). Designing for interpretation. In *Proceedings of the HCI International.* Las Vegas, Nevada.

Sloterdijk, P. (2001). Kränkung durch Maschinen. In P. Sloterdijk (Ed.), *Nicht gerettet, Versuche nach Heidegger* (pp. 338-366). Frankfurt am Main: Suhrkamp Verlag.

Sloterdijk, P. (2002). *Luftbeben – An den Quellen des Terrors.* Frankfurt am Main: Suhrkamp Verlag.

Spinuzzi, Clay (2002). A Scandinavian challenge, a US response: Methodological assumptions in Scandinavian and US prototyping approaches. In *Proceedings of the 20th annual international conference on Computer Documentation* (pp. 208-215).

Star, Susan Leigh (1991). Invisible work und silenced dialogues in knowledge representation. In I.V. Eriksson, B.A. Kitchenham, & K.G. Tijdens (Eds.), *Women, work and computerization: Understanding and overcoming bias in work and education* (pp. 81-92). Amsterdam: Elsevier Science Publishers.

Stephenson, N. (1992). *Snow crash.* Bantam Books

Stephenson, Neal (1995). The Diamond Age or, A Young Lady's Illustrated Primer. Bantam Books.

Suchman, L. (1994). Supporting articulation work: Aspects of a feminist practice of technology production. In A. Adam, J. Emms, E. Green, & J. Owen (1994). *Women, work and computerization. Breaking old boundaries – building new forms* (pp. 7-21). Amsterdam: Elsevier Science, pp. 7-21. Also in: R. Kling (Ed.) (1996), Computerization *and controversy. Value conflicts and social choices* (2ⁿᵈ Edition) (pp. 407-425). San Diego: Academic Press.

Svanæs, Dag (1999). *Understanding interactivity: Steps to a phenomenology of human-computer interaction*. Trondheim, Norway: Norges Teknisk-Naturvitenskapelige Universitet (NTNU). Retrieved from, http://www.idi.ntnu.no/~dags/interactivity.pdf

Thagard, P. (2004). What is doubt and when is it reasonable? In M. Ezcurdia, R. Stainton, & C. Viger (Eds.), *New essays in the philosophy of language and mind. Canadian Journal of Philosophy, Supplementary Volume 30*, 391-406. Retrieved from, http://cogsci.uwaterloo.ca/Articles/doubt.html

Turk, M. (2004). Computer vision in the interface. *Communications of the ACM, 47*(1), 60-67.

Wagner, I. (1994). Hard times. The politics of women's work in computerised environments. In A. Adam, J. Emms, E. Green, & J. Owen (Eds.), *Women, work and computerization. Breaking old boundaries – building new forms* (pp. 23-34). Amsterdam: Elsevier Science.

Wahlster, W. et al. (2004, September). Grand challenges in the evolution of the information society. *ISTAG Report*. European Communities. Retrieved from, ftp://ftp.cordis.europa.eu/pub/ist/docs/2004_grand_challenges_web_en.pdf

Weiser, M. (1991). The computer for the 21st century. *Scientific American, 265*(3), 94-104. Reprinted in *IEEE: Pervasive Computing*, January-March 2002, pp. 19-25. Retrieved from, http://www.ubiq.com/hypertext/weiser/SciAmDraft3.html

Weiser, M. (1993). Some computer science issues in ubiquitous computing. *Communications of the ACM, 36*(7), 75-84.

Weiser, M. (1994). The world is not a desktop. *ACM SIGCHI Interactions 1*(1), 7-8.

Weiser, M., Brown, J.S. (1995). Designing calm technology. In P.J. Denning & R.M. Metcalfe (Eds.) *Beyond calculation – The next fifty years of computing*. Copernicus/Springer-Verlag. Retrieved from, http://sandbox.xerox.com/hypertext/weiser/calmtech/calmtech.htm http://www.ubiq.com/hypertext/weiser/acmfuture2endnote.htm

Winograd, T. (1997). The design of interaction. In P.J. Denning, & R.M. Metcalfe (Eds.), *Beyond calculation – The next fifty years of computing* (pp. 149-161). New York: Copernicus, Springer-Verlag.

You, H-c. & Chen, K. (2006). Applications of affordance and semantics in product design. *Design Studies, 28*, 23-38.

Zimmerman, M. E. (1990). *Heidegger's confrontation with modernity. Technology, politics, art*. Bloomington, Indiana: University Press.

KEY TERMS

Ambient Intelligence: ISTAG 1999 states: "Ambient Intelligence should be the result of the convergence of three key technologies: 'Ubiquitous Computing', 'Ubiquitous Communication', and 'Intelligent User-Friendly Interfaces'. AmI is unobtrusive and often invisible, being embedded in everyday objects such as furniture, clothes, vehicles, roads and smart materials. Interaction is relaxing and enjoyable for the citizen, and does not involve a steep learning curve; otherwise stated, the dominant mode of interaction will become laid-back rather than lean-forward. The technology is all around us but almost invisible: it is everywhere and yet in our consciousness is nowhere unless we need it. The resulting landscape is embedded, personalized, adaptive, and anticipatory. People will be surrounded by intelligent and intuitive interfaces recognizing and responding to the presence of individuals. AmI is presponsive instead of being simply responsive."

Critical Transformative Room: In a Critical Transformative Room two ore more actors mutually interact about fear, doubt, change, truth and any other emotionality and sociability within an application frame. A Critical Transformative Room creates a space where the preferred interpretation of the actions of the artificial actors can be negotiated by the human actors. In a Critical Transformative Room doubt can occur as a constructive strategy and can be effective in a change of the acting itself. Creating such a room requires actors who already have a habit of causing doubt and who accept that truth always is situated.

Emotional and social: Artificial intelligent tools and environments do not have emotions, they simulate emotionality. User emotions connected with the diverse invisibilities of artificial intelligent tools and environments are "frozenness" and "despair" (see Figure 1: Critical Transformative Room "Use–Design"). "Doubt" and "trust" are the basic emotions for sociability. Making a user feel "in-security" and "in-control" at the same time, is impossible. Users might express their emotions in "situated ratings" to give feedback to artificial products and their designers.

Invisibility and Visibility: The term "invisible" includes anything, what humans cannot or can only partly cognize using their senses: hearing, seeing, touching, smelling and tasting. Making invisible is "veiling", making visible is "unveiling". The visibility of artificial actors is limited within the technical constraints of their construction. But their invisibility is unlimited.

Mental Invisibility: Artificial products are mental invisible if they are taken for granted, when they are thought of as a natural part of daily life. Their evident and continuous availability causes their disappearance in the complexity of our environment. Humans integrate the ready-made technological acting in their routine acting and accept it without reflection and emotions. Mental invisibility can be seen as precondition for the acceptance, the stabilization of use, and the domestication of technology, but it should not be the frozen final-state of human actors.

Methodological Invisibility: Methodological invisibility on the users' side is caused by the designers closing almost any options for "post-design by user". Designers focus on security, non-ambiguity and are afraid of the complex and the unpredictable in the user world. By the use of expert speak, syntax-level programming languages, and mathematically over-abstracted methods within a closed interaction world of "we-can makers", the dominance of design over use is established. Methodological invisibility on the designers' side occurs, when these ICT professionals are frequently not designing, but using established methods and theories without appropriate doubt.

Physical Invisibility: Physical invisibility of sensing, computing, transmitting and acting hardware is driven by two trends. One is the continued process of miniaturization - down to nanotechnological intelligent dust. The other is global wireless Internet access which allows such devices to be included in almost any object of everyday life.

Compilation of References

Aarts, E. (2004). Ambient Intelligence: A Multimedia Perspective. In *IEEE Multimedia* (pp. 12-19).

Abele, A. and Becker, P. (1991). *Wohlbefinden. Theorie – Empirie – Diagnostik.* Weinheim: Juventa.

Abeles, M., Bergman, H., Gat, I., Meilljson, I., Seidemann, E., Tishby, N., & Vaadia, E. (1995). Cortical activity flips among quasi-stationary states. In *Proceedings of the National Academy of Sciences of the United States of America, Vol. 92* (pp. 8616-8620).

Adi, T. (2007). A theory of semantics based on Old Arabic. In R. Gudwin and J. Queiroz (Eds.), *Semiotics and intelligent systems development* (pp. 176-209). Hershey, PA: Idea Group, Inc.

Adi, T., & Ewell, O. K. (1987). Comprehension of natural language by machine. Retrieved July 2008, from http://www.readware.com/papers/machcomp.rtf

Adi, T., & Ewell, O. K. (1987). Letter semantics in Arabic morphology. In *Proceedings of the Morphology Workshop of the 1987 Linguistic Institute Conference, Stanford, CA.* Tokyo: Stanford University Press. Retrieved July 2008, from http://www.readware.com/papers/ltr_sem.doc

Adi, T., & Ewell, O. K. (1996). Where human genius comes from. Retrieved September 10, 2008, from http://www.readware.com/papers/ls96.htm

Adi, T., Ewell, O. K., Adi, P. and Vogel, T. (2008). A new theory of cognition and software implementations in information technology. Accepted for publication in Journal of Information Technology Research (JITR). Hershey, PA: Idea Group, Inc.

Adolphs, R., Tranel, D., & Damasio, A. R. (1998). The human amygdale in social judgement. *Nature, 393*(6684), 470-474.

Aghaee, N. & Ören, T. (2003). Towards fuzzy agents with dynamic personality for human behavior simulation. *2003 Summer Computer Simulation Conference* (pp 3-10).

Ainsworth, M. D. S. (1989). Attachments beyond infancy. *American Psychologist, 44*(4), 709-716.

Alchourron, C., Gärdenfors, P., & Makinson, D. (1985). On the logic of theory change: Partial meet contraction and revision functions. *Journal of Symbolic Logic, 50,* 510-530.

Aleven, V., McLaren, B., Sewall, J., & Koedinger, K. (2006). The cognitive tutor authoring tools (CTAT): Preliminary evaluation of efficiency gains. In *Proceedings of ITS 2006.*

Alexander, J., Fabricius, W., Fleming, V., Zwahr, M., & Brown, S. (2003). The development of metacognitive causal explanations. *Learning and Individual Differences, 13,* 227-238.

Allen, C., Wallach, W., & Smith, I. (2006). Why machine ethics? *IEEE Intelligent Systems,* (pp. 12-17).

Allen, D. (2003). *Getting things done.* US: Viking Books.

Alpaydin, E. (2004). *Introduction to machine learning.* Cambridge, MA: The MIT Press.

Anderson, A. K., & Phelps, E. A. (2002). Is the human amygdale critical for the subjective experience of emotion? Evidence of intact dispositional affect in patients with amygdale lesions. *Journal of Cognitive Neuroscience, 14*(5), 709-720.

Anderson, J. R., & Lebiere, C. (1998). *The atomic components of thought.* Mahwah, NJ: Lawrence Erlbaum Associates, Inc.

Anderson, J. R., Corbett, A. T., Koedinger, K. R., & Pelletier, R. (1995). Cognitive tutors: Lessons learned. *The Journal of the Learning Sciences, 4*(2), 167-207.

Anderson, J., Boyle, C., Farrell, R., & Reiser, B. (1987). Cognitive principles in the design of computer tutors. In: P. Morris (Ed.), *Modeling cognition* (pp. 93-133). New York: John Wiley.

Anderson, J.A. (1995). *An introduction to neural networks.* Cambridge, MA: MIT Press.

Anderson, J.R. (2000). *Learning and memory: an integrated approach.* New York, NY: John Wiley & Sons.

Anderson, M., Anderson, S., & Armen C. (2004). Towards machine ethics. *AAAI-04 Workshop on Agent Orgnizations: Theory and Practice.* San José, California.

Andre, E., Klesen, M., Gebhard, P., Allen, S., & Rist, T. (2001). Integrating models of personality and emotions in lifelike characters. In A. Paiva (Ed.), *Affective interactions: Towards a new generation of computer interfaces* (pp. 150-165). New York: Springer-Verlag.

Araujo A. F. R. (1994). *Memory, emotions, and neural networks: Associative learning and memory recall influenced by affective evaluation and task difficulty.* Unpublished doctoral dissertation, University of Sussex, England.

Araya, Agustln A. (1995). Questioning ubiquitous computing. In *Proceedings of the ACM 23rd Annual Conference on Computer Science.* ACM Press.

Arbib, M.A, & Fellous, J.M. (2004). Emotions: from brain to robot. *Trends in Cognitive Sciences, 8,* 554-561.

Arbib, M.A., & Rizzolatti. R. (1997). Neural expectations: A possible evolutionary path from manual skills to language. *Communication and Cognition, 29,* 393-423.

Arkin, R. (2007). *Governing lethal behavior: embedding ethics in a hybrid deliberative/reactive robot architecture.* Technical Report GIT-GVU-07-11.

Arkin, R. C. (2005). Moving up the food chain: motivation and emotion in behavior-based robots. In J. Fellous & M. Arbib (Eds.), *Who needs emotions: The brain meets the robot* (pp. 425-270). New York, NY: Oxford University Press.

Arkin, R.C. (1989). Motor schema-based mobile robot navigation. *The International Journal of Robotics Research, 8*(4), 92-112.

Arnold, M. (1970). *Feelings and emotions, the Loyola symposium.* New York: Academic Press

Arnold, M. B. (1950). An excitatory theory of emotion. In M. L. Reymert (Ed.), *Feelings and emotions: The Mooseheart symposium* (pp. 11-33). McGraw-Hill, Inc.

Aron, A., Fisher, H., Mashek, D.J., Strong, G., Li, H., & Brown, L.L. (2005). Reward, Motivation, and Emotion Systems Associated With Early-Stage Intense Romantic Love. *Journal of Neurophysiology, 94,* 327-337.

Aronson, E. (1996). *The social animal.* (Seventh edition). New York: W. H. Freeman.

Arun, C. (1997). A computational architecture to model human emotions. *Proceedings of International Conference on Intelligent Information System* (pp. 86-89). Grand Bahamas Island, Bahamas.

Asimov, I. (1950). *I, Robot.* New York: Gnome Press.

Astleitner, H. (2001). Designing emotionally sound instruction. *Journal of Instructional Psychology, 28,* 209-219.

Aubé, M. (1997). Toward computational models of motivation: A much needed foundation for social sciences and education. *Journal of Artificial Intelligence in Education, 8*(1), 43-75.

Aubé, M. (1997). *Les émotions comme opérateurs des engagements: Une métaphore pour les structures de contrôle dans les systèmes multi-agents* [Emotions as commitments operators: A metaphor for control structures in multi-agents systems]. Unpublished doctoral dissertation, Université de Montréal, Montréal.

Aubé, M. (1998). A commitment theory of emotions. In D. Canamero (Ed.), *Emotional and intelligent: The tangled knot of cognition. Papers from the 1998 AAAI Fall Symposium* (pp. 13-18). Menlo Park, California: AAAI Press.

Aubé, M. (2001). From Toda's urge theory to the commitment theory of emotions. *Grounding emotions in adaptive systems*, Special issue of *Cybernetics and Systems: An International Journal, 32*(6), 585-610.

Aubé, M. (2005). Beyond needs: Emotions and the commitments requirement. In D. N. Davis (Ed.), *Visions of mind: Architectures for cognition and affect* (pp. 21-44). Hershey, PA: Idea Group., Inc.

Aubé, M., & Senteni, A. (1995). A foundation for commitments as resource management in multi-agents systems. In T. Finin & J. Mayfield (Eds.), *Proceedings of the CIKM Workshop on Intelligent Information Agents*. Baltimore, Maryland.

Aubé, M., & Senteni, A. (1996). Emotions as commitments operators: A foundation for control structure in multi-agents systems. In W. Van de Velde & J. W. Perram (Eds.), *Agents breaking away, Proceedings of the 7th European Workshop on MAAMAW, Lecture Notes on Artificial Intelligence, No. 1038* (pp. 13-25). Berlin: Springer.

Aubé, M., & Senteni, A. (1996). What are emotions for? Commitments management and regulation within animals/animats encounters. In P. Maes, M. Mataric, J.-A. Meyer, J. Pollack, & S. W. Wilson (Eds.), *From animals to animats 4: Proceedings of the Fourth International Conference on Simulation of Adaptive Behavior* (pp. 264-271). Cambridge, MA: The MIT Press/Bradford Books.

Austermann, A., Esau, N., Kleinjohann, L., & B. Kleinjohann (2005). Fuzzy emotion recognition in natural speech dialogue. *Robot and Human Interactive Communication IEEE 14th workshop*.

Averill, J. R. (1980). A constructivist view of emotion. In R. Plutchik & H. Kellerman (Eds.), *Emotion: Theory, research, and experience: Vol. 1. Theories of emotions* (pp. 305-339). New York: Academic Press.

Avila-García, O. & Cañamero, L. (2005). Hormonal modulation of perception in motivation-based action selection architectures. In *Proceedings of the AISB'05 Convention: Vol. 2* (pp. 9-16). Hertfordshire, UK: AISB Press.

Axelrod, R. (1984). *The evolution of cooperation*. New York: Basic Books.

Axelrod, R., & Dion, D. (1988). The further evolution of cooperation. *Science, 242*(4884), 1385-1390.

Aylett, R. S. (2006). Emotion as an integrative process between non-symbolic and symbolic systems in intelligent agents. In *Proceedings of the AISB'06 Symposium of Brain and Mind: Integrating high level cognitive processes with brain mechanisms and functions in a working robot* (pp. 43-47). Bristol, England: AISB Press.

Bach, J. (2003). The MicroPsi agent architecture. In *Proceedings of ICCM-5, International Conference on Cognitive Modeling* (pp. 15-20). Bamberg, Germany: ICCM Press.

Baddeley, A. (1990). *Human memory: Theory and practice*. Boston: Allyn and Bacon.

Baerends, G.P. (1976). The functional organization of behaviour. *Animal Behaviour, 24*, 726-738.

Balch, T. (2000). TeamBots software and documentation. Retrieved May 18, 2008, from http://www.cs.cmu.edu/~trb/TeamBots/

Baldi, P. (2004). Surprise: a shortcut for attention? In L. Itti, G. Rees & J. Tsotsos (Eds.), *Neurobiology of Attention* (pp. 24-28). San Diego, CA: Elsevier Science.

Balkenius, C. (1993). *The roots of motivation*. In J.-A. Mayer, H.L. Roitblat, & S.W. Wilson (Eds.), *From Animals to Animats 2*. MIT Press/Bradford Books.

Bandai. (2000). Tamagotchi. Retrieved January 2000, from http://www.bandai.com/

Banik, S. C., Watanabe, K., & Izumi, K. (2007). Intelligent behavior generation of job distributed mobile robots through emotional interaction. In *Proceedings of 13th International Conference on Advanced Robotics* (pp. 1215-1219). Jeju, Korea.

Banik, S. C., Watanabe, K., Maki K. Habib & Izumi, K. (2008). An emotion-based task sharing approach for a cooperative multiagent robotic system. In *Proceedings of IEEE International Conference on Mechatronics and Automation* (WC1-4). Takamatsu, Japan.

Barberá, E., & Ramos, A. y Sarrió, M. (2000). Mujeres directivas ante el tercer milenio: el proyecto Nowdi XXI. *Papeles del psicólogo, 75*. http://www.papelesdelpsicologo.es/vernumero.asp?id=820.

Barceló, M. (2005). *Inteligencia artificial*. Barcelona. Servicio de publicaciones de la UOC.

Bar-On, R. (1997). *The emotional quotient inventory (EQ-i): Technical manual*. Toronto: Multi-Health Systems.

Baron-Cohen, S., Ring, H. A., Bullmore, E. T., Wheelwright, S., Ashwin, C., & Williams, S. C. R. (2000). The amygdala theory of autism. *Neuroscience and Biobehavioral Reviews, 24*(3), 355-364.

Barrett, L.F., Mesquita, B., Ochsner, K.N., & Gross, J.J. (2007). The Experience of Emotion. *Annual Review of Psychology, 58*, 373-403.

Barrett, L.F., Mesquita, B., Ochsner, K.N., & Gross, J.J. (2007). The experience of emotion. *Annual Review of Psychology, 58*, 373-403.

Barro, R.J. (1977). Unanticipated money growth and unemployment in the United States. American Economic Review *67*, 101–115.

Bartlett, F.C. (1932). *Remembering*. Cambridge: Cambridge University Press.

Bartneck, C. (2001). How convincing is Mr. Data's smile: Affective expressions of machines. *User Modeling and User-Adapted Interaction, 11*, 279-295. | DOI: 10.1023/A:1011811315582

Bartneck, C. (2002). *eMuu - an embodied emotional character for the ambient intelligent home*. Ph.D. thesis, Eindhoven University of Technology, Eindhoven.

Bartneck, C. (2002). Integrating the OCC model of emotions in embodied characters. In *Proceedings of the Workshop on Virtual Conversational Characters: Applications, Methods, and Research Challenges*, Melbourne.

Bartneck, C. (2003). Interacting with an embodied emotional character. In *Proceedings of the Design for Pleasurable Products Conference (DPPI2004), Pittsburgh* (pp. 55-60). | DOI: 10.1145/782896.782911

Bartneck, C., & Lyons, M. J. (2007). HCI and the Face: Towards an Art of the Soluble. In J. Jacko (Ed.), *Human-computer interaction, part 1, HCII2007, LNCS 4550* (pp. 20-29). Berlin: Springer. | DOI: 10.1007/978-3-540-73105-4_3

Bartneck, C., & Okada, M. (2001). Robotic user interfaces. In *Proceedings of the Human and Computer Conference (HC2001), Aizu* (pp. 130-140).

Bartneck, C., & Reichenbach, J. (2005). Subtle emotional expressions of synthetic characters. *The International Journal of Human-Computer Studies, 62*(2), 179-192. | DOI: 10.1016/j.ijhcs.2004.11.006

Bartneck, C., & Suzuki, N. (2005). Subtle Expressivity for Characters and Robots. *International Journal of Human Computer Studies, 62*(2), 159-160. | DOI: 10.1016/j.ijhcs.2004.11.004

Bartneck, C., Kanda, T., Ishiguro, H., & Hagita, N. (2007). Is the uncanny valley an uncanny cliff? In *Proceedings of the 16th IEEE International Symposium on Robot and Human Interactive Communication, RO-MAN 2007, Jeju, Korea* (pp. 368-373). | DOI: 10.1109/ROMAN.2007.4415111

Bartneck, C., Reichenbach, J., & Breemen, A. (2004). In your face, robot! The influence of a character's embodiment on how users perceive its emotional expressions. In *Proceedings of the Design and Emotion 2004, Ankara*.

Bass, B.M. (1985). *Leadership and performance beyond expectations*. New York: The Free Press.

Bassili, J. N. (1976). Temporal and spatial contingencies in the perception of social events. *Journal of Personality and Social Psychology, 33*(6), 680-685.

Bates, J. (1994). The role of emotion in believable agents. *Communications of the ACM, 37*(7), 122-125.

Bates, J., Loyall, A. B., & Reilly, W. S. (1992). *An architecture for action, emotion, and social behaviour*. Technical Report CMU-CS-92-144, School of Computer Science, Carnegie Mellon University.

Batson, C. D., Shaw, L. L., & Oleson, K. C. (1992). Differentiating affect, mood, and emotion. *Emotion*, 294-326.

Baumeister, R. F., & Leary, M. R. (1995). The need to belong: Desire for interpersonal attachments as a fundamental human motivation. *Psychological Bulletin, 117*(3), 497-529.

Baylor, A. L. (2003). *The impact of three pedagogical agent roles*. Florida State University. Retrieved May 31, 2008, from http://garnet.acns.fsu.edu/~abaylor/PDF/baylor_aamas.pdf .

Baylor, A.L., Shen, E., & Huang, X. (2003). Which pedagogical agent do learners choose? The effects of gender and ethnicity. In *Proceedings of the World Conference on E-learning in Corporate, Government, Healthcare & Higher Education, Assoc. for the Advancement of Computing in Education* (pp. 1507-1510).

Beaudry, É., Brosseau, Y., Côté, C., Raïevsky, C., Létourneau, D., Kabanza, F., & Michaud, F. (2005). Reactive planning in a motivated behavioural architecture. In *Proceedings of the Twentieth National Conference on Artificial Intelligence* (AAAI-05) (pp. 1242-1247). Menlo Park, California: AAAI Press.

Benjamin, M., McKeachie, W., Lin, Y.-G., & Holinger, D. (1981). Test anxiety: deficits in information processing. *Journal of Educational Psychology, 73*, 816-824.

Berkowitz, L. (2000). *Causes and consequences of feelings.* Cambridge, England: Cambridge University Press.

Berlyne, D. E. (1960). *Conflict, arousal and curiosity.* New York: McGraw-Hill.

Beslay, L., & Hakala, H. (2005). Digital territory: Bubbles. In P.T Kidd (Ed.), European visions for the knowledge age – A quest for new horizons in the information society. Retrieved from, http://cybersecurity.jrc.es/docs/DigitalTerritoryBubbles.pdf

Besson, M., Faita, F., Peretz, I., Bonnel, A. M., & Requin, J. (1998). Singing in the brain: Independence of lyrics and tunes. *Psychological Science, 9*(6), 494–498.

Betz, M., O'Connell, L., & Shepard J.M.. (1989). Gender differences in proclivity unethical behaviour. *Journal of Business Ethics, 8*, 321-324.

Beyer, H., & Holtzblatt, K. (1993). Making customer-centered design work for teams. *Communications of the ACM, 36*(10), 92-103.

Bickmore, T., & Picard, R. (2004). Towards caring machines. In *CHI '04: Extended abstracts on human factors in computing systems* (pp. 396-403). New York: ACM Press.

Biederman, I., & Vessel, E. A. (2006). Perceptual pleasure and the brain. *American Scientist, 94*(3), 247-255.

Bigand, E., Vieillard, S., Madurell, F., Marozeau, J., & Dacquet, A. (2005). Multidimensional scaling of emotional responses to music: The effect of musical expertise and of the duration of the excerpts. *Cognition & Emotion, 19*(8), 1113–1139.

Bilimoria, D., & Piderit, S.K. (1994). Board committee membership: Effects of sex-based bias. *Academy of Management Journal, 37*(6), 1453-77.

Biocca, F. (1997). The cyborg's dilemma: embodiment in virtual environments. In *Proceedings of the Second International Conference on Cognitive Technology - "Humanizing the Information Age", Aizu* (pp. 12-26). | DOI: 10.1109/CT.1997.617676

Blakermore, S.J., Winston, J., & Frith, U. (2004). Social cognitive neuroscience: where are we heading? *Trends in Cognitive Science, 5*, 216-222.

Blaney, P.H. (1986). Affect and memory: A review. *Psychological Bulletin, 99*(2), 229-246.

Blank, Carlos (2000). Penrose y la inteligencia artificial. *Episteme, 20*(1), 29-49.

Bless, H., & Schwarz, N. (1999). Mood, its impact on cognition and behavior. *Blackwell encyclopedia of social psychology.* Oxford, England: Blackwell.

Bless, H., Schwarz, N., &Wieland, R. (1996). Mood and the impact of category membership and individuating information. *European Journal of Social Psychology, 26*, 935-959.

Bloch, S. (1989). Émotion ressentie, émotion recréée. *Science et Vie, Hors série, 168*, 68-75.

Bloch, S., Lemeignan, M., & Aguilera, N. (1991). Specific respiratory patterns distinguish among human basic emotions, *International Journal of Psychophysiology, 11*(2), 141-154.

Bloch, S., Orthous, P., & Santibanez-H, G. (1987). Effector patterns of basic emotions: A psychophysiological method for training actors. *Journal of Social and Biological Structures, 10*(1), 1-19.

Block, N. (1981). Psychologism and Behaviourism. *The Philosophical Review LXXXX, 1,* 5-43.

Block, N. (1995). On a confusion about a function of consciousness. *Behavioral and Brain Sciences, 18,* 265-66.

Blood, A. J., & Zatorre, R. J. (2001). Intensely pleasurable responses to music correlate with activity in brain regions implicated in reward and emotion. *Proceedings of the National Academy of Sciences of the United States of America*, *98*(20), 11818–11823.

Bloom, B. S. (1984). The 2-sigma problem: The search for methods of group instruction as effective as one to-one tutoring. *Educational Researcher, 13*, 4-16.

Boden, M. (1995). Creativity and unpredictability. *Stanford Humanities Review, 4*(2), 123-139.

Bødker, S. (2006). When second wave HCI meets third wave challenges. In *Proceedings of the 4th Nordic conference on Human-computer interaction: changing roles* (pp. 1-8). Oslo, Norway.

Bødker, S., & Greenbaum, J. (1993). Design of information systems: Things versus people. In E. Green, J. Owen, & D. Pain (Eds.), *Gendered by design? Information technology and office systems* (pp. 53-63). London: Taylor & Francis.

Bødker, S., Ehn, P., Sjögren, D., & Sundblad, Y. (2000, October). Co-operative Design – perspectives on 20 years with "the Scandinavian IT Design Model". In *Proceedings of NordiCHI 2000. Report number CID-104*. Stockholm, Sweden: Royal Institute of Technology, Centre for User Oriented IT Design. Retrieved from, http://cid.nada.kth.se/pdf/cid_104.pdf

Boekaerts, M. (1997). Self-regulated learning: A new concept embraced by researchers, policy makers, educators, teachers and students. *Learning and Instruction, 7*(2), 161-186.

Boekaerts, M. (2003). Toward a model that integrates motivation, affect, and learning. *British Journal of Educational Psychology Monograph Series, 2*, 173-189.

Bohn, J., Coroamă, V., Langheinrich, M., Mattern, F. & Rohs, M. (2001). *Ethics and Information Technology, 3*, 157-169. Retrieved from, http://www.vs.inf.ethz.ch/publ/papers/socialambient.pdf

Bondarev, A. (2002). *Design of an emotion management system for a home robot*. Master, Eindhoven University of Technology, Eindhoven.

Bonny, H. L. (2002). *Music consciousness: The evolution of guided imagery and music* (L. Summer, Ed.). Barcelona Publishers.

Borenstein, J., & Koren, Y. (1991). The vector field histogram – fast obstacle avoidance for mobile robots. *IEEE Journal on Robotics and Automation, 7*(3), 278-288.

Boucher, J. D. (1983). Antecedents to emotions across cultures. In S. H. Irvine & J. W. Berry (Eds.), *Human Assessment and Cultural Factors* (pp. 407-420). New York: Plenum.

Bowlby, J. (1969). *Attachment and loss. Vol. 1: Attachment*. London: Penguin Books.

Bowlby, J. (1973). *Attachment and loss. Vol. 2: Separation, anxiety, and anger*. London: Penguin Books.

Bowlby, J. (1980). *Attachment and loss. Vol. 3: Loss, sadness, and depression*. London: Penguin Books.

Brake, M.L. & Tessmer, A. (2004). Robots and girls. *Antennas and Propagation Magazine, IEEE, 46*(1), 142-143.

Bratman, M. E., Israel, D. J., & Pollack, M. E. (1988). Plans and resource-bounded practical reasoning. *Computational Intelligence, 4*(4), 349-355. | DOI: 10.1111/j.1467-8640.1988.tb00284.x

Bratman, M., Israel, D., & Pollack, M. (1988). Plans and resource-bounded practical reasoning. *Computational Intelligence, 4*(4), 349–355.

Brave, S., & Nass, C. (2002). Emotion in human-computer interaction. In A.Sears & J.A A. Jacko (Eds.), *The human-computer interaction handbook:Fundamentals, evolving technologies   and emerging applications* (pp. 77-93). NJ: Lawrence Erlbaum Associates, Inc.

Brave, S., & Nass, C. (2003). Emotion in human-computer interaction. In J. Jacko, & A. Sears (Eds.), *Handbook of human-computer interaction*. (pp. 81-96). Mahwah, NJ, USA: Lawrence Erlbaum Associates.

Brave, S., Nass, C., & Hutchinson, K. (2005). Computers that care: Investigating the effects of orientation of emotion exhibited by an embodied computer agent. *International Journal of Human-Computer Studies, 62*, 161-178.

Brave, S., Nass, C., & Hutchinson, K. (2005). Computers that care: investigating the effects of orientation of emotion exhibited by an embodied computer agent. *International Journal of Human-Computer Studies, 62*(2), 161-178.

Brazeal, C. (2003). Emotion and sociable humanoid robots. *International Journal of Human-Computer Studies, 59*(1-2), 119-155.

Brazeal, C., Buschbaum, D., Gray, J., Gatenby, D., & Blumberg, B. (2005). Learning from and about others: Towards using imitation to bootstrap the social understanding of others by robots. *Artificial, Life, 11*(1-2), 79-98.

Breazeal (2002). *Designing sociable robots.* MIT Press.

Breazeal, C. & Scassellati, B. (1999). How to build robots that make friends and influence people. *Proceedings of the IEEE/RSJ International Conference on Intelligent Robots and Systems*, Knyoju, Japan.

Breazeal, C. (2002). *Designing sociable robots.* Cambridge, MA: MIT Press.

Breazeal, C. (2003). Emotion and sociable humanoid robots. *International Journal of Human-Computer Studies, 59*, 119-155.

Breazeal, C. (2003). Toward sociable robots. *Robotics and Autonomous Systems, 42*, 167-75.

Breazeal, C. (2004). Function meets style: Insights from emotion theory applied to HRI. *IEEE Transactions on Systems, Man and Cybernetics, 34*(2), 187-194.

Breazeal, C. (2006). Human-robot partnership. In S. Coradeschi, H. Ishiguro, M. Asada, S. Shapiro, M. Theilscher, C. Breazeal, M. Mataric, & H. Ishida (Eds.), Trends and Controversies: Human-Inspired Robots. *IEEE Intelligent Systems 21*(4), 79-81. Retrieved April 18, 2008, from http://robotics.usc.edu/~maja/publications/special-issue-ieeeintsys06.pdf

Breazeal, C., Brooks, A., Gray, J., Hoffman, G., Kidd, C., Lee, H., Lieberman, J., Lockerd, A., & Chilongo, D. (2004). Tutelage and collaboration for humanoid robots. *International Journal of Humanoid Robots, 1*(2), 315-48.

Breazeal, C., Hoffman, G., & Lockerd, A. (2004). Teaching and working with robots as a collaboration. In *Proceedings of AAMAS 2004* (pp. 1030-1037).

Breemen, A., Yan, X., & Meerbeek, B. (2005). iCat: an animated user-interface robot with personality. In *Proceedings of the Fourth International Conference on Autonomous Agents & Multi Agent Systems, Utrecht.* | DOI: 10.1145/1082473.1082823

Brehm, J. W. (1999). The intensity of emotion. *Personality and Social Psychology Review, 3*, 2-22.

Brick, T., & Scheutz, M. (2007). Incremental natural language processing for HRI. In *Proceedings of the Second ACM IEEE International Conference on Human-Robot Interaction* (pp. 263-270).

Brick, T., Schermerhorn, P., & Scheutz, M. (2007). Speech and action: Integration of action and language for mobile robots. In *Proceedings of the 2007 IEEE/RSJ International Conference on Intelligent Robots and Systems* (pp. 1423-1428).

Broekens, J. (2007). Emotion and reinforcement: Affective facial expressions facilitate robot learning. *LNAI Special Volume on AI for Human Computing* (pp. 113-132). Hyderabad, India: Springer.

Brooks, R. (1986). A robust layered control system for a mobile robot. *IEEE Journal of Robotics and Automation 2*(1),14-23.

Brooks, R. A. (1986). A robust layered control system for a mobile robot. *IEEE Journal of Robotics and Automation, 2*(1), 14-23.

Brooks, R. A. (1991). Intelligence without reason. In *Proceedings of the 12th International Joint Conference on Artificial Intelligence (IJCAI-91),* (pp. 569-595).

Brooks, R. A. (1991). Intelligence without representation. *Artificial Intelligence, 47*(1-3), 139-159.

Brooks, R.A. (1991). Intelligence without representation. *Artificial Intelligence, 47*, 139-159.

Brown, J. S., & Farber, I. E. (1951). Emotions conceptualized as intervening variables - with suggestions towards a theory of frustration. *Psychological Bulletin, 48*, 465-495.

Bui, T. D., Heylen, D., Poel, M., & Nijholt, A. (2002). ParleE: An adaptive plan based event appraisal model of emotions. *Lecture Notes on Artificial Intelligence, 2479*, 129-143.

Bui, T.D., Heylen, D., & Poel, M. (2002). ParleE: An adaptive plan-based event appraisal model of emotions. In G. L. M. Jarke, J. Koehler (Eds.), *Procs. KI 2002: Advances in Artificial Intelligence.*

Bumby, K.E., & Dautenhahn, K. (1999). Investigating children's attitudes towards robots: A case study. *Third Cognitive Technology Conference*, San Francisco CA.

Burgdorf, J., & Panksepp, J. (2006). The neurobiology of positive emotions. *Neuroscience and Biobehavioral Reviews, 30*, 173-187.

Burghouts G.J., R. op den Akker, Heylen D., Poel M., & Nijholt A. (2003). *An action selection architecture for an emotional agent.*

Burleson, W. & Picard, R.W. (2007). Gender-specific approaches to developing emotionally intelligent learning companions. *Intelligent Systems, 22*(4), 62-69.

Burns, J. (2006). The social brain hypothesis of schizophrenia. *World Psychiatry, 5*(2), 77-81.

Butler, E., Egloff, B., Wilhem, F. H., Smith, N. C., Erickson, E. A., & Gross, J. J. (2003). The social consequences of expressive suppression. *Emotion, 3*(1), 48-67.

Cagan, P. (1956). The monetary dynamics of hyperinflation. In M. Friedman, *Studies in the Quantity Theory of Money*. Chicago: University of Chicago Press.

Callejas, Z., & López-Cózar, R. (2008). Influence of contextual information in emotion annotation for spoken dialogue systems. *Speech communication, 50*, 416-433.

Calvo, P. & Gomila, A., eds. (2008). *Handbook of cognitive science: Embodied approaches*. Elsevier.

Campbell, K.K. (1970). *Body and mind*. New York: Doubleday.

Cañamero, D. (1998). Issues in the design of emotional agents. In D. Cañamero (Ed.), *Emotional and intelligent: The tangled knot of cognition. Papers from the 1998 AAAI Fall Symposium* (pp. 49-54). Menlo Park, California: AAAI Press.

Cañamero, D. (2003). Designing emotions for activity selection in autonomous agents. In R. Trappl, P. Petta, & S. Payr, (Eds.), *Emotions in humans and artifacts.* Cambridge, MA: The MIT Press.

Cañamero, L. (2005). Emotion understanding from the perspective of autonomous robots research. *Neural Network, 18*, 445-455.

Cannon, W.B. (1920). The James-Lange theory of emotions: A critical examination and an alternative theory. *The American Journal of Psychology, 39*(¼),106-124.

Caprara, G.V., & Cervone, D. (2000). *Personality: Determinants, dynamics and potentials*. Cambridge University Press.

Capurro, R. (1992). Informatics and hermeneutics. In C. Floyd, H. Züllighoven, R. Budde, & R. Keil-Slawik (Eds.), *Proceedings of Software Development and Reality Construction (September 1988)* (pp. 363-375). Heidelberg, Germany: Springer-Verlag.

Carney, D., & Colvin, C. (2005). *The circumplex structure of emotive social behavior.* In preparation.

Carpenter, R. (2007). Jabberwacky: Communication, companionship, intelligence. Retrieved February 12, 2007, from http://www.jabberwacky.com/

Carroll, C.D. (2003). Macroeconomic expectations of households and professional forecasters. *Quarterly Journal of Economics.*

Carver, C. S., & Scheier, M. F. (1990). Origins and functions of positive and negative affect: A control process view. *Psychological Review, 97*(1), 19-35.

Casacuberta, D. (2000). *Qué es una emoción*. Barcelona: Crítica.

Casacuberta, D. (2004). Dj el niño: expressing synthetic emotions with music. *AI & Society, 18*(3), 257–263.

Casacuberta, David (2000). *¿Qué es una emoción?* Barcelona. Crítica 2000.

Cassady, J. (2004). The influence of cognitive test anxiety across the learning-testing cycle. *Learning and Instruction, 14*(6).

Cassell, J., Sullivan, J., Prevost, S., & Churchill, E. (2000). *Embodied conversational agents*. Cambridge: MIT Press.

Cassell, J., Sullivan, J., Prevost, S., & Churchill, E. (Eds.). (2000). *Embodied conversational agents*. Cambridge, MA: MIT Press.

Castelfranchi, C. (2000). Affective appraisal versus cognitive evaluations in social emotions and interactions. In A. Paiva (Ed.), *Affective interactions: Towards a new generation of affective interfaces.* (pp. 76-106). New York: Springer.

Castelfranchi, C. (2005). Mind as an anticipatory device: for a theory of expectations. In *Proceedings of the First International Symposium on Brain, Vision, and Artificial Intelligence (BVAI 2005)* (Vol. 3704, pp. 258–276).

Castelfranchi, C., Falcone, R., & Piunti, M. (2006). Agents with anticipatory behaviors: To be cautious in a risky environment. In *Proceedings of the 17th European Conference on Artificial Intelligence (ECAI'06)* (pp. 693-694).

Castelfranchi, C., Miceli, M., & Conte, R. (1991). Limits and levels of cooperation: Disentangling various types of prosocial interaction. In Y. Demazeau & J. P. Muller (Eds.), *Decentralized AI-2* (pp. 147-157). B. V. Amsterdam, The Netherlands: Elsevier Science Publishers.

Cerami, F. (2006). Miss Digital World. Retrieved August 4th, from http://www.missdigitalworld.com/

Chalmers, D.J. (1995). Facing up to the problem of consciousness. *Journal of Consciousness Studies, 2,* 200-19.

Chalmers, D.J. (1996). *The conscious mind.* New York: Oxford University Press.

Chalmers, D.J. (2002). Consciousness and its place in nature. In D.J. Chalmers (Ed.), *Philosophy of mind: Classical and contemporary readings.* Oxford, UK: Oxford.

Chalmers, M. (2004). Coupling and heterogeneity in ubiquitous computing. In *Reflective HCI – Towards a Critical Technical Practice (CHI Workshop).* Retrieved from, http://www.dcs.gla.ac.uk/~matthew/papers/ReflectiveHCI2004.pdf

Chalmers, M. (2004). *A historical view of context. Computer supported cooperative work, 13*(3-4), 223-247. Retrieved from, http://www.equator.ac.uk/var/uploads/M.Chalmers2004.pdf

Champanard, A.J. (2007). Evolving with creatures' AI: 15 tricks to mutate into your own game. AIGameDev.com Reviews, October 21, 2007. Retrieved May 17, 2008, from http://aigamedev.com/reviews/creatures-ai

Chan, C., Lyons, M. J., & Tetsutani, N. (2003). Mouthbrush: drawing and painting by hand and mouth. In *Proceedings of the Fifth International Conference on Multimodal Interfaces, Vancouver* (pp. 277-280). | DOI: 10.1145/958432.958482

Chan, T.W. (1996). Learning companion systems, social learning systems, and intelligent virtual classroom. Invited Talk, World Conference on Artificial Intelligence in Education, Washington, DC, USA. *Journal of Artificial Intelligence in Education, 7*(2), 125-159.

Changchun Liu, Rani, P., & Sarkar, N (2006). Affective state recognition and adaptation in human-robot interaction: a design approach. *Intelligent Robots and Systems. 2006 IEEE/RSJ International Conference.* (pp. 3099-3106).

Charlesworth, W. R. (1969). The role of surprise in cognitive development. In D. Elkind & J. H. Flavell (Eds.), *Studies in cognitive development* (pp. 257-314). Oxford: Oxford University Press.

Charlesworth, W. R., & Kreutzer, M. A. (1973). Facial expressions of infants and children. In P. Ekman (Ed.), *Darwin and facial expression: A century of research in review* (pp. 91-167). New York: Academic Press.

Chi, M. T. H., Bassok, M., Lewis, M. W., Reimann, P., & Glaser, R. (1989). Self-explanations: How students study and use examples in learning to solve problems. *Cognitive Science, 13*(2), 145-182.

Chown, E. (1993). The adaptive power of affect: Learning in the SESAME architecture. In J. A. Meyer, H. L. Roitblat, & S. Wilson (Eds.), *From Animals to Animats 2: Proceedings of the Second International Conference on Simulation Adaptive Behavior* (pp. 515). Cambridge, MA: MIT Press.

Cialdini, R. B. (1984). *Influence.* New York: William Morrow and Company.

Cialdini, R. B., Vincent, J. E., Lewis, S. K., Catalan, J., Wheeler, D., & Darby, B. L. (1975). Reciprocal concessions procedure for inducing compliance: The door-in-the-face technique. *Journal of Personality and Social Psychology, 31*(2), 206-215.

Ciarrochi J., & Mayer J.D. (2007). Applying emotional intelligence. *Psychology Press.* New York.

Cipresso P., & Villamira M.A. (2007). A spettative razionali e microfondazione per ecomomie in situazione di iperinflazione. In *Proceedings of WIVACE 2007.*

Cipresso P., Balgera A., & Villamira M.A. (2008). Agent-based computational economics and emotions for decision-making processes. In *Selected Proceedings of the IAREP/SABE 2008 World Conference at LUISS in Rome.*

Cipresso P., Villamira M.A. (2007). Shaping the "post-carbon" society: changes at systemic level in transport, housing and consumer behaviour, an Agent-based Computational Economics approach. In *Proceedings of International Association for Research in Economic Psychology Conference*, Ljubljana, Slovenia.

Clark, D. M., & Teasdale, J. D. (1985). Constraints on the effect of mood on memory. *Journal of Personality and Social Psychology, 48*, 1595–1608.

Clark, W.C., & Grunstein, M. (2000). *Are we hardwired? The role of genes in human behavior.* Oxford: OUP.

Clement, A. & Van den Besselaar, P. (1993, June). A retrospective look at PD projects. *Communications of the ACM, 36*(6), 29-37.

Clore, G.L., Gasper, K., & Conway, H. (2001). Affect as information. In J.P. Forgas (Ed.), *Handbook of Affect and Social Cognition* (pp. 121-144).

Cohen, R. A. (2000). Ethics and cybernetics: Levinasian reflections. *Ethics and Information Technology, 2*, 27-35.

Colby, K.M., Hilf, F.D., Weber, S., & Kraemer, H.C. (1972). Turing-like indistinguishability tests for the validation of a computer simulation of paranoid processes. *Artificial Intelligence, 3*, 199-221.

Colwill, J. & Townsend, J. (1999). Women, leadership and information technology. The impact of women leaders in organizations and their in integrating information technology with corporate strategy. *The Journal of Management Development, 18*(3), 207-216.

Conati, C., & Klawe, M. (2002). Socially intelligent agents in educational games. In K. Dautenhahn, A.H. Bond, L. Cañamero, & B. Edmonds (Eds.), *Socially intelligent agents - Creating relationships with computers and robots* (pp. 213-221). Kluwer Academic Publishers.

Cook, N.D. (2000). On defining awareness and consciousness: The importance of the neuronal membrane. In *Proceedings of the Tokyo-99 Conference on Consciousness.* Singapore: World Scientific.

Cook, N.D. (2002). Bihemispheric language: How the two hemispheres collaborate in the processing of language. In T. Crow (Ed.), *The speciation of modern Homo sapiens.* London, UK: Proceedings of the British Academy, v. 106 (ch. 9).

Cook, N.D. (2002). *Tone of voice and mind: The connections between intonation, emotion, cognition and consciousness.* Amsterdam, Netherlands: John Benjamins.

Cook, N.D. (2008). The neuron-level phenomena underlying cognition and consciousness: Synaptic activity and the action potential. *Neuroscience, 153*(3), 556-70.

Corbett, A., & Anderson, J. R. (1995). Knowledge tracing: modeling the acquisition of procedural knowledge. *User Modeling and User-Adapted Interaction, 4*, 253–278.

Coricelli, G., Dolan, R.J., & Sirigu, A. (2007). Brain, emotion and decision making: the paradigmatic example of regret. *Trends in Cognitive Sciences, 11*, 258-265.

Cosmides, L. (1989). The logic of social exchange: Has natural selection shaped how humans reason? Studies with the Wason selection task. *Cognition, 31*(3), 187-276.

Costa, P. T., & McCrae, R. R. (1992). Normal personality assessment in clinical practice: The NEO personality inventory. *Psychological Assessment, 4*(1), 5-13.

Coyne, R. (1995). *Designing information technology in the postmodern age: From method to metaphor.* Cambridge: MIT Press..

Crutzen C. K. M. (2006, December). Invisibility and the meaning of ambient intelligence. *International Review of Information Ethics, 6*, 52-62. Retrieved from, http://www.i-r-i-e.net/inhalt/006/006_Crutzen.pdf

Crutzen, C. K. M. (2000). *Interactie, een wereld van verschillen. Een visie op informatica vanuit genderstudies* (p. 417). Dissertation, Open University of the Netherlands. Retrieved from, http://www.cecile-crutzen.de/Downloads/2000-Dissertatie-Interactie-een-wereld-van-verschillen.pdf

Crutzen, C. K. M. (2007). Ambient intelligence between heaven and hell: A transformative critical room?

In I. Zorn, S. Maass, E. Rommes, C. Schirmer, & H. Schelhowe (Eds.), *Gender designs it – Construction and deconstruction of information society technology* (pp. 65-78). Wiesbaden, Germany: VS Verlag für Sozialwissenschaften.

Crutzen, C. K. M., & Hein, H.-W.(2001). Die bedenkliche Dienlichkeit und Sicherheit von Softwaresystemen und die erlebte Verläßlichkeit. 31. Jahrestagung der Gesellschaft für Informatik/Österreichische Computer Gesellschaft Jahrestagung 2001, Wien, Workshop "Erkenntnistheorie - Semiotik - Ontologie: Die Bedeutung philosophischer Disziplinen für die Softwaretechnik". In K. Bauknecht, W. Brauer, & T. Mück. (Eds.), *Informatik 2001. Wirtschaft und Wissenschaft in der Network Economy – Visionen und Wirklichkeit, Band II.* (pp. 782-787). Wien, Österreichische Computer Gesellschaft.

Crutzen, C. K. M., & Kotkamp, E. (2006b). Questioning gender, transformative critical rooms. In E. Trauth (Ed.), *Encyclopedia of gender and information technology.* Hershey, PA: Information Science Reference.

Crutzen, C. K. M., Kotkamp, E. (2006a). Questioning gender, deconstruction and doubt. In E. Trauth (Ed.), *Encyclopedia of gender and information technology.* Hershey, PA: Information Science Reference.

Csikszentmihalyi, M. (1990). *Flow: The psychology of optimal experience.* New York: Harper and Row.

Cumming, G., Finch, S., & Thomason, N. (1999). Educational design for effective learning: Building and using a computer-based learning environment for statistical concepts. In G. Cumming, T. Okamoto, & L. Gomez (Eds.), *Advanced research in computers and communications in education* (pp.558-565). Amsterdam: IOS Press.

Custódio, L., Ventura, R., & Pinto-Ferreira, C. (1999). Artificial emotions and emotion-based control systems. In *Proceedings of 7th IEEE International Conference on Emerging Technologies and Factory Automation.* Vol. 2 (pp. 1415-1420). Barcelona, Spain.

Custòdio, L., Ventura, R., & Pinto-Ferreira, C. (1999). Artificial emotions and emotion-based control systems. *7th IEEE International Conference on Emerging Technologies and Factory Automation* (pp. 1415-1420). Barcelona, Spain.

Cyberlife Technology Ltd. (1997). *Creatures.* Computer game, multiple platforms. Virgin Interactive Entertainment.

Cycorp. (2007). Cyc. Retrieved February 2007, from http://www.cyc.com/

d'Inverno, M., & Luck, M. (1996). Understanding autonomous interaction. In W. Wahlster (Ed.), *12th European Conference on Artificial Intelligence* (pp. 529-533). Budapest, Hungary: John Wiley & Sons.

d'Inverno, M., Luck, M., & Wooldridge, M. (1997, August). *Cooperation structures.* Paper presented at 15th International Joint Conference on Artificial Intelligence, Nagoya, Japan.

Dailey, M. N., Cottrell, G. W., Padgett, C., & Adolphs, R. (2002). EMPATH: A neural network that categorizes facial expressions. *Journal of Cognitive Neuroscience, 14*(8), 1158-1173. | DOI: 10.1162/089892902760807177

Dalla Bella, Peretz, I., Rousseau, L., & Gosselin, N. (2001). A developmental study of the affective value of tempo and mode in music. *Cognition, 80*(3), 1–10.

Damasio, A. (1994). *Descartes' Error: Emotion, Reason and the Human Brain.* Avon Books, New York.

Damasio, A. (1999). *The feeling of what happens: bodies, emotion and the making of consciousness.* Heinemann.

Damasio, A. (2000). A second chance for emotion. In R. D. Lane & L. Nadel (Eds.), *Cognitive neuroscience of emotion* (pp. 12-23). New York: Oxford University Press.

Damasio, A. R. (1995). *L'error de Descartes: la raison des émotions.* Paris: Odile Jacob.

Damasio, A.R. (1996). *Descartes' error – Emotion, reason and the human brain.* London: Papermac.

Damasio, A.R. (1999). *The feeling of what happens: Body and emotion in the making of consciousness.* New York: Harcourt, Brace & Co.

Damasio, A.R., Grabowski, T.J., Bechara, A., Damasio, H., Ponto, L.L.B., Parvizi, J., & Hichwa, R.D. (2000). Subcortical and cortical brain activity during the feeling of self-generated emotions. *Nature Neuroscience, 3,* 1049-56.

Dancy, J. (2004). *Ethics without principles*. Clarendon Press.

Dapretto, M., Davies, M. S., Pfeifer, J. H., Scott, A. A., Sigman, M., Bookheimer, S. Y., & Iacoboni, M. (2006). Understanding emotions in others: Mirror neuron dysfunction in children with autism spectrum disorders. *Nature Neuroscience, 9*(1), 28-30.

Darwall, S. (2006) *The second-person standpoint. Morality, respect and accountability*. Cambridge, MA: Harvard University Press.

Darwin, C. (1872). *The expression of the emotions in man and animals*. London,: J. Murray.

Darwin, C. (1899). *The expression of emotions in man and animals*. New York: D. Appleton and Company.

Darwin, C. (1965). *The expression of the emotions in man and animals.* Chicago: The University of Chicago Press. (Original work published 1872)

Davidson, R. J. (1994). On emotion, mood, and related affective constructs. In P. Ekman & R. J. Davidson (Eds.), *The nature of emotion: Fundamental questions* (pp. 51-55). Oxford: Oxford University Press.

Davies, S. (2001). Philosophical perspectives on music's expressiveness. In P. N. Juslin & J. A. Sloboda (Eds.), *Music and emotion: Theory and research.* Oxford: Oxford University Press.

Davis, D. (2002). Modeling emotion in computational agents. *International Conference on Artificial Intelligence and Applications.*

Davis, D. Chalabi, T. & Berbank-Green, B. (1999). Towards an architecture for Artificial life agents II. New Frontiers in Computational Intelligence and Its Applications, ISO Press.

De Silva, C. G., Lyons, M. J., Kawato, S., & Tetsutani, N. (2003). Human factors evaluation of a vision-based facial gesture interface. In *Proceedings of the Conference on Computer Vision and Pattern Recognition Workshop* (pp. 52). | DOI: 10.1109/CVPRW.2003.10055

Dealmeida, L. Da Silva, B. & Bazzan, A. (2004). *Towards a physiological model of emotions: First Step*. America Association for Artificial Intelligence.

DeLancey, C. (2001). *Passionate engines: What emotions reveal about mind and artificial intelligence. Oxford:* Oxford University Press.

DeLancey, C. (2002). *Passionate engines: What emotions reveal about mind and artificial intelligence.* Oxford, UK: Oxford University Press.

Deniz, O. (2006). *An engineering approach to sociable robots.* Doctoral dissertation, Universidad de Las Palmas de Gran Canaria.

Deniz, O., Hernández, M., Lorenzo, J., & Castrillon, M. (2007). An engineering approach to sociable robots. *Journal of Experimental & Theoretical Artificial Intelligence, 19*(4), 285-306.

Dennett, D. C. (1987). *The intentional stance.* Cambridge, MA: MIT Press.

Denton, D. (2006). *Emotions: The dawning of consciousness.* Oxford: OUP.

Derbaix, C., & Vanhamme, J. (2003). Inducing word-of-mouth by eliciting surprise - a pilot investigation. *Journal of Economic Psychology, 24*, 99-116.

Derks, D., Fischer, A.H., & Bos, A.E.R. (2008). The role of emotion in computer-mediated communication: A review. *Computers in Human Behavior, 24*, 766-785.

Desai, M. M. (1939). Surprise: A historical and experimental study. *British Journal of Psychology, Monograph Supplements, 22.*

Dewey, J. (1916). Education as growth. In *Democracy and education.* Retrieved from, http://www.ilt.columbia.edu/publications/dewey.html

Dias, J., & Paiva, A. (2005). Feeling and Reasoning: a computational model. In *EPIA, 12th Portuguese Conference on Artificial Intelligence* (pp 127-140). Berlin/Heidelberg: Springer.

Dillenbourg, P., Baker, M., Blaye, A., & O'Malley, C. (1995). The evolution of research on collaborative learning. In P. Reimann & H. Spada (Eds.), *Learning in humans and machines. Towards an interdisciplinary learning science* (pp. 189-211). London: Pergamon.

Dimberg, U. (1982). Facial reactions to facial expressions. *Psychophysiology, 19*(6), 643-647.

Dimberg, U. (1988). Facial electromyography and emotional reactions. *Psychophysiology, 27*(5), 481-494.

Dörner D., & Hille, K. (1995). Artificial souls: Motivated emotional robots. In *Proceedings of the IEEE International Conference on Systems, Man and Cybernetics* (pp. 3828-3832). Vancouver, BC, Canada: IEEE Press.

Dorsch, T. (2008). Development of an ambient emotional responsive character. In *NAMU Lab.,* vol. BSc. Tampere: Tampere University of Technology (TUT) - in cooperation with Studiengang Virtual Design, Fachhochschule Kaiserslautern.

Downie, J. S. (2006). The music information retrieval evaluation exchange (MIREX). *D-Lib Magazine, 12*(12).

Doya, K. (1999). What are the computations of the cerebellum, the basal ganglia and the cerebral cortex? *Neural Networks,. 12,* 961-974.

Dreyfus, H.L. (1991). *Being-in-the-world. A commentary on Heidegger's* Being and Time, *Division I.* Cambridge, MA: MIT Press.

Dubois, D., & Prade, H. (1988). *Possibility theory.* New York: Plenum Press.

Ducatel, K., Bogdanowicz, M., Scapolo, F., Leijten, J., & Burgelman J.-C. (2001). *Scenarios for ambient intelligence 2010*, ISTAG Report, European Commission, Institute for Prospective Technological Studies, Seville. Retrieved August 25, 2008, from ftp://ftp.cordis.lu/pub/ist/docs/istagscenarios2010.pdf.

Duclos, S. E., & Laird, J. D. (2001). The deliberate control of emotional experience through control of expressions. *Cognition and Emotion, 15*(1), 27-56.

Duffy, B.R. (2003). Anthropomorphism and the social robot. *Robotics and Autonomous Systems, 42,* 177-190.

Dweck, C. S. (1986). Motivational processes affecting learning. *American Psychologist, 41*(10), 1040-1048.

Dyer, M. G. (1987). Emotions and their computations: Three computer models. *Cognition and Emotion, 1*(3), 323-347.

Eberts, R. E. (1997). Computer-based instruction. In M. G. Helander, T. K. Landauer, & P. V. Prabhu (Eds.), *Hand-*

book of Human-Computer Interaction (pp. 825–847). Amsterdam, The Netherlands: Elsevier.

Edelman, G., & Tononi, G. (2000). *A universe of consciousness: How matter becomes imagination.* NY: Basic Books.

Edelman, G.M. & Tononi, G.A. (2000). *A universe of consciousness.* New York: Basic Books.

Edmonds, B. (2008). The social embedding of intelligence: Towards a machine that could pass the turing test. In: R. Epstein, G. Roberts & G. Beber (Eds.), *Parsing the Turing Test: Philosophical and methodological issues in the quest for the thinking computer.* Springer Science.

Egges, A., Kshirsagar, S., & Magnenat-Thalmann, N. (2004). Generic personality and emotion simulation for conversational agents: *Computer animation and virtual worlds, 15*(1), 1-13.

Ehn, P. (1993). Scandinavian design: On participation and skill. In D. Schuler, & A. Namioka (Eds.), *Participatory design – Principles and practices* (pp. 41-78). Lawrence Erlbaum Associates.

Eibl-Eibesfeldt, I. (1973). The expressive behavior of the deaf-and-blind-born. In M. Von Cranach & I. Vine (Eds.), *Social communication and movement. Studies of interaction and expression in man and chimpanzee* (pp. 163-194). New York: Academic Press.

Eibl-Eibesfeldt, I. (1975). *Ethology: The biology of behavior.* (2nd edition). New York: Holt, Rinehart and Winston.

Ekman, P. (1982). *Emotion in the human face.* New York: Cambridge University Press.

Ekman, P. (1984). Expression and the nature of emotion. In K. R. Scherer & P. Ekman (Eds.), *Approaches to emotion* (pp. 319-343). Hillsdale, N.J.: Erlbaum.

Ekman, P. (1985). *Telling lies: Clues to deceit in the marketplace, politics, and marriage.* New York: W.W. Norton.

Ekman, P. (1992). An argument for basic emotions. *Cognition & Emotion, 6*(3), 169–200.

Ekman, P. (1993). Facial expression and emotion. *American Psychologist, 48*(4), 384-392.

Ekman, P. (1994). Moods, emotions, and traits. In P. Ekman & R. J. Davidson (Eds.), *The nature of emotion: Fundamental questions* (pp. 56-58). Oxford: Oxford University Press.

Ekman, P. (1999). Basic emotions. In T. Dalgleish & T. Power (Eds.), *The handbook of cognition and emotion* (pp. 45-60). New York, NY: Wiley.

Ekman, P. (2000). Facial expressions. In T. Dalgleish & M. J. Power (Eds.), *Handbook of cognition and emotion* (pp. 301-320). New York: John Wiley & Sons Ltd.

Ekman, P. (2003). *Emotions revealed. Recognizing faces and feelings to improve communication and emotional life*. New York: Henry Holt and Company, LLC.

Ekman, P. (Ed.). (1982). *Emotion in the human face*. Cambridge, England: Cambridge University Press.

Ekman, P., & Friesen, W. V. (1975). *Unmasking the face*. Englewood Cliffs: Prentice Hall.

Ekman, P., & Friesen, W. V. (1975). *Unmasking the face: A guide to recognizing emotions from facial expressions*. Englewood Cliffs, NJ: Prentice-Hall.

Ekman, P., & Friesen, W. V. (1975). *Unmasking the face: A guide to recognizing emotions from facial clues*. Englewood Cliffs, NJ: Prentice-Hall.

Ekman, P., Friesen, W. V., & & Hager, J. V. (2002). *Facial action coding system (2nd Ed.)*. Salt Lake City, Utah: Research Nexus eBook.

Ekman, P., Friesen, W. V., & Ellsworth, P. (1972). *Emotion in the human face: guidelines for research and an integration of findings*. New York: Pergamon Press.

Ekman, P., Friesen, W., & Hager, J. (n.d.). Facial Action Coding System (FACTS). Retrieved from, http://face-and-emotion.com/dataface/facs/new_version.jsp

Ekman, P., Levenson, R. W., & Friesen, W. V. (1983). Autonomous nervous system activity distinguishes between emotions. *Science, 221*(4616), 1208-1210.

Elias, M. J., Zins, J. E., Weissberg, R. P., Frey, K. S., Greenberg, M. P., Haynes, N. M., Kessler, R., Schwab-Stone, M. E., & Shriver, T. P. (1997). *Promoting social and emotional learning. Guidelines for educators*. Association for Supervision and Curriculum Development: USA.

Eliott, C. (1992). *The affective reasoner: A process model of emotions in a multi-agent system*. PhD thesis, Institute for the Learning Sciences, Northwestern University.

Elliott, C. (1994). *The affective reasoning project*. DePaul University. Retrieved April 18, 2008, from http://condor.depaul.edu/~elliott/arback.html

Elliott, C. (1997). *Hunting for the Holy Grail with "emotionally intelligent" virtual actors*. Institute for Applied Artificial Intelligence, De Paul University.

Elliott, C. D. (1992). *The affective reasoner: A process model of emotions in a multi-agent system*. Ph.D. thesis, The Institute for the Learning Sciences, Northwestern University, Evanston, Illinois.

Elliott, C., Rickel, J., & Lester, J. (1999). Lifelike pedagogical agents and affective computing: An exploratory synthesis. In M. Wooldridge & M. Veloso (Eds.), *Artificial intelligence today*, (pp. 195-212). Berlin: Springer-Verlag.

Ellis, P. M., & Bryson, J. J. (2005). The significance of textures for affective interfaces. In J. G. Carbonell & J. Siekmann (Eds.), *Intelligent virtual agents* (Vol. 3661/2005, pp. 394-404). Berlin: Springer. | DOI: 10.1007/11550617_33

Ellsworth, P. C., & Scherer, K R. (2003). Appraisal processes in emotion. In R. J. Davidson, K. R. Scherer, & H. H. Goldsmith (Eds.), *Handbook of affective sciences* (pp. 572-595). New York: Oxford University Press.

Ellsworth, P. C., & Smith, C. A. (1988). From appraisal to emotion: Differences among unpleasant feelings. *Motivation and Emotion, 12*(3), 271-302.

Ellsworth, P. C., & Smith, C. A. (1988). Shades of joy: Patterns of appraisal differentiating pleasant emotions. *Cognition and Emotion, 2*(4), 301-331.

Elman J.L. (1990). Finding structure in time. *Cognitive Science, 14.*

El-Nasr, M. (1998). *Modeling emotions dynamics in intelligent agents*, Texas A&M University.

El-Nasr, M. S., Ioerger, T., & Yen, J. (2000). FLAME: Fuzzy logic adaptive model of emotions. *Autonomous Agents and Multi-Agent Systems, 3*(3), 219-257.

El-Nasr, M. S., Yen, J., & Ioerger, T. R. (2000). FLAME - Fuzzy Logic Adaptive Model of Emotions. *Autonomous Agents and Muti-Agent Systems, 3*(3), 219-257.

Escaja, T. (2003). Escritura tecnetoesquelética e hipertexto Espéculo. *Revista de estudios literarios de la Universidad Complutense de Madrid.* N° 24. Retrieved June 18, 2008, from http://www.ucm.es/info/especulo/numero24/ciberpoe.html.

Eustache, F., & Desgranges, B. (2008). MNESIS: Towards the integration of current multisystem models of memory. *Neuropsychology Review, 18*(1), 53-69.

Evans, D. (2001). *Emotion: The science of sentiment.* Oxford, England: Oxford University Press.

Eysenck, H. J. (1990). *Biological dimensions of personality. Handbook of personality: Theory and research.* New York: Guilford.

Farnsworth, P. R. (1954). A study of the hevner adjective list. *The Journal of Aesthetics and Art Criticism, 13*(1), 97–103.

Fasel, B., & Luettin, J. (2003). Automatic facial expression analysis: a survey. *Pattern Recognition, 36*(1), 259-275. | DOI: 10.1016/S0031-3203(02)00052-3

Feenberg A. (1996). *Summary remarks on my approach to the philosophical study of technology.* Retrieved from, http://www-rohan.sdsu.edu/faculty/feenberg/Method1.htm

Fehr, B., & Russell, J. A. (1984). Concept of emotion viewed from a prototype perspective. *Journal of Experimental Psychology: General, 113*(3), 464-486.

Fehr, B., & Russell, J. A. (1984). Concept of emotion viewed from a prototype perspective. *Journal of Experimental Psychology: General, 113*(3), 464–486.

Fellous, J. M. From human emotions to robot emotions. In *Proceedings of the 2004 AAAI Spring Symposium: Architectures for Modeling Emotions: Cross-Disciplinary Foundations* (pp. 37–47). Palo Alto, CA: AAAI Press.

Fellous, J.-M. (1999). Neuromodulatory basis of emotion. *The Neuroscientist, 5*(5), 283-94.

Fellous, J.-M., & Arbib, M.A. (2005). *Who needs emotions? The brain meets the robot.* Oxford University Press.

Fernadez-Duque, D., Baird, J., & Posner, M. (2000). Awareness and Metacognition, *Consciousnes and Cognition, 9,* 324-326.

Fischer, K. W., Shaver, P.R., & Carnochan, P. (1990). How emotions develop and how they organise development. *Cognition and Emotion, 4*(2), 81-127.

Fiser, J., Chiu, C., & Weliky, M. (2004). Small modulation of ongoing cortical dynamics by sensory input during natural vision. *Nature, 431,* 573-578.

Fisher, I. (1930). *The Theory of interest.* The Macmillan Company.

Floyd, C., Mehl, W., Reisen, F., Schmidt, G., & Wolf, G. (1989). Out of Scandinavia: Alternative approaches to software design and system development. *Human-Computer Interaction 4,* 253-350.

Fogg, B. J. (2003). *Persuasive technology: using computers to change what we think and do.* Amsterdam; Boston: Morgan Kaufmann Publishers.

Fong, T., Nourbakhsh, I., & Dautenhahn, K. (2003). A survey of socially interactive robots. *Robotics and Autonomous Systems, Special issue on Socially Interactive Robots, 42*(3-4), 143-166.

Fox, D., Burgard, W., & Thrun, S. (1997). The dynamic window approach to collision avoidance. *IEEE Robotics and Automation Magazine, 4*(1), 23-33.

Fox, M.D., Snyder, A.Z., Vincent, J.L., Corbetta, M., Van Essen, D.C., & Raichle, M.E. (2005). The human brain is intrinsically organized into dynamic, anticorrelated functional networks. In *Proceedings of the National Academy of Sciences of the United States of America, Vol. 102* (pp. 9673-9678).

Fractal.org. (n.d.). The Nature of Emotions by Plutchik. Retrieved from, http://www.fractal.org/Bewustzijns-Besturings-Model/Nature-of-emotions.htm

Freedman, J. L., Wallington, S. A., & Bless, E. (1967). Compliance without pressure: The effect of guilt. *Journal of Personality and Social Psychology, 7*(2), 117-124.

Freedman, J., & Fraser, S. (1966). Compliance without pressure: The foot-in-the-door technique. *Journal of Personality and Social Psychology, 4*(2), 195-202.

French, R (1990). Subcognition and the limits of the Turing Test. *Mind, 99*(393), 53-65.

Friberg, A., Bresin, R., & Sundberg, J. (2006). Overview of the KTH rule system for musical performance. *Advances in Cognitive Psychology, 2*(2-3), 145–161.

Fridja, N. (1987). *The emotions: Studies in emotion and social interaction.* New York: Cambridge Universty Press.

Fridja, N., & Swagerman, J. (1987). Can computers feel? Theory and design of an emotional sysem. *Cognition and Emotion, 1*(3), 235-257.

Friedewald, M., & Da Costa, O. (2003). *Science and technology roadmapping: Ambient intelligence in everyday life (Aml@Life). JRC/IPTS - ESTO Study,* July 2003. Retrieved from, http://forera.jrc.ec.europa.eu/documents/SandT_roadmapping.pdf

Friedewald, M., Vildjiounaite, E., & Wright, D. (Eds.) (2006). The brave new world of ambient intelligence: An analysis of scenarios regarding privacy, identity and security issues. In Security in Pervasive Computing, Lecture Notes in Computer Science 3934. Berlin: Springer-Verlag, pp. 119-133.

Frijda, N. (1986). *The emotions.* Cambridge University Press.

Frijda, N. H. (1989). Les théories des émotions : Un bilan. In B. Rimé, & K. R. Scherer (Eds.), *Les émotions* (pp. 21-72). Paris: Delachaux et Niestle.

Frijda, N. H. (1989). The functions of emotional expression. In J. P. Forgas & J. M. Innes (Eds.), *Recent advances in social psychology: An international perspective* (pp. 205-217). Amsterdam: North-Holland.

Frijda, N. H. (1993). Moods, emotion episodes, and emotions. In M. Lewis & J. M. Haviland (Eds.), *Handbook of emotions* (pp. 381-403). New York: The Guilford Press.

Frijda, N. H. (1994). Varieties of affect: emotions and episodes, moods, and sentiments. In P. Ekman, & R. J. Davidson (Eds.), *The Nature of Emotion* (pp. 59-67). New York: Oxford University Press.

Frijda, N. H., Kuipers, P., & ter Schure, E. (1989). Relations among emotion, appraisal, and emotional action readiness. *Journal of Personality and Social Psychology, 57*(2), 212-228.

Frijda, N. H. (1987). *The emotions (studies in emotion and social interaction).* Cambridge University Press.

Fromme, D. K., & O'Brien, C. S. (1982). A dimensional approach to the circular ordering of the emotions. *Motivation and Emotion, 6*(4), 337-363.

Funge, J. (2004). *Artificial intelligence for computer games: an introduction.* A K Peters.

Fussell, S. R. (2002). The verbal communication of emotions: introduction and overview. In S.R. Fussell (Ed.), *The verbal communication of emotions: interdisciplinary perspectives* (pp. 1-16). Mahwah, N.J.: L. Erlbaum Associates.

Gadanho, S. C. (2002). Emotional and cognitive adaptation in real environments. *Symposium ACE'2002 of the 16th European Meeting on Cybernetics and Systems Research.*

Gadanho, S., & Hallam, J. (2001). Emotion-triggered learning in autonomous robot control. *Cybermetics and Systems, 32,* 531-559.

Gadanho, S., & Hallam, J. (2001). Emotion-triggered learning in autonomous robot control. *Cybernetics and Systems: an International Journal, 5*(32), 531-559.

Gadanho, S.C., & Hallam, J. (2001). Robot learning driven by emotions. *Adaptive Behavior, 9*(1), 42-64.

Gage, A. (2004). Multi-robot task allocation using affect. Doctoral dissertation, University of South Florida, USA.

Gage, J. (1993). *Color and culture: Practice and meaning from antiquity to abstraction.* Boston, Toronto, & London: Little, Brown, & Co.

Gaggioli, A. (2005). Optimal experience in ambient intelligence. In G. Riva, F. Vatalaro, F. Davide, M. Alcañiz (Eds.), *Ambient Intelligence.* IOS Press.

Gardner, H. (1983). *Frames of the mind.* New York: Basic Books.

Gelambí, M. (2004). *La gestión transversal de género como reto para las empresas.* Tarragona. Universitat Rovira y Virgili. CIES.

Gerbrandy, J., & Groeneveld, W. (1997). Reasoning about information change. *Journal of Logic, Language, and Information, 6*, 147-196.

Gibbard, A. (1990). *Wise choices, apt feelings: a theory of normative judgment.* Harvard University Press.

Gibson, J. (1977). The theory of affordances. In R.E. Shaw, & J. Bransford (Eds.), *Perceiving, acting, and knowing: Toward an ecological psychology* (pp. 67-82). Hillsdale, NJ: Lawrence Erlbaum Associates.

Gibson, J. (1979). The ecological approach to visual perception. Boston, MA: Houghton Mifflin Company.

Gibson, J. (1982). The theory of affordances and the design of the environment. In E. Reed, & R. Jones (Eds.), *Reasons for realism: Selected essays of James J. Gibson* (pp. 413-416). Hillsdale, NJ: Lawrence Erlbaum Associates.

Gibson, J. J. (1966). *The senses considered as perceptual systems.* Boston: Houghton Mifflin.

Gibson, J. J. (1977). The theory of affordances. In R. Shaw & J. Bransford (Eds.), *Perceiving, acting and knowing. Toward an ecological psychology* (pp. 67-82). Hillsdale, N.J.: Erlbaum.

Giddens, A. (2003). *The sociology.* London: Pluto Press.

Gigerenzer, G., & Hug, K. (1992). Domain-specific reasoning: Social contracts, cheating, and perspective change. *Cognition, 43*(2), 127-171.

Gilbert, L., & Moore, D. (1998). Building interactivity into web courses: Tools for social and instructional interaction. *Educational Technology, 38*(3), 29-35.

Gluck, M., Mercado, E., & Myers, C. (2008). *Learning and memory: From brain to behavior.* New York: Worth Publishers.

Glynn, S. M., & Koballa, T. R. (2006). Motivation to learn science. In J. Mintzes and W. Leonard (Eds.), *Handbook of college science teaching.* Arlington, VA: NSTA Press.

Gockley, R., Bruce, A., Forlizzi, J., Michalowski, M., Mundell, A., Rosenthal, S., Sellner, B., Simmons, R., Snipes, K., Shultz, A., & Wang, J. (2005). Designing robots for long-term social interaction. *2005 IEEE International Conference on Robotics and Automation.*

Goddard, C. (2002). Explicating emotions across languages and cultures: a semantic approach. In S.R. Fussell (Ed.), *The verbal communication of emotions: interdisciplinary perspectives* (pp. 19-53). Mahwah, N.J.: L. Erlbaum Associates.

Goddard, C. and Wierzbicka, A. (2007). Semantic primes and cultural scripts in language learning and intercultural communication. In G. Palmer & F. Sharifian (Eds.), *Applied cultural linguistics: implications for second language learning and intercultural communication* (pp. 105-124). Amsterdam: John Benjamins.

Goethe, J. W. von. (1840). *Goethe's theory of colours* (C.L. Eastlake, tr.). London, UK: Murray.

Goldberg, D., & Matarić, M. J. (1997). Interference as a tool for designing and evaluating multi-robot controllers. In *Proceedings of the National Conference on Artificial Intelligence (AAAI),* (pp. 637-642).

Goldberg, D., & Matarić, M. J. (2002). Design and evaluation of robust behavior-based controllers for distributed multi-robot collection tasks. In T. Balch, & L. E. Parker (Eds.), *Robot teams: From diversity to polymorphism,* (pp. 315-344), AK Peters.

Goleman, D. (1995). *Emotional intelligence.* New York: Bantam Books.

Goleman, D. (1998). *Working with emotional intelligence.* New York: Bantam Books.

Gómez, E. (2006). *Tonal description of music audio signals.* Doctoral dissertation, Universitat Pompeu Fabra.

Gopych, P. (2002). Computer modeling of feelings and emotions: a quantitative neural network model of the feeling-of-knowing. *Kharkiv University Bulletin no. 550.*

Gordon, R. (1987). *The structure of emotions.* Cambridge, UK: Cambridge University Press.

Gosselin, N., Peretz, I., Noulhiane, M., Hasboun, D., Beckett, C., Baulac, M., et al. (2005). Impaired recognition of scary music following unilateral temporal lobe excision. *Brain, 128*(3), 628–640.

Gould, E., Reeves, A., Graziano, M., & Gross, C. (1999). Neurogenesis in the neocortex of adult primates. *Science, 286*, 548-52.

Gouyon, F., Herrera, P., Gómez, E., Cano, P., Bonada, J., Loscos, A., et al. (2008). Content processing of music audio signals. In P. Polotti & D. Rocchesso (Eds.), *Sound to sense, sense to sound: A state of the art in sound and music computing* (pp. 83–160). Berlin: Logos Verlag Berlin GmbH.

Gratch, J. & Marsella, S. (2001). Tears and Fears: Modeling emotions and emotional behaviors in synthetic agents. *5th International Conference on Autonomous Agents.*

Gratch, J. (2000). Émile: Marshalling passions in training and education. In *Proceedings of the 4th International Conference on Autonomous Agents* (pp. 325-332). Barcelona, Spain.

Gratch, J., & Marsella, S. (2004). A domain-independent framework for modeling emotion. *Journal of Cognitive Systems Research, 5*(4), 269-306.

Greenbaum, J. (1991). Toward participatory design: The head and the heart revisited. In *IFIP TC9/WG 9.1 Conference on Women, Work and Computerization*, Helsinki, Finland; Amsterdam, The Netherlands: Elsevier Science Publishers.

Gregory, R.L. (ed.) (1987). The Oxford companion to the mind. Oxford, UK: Oxford University Press.

Grewe, O., Nagel, F., Kopiez, R., & Altenmüller, E. (2007). Emotions over time: synchronicity and development of subjective, physiological, and facial affective reactions to music. *Emotion, 7*(4), 774–788.

Grey, J.R. (2004). Integration of emotion and cognitive control. *Current Directions in Psychological Science, 13*, 46-48.

Gros, C. (2005). Self-Sustained Thought Processes in a Dense Associative Network. In U. Furbach (Ed.), *Proceedings of the 28th Annual German Conference on Artificial Intelligence (KI 2005), Springer Lecture Notes in Artificial Intelligence, Vol. 3698* (pp. 366-379).

Gros, C. (2007). Neural networks with transient state dynamics. *New Journal of Physics, 9*, 109-128.

Gros, C. (2008). *Complex and adaptive dynamical systems, a primer.* Springer.

Gros, C., & Kaczor, G. (2008). Learning in cognitive systems with autonomous dynamics. *Proceedings of the International Conference on Cognitive Systems, Karlsruhe 2008.* IEEE.

Gross, J. J., & John, O. P. (2003). Individual differences in two emotion regulation processes: Implications for affect, relationships, and wellbeing. *Journal of Personality & Social Psychology, 85*(2), 348-362.

Grosser, K. & Moon, J. (2005). The role of corporate social responsibility in gender mainstreaming. *International Feminist Journal of Politics, 7*(4), 532-554.

Guaus, E., & Herrera, P. (2006). Music genre categorization in humans and machines. In *Proceedings of the 121st Convention of the Audio Engineering Society.*

Gurtner, J-L., Monnard, I., & Genoud, P. A. (2001). Towards a Multilayer model of context and its impact on motivation. In S. Volet, & S. Jarvela, (Eds.), *Motivation in learning contexts: theoretical and methodological implications* (pp. 189-208). Oxford: Elsevier Pergamon.

Haegen, Rina Van der (1989). *In het spoor van seksuele differentie* (p. 104). Nijmegen, The Nederlands: Sun.

Haist, F., Gore, J.B., & Mao, H. (2001). Consolidation of memory over decades revealed by functional magnetic resonance imaging. *Nature Neuroscience, 4*, 1139-1145.

Hallnäs, L., & Redström, J. (2001). Slow technology – Designing for reflection. Personal *and Ubiquitous Computing, 5*, 201-212.

Halpern, J. (2003). *Reasoning about uncertainty.* Cambridge, MA: MIT Press.

Hamming, R.W. (1980). *Coding and information theory.* Englewood Cliffs, NJ: Prentice-Hall.

Hanard, S. (1992). The Turing Test is not a trick: Turing indistinguishability is a scientific criterion. *SIGART Bulletin 3*(4), 9-10.

Hanard, S. (2001). Minds, Machines and Turing: The indistinguishability of indistinguishable. *Journal of Logic, Language, and Information* – special issue on Alan Turing and Artificial Intelligence. Retrieved December 18, 2006, from http://www.wkap.nl/journalhome.htm/0925-8531.

Hansen, C. H., & Hansen, R. D. (1988). Finding the face in the crowd: An anger superiority effect. *Journal of Personality and Social Psychology, 54,* 917-924.

Hansson, S. O., & Wassermann, R. (2002). Local change. *Studia Logica, 70,* 49-76.

Hara, F., & Kobayashi, H. (1996). A face robot able to recognize and produce facial expression. In *Proceedings of the IEEE/RSJ International Conference on Intelligent Robots and Systems '96, IROS 96, Osaka* (pp. 1600-1607). | DOI: 10.1109/IROS.1996.569026

Haraway, D. J. (1991). *Simians, cyborgs and women: the reinvention of nature.* New York: Routledge.

Hare, R. D. (1993). *Without conscience: The disturbing world of psychopaths among us.* New York: The Gilford Press.

Harnad, S. (2001). What's wrong and right about searle's chinese room argument? In: M. Bishop & J. Preston (Eds.) *Essays on Searle's Chinese room argument.* Oxford University Press.

Harré, R. (1986). *The social construction of emotions.* Oxford: Blackwell.

Harter, S. (1988). *Manual for the self-perception profile for adolescents.* Denver, CO: University of Denver Press.

Hasselmo, M. E., Rolls, E. T., & Baylis, G. C. (1989). The role of expression and identity in the face-selective response of neurons in the temporal visual cortex of the monkey. *Behavioural Brain Research, 32*(3), 203-218.

Hatfield, E., Cacioppo, J. T., & Rapson, R. L. (1994). *Emotional contagion.* Cambridge, England: Cambridge University Press.

Hayes, P. J. (1985). The second naive physics manifesto. In J. R. Hobbs & R. C. Moore (Eds.), *Formal Theories of the Commonsense World.* Norwood, New Jersey: Ablex.

Hazan, C., & Shaver, P. (1987). Romantic love conceptualized as an attachment process. *Journal of Personality and Social Psychology, 52*(3), 511-524.

Hebb, D. O. (1949). *The organization of behavior: A neuropsychological theory.* New York: Wiley.

Heckhausen, H. (1989). *Motivation und handeln.* Berlin: Springer.

Hegselmann, R. & Flache, A. (1998). Understanding complex social dynamics: A plea for cellular automata based modeling. *Journal of Artificial Societies and Social Simulation.*

Heidegger, M. (1926). Sein und Zeit. Used edition: Tübingen, Germany, Max Niemeyer Verlag, 17. Auflage, 1993.

Heidegger, M. (1936). Der Ursprung des Kunstwerkes. Used edition: Stuttgart, Germany, Philipp Reclam jun., 1960.

Heidegger, M. (1962). Die Technik und die Kehre. Stuttgart, Germany: Günther Neske Verlag.

Hein, H.-W. (1999). Big Brother is scanning you. *Spektrum der Wissenschaft, 3,* 106-108.

Heise, D. (1979). *Understanding events: Affect and the construction of social action.* New York: Cambridge University Press.

Henninger, A., Jones, R., & Chown, E., (2003). Behaviours that emerge from emotion and cognition: implementation and evaluation of symbolic-connectionist architecture. In *Proceedings of the Second International Joint Conference on Autonomous Agents and Multiagent Systems* (pp. 321-328). Melbourne, Australia.

Hernández, D., Deniz, O., Lorenzo, J., & Hernández, M. (2004). *BDIE: A BDI like architecture with emotional capabilities.* AAAI Spring Symposium, Stanford, CA.

Herrera, P., Bello, J., Widmer, G., Sandler, M., Celma, O., Vignoli, F., et al. (2005). SIMAC: Semantic interaction with music audio contents. In *Proceedings of the 2nd European Workshop on the Integration of Knowledge, Semantics and Digital Media Technologies* (pp. 399–406). London, UK.

Hevner, K. (1936). Experimental studies of the elements of expression in music. *The American Journal of Psychology, 48*(2), 246–268.

Hicks, R. (2007). The no inference engine theory. *Decision Support Systems, 43*(2).

Higgins, E. T. (1989). Self-discrepancy: A theory relating self and affect. *Psychological Review, 94,* 319-340.

Hillman, J. (1960). *Emotion: A comprehensive phenomenology of theories and their meanings for therapy.* Evanston, IL: Northwestern Univ. Press.

Hinde. R.A. (1970). *Animal behavior: a synthesis of ethology and comparative psychology.* (2ⁿᵈ Ed). London: McGraw-Hill.

Hochschild, A. R. (1979). Emotion work, feeling rules, and social structure. *American Journal of Sociology, 85*(3), 551-575.

Hochschild, A. R. (1983). *The managed heart: The commercialization of human feelings.* Berkeley: University of California Press.

Hoffman, H. S. (1974) Fear-mediated processes in the context of imprinting. In M. Lewis & L. A. Rosenblum (Eds.), *The origins of fear* (pp. 25-48). New York: John Wiley and Sons.

Hollinger, G. A., Georgiev, Y., Manfredi, A., Maxwell, B.A., Pezzementi, Z.A., & Mitchell, B. (2006). Design of a social mobile robot using emotion-based decision mechanisms. *IEEE/RSJ International Conference on Intelligent Robots and Systems* (pp. 3093-3098). Beijing, China: IEEE Press.

Honda. (2002). Asimo. Retrieved from, http://www.honda.co.jp/ASIMO/

Honing, H., & Ladinig, O. (2008). The potential of the internet for music perception research: A comment on lab-based versus web-based studies. *Empirical Musicology Review, 3*(1), 4–7.

Hornecker, E. (2004). Tangible user interfaces als kooperationsunterstützendes medium. Dissertation Fachbereich Mathematik & Informatik, Universität Bremen. Retrieved from, http://deposit.ddb.de/cgi-bin/dokserv?idn=975431153

Horstmann, G. (2002). Evidence for attentional capture by a surprising color singleton in visual search. *Psychological Science, 13*, 499-505.

Howitt, P. (2006), The microfoundations of the Keynesian multiplier process. *Journal of Economic Interaction and Coordination*, 33-44.

Hu, X., Downie, S. J., Laurier, C., Bay, M., & Ehmann, A. F. (2008). The 2007 MIREX audio mood classification task: Lessons learned. In *Proceedings of the 9th International Conference on Music Information Retrieval* (pp. 462–467). Philadelphia, PA, USA.

Huang, Z.Y., & Fewell, J.H. (2002). Modeling insect societies: from genes to colony behavior. *Trends in Ecology & Evolution, 17*(9), 403-404.

Hudlicka, E. (2003). To feel or not to feel: The role of affect in human-computer interaction. *International Journal of Human-Computer Studies, 59*, 1-32.

Hudlicka, E., & Fellous, J.M. (2008). *The emotion Homepage.* Retrieved from, http://emotion.nsma.arizona.edu

Huebner, R. (2000, July). Postmortem: Nihilistic software's vampire: the masquerade — redemption. *Game Developer Magazine*, 44-51.

Huhns, M. N., & Mohammed, A. M. (1999). Benevolent agent. *IEEE Internet Computing, 3*(2), 96-98.

Huhns, M. N., & Stephens, L. M. (1999). Multiagent systems and societies of agents. In G. Weiss (Ed.), *Multiagent systems: A modern approach to distributed artificial intelligence* (pp. 79-120). Cambridge, MA: MIT Press.

Humaine. (n.d.). Humaine emotion research net. Retrieved from, http://emotion-research.net/

Hume, D. (1739/1978). *A treatise of human nature. (Edited by L. A. Selby-Bigge).* Oxford: Oxford University Press.

Huron, D. (2006). *Sweet anticipation: Music and the psychology of expectation.* Cambridge: The MIT Press.

Huron, D. (2006). *Sweet anticipation: Music and the psychology of expectation.* Cambridge: MIT Press.

Hutchins, E. (1995). Cognition in the wild. Cambridge, MA: MIT Press.

Hutchinson, R. R. (1972). The environmental causes of aggression. In J. K. Coles & D. D. Jenson (Eds.), *Nebraska Symposium on Motivation 1972: Vol. 20* (pp. 155-181). Lincoln: University of Nebraska Press.

Iacoboni, M., & Mazziotta, J. C. (2007). Mirror neuron system: Basic findings and clinical applications. *Annals of Neurology, 62*(3), 213-218.

Iacoboni, M., Molnar-Szakacs, I., Gallese, V., Buccino, G., Mazziotta, J. C., & Rizzolatti, G. (2005). Grasping the intentions of others with one's own mirror neuron system. *PLoS Biology, 3*(3), e79, 0001-0007.

IBM (n.d.). Retrieved from, http://www.ibm.com

Ihde, D. (1986). *Experimental phenomenology. An introduction.* Albany, NY: State University of New York Press.

Illeris, K. (2003). *From vocational training to workplace learning.* Roskilde Universitetscenter, Copenhagen. Retrieved April 18, 2008, from http://www.ruc.dk/upload/application/pdf/08f567a4/glasgow.pdf

Insel, T. R. (2003). The neurobiology of affiliation: implications for autism. In R. J. Davidson, K. R. Scherer, & H. H. Goldsmith (Eds.), *Handbook of affective sciences* (pp. 1010-1020). New York: Oxford University Press.

Ioannou, S., Raouzaiou, A., Tzouvaras, V., Mailis, T., Karpouzis, K., & Kollias S. (2005). Emotion recognition through facial expression analysis based on a neurofuzzy network. *Neural Networks, 18*(4), 423-435.

Isen, A. M. (2004). Positive affect and decision making. In M. Lewis, & J. M. Haviland Jones (Eds.), *Handbook of emotions* (2nd ed.) (pp. 417-435). New York: The Guilford Press.

Ishiguro, H. (2005). Android science - Towards a new cross-interdisciplinary framework. In *Proceedings of the CogSci Workshop Towards Social Mechanisms of Android Science, Stresa* (pp. 1-6).

Ishii, K. (2006). Cognitive robotics to understand human beings. *Science & Technology Trends. Quarterly Review, 20*, 11-32.

ISTAG (1999). Orientations for Workprogramme 2000 and beyond. *European Communities.* Retrieved from, ftp://ftp.cordis.europa.eu/pub/ist/docs/istag-99-final.pdf

ISTAG (2001). IST2001: Technologies serving people. Four parts. *European Communities.* Retreived from, http://cordis.europa.eu/ist/library.htm

Itti, L., & Baldi, P. (2006). Bayesian surprise attracts human attention. *Advances in Neural Information Processing Systems (NIPS 2005), 19*, 1-8.

Iversen, O.S., Kanstrup, A.M., & Petersen, M.G. (2004). A visit to the "new Utopia": Revitalizing democracy, emancipation and quality in co-operative design. In *Proceedings of the Third Nordic Conference on Human-Computer Interaction* (pp. 171-179).

Iversena, S.D., & Iversena, L.L. (2007). Dopamine: 50 years in perspective. *Trends in Neurosciences, 30*, 88-193.

Izard, C. E. (1971). *The face of emotion.* New York: Appleton-Century Crofts.

Izard, C. E. (1977). *Human emotions.* New York: Plenum.

Izard, C. E. (1991). *The psychology of emotions.* NY: Plenum Press.

Izard, C. E. (1993). Four systems for emotion activation: Cognitive and noncognitive processes. *Psychological Review, 100*(1), 68-90.

Jain, A.K., & Ross, A. (2004). Multibiometric systems. *Communications of the ACM, 47*(1), 34-44.

Jakobson, R. (1937). Six lectures on sound and meaning. In *Lectures on sound & meaning*, MIT Press, Cambridge, Mass.

James, W. (1884). What is an emotion? *Mind, 9*, 188–205.

Jaques, P. A., Bocca, E., & Viccari, R. (2003). Considering student's emotions in computational educational systems. In *Simpósio Brasileiro de Informática na Educação, Rio de Janiero. Anais do Simpósio Brasileiro de Informática na Educação.* Rio de Janeiro: UFRJ, 2003 (pp. 543-552). Retrieved April 18, 2008, from http://www.inf.unisinos.br/~pjaques/papers/jaques_sbie_2003.pdf

Järvelä, S., Lehtinen, E., & Salonen, P. (2000). Socio-emotional orientation as a mediating variable in the teaching-learning interaction: implications for instructional design. *Scandinavian Journal of Educational Research, 44*, 293-306.

Järvenoja, H., & Järvelä, S. (2005). How students describe the sources of their emotional and motivational experiences during the learning process: A qualitative approach. *Learning and Instruction, 15*(5), 465-480.

Jennings, N. R. (1993). Commitments and conventions: The foundation of coordination in multi-agent systems. *Knowledge Engineering Review, 8*(3), 223-250.

Jennings, N. R., Sycara, K., & Wooldridge, M. (1998). A roadmap of agent research and development. *Autonomous Agents and Multi-Agent Systems Journal, 1*, 275–306.

Jerusalem, M., & Pekrun, R. (Eds.). (1999). *Emotion, motivation und leistung.* Gottingen, Bern, Toronto, Seattle: Hogrefe.

Jiang, H., & Vidal, J. M. (2006). From rational to emotional agents. In *Proceedings of the American Association for Artificial Intelligence (AAAI). Workshop on Cognitive Modeling and Agent-based Social Simulation.*

Johnson, W. L., Rickel, J. W., & Lester, J. C. (2000). Animated pedagogical agents: face-to-face interaction in interactive learning environments. *International Journal of Artificial Intelligence in Education, 11*, 47-78.

Johnson-Laird, P. N., & Oatley, K. (1989). The language of emotions: An analysis of a semantic field. *Cognition and Emotion, 3*(2), 81-123.

Johnston, O., & Thomas, F. (1995). *Disney animation: The illusion of life.* New York: Hyperion.

Jonas, H. (1987). *Technik, Medizin und Ethik.* Frankfurt am Main: Insel Verlag.

Jonassen David H., Jane Howland, Joi Moore, and Rose M. Marra (2002), *Learning to solve problems with technology: A constructivist perspective* (2nd Ed.). Prentice Hall.

Judea, P. (1984). *Heuristics: Intelligent search strategies for computer problem solving.* Reading, MA: Addison-Wesley.

Juslin, P. N., & Västfjäll, D. (2008). Emotional responses to music: The need to consider underlying mechanisms. *Behavioral and Brain Sciences, 31*(5).

Juslin, P., & Laukka, P. (2004). Expression, perception, and induction of musical emotions: A review and a questionnaire study of everyday listening. *Journal of New Music Research, 33*(3), 217–238.

Kahneman, D. Wakker, P.P., & Sarin, R. (1997). Back to Bentham? Explorations of experienced utility. *Quarterly Journal of Economics, 112*, 375-405.

Kahneman, D., & Tversky, A. (1982). Variants of uncertainty. *Cognition, 11*, 143-157.

Kalenka, S., & Jennings, N. R. (1999). Socially responsible decision making by autonomous agents. In Kepa, K., Ernest, S., & Xabier, A. (Eds.), *Cognition, Agency and Rationality* (pp.135-150). Dordrecht, Netherlands: Kluwer Academic Publishers.

Kanda, T., Hirano, T. & Eaton D. (2004). Interactive robots as social partners and peer tutors for children: A field trial. *Human Computer Interaction, 19*, 61-84.

Kappas, A., Bherer, F., & Thériault, M. (2000). Inhibiting facial expressions: Limitations to the voluntary control of facial expressions of emotion. *Motivation and Emotion, 24*(4), 259-268.

Karl, A., Birbaumer, N., Lutzenberger, W., Cohen, L.G., & Flor, H. (2001). Reorganization of motor and somatosensory cortex in upper extremity amputees with phantom limb pain. *The Journal of Neuroscience, 21*, 3609-18.

Karunaratne, S., & Yan, H. (2001, May). Interactive emotional response computation for scriptable multimedia actors. In *Proceedings of 2001 International Symposium on Intelligent Multimedia, Video and Speech Processing,* Hong Kong, China.

Kearsley, G. (1993). Intelligent agents and instructional systems: Implications of a new paradigm. *Journal of Artificial Intelligence in Education, 4*(4), 295-304.

Keller, J. M. (1979). Motivation and instructional design: A theoretical perspective. *Journal of Instructional Development, 2*(4), 26-34.

Keller, J. M. (1999). Using the ARCS motivational process in computer-based instruction and distance education. *New Directions for Teaching and Learning, 78*, 39-47.

Keltner, D., Ekman, P., Gonzaga, G. C., & Beer, J. (2003). Facial expression of emotion. In R. J. Davidson, K. R. Scherer, & H. H. Goldsmith (Eds.), *Handbook of affective sciences* (pp. 415-432). New York: Oxford University Press.

Kemper, T. (1992). Richard S. Lazarus's emotion and adaptation review. *Contemporary Sociology, 21*(4), 522-523.

Kenealy, P. (1988). Validation of a music mood induction procedure: Some preliminary findings. *Cognition & Emotion, 2*(1), 41–48.

Kenet, T., Bibitchkov, D., Tsodyks, M., Grinvald, A., & Ariell, A. (2003). Spontaneously emerging cortical representations of visual attributes. *Nature, 425*, 954-956.

Kerr, N. L., & Kaufman-Gilliland, C. M. (1994). Communication, commitment, and cooperation in social dilemmas. *Journal of Personality and Social Psychology, 66*(3), 513-529.

Kim E.H., Hyun, K.H. & Kwak, Y.K. (2005). Robust emotion recognition feature, frequency range of meaningful signal. *Robot and Human Interactive Communication IEEE 14th workshop.*

Kim, Y., Schmidt, E., & Emelle, L. (2008). Moodswings: A collaborative game for music mood label collection. In *Proceedings of the 9th International Conference on Music Information Retrieval* (pp. 231–236). Philadelphia, PA, USA.

Kirk, R. (1974). Zombies versus materialists. *Aristotelian Society, 48* (suppl.), 135-52.

Kirkup, G., et al. (2000). *The gendered cyborg: A reader.* New York: Routledge.

Kitano, H., Tadokoro, S., & Noda, I. (1999, October). RoboCup-rescue: Search and rescue in large scale disasters as a domain for autonomous agents research. In *Proceedings of IEEE Conference on Systems, Men and Cybernetics, 6*, 739-743.

Kivy, P. (1989). *Sound sentiment: An essay on the musical emotions.* Temple University Press.

Klein, J., Moon, Y., & Picard, R. (1999). This computer responds to user frustration. In *Proceedings of the Conference on Human Factors in Computing Systems* (pp. 242-243). Pittsburgh: ACM Press.

Klein, J., Moon, Y., & Picard, R.W. (2002). This computer responds to user frustration: Theory, design, and results. *Interacting with Computers, 14*, 119-140.

Kleinginna, P.R., & Kleinginna, A.M. (1981). A categorized list of emotion definitions, with suggestions for a consensual definition. *Motivation & Emotion, 5*(4), 345-79.

Klinger, E. (1975). Consequences of commitment to and disengagement from incentives. *Psychological Review, 82*(1), 1-25.

Knudsen, E.J., du Lac, S., & Esterly, S.D. (1987). Computational maps in the brain. *Annual Review of Neuroscience, 10*, 41-65.

Koda, T. (1996). *Agents with faces: A study on the effect of personification of software agents.* Unpublished Masters Thesis, MIT Media Lab, Massachusetts Institute of Technology, Cambridge, MA.

Koedinger, K., & Aleven, V. (2007). Exploring the assistance dilemma in experiments with cognitive tutors. *Educational Psychology Review 19*, 239-264.

Koedinger, K., Aleven, V., Heffernan, N., McLaren, B., & Hockenberry, M. (2004). Opening the door to nonprogrammers: authoring intelligent tutor behavior by demonstration. In *Proceedings of ITS-2004* (pp. 162-174). Berlin: Springer

Koedinger, K., Anderson, J., Hadley, W., & Mark, M. (1997). Intelligent tutoring goes to school in the big city. *International Journal of Artificial Intelligence in Education, 8*, 30-43

Koelsch, S., Fritz, T., Cramon, D. Y. V., Müller, K., & Friederici, A. D. (2006). Investigating emotion with music: an fmri study. *Human Brain Mapping, 27*(3), 239–250.

Kolodner, J.L. (1984). *Retrieval and organization strategies in conceptual memory: A computer model.* Northvale, NJ: Lawrence Erlbaum Associates.

Kolodner, J.L. (1993). *Case-based reasoning.* San Francisco, CA: Morgan Kaufmann.

Kort, B., & Reilly, R. (2002). An affective module for an intelligent tutoring system. In S. A. Cerri, G. Gouarderes, & F. Paraguacu (Eds.), *Intelligent Tutoring Systems 2002 LNCS 2363* (pp. 955-962). Springer-Verlag.

Kostakos, V., O'Neill, E. (2004). Pervasive computing in emergency situations. In *Proceedings of the Thirty-Seventh Annual Hawaii International Conference on System Sciences, January 5-8, 2004,* Computer Society Press.

Kramer, A., A.D.I., Lim, S., Kuo, J., Lee, S-L, & Kiesler, S. (2005). Eliciting information from people with a gendered humanoid robot powers. *Robot and Human Interactive Communication, ROMAN 2005. IEEE International Workshop*, 158-163.

Krikke, J., & Alfonsi, B. (2006). In the News. *Intelligent Systems, IEEE, 21*, 102-104.

Kringelbach, M.L. (2005). *The Human Orbitofrontal Cortex: Linking Reward to Hedonic Experience. Nature Reviews of Neuroscience, 6*, 691-702.

Kripke, S.A. (1980). *Naming and necessity.* Cambridge, MA: Harvard University Press.

Krumhansl, C. L. (1997). An exploratory study of musical emotions and psychophysiology. *Canadian Journal of Experimental Psychology, 51*(4), 336–353.

Kubrick, S. (1968). *2001: A Space Odyssey* (movie).

Kuhl, J. (1986). Motivation and information. In R. M. Sorrentino, & E.T. Higgins (Eds.), *Handbook of Motivation and Cognition* (pp. 404-434). Chichester: Wiley.

Kühnlenz, K., & Buss, M. (2004). Towards an emotion core based on a hidden Markov model. In *Proceedings of the 13th International Workshop on Robot and Human Interactive Communication* (pp. 119-124). Kurashiki, Okayama, Japan.

Kumar, R., Rosé, C., Aleven, V., Iglesias, A., & Robinson, A. (2006). Evaluating the effectiveness of tutorial dialogue instruction in an exploratory learning context. In Proceedings *ITS 2006.* (in Press).

Laird, J. E., Newell, A., & Rosenbloom, P. S. (1987). Soar: An architecture for general intelligence. *Artificial Intelligence, 33*, 1-64.

Laird, L., & Gresler, C. (1990). William James and the mechanism of emotional experience. *Journal of Personality and Social Psychology,16*, 636-651.

Lange, C.J. (1885). *Om sindsbevaegelser: Et psyko-fysiologisk studie.* Copenhagen: Jacob Lunds.

Langheinrich, M. (2005). Personal privacy in ubiquitous computing tools and system support. Dissertation of the Swiss Federal Institute of Technology, Zürich. Retrieved from, http://www.vs.inf.ethz.ch/publ/papers/langheinrich-phd-2005.pdf

Larsen, R. J., & Diener, W. (1992). Promises and problems with the circumplex model of emotion. *Review of Personality and Social Psychology, 13,* 25-59.

Larsen, R. J., Kasimatis, M., & Frey, K. (1992). Facilitating the furrowed brow: A nonobtrusive test of the facial feedback hypothesis applied to unpleasant effect. *Cognition and Emotion, 6*(5), 321-338.

Laughlin, C.D., Jr., McManus, J., & d'Aquili, E.G. (1990). Brain, symbol and experience: Toward a neurophenomenology of consciousness. Boston, MA: New Science Library.

Laukenmann, M. (2007). An investigation of the influence of emotional factors on learning in physics instruction. *International Journal of Science Education, 25*(4), 489 – 507.

Laurier, C., & Herrera, P. (2007). Audio music mood classification using support vector machine. In *Proceedings of the 8th International Conference on Music Information Retrieval.* Vienna, Austria.

Laurier, C., & Herrera, P. (2008). Mood cloud: A real-time music mood visualization tool. In *Proceedings of the 2008 Computers in Music Modeling and Retrieval Conference* (pp. 163–167). Copenhagen, Danemark.

Laurier, C., Grivolla, J., & Herrera, P. (2008). Multimodal music mood classification using audio and lyrics. In *Proceedings of the International Conference on Machine Learning And Applications.* San Diego, CA, USA.

Lazarus, R. (1991). *Emotion and adaptation.* New York: Oxford University Press.

Lazarus, R. (2006): *Stress and emotion: a new synthesis.* New York: Springer.

Lazarus, R. S. (1966). *Psychological stress and the coping process,* McGraw-Hill, New-York.

Lazarus, R. S. (1991). Progress on a cognitive-motivational-relational theory of emotion. *American Psychologist, 46*(8), 819-834.

Lazarus, R. S. (1991). *Emotion and adaptation.* New York: Oxford University Press.

Lazarus, R. S. (1991). Cognition and motivation in emotion. *American Psychologist, 46*(4), 352-367.

Lazarus, R. S. (1999). *Stress and emotion a new synthesis*. New York: Springer.

Lazarus, R. S., & Folkman, S. (1984). *Stress, appraisal, and coping*. New York: Springer.

Lazarus, R. S. (1991). *Emotion and adaptation*. Oxford: Oxford University Press.

Lazarus, R.S., Kanner, A.D. & Folkman, S. (1980). Emotions: A cognitive – phenomenological analysis, IN (ULICH 1985)

Leary, T. (1957). *Interpersonal diagnosis of personality*. New York: Ronald Press.

LeBaron, B. (2006). Agent based computational finance: suggested readings and early research. *Journal of Economic Dynamics and Control*.

Leber, A.B., Turk-Browne, N.B., & Chun, M.M. (2008). Neural predictors of moment-to-moment fluctuations in cognitive flexibility. *PNAS, 105*(36), 13592–13597.

LeDoux J. (1998). Fear and the brain: Where have we been, and where are we going? *Biological-Psychiatry, 44*, 12.

LeDoux, J. (1996). *The emotional brain: The mysterious underpinnings of emotional life*. New York: Simon & Schuster.

LeDoux, J. E. (1989). Cognitive-emotional interactions in the brain. *Cognition and Emotion, 3*(4), 267-289.

LeDoux, J. E. (1996). *The emotional brain: The mysterious underpinnings of emotional life*. New York: Simon and Schuster.

LeDoux, J.E. (1998). Fear and the brain: Where have we been and where are we going? *Biological Psychiatry, 44*, 1229-1238.

Lee S-L., Kiesler, S., Lau, I.Y., & Chiu, C.Y. (2005). Human mental models of humanoid robots. *2005 IEEE International Conference on Robotics and Automation*.

Lee, M., & Franklin, S. (1998). An architecture for emotion. *AAAI Fall Symposium Emotional and Intelligent: The Tangled Knot of Cognition*. (pp. 122-128). Menlo Park, CA: AAAI Press.

Lee-Johnson, C. P., & Carnegie, D. A. (2007). Emotion-based parameter modulation for a hierarchical mobile robot planning and control architecture. In *Proceedings of the IEEE/RSJ International Conference on Intelligent Robots and Systems* (pp. 2839-2844). San Diego, CA: IEEE Press.

Lee-Johnson, C. P., & Carnegie, D. A. (in press). Mobile robot navigation modulated by artificial emotions. *IEEE Transactions on Systems, Man and Cybernetics: Part B*.

Leijonhufvud, A. (2006). Agent-based macro. In L. Tesfatsion & K.L. Judd (Ed.), *Handbook of Computational Economics* (Vol. 2, pp. 1625-37). Amsterdam: North-Holland.

Lepper, M. R., & Malone, T. W. (1987). Intrinsic motivation and instructional effectiveness in computer based education. In R. E. Snow & M. J. Farr (Eds.), *Aptitude, learning and instruction: Volume III Cognitive and affective process analyses*. Hillsdale, NJ: Erlbaum.

Lester, J. C., Converse, S. A., Kahler, S. E., Barlow, S. T., Stone, B. A., & Bhogal, R. S. (1997). The persona effect: Affective impact of animated pedagogical agents. In *Proceedings of CHI '97* (pp. 359-366). New York: ACM Press.

Levenson, R. W. (1994). Emotional control: Variations and consequences. In P. Ekman & R. J. Davidson (Eds.), *The nature of emotion: Fundamental questions* (pp. 273-279). Oxford: Oxford University Press.

Levenson, R. W., & Ruef, A. M. (1992) Empathy: A physiological substrate. *Journal of Personality and Social Psychology, 63*(2), 234-246.

Levitin, D. (2007). Life soundtracks: The uses of music in everyday life. *Report prepared for the exclusive use of Philips Consumer Electronics B.V., Eindhoven, The Netherlands, http://www.yourbrainonmusic.com*.

Levy, D. (2007). *Love, Sex and Robots – the evolution of human-robot relationships* (uncorrected proof). London: Duckworth.

Lewis M, Haviland-Jones J.M., & L. Feldman Barrett (Eds.). (2008). Handbook of emotions (3rd Ed.). New York: Psychology Press.

Lewis, M.D. (2005). Bridging emotion theory and neurobiology through dynamic systems modeling. *Behavioral and Brain Sciences, 28*, 169-245.

Lewis, M.D. (2005). Self-organizing individual differences in brain development. *Developmental Review, 25*, 252-277.

Li, L. (1999). *Action theory and cognitive psychology in industrial design: User models and user interfaces.* Dissertation. Braunschweig, Germany: Hochschule für Bildende Künste. Retrieved from, http://www.hbk-bs.de/bibliothek/ediss/data/19990630a

Li, T., & Ogihara, M. (2003). Detecting emotion in music. In *Proceedings of the 4th International Conference on Music Information Retrieval* (pp. 239–240). Baltimore, MD, USA.

Li, T., Ma, Y., Qiu, Y., & Yue, P. (2007, February). Modeling personality, emotion and mood for a pedagogical agent. In *Proceedings of Artificial Intelligence and Applications 2007*, Innsbruck, Austria. Calgary AB, Canada: Acta Press.

Li, T., Qiu, Y., Yue, P., & Zhong, G. (2007). Exploiting model of personality and emotion of learning companion agent. *International Conference on Computer Systems and Applications* (pp. 860-865).

Lieberman, H., & Selker, T. (2003). Agents for the User Interface. In J. Bradshaw (Ed.), *Handbook of agent technology.* Boston: The MIT Press.

Lieberman, M.D. (2007). Social Cognitive Neuroscience: A Review of Core Processes. *Annual Review of Psychology, Vol. 58*, 259-289.

Linder, C., & Marshall, D. (1997). Introducing and evaluating metacognitive strategies in large-class introductory physics teaching. In C. Rust (Ed.), *Improving student learning: Improving students as learners* (pp. 411-422). Oxford, UK: Oxford Centre for Staff and Learning Development.

Lisetti, C., & Nasoz, F. (2002). MAUI: A multimodal affective user interface. In *Proceedings of the ACM Multimedia International Conference* (pp. 161-170). Juan-les-Pins, France.

Little, D. (1991). *Learner Autonomy: Definition, issues and problems.* Dublin: Authentik.

Liu, K., & Picard, R. (2005). Embedded empathy in continuous, interactive health assessment. *Affective computing.* Retrieved April 18, 2008, from http://affect.media.mit.edu/pdfs/05.liu-picard.pdf

Llinas, R.R. (1988). The intrinsic electrophysiological properties of mammalian neurons. *Science, 242*, 1654-64.

Loebner Results (2003). University of Surrey. Retrieved February 9, 2008, from http://loebner03.hamill.co.uk/

Loebner, H. (2008). Home page of the Loebner Prize in artificial intelligence. Retrieved February 12, 2007, from http://www.loebner.net/Prizef/loebner-prize.html.

Logan, B. (2000). Mel frequency cepstral coefficients for music modeling. In *Proceeding of the 1st International Symposium on Music Information Retrieval.* Plymouth, MA, USA.

Lorenz, K. (1950). The comparative method in studying innate behavior patterns. *Symposia of the Society for Experimental Biology, 4*, 221-268.

Lorini, E., & Castelfranchi, C. (2006). The unexpected aspects of surprise. *International Journal of Pattern Recognition and Artificial Intelligence, 20*, 817-835.

Lorini, E., & Castelfranchi, C. (2007). The cognitive structure of Surprise: looking for basic principles. *Topoi: An International Review of Philosophy, 26*(1), 133-149.

Lorini, E., & Piunti, M. (2007). The benefits of surprise in dynamic environments: from theory to practice. In A. Paiva, R. Prada & R. W. Picard (Eds.), *Proceedings of the Second International Conference on Affective Computing and Intelligent Interaction* (Vol. 4738, pp. 362-373). Berlin: Springer.

Losonczy, A., Makara, J.K., & Magee, J.C. (2008). Compartmentalized dendritic plasticity and input feature storage in neurons. *Nature, 452*, 436-40.

Lovett, M. C., Daily, L. Z., & Reder, L. M. (2000). A source activation theory of working memory: Cross-task prediction of performance in ACT-R. *Cognitive Systems Research, 1*, 99-118.

Lowenstein, G. (1994). The psychology of curiosity: A review and reinterpretation. *Psychological Bulletin, 116*(1), 75-98.

Loyall, A. B. (1997). *Believable agents: Building interactive personalities.* Ph.D. Thesis. Technical Report CMU-CS-97-123. School of Computer Science, Carnegie Mellon University, Pittsburgh, PA..

Lu, D., Liu, L., & Zhang, H. (2006). Automatic mood detection and tracking of music audio signals. *IEEE Transactions on Audio, Speech, and Language Processing, 14*(1), 5–18.

Luck, G., Riikkilä, K., Lartillot, O., Erkkilä, J., & Toiviainen, P. (2006). Exploring relationships between level of mental retardation and features of music therapy improvisations: a computational approach. *Nordic Journal of Music Therapy, 15*(1), 30–48.

Lucky, R. (1999, March). Connections – Everything will be connected to everything else. *IEEE Spectrum Reflections Column.* Retrieved from, http://www.argreenhouse.com/papers/rlucky/spectrum/connect.shtml

Lugmayr, A. (2006). From ambient media towards biomedia. Paper presetned at *MindTrek Conference 2006,* Tampere

Lugmayr, A. (2006). The future is "ambient." In R. Creutzburg, J. H. Takala, and C. W. Chen, (Eds.), *Proceedings of SPIE Vol. 6074, 607403 Multimedia on Mobile Devices II.* vol. 6074. San Jose: SPIE.

Lugmayr, A. (2007, July-August). Ambient Media. *Novatica, 33.* Retrieved from, http://www.ati.es/novatica/infonovatica_eng.html

Lugmayr, A. (2008). Ambient (intelligent) media and beyond. Paper presented at *European Interactive TV Conference (EuroITV) 2008,* Salzburg, Austria.

Lugmayr, A. (2008). Ambient media and beyond. Paper presented at *1st International Conference on Designing Interactive User Experiences for TV and Video (uxTV) 2008.* Silicon Valley, CA.

Lugmayr, A. (in press). *Ambient media and beyond.* New York: Springer-Verlag.

Lugmayr, A., Pohl, A., Mühlhäuser, M., Kallenbach, J., & Chorianopoulos, K. (2007). Ambient media and home entertainment. In G. Lekakos, K. Chorianopoulos, & G. Doukidis (Eds.), *Interactive Digital Television: Technologies and Applications.* Hershey, PA: Idea Group Publishing.

Lugmayr, A., Pohl, A., Mühlhäuser, M., Negru, D., Kallenbach, J., Köbler, F., et al. (2006). Ambient media and home entertainment (workshop review). In *Proceed-*

ings of the 4th Euro iTV Conference. Athens, Greece: ELTRUN/AUEB.

Lund, H. H., & Nielsen, J. (2002). An edutainment robotics survey. In *Proceedings of the Third International Symposium on Human and Artificial Intelligence Systems: The Dynamic Systems Approach for Embodiment and Sociality, Fukui.*

Lutz, A., & Thompson, E. (2003). Neurophenomenology: Integrating subjective experience and brain dynamics in the neuroscience of consciousness. *Journal of Consciousness Studies, 10*(9/10), 31-52.

Lutz, C. (1988). Ethnographic perspectives on the emotion lexicon. In V. Hamilton, G. H. Bower, & N. H. Frijda (Eds.), *Cognitive perspectives on emotion and motivation* (pp. 399-419). Dordrecht: Kluwer.

Lyons, M. J. (2004). Facial gesture interfaces for expression and communication. In *Proceedings of the IEEE International Conference on Systems, Man and Cybernetics, The Hague* (pp. 598- 603). | DOI: 10.1109/ICSMC.2004.1398365

Lyons, M. J., & Tetsutani, N. (2001). Facing the music: a facial action controlled musical interface. In *Proceedings of the Conference on Human Factors in Computing Systems CHI2001, Seattle* (pp. 309-310). | DOI: 10.1145/634067.634250

Lyons, M. J., Akamatsu, S., Kamachi, M., & Gyoba, J. (1998). *Coding Facial Expressions with Gabor Wavelets.* Proceedings of the Third IEEE International Conference on Automatic Face and Gesture Recognition, Nara pp. 200-205. | DOI: 10.1109/AFGR.1998.670949

Lyons, M. J., Budynek, J., & Akamatsu, S. (1999). Automatic Classification of Single Facial Images. *IEEE Transactions Pattern Analysis and Machine Intelligence, 21*(12), 1357-1362. | DOI: 10.1109/34.817413

Lyons, M. J., Chan, C., & Tetsutani, N. (2004). *MouthType: Text Entry by Hand and Mouth.* Proceedings of the Conference on Human Factors in Computing Systems CHI2004, Austria pp. 1383-1386. | DOI: 10.1145/985921.986070

Lyons, M. J., Funk, M., & Kuwabara, K. (2005). Segment and browse: A strategy for supporting human monitoring of facial expression behaviour. In *Lecture notes in com-*

puter science - human-computer interaction - INTERACT 2005 (Vol. 3585/2005, pp. 1120-1123). Rome: Springer. | DOI: 10.1007/11555261_119

Lyons, M. J., Kluender, D., & Tetsutani, N. (2005). Supporting empathy in online learning with artificial expressions. *Journal of Educational Technology & Society, 8*(4), 22-30.

Lyons, W. (1986). *The disappearance of introspectionism.* Cambridge, MA: MIT Press.

MacDorman, K. F. (2006). Subjective ratings of robot video clips for human likeness, familiarity, and eeriness: An exploration of the uncanny valley. In *Proceedings of the ICCS/CogSci-2006 Long Symposium: Toward Social Mechanisms of Android Science, Vancouver.*

Macedo, L. (2006). *The Exploration of Unknown Environments by Affective Agents.* Unpublished PhD, University of Coimbra, Coimbra.

Macedo, L., & Cardoso, A. (2001). Creativity and surprise. In G. Wiggins (Ed.), *Proceedings of the AISB'01 Symposium on Creativity in Arts and Science* (pp. 84-92). York, UK: The Society for the Study of Artificial Intelligence and Simulation Behaviour.

Macedo, L., & Cardoso, A. (2001). Modelling forms of surprise in an artificial agent. In J. Moore & K. Stenning (Eds.), *Proceedings of the 23rd Annual Conference of the Cognitive Science Society* (pp. 588-593). Edinburgh, Scotland, UK: Erlbaum.

Macedo, L., & Cardoso, A. (2002). Assessing creativity: the importance of unexpected novelty. In *Proceedings of the ECAI'02 Workshop on Creative Systems: Aproaches to Creativity in AI and Cognitive Science,* (pp. 31-37). Lyon, France: University Claude Bernard - Lyon.

Macedo, L., & Cardoso, A. (2003). A model for generating expectations: the bridge between memory and surprise. In C. Bento, A. Cardoso & J. Gero (Eds.), *Proceedings of the 3rd Workshop on Creative Systems: Approaches to Creativity in AI and Cognitive Science, International Joint Conference on Artificial Intelligence* (pp. 3-11). Acapulco, Mexico: IJCAI03.

Macedo, L., & Cardoso, A. (2004). Exploration of unknown environments with motivational agents. In N. Jennings & M. Tambe (Eds.), *Proceedings of the Third International Joint Conference on Autonomous Agents and Multiagent Systems* (pp. 328 - 335). New York: IEEE Computer Society.

Macedo, L., & Cardoso, A. (2005). The role of surprise, curiosity and hunger on the exploration of unknown environments. In *Proceedings of the 12th Portuguese Conference on Artificial Intelligence.* Covilhã, Portugal.

Macedo, L., Cardoso, A., & Reisenzein, R. (2006). A surprise-based agent. In R. Trappl (Ed.), *Proceedings of the 18th European Meeting on Cybernetics and Systems Research* (pp. 583-588). Vienna, Austria: Austrian Society for Cybernetic Studies.

Macedo, L., Reisenzein, R., & Cardoso, A. (2004). Modeling forms of surprise in artificial agents: empirical and theoretical study of surprise functions. In K. Forbus, D. Gentner & T. Regier (Eds.), *Proceedings of the 26th Annual Conference of the Cognitive Science Society* Chicago, Illinois, USA: Lawrence Erlbaum Associates, Inc.

MacFadden, R. J. (2005). Souls on ice: Incorporating emotion in web-based education. In R. J. MacFadden, B. Moore, M. Herie, & D. Schoech (Eds.), *Web-based education in the human services: Models, methods, and best practices.* (pp. 79-98). New York, London, Victoria: The Haworth Press.

MacFadden, R. J., Herie, A. M., Maiter, S., & Dumbrill, G. (2005). Achieving high touch in high tech: a constructivist, emotionally-oriented model of web-based instruction. In R. Beaulaurier & M. Haffey (Eds.), *Technology in Social Work Education and Curriculum. The High Tech, High Touch Social Work Educator* (pp. 21-41). New York: Haworth Press.

MacLean, P. D. (1993). Cerebral evolution of emotion. In M. Lewis & J. M. Haviland (Eds.), *Handbook of emotions* (pp. 67-83). New York: The Guilford Press.

MacLennan, B.J. (1994). Continuous computation and the emergence of the discrete. In K.H. Pribram (Ed.), *Rethinking neural nets: Quantum fields and biological data* (pp. 199-232). Hillsdale, NJ: Lawrence-Erlbaum.

MacLennan, B.J. (1995). The investigation of consciousness through phenomenology and neuroscience. In J. King & K.H. Pribram (Eds.), *Scale in conscious experience: Is the brain too important to be left to specialists to study?* (pp. 25-43). Hillsdale, NJ: Lawrence Erlbaum.

MacLennan, B.J. (1996). The elements of consciousness and their neurodynamical correlates. *Journal of Consciousness Studies, 3* (5/6), 409-24. Reprinted in J. Shear (Ed.), *Explaining consciousness: The hard problem* (pp. 249-66). Cambridge, MA: MIT, 1997.

MacLennan, B.J. (1996). *Protophenomena and their neurodynamical correlates* (Technical Report UT-CS-96-331). Knoxville, TN: University of Tennessee, Knoxville, Department of Computer Science. Available: www.cs.utk.edu/~mclennan

MacLennan, B.J. (1999). Neurophenomenological constraints and pushing back the subjectivity barrier. *Behavioral and Brain Sciences, 22*, 961–63.

MacLennan, B.J. (1999) *The protophenomenal structure of consciousness with especial application to the experience of color: Extended version* (Technical Report UT-CS-99-418). Knoxville, TN: University of Tennessee, Knoxville, Department of Computer Science. Available: www.cs.utk.edu/~mclennan

MacLennan, B.J. (2003). Color as a material, not an optical, property. *Behavioral and Brain Sciences, 26*, 37-8.

MacLennan, B.J. (2004). Natural computation and non-Turing models of computation. *Theoretical Computer Science, 317*, 115-45.

MacLennan, B.J. (2008). Consciousness: Natural and artificial. *Synthesis Philosophica, 22*(2), 401-33.

MacLennan, B.J. (2008). Protophenomena: The elements of consciousness and their relation to the brain. In A. Batthyány, A. Elitzur & D. Constant (Eds.), *Irreducibly conscious: Selected papers on consciousness* (pp. 189-214). Heidelberg & New York: Universitäts-verlag Winter.

Maes, P. (1993). Behavior-Based Artificial Intelligence. *From animals to animats 2. Proceedings of the Second International Conference on Simulation of Adaptive Behavior.* Cambridge, MA: MIT Press.

Maes, P. (1994). *Agents that reduce work and information overload.* Communications of the ACM *37*(7), 30-40.

Maes, P. (1995). Modeling adaptive autonomous agents. In C. G. Langton (Ed.), *Artificial Life: An over view* (pp. 176-181). Cambridge, MA: The MIT Press.

Maes, P. (Ed.). (1991). *Designing autonomous agents: Theory and practice from biology to engineering and back.* Cambridge: MIT Press.

Magnumlanguage (n.d.). Retrieved from, http://www.magnumlanguage.com/magnum.asp.

Magnus, M. (2001). *What's in a word: Studies in phonosemantics,* Doctoral dissertation, University of Trondheim, Norway. Retrieved from the web September 10, 2008 http://www.trismegistos.com/Dissertation/

Mahmood, A. K., & Ferneley, E. (2004). Can avatars replace the trainer? A case study evaluation. In *Proceedings of the the International Conference on Enterprise Information Systems (ICEIS), Porto* (pp. 208-213).

Majumdar A., Sowa J., & Stewart J. (2008). Pursuing the goal of language understanding. In Eklund, P. & Haemmerlé, O. (Eds.) *Proceedings of the 16th ICCS.* Berlin: Springer-Verlag.

Makri-Botsari, E. (2001). Causal links between academic intrinsic motivation, self-esteem, and unconditional acceptance by teachers in high school students. In R. Riding & S. Rayner (Eds.), *International perspectives on individual differences. Vol. 2: Self-perception* (pp.209-220). Westport, CT: Ablex Publishing.

Malatesta, C. Z., & Haviland, J. M. (1982). Learning display rules: The socialization of emotion expression in infancy. *Child Development, 53*(4), 991-1003.

Mandel, M. I., & Ellis, D. P. (2007). A web-based game for collecting music metadata. In *Proceedings of the 8th International Conference on Music Information Retrieval* (pp. 365–366). Vienna, Austria.

Mandel, M., Poliner, G., & Ellis, D. (2006). Support vector machine active learning for music retrieval. *Multimedia Systems, 12*(1), 3–13.

Mandler, G. (1984). *Mind and body: Psychology of emotion and stress.* New York: W. W. Norton.

Mandler, G. (1997). *Human nature explored.* New York: Oxford University Press.

Mankiw, N.G., & Ricardo, R (2001). *Sticky information: A model of monetary nonneutrality and structural slumps* (NBER Working Paper Number 8614).

Mar, R. A. & Oatley, K. (2008). The function of fiction is the abstraction and simulation of social experience. *Perspectives on Psychological Science, 3*(3), 173-192.

Marder E. & Goaillard J.M.(2006). *Variability, compensation and homeostasis in neuron and network function.* Nature Reviews of Neuroscience, Vol. 7, pp. 563-574.

Margulies, A. (1993). Empathy, virtuality and the birth of complex emotional states: Do we find or do we create feelings in the other. In S. L. Albon, D. Brown, E. J. Khantzian & J. E. Mack (Eds.), *Human feelings: Explorations in affect development and meaning.* The Analytic Press.

Maria, K.A., & Zitar, R.A. (2007). Emotional agents: A modeling and an application. *Information and Software Technology, 49,* 695-716.

Marsh, H.W. (1990). The structure of academic self-concept, the Marsh/Shavelson model. *Journal of Educational Psychology, 82,* 623-636.

Martens, R., Gulikers, J., & Bastaens, T. (2004). The impact of intrinsic motivation on e-learning in authentic computer tasks. *Journal of Computer Assisted Learning, 20*(5), 368-376.

Martinez, M. (2000). *Successful web learning environments: new design guidelines.* (ERIC Document No. ED 446745). Retrieved April 18, 2008, from http://eric.ed.gov/ERICDocs/data/ericdocs2sql/content_storage_01/0000019b/80/16/99/b3.pdf

Martinho, C., Paiva, A., & Gomes, M. (2000). Emotions for a Motion: Rapid Development of Believable Panthematic Agents in Intelligent Virtual Environments. *Applied artificial intelligence, 14*(1), 33-68.

Marx, G. T. (2001). Murky conceptual waters: The public and the private. *Journal Ethics and Information Technology, 3*(3).

Mascolo, M. F., & Fischer, K. W. (1995). Developmental transformations in appraisals for pride, shame, and guilt. In J. P. Tangney & K. W. Fischer (Eds.), *Self-conscious emotions. The psychology of shame, guilt, embarrassment, and pride* (pp. 64-113). New York: The Guilford Press.

Masuch, M., Hartman, K., & Schuster, G. (2006). Emotional agents for interactive environments. In *C5'06: Proceedings of the Fourth International Conference on Creating, Connecting and Collaborating through Computing* (pp. 96-102).

Mateas, M., & Stern, A. (2003, March). *Facade: An experiment in building a fully-realized interactive drama.* Paper presented at the game design track of the Game Developer's Conference, San Jose, CA.

Mateas, M., & Stern, A. (2004). *A behavior language: Joint action and behavioral idioms.* In H. Prendinger,& M. Ishizuka (Eds.), *Life-like characters. tools, affective functions, and applications. Cognitive technologies.* Berlin, Heidelberg: Springer Verlag.

Mathes, E. W., Adams, H. E., & Davies, R. M. (1985). Jealousy: Loss of relationship rewards, loss of self-esteem, depression, anxiety, and anger. *Journal of Personality and Social Psychology, 48*(6), 1552-1561.

Matsumoto, D. (1990). Cultural similarities and differences in display rules. *Motivation and Emotion, 14*(3), 195-214.

Matt, J., Leuthold, H., & Sommer, W. (1992). Differential effects of voluntary expectancies on reaction times and event-related potentials: Evidence for automatic and controlled expectancies. *Journal of Experimental Psychology: Learning, Memory and Cognition, 18,* 810-822.

Mavrommati, I. (2002). e-Gadgets case description. In *Doors of Perception 7: Flow.* Retrieved from, http://flow.doorsofperception.com/content/mavrommati_trans.html

Maxis Software, Inc. (2000). *The Sims.* Computer game, PCElectronic Arts, Inc.

Mayer, J. D., & Salovey, P. (1993). The intelligence of emotional intelligence. *Intelligence, 17*(4), 433-442.

Mayer, J.D., & Salovey, P. (1995). Emotional intelligence and the construction and regulation of feelings. *Applied and Preventive Psychology, 4,* 197-208.

Mayer, J. D., Salovey, P., & Caruso, D. R. (2000). Models of emotional intelligence. *Handbook of intelligence.* Cambridge, UK: Cambridge University Press.

Mayer, J.D. (2000). Emotion, intelligence, emotional intelligence. *The handbook of affect and social cognition.* Mahwah, New Jersey: Lawrence Erlbaum and Associates.

Mayer, J.D., & Geher, G. (1996). Emotional intelligence and the identification of emotion. *Intelligence, 22*, 89-113.

Mayer, J.D., Caruso, D., & Salovey, P. (1999). Emotional intelligence meets traditional standards for an intelligence. *Intelligence, 27*, 267-298.

Mayer, J.D., Salovey, P., & Caruso, D.R. (2000). Models of emotional intelligence. In R.J. Sternberg (Ed.), *Handbook of Intelligence* (pp. 396-420). Cambridge, England: Cambridge University Press.

McCall, R.J. (1983). *Phenomenological psychology: An introduction. With a glossary of some key Heideggerian terms.* Madison, WI: University of Wisconsin Press.

McCarthy, J. (1974). Review of "Artificial Intelligence: A General Survey". *Artificial Intelligence, 5*(3). Retrieved May 18, 2008, from http://www-formal.stanford.edu/jmc/reviews/lighthill/lighthill.html

McCauley, L., Franklin, S., & Bogner. M. (2000). An emotion-based "conscious" software agent architecture. In A. Paiva (Ed.) *Affective interactions. Towards a new generation of computer interfaces* (pp. 107-120). Berlin: Springer.

McCauley, T. L., & Franklin, S. (1998). An architecture for emotion. *AAAI Fall Symposium* (pp. 122-127). Menlo Park, California: AAAI Press.

McCormick, B.H., DeFanti, T.A., & Brown, M.D. (eds.) (1987). *Visualization in Scientific Computing.* US: ACM Press.

McCrae, R. R., & Costa, P. T. (1996). Toward a new generation of personality theories: theoretical contexts for the five-factor model. *Five-Factor Model of Personality*, 51-87.

McCrae, R., & John, O. (1992). An introduction to the five-factor model and its application. *Journal of Personality, 60*(2), 175-215.

McDermott, D. (1997, May 14th). Yes, Computers Can Think. *New York Times.*

McDougall, W. (1908/1960). *An introduction to social psychology.* London: Methuen.

McFarland, D. (1991). What it means for robot behaviour to be adaptive. In J.A. Meyer and S.W. Wilson (Eds.), *From animals to animats. Proceedings of the first international conference on simulation of adaptive behavior.* Cambridge, MA: MIT Press.

McGaugh, J. (2003). *Memory and emotion: the making of lasting memories.* New York: Columbia University Press.

McKinney, C. H., Antoni, M. H., Kumar, M., Tims, F. C., & Mccabe, P. M. (1997). Effects of guided imagery and music (gim) therapy on mood and cortisol in healthy adults. *Health Psychology, 16*(4), 390–400.

Mealey, L. (1995). The sociobiology of sociopathy: An integrated evolutionary model. *Behavioral and Brain Sciences, 18*(3), 523-599.

Medawar, P. B. (1967). *The art of the soluble.* London: Methuen.

Mehrabian, A., & Russell, J. (1974). *An approach to environmental psychology.* Cambridge, MA: MIT Press.

Menon, V., & Levitin, D. J. (2005). The rewards of music listening: response and physiological connectivity of the mesolimbic system. *Neuroimage, 28*(1), 175–184.

Merrill, D. C., Reiser, B. J., Ranney, M., & Trafton, J. G. (1992). Effective tutoring techniques: Comparison of human tutors and intelligent tutoring systems. *Journal of the Learning Sciences, 2*(3), 277-305.

Mewes, F. (2002). Regulations for the human park: On Peter Sloterdijk's Regeln für den Menschenpark. *Gnosis, 6*(1). Retrieved from, http://artsandscience.concordia.ca/philosophy/gnosis/vol_vi/Sloterdijk.pdf

Meyer, L. B. (1956). *Emotion and meaning in music.* Chicago: University Of Chicago Press.

Meyer, W.-U. (1988). Die Rolle von Überraschung im Attributionsproze\"s [The role of surprise in the attribution process]. *Psychologische Rundschau, 39*, 136-147.

Meyer, W.-U., & Niepel, M. (1994). Surprise. *Encyclopedia of human behavior* (pp. 353-358).

Meyer, W.-U., Reisenzein, R., & Niepel, M. (2000). Überraschung [Surprise]. *Emotionspsychologie: Ein Handbuch* (pp. 253-263).

Meyer, W.-U., Reisenzein, R., & Schützwohl, A. (1997). Towards a process analysis of emotions: The case of surprise. *Motivation and Emotion, 21*, 251-274.

Miceli, M., & Castelfranchi, C. (2002). The mind and the future: The (negative) power of expectations. *Theory & Psychology, 12*, 335-366.

Michalowski, M. P., Sabanovic, S., & Kozima, H. (2007). A dancing robot for rhythmic social interaction. *In Proceedings of the ACM/IEEE International Conference on Human-Robot Interaction, Arlington, Virginia, USA* (pp. 89-96). | DOI: 10.1145/1228716.1228729

Michaud, F., Côté, C., Létourneau, D., Brosseau, Y., Valin, J., Beaudry, É., et al. (2007). Spartacus attending the 2005 AAAI conference. *Autonomous Robots, Special Issue on the AAAI Mobile Robot Competitions and Exhibition, 22*(4), 369-384.

Michaud, F., Robichaud, E., & Audet, J. (2001). Using motives and artificial emotions for prolonged activity of a group of autonomous robots. *AAAI Fall Symposium on Emotional and Intelligent II: The Tangled Knot of Social Cognition* (pp. 85-90). Cape Code, MA.

Michotte, A. E. (1950). The emotions regarded as functional connections. In M. Reymert (Ed.), *Feelings and emotions. The Mooseheart symposium* (pp. 114-126). New York: McGraw-Hill.

Militiadou, M., & Savenye, W. (2003). Applying social cognitive constructs of motivation to enhance student success in online distance education. *AACE Journal, 11*(1), 78-95.

Millington, I. (2006). *Artificial intelligence for games.* San Francisco, CA: Morgan Kaufmann.

Minsky, M. (1986). *The society of mind.* New York: Simon and Schuster.

Minsky, M. (1987). *The society of mind.* London: William Heinemann Ltd.

Minsky, M. (2007). Once more with feelings. In interview with Amanda Gefter. *New Scientist, February,* 48-49

Minsky, M. (2007). *The emotion machine: Commonsense thinking, artificial intelligence, and the future of the human mind.* New York: Simon & Schuster.

Mitchell, T. (1997). *Machine learning.* McGraw Hill.

Mohammed, A. M., & Huhns, M. N. (2001). Multiagent benevolence as a social norm. In Conte R., & Dellarocas,

C. (Ed.), *Social order in multiagent systems* (pp. 65-83). Boston, MA: Kluwer Academic Publishers.

Moller, J., & Koller, O. (Eds). (1996). *Emotionen, kognitionen und schulleistung.* Weinheim: Psychologie Verlags Union.

Montemerlo, M., Pineau, J., Roy, N., Thrun, S. & Verma, V. (2002). Experiences with a mobile robotic guide for the elderly. *18th National Conference on Artificial Intelligence* (pp. 587-592).

Moreno, R., Mayer, R. E., Spires, H. A., & Lester, J. C. (2001). The case for social agency in computer-based teaching: do students learn more deeply when they interact with animated pedagogical agents? *Cognition and Instruction, 19*, 177-213.

Morgado, L., & Gaspar, G. (2005). Emotion based adaptive reasoning for resource bounded agents. In *AAMAS '05: Proceedings of the fourth International Joint Conference on Autonomous Agents and Multi-Agent Systems* (pp. 921–928). New York: ACM Press.

Mori, M. (1970). The uncanny valley. *Energy, 7,* 33-35.

Morris, C. (1997). Psychology: An introduction. México: Editorial Prentice Hall..

Morrison, D., Wang, R., & Liyanage C. De Silva. (2007). Ensemble methods for spoken emotion recognition in call-centres. *Speech Communication, 49,* 98-112.

Moshkina, L., & Arkin, R. C. (2005). Human perspective on affective robotic behavior: A longitudinal study. In *Proceedings of the IEEE/RSJ International Conference on Intelligent Robots and Systems* (pp. 1444-1451). Edmonton, AB, Canada: IEEE Press.

Moshkina, L., & Arkin, R.C. (2003). On TAMEing robots. In *IEEE International Conference on Systems, Man and Cybernetics, Vol. 4* (pp. 3949–3959).

Mullennix, J.W., Stern, S.E., Wilson, S.J., & Dyson, C. (2003). Social perception of male and female computer synthesized speech. *Computers in Human Behavior, 19,* 407-424.

Munduate, L. (2003). Género y liderazgo. Diferencias entre hombres y mujeres en el acceso a los puestos directivos. *Revista de Psicología Social, 18*(3), 309-314.

Murphy, R. R., Lisetti, C. L., Tardif, R., Irish, L., & Gage, A. (2002). Emotion-based control of cooperating heterogeneous mobile robots. *IEEE Transactions on Robotics and Autotomation, 18*(5), 744-757.

Murray, I.R., & Arnott, J.L. (2008). Applying an analysis of acted vocal emotions to improve the simulation of synthetic speech. *Computer Speech & Language, 22*, 107-129.

Muth J.F. (1961). Rational expectations and the theory of price movements. *Econometrica, 29*, 315-335.

Mynatt, E. D., Rowan, J., Craighill, S., & Jacobs, A. (2001) Digital family portraits: Providing peace of mind for extended family members. In *Proceedings of the ACM Conference on Human Factors in Computing Systems (CHI 2001)* (pp. 333-340). Seattle, Washington: ACM Press.

Nagel, T. (1974). What is it like to be a bat? *The Philosophical Review, 83*(4), 435-450.

Nair, R., Tambe, M., & Marsella, S. (2005). The role of emotions in multi-agent teamwork: A preliminary investigation. In J.-M. Fellous & M. Arbib (Eds.), *Who needs emotions: The brain meets the robots* (pp. 311-329). Oxford: Oxford University Press.

Naqvi, N., Shiv, B., & Bechara, A. (2006). The role of emotion in decision making: a cognitive neuroscience perspective. *Current Directions in Psychological Science, 15*, 260-264.

NASA. (n.d.). Autogenic-Feedback System-2 (AFS-2). In *NASA Tech. Briefs.* Retrieved from, http://www.techbriefs. com/index.php?option=com_staticxt&staticfile=Briefs/ Jan01/ARC140481.html.

Nass, C., Moon, Y., & Green, N. (1997). Are machines gender neutral? Gender-stereotypic responses to computers with voices. *Journal of Applied Social Psychology, 27*, 864-876.

Nass, C., Steuer, J., Tauber, E., & Reeder H. (1993). Anthropomorphism, agency, & ethopoeia: Computers as social actors. *InterCHI '93*, Amsterdam.

Neal, M.J., & Timmis, J. (2003). Timidity: A useful mechanism for robot control? *Informatica, 27*(4), 197-204.

NEC. (2001). PaPeRo. Retrieved from, http://www.incx. nec.co.jp/robot/

Nehaniv, C. (1998). The first, second and third person emotions: Grounding adaptation in a biological and social world. *5th International Conference of the society for adaptive behavior (SAB).* Retrieved from http://www. ofai.at/~paolo.petta/conf/sab98/final/nehaniv.ps.gz.

Nesse, R. M. (1990). Evolutionary explanations of emotions. *Human Nature, 1*(3), 261-289.

Nesse, R. M. (2004). Natural selection and the elusiveness of happiness. *Philosophical Transactions of the Royal Society B, 359*(1449), 1333-1349.

Nesse, R. M. (2007). Runaway social selection for displays of partner value and altruism. *Biological Theory, 2*(2), 143-155.

Newell, A. (1990). *Unified theories of cognition.* Cambridge, MA: Harvard University Press.

Nichols, S. (2004). *Sentimental rules.* Oxford University Press.

Nielsen, J., & Loranger, H. (2006). Prioritizing web Usability. Berkeley, CA: New Riders Press.

Niepel, M. (2001). Independent manipulation of stimulus change and unexpectedness dissociates indices of the orienting response. *Psychophysiology, 38*, 84-91.

Norman, D. (1988). The psychology of everyday things. New York: Basic Books Inc.

Norman, D. (1998). *The invisible computer: Why good products can fail, the personal computer is so complex, and information appliances are the solution.* Cambridge, MA: MIT Press.

Norman, D. (2005). Human-centered design considered harmful. *ACM SIGCHI Interactions 12*(4), 14-19.

North, A. C., & Hargreaves, D. J. (1997). Music and consumer behaviour. In D. J. Hargreaves & A. C. North (Eds.), *The social psychology of music* (pp. 268–289). Oxford: Oxford University Press.

North, A. C., Hargreaves, D. J., & O'Neill, S. A. (2000). The importance of music to adolescents. *British Journal of Educational Psychology*, 255–272.

Nowak, K. L. & Rauh, C. (2005). The influence of the avatar on online perceptions of anthropomorphism, androgyny, credibility, homophily, and attraction. *Journal of Computer-Mediated Communication, 11*(1).

Nummenmaa, L., & Niemi, P. (2004). Inducing affective states with success–failure manipulations: a metaanalysis. *Emotion, 4*, 207-214.

Nussbaum, C. O. (2007). *The musical representation: Meaning, ontology, and emotion* (1st ed.). Cambridge: The MIT Press.

Nwana, H. S. (1996). Software agents: An overview. *Knowledge Engineering Review, 11*(3), 1-40.

O'Keefe, D. J., & Figge, M. (1997). A guilt-based explanation of the door-in-the-face influence strategy. *Human Communication Research, 24*(1), 64-81.

O'Reagan, K. (2003). Emotion and E-Learning. *Journal of Asynchronous Learning Networks (JALN), 7*(3). Retrieved August 10, 2008, from http://www-etud.iro.umontreal.ca/~chalfoup/publications/W7-Chalfoun-Chaffar-Frasson-ITS-Workshop-2006-FINAL.pdf.

O'Reilly, W. S. N. (1996). *Believable social and emotional agents*. Ph.D. Thesis, Carnegie Mellon University, Pittsburgh, PA.

Oatley, K. (1992). *Best laid schemes: The psychology of emotions*. Cambridge, England: Cambridge University Press.

Oatley, K. (1996). Emotions: Communications to the self and others. In R. Harré & W.G. Parrott (Eds.), *The emotions: Social, cultural, and biological dimensions* (pp. 312-316). London: Sage.

Oatley, K. (1999). Why fiction may be twice as true as fact: Fiction as cognitive and emotional simulation. *Review of General Psychology, 3*(2), 101-117.

Oatley, K. (2000). Shakespeare's invention of theatre as simulation that runs on minds. In A. Sloman (Ed.), *Proceedings of the AISB-2000 Workshop: How to Design a Functioning Mind* (pp. 102-110). Birmingham, UK: Society for the Study of Artificial Intelligence and Simulation of Behaviour.

Oatley, K. (2003). Creative expression and communication of emotions in the visual and narrative arts. In R.

J. Davidson, K. R. Scherer, & H. H. Goldsmith (Eds.), *Handbook of Affective Sciences* (pp. 481-502). New York: Oxford University Press.

Oatley, K. (2004). From the emotions of conversation to the passions of fiction. In A. S. R. Manstead, N. Frijda, & A. Fisher (Eds.), *Feelings and emotions. The Amsterdam symposium* (pp. 98-115). Cambridge, UK: Cambridge University Press.

Oatley, K., & Johnson-Laird, P. N. (1987). Towards a cognitive theory of emotions. *Cognition and Emotion, 1*(1), 29-50.

Oatley, K., & Mar, R. A. (2005). Evolutionary pre-adaptation and the idea of character in fiction. *Journal of Cultural and Evolutionary Psychology, 3*(2), 179-194.

Ochsner, K.N. & Gross, J.J. (2005). The cognitive control of emotions. *Trends in Cognitive Sciences, 9*, 241-249.

Ohlen, J., Zeschuk, G., & Muzyka, R. (2001, March). Postmortem: BioWare's Baldur's gate II. *Game Developer Magazine*, 54-66.

Öhman, A. (1986). Face the beast and fear the face: Animal and social fears as prototypes for evolutionary analyses of emotion. *Psychophysiology, 23*(2), 123-145.

Öhman, A., & Dimberg, U. (1978). Facial expressions as conditioned stimuli for electrodermal responses: A case of "preparedness"? *Journal of Personality and Social Psychology, 36*(11), 1251-1258.

Ohman, A., Flykkt, A., & Lundqvist, D. (2000). Unconscious emotion: Evolutionary perspectives, psychophysiological data and neuropsychological mechanisms. In R. D. Lane & L. Nadel (Eds.), *Cognitive neuroscience of emotion* (pp. 296-327). New York: Oxford University Press.

Ortony, A. (2002). On making believable emotional agents believable. In R. Trappl, P. Petta, & S. Payr (Eds.), *Emotions in humans and artifacts* (pp. 189-211). Cambridge, MA: MIT Press.

Ortony, A. (2003). On making believable emotional agents believable. In R. P. Trapple, P. (Ed.), *Emotions in humans and artefacts*. Cambridge: MIT Press.

Ortony, A. (2003). On making believable emotional agents believable. In *Emotions in humans and artifacts* (pp. 189-212) Cambridge, Massachusetts; London, England: MIT Press.

Ortony, A., & Partridge, D. (1987). Surprisingness and expectation failure: what's the difference? In *Proceedings of the 10th International Joint Conference on Artificial Intelligence* (pp. 106-108). Milan, Italy: Morgan Kaufmann.

Ortony, A., & Turner, T. J. (1990). What's basic about basic emotions? *Psychological Review, 97*(1), 315-331.

Ortony, A., & Turner, W. (1990). What's basic about basic emotions? *Psychological Review, 97*, 315–31.

Ortony, A., Clore, G. L., & Foss, M. A. (1987). The referential structure of the affective lexicon. *Cognitive Science, 11*, 341-364.

Ortony, A., Clore, G., & Collins, A. (1988). *The cognitive structure of emotions*. Cambridge, UK: Cambridge University Press.

Ortony, A., Clore, G., & Collins, A. (1990). *The cognitive structure of emotions*. Cambridge, U.K.: Cambridge University Press.

Ortony, A., Clore, G.L., & Collins, A. (1988). *The cognitive structure of emotions*. Cambridge University Press.

Oulasvirta, A., & Salovaara, A. (2004). A cognitive meta-analysis of design approaches to interruptions in intelligent environments. In *Proceedings of CHI 2004, Late Breaking Results* (pp.1155-1158). Vienna, Austria. Retrieved from, http://www.hiit.fi/~asalovaa/articles/oulasvirta-chi2004-p1155.pdf

Oviatt, S., Darrell, T., & Flickner, M. (Eds.) (2004). Multimodal interfaces that flex, adapt, and persist. *Communications of the ACM, 47*(1), 30-33.

Oxford (n.d.). Oxford Reference ONLINE. Retrieved from, http://www.oxfordreference.com/.

Paiva A., Dias, J., Sobral, D., Aylett, R., Woods, S., Hall, L., & Zoll, C. (2005). Learning by feeling: Evoking empathy with synthetic characters. *Applied Artificial Intelligence, 19*(3-4), 235-266(32). Taylor and Francis Ltd.

Paiva, A., Costa, M., Chaves, R, Piedade, M., Mourão, D., Sobral, D., et al. (2003). SenToy: An affective sympathetic interface. *Int. J. Hum.-Comput. Stud., 59*, 227-235.

PalCom (2007). Palpable computing: A new perspective on ambient computing. *Deliverable, 54*(2.2.3) Open Architecture. Retrieved from, http://www.ist-palcom.org/publications/

PalCom (2008). Retrieved from, http://www.ist-palcom.org/

Panaoura, A., & Filippou, G. (2007). *Cognitive Development, 22*(2), 149-164.

Panksepp, J. (1982). Toward a general psychobiological theory of emotions. *Behavioral and Brain Sciences, 5*(3), 407-467.

Panksepp, J. (1998). *Affective neuroscience. The foundations of human and animal emotions*. New York: Oxford University Press.

Panksepp, J. (2004). *Affective neuroscience: The foundations of human and animal emotions*. New York: Oxford University Press.

Panksepp, J. (2004). Basic affects and the instinctual emotional systems of the brain. In A. S. R. Manstead, N. Frijda, & A. Fisher (Eds.), *Feelings and emotions. The Amsterdam symposium* (pp. 174-193). Cambridge: Cambridge University Press.

Panksepp, J., & Bernatzky, G. (2002). Emotional sounds and the brain: the neuro-affective foundations of musical appreciation. *Behavioural Processes*, 133–155.

Pantic, M., & Rothkrantz, L. J. M. (2000). Automatic analysis of facial expressions: the state of the art. *IEEE Transactions on Pattern Analysis and Machine Intelligence, 22*(12), 1424 - 1445 |DOI: 10.1109/34.895976

Parker, L. E. (1994). Alliance: An architecture for fault tolerant, cooperative control of heterogeneous mobile robots. In *Proceedings of IEEE/RSJ/GI International Conference on Intelligent Robots and Systems* (pp. 776-783), Munich, Germany.

Parker, L. E. (1998). Alliance: An architecture for fault tolerant multirobot cooperation. *IEEE Trans. on Robotics and Automation, 14*(2), 220-240.

Parker, L.E. (1998). Alliance: An architecture for fault-tolerant multi-robot cooperation. *IEEE Transactions on Robotics and Automation, 14*(2), 220-240.

Parr, L.A., Waller, B.M., & Fugate, J. (2005). Emotional communication in primates: implications for neurobiology. *Current Opinion in Neurobiology, 15*, 716-720.

Parrott, W. G., & Smith, S. F. (1991). Embarrassment: Actual vs. typical cases, classical vs. prototypical representations. *Cognition and Emotion, 5*(5-6), 467-488.

Partala, T., & Surakka, V. (2004). The effects of affective interventions in human-computer interaction. *Interacting with Computers, 16*, 295-309.

Patel, A. D. (2007). *Music, language, and the brain.* Oxford: Oxford University Press.

Peirce, C. S. (1877, November). The fixation of belief. *Popular Science Monthly, 12*, 1-15.

Peirce, C. S. (1960). *Collected papers of Charles Sanders Peirce.* Cambridge: Harvard University Press.

Pekrun, R. (2005). Progress and open problems in educational emotion research. *Learning and Instruction, 15*, 497-506.

Pelachaud, C. (2005). Multimodal expressive embodied conversational agents. In *Proceedings of the 13th Annual ACM International Conference on Multimedia, Hilton, Singapore* (pp. 683 - 689). | DOI: 10.1145/1101149.1101301

Penrose, R. (1995). *La nueva mente del emperador.* Barcelona. Grijalbo-Mondadori.

Peot , M., & Smith, D. (1992). Conditional nonlinear planning. In *Artificial Intelligence Planning Systems: Proceedings of the First International Conference*, June 15-17, 1992, College Park, Maryland. San Francisco, CA: Morgan Kaufmann.

Pereira, D., Oliveira, E., Moreira, N., & Sarmento, L. (2005). Towards an architecture for emotional BDI agents. In *EPIA'05: Proceedings of 12th Portuguese Conference on Artificial Intelligence* (pp. 40-47).

Peretz, I., Gagnon, L., & Bouchard, B. (1998). Music and emotion: perceptual determinants, immediacy, and isolation after brain damage. *Cognition, 68*(2), 111–141.

Peters, M. (1998). Towards artificial forms of intelligence, creativity, and surprise. In *Proceedings of the Twentieth Annual Conference of the Cognitive Science Society* (pp. 836-841). Madison, Wisconsin, USA: Erlbaum.

Petersen, M.G. (2004). Remarkable computing – the challenge of designing for the home. *CHI*, 1445-1448.

Petta, P., & Cañamero, L. (2001). Grounding emotions in adaptive systems: volume II. *Cybernetics and Systems: An International Journal, 32*(6), 581-583.

Pezzo, M. V. (2003). Surprise, defence, or making sense: What removes hindsight bias? *Memory, 11*, 421-441.

Phelps, E.A. (2006). Emotion and cognition: Insights from studies of the human amygdala. *Annual Review of Psychology, 52*, pp. 27-53.

Philips Research (2003). 365 days – Ambient Intelligence research in HomeLab. www.research.philips.com/technologies/misc/homelab/downloads/homelab_365.pdf

Philips. iCat http://www.research.philips.com/newscenter/pictures/041209-icat.html, http://www.research.philips.com/technologies/syst_softw/robotics/index.html.

Piaget, J. (1989). Les relations entre l'intlligence et l'affectivité dans le développement de l'enfant. In B. Rimé, & K. R. Scherer (Eds.), *Les émotions.* (pp. 75-96). Paris: Delachaux et Niestle.

Picard, R. (1995). *Affective computing.* Cambridge, MA: MIT Press.

Picard, R. (1997). *Affective computing.* Cambridge, MA: MIT Press.

Picard, R. W. (2000). *Affective computing.* Cambridge: MIT Press.

Picard, R. W., & Wexelblat, A. (2002). Future interfaces: Social and emotional. *Extended Abstracts of The CHI 2002- Conference on Human Factors in Computing Systems* (pp. 698-699). New York: ACM Press.

Picard, R.W. (2000). Synthetic emotion. *Computer Graphics and Applications IEEE, 20*(1), 52-53.

Picard, R.W., Vyzas, E. & Healey, J. (2001). Toward machine emotional intelligence: analysis of affective physiological state. *Pattern Analysis and Machine Intelligence, IEEE Transactions*, 23 (10), 1175-1191.

Picard. R. (1997). *Affective computing.* MIT Press.

Pignatiello, M. F., Camp, C. J., & Rasar, L. (1986). Musical mood induction: An alternative to the velten technique. *Journal of Abnormal Pychology, 95*(3), 295–297.

Pines, S. (1986). Ibn al-Haytham's critique of Ptolemy. In *Studies in Arabic versions of Greek texts and in mediaeval science, Vol. II.* Leiden, The Netherlands: Brill.

Pinker, S. (2008). Institute of Social Psychology 'Psychology as Social Science' public lecture, London School of Economics. *Stuff of Thought: Language as a window into human nature.* June 9, London, UK.

Pinker, S. 1997. *How the mind works.* New York: W. W. Norton and Company.

Pintrich, P., & Schunk, D. (2002). *Motivation in education: Theory, research and applications.* Upper Saddle River, NJ: Prentice-Hall Merrill.

Pitchford, I. (2001). The origins of violence: Is psychopathy an adaptation? *The Human Nature Review, 1,* 28-36.

Piva, S., Singh, R., Gandetto M., & Regazzoni, C. S. (2005). A Context-based Ambient Intelligence Architecture. In P. Remagnino, G.L. Foresti, & T. Ellis (Eds.), *Ambient intelligence: A novel paradigm* (pp. 63-87). New York: Springer.

Piza, H. I., Zúñiga, F., & Ramos, F. F. (2004). A platform to design and run dynamic virtual environments. In *Proceedings of the 2004 International Conference on Cyberworlds* (pp. 78-85).

Plant, S. (2000). On the matrix: Cyberfeminist simulations. In G. Kirkup, L. Janes, K. Woodward, & F. Hovenden (Eds.), *The gendered cyborg* (pp. 265-275). New York: Routledge.

Plutchik, R. (1980). A general psychoevolutionary theory of emotion. In R. Plutchik, & H. Kellerman (Eds.), *Emotion: Theory, research, and experience: Vol. 1. Theories of emotion* (pp. 3-33). New York: Academic.

Plutchik, R. (1980). *Emotion: A psychoevolutionary synthesis.* New York: Harper & Row.

Plutchik, R. (1983). A general phycoevolutionary theory of emotion. In R. Plucthik & H. Kellerman (Eds.), *Emotion: Theory, research and experience: Vol. 1. Theories of emotion* (pp. 3-33). New York: Academic Press.

Plutchik, R. (2000). *Emotions in the practice of psychotherapy: Clinical implications of affect theories.* New York: American Psychological Association.

Plutchik, R. (2001). The nature of emotions. *American Scientist, 89*(4), 344-350.

Plutchik, R. (2003). *Emotions and life: Perspectives from psychology, biology, and evolution.* New York: American Psychological Association.

Plutchik, R., & Conte, H.R. (Eds.). (1997). *Circumplex models of personality and emotions.* Washington, DC: American Psychological Association.

Plutchik, R., & Kellerman, H. (1990). *Emotion Theory, Research, and Experience vol. 1-5.* Academic Press.

Pokahr, A., Braubach, L., & Lamersdorf, W. (2005). JADEX: a BDI reasoning engine. In R. H. Bordini, M. Dastani, J. Dix & A. El Fallah-Seghrouchni (Eds.), *Multi-agent programming: Languages, platforms and applications* (pp. 149-174). New York: Springer.

Popper, K (2002). *Conjectures and refutations: the growth of scientific knowledge.* London & New York: Routledge.

Power M., & Dalgleish T. (2008). *Cognition and emotion. From order to disorder.* New York: Psychology Press.

Powers, Aaron, Kramer, A.D., Lim, S., Kuo, J., Lee S-L., & Kiesler, S. (2005). Eliciting information from people with a gendered humanoid robot. *2005 IEEE International Workshop on Robots and Human Interactive Communication.*

Prendinger, H., & Ishizuka, M. (2002). Scripting the bodies and minds of life-like characters. In M. Ishizuka & A. Sattar (Eds.), *PRICAI 2002: Trends in Artificial Intelligence: 7th Pacific Rim International Conference on Artificial Intelligence* (pp. 571-580). Springer.

Prendinger, H., & Ishizuka, M. (2005). The empathic companion: A character-based interface that addresses users' affective states. *International Journal of Applied Artificial Intelligence, 19,* 297-285.

Prendinger, H., & Ishizuka, M. (2005). The empathic companion: A character-based interface that addresses users' affective states. *Applied Artificial Intelligence, 19*(3-4), 267-285.

Prinz, J. (2006). *Gut reactions: A perceptual theory of emotion.* New York: Oxford University Press.

Provine, R. R. (1992). Contagious laughter: Laughter is a sufficient stimulus for laughs and smiles. *Bulletin of the Psychonomic Society, 30*(1), 1-4.

Provine, R. R. (2000). *Laughter: A scientific investigation.* New York: Penguin Books.

Punie, Y. (2003). *A social and technological view of ambient intelligence in everyday life: What bends the trend?* The European Media and Technology in Everyday Life Network, 2000-2003, Institute for Prospective Technological Studies, Directorate General Joint Research Centre, European Commission. Retrieved from, http://www.lse.ac.uk/collections/EMTEL/reports/punie_2003_emtel.pdf

Purdy, J.E., Markham, M.R., Schwartz, B.L., & Gordon, W. (2001). *Learning and memory.* Belmont, CA: Wadsworth.

Pynadath, D. V., & Marsella, S. (2005). PsychSim: modeling theory of mind with decision-theoretic agents. In *Proceedings of the International Joint Conference on Artificial Intelligence* (pp. 1181-1186).

Pyszczynski, T. A., & Greenberg, J. (1987). Toward an integration of cognitive and motivational perspectives on social inference: A biased hypothesis-testing model. *Advances in Experimental Social Psychology.*

Rakic, P. (2002). Neurogenesis in adult primate neocortex: An evaluation of the evidence. *Nature Reviews Neuroscience, 3*(1), 65-71.

Ramachandran, V.S. (2004). *A brief tour of human consciousness.* New York: Pi Press, Pearson Education.

Ramos, A. (2004). *Liderazgo transformacional: un estudio desde la psicología de género.* Doctoral Thesis. Universitat de Valencia.

Rao, A. S., & Georgeff, M. P. (1995). BDI Agents: From theory to practice. In V. Lesser & L. Gasser (Eds.), *Proceedings of the First International Conference on Multi-Agent Systems*, ICMAS '95 (pp. 312-319). California: AAAI Press.

Raouzaiou, A., Spyrou, E., Karpouzis K., & Kollias S. (2005). Emotion synthesis: An intermediate expressions' generator system in the mpeg-4 framework. *International Workshop VLBV05*, Sardinia, Italy. Retrieved April 18, 2008, from http://www.image.ece.ntua.gr/php/publications.php?from=2005&srchtype=c&to=2005

Raskin, J. (2000). The humane interface. Reading, MA: Addison-Wesley.

Raufaste, E., Da Silva Neves, R., & Mariné, C. (2003). Testing the descriptive validity of possibility theory in human judgments of uncertainty. *Artificial Intelligence, 148,* 197-218.

Real academia Española (2008). *Emotion definition.* Retrieved January 04, 2008, from http://buscon.rae.es/draeI/SrvltConsulta TIPO_BUS=3&LEMA= emoción

Reilly, W. (1996). *Believable Social and Emotional Agents.* Technical Report CMU-CS-96-138, School of Computer Science, Carnegie Mellon University, Pittsburgh, PA, USA.

Reilly, W. (1996). *Believable social and emotional agents.* Unpublished PhD Thesis, School of Computer Science, Carnegie Mellon University, Pittsburgh, PA.

Reilly, W. S. N. (1996). *Believable social and emotional agents.* Unpublished Ph.D. Thesis. Carnegie Mellon University, Pittsburgh, PA..

Reilly, W. S., & Bates, J. (1992). *Building emotional agents.* School of Computer Science Technical Report CS-92-143, Carnegie Mellon University.

Reisenzein, R. (1995). On Oatley and Johnson-Laird's theory of emotions and hierarchical structures in the affective lexicon. *Cognition and Emotion, 9,* 383-416.

Reisenzein, R. (2000). Exploring the strength of association between the components of emotion syndromes: The case of surprise. *Cognition and Emotion, 14,* 1-38.

Reisenzein, R. (2000). The subjective experience of surprise. In *The message within: The role of subjective experience in social cognition and behavior* (pp. 262-279). Philadelphia, PA: Psychology Press.

Reisenzein, R. (2001). Appraisal processes conceptualized from a schema-theoretic perspective: Contributions to a process analysis of emotions. In K. Scherer, A. Schorr & T. Johnstone (Eds.), *Appraisal processes in emotion: Theory, Methods, Research* (pp. 187-201). Oxford: Oxford University Press.

Reisenzein, R. (2007). What is a definition of emotion? And are emotions mental-behavioral processes? *Social Science Information, 46*, 424-428.

Reisenzein, R. (2008). Emotions as metarepresentational states of mind: Naturalizing the belief-desire theory of emotion. *Cognitive Systems Research, 9.*

Reisenzein, R., & Junge, M. (2006). *Überraschung, Enttäuschung und Erleichterung: Emotionsintensität als Funktion von subjektiver Wahrscheinlichkeit und Erwünschtheit [Surprise, disappointment and relief: Emotion intensity as a function of subjective probability and desire strength].* Paper presented at the 45th Congress of the German Psychological Association (DGPs).

Reisenzein, R., Bördgen, S., Holdtbernd, T., & & Matz, D. (2006). Evidence for strong dissociation between emotion and facial displays: The case of surprise. *Journal of Personality and Social Psychology, 91*, 295-315.

Report of the Technology Enhanced Learning Committee (2004). *Report of the technology enhanced learning committee.* The University of Texas at Austin. Retrieved April 18, 2008, from http://www.utexas.edu/provost/research/TEL_Report_2004.pdf

Rhodes, R. ,& Lawler, J. (1981), Athematic metaphors. In *Papers from the 17th Annual Meeting of the Chicago Linguistics Society*, Chicago.

Ribot, T. A. (1896). *La psychologie des sentiments [The psychology of emotions].* Paris: Alcan.

Richey, R. C. (2008). Reflections on the 2008 AECT Definitions of the Field. *TechTrends. 52*(1) 24-25.

Rickel, J., & Johnson, W. L. (1999). Animated agents for procedural training in virtual reality: Perception, cognition, and motor control. *Applied Artificial Intelligence, 13*(4-5), 343- 382.

Ridgeway C. (1993). Gender, status, and the social psychology of expectations. In P. England (Ed.), *Theory on gender/feminism on theory* (pp. 175-197). New York: Aldine.

Rieber, L. P., Smith, L., & Noah, D. (1998). The value of serious play. *Educational Technology, 38*(6), 29-37.

Ritchie, G. (1999). Developing the incongruity-resolution theory. In *Proceedings of the AISB. Symposium on Creative Language* (pp. 78-85). Edinburgh, Scotland.

Rivard, F., Bisson, J., Michaud, F., & Létourneau, D. (2008). Ultrasonic relative positioning for multi-robot systems. In *Proceedings of IEEE International Conference on Robotics and Automation.*

Rizzolati, G., & Craighero, L. (2004). The mirror-neuron system. *Annual Review of Neuroscience, 27*, 169–192.

Rizzolatti, G., Fadiga, L., Gallese, V., & Fogassi, L. (1996). Premotor cortex and the recognition of motor actions. *Cognitive Brain Research, 3*(2), 131-41.

Rizzolatti. G., & Fogassi, L. (2007). Mirror neurons and social cognition. In R. I. M. Dunbar & L. Barrett (Eds.), *The Oxford Handbook of evolutionary psychology* (pp. 179-195). New York: Oxford University Press.

Rizzolatti. G., Fogassi, L., & Gallese, V. (2001). Neurophysiological mechanisms underlying the understanding and imitation of action. *Nature Reviews Neuroscience, 2*(9), 661-70.

Robins, B., Dautenhahn, K., Boekhorst, R., & Billard, A. (2005). Robotic assistants in therapy and education of children with autism: can a small humanoid robot help encourage social interaction skills? *Universal Access in the Information Society, 4*(2), 105-120. | DOI: 10.1007/s10209-005-0116-3

Robinson, D. T, SmithLovin, L., & Wisecup, A. (2006). Affect control theory. In J. E. Stets, & J. H. Turner (Eds.), *Handbook of the sociology of emotions* (pp. 179-202). New York: Springer.

Rogers, C. (1969). *Freedom to learn: A view of what education might become.* Columbus, Ohio: Charles Merrill.

Rolls, E.T. (2002). Emotion, neural basis of. In N.J. Smelsner & P.B. Baltes (Eds.), *International encyclopedia of the social and behavioral sciences* (pp. 4444-9). Amsterdam, Netherlands: Pergamon.

Rolls, E.T. (2005). *Emotion explained.* Oxford University Press.

Rolls, E.T. (2006). Brain mechanisms of emotion and decision-making. *International Congress Series, 1291*, 3-13. Amsterdam: Elsevier.

Rolls, E.T. (2007). A neurobiological approach to emotional intelligence. In G. Matthews, M. Zeidner & R.D.

Roberts (Eds.), *The science of emotional intelligence* (pp. 72-100). Oxford, UK: Oxford Univ. Press.

Roseman, I. J., Aliki Antoniou, A., & Jose, P. E. (1996). Appraisal determinants of emotions: Constructing a more accurate and comprehensive theory. *Cognition and Emotion, 10*(3), 241-277.

Roseman, I. J., Jose, P. E., & Spindel, M. S. (1990). Appraisals of emotion-eliciting events: testing a theory of discrete emotions. *Journal of Personality and Social Psychology, 59*(2), 899-915.

Rosenberg, M. (1982). Psychological selectivity in self-esteem formation. In M. Rosenberg and H.B. Kaplan (Eds.)., *Social psychology of the self-concept* (pp. 535–546). Arlington Heights, IL: Harlan Davidson.

Rosenbloom, P., Laird, J., & Newell, A. (1993). *The soar papers: Research on integrated intelligence*. Cambridge: MIT Press.

Rosenblum, L. A., & Alpert, S. (1974). Fear of strangers and specificity of attachment in monkeys. In M. Lewis & L. A. Rosenblum (Eds.), *The origins of fear* (pp. 165-193). New York: John Wiley and Sons.

Rosener, J.B. (1990). Ways women lead. *Harvard Business Review, 68*, 119-120.

Ross, M. & Holmberg D. (1990). Recounting the past: Gender differences in the recall of events in the history of a close relationship. In J.M. Olson, & M.P. Zanna (Eds.), *Self-inferences processes: The Ontario Symposium,* (pp. 135-152). Hillsdale, NJ: Erlbaum, 135-152.

Roßnagel, A. (2007). Datenschutz in einem informatisierten Alltag. Friedrich-Ebert-Stiftung, Berlin. Retrieved from, http://library.fes.de/pdf-files/stabsabteilung/04548.pdf

Rouvroy, A., Poullet, Y. (in press). The right to informational self-determination and the value of self-development—Reassessing the importance of privacy for democracy. In *Reinventing Data Protection, Proceedings of the International Conference (Brussels, 12-13 October 2007).* Springer. Retrieved from, http://works.bepress.com/antoinette_rouvroy/7

Rozin, P., & Fallon, A. E. (1987). A perspective on disgust. *Psychological Review, 94*(1), 23-41.

Rozin, P., Haidt, J., & McCauley, C. R. (1993). Disgust. In M. Lewis & J. M. Haviland (Eds.), *Handbook of emotions* (pp. 575-594). New York: The Guilford Press.

Ruch, W. (1993). Exhilaration and humor. In M. Lewis & J. M. Haviland (Eds.), *Handbook of emotions* (pp. 605-616). New York: The Guilford Press.

Rudrauf, D., Lutz, A., Cosmelli, D., Lachaux, J.-L., & Le Van Quyen, M. (2003). From autopoiesis to neurophenomenology: Francisco Varela's exploration of the biophysics of being. *Biological Research, 36*(1), 27-65.

Ruebenstrunk, G. (1998). *Emotional computers: computer models of emotions and their meaning for emotion-psychological research.* Unpublished dissertation, University of Bielefeld, Germany. Retrieved June 15, 2008 from http://www.ruebenstrunk.de/emeocomp/content.htm

Ruebenstrunk, G. (2004, January). Emotional machines. Paper presented at workshop at V2_Lab (Institute for Unstable Media). Rotterdam, The Netherlands. Retrieved June 15, 2008, from http://www.ruebenstrunk.de/Rotterdam.doc

Ruebenstrunk, G. (2004, November). Affective systems. Paper presented as moderator at workshop on affective systems, Dutch Electronics Arts Festival (DEAF 04). Rotterdam, The Netherlands. Retrieved on June 15, 2008, from http://www.ruebenstrunk.de/presentation4.ppt

Ruffman, T., & Keenan, T. R. (1996). The belief-based emotion of surprise: The case for a lag in understanding relative to false belief. *Developmental Psychology, 32*, 40-49.

Rumelhart, D. E. (1984). Schemata and the cognitive system. *Handbook of social cognition* (pp. 161-188).

Russell, J. (1980). A circumplex model of affect. *Journal of Personality and Social Psychology, 39*(6), 1161–1178.

Russell, J. A. (1979). Affective space is bipolar. *Journal of Personality and Social Psychology, 37*(3), 345-356.

Russell, J. A. (1980). A circumplex model of affect. *Journal of Personality and Social Psychology, 39*(6), 1161-1178.

Russell, J. A. (1991). In defense of a prototype approach to emotion concepts. *Journal of Personality and Social Psychology, 60*(1), 37-47.

Russell, S., & Norvig, P. (1995). *Artificial intelligence - a modern approach.* Englewood Cliffs, NJ: Prentice Hall.

Ruys, K.I., & Stapel, D.A. (2008). The secret life of emotions. *Psychological Science, 19*(4), 385-391. Blackwell Publishing.

Saarni, L. (1990). Emotional competence: how emotions and relationships become integrated. In R. A. Thompson (Ed.), *Socioemotional development.* Lincoln, NE: University of Nebraska Press.

Sackett, G. P. (1966). Monkeys reared in isolation with pictures as visual input: Evidence for an innate releasing mechanism. *Science, 154,* 1468-1473.

Sacks, O. (2007). *Musicophilia: Tales of music and the brain.* New York: Knopf Publishing Group.

Sacks, O., & Freeman, A. (1994). An anthropologist on mars. *Journal of Consciousness Studies, 1*(2), 234–240.

Saffo, P. (1996). The consumer spectrum. In T. Winograd (Ed.), *Bringing design to software* (pp. 87-99). Reading, MA: Addison-Wesley.

Sagi, A., & Hoffman, M. L. (1976). Empathic distress in the newborn. *Developmental Psychology, 12*(2), 175-76.

Salomon, G. (1992). Effects with and of computers and the study of computer-based learning environments. In E. DeCorte, M. C. Linn, H. Mandl, & L. Verschaffel, (Eds.), *Computer-based learning environments and problem solving* (pp. 249-263). Berlin: Springer-Verlag.

Salovey, P., & Meyer, J. P. (1990). Emotional intelligence. *Imagination, Cognition and Personality, 9,* 185-211.

Salovey, P., & Sluyter, D. J. (1997). *Emotional development and emotional intelligence.* New York: Basic Books.

Saltzman, M. (Ed.) (1999). *Game design: Secrets of the sages.* Indianapolis, IN: Brady Publishing.

Santamaria, J.C. (1997). Learning adaptive reactive agents. Unpublished doctoral dissertation. Georgia Institute of Technology, Atlanta, GA..

Sargent, T.J. (1993). *Bounded rationality in macroeconomics.* Oxford: Oxford University Press.

Sartre, J. (2001). *Sketch for a theory of the emotions.* New York: Routledge.

Saussure, Ferdinand de (1916). *Cours de linguistique générale.* Paris: Payot.

Saygin, A.P., & Cicekli, I. (2002). Pragmatics in human-computer conversations. *Journal of Pragmatics, 34,* 227-258.

Scerri, P., Pynadath, D. V., & Tambe, M. (2002). Towards adjustable autonomy for the real world. *Journal of Artificial Intelligence Research, 17,* 171-228.

Schank, R. (1986). *Explanation patterns: understanding mechanically and creatively.* Hillsdale, NJ: Lawrence Erlbaum Associates.

Scheeff, M., Pinto, J., Rahardja, K., Snibbe, S., & Tow R. (2000). Ex with Sparky: A social robot. *Proceedings of the Workshop on Interactive Robot Entertainment.*

Scheman, N. (1993). *Engenderings: Constructions of knowledge, authority, and privilege.* New York: Routledge.

Scherer, K. R. (1988). Criteria for emotion-antecedent appraisal: A review. In V. Hamilton, G. H. Bower, & N. H. Frijda (Eds.), *Cognitive perspectives on emotion and motivation* (pp. 89-126). Dordrecht: Kluwer.

Scherer, K. R. (1993). Studying the emotion-antecedent appraisal process: An expert system approach. *Cognition and Emotion, 7*(3), 325-355.

Scherer, K.R. (1994). Emotion serves to decouple stimulus and response. In P. Ekman & R. J. Davidson (Eds.), *The nature of emotion: Fundamental questions* (pp. 127-130). Oxford: Oxford University Press.

Scherer, K. R. (2001). Appraisal considered as a process of multi-level sequential checking. In K. R. Scherer, A. Schorr, & T. Johnstone, (Eds), *Appraisal processes in emotion: Theory, methods, research* (pp. 92-120). New York: Oxford University Press.

Scherer, K. R. (Ed.). (1988). *Facets of emotion: Recent research.* Hillsdale, N.J.: Erlbaum.

Scherer, K. R., & Tannenbaum, P. H. (1986). Emotional experiences in everyday life: A survey approach. *Motivation and Emotion, 10*(4), 295-314.

Scherer, K. R., Schorr, A., & Johnstone, T. (2001). *Appraisal theories of emotions: Theories, methods, research,* New York: Oxford University Press.

Scherer, K. R., Wallbott, H. G., & Summerfield, A. B. (Eds.). (1986). *Experiencing emotion: A cross-cultural study.* Cambridge, England: Cambridge University Press.

Scherer, K. R. (1991). Emotion expression in speech and music. In J. Sundberg, L. Nord, & R. Carlson (Eds.), *Music, language, speech, and brain* (pp. 146–156). London: MacMillian.

Scherer, K. R., & Zentner, M. R. (2001). Emotional effects of music: Production rules. In P. N. Juslin & J. A. Sloboda (Eds.), *Music and emotion: Theory and research* (pp. 361–392). Oxford: Oxford University Press.

Schermerhorn, P., Kramer, J., Brick, T., Anderson, D., Dingler, A., & Scheutz, M. (2006). DIARC: A testbed for natural human-robot interactions. In *Proceedings of AAAI 2006 Robot Workshop.*

Schermerhorn, P., Scheutz, M., & Crowell., C.R. (2008). Robot social presence and gender: Do females view robots differently than males? In *Proceedings of the Third ACM IEEE International Conference on Human-Robot Interaction*, Amsterdam (pp. 263-270).

Scheutz (2001). The evolution of simple affective states in multi-agent environments. In D. Cañamero (Ed.), *Proceedings of AAAI Fall Symposium* (pp. 123–128).

Scheutz, M. (2002). Affective action selection and behavior arbitration for autonomous robots. In H. Arabnia (Ed.), *Proceedings of the 2002 International Conference on Artificial Intelligence* (pp. 334-340).

Scheutz, M. (2004). How to determine the utility of emotions. In *Proceedings of AAAI Spring Symposium,*

Scheutz, M. (2004, July). Useful roles of emotions in artificial agents: A case study from artificial life. In L. Deborah & G.F. McGuinness (Eds.), *AAAI conference* (pp. 42-48). California: AAAI Press.

Scheutz, M., & Andronache, V. (2004). Architectural mechanisms for dynamic changes of behavior selection strategies in behavior-based systems. *IEEE Transactions of System, Man, and Cybernetics Part B, 34*(6), 2377-2395.

Scheutz, M., & Schermerhorn, P. (in press). Dynamic robot autonomy: Investigating the effects of robot decision-making in a human-robot team task.

Scheutz, M., Eberhard, K., & Andronache, V. (2004). A parallel, distributed, realtime, robotic model for human reference resolution with visual constraints. *Connection Science, 16*(3), 145-167.

Scheutz, M., McRaven, J., & Cserey, G. (2004). Fast, reliable, adaptive, bimodal people tracking for indoor environments. In *IEEE/RSJ International Conference on Intelligent Robots and Systems (IROS)* (pp. 1340-1352).

Scheutz, M., Schermerhorn, P., Kramer, J., & Anderson, D. (2007). First steps toward natural human-like HRI. *Autonomous Robots, 22*(4), 411-423.

Scheutz, M., Schermerhorn, P., Kramer, J., & Middendorff, C. (2006). The utility of affect expression in natural language interactions in joint human-robot tasks. In *Proceedings of the 1st ACM International Conference on Human-Robot Interaction* (pp. 226–233).

Scheutz, M., Schermerhorn, P., Middendorff, C., Kramer, J., Anderson, D., & Dingler, A. (2005). Toward affective cognitive robots for human-robot interaction. In *AAAI 2005 Robot Workshop* (pp. 1737-1738).

Schiano, D. J., Ehrlich, S. M., & Sheridan, K. (2004). Categorical imperative not: facial affect is perceived continously. In *Proceedings of the CHI2004, Vienna* (pp. 49-56).

Schiano, D. J., Ehrlich, S. M., Rahardja, K., & Sheridan, K. (2000). Face to interface: facial affect in (hu)man and machine. In *Proceedings of the CHI 2000, Den Hague* (pp. 193-200).

Schimmack, U., & Colcombe, S. (2007). Eliciting mixed feelings with the paired-picture paradigm: A tribute to Kellogg (1915). *Cognition and Emotion, 21*, 1546-1553.

Schlosberg, H. (1954). Three dimensions of emotion. *Psychological Review, 61*(2), 81-88.

Schlossberg, H. (1952). The description of facial expressions in terms of two dimensions. *Journal of Experimental Psychology, 44*(2).

Schmidhuber, J. (2006). Developmental robotics, optimal artificial curiosity, creativity, music, and the fine arts. *Connection Science, 18*, 173-187.

Schmidt, A. (2005). Interactive context-aware systems interacting with ambient intelligence. In G. Riva, F. Vatalaro, F. Davide, & M. Alcañiz (Eds.), *Ambient intelligence* (Part 3, pp. 159-178). IOS Press. Retrieved from, http://www.emergingcommunication.com/volume6.html

Schneider, D. (2004). Conception and implementation of rich pedagogical scenarios through collaborative portal sites. In M. Tokoro & L. Steels (Eds.), *The Future of Learning II, Sharing representations and Flow in Collaborative Learning Environments.* IOS Press.

Schneider-Fontan, M., & Mataric, M. (1998). Territorial multi-robot task division. *IEEE Transaction on Robotics and Automation, 14*, 815-822.

Schraagen, J. M., Chipman, S. F., Shalin, V. L. (2000). *Cognitive task analysis.* Mawah, NJ: Lawrence Erlbaum Associates.

Schubert, E. (1999). *Measurement and time series analysis of emotion in music.* Doctoral dissertation, University of New South Wales.

Schuller, B., Arsic, D., Wallhoff, F., & Rigoll, G. (2006). Emotion recognition in the noise applying large acoustic feature sets. *Speech Prosody 2006, ISCA*, Dresden, Germany.

Schultz, P. A. (1994). Goals as the transactive point between motivation and cognition. In P. R. Pintrich, D. R. Brown, & L. E. Weinstein (Eds.), *Student motivation, cognition and learning. Essays in honor of Wilbert J. McKeachie* (pp. 135-156). Hillsdale, NJ: Erlbaum.

Schulz, F. v. T. (1981). *Miteinander Reden - Stoerungen und Klaerungen.* Reinbeck bei Hamburg: Rowolth Taschenbuch Verlag GmbH.

Schützwohl, A. (1998). Surprise and schema strength. *Journal of Experimental Psychology: Learning, Memory, and Cognition, 24*, 1182-1199.

Schwab, B. (2004). *AI game engine programming.* Hingham, Massachusetts: Charles River Media.

Schwarz, N. (2000). Emotion, cognition and decision making. *Cognition and Emotion. 14*(4), 433-440.

Schwienhorst, K. (2002). The state of VR: A meta-analysis of virtual reality tools in second language acquisition. *Computer Assisted Language Learning, 15*(3), 221-239. | DOI: 10.1076/call.15.3.221.8186

Searle, J. (1983). *Intentionality.* Cambridge: Cambridge University Press.

Searle, J. R. (1980). Minds, brains and programs. *Behavioral and Brain Sciences, 3*(3), 417-457.

Seels, B. & Richey, R. (1994). *Instructional Technology: The definitions and domains of the field.* Washington D.C.: Association for Educational Communications and Technology.

Selker, T. (1994). COACH: A teaching agent that learns. *Communications of the ACM, 37*(7), 92-99.

Sengers, P., & Gaver, B. (2005, July). Designing for interpretation. In *Proceedings of the HCI International.* Las Vegas, Nevada.

Serrà, J., Gomez, E., Herrera, P., & Serra, X. (2008). Chroma binary similarity and local alignment applied to cover song identification. *IEEE Transactions on Audio, Speech, and Language Processing, 16*(6), 1138–1151.

Shackle, G. (1969). *Decision, order and time in human affairs* (2nd ed.). Cambridge, UK: Cambridge University Press.

Shafer, G. (1976). *A mathematical theory of evidence.* Princeton, NJ: Princeton University Press.

Shah, H. (2005). Alice: An Ace in Digitaland. *Special issue of on-line journal TripleC: Cognition, Communication and Cooperation – selected papers from 2005 European Computing and Philosophy Conference, 4*(2), 284-292. Retrieved from, http://triplec.uti.at/articles.php

Shah, H., & Warwick, K. (2008). Can a machine tell a joke? *European conference on computing and philosophy.* Montpellier, France, 16-18 June.

Shah, H., & Warwick, K. (in press) Constraining Random dialogue in a modern eliza. In C.T.A. Schmidt (Ed.), *Essays on computers and philosophy: From man through to artefacts to man.* AAAI / MIT

Shand, A. F. (1914). *The foundations of character*. London: Macmillan.

Shannon, C. (1948). A mathematical theory of communication. *Bell System Technical Journal, 27*, 379-423 and 623-656.

Shapiro, L. (2004). *The mind incarnate*. MIT Press.

Sharon, T. (n.d.). The Smile Detector. Retrieved from, http://xenia.media.mit.edu/~taly/mas630/smiley.html.

Sharpsteen, D. J. (1991). The organization of jealousy knowledge: Romantic jealousy as a blended emotion. In P. Salovey (Ed.). *The psychology of jealousy and envy* (pp. 31-51). New York: The Guilford Press.

Shaver, P. R., Wu, S., & Schwartz, J. (1992). Cross-cultural similarities and differences in emotion and its representation: A prototype approach. *Review of Personality and Social Psychology, 13,* 175-212.

Shaver, P.R., Schwartz, J., Kirson, D., & O'Connor, C. (1987). Emotion knowledge: Further exploration of a prototype approach. *Journal of Personality and Social Psychology, 52*(6), 1061-1086.

Sheets-Johnstone, M. (1999). Emotion and movement: A beggining empirical-phenomenological analysis of their relationship. *Journal of Consciousness Studies*, 6, 259-277.

Shi, Y.-Y., Zhu, X., Kim, H.-G., & Eom, K.-W. (2006). A tempo feature via modulation spectrum analysis and its application to music emotion classification. In *Proceedings of the IEEE International Conference on Multimedia And Expo* (pp. 1085–1088). Toronto, Canada.

Shoham, Y., & Tennenholtz, M. (1995). On social laws for artificial agent societies: Off-line design. *Artificial Intelligence, 73*(1-2), 231-252.

Short, J., Williams, E., & Christie, B. (1976). *The social psychology of telecommunication*. London: Wiley.

Shugrina, M., Betke, M., & Collomosse, J. (2006). Empathic painting: interactive stylization through observed emotional state. In *Proceedings of the 4th International Symposium on Non-Photorealistic Animation and Rendering, Annecy, France* (pp. 87 - 96). | DOI: 10.1145/1124728.1124744

Shweder, R. (1994). You're not sick, you're just in love: emotion as an interpretive system. In P. Ekman & R.J. Davidson (Eds.), *The nature of emotion: fundamental questions* (pp. 32-44). New York: Oxford University Press.

Shweder, R. A., & LeVine, R. A. (Eds.). (1984). *Culture theory: Essays on mind, self, and emotion*. Cambridge, England: Cambridge University Press.

Siino R.M. & Hinds, P.J. (2005). Robots, gender & sensemaking: Sex segregation's impact on workers making sense of a mobile autonomous robot. *Proceedings of the 2005 IEEE International Conference on Robotics and Automation*, Barcelona, Spain.

Simmons, R. (1996). The curvature-velocity method for local obstacle avoidance. In *Proceedings of the IEEE International Conference on Robotics and Automation* (pp. 3375-3382). Minneapolis, MN: IEEE Press.

Simon, H. (1997). *Models of bounded rationality, Vol. 3*. MIT Press.

Simon, H. A. (1967). Motivational and emotional controls of cognition. *Psychological Review, 74*(1), 29-39.

Simon, H.A. (1983). *Reason in human affairs*. Stanford, CA: Stanford University Press.

Singer, T., Seymour, B., O'Doherty, J., Kaube, H., Dolan, R.J., & Frith,C.D. (2004). Empathy for pain involves the affective but not sensory components of pain. *Science, 303*, 1157-1162.

Singh, M. P. (1999). An ontology for commitments in multiagent systems: Toward a unification of normative concepts. *Artificial Intelligence and Law, 7*(1), 97-113.

Skowronek, J., McKinney, M., & Van de Par, S. (2007). A demonstrator for automatic music mood estimation. In *Proceedings of the 8th International Conference on Music Information Retrieval* (pp. 345–346). Vienna, Austria.

Sloboda, J. (1999). Everyday uses of music listening: A preliminary study. In S. W. Yi (Ed.), *Music, mind and science* (pp. 354–369). Seoul National University Press.

Sloman, A. (1999). Architectural requirements for human-like agents both natural and artificial. In K. Dautenhahn (Ed.), *Human cognition and social agent technology, advances in consciousness research*. Amsterdam: John Benjamins Publishing Company.

Sloman, A. (2001). Beyond shallow models of emotion. *Cognitive Processing, 2*(1), 177–198.

Sloman, A. (2008). *Questions about emotions.* Retrieved 06-2008, from http://www.cs.bham.ac.uk/research/projects/cogaff/misc/emotions-questions.html

Sloman, A. Chrisley, R., & Scheutz, M. (2003). The architectural basis of affective states and processes. University of Birmingham, University of Sussex, University of Notre Dame.

Sloman, A., & Croucher, M. (1981). *Why robots will have emotions.* University of Sussex, School of Cognitive and Computing Sciences.

Sloman, A., & Croucher, M. (1981).Why robots will have emotions. In *Proceedings of the 7th International Joint Conference on AI. US:* Morgan-Kaufman.

Sloman, A., Chrisley, A., & Scheutz, M. (2005). The architectural basis of affective states and processes. In J.M. Fellous & M.A. Arbib (Eds.), *Who needs emotions? The Brain Meets the Machine* (pp. 201-244). New York: Oxford University Press.

Sloman, A., Chrisley, R., & Scheutz, M. (2005). The architectural basis of affective states and processes. In J. Fellous & M. Arbib (Eds.), *Who needs emotions: The brain meets the robot* (pp. 203-244). New York: Oxford University Press.

Sloterdijk, P. (2001). Kränkung durch Maschinen. In P. Sloterdijk (Ed.), *Nicht gerettet, Versuche nach Heidegger* (pp. 338-366). Frankfurt am Main: Suhrkamp Verlag.

Sloterdijk, P. (2002). *Luftbeben – An den Quellen des Terrors.* Frankfurt am Main: Suhrkamp Verlag.

Smith, A. (1795/1982). The history of astronomy. *Essays on philosophical subjects, ed. W. P. D. Wightman & J. C. Bryce, vol. 3 of the Glasgow Edition of the Works and Correspondence of Adam Smith,* 5-32.

Smith, C. A., & Ellsworth, P. C. (1985). Patterns of cognitive appraisal in emotion. *Journal of Personality and Social Psychology, 48*(4), 813-838.

Snowdon, B., & Vane H. (2002). An encyclopedia of macroeconomics. Edward Elgar Publishing.

Snowdon, C. T. (2003). Expression of emotion in nonhuman animals. In R. J. Davidson, K. R. Scherer, & H. H. Goldsmith (Eds.), *Handbook of affective sciences* (pp. 457-480). New York: Oxford University Press.

Sokolov, E. N. (1963). Higher nervous functions. The orienting reflex. *Annual Review of Physiology, 26,* 545-580.

Soldato (del), T. (1992). Detecting and reacting to the learner's motivational state. In *Proceedings of International Conference on Intelligent Tutoring Systems* (pp. 567-574). Berlin: Springer.

Solé, R., & Goodwin, B. (2002). *Signs of life: How complexity pervades biology.* New York: HarperCollins Publishers.

Soller, A. (2001). Supporting social interaction in an intelligent collaborative learning system. *Intelligence Journal of Artificial Intelligence in Education,* [S. l.], v. 11.

Solomon, R.C. (1977). The Logic of Emotion. In *Symposium Papers to be Read at the Meeting of the Western Division of the American Philosophical Association April 28-30, Vol. 11* (pp. 41-49). Chicago: Blackwell Publishing.

Sommer, W., Leuthold, H., & Matt, J. (1998). The expectancies that govern the P300 amplitude are mostly automatic and unconscious. *Behavioral and Brain Sciences, 21,* 149-150.

Sony. (1999). Aibo. Retrieved January 1999, from http://www.aibo.com

Sordo, M., Laurier, C., & Celma, O. (2007). Annotating music collections: How content-based similarity helps to propagate labels. In *Proceedings of the 8th International Conference on Music Information Retrieval* (pp. 531–534). Vienna, Austria.

Sowa, J. (1990). Crystallizing theories out of knowledge soup. In Zbigniew, W. R. & Zemankova, M. (Eds.), *Intelligent systems: state of the art and future directions.* New York: Ellis Horwood. Retrieved July 2008, from http://www.jfsowa.com/pubs/crystal.htm

Sowa, J. (2000). Ontology, metadata, and semiotics. Presented at ICCS'2000 in Darmstadt, Germany, on August 14, 2000. In Ganter, B. & Mineau, G. W. (Eds.), *Conceptual structures: logical, linguistic, and computational issues.* Lecture notes in AI #1867, 55-81. Berlin: Springer-Verlag. Retrieved July 2008, from http://www.jfsowa.com/ontology/ontometa.htm

Sowa, J. (2006). The challenge of knowledge soup. In Ramadas, J. & Chunawala, S. (Eds.), *Research trends in science, technology and mathematics education* (pp. 55-90). Mumbai: Homi Bhabha Centre. Retrieved July 2008, from http://www.jfsowa.com/pubs/

Sowa, J. (2008). From an e-mail to Tom Adi dated July 10, 2008.

Spackman, M.P., & Miller, D. (2008). Embodying emotions: What emotion theorists can learn from simulations of emotions. *Minds & Machines, 18*, 357-372.

Spector, W. (2000, November). Postmortem: Ion Storm's deus ex. *Game Developer Magazine*, 50-58.

Sperling, R., Howard, B., & Staley, R. (2004). Metacognition and self-regulated learning constructs. *Educational Research and Evaluation, 10*(2), 117-139.

Spinoza, B. (1677). *Ethique [Ethica ordine geometrico demonstrata]* (F. Alquié Trans.). (2nd ed.). Paris: Presses universitaires de France, 1966.

Spinuzzi, Clay (2002). A Scandinavian challenge, a US response: Methodological assumptions in Scandinavian and US prototyping approaches. In *Proceedings of the 20th annual international conference on Computer Documentation* (pp. 208-215).

Standifer, C. (1995). Personal communication.

Star, Susan Leigh (1991). Invisible work und silenced dialogues in knowledge representation. In I.V. Eriksson, B.A. Kitchenham, & K.G. Tijdens (Eds.), *Women, work and computerization: Understanding and overcoming bias in work and education* (pp. 81-92). Amsterdam: Elsevier Science Publishers.

Steels, L. (1995). The artificial life roots of artificial intelligence. In C.G. Langton (Ed.), *Artificial Life: An overview*. Cambridge, MA: MIT Press.

Steels, L., & Brooks, R. (Eds.). (1995). *The artificial life route to artificial intelligence*. Hillsdale, NJ: Erlbaum.

Steffens, B. (2007). *Ibn Al-Haytham: first scientist.* Greensboro, NC: Morgan Reynolds

Stein, N. L., Trabasso, T., & Liwag, M. (1993). The representation and organization of emotional experience: Unfolding the emotion episode. In M. Lewis & J. M.

Haviland (Eds.), *Handbook of emotions* (pp. 279-300). New York: The Guilford Press.

Stephenson, N. (1992). *Snow crash*. Bantam Books

Stephenson, Neal (1995). The Diamond Age or, A Young Lady's Illustrated Primer. Bantam Books.

Stets, J. E. (2003). Emotions and sentiments. In J. Delamater (Ed.), *Handbook of social psychology* (pp 309-335) New York: Springer.

Storm, C., & Storm, T. (1987). A taxonomic study of the vocabulary of emotions. *Journal of Personality and Social Psychology, 53*(4), 805-816.

Stout, M. (2005). *The sociopath next door.* New York: Broadway Books.

Stoytchev, A., & Tanawongsuwan, R. (1998, July). Pepe: PErsonal PEt. In *Video Proceedings of the AAAI-98 Mobile Robot Exhibition*, Madison, WI.

Strack, F., Martin, L. L., & Stepper, S. (1988). Inhibiting and facilitating conditions of the human smile: A nonobtrusive test of the facial feedback hypothesis. *Journal of Personality and Social Psychology, 54*(5), 768-777.

Strawson, P.F. (1968). *Freedom and Resentment*. Londres: Methuen.

Studdard, P. (1995). *Representing human emotions in intelligent agents*. Unpublished Masters Thesis. The American University, Washington, DC.

Suchman, L. (1994). Supporting articulation work: Aspects of a feminist practice of technology production. In A. Adam, J. Emms, E. Green, & J. Owen (1994). *Women, work and computerization. Breaking old boundaries—building new forms* (pp. 7-21). Amsterdam: Elsevier Science, pp. 7-21. Also in: R. Kling (Ed.) (1996), Computerization *and controversy. Value conflicts and social choices* (2nd Edition) (pp. 407-425). San Diego: Academic Press.

Sugeno, M. (1985). *Industrial applications of fuzzy control*. New York: Elsevier Science.

Suh, K. S. (1999). Impact of communication medium on task performance and satisfaction: An examination of media-richness theory. *Information & Management, 35*(3), 295-312.

Suls, J. M. (1971). A two-stage model for the appreciation of jokes and cartoons: An information-processing analysis. In J. H. Goldstein & P. E. McGhee (Eds.), *The psychology of humor* (pp. 81-100). New York: Academic Press.

Sur, M. (2004). Rewiring cortex: Cross-modal plasticity and its implications for cortical development and function. In G.A. Calvert, C. Spence & B.E. Stein (Eds.), *Handbook of multisensory processing* (pp. 681-94). Cambridge, MA: MIT Press.

Sutton, R.S., & Barto, A.G. (1998). *Reinforcement learning: an introduction.* Cambridge, MA: MIT Press.

Svanæs, Dag (1999). *Understanding interactivity: Steps to a phenomenology of human-computer interaction.* Trondheim, Norway: Norges Teknisk-Naturvitenskapelige Universitet (NTNU). Retrieved from, http://www.idi.ntnu.no/~dags/interactivity.pdf

Swann, W., Chang-Schneider, C., & Larsen McClarty, K. (2007). Do people's self-views matter? Self-concept and self-esteem in everyday life. *American Psychologist, 62*(2), 84-94.

Swartout, W. et al. (2006). Towards virtual humans. *AI Magazine, 27*(1).

Tambe, M. (1997). Towards flexible teamwork. *Journal of Artificial Intelligence Research, 7,* 83-124.

Tamura, T., Yonemitsu, S., Itoh, A., Oikawa, D., Kawakami, A., Higashi, Y., et al. (2004). Is an entertainment robot useful in the care of elderly people with severe dementia? *The Journals of Gerontology Series A: Biological Sciences and Medical Sciences, 59:M83-M85*

Tangney, J. P., & Fischer, K. W. (Eds.). (1995) *Self-conscious emotions. The psychology of shame, guilt, embarrassment, and pride.* New York: The Guilford Press.

Tao, J., & Tan, T. (2005). *Affective Computing: A Review.* Affective Computing and Intelligent Interaction. LNCS 3784: 981–995, Springer.

Teigen, K. H., & Keren, G. B. (2003). Surprises. Low probabilities or high contrasts? *Cognition, 87,* 55-71.

Terna P., Boero R., Morini M., & Sonnessa M. (2006). Modelli per la complessità. *La simulazione ad agenti in economia,* Bologna, Il Mulino.

Tesfatsion, L. (2006). Agent based computational economics: A constructive approach to economic theory. In L. Tesfatsion & K.L. Judd (Eds.), *Handbook of computational economics*, Vol. 2. North-Holland, Amsterdam.

Tesser, A., Gatewood, R., & Driver, M. (1968). Some determinants of gratitude. *Journal of Personality and Social Psychology, 9*(3), 233-236.

Thagard, P. (2004). What is doubt and when is it reasonable? In M. Ezcurdia, R. Stainton, & C. Viger (Eds.), *New essays in the philosophy of language and mind. Canadian Journal of Philosophy, Supplementary Volume 30,* 391-406. Retrieved from, http://cogsci.uwaterloo.ca/Articles/doubt.html

Thalmann, D. Raupp, S. & Kallmann, M. (1999). *Virtual human's behavior: Individuals, groups and crowds.* Swiss Federal Institute of Technology.

Thayer, R. E. (1989). *The biopsychology of mood and arousal.* Oxford: Oxford University Press.

Thayer, R. E. (1996). *The origin of everyday moods: Managing energy, tension, and stress.* Oxford: Oxford University Press.

The Logical Language Group (LLG). (1987). *Lojban.* Retrieved from, http://www.lojban.org

Thompson, R. A. (1989). Causal attributions and children's emotional understanding. In C. Saarni & P. L. Harris (Eds.), *Children's understanding of emotion* (pp. 117-150). Cambridge, England: Cambridge University Press.

Thrun, S. (2003). Robotic mapping: A survey. In G. Lakemeyer & B. Nebel (Eds.), *Exploring artificial intelligence in the new millennium* (pp. 1-35). San Francisco: Morgan Kaufmann.

Thrun, S., Beetz, M., Bennewitz, M., Burgard, W., Cremers, A.B., Dellaert, F., Fox, D., Hähnel, D., Rosenberg, C., Roy, N., Schulte J., & Schulz D. (2000). Probabilistic algorithms and the interactive museum tourguide robot minerva. *International Journal of Robotics Research, 19*(11), 972-999.

Tinbergen, N. (1950). The hierarchical organization of nervous mechanisms underlying instinctive behavior. *Symposia of the Society for Experimental Biology, 4,* 305-312.

Tinbergen, N. (1951). *The study of instinct*. Clarendon Press.

Toates, F. (1986). *Motivational systems*. Cambridge: Cambridge University Press.

Toates, F. (1988). Motivation and emotion from a biological perspective. In V. Hamilton, G. H. Bower, & N. H. Frijda (Eds.), *Cognitive perspectives on emotion and motivation* (pp. 3-35). Dordrecht: Kluwer.

Tobii Technology. (2007). Tobii Technology. Retrieved February 2007, from http://www.tobii.com/

Toda, M. (1985). Emotions viewed as tightly organized, genetically determined system of behavior-selection programs. In J. T. Spence & C. E. Izard (Eds.), *Motivation, Emotion, and Personality* (pp. 261-273). North-Holland: Elsevier Science Publishers.

Tomasello, M., Carpenter, M., Call, J., Behne, T., & Moll, H. (2005). Understanding and sharing intentions: The origins of cultural cognition. *Behavioral and Brain Sciences, 28,* 675-735.

Tomkins, S. S. (1962). *Affect, imagery, consciousness. Volume I. The positive affects*. New York: Springer.

Tomkins, S. S. (1980). Affect as amplification: some modifications in theory. In R. Plutchik & H. Kellerman (Eds.), *Emotion: Theory, research and experience*. New York: Academic Press.

Tomlinson, B. & Blumberg, B. (2002). Social synthetic characters. *Computer Graphics, 26,* 5-7.

Tomlinson, Jr., W. (2002). *Synthetic social relationships for computational entities*. Unpublished doctoral dissertation, Massachusetts Institute of Technology, Cambridge.

Tozour, P. (2002). The evolution of game AI. In S. Rabin (Ed.), *AI Game programming wisdom*. Hingham, MA: Charles River Media.

Trainor, L. J., Tsang, C. D., & Cheung, V. H. (2002). Preference for sensory consonance in 2- and 4-month-old infants. *Music Perception, 20*(2), 187–194.

Trevarthen, C. (1984). Emotions in infancy: Regulators of contact and relationships with persons. In K. R. Scherer & P. Ekman (Eds.), *Approaches to emotion* (pp. 129-157). Hillsdale, N.J.: Erlbaum.

Tribus, M. (1961). *Thermostatics and thermodynamics*. Princeton, NJ: van Nostrand.

Trivers, R. L. (1971). The evolution of reciprocal altruism. *The Quarterly Review of Biology, 46*(1), 35-57.

Tulving, E., & Craik, F.I.M. (2000). *The Oxford handbook of memory*. New York: Oxford University Press.

Turing, A. (1950). Computing machinery and intelligence. *Mind, 59,* 433-460.

Turing, A.M., Braithwaite, R., Jefferson, G., & Newman, M. (1952) Can automatic calculating machines be said to think? In J. Copeland (Ed.), *The Essential Turing – the ideas that gave birth to the computer age* (pp 487- 506). Clarendon Press: Oxford.

Turk, M. (2004). Computer vision in the interface. *Communications of the ACM, 47*(1), 60-67.

Turner, J. H. (1997). The evolution of emotion: The nonverbal basis of human social organization. In U. Segerstråle & P. Molar (Eds.), *Nonverbal communication: Where nature meets culture* (pp. 211-223). Mahwah, NJ: Erlbaum.

Turrigiano, G.G. & Nelson, S.B. (2004). Homeostatic plasticity in the developing nervous system. *Nature Reviews of Neuroscience, 5,* 97-107.

Txopitea, A. (2008). Retrieved May 30, 2008, from www.cyberpoetry.net/index.html.

Tzanetakis, G., & Cook, P. (2002). Musical genre classification of audio signals. *IEEE Transactions on Audio, Speech and Language Processing, 10*(5), 293–302.

Ulich, D. (1985). El Sentimiento, Introducción a la psicología de la emoción. Barcelona. Editorial Herder.

Urban, C. (1997). *PECS: A reference model for human-like agents*. University of Passau.

Vallverdú, J. (2005). Robots: la frontera de un nuevo arte. *Cuadernos del Minotauro, 1,* 21-30.

Vallverdú, J. (2006). Choosing between different AI approaches? The scientific benefits of the confrontation, and the new collaborative era between humans and machines. *TripleC, 4*(2), 209-216.

Vallverdú, J. (2007). ¿Por qué motivos crearemos máquinas emocionales? *Astrolabio, Revista internacional de filosofía, 5,* 44-52.

Vallverdú, J. (2007). *Una ética de las emociones*. Barcelona: Anthropos.

Vallverdú, J., & Casacuberta, D. (2008). The panic room. On synthetic emotions. In A. Briggle, K. Waelbers & P. Brey (Eds.), *current issues in computing and philosophy* (pp. 103-115). The Netherlands: IOS Press.

Vallverdú, J., & Casacuberta, D. (2008, June). *Modelling synthetic emotions: TPR 2.0.* (ECAP08). Paper presented at the *International Meeting of the European Association for Philosophy and Computing*, Montpellier, France.

van Ditmarsch, H. P., van der Hoek, W., & Kooi, B. P. (2007). Dynamic epistemic logic. In *Synthese Library* (Vol. 337). Berlin: Springer.

Van Kesteren, A. et al. (2000). *Simulation of emotions of agents in virtual environments using neural networks*. University of Twente

VanLehn, K. (2006). The behavior of tutoring systems. *International Journal of Artificial Intelligence in Education, 16*, 227-265.

Vanlehn, K., Lynch, C., Schultz, K., Shapiro, J. A., Shelby, R. H., & Taylor, L. (2005). The Andes physics tutoring system: Lessons learned. *International Journal of Artificial Intelligence in Education, 15*(3), 147-204.

Varela, F.J. (1996). Neurophenomenology: A methodological remedy to the hard problem. *Journal of Consciousness Studies, 3*, 330-50. Reprinted in: J. Shear (Ed.), *Explaining consciousness: The hard problem of consciousness* (pp. 337-58). Cambridge, MA: MIT Press, 1997.

Vaughan, R. T., Gerkey, B. P., & Howard, A. (2003). On device abstractions for portable, reusable robot code. In *Proceedings IEEE/RSJ International Conference on Intelligent Robots and Systems* (pp. 2421-2427).

Velásquez, J. (1997). Modeling emotions and other motivations in synthetic agents. In *Proceedings of the Fourteenth National Conference on Artificial Intelligence* (pp. 10-15) Menlo Park, CA: AAAI Press. Retrieved April 18, 2008, from http://citeseer.ist.psu.edu/103027.html

Velásquez, J. (1998). A computational framework for emotion-based control. *Workshop on Grounding Emotions in Adaptive Systems, Fifth International Conference on Simulation of Adaptive Behaviors* (SAB'98), Zurich, 21 août 1998.

Velásquez, J. D. (1997). Modeling emotions and other motivations in synthetic agents. In *Proceedings of the 14th National Conference on Artificial Intelligence* (pp. 10-15). Providence, RI.

Velásquez, J. D. (1998). A computational framework for emotion-based control. In *Proceedings of Fifth International Conference on Simulation of Adaptive Behaviors (SAB'98),*

Velásquez, J. D., & Maes, P. (1997). Cathexis: A computational model of emotions. In *Proceedings of the 1st International Conference on Autonomous Agents* (pp. 518-519). CA: Marina del Rey.

Velásquez, J., (1998). Modeling emotion-based decision-making. In D. Cañamero (Ed.), *Proceedings of the 1998 AAAI Fall Symposium. Emotional and Intelligent: the Tangled Knot of Cognition* (pp. 164–169). Retrieved April 18, 2008, from http://www.ai.mit.edu/people/jvelas/papers/velasquez-fs98.ps

Verruggio, J. M. (2007) *European research network's roboethics roadmap*. European Union.

Ververidis, D., & Kotropolos, C. (2004). *Automatic emotional speech classification*. Paper presented at the IEEE International Conference on Acoustics, Speech and Signal Processing.

Viccari, R. M., Jaques, P. A., & Verdin, R. (2008). *Agent-based tutoring systems by cognitive and affective modeling*. Hershey, PA: IGI Global.

Vieillard, S., Peretz, I., Gosselin, N., Khalfa, S., Gagnon, L., & Bouchard, B. (2008). Happy, sad, scary and peaceful musical excerpts for research on emotions. *Cognition & Emotion, 22*(4), 720–752.

Vilarroya, Óscar (2002). *Palabra de robot: Inteligencia artificial y comunicación*. Estudi General. Premio Europeo de Divulgación Científica.

Villamira M.A. (in press). Comunicare, FrancoAngeli, Milano.

Villamira M.A., & Cipresso P. (2008). Bio-inspired ICT for evolutionary emotional intelligence. In *Artificial life and evolutionary computation*.

Volet, S. (2001). Understanding learning and motivation in context. A multidimensional and multi-level cognitive-situative perspective. In S. Volet & S. Järvelä (Eds.), *Motivation in learning contexts: Theoretical and methodological implications* (pp. 57-82). Amsterdam: Pergamon Press.

Vygotsky, L.S. (1978). *Mind in society: The development of higher psychological processes.* Cambridge MA: Harvard University Press.

Wagner, I. (1994). Hard times. The politics of women's work in computerised environments. In A. Adam, J. Emms, E. Green, & J. Owen (Eds.), *Women, work and computerization. Breaking old boundaries – building new forms* (pp. 23-34). Amsterdam: Elsevier Science.

Wahlster, W. et al. (2004, September). Grand challenges in the evolution of the information society. *ISTAG Report.* European Communities. Retrieved from, ftp://ftp.cordis.europa.eu/pub/ist/docs/2004_grand_challenges_web_en.pdf

Wakeford, N. (2000). Gender and the landscapes of computing in an internet café. In Kirkup, G., Janes, L., Woodward, K., & Hovenden, F. (Eds.), *The gendered cyborg* (pp. 291-304). New York: Routledge.

Walker-Andrews, A. S. (1986). Intermodal perception of expressive behaviors: Relation of eye and voice? *Developmental Psychology, 22*(3), 373-377.

Wallace, R. (2007). A.L.I.C.E – artificial linguistic internet computer entity. Retrieved November 23, 2007, from http://www.alicebot.org

Walzer, M. (1977). *Just and unjust wars.* Basic Books.

Warren, D., Shen E., Park, S., Baylor, A. L., & Perez, R. (2005). Adult learner perceptions of affective agents. In C.K. Looi, G. McCalla, B. Bredeweg & J. Breuker (Eds.), *Artificial intelligence in education: Supporting learning through intelligent and socially informed technology* (Vol. 125, pp. 944-946). Amsterdam: IOS Press.

Watson, J. (1913). Psychology as the behaviorist views it. *Psychological Review, 22*.

Watson, J. B. (1919). *Psychology, from the standpoint of a behaviorist.* Philadelphia: Lippincott.

Watson, J. Rayner, R. (1920). Conditioned emotional reactions. *Journal of Experimental Psychology, 3*.

Watt, S. (1995, November). A brief naive psychology manifesto. *INFORMATICA, 19* http://www.comp.rgu.ac.uk/staff/sw/stuarts_papers/naiveshort.htm

Wehrle, T. (1998). Motivations behind modeling emotional agents: Whose emotion does your robot have? In C. Numaoka, L. D. Cañamero & P. Petta (Eds.), *Grounding emotions in adaptive systems.* Zurich: 5th International Conference of the Society for Adaptive Behavior Workshop Notes (SAB'98).

Weick, K.E. (1995). *Sensemaking in organizations.* Newbury Park, CA: Sage.

Weiler, A. (2004). Information-seeking behavior in Generation Y students: Motivation, critical thinking, and learning theory. *The Journal of Academic Librarianship, 31*(1), 46-53.

Weiner, B. (1985). "Spontaneous" causal thinking. *Psychological Bulletin, 97*, 74-84.

Weiner, B. (1985). An attributional theory of achievement motivation and emotion. *Psychological Review, 92*(4), 548-573.

Weiner, B., & Graham, S. (1989). Understanding the motivational role of affect: Life-span research from an attributional perspective. *Cognition and Emotion, 3*(4), 401-419.

Weiser, M. (1991). The computer for the 21st century. *Scientific American, 265*(3), 94-104. Reprinted in *IEEE: Pervasive Computing,* January-March 2002, pp. 19-25. Retrieved from, http://www.ubiq.com/hypertext/weiser/SciAmDraft3.html

Weiser, M. (1993). Some computer science issues in ubiquitous computing. *Communications of the ACM, 36*(7), 75-84.

Weiser, M. (1994). The world is not a desktop. *ACM SIGCHI Interactions 1*(1), 7-8.

Weiser, M., Brown, J.S. (1995). Designing calm technology. In P.J. Denning & R.M. Metcalfe (Eds.) *Beyond calculation – The next fifty years of computing.* Copernicus/Springer-Verlag. Retrieved from, http://sandbox.xerox.com/hypertext/weiser/calmtech/calmtech.htm http://www.ubiq.com/hypertext/weiser/acmfuture2endnote.htm

Weld, D. S., Anderson, C.R., & Smith, D.E. (1998). Extending Graphplan to handle uncertainty & sensing actions. In *Proceedings of AAAI 1998.* AAAI Press.

Wieczorkowska, A., Synak, P., Lewis, R., & Raś. (2005). Extracting emotions from music data. In *Foundations of intelligent systems* (pp. 456–465). Springer-Verlag.

Wierzbicka, A. (1996). *Semantics: primes and universals.* Oxford: Oxford University Press.

Wierzbicka, A. (1999). *Emotions across languages and cultures: Diversity and universals.* Cambridge, UK: Cambridge University Press.

Wilhelm, T., Bohme, H.J., Grofi, H.M., & Backhaus, A. (2004). Statistical and neural methods for vision-based analysis of facial expressions and gender. In *Systems, Man and Cybernetics, 2004 IEEE International Conference,* 3, (pp. 2203-2208).

Willeke, T., Kunz, C., & Nourbakhsh, I. (2001). The history of the mobot museum robot series: An evolutionary study. In *Proceedings of FLAIRS 2001.*

Wilson, E. O. (1971). *The insect societies.* Cambridge: Harvard University Press.

Wilson, E.O. (2008). One giant leap: How Insects achieved altruism and colonial life. *BioScience, 58*(1), 17-25.

Winkielman , P. & Berridge, K. (2004). Unconscious emotion. In *Current Directions in Psychological Science, 13*(3),120-123. Blackwell Synergy.

Winograd, T. (1997). The design of interaction. In P.J. Denning, & R.M. Metcalfe (Eds.), *Beyond calculation – The next fifty years of computing* (pp. 149-161). New York: Copernicus, Springer-Verlag.

Wiratanaya, A., Lyons, M. J., & Abe, S. (2006). An interactive character animation system for dementia care. In *Proceedings of the ACM SIGGRAPH 2006 Research posters, Boston, Massachusetts* (pp. Article No. 82). | DOI: 10.1145/1179622.1179717

Witten, I. H., & Frank, E. (1999). *Data Mining: Practical Machine Learning Tools and Techniques with Java Implementations.* Morgan Kaufmann.

Wolfram, S. (2002). *A new kinf of science.* Canada: Wolfram Media, Inc.

Wong, P. T. P., & Weiner, B. (1981). When people ask "why" questions, and the heuristics of attributional search. *Journal of Personality and Social Psychology, 40*(4), 650-663.

Wood, J. V., Saltzberg, J. A., & Goldsamt, L. A. (1990). Does affect induce self-focused attention? *Journal of Personality and Social Psychology, 58*(5), 899–908.

Woodcock, S. (2000). *AI roundtable moderator's report.* Report on the AI Roundtable of the Game Developer's Conference, San Jose, CA. Retrieved May 17, 200,8 from http://www.gameai.com/cgdc00notes.html

Woodcock, S. (2000, August). Game AI: The state of the industry. *Game Developer's Magazine,* 24-32.

Wooldridge, M. (2002). *An introduction to multiagent systems.* West Sussex: John Wiley & Sons.

World Wide Web Consortium (W3C). (2006). W3C Emotion Incubator Group. Retrieved from, http://www.w3.org/2005/Incubator/emotion/

Wosnitza, M., & Nenniger, P. (2001). Perceived learning environments and use of learning-strategies. The mediating role of motivation for the self-direction in learning. In S. Volet & S. Järvelä (Eds.), *Motivation in learning contexts: Theoretical and methodological implications* (pp. 171-187). Amsterdam: Pergamon Press.

Wosnitza, M., & Volet, S. (2005). Origin, direction and impact of emotions in social online learning. *Learning and Instruction, 15*(5), 449-464.

Wundt, W. (1863). *Vorlesungen über die Menschen- und Tierseele [Lectures on the mind of man and animals].* Leipzig: Voss.

Yang, Y. H., Lin, Y. C., Cheng, H. T., & Chen, H. H. (2008). Mr.emo: Music retrieval in the emotion plane. In *Proceedings of the ACM International Conference on Multimedia.* Vancouver, BC, Canada.

Yang, Y. H., Lin, Y. C., Su, Y. F., & Chen, H. H. (2008). A regression approach to music emotion recognition. *IEEE Transactions on Audio, Speech, and Language Processing, 16*(2), 448–457.

Yeung, A.S., Wong, E. (2004). *Teacher self-concept enhancement: Effects of an in-service training program in Hong Kong.* Hong Kong: The Hong Kong Institute of Education.

Yip, J.A., & Martin, R.A. (2006). Sense of humor, emotional intelligence, and social competence. *Journal of Research in Personality, 40,* 1202-1208.

You, H-c. & Chen, K. (2006). Applications of affordance and semantics in product design. *Design Studies, 28,* 23-38.

Zadeh, L. (1975). The concept of a linguistic variable and its applications to approximate reasoning. *Information Sci. 8.*

Zadeh, L. A. (2002). From computing with numbers to computing with words—from manipulation of measurements to manipulation of perceptions. *International Journal of Applied Mathematics and Computer Sciences, 12*(3), 307-324.

Zajonc, R. (1984). On the primary affect. *American Psychologist, 39*(1), 117-123.

Zanbaka C., Goolkasian, P., & Hodges, L. (2006). Can a virtual cat persuade you? The role of gender and realism in speaker persuasiveness. In *Proceedings of the SIGCHI conference on Human Factors in computing systems* (pp. 1153-1162). Montréal, Québec, Canada.

Zanbaka, C., Goolkasian, P., & Hodges, L. (2006). Can a virtual cat persuade you? The role of gender and realism in speaker persuasiveness. In *Proceedings of the SIGCHI Conference on Human Factors in Computing Systems, Montreal, Quebec, Canada.* | DOI: 10.1145/1124772.1124945

Zapata-Rivera, J. D., & Greer, J. (2001). SMODEL Server: Student modelling in distributed multi-agent tutoring systems. In J. D. Moore, C. L. Redfield, & W. L. Johnson (Eds.), *Artificial intelligence in education* (pp.446-455). Amsterdam: IOS Press.

Zhai, S., Morimoto, C., & Ihde, S. (1999). *Manual and gaze input cascaded (MAGIC) pointing.* In *Proceedings of the SIGCHI conference on Human factors in computing systems: the CHI is the limit, Pittsburgh* (pp. 246-253). | DOI: 10.1145/302979.303053

Zhang, T. & Covaci, S. (2002). Adaptive behaviors of intelligent agents based on neural semantic knowledge. *Symposium on Applications and the Internet (SAINT '02).*

Zimmerman, M. E. (1990). *Heidegger's confrontation with modernity. Technology, politics, art.* Bloomington, Indiana: University Press.

Zúñiga, F., Ramos, F. F., & Piza, I. (2005). GeDA-3D agent architecture. *In Proceedings of the 11th International Conference on Parallel and Distributed Systems, 2,* 201-205.

About the Contributors

Jordi Vallverdú is an associate professor for philosophy of science & computing at Universitat Autònoma de Barcelona. He holds a PhD. in philosophy of science (UAB) and a master in history of sciences (physics dept. UAB). After a short research stay as fellowship researcher at Glaxco-Wellcome Institute for the History of Medicine-London (1997) and research assistant of Dr. Jasanoff at J.F.K. School of Government – Harvard University (2000), he worked in computing epistemology issues, bioethics (because of the emotional aspects of cognition; he is listed as EU Biosociety Research Expert) and, especially, on synthetic emotions. He co-leads a research group on this last topic, SETE (Synthetic Emotions in Technological Environments), with which has published several book chapters about computational models of synthetic emotions and their implementation into social robotic systems. "

David Casacuberta is a philosophy of science professor in the Universidad Autònoma de Barcelona (Spain). He has a PhD in philosophy and a master degree in cognitive sciences and language. His current line of research is the cognitive and social impact of new media, and specially, how the inclusion of artificial intelligence and artificial emotions can produce innovative, more interactive and radically different new types of media.

* * *

Tom Adi was an assistant professor for computer science in the 1980's. He taught at universities in Jordan and Saudi Arabia. He received a PhD in industrial computer science in 1978 from Johannes Gutenberg University in Mainz, Germany. While designing a machine translation software in 1985, he discovered a theory of semantics (published in Semiotics and Intelligent Systems Development, 2007). Based on this semantics, he developed a theory of cognition. In a nutshell, the sounds in the names of things point to models of those things. A paper about these theories and their implementations in the software Readware appears in 2009 in the *Journal of Information Technology Research*. As chief scientist of Management Information Technologies, Inc., he is currently working on theories (ontologies) for mental processes, socio-legal systems, emotions, health and disease, and spiritual relations.

Alberto Amengual graduated in computer science in 1995 after which he worked in the IT industry in Spain for several years, and he worked as part-time faculty at the University of the Balearic Islands. In 2003 he started a dissertation in Natural Language Processing. From 2004, he enjoys an ICSI Fellowship for Spanish Technologists, funded by the Spanish Ministry of Science. In Berkeley he changed the focus of his dissertation, finally aimed at building computational models of human motivation, more specifically of attachment behavior, under the direction of professors Main and Hesse from the Department of Psychology at the University of California at Berkeley. He is currently in the final stage of his PhD.

Michel Aubé is a professor at the Université de Sherbrooke, Canada, since 1983, where he has been teaching cognitive science, theories of emotions, teacher training, and the integration of computers in education. Since 2004, he has been lent by his Faculty to the Quebec Ministry of Education as a consultant in designing the new curriculum for elementary and secondary schools. He obtained his master's degree in cognitive psychology from the University of Toronto, and his PhD in education sciences from the Université de Montréal. His doctoral studies bear upon the design of a computational model of emotions, called "The Commitment Theory of Emotions". He is also involved in the design and implementation of websites dedicated to the scientific training of children from elementary schools, by putting them in contact with adult scientists. His research interests are distributed along three main axes: development of a robust computational model of emotions; use of computer technologies to foster scientific thinking in children; use of computer technologies in building online distance-training systems for teachers.

Sajal Chandra Banik received BSc in mechanical engineering from Bangladesh University of Engineering and Technology (BUET), Bangladesh in September, 1998. He got MSc in mechatronics from Technical University of Hamburg-Harburg (TUHH), Germany in April, 2005. From October, 2005 he is a PhD student in the Department of Advanced System Control Engineering, Saga University. From May, 1999 to August, 2002, he was a lecturer in the Department of Mechanical Engineering, Chittagong University of Engineering and Technology (CUET), Bangladesh. During the masters course, he was also a part time research assistant in the Department of Machine Element and Material Handling, Helmut Schmidt University, Hamburg, Germany from January, 2004 to April, 2005. Since July 2005, he has been with the Department of Mechanical Engineering, CUET as an assistant professor. His main research interests are human adaptive and friendly Mechatronics, service robots, Biorobotics, Multiagent system, Human-robot interaction, emotional robotics.

Christoph Bartneck is an assistant professor in the Department of Industrial Design at the Eindhoven University of Technology. He has a background in industrial design and human-computer interaction, and his projects and studies have been published in various journals, newspapers, and conferences. His interests lie in the fields of social robotics, design science, and multimedia applications. He has worked for several companies including the Technology Centre of Hannover (Germany), LEGO (Denmark), Eagle River Interactive (USA), Philips Research (Netherlands), and ATR (Japan).

Gloria Bueno received her MsC from Universidad Complutense de Madrid in 1993, and her PhD from Coventry University in 1998. From 1998 to 2000 Gloria worked as a postdoctoral researcher at Université Louis Pasteur, Strasbourg. In 2000-2001 she worked at CNRS-Institut de Physique Biologique-Hôpital Civil and from 2001 to 2003 she was a senior researcher at CEIT (Centro de Estudios e Investigaciones Técnicas de Gipuzkoa), San Sebastián, Spain. She is currently an associate professor at Universidad de Castilla-La Mancha, Spain. Her main research interests include image processing – particularly for biomedical engineering applications- computer vision, artificial intelligence, modeling and simulation.

Amílcar Cardoso is associate professor at the Department of Informatics Engineering and director of the Centre for Informatics and Systems of the University of Coimbra, where coordinates the Cognitive and Media Systems Group. He has developed, in the nineties, pioneering work on Computational Creativity, an area where he has assumed relevant organisational and networking roles and where has a significant record of publications, particularly in computer models of creativity phenomena inspired both in psychological and evolutionary theories. His main current research interests include also affective computing and multi-agent systems, particularly in contexts of creative systems, human-machine interaction and social simulation.

Dale Carnegie (IEEE senior member) received his MSc with first class honours in physics and electronics and his PhD in computer science from the University of Waikato in Hamilton, New Zealand. He is currently a professor of Computer Systems Engineering at Victoria University of Wellington, New Zealand where he heads the Mechatronics Research Group and co-ordinates the Computer Systems Engineering Programme. His research interests are in the areas of autonomous mobile robotics, sensors, embedded controllers and applied artificial intelligence.

Rocío Carrasco Carrasco is currently a lecturer at the University of Huelva, Spain. In 1999 she graduated in English Studies at the University of Zaragoza. She obtained her MA in masculinity and science fiction cinema from the University of Huelva, and is soon to receive her PhD in the same field. Her current research deals with gender representation in US Science Fiction Films. She has published scientific articles on postmodernism, gender and science fiction. Her book *New Heroes on Screen. Prototypes of Masculinity in Contemporary Science Fiction Cinema* was published by Huelva University Press in 2006.

Cristiano Castelfranchi is full professor of Cognitive Sciences at the University of Siena, Department of Communication Science and, director of the Institute of Cognitive Sciences and Technologies of the National Research Council, in Rome, Italy. His interests cover multi-agent systems research, cognitive modelling and social psychology. Cristiano Castelfranchi is of the pioneers of Distributed AI in Italy and Europe. He has published extensively in cognitive psychology, in artificial intelligence, and in social theory and simulation. He has published 3 books in English and 7 books in Italian, more than 200 conference and journal articles on cognitive, computational and formal-theoretical models of social interaction and social mind. He has been an invited speaker at several international conferences in the fields of Artificial Intelligence and Cognitive Sciences (ex. IJCAI'97, EuroCogSci'07).

Modesto Castrillon is an assistant professor at the Department of Computer Science and a research member of the Institute of Intelligent Systems and Numerical Applications in Engineering at the ULPGC (University of Las Palmas de Gran Canaria), Spain. His research interests include facial detection and recognition, and computer vision for human-computer interaction. He holds since 2003 a PhD from the ULPGC, and is member of AEPIA, AERFAI and the IEEE.

Pietro Cipresso, MEc, PhD candidate, graduated at Bocconi University (Milan) in economics with specialization in statistics and operational research. Currently he is research fellow and teaching associate at Institute of Human, Language and Environmental Sciences, IULM University - Milan and PhD candidate, in the same University, in Communication and New Technologies. Cipresso has been business and technology consulting in multinational companies for ten years. Now, he is mainly involved in research on AI, ALife, agent-based computational economics (ACE), economic psychology, communication, complex systems, computational models of emotional/cognitive processes and bio-signals processing. Cipresso has attended international School in Milan, Budapest, Lion and Paris. He has talked to many international scientific conference about his researches.

Cecile K. M. Crutzen studied mathematics at the University Aachen (Germany) and didactics at the University Eindhoven (The Netherlands). She is associate professor at the Computer Science faculty of the Open University of the Netherlands. Her research is situated in the field of people, society and computers and focussed on computer science and genderstudies, especially in e-learning, ambient intelligence, and object orientation. Her PhD, "Interaction, a World of Differences" was interdisciplinary in computer science and genderstudies, too.

Jean-Marie Dembele, PhD candidate in computer science at Cheikh Anta Diop University. He is also assistant professor in Gaston Berger University (www.ugb.sn). The formation received in both computer science and mathematics has provided the ability to couple mathematical modeling and computer science paradigms and resources of simulation. His main field of interest is agent-based modeling, applied, in his PhD program, to physical systems, described by partial differential equations (transport phenomena, lagrangian models of fluids dynamics, coastal erosion, etc.). He is also interested in dynamical social networks and interacting agents. Dembele made productive collaborations with Collegues with different backgrounds (economics, psychology, etc.), to gain a multidisciplinarity in developing modeling tools.

Oscar Deniz: He received his MsC and PhD from Universidad de Las Palmas de Gran Canaria, Spain, in 1999 and 2006, respectively. He has been associate professor at Universidad de Las Palmas de Gran Canaria from 2003 to 2007 and currently at Universidad de Castilla-La Mancha, Spain. His main research interests are human-robot interaction and computer vision. He is a research fellow of the Institute of Intelligent Systems and Numerical Applications in Engineering and member of IEEE, AEPIA and AERFAI.

Tillmann Dorsch describes himself as an innovative and creative thinker. He is a passional 3D artist and likes working in cross-functional teams with scientists, architects and other designers. In his working he is dealing with animations, visualizations, games, graphic-, screen- and interaction-design. (www. tillmann-dorsch.de). In 2004 he finished successfully his education as a graphic design at the Akademie für Kommunikation in Stuttgart (Germany). Afterwards he started his studies "virtual design" at the University of Applied Science Kaiserslautern (Germany) which he completed at the Tampere University of Technology (TUT, Finland) in 2008. The topic of his bachelor thesis was "Development of an Ambient Emotional Responsive Character". He was examining methods to design and measure emotions and movements. Within the practical part he collaborated with Pablo Roman Humanes to realize a virtual character which reacts to his surrounding by motion tracking and gives emotional feedback to the user of the system in real-time. (www.emodo.kilu.de). His passions in private live are photography, video games, architecture, art&design, sports and nature. In 2008 he won a spezial price in photo competition ("blende 2008").

Anthony G. Francis, Jr. studies human and other minds to help create intelligent machines and emotional robots. He received his PhD from Georgia Tech in 2000 applying principles of human memory to information retrieval and continued this work at Enkia Corporation. His academic research also includes work on emotional robotics for Georgia Tech and Yamaha; his software industry experience includes military, law enforcement and public health projects. He has published ten papers, one book chapter, a science fiction short story, and a webcomic. He currently works as a search quality engineer at Google on projects to debug and extend Google's core ranking algorithms. More details about his research can be found at his blog at http://www.dresan.com/.

Mercedes García Ordaz is a professor at the Department of Financial Economy, Accounting and Operations Research of the University of Huelva, where she has lectured for 20 years. She has published numerous works on accounting and communication. She has obtained The Rainbow Research Award. She has published more than 100 scientific works.

After completing a PhD dissertation on "The Computational Theory of the Mind", in 1990, **Antoni Gomila** got a postdoc Fulbright grant from the Spanish Government, to work with Jerry Fodor at Rutgers University. He's got positions at the University of Salamanca, La Laguna and the Balearic Islands, where he teaches "Thinking and Language" since 2000. He's published papers on questions on the foundations of psychology, on meaning, language evolution and on theory of mind. He's just edited, with Paco Calvo, the *Handbook of Cognitive Science: an Embodied Approach* (Elsevier 2008).

Dorel V. Gorga is a researcher and PhD student in the unit of TECFA, active in the field of educational technology, at the School of Psychology and Education, University of Geneva, Switzerland. His research interests focus on e-learning and affective computing. More particularly: computational models of emotion in educational technology, activity-based instructional designs and integration of technological innovations into communities of practice. Recent publications include articles on the knowledge management within communities of practice and the pedagogical approaches related to collaborative learning.

Claudius Gros holds a chair in theoretical physics at the J.W. Goethe University Frankfurt. He received his degree in theoretical physics from the ETH-Zürich in 1985, where he also completed his PhD studies in theoretical condensed matter physics in 1988. Since then and till 2004 the focus of his research has been the theory of correlated electron systems and of high temperature superconductivity, resulting in over 80 scientific journal publications. Since 2004 C. Gros studies cognitive systems, with the aim to develop an overall framework for an evolvable cognitive system base on biologically inspired principles. He proposed in this context the notion of transient state dynamics for the modelling of the self-sustained and autonomously generated neural activity in the brain.

Maki K. Habib obtained his PhD Eng in intelligent robotics from the University of Tsukuba, Japan. He was a selected research scientist at RIKEN, Japan, and senior researcher at RISO-Laboratories, Japan, and visiting researcher at EPFL-Lausanne, Switzerland. He was a visiting expert under Asian Development Bank (ADB), Associate Professor at UTM, Malaysia, and a Senior Manager at MCRIA, Malaysia. Then, he was a senior research scientist with GMD, Japan, leading Telecooperation group, Associate Professor with Monash University and leading the Mechatronics Engineering Programme. He was appointed as a professor of Robotics and Mechatronics at Swinburne University. Then, he was an invited Professor at KAIST, Korea. Currently he is a full professor at the American University in

Cairo and a Visiting professor at Saga University, Japan. His main area of research are focusing on human adaptive and friendly mechatronics, autonomous navigation, service robots and humanitarian demining, telecooperation, distributed teleoperation and collaborative control, wireless sensor networks and ambient intelligence, biomimetic robots.

Hans-Werner Hein 1975 finished his informatics diploma at the University Karlsruhe (Germany), focussed on Artificial Intelligence, received 1982 the Dr.-Ing. degree at the University Erlangen-NŸrnberg for research on "Understanding Continuous Speech". At the research institute GMD, Sankt Augustin, he headed R&D projects on "Expert Systems" and "Multi-modal Adaptive Human-Machine Interfaces". He founded and headed a research group "Machine Intelligence" at the University Dortmund Robotics Institute. Since 1994 he is independent researcher and consultant focussed on human-machine-relation topics: biometrics, trust management, privacy profiles, dependable agents, ambient intelligence, cyborgetics. HWH since long is engaged in didactically enlightening all types of IT consumers, and co-operates in special IT activities for highly skilled children.

Perfecto Herrera holds a degree in Psychology by the University of Barcelona (1987), where he also worked as software developer and assistant professor. He has also got courses on computer music, sound engineering and audio postproduction and enrolled in a Technology doctoral program, where he is now finishing his PhD Thesis. He has been working in the MTG since its inception around 1996, first as the responsible for the sound laboratory/studio, then as a researcher. He worked in the MPEG-7 standardization initiative between 1999 and 2001. Then he collaborated in the EU-IST funded CUIDA-DO project, contributing to the research and development of tools for indexing and retrieving music and sound collections. This work was somehow continued and expanded as scientific coordinator for the Semantic Interaction with Music Audio Contents (SIMAC) project, again funded by the EU-IST. He is currently the head of the Department of Sonology in the Higher Music School of Catalonia (ESMUC), where he teaches music technology and psychoacoustics. His main research interests are music content processing, classification, and music perception and cognition.

Pilar Herrero is an associate professor at the Universidad Politécnica de Madrid, in Spain. European PhD in Computer Science and Extraordinary Prize of Doctorate (Extraordinary PhD Award), in the last few years, she has also been involved in the organization of more than 10 international events, such as conferences and workshops, as a Steering Committee member, networks of excellence, and she has also been part of more than 50 Program Committees. Pilar has more than 70 international publications, some of them in prestigious international journals that are listed as Journal Citation Reports (JCRs). Editor, of more than 15 international publications and special issues in prestigious journals and several proceedings books, since 2005 she has been involved in the organization board of the On The Move (OTM) Federated Conferences as Workshops general chair, and since then she has coordinated more than 45 international workshops and events.

Mario Hernandez: He received his Graduate in Electrical Engineering and PhD in computer science from the Universidad de Las Palmas de Gran Canaria. He is currently a full professor of Computer Science and Engineering at the Computer Science and Systems Department of the Las Palmas de Gran Canaria University. His current research interests span autonomous systems, knowledge-based systems, active vision, visual learning, scene analysis, mobile robotics and interactive robotic systems. He has been the author or coauthor of more than 60 research papers and chapters. He is member of the International Association of Pattern Recognition (IAPR), the Asociación Española de Reconocimiento de Formas y Análisis de Imágenes (AERFAI) and the Asociación Española para la Inteligencia Artificial (AEPIA).

Kiyotaka Izumi received a BE degree in electronic engineering from Nagasaki Institute of Applied Science in 1991, a ME degree in electrical engineering from Saga University in 1993, and a DE degree in Faculty of Engineering Systems and Technology from the Saga University in 1996. From April, 1996 to March, 2001, he was a research associate in the Department of Mechanical Engineering at Saga University. From April, 2001, he was with the Department of Advanced Systems Control Engineering, Graduate School of Science and Engineering, Saga University. From August, 2004, he is an Associate Professor in the Department of Advanced Systems Control Engineering, Graduate School of Science and Engineering, Saga University. His research interests are in intelligent control, fuzzy control, evolutionary computation, and their applications to the robot control.

Christopher Lee-Johnson completed a BTech (Hons, first class) in electronic engineering and an MSc (Hons, first class) in physics and electronics at the University of Waikato, Hamilton, New Zealand. He is currently a doctoral candidate at Victoria University of Wellington, New Zealand. His research interests include mobile robot planning and control, cognition and emotion, and biologically-inspired intelligent systems.

Cyril Laurier is a computer science engineer graduated from the IMAC school in Paris, and holds a master degree in acoustics, signal processing and computer science applied to Music (from IRCAM). He worked as a developer and project manager at IK Multimedia, one of the most successful company in the computer music software industry. He has been working at the Music Technology Group (MTG, UPF Barcelona) since 2006 as a PhD candidate. He is also involved in the EU-IST funded PHAROS project and in coordinating the music information retrieval development team at the MTG. His main research topic is music audio analysis, classification, and especially emotions and mood in music.

Javier Lorenzo is an associate professor at the Department of Computer Science and a research member of the Institute of Intelligent Systems and Numerical Applications in Engineering of the University of Las Palmas de Gran Canaria (ULPGC), Spain. He is currently teaching graduate courses in Computer Vision, Pattern Recognition and Artificial Intelligence at Facultad de Informática and Escuela Técnica Superior de Ingenieros Industriales. He received his PhD in computer science in 2001 on feature selection in machine learning. Since 2001, his research interests have been in computer vision applied to human-computer interaction, bioinspired computer vision systems, machine learning and web usage mining. Dr. Lorenzo has been co-author of chapters in the books *Pattern Recognition and Image Analysis* (AERFAI, 1998) and *Artificial Intelligence* (Inteligencia Artificial, McGraw-Hill, 2008). He has also participated as research member and project coordinator in several research projects.

Emiliano Lorini received the MS degree in artificial intelligence in 2005 from Université Paul Sabatier, Toulouse, France and the PhD in cognitive sciences from the University of Siena, Italy. He is currently post-doctoral student at the Institut the Recherche en Informatique de Toulouse-IRIT (France) and research fellow of the Institute of Cognitive Sciences and Technologies (CNR, Rome) at the Division of Artificial Intelligence, Cognitive Modelling and Interaction. His research is focused on several topics in the fields of artificial intelligence, multi-agent systems and cognitive sciences. In particular, he is interested in cognitive theories of emotions, theory of intention and intentional action, formal models of trust and reputation, theory of social power and collective action, deontic logic.

Artur Lugmayr describes himself as a creative thinker and his scientific work is situated between art and science. His vision can be expressed as to create media experiences on future emerging media technology platforms. He is the head and founder of the New AMbient MUltimedia (NAMU) research group at the Tampere University of Technology (Finland) which is part of the Finnish Academy Centre of Excellence of Signal Processing from 2006 to 2011 (http://namu.cs.tut.fi). He is holding a Dr.-Techn. degree from the Tampere University of Technology (TUT, Finland), and is currently engaged in Dr.-Arts studies at the School of Motion Pictures, TV and Production Design (UIAH, Helsinki). He chaired the ISO/IEC ad-hoc group "MPEG-21 in broadcasting"; won the NOKIA Award of 2003 with the text book "Digital interactive TV and Metadata" published by Springer-Verlag in 2004; representative of the Swan Lake Moving Image & Music Award (http://www.swan-lake-award.org/); board member of MindTrek (http://www.mindtrek.org), EU project proposal reviewer; invited key-note speaker for conferences; organizer and reviewer of several conferences; and has contributed one book chapter and written over 25 scientific publications. His passion in private life is to be a notorious digital film-maker. He is founder of the production company LugYmedia Inc. (http://www.lugy-media.tv). More about him in Google.

Michael J. Lyons is a professor of Image Arts and Sciences at Ritsumeikan University in Kyoto Japan. He has conducted research in human-computer interaction, pattern recognition, visual perception, and the self-organization of complex systems, including many works on several aspects of facial information processing. His work has been published at conference and in journals such as SIGGRAPH, CHI, IEEE Face and Gesture Recognition, and IEEE PAMI. Prior to his current position he was for many years a senior research scientist at the Advanced Telecommunications Research Laboratories in Kyoto, and has been a member of the teaching and research faculties of the University of Southern California and the California Institute of Technology. He holds the PhD and MSc degree in physics from the University of British Columbia, and the BSc degree from McGill University, also in physics.

Luis Macedo is assistant professor at the Department of Informatics Engineering of the University of Coimbra, and member of the Cognitive and Media Systems Group of the Centre for Informatics and Systems of the University of Coimbra, Portugal. He graduated in informatics engineering, obtained the MSc degree in systems and information technologies, and the PhD in informatics engineering. His main interests lie in the fields of artificial intelligence and cognitive science, especially multi-agent systems, social simulation, cognitive agents, affective computing, computational neuroscience, and planning and decision-making under uncertainty. He has published various articles on these and other topics.

Bruce MacLennan received his BS (1968, mathematics, honors) from Florida State and his MS (1974) and PhD (1975) in computer science from Purdue. He was a senior software engineer for Intel (1975–9) and later assistant professor (1979–83), associate professor (1983–7), and acting chair (1984–5) of the Computer Science Department of the Naval Postgraduate School. Since 1987 he has been in the Department of Electrical Engineering and Computer Science of the University of Tennessee, Knoxville. Much of MacLennan's academic research has been directed toward understanding the mind in a way integrating both psychological and physical reality. Since the mid-1980s, his research has focused on new approaches to robotic artificial intelligence based on neuroscience and informed by phenomenological philosophy and psychology. His research focus is basic science: what can AI reveal about natural intelligence and the relation of mind and matter? In connection with this work he has published several papers on the neurophenomenology of consciousness and color vision. MacLennan has more than 60 refereed journal articles and book chapters and has published two books. He has made more 60 invited or refereed presentations, most recently in Bologna and Sheffield. He is a fellow of the Institute for Advanced Studies, Collegium Budapest.

Francisco José Martínez López is a full professor at Department of Financial Economy, Accounting and Operations Research of the University of Huelva, where he has lectured for 20 years. He currently lectures on Information Technologies, Computer Science and Information Systems at the Faculty of Management Sciences. He holds a PhD in economic and management sciences (with honours). He has given conferences at numerous institutions, courses and masters, as well as more than 30 doctorate courses in Spanish, European and American Universities. He is the director and main researcher of numerous scientific projects, both national and international. He is the author and co-author of more than 200 scientific works. He has been chancellor of the University of Huelva and president of the Economic and Social Council of Huelva.

Manish Mehta is a PhD student under the Human-Centered Computing program at Georgia Institute of Technology. His research interests include Interactive game characters and interactive narrative. Before joining Georgia Tech, he worked on a project that demonstrated natural, fun and experientially rich communication between humans (esp. children and adolescent) and embodied historical and literary characters from the fairy tale universe of Hans Christian Andersen. Currently, he is working on developing a wiki environment for authoring virtual characters using second life as the virtual world. More details about his projects can be found at http://www.cc.gatech.edu/~mehtamal/.

François Michaud (M'90) received his bachelor's degree ('92), master's degree ('93) and PhD degree ('96) in electrical engineering from the Université de Sherbrooke, Québec Canada. After completing postdoctoral work at Brandeis University, Waltham MA ('97), he became a faculty member in the Department of Electrical Engineering and Computer Engineering of the Université de Sherbrooke, and founded LABORIUS, a research laboratory working on designing intelligent autonomous systems that can assist humans in living environments. His research interests are in architectural methodologies for intelligent decision-making, design of autonomous mobile robotics, cognitive architectures, social robotics, robot for children with autism, robot learning and intelligent systems. Prof. Michaud is the Canada Research Chairholder in Autonomous Mobile Robots and Intelligent Systems. He is a member of IEEE, AAAI and OIQ (Ordre des ingénieurs du Québec). In 2003 he received the Young Engineer Achievement Award from the Canadian Council of Professional Engineers.

Hector Rafel Orozco Aguirre graduated in 2003 from the University of Guadalajara as computer engineer specialized in system software. In 2006 he obtained his master's degree in electric engineering and computer systems at CINVESTAV Guadalajara. His thesis named "Virtual Tracking and Monitoring in Neurosurgery" gave support to the project number 49 of the Sectorial Found for Investigation in Health and Social Security (Economic Neuronavigator of Multiple Use). At present, Rafael Orozco is studying to obtain the doctor's degree at CINVESTAV Guadalajara, he continues his reseach work at the

Virtual Reality Laboratory of the Federal Polytechnic School of Lausanne, Switzerland. Rafael Orozco has several years of teaching experience at the University of Guadalajara, and Occidental Technological Institute for Advanced Studies (ITESO, Jesuit University of Guadalajara). He also gave courses which formed part of the PAFTI program at CINVESTAV Guadalajara in such topics as development of web applications and the use of Java technology.

Sarantos Psycharis was born at Montreal ,1961. He holds a PhD ,University of Glasgow 1988,in the field of Computational Physics and an Msc in Information Technology, University of Athens, 2002. He has been Lecturer at the Pedagogical Department of Primary Education, Aegean University and currently he is appointed as Associate Professor at the School of Pedagogical and Technological Education in Athens in the field of ICT in Education. He has published numerous articles in Physics, Didactics of Physics, Science Education and ICT in Education. His main interests include the new insights of the use of ICT in education, mainly connected with the algorithmic thinking and the shift from computational–physics education to computational physics–education.

Clément Raïevsky received his master's degree (2002) in computer science from Université Pierre et Marie Curie, Paris. Since 2003, he is pursuing a PhD in computer engineering at LABORIUS. His research interests are artificial intelligent decision-making, agent coordination and artificial emotions.

Ashwin Ram is an associate professor and director of the Cognitive Computing Lab in the College of Computing at Georgia Tech, an associate professor of Cognitive Science, and an adjunct professor in Psychology at Georgia Tech and in MathCS at Emory University. He received his PhD from Yale University in 1989, his MS from University of Illinois in 1984, and his BTech from IIT Delhi in 1982. He has published 2 books and over 100 scientific articles in international forums. He is a founder of Enkia Corporation which provides AI software for information assurance and decision support. More details about his research can be found at http://www.cc.gatech.edu/faculty/ashwin.

Felix Francisco Ramos Corchado studied his Phd from Compiègne Technologic University in France. He has 15 years experience working in educations, research, technology development and creation of new groups of research. Academically, professor Ramos started his work as a researcher in 1988, working for Electric and Mechanic Department of the IPN and the Engineering Department of the National University of Mexico. In 1989 he joined Statistic and Calculi Department of the Postgraduate College as a researcher on information systems. In 1997 he joined computer science department of CINVESTAV as a full time researcher. In 2000 created the International Symposium on Advanced Distributed Systems. From 1999 to 2002 he led the Computer Chapter of the IEEE. Prof. Ramos research interests include: multiagent systems, animation of synthetic characters, virtual and augmented virtual reality, is part of scientific committee of different international journals and symposiums around the world and currently is member of the Mexican research System.

Luis Alfonso Razo Ruvalcaba graduated with honours from university as computer engineer and continued his studies at CINVESTAV Guadalajar where he joind the GeDa-3D development group. In 2007 he defended his thesis named "Behavior and Personality Algorithms for Emotional Agents" and obtained master's degree in computer science. As active participant of Distributed Systems Research Group of CINVESTAV Guadalajara Luis Razo has become a co-author of two articles related to emotional agent topics and one chapter of the present book. He also has 5 years teaching experience; he is a lecturer at the University of Guadalajara in such subjects as distributed systems, algorithms and programming., development of software for mobile devices over J2ME and Symbian Platform. At present he is studying at CINVESTAV Guadalajara and INP Grenoble to obtain the doctor's degree in computer science. He wants to orient his future research work towards met-analysis, characterization, meta-models and model oriented engineering; his aim is to develop, deepen and enrich these topics. To reach this aim he is going to dedicate one year to research work in the LCIS-Laboratory of INP Grenoble in Valence, France.

Rainer Reisenzein is full professor of General Psychology at the Institute of Psychology of the University of Greifswald, Germany. His research focuses on theoretical and empirical questions of emotion psychology, including the subjective experience of emotion, the relation of cognition and emotion, the facial expression of emotion, the emotion of surprise, and the history of emotion psychology. He has published numerous journal articles and book chapters on these and other topics, has edited special issues of journals, and is co-author of a three-volume German text book on emotions. He has been an invited speaker at the 2005 conference of the *International Society for Research on Emotions*, and is currently on the editorial board of the journals *Emotion, Cognition and Emotion*, and *Experimental Psychology*.

Olinto Rodriguez is an aggregate professor at the Universidad del Zulia in Maracaibo, Venezuela. His interests include the use of intelligent agents in computing, cryptography, databases and data mining. In the university, Olinto has been tutor of at least 40 end of career projects. He is a software consultant in several organizations since 1992. Currently, he is doing his PhD at the Universidad Politécnica de Madrid and his work is based on the use of collaborative agents and the reaction of agents.

Sigerist Rodriguez is an assistant professor at the Universidad del Zulia in Maracaibo, Venezuela. Currently he is doing his PhD at the Universidad Politécnica de Madrid. His interests include intelligent agents behavior, machine learning and emotion inclusion in agents. He is the curriculum commission coordinator at the Universidad del Zulia's computing science department.

Huma Shah is a research scientist investigating the Turing Test, her study is currently supervised by professor Kevin Warwick at the School of Systems Engineering, The University of Reading, UK. She has been involved in organising the 2006 and 2008 Loebner Prizes for Artificial Intelligence, a science contest that stages Turing's imitation game. With professor Warwick, she believes the 'canonical Turing Test' is one that involves a five minutes, unrestricted conversation, parallel-paired comparison of a machine with a human. She believes that current entries into the Loebner Prize are missing the 'Turing schoolmaster', and that the developers, 'Turing mechanics' could improve their systems with an interdisciplinary approach to passing the imitation game. She believes that passing the Turing Test is on the road to true AI, for it would involve inculcating emotional intelligence into artificial systems.

Matthias Scheutz received the MSc.E. degrees in formal logic and computer engineering from the University of Vienna and the Vienna University of Technology, respectively, in 1993, and the MA and PhD in philosophy at the University of Vienna, Austria, in 1989 and 1995, respectively. He also received the joint PhD in cognitive science and computer science from Indiana University Bloomington in 1999.

He is an associate professor in the Cognitive Science Program and the School of Informatics at Indiana University Bloomington and director of the Human-Robot Interaction Laboratory. He has over 100 peer-reviewed publications in artificial intelligence, artificial life, agent-based computing, cognitive modeling, foundations of cognitive science, and robotics. His current research interests include agent-based modeling, complex cognitive and affective robots for human-robot interaction, computational models of human language processing for mono- and bilinguals, distributed agent architectures, and interactions between affect and cognition.

Paul Schermerhorn received a BA from Goshen College (Goshen, IN) in 1995, double-majoring in accounting and psychology. He then pursued graduate studies in the Department of Philosophy at Northern Illinois University (DeKalb, IL), completing the MA In 1999. In 2002, he received a MS in Computer Science and Engineering at the University of Notre Dame (Notre Dame, IN) for research focusing on runtime systems for intelligent memory devices. He completed the PhD at Notre Dame in the field of agent-based modeling in 2006, and is currently a post-doctoral researcher in the Human- Robot Interaction Laboratory at Indiana University Bloomington. His research interests include affective robot control systems and agent-based modeling of social interactions in biological agents.

Daniel K. Schneider is senior lecturer and researcher at TECFA, a research and teaching unit in the faculty of psychology and education, University of Geneva. Holding a PhD in political science, he has been working in educational technology since 1988 and participated in various innovative pedagogical and technological projects. He has been a prime mover towards the introduction of creative pedagogical strategies and ICT technologies. His current R&D interests focus on modular, flexible and open Internet architectures supporting rich and effective educational designs. Within TECFA's blended master program in educational technology, he teaches educational information and communication systems, interactive multimedia, virtual environments and research methodology.

Marco Villamira, MD, PhD, full professor of General Psychology and head of the Institute of Human, Language and Environmental Sciences. Currently, his main interests deal with complex systems, agent-based models, AI, ALife and the relations between emotions, perception, cognition and consciousness.

Kevin Warwick is professor of Cybernetics at the University of Reading, England, where he carries out research in artificial intelligence, control, robotics and biomedical engineering. At 22 he took his first degree at Aston University, followed by a PhD and a research post at Imperial College, London. He subsequently held positions at Oxford, Newcastle and Warwick universities before being offered the Chair at Reading, at the age of 33. He has been awarded higher doctorates (DScs) both by Imperial College and the Czech Academy of Sciences, Prague. He was presented with The Future of Health technology Award from MIT (USA), was made an Honorary Member of the Academy of Sciences, St.Petersburg and received The IEE Achievement Medal in 2004. In 2000 Kevin presented the Royal Institution Christmas Lectures, entitled "The Rise of The Robots".

Keigo Watanabe received the BE and ME degrees in mechanical engineering from the University of Tokushima, Tokushima, Japan, in 1976 and 1978, respectively, and the DE degree in aeronautical engineering from Kyushu University, Fukuoka, Japan, in 1984. From 1980 to March 1985, he was a research associate at Kyushu University. From April 1985 to March 1990, he was an associate professor at the College of Engineering, Shizuoka University, Shizuoka, Japan. From April 1990 to March 1993, he was an associate professor, and from April 1993 to March 1998, he was a full professor in the Department of Mechanical Engineering, Saga University, Saga, Japan. Since April 1998, he has been with the Department of Advanced Systems Control Engineering, Graduate School of Science and Engineering, Saga University. He has published more than 570 technical papers in transactions, journals, and international conference proceedings, and is the author or editor of 25 books. His research interests are in intelligent signal processing and control using softcomputing, bio-inspired robotics, and nonholonomic systems.

Index